...more resources, visit the Web site for

The American Promise

bedfordstmartins.com/roark

FREE Online Study Guide

Get instant feedback on your progress with

- Chapter self-tests
- Key terms review
- Map quizzes
- Timeline activities
- Note-taking outlines

FREE History research and writing help

Refine your research skills and find plenty of good sources with

- Suggested references for each chapter compiled by the textbook authors
- A database of useful images, maps, documents, and more at *Make History*
- A guide to online sources for history
- Help with writing history papers
- A tool for building a bibliography
- Tips on avoiding plagiarism

The
American
Promise
A History of
the United States

FIFTH EDITION

CANADA

MINNESOTA

Lake Superior

St. Paul
Minneapolis

WISCONSIN

Lake Michigan

Lake Huron

MAINE

Augusta

VERMONT
Burlington   Montpelier

Mt. Washington
(6,288 ft.; 1,917 m)   Concord

Portland

NEW
HAMPSHIRE

Manchester

Boston
MASS.

Lake Ontario

Albany

Hartford

Providence

R.I.

CONNECTICUT

NEW
YORK

Buffalo

MICHIGAN

Milwaukee   Lansing

Madison

Detroit

Chicago

Lake Erie

Cleveland

PENNSYLVANIA

Hudson River

New York

IOWA

Des Moines

CENTRAL
LOWLAND

Omaha

Missouri River

INDIANA

Springfield

MISSOURI

ILLINOIS

Kansas City
Topeka

St. Louis

Jefferson
City

Indianapolis

OHIO

Columbus

Cincinnati

Charleston

Frankfort

Louisville

Ohio River

KENTUCKY

Cumberland
River

Wheeling

Pittsburgh

W.
VA.

Harrisburg

APPALACHIAN MTS.

Trenton

Philadelphia

NEW JERSEY

Dover

Baltimore

DELAWARE

Annapolis

WASHINGTON, D.C.

MARYLAND

Potomac
River

Richmond

Chesapeake
Bay

VIRGINIA

Norfolk

Raleigh

ATLANTIC
OCEAN

Tulsa

ARKANSAS

Little
Rock

Mississippi River

Knoxville
Nashville

Mt. Mitchell
(6,684 ft.; 2,037 m)

Memphis

Tennessee River

NORTH CAROLINA

Charlotte

SOUTH CAROLINA

Columbia

TIDEWATER

TENNESSEE

Birmingham

Atlanta

Charleston

ALABAMA

GEORGIA

Dallas

MISSISSIPPI

Jackson

Alabama River

Montgomery

LOUISIANA

Baton Rouge

Houston   New Orleans

Jacksonville

Tallahassee

Orlando

FLORIDA

Lake
Okeechobee

Miami

Gulf
of
Mexico

BAHAMAS

THE
UNITED STATES

Elevation
Feet   Meters

Over 13,001   Over 3,001

6,561–13,000   2,001–3,000

3,281–6,560   1,001–2,000

1,641–3,280   501–1,000

661–1,640   201–500

0–660   0–200

Below   Below
sea level   sea level

67°W   65°W

ATLANTIC OCEAN

San Juan

PUERTO
RICO

18°N

VIRGIN
ISLANDS

Caribbean Sea

0   50   100 miles

0   50   100 kilometers

CUBA

0   150   300 miles

0   150   300 kilometers

90°W   80°W   70°W

THE CONTEMPORARY WORLD

80°N

Greenland
(Den.)

ALASKA

ICELAND

60°N

CANADA

UNITED
KINGDOM

IRELAND

FRANCE

40°N

UNITED STATES

SPAIN

PORTUGAL

ATLANTIC
OCEAN

Azores
(Port.)

MOROCCO

Canary Is.
(Sp.)

A

Western Sahara
(Mor.)

20°N

Hawaii

MEXICO

BAHAMAS

DOMINICAN
REPUBLIC

HAITI

Puerto Rico (U.S.)

CUBA

ST. KITTS AND NEVIS

JAMAICA

ANTIGUA AND BARBUDA

BELIZE

Guadeloupe (Fr.)

DOMINICA

GUATEMALA

HONDURAS

Martinique (Fr.)

ST. VINCENT AND THE GRENADINES

EL SALVADOR

NICARAGUA

ST. LUCIA

BARBADOS

GRENADA

COSTA RICA

TRINIDAD AND TOBAGO

MAURITANIA

CAPE
VERDE

SENEGAL

MALI

GAMBIA

GUINEA-BISSAU

GUINEA

SIERRA LEONE

LIBERIA

CÔTE D'IVOIRE

BURKINA FASO

GHANA

PANAMA

VENEZUELA

GUYANA

SURINAME

French Guiana (Fr.)

PACIFIC OCEAN

COLOMBIA

0°

Equator

Galápagos Is.
(Ec.)

ECUADOR

PERU

BRAZIL

SAMOA

BOLIVIA

20°S

TONGA

PARAGUAY

CHILE

ATLANTIC
OCEAN

Easter I.
(Chile)

URUGUAY

N
W   E
S

ARGENTINA

0   1,500   3,000 miles
0   1,500   3,000 kilometers

40°S

Falkland Is.
(U.K.)

60°S

80°S

160°W   140°W   120°W   100°W   80°W   60°W   40°W   20°W

ARCTIC OCEAN

NORWAY
SWEDEN
FINLAND
ESTONIA
LATVIA
LITHUANIA
DEN.
NETH.
GERMANY POLAND BELARUS
BEL.
LUX. CZ.
SLK. UKRAINE
AUS. HUNG. MOLDOVA
SLN. ROMANIA
SWITZ. ITALY CR. SE.
B.H. BULGARIA
MO. KO.
ALB. MAC.
GREECE
TUNISIA MALTA
CYPRUS
ISRAEL
Gaza Strip

RUSSIAN FEDERATION

KAZAKHSTAN

MONGOLIA

GEORGIA
ARMENIA
TURKEY
AZERBAIJAN
SYRIA
LEBANON
IRAQ
West Bank
JORDAN
KUWAIT
SAUDI ARABIA
QATAR
UNITED ARAB
EMIRATES

UZBEKISTAN
KYRGYZSTAN
TURKMENISTAN TAJIKISTAN

AFGHANISTAN

IRAN

PAKISTAN

BAHRAIN

OMAN

CHINA

N. KOREA
S. KOREA
JAPAN

PACIFIC OCEAN

BHUTAN
NEPAL
BANGLADESH
INDIA
MYANMAR
(BURMA)
LAOS
VIETNAM
THAILAND
CAMBODIA

Taiwan

ERIA
LIBYA
EGYPT

NIGER
CHAD
SUDAN
ERITREA
YEMEN
DJIBOUTI

NIGERIA
BENIN
TOGO
CENTRAL
AFRICAN REP.
SOUTH
SUDAN
ETHIOPIA
SOMALIA

MALDIVES

SRI
LANKA

PHILIPPINES

Mariana Is.
(U.S.)

Guam
(U.S.)

MARSHALL
IS.

CAMEROON
EQ.
GUINEA
GABON
CONGO
SÃO
TOMÉ
& PRÍNCIPE
DEM. REP. OF
THE CONGO
UGANDA
RWANDA
KENYA
BURUNDI
TANZANIA

COMOROS

SEYCHELLES

BRUNEI

MALAYSIA

SINGAPORE

PALAU

FEDERATED STATES
OF MICRONESIA

NAURU

KIRIBATI

INDONESIA

PAPUA
NEW
GUINEA

TUVALU

SOLOMON
IS.

ANGOLA
ZAMBIA
MALAWI
ZIMBABWE
MADAGASCAR
NAMIBIA
BOTSWANA

INDIAN OCEAN

TIMOR
LESTE

VANUATU

FIJI

MAURITIUS

New Caledonia
(Fr.)

AUSTRALIA

MOZAMBIQUE
SOUTH
AFRICA
SWAZILAND
LESOTHO

NEW
ZEALAND

Tasmania
(AUST.)

ABBREVIATIONS

ALB.	ALBANIA
AUS.	AUSTRIA
BEL.	BELGIUM
B.H.	BOSNIA AND HERZEGOVINA
CR.	CROATIA
CZ.	CZECH REPUBLIC
DEN.	DENMARK
HUNG.	HUNGARY
KO.	KOSOVO
LUX.	LUXEMBOURG
MAC.	MACEDONIA
MO.	MONTENEGRO
NETH.	NETHERLANDS
SE.	SERBIA
SLK.	SLOVAKIA
SLN.	SLOVENIA
SWITZ.	SWITZERLAND

ANTARCTICA

20°E   40°E   60°E   80°E   100°E   120°E   140°E   160°E

The American Promise

A History of the United States

FIFTH EDITION

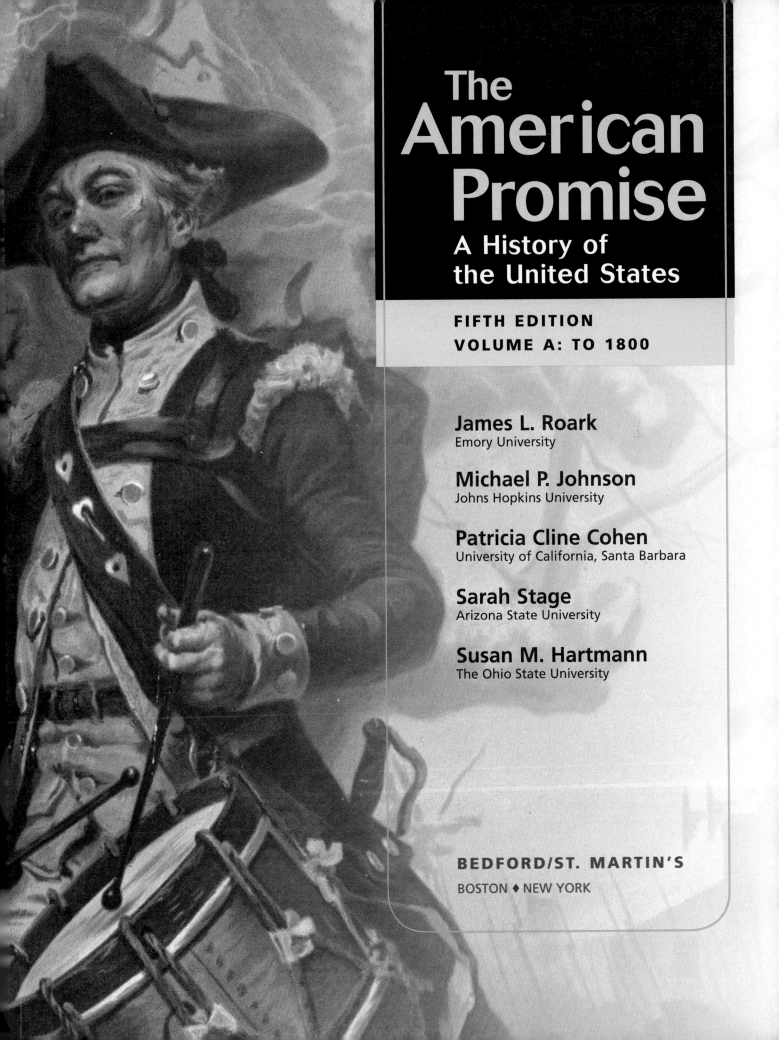

The American Promise

A History of the United States

FIFTH EDITION
VOLUME A: TO 1800

James L. Roark
Emory University

Michael P. Johnson
Johns Hopkins University

Patricia Cline Cohen
University of California, Santa Barbara

Sarah Stage
Arizona State University

Susan M. Hartmann
The Ohio State University

BEDFORD/ST. MARTIN'S
BOSTON ♦ NEW YORK

FOR BEDFORD/ST. MARTIN'S

Publisher for History: Mary Dougherty
Executive Editor for History: William J. Lombardo
Director of Development for History: Jane Knetzger
Developmental Editor: Michelle McSweeney
Senior Production Editor: Bridget Leahy
Assistant Production Manager: Joe Ford
Senior Marketing Manager for U.S. History: Amy Whitaker
Editorial Assistants: Jennifer Jovin and Laura Kintz
Production Assistants: Elise Keller and Victoria Royal
Copy Editor: Linda McLatchie
Indexer: Leoni Z. McVey
Photo Researchers: Pembroke Herbert and Sandi Rygiel, Picture Research Consultants, Inc.
Permissions Manager: Kalina K. Ingham
Senior Art Director: Anna Palchik
Text Designer: Tom Carling, Carling Design, Inc.
Cover Designer: Billy Boardman
Cover Art: The Continentals, 1875, by Frank Blackwell Mayer. Two soldiers of the Continental Army color guard, playing fife and drum, marching in winter. Library of Congress Prints and Photographs Division, Washington, D.C.
Cartography: Mapping Specialists Limited
Composition: Cenveo Publisher Services
Printing and Binding: RR Donnelley and Sons

President: Joan E. Feinberg
Editorial Director: Denise B. Wydra
Director of Marketing: Karen R. Soeltz
Director of Production: Susan W. Brown
Associate Director, Editorial Production: Elise S. Kaiser
Managing Editor: Elizabeth M. Schaaf

Library of Congress Control Number: 2011939422

Manufactured in the United States of America.

7   6   5   4   3   2
f   e   d   c   b   a

For information, write: Bedford/St. Martin's, 75 Arlington Street, Boston, MA 02116 (617-399-4000)

ISBN: 978–0–312–66312-4 (Combined Edition)
ISBN: 978–0–312–56953-2 (Loose-leaf Edition)
ISBN: 978–0–312–66313-1 (Vol. 1)
ISBN: 978–0–312 56948 8 (Loose-leaf Edition)
ISBN: 978–0–312–66314-8 (Vol. 2)
ISBN: 978–0–312–56946-4 (Loose-leaf Edition)
ISBN: 978–0–312–56954-9 (Vol. A)
ISBN: 978–0–312–56947-1 (Vol. B)
ISBN: 978–0–312–56944-0 (Vol. C)

Preface

As authors, we continue to be deeply gratified that *The American Promise* is one of the most widely adopted texts for the U.S. history survey, reaching students at all levels and helping instructors in all classroom environments. We know from years of firsthand experience that the survey course is the most difficult to teach and the most difficult to take, and we remain committed to making this book the most teachable and readable introductory American history text available. In creating this fifth edition, we set out to develop a resource that is both recognizable and new.

Our experience as teachers continues to inform every aspect of our text, beginning with its framework. We have found that students need *both* the structure a political narrative provides *and* the insights gained from examining social and cultural experience. To write a comprehensive, balanced account of American history, we focus on the public arena — the place where politics intersects social and cultural developments — to show how Americans confronted the major issues of their day and created far-reaching historical change. To engage students in the American story and to portray fully the diversity of the American experience, we stitch into our narrative the voices of hundreds of contemporaries, provide a vivid and compelling art program, and situate American history in the global world in which students live. To help students read, understand, and remember American history, we provide the best in pedagogical aids. While this edition rests solidly on our original goals and premises, the book has also changed, largely in response to adopters who helped us see new ways that the book could work for their students.

Users of past editions have emphasized the central role that *The American Promise* plays in their introductory courses — both as an in-class tool for them to teach from and as a resource for students to study from independently. Our goal in this fifth edition was to make our text even more successful for all students and instructors, whether they are using it in class or at home, whether in print or online. Within the book's covers, we added more contemporary voices to enliven the narrative, more visuals that promote analytical skills, and more pedagogy to facilitate independent study and class discussion. In an effort to assist instructors to help their students meet specific learning objectives, our new pedagogy highlights historical interrelationships and causality, underscores the importance of global contexts in U.S. history, and models historical thinking.

To extend the text, our array of multimedia and print supplements has never been more abundant or more impressive. A range of options — from video clips to lecture kits on CD-ROM and much more — offers instructors endless combinations to tailor *The American Promise* to fit the needs of their classroom. (See pages xii–xv.) Students of all learning styles have more ways than ever to enhance their traditional textbook experience and make history memorable. The e-book, for example, allows students to zoom in on and more closely examine the text's hundreds of historical photographs and artifacts. The book companion site links to even more primary documents, including images, texts, and audiovisual files, and its Online Study Guide provides Web-based self tests, map exercises, and visual activities. By seamlessly connecting our text to its rich storehouse of digital resources, these supplements help students better understand the people whose ideas and actions shaped their times and whose efforts still affect our lives.

Our title, *The American Promise*, reflects our agreement with playwright Arthur Miller's conviction that the essence of America has been its promise. For millions, the nation has held out the promise of a better life, unfettered worship, equality before the law, representative government, democratic politics, and other freedoms seldom found elsewhere. But none of these promises has come with guarantees. As we see it, much of American history is a continuing struggle over the definition and realization of the nation's promise. Who are we, and what do we want to be? Abraham Lincoln, in the midst of what he termed the "fiery trial" of the Civil

War, pronounced the nation "the last best hope of Earth." Kept alive by countless sacrifices, that hope has been marred by compromises, disappointments, and denials, but it still lives. We believe that our new edition of *The American Promise,* with its increased attention to human agency, will continue to show students that American history is an unfinished story and to make them aware of the legacy of hope bequeathed to them by generations of Americans stretching back more than four centuries, a legacy that is theirs to preserve and build on.

Features

We know that a history survey textbook may be unfamiliar or challenging for many students. The benefit of this full-length format is that we have room to give students *everything* they need to succeed. Our book is designed to pique students' interest and to assist them in every way in their reading, reviewing, and studying for exams. We are pleased to draw your attention to three aspects of our textbook that make *The American Promise* stand out from the crowd — our visual program, pedagogical support, and special features.

Visuals. From the beginning, readers have proclaimed this textbook a visual feast, richly illustrated in ways that extend and reinforce the narrative. The fifth edition offers more than eight hundred contemporaneous **illustrations** — one-third of them new — along with innovative techniques for increasing visual literacy. Twelve new **Visualizing History** features show students how to examine the evidence through a wide spectrum of historic objects, including archaeological artifacts, furniture, paintings, photographs, advertisements, clothing, and political cartoons. In addition, one picture in each chapter includes a special **visual activity caption** that reinforces the skill of image analysis. More than three hundred **artifacts** — from dolls and political buttons to guns and sewing machines — emphasize the importance of material culture in the study of the past and make the historical account tangible.

Our highly regarded and thoroughly redesigned **map program,** with more than 170 maps in all, rests on the old truth that "History is not intelligible without geography." Each chapter offers, on average, four **full-size maps** showing major developments in the narrative and two or three **spot maps** embedded in the narrative that emphasize an area of detail from the discussion. To help students think critically about the role of geography in American history, we include **two critical-thinking map exercises** per chapter. Revised maps in the fifth edition illustrate new scholarship on topics such as the Comanche empire in the American Southwest and highlight recent events in the Middle East. Another unique feature is our brief **Atlas of the Territorial Growth of the United States,** a series of full-color maps at the end of each volume that reveals the changing cartography of the nation.

Throughout the text, a host of tables, figures, and other graphics enhance and reinforce the content. **Thematic chronologies** summarize complex events and highlight key points in the narrative. To support our emphasis on the global context of U.S. history, **Global Comparison figures** showcase data with a focus on transnational connections. In addition, occasional **Promise of Technology** illustrations examine the ramifications — positive and negative — of technological developments in American society and culture.

Pedagogy. As part of our ongoing efforts to make *The American Promise* the most teachable and readable survey text available, we paid renewed attention to imaginative and effective pedagogy. Each chapter begins with a concise but colorful **opening vignette** that invites students into the narrative with lively accounts of individuals or groups who embody the central themes of the chapter. New vignettes in this edition include the Grimké sisters speaking out against slavery, Frederick Jackson Turner proclaiming his frontier hypothesis, migrant mother Frances Owens struggling to survive in the Great Depression, and the experience of Vietnam War veteran Frederick Downs Jr. Each vignette ends with a **narrative overview** of all of the chapter's main topics. Major sections within each chapter have **introductory paragraphs** that preview the subsections that follow and conclude with **review questions** to help students check their comprehension of main ideas. **Running heads** with dates and topical headings remind students of chronology, and **callouts** draw attention to interesting quotations from a wide range of American voices. In addition, **key terms,** set in boldface type and grouped together at the end of the chapter, highlight important people, events, and concepts. All chapters culminate in a **conclusion,** which reexamines central ideas and provides a bridge to the next chapter, and a **Selected Bibliography,** which lists important books to jump-start student research and to show students that our narrative comes from scholarship.

The two-page **Reviewing the Chapter** section at the end of each chapter provides a thorough review guide to ensure student success. A list of **Key Terms**, grouped according to chapter headings, provides a starting point for self study and suggests important relationships among major topics, while an illustrated chapter **Timeline** gives clear chronological overviews of key events. Three sets of questions prompt students to think critically and to make use of the facts they have mastered. **Review Questions,** repeated from within the narrative, focus on a specific topic or event, and **Making Connections** questions prompt students to think about broad developments within the chapter. An **all-new set of Linking to the Past** questions cross-reference developments in earlier chapters, encouraging students to make comparisons, see causality, and understand change over longer periods of time. **Online Study Guide cross-references** at the end of the review section point students to free self-assessment quizzes and other study aids.

Special Features. We have been delighted to learn that students and instructors alike use and enjoy our special features. Many instructors use them for class discussion or homework, and students report that even when the special features are not assigned, they read these features on their own because they find them interesting, informative, and exceptional entry points back into the narrative text itself. Each boxed feature concentrates on a historical thinking skill or a habit of mind. We include features that focus on analyzing written or visual primary source evidence, and other features that pose intriguing questions about the past or America's relation to the world and thereby model historical inquiry, the curiosity at the heart of our discipline. For this edition, we have added a **new Visualizing History** feature to many chapters. Images such as Native American weaponry, Puritan furniture, nineteenth-century paintings, photographs by progressive reformers, early-twentieth-century advertisements, and twenty-first-century political cartoons are all presented as sources for examination. By stressing the importance of historical context and asking critical questions, each of these new features shows students how to mine visual documents for evidence in order to reach conclusions about the past.

Fresh topics and the addition of questions in our four enduring special features further enrich this edition. Each biographical **Seeking the American Promise** essay explores a different promise of America — the promise of home ownership or the promise of higher education, for example — while recognizing that the promises fulfilled for some have meant promises denied to others. New subjects in this edition include indentured servant Anne Orthwood and her struggle in colonial America, progressive reformer Alice Hamilton, World War I servicewoman Nora Saltonstall, Chinese scientist Qian Xuesen and his encounter with anticommunism in America, and Vietnamese immigrant-turned-politician Joseph Cao. In addition to these new topics, all Seeking the American Promise features now conclude with a **new set of Questions for Consideration** that help students explore the subject further and understand its significance within the chapter and the book as a whole.

Each **Documenting the American Promise** feature juxtaposes three or four primary documents to show varying perspectives on a topic or an issue and to provide students with opportunities to build and practice their skills of historical interpretation. Feature introductions and document headnotes contextualize the sources, and **Questions for Analysis and Debate** promote critical thinking about primary sources. New topics in this edition are rich with human drama and include "Hunting Witches in Salem, Massachusetts," "Mill Girls Stand Up to Factory Owners," and "The Press and the Pullman Strike."

Historical Questions essays pose and interpret specific questions of continuing interest in order to demonstrate various methods and perspectives of historical thinking. **New question sets** accompanying each of these features focus on a particular mode of inquiry: **Thinking about Evidence, Thinking about Beliefs and Values,** and **Thinking about Cause and Effect.** New to this edition is the feature "How Did America's First Congress Address the Question of Slavery?"

Beyond America's Borders features consider the reciprocal connections between the United States and the wider world and challenge students to think about the effects of transnational connections over time. With the goal of widening students' perspectives and helping students see that this country did not develop in isolation, these features are enhanced by new end-of-feature questions, **America in a Global Context.** New essays in this edition include "European Nations and the Peace of Paris, 1783" and "Global Prosperity in the 1850s."

Updated Scholarship

We updated the fifth edition in myriad ways to reflect our ongoing effort to offer a comprehensive text that braids all Americans into the national narrative and to frame that national narrative in a more global perspective. To do so, we have paid particular attention to the most recent scholarship and, as always, appreciated and applied many suggestions from our users that keep the book fresh, accurate, and organized in a way that works best for students.

In Volume One, we focused our attention on Native Americans, especially in the West, because of the publication of exciting new scholarship. In Chapter 6, we have incorporated into the narrative more coverage of Indians and their roles in various conflicts between the British and the colonists before the Revolution. Chapter 9 expands the coverage of American conflicts with Indians in the Southwest, adding new material on Creek chief Alexander McGillivray. Chapter 10 greatly increases the coverage of Indians in the West, with a new section devoted to the Osage territory and the impressive Comanche empire known as Comanchería. In addition, several new Visualizing History features — on ancient tools used in Chaco Canyon, on Aztec weaponry and its weaknesses in the face of Spanish steel, on Mohawk clothing and accessories, and on gifts exchanged between Anglos and Indians on the Lewis and Clark trail — highlight the significance of Native American material culture over the centuries.

Volume Two also includes expanded attention to Native Americans — particularly in Chapter 17, where we improved our coverage of Indian schools, assimilation techniques used by whites, and Indian resistance strategies — but our main effort for the fifth edition in the second half of the book has been to do more of what we already do best, and that is to give even more attention to women, African Americans, and the global context of U.S. history. In the narrative, we have added coverage of women as key movers in the rise of the Lost Cause after the Civil War, and we consider the ways in which the GI Bill disproportionately benefited white men after World War II. New features and opening vignettes focus on widely recognized as well as less well-known women who both shaped and were shaped by the American experience: the depression-era struggle of Florence Owens (the face of the famous Dorothea Lange photograph *Migrant Mother*), the workplace reforms set in motion by progressive activist Alice Hamilton, and the World War I

service of overseas volunteer Nora Saltonstall. Chapter 16 includes new coverage of the Colfax massacre, arguably the single worst incidence of brutality against African Americans during the Reconstruction era. Chapter 27 provides new coverage of civil rights activism and resistance in northern states, and Chapter 28 increases coverage of black power and urban rebellions across the country. A new Visualizing History feature in Chapter 16 examines the Winslow Homer painting *A Visit from the Old Mistress*.

Because students live in an increasingly global world and need help making connections with the world outside the United States, we have continued our efforts to incorporate the global context of American history throughout the fifth edition. This is particularly evident in Volume Two, where we have expanded coverage of transnational issues in recent decades, such as the 1953 CIA coup in Iran, the U.S. bombing campaign in Vietnam, and U.S. involvement in Afghanistan.

In addition to the many changes noted above, in both volumes we have updated, revised, and improved the fifth edition in response to both new scholarship and requests from instructors. New and expanded coverage areas include, among others, taxation in the pre-Revolutionary period and the early Republic, the Newburgh Conspiracy of the 1780s, the overbuilding of railroads in the West during the Gilded Age, the 1918–1919 global influenza epidemic, finance reform in the 1930s, post–World War II considerations of universal health care, the economic downturn of the late 2000s, the Obama presidency, and the most recent developments in the Middle East.

Acknowledgments

We gratefully acknowledge all of the helpful suggestions from those who have read and taught from previous editions of *The American Promise*, and we hope that our many classroom collaborators will be pleased to see their influence in the fifth edition. In particular, we wish to thank the talented scholars and teachers who gave generously of their time and knowledge to review this book: Patricia Adams, *Chandler-Gilbert Community College*; Susan Agee, *Truckee Meadows Community College*; Jennifer Bertolet, *George Washington University*; Michael Bryan, *Greenville Technical College*; Kim Burdick, *Delaware Technical and Community College*; Monica Butler, *Seminole State College, Sanford*; Andria Crosson, *University of Texas San Antonio*; Lawrence Devaro, *Rowan University and Camden County College*;

Philip DiMare, *California State University, Sacramento*; Dorothy Drinkard-Hawkshawe, *East Tennessee State University*; Edward (Jim) Dudlo, *Brookhaven College*; John Duke, *Alvin Community College*; Aaron Edstrom, *University of Texas El Paso*; Brian Farmer, *Amarillo College*; Rafaele Fierro, *Tunxis Community College*; José Garcia, *University of Central Florida*; Cecilia Gowdy-Wygant, *Front Range Community College Westminster*; William Grose, *Wythevilla Community College*; Stephanie Lee Holyfield, *University of Delaware*; Johanna Hume, *Alvin Community College*; W. Sherman Jackson, *Miami University*; Michael Jacobs, *University of Wisconsin Baraboo/ Sauk County*; Kevin Kern, *University of Akron*; Barbara Martin, *University of Southern Indiana*; Alfonso John Mooney, *University of Oklahoma*; Christopher Paine, *Lake Michigan College*; George Sochan, *Bowie State University*; Joyce Thierer, *Emporia State University*; Kathryn Wells, *Central Piedmont Community College*; Steven White, *Bluegrass Community and Technical College*; and Tom Zeiler, *University of Colorado at Boulder*.

A project as complex as this requires the talents of many individuals. First, we would like to acknowledge our families for their support, forbearance, and toleration of our textbook responsibilities. Pembroke Herbert and Sandi Rygiel of Picture Research Consultants, Inc., contributed their unparalleled knowledge, soaring imagination, and diligent research to make possible the extraordinary illustration program.

We would also like to thank the many people at Bedford/St. Martin's who have been crucial to this project. No one contributed more than freelance developmental editor Michelle McSweeney, who managed the entire revision and oversaw the development of each chapter. The results of her dedication to excellence and commitment to creating the best textbook imaginable are evident on every page. We greatly appreciate the acute intelligence, attention to detail, and limitless tolerance for the authors' eccentricities that Michelle brought to this revision. We thank freelance editors Jan Fitter and Shannon Hunt for their help with the manuscript. Thanks also go to editorial assistant Laura Kintz for her assistance preparing the manuscript and to associate editor Jennifer Jovin, who provided unflagging assistance and who coordinated the supplements. We are also grateful to Jane Knetzger, director of development for history; William J. Lombardo, executive editor for history; and Mary Dougherty, publisher for history, for their support and guidance. For their imaginative and tireless efforts to promote the book, we want to thank Jenna Bookin Barry, Amy Whitaker, John Hunger, Sean Blest, and Stephen Watson. With great skill and professionalism, Bridget Leahy, senior production editor, pulled together the many pieces related to copyediting, design, and composition, with the able assistance of Elise Keller and the guidance of managing editor Elizabeth Schaaf and assistant managing editor John Amburg. Senior production supervisor Joe Ford oversaw the manufacturing of the book. Designer Tom Carling, copyeditor Linda McLatchie, and proofreaders Janet Cocker and Mary Lou Wilshaw-Watts attended to the myriad details that help make the book shine. Leoni McVey provided an outstanding index. The book's gorgeous covers were designed by Billy Boardman. New media editor Marissa Zanetti made sure that *The American Promise* remains at the forefront of technological support for students and instructors. Editorial director Denise Wydra provided helpful advice throughout the course of the project. Finally, Charles H. Christensen, former president, took a personal interest in *The American Promise* from the start, and Joan E. Feinberg, president, guided all editions through every stage of development.

Versions and Supplements

Adopters of *The American Promise* and their students have access to abundant extra resources, including documents, presentation and testing materials, the acclaimed Bedford Series in History and Culture volumes, and much much more. See below for more information, visit the book's catalog site at **bedfordstmartins .com/roark/catalog**, or contact your local Bedford/ St. Martin's sales representative.

Get the Right Version for Your Class

To accommodate different course lengths and course budgets, *The American Promise* is available in several different formats, including three-hole punched loose-leaf Budget Books versions and e-books, which are available at a substantial discount.

- **Combined edition** (Chapters 1–31) — available in hardcover, loose-leaf, and e-book formats

- **Volume 1: To 1877** (Chapters 1–16) — available in paperback, loose-leaf, and e-book formats

- **Volume 2: From 1865** (Chapters 16–31) — available in paperback, loose-leaf, and e-book formats

- **Volume A: To 1800** (Chapters 1–10) — available in paperback format

- **Volume B: 1800–1900** (Chapters 10–20) — available in paperback format

- **Volume C: From 1900** (Chapters 21–31) — available in paperback format

The online, interactive **Bedford e-Book** can be examined or purchased at a discount at **bedfordstmartins.com/ebooks**. Your students can also purchase *The American Promise* in other popular e-book formats for computers, tablets, and e-readers.

Online Extras for Students

The book's companion site at **bedfordstmartins .com/roark** gives students a way to read, write, and study, and to find and access quizzes and activities, study aids, and history research and writing help.

FREE Online Study Guide. Available at the companion site, this popular resource provides students with quizzes and activities for each chapter, including multiple-choice self-tests that focus on important concepts; flashcards that test students' knowledge of key terms; timeline activities that emphasize causal relationships; and map quizzes intended to strengthen students' geography skills. Instructors can monitor students' progress through an online Quiz Gradebook or receive email updates.

FREE Research, Writing, and Anti-plagiarism Advice. Available at the companion site, Bedford's **History Research and Writing Help** includes the textbook authors' **Suggested References** organized by chapter; **History Research and Reference Sources,** with links to history-related databases, indexes, and journals; **More Sources and How to Format a History Paper,** with clear advice on how to integrate primary and secondary sources into research papers and how to cite and format sources correctly; **Build a Bibliography,** a simple Web-based tool known as The Bedford Bibliographer that generates bibliographies in four commonly used documentation styles; and **Tips on Avoiding Plagiarism,** an online tutorial that reviews the consequences of plagiarism and features exercises to help students practice integrating sources and recognize acceptable summaries.

Resources for Instructors

Bedford/St. Martin's has developed a wide range of teaching resources for this book and for this course. They range from lecture and presentation materials and assessment tools to course management options. Most can be downloaded or ordered at **bedfordstmartins.com/roark/catalog**.

HistoryClass for The American Promise. HistoryClass, a Bedford/St. Martin's Online Course

Space, puts the online resources available with this textbook in one convenient and completely customizable course space. There you and your students can access an interactive e-book and primary sources reader; maps, images, documents, and links; chapter review quizzes; interactive multimedia exercises; and research and writing help. In HistoryClass you can get all our premium content and tools and assign, rearrange, and mix them with your own resources. For more information, visit **yourhistoryclass.com**.

Bedford Coursepack for Blackboard, WebCT, Desire2Learn, Angel, Sakai, or Moodle. We have free content to help you integrate our rich content into your course management system. Registered instructors can download coursepacks with no hassle and no strings attached. Content includes our most popular free resources and book-specific content for *The American Promise*. Visit **bedfordstmartins.com/coursepacks** to see a demo, find your version, or download your coursepack.

Instructor's Resource Manual. The instructor's manual offers both experienced and first-time instructors tools for preparing lectures and running discussions. It includes chapter review material, teaching strategies, and a guide to chapter-specific supplements available for the text.

Guide to Changing Editions. Designed to facilitate an instructor's transition from the previous edition of *The American Promise* to the current edition, this guide presents an overview of major changes as well as of changes in each chapter.

Computerized Test Bank. The test bank includes a mix of fresh, carefully crafted multiple-choice, matching, short-answer, and essay questions for each chapter. It also contains the Historical Question, Documenting the American Promise, Seeking the American Promise, and Beyond America's Borders questions from the textbook and model answers for each. The questions appear in Microsoft Word format and in easy-to-use test bank software that allows instructors to easily add, edit, re-sequence, and print questions and answers. Instructors can also export questions into a variety of formats, including WebCT and Blackboard.

***The Bedford Lecture Kit*: Maps, Images, Lecture Outlines, and i>clicker Content.** Look good and save time with *The Bedford Lecture Kit*. These presentation materials are downloadable individually from the Instructor Resources tab at **bedfordstmartins.com/roark/catalog** and are available on *The Bedford Lecture Kit* Instructor's Resource CD-ROM. They provide ready-made and fully customizable PowerPoint multimedia presentations that include lecture outlines with embedded maps, figures, and selected images from the textbook and extra background for instructors. Also available are maps and selected images in JPEG and PowerPoint formats; content for i>clicker, a classroom response system, in Microsoft Word and PowerPoint formats; the *Instructor's Resource Manual* in Microsoft Word format; and outline maps in PDF format for quizzing or handing out. All files are suitable for copying onto transparency acetates.

***Make History* — Free Documents, Maps, Images, and Web Sites.** *Make History* combines the best Web resources with hundreds of maps and images, to make it simple to find the source material you need. Browse the collection of thousands of resources by course or by topic, date, and type. Each item has been carefully chosen and helpfully annotated to make it easy to find exactly what you need. Available at **bedfordstmartins .com/makehistory**.

Reel Teaching: Film Clips for the U.S. History Survey. This DVD provides a large collection of short video clips for classroom presentation. Designed as engaging "lecture launchers" varying in length from 1 to 15 or more minutes, the 59 documentary clips were carefully chosen for use in both semesters of the U.S. survey course. The clips feature compelling images, archival footage, personal narratives, and commentary by noted historians.

America in Motion: Video Clips for U.S. History. Set history in motion with *America in Motion*, an instructor DVD containing dozens of short digital movie files of events in twentieth-century American history. From the wreckage of the battleship *Maine*, to FDR's Fireside Chats, to Oliver North testifying before Congress, *America in Motion* engages students with dynamic scenes from key events and challenges them to think critically. All files are classroom-ready, edited for brevity, and easily integrated with PowerPoint or other presentation software for electronic lectures or assignments. An accompanying guide provides each clip's historical context, ideas for use, and suggested questions.

***The American Promise* via Dallas Tele-Learning Distance Learning Courses.** *The*

American Promise has been selected as the textbook for the award-winning U.S. history video-based courses *Shaping America: U.S. History to 1877* and *Transforming America: U.S. History since 1877* by Dallas TeleLearning at the LeCroy Center for Educational Telecommunications, Dallas County Community College District. Guides for students and instructors fully integrate the narrative of *The American Promise* into each course. For more information on these distance-learning opportunities, visit the Dallas TeleLearning Web site at **http://telelearning.dcccd.edu**, email **learn@dcccd.edu**, or call 972-669-6650.

Videos and Multimedia. A wide assortment of videos and multimedia CD-ROMs on various topics in U.S. History is available to qualified adopters through your Bedford/St. Martin's sales representative.

Package and Save Your Students Money

For information on free packages and discounts up to 50%, visit **bedfordstmartins.com/roark/catalog**, or contact your local Bedford/St. Martin's sales representative.

Bedford e-Book. The e-book for this title, described above, can be packaged with the print text at a discount.

Reading the American Past, **Fifth Edition.** Edited by Michael P. Johnson, one of the authors of *The American Promise*, and designed to complement the textbook, *Reading the American Past* provides a broad selection of over 150 primary source documents, as well as editorial apparatus to help students understand the sources. Available free when packaged with the print text.

Reading the American Past e-Book. The reader is also available as an e-book. When packaged with the print or electronic version of the textbook, it is available for free.

The Bedford Series in History and Culture. More than one hundred fifty titles in this highly praised series combine first-rate scholarship, historical narrative, and important primary documents for undergraduate courses. Each book is brief, inexpensive, and focused on a specific topic or period. For a complete list of titles, visit **bedfordstmartins.com/history/series**. Package discounts are available.

Rand McNally Atlas of American History. This collection of more than eighty full-color maps illustrates key events and eras from early exploration, settlement, expansion, and immigration to U.S. involvement in wars abroad and on U.S. soil. Introductory pages for each section include a brief overview, timelines, graphs, and photos to quickly establish a historical context. Available for $3.00 when packaged with the print text.

Maps in Context: A Workbook for American History. Written by historical cartography expert Gerald A. Danzer (University of Illinois at Chicago), this skill-building workbook helps students comprehend essential connections between geographic literacy and historical understanding. Organized to correspond to the typical U.S. history survey course, *Maps in Context* presents a wealth of map-centered projects and convenient pop quizzes that give students hands-on experience working with maps. Available free when packaged with the print text.

The Bedford Glossary for U.S. History. This handy supplement for the survey course gives students historically contextualized definitions for hundreds of terms—from *abolitionism* to *zoot suit*—that they will encounter in lectures, reading, and exams. Available free when packaged with the print text.

U.S. History Matters: A Student Guide to World History Online. This resource, written by Alan Gevinson, Kelly Schrum, and the late Roy Rosenzweig (all of George Mason University), provides an illustrated and annotated guide to 250 of the most useful Web sites for student research in U.S. history as well as advice on evaluating and using Internet sources. This essential guide is based on the acclaimed "History Matters" Web site developed by the American Social History Project and the Center for History and New Media. Available free when packaged with the print text.

Trade Books. Titles published by sister companies Hill and Wang; Farrar, Straus and Giroux; Henry Holt and Company; St. Martin's Press; Picador; and Palgrave Macmillan are available at a 50% discount when packaged with Bedford/St. Martin's textbooks. For more information, visit **bedfordstmartins.com/tradeup**.

A Pocket Guide to Writing in History. This portable and affordable reference tool by Mary Lynn Rampolla provides reading, writing, and research advice useful to students in all history courses. Concise yet comprehensive advice on approaching typical history assignments, developing critical reading skills, writing effective history papers, conducting research, using and documenting sources, and avoiding plagiarism—enhanced with practical tips and examples throughout—have made this slim reference a best-seller. Package discounts are available.

A Student's Guide to History. This complete guide to success in any history course provides the practical help students need to be effective. In addition to introducing students to the nature of the discipline, author Jules Benjamin teaches a wide range of skills from preparing for exams to approaching common writing assignments, and explains the research and documentation process with plentiful examples. Package discounts are available.

Going to the Source: The Bedford Reader in American History. Developed by Victoria Bissell Brown and Timothy J. Shannon, this reader's strong pedagogical framework helps students learn how to ask fruitful questions in order to evaluate documents effectively and develop critical reading skills. The reader's wide variety of chapter topics that complement the survey course and its rich diversity of sources—from personal letters to political cartoons—provoke students' interest as it teaches them the skills they need to successfully interrogate historical sources. Package discounts are available.

America Firsthand. With its distinctive focus on ordinary people, this primary documents reader, by Anthony Marcus, John M. Giggie, and David Burner, offers a remarkable range of perspectives on America's history from those who lived it. Popular Points of View sections expose students to different perspectives on a specific event or topic, and Visual Portfolios invite analysis of the visual record. Package discounts are available.

Brief Contents

Contents

CHAPTER 1
Ancient America,
Before 1492   2

CHAPTER 2
Europeans Encounter the
New World, 1492–1600   30

CHAPTER 5
Colonial America in the Eighteenth Century, 1701–1770 122

CHAPTER 6
The British Empire and the Colonial Crisis, 1754–1775 156

CHAPTER 9

The New Nation Takes Form, 1789–1800   258

CHAPTER 10

Republicans in Power, 1800–1824   288

Maps, Figures, and Tables

Maps

Figures and Tables

Special Features

The
American
Promise

A History of
the United States

FIFTH EDITION

**MISSISSIPPIAN
WOODEN MASK**

Sometime between
AD 1200 and 1350, a Native
American among the Mississippian people in what is now central
Illinois fashioned this mask from red cedar. A thin sheet of copper that
originally covered the mask has eroded away, leaving a greenish
residue streaking the face. Influenced by the culture of the vast
ceremonial site at Cahokia, shown in an artist's rendering in the
background, the people who used the mask in rituals probably
intended it to depict the face of both worldly and supernatural power.
The haunting visage evokes the long history of ancient Americans and
their impressive achievements.

Mask photograph: © 2002 John Bigelow Taylor www.johnbigelowtaylor.com. Illinois State Museum,
Springfield, Cat. No. 273; background: Richard Schlecht/National Geographic Stock.

1

Ancient America
Before 1492

NOBODY TODAY KNOWS HIS NAME. BUT ALMOST A THOUSAND YEARS ago, more than four hundred years before Europeans arrived in the Western Hemisphere, many ancient Americans celebrated this man — let's call him Sun Falcon. They buried Sun Falcon during elaborate rituals at Cahokia, the largest residential and ceremonial site in ancient North America. (In this chapter, ancient North America refers to the giant landmass north of present-day Mexico.) Located near the eastern shore of the Mississippi River in what is now southwestern Illinois, Cahokia stood at the spiritual and political center of the world in the eyes of the 15,000 or 20,000 ancient Americans who lived there and thousands more in the hinterlands nearby. The way Cahokians buried Sun Falcon suggests that he was a very important person who represented spiritual and political authority.

What we know about Sun Falcon and the Cahokians who buried him has been discovered by archaeologists — scientists who study artifacts, or material objects, left behind by ancient peoples. Cahokia attracted the attention of archaeologists because of the hundreds of earthen mounds that ancient Americans built in the region. The largest surviving mound, Monks Mound, is a huge terraced pyramid rising one hundred feet from a base that covers sixteen acres (an acre is about the size of a football field), making it the biggest single structure ever built by ancient North Americans.

Atop the four terraces — or platforms — on Monks Mound, political and religious leaders performed ceremonies watched by thousands of Cahokia residents and visitors who stood on a fifty-acre plaza at the base of the mound. Exactly what the leaders did in these ceremonies is unknown. Whatever they did was probably designed to demonstrate to onlookers the leaders' access to supernatural forces. Large garbage pits beside the plaza contain the bones of thousands of butchered deer, remnants of giant feasts that probably accompanied these ceremonies. At the far edge of the plaza, about a half mile from the base of Monk's Mound, Cahokians buried Sun Falcon in an oblong mound about 6 feet high and 250 feet long.

Before Cahokians lowered Sun Falcon into his grave sometime around AD 1050, they first placed the body of another man facedown in the dirt. On top of that man, Cahokians draped a large cape made of twenty thousand shell beads crafted into the likeness of a bird. They then put Sun Falcon faceup on the beaded cape with his head pointing southeast, aligned with the passage of the sun across the sky during the summer solstice at Cahokia. Experts speculate that Cahokians believed that Sun Falcon looked upward toward the life-giving light of the sun while the man

3

beneath the beaded cape communicated with the dark interior of the earth. The people who buried Sun Falcon, it appears, sought to pay homage not only to him but also to the awe-inspiring forces of darkness and light, of earth and sun, that governed their lives.

To accompany Sun Falcon, Cahokians also buried hundreds of arrows with exquisitely crafted arrowheads, thousands of shell beads, and other rare and valuable artifacts that they believed Sun Falcon would find useful in the afterlife. Near the artifacts, Cahokians buried the bodies of seven other adults, including at least one person killed at the grave site, who probably were relatives or servants of Sun Falcon. Not far away, archaeologists discovered several astonishing mass graves. One contained 53 women, all but one between the ages of fifteen and twenty-five, who had been sacrificed by poison, strangulation, or having their throats slit. Other graves contained 43 more sacrificed women, 4 men whose arms had been tied together at the elbows and whose heads and hands had been chopped off, and 39 other men and women who had been executed at the burial site. In all, more than 270 people were buried in the mound with Sun Falcon.

To date, archaeologists have found no similar burial site in ancient North America. However, they have excavated only a tiny fraction of Cahokia. Who knows what remains to be discovered there and elsewhere?

Nobody knows exactly who Sun Falcon was or why Cahokians buried him as they did. Archaeologists believe that Sun Falcon's burial and the human sacrifices that accompanied it were major public rituals that communicated to the many onlookers the fearsome power he wielded, the respect he commanded, and the authority his survivors intended to honor and maintain. Much remains unknown and unknowable about him and his fellow Cahokians, just as it does with other ancient Americans. The history of ancient Americans is therefore necessarily incomplete and controversial. Still, archaeologists have learned enough to understand where ancient Americans came from and many basic features of the complex cultures they created and passed along to their descendants, who dominated the history of America until 1492.

Cahokia Burial
The excavation of the ceremonial burial site at Cahokia revealed the remains of a man—presumably a revered leader—whom Cahokians buried atop a large cape or blanket in the shape of a bird, probably a raptor. Archaeologists superimposed the grid of white lines to record the precise location of each object. Covering the cape are more than 20,000 beads made of shells sewn onto an underlying fabric or animal skin (not visible). Nearby in the same mound, excavators found mass graves of scores of other Cahokians, many of them executed just before burial, evidently during ceremonies to honor their leader. Courtesy Illinois State Museum: archival photograph.

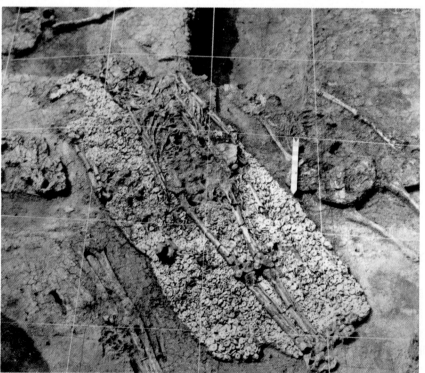

▶ Archaeology and History

Archaeologists and historians share the desire to learn about people who lived in the past, but they usually employ different methods to obtain information. Both archaeologists and historians study **artifacts** as clues to the activities and ideas of the humans who created them. They concentrate, however, on different kinds of artifacts. **Archaeologists** tend to focus on physical objects such as bones, spear points, pots, baskets, jewelry, clothing, and buildings. Historians direct their attention mostly to writings, including personal and private jottings such as letters and diary entries, and an enormous variety of public documents, such as laws, speeches, newspapers, and court cases. Although historians are interested in other artifacts and archaeologists do not neglect written sources if they exist, the characteristic concentration of historians on writings and of archaeologists on other physical objects denotes a rough cultural and chronological boundary between the human beings studied by the two groups of scholars, a boundary marked by the use of writing.

Writing is defined as a system of symbols that record spoken language. Writing originated among ancient peoples in China, Egypt, and Central America about eight thousand years ago, within the most recent 2 percent of the four hundred millennia that modern human beings (*Homo sapiens*) have existed. Writing came into use even later in most other places in the world. The ancient Americans who buried Sun Falcon at Cahokia about AD 1050 and all those who inhabited North America in 1492 possessed many forms of symbolic representation, but not writing.

The people who lived during the millennia before writing were biologically nearly identical to us. But unlike us, they did not use writing to communicate across space and time. They invented hundreds of spoken languages; they moved across the face of the globe, learning to survive in almost every natural environment; they chose and honored leaders; they traded, warred, and worshipped; and, above all, they learned from and taught one another. Much of what we would like to know about their experiences remains unknown because it took place before writing existed.

North Americans in 1492 possessed many forms of symbolic representation, but not writing.

Archaeologists specialize in learning about people who did not document their history in writing. They study the millions of artifacts these people created. They also scrutinize soil, geological strata, pollen, climate, and other environmental features to reconstruct as much as possible about the world ancient peoples inhabited. Although no documents chronicle ancient Americans' births and deaths or pleasures and pains, archaeologists have learned to make artifacts, along with their natural and human environment, reveal a great deal about the people who used them.

This chapter relies on studies by archaeologists to sketch a brief overview of ancient America, the long first phase of the history of the United States. Ancient Americans and their descendants resided in North America for thousands of years before Europeans arrived. For their own reasons and in their own ways, they created societies and cultures of remarkable diversity and complexity. Because they did not use written records, their

Mexican Stone Tablet

In 2006, Mexican archaeologists announced the discovery of this stone tablet inscribed with the earliest evidence of writing in the Western Hemisphere. About three thousand years ago, somebody in what is now the Mexican state of Veracruz incised this stone with sixty-two characters, barely visible in this photograph. Experts have not yet deciphered the writing, but the repetition of certain characters has led some experts to speculate that it records poetry.

© Michael D. Coe.

history cannot be reconstructed with the detail and certainty made possible by writing. But it is better to abbreviate and oversimplify ancient Americans' history than to ignore it.

> **REVIEW**   Why do historians rely on the work of archaeologists to write the history of ancient North America?

▶ The First Americans

The first human beings to arrive in the Western Hemisphere emigrated from Asia. They brought with them hunting skills, weapon- and tool-making techniques, and a full range of other forms of human knowledge developed millennia earlier in Africa, Europe, and Asia. These first Americans hunted large mammals, such as the mammoths they had learned in Europe and Asia to kill, butcher, and process for food, clothing, building materials, and many other purposes.

Most likely, these first Americans wandered into the Western Hemisphere more or less accidentally, hungry and in pursuit of their prey.

African and Asian Origins

Human beings lived elsewhere in the world for hundreds of thousands of years before they reached the Western Hemisphere. They lacked a way to travel to the Western Hemisphere because millions of years before humans existed anywhere on the globe, North and South America became detached from the gigantic common landmass scientists now call **Pangaea**. About 240 million years ago, powerful forces deep within the earth fractured Pangaea and slowly pushed continents apart to approximately their present positions (Map 1.1). This process of **continental drift** encircled the land of the Western Hemisphere with large oceans that isolated it from the other continents long before early human beings (*Homo erectus*) first appeared in Africa about two million years ago. (Hereafter in this chapter, the

MAP ACTIVITY

Map 1.1   Continental Drift
Massive geological forces separated North and South America from other continents eons before human beings evolved in Africa 1.5 million years ago.

READING THE MAP: Which continents separated from Pangaea earliest? Which ones separated from each other last? Which are still closely connected to each other?
CONNECTIONS: How does continental drift explain why human life developed elsewhere on the planet for hundreds of thousands of years before the first person entered the Western Hemisphere 15,000 years ago?

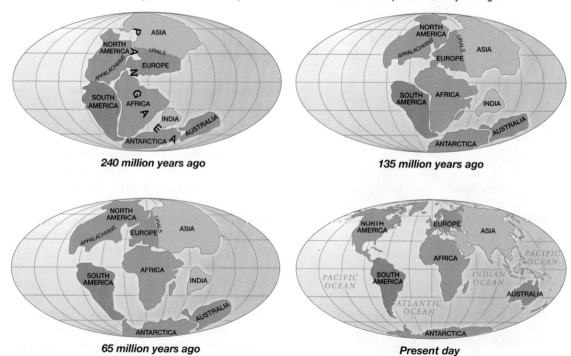

240 million years ago

135 million years ago

65 million years ago

Present day

abbreviation *BP* — archaeologists' notation for "years before the present" — is used to indicate dates earlier than two thousand years ago. Dates more recent than two thousand years ago are indicated with the common and familiar notation *AD* — for example, AD 1492.)

More than 1.5 million years after *Homo erectus* appeared, or about 400,000 BP, modern humans (*Homo sapiens*) evolved in Africa. All human beings throughout the world today are descendants of these ancient Africans. Their DNA was the template for ours. Slowly, over many millennia, **Homo sapiens** migrated out of Africa and into Europe and Asia. Unlike North and South America, Europe and Asia retained land connections to Africa, allowing ancient humans to migrate on foot. Sometimes ancient people navigated rivers and lakes in small boats, but these vessels could not survive battering by the winds and waves of the enormous oceans isolating North and South America from the Eurasian landmass. For roughly 97 percent of the time *Homo sapiens* have been on

Beringia

earth, none migrated to the Western Hemisphere.

Two major developments made it possible for ancient humans to migrate to the Western Hemisphere. First, people successfully adapted to the frigid environment near the Arctic Circle. Second, changes in the earth's climate reconnected North America to Asia.

By about 25,000 BP, *Homo sapiens* had spread from Africa throughout Europe and Asia. People, probably women, had learned to use bone needles to sew animal skins into warm clothing that permitted them to become permanent residents of extremely cold regions such as northeastern Siberia. A few of these ancient Siberians clothed in animal hides walked to North America on land that now lies submerged beneath the sixty miles of water that currently separates easternmost Siberia from westernmost Alaska. A pathway across this watery chasm opened during the last global cold spell — the Wisconsin glaciation, which endured from about 25,000 BP to 14,000 BP — when snow piled up in glaciers, causing the sea level to drop as much

FIGURE 1.1 Human Habitation of the World and the Western Hemisphere
These clock faces illustrate the long global history of modern humans (left) and of human history in the Western Hemisphere since the arrival of the first ancient Americans (right). If the total period of human life on earth is considered, American history since the arrival of Columbus in 1492 comprises less than one minute (or one-tenth of 1 percent) of modern human existence. And if the total period of human life in the New World is converted from millennia to a 12-hour clock, ancient American history makes up the first 11½ hours, and all history since the arrival of the Europeans in 1492 occupies only the last half hour.

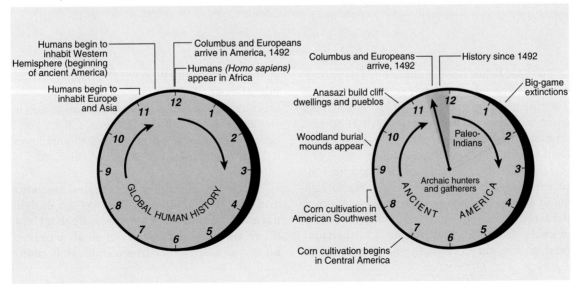

Who Were the First Americans?

To learn who the first Americans were and when they arrived requires following a trail that has grown very cold during the past 15,000 or 20,000 years.

After millennia of erosion and environmental change, much of the land they walked, hunted, and camped on is now submerged and inaccessible beneath the Bering Sea and along the Atlantic and Pacific coasts, where rising sea levels have flooded wide, previously exposed coastal plains. Most of the numerous Paleo-Indian sites archaeologists have excavated were occupied more than a hundred centuries after the first migrants arrived. These sites often yield spear points and large animal bones, but Paleo-Indian human skeletal remains are very rare. And yet evidence that Paleo-Indians inhabited the Western Hemisphere is overwhelming and indisputable. Human craftsmanship is the only credible explanation for Clovis points, and carbon dating establishes that the oldest Clovis sites are about 13,500 years old.

Scattered and controversial evidence suggests, however, that Clovis peoples were not the first arrivals. The Monte Verde excavation in Chile has persuaded many archaeologists that the first Americans resided in South America sometime between 14,750 BP and 14,000 BP. This site and a few other likely pre-Clovis sites in North America, most notably Meadowcroft in Pennsylvania, contain no Clovis-era artifacts, suggesting that their inhabitants arrived earlier and differed from the later Clovis peoples. But if the first Americans already lived in Chile and Pennsylvania 14,000 or more years ago, when did they first arrive and from where?

Some experts hypothesize that pre-Clovis peoples sailed or floated across the Pacific from Australia or Antarctica. Most scholars consider those ideas far-fetched. The Pacific is too wide and tempestuous for these ancient peoples and their small boats to have survived a long transoceanic trip.

Ancient Siberians had the means (hunting skills and adaptation to the frigid climate), motive (pursuit of game animals), and opportunity (the Beringian land bridge) to become the first humans to arrive in America, and most archaeologists believe they did just that. But when they came is difficult to determine, since the Beringian land bridge existed for thousands of years. The extreme rarity of the earliest archaeological sites in North America also makes it difficult to estimate with confidence when pre-Clovis hunters arrived. A rough guess is 15,000 BP, although it might have been earlier. The scarcity of pre-Clovis sites discovered so far strongly suggests that these ancient Americans were few in number (compared to the much more numerous Clovis-era Paleo-Indians), very widely scattered, and ultimately unsuccessful in establishing permanent residence in the hemisphere. Although they and their descendants may have survived in America for a millennium or more, pre-Clovis peoples appear to have died out. The sparse archaeological evidence discovered to date does not suggest that they evolved into Clovis peoples. Although Clovis peoples evidently were not the first humans to arrive in the Western Hemisphere, they probably represent the first Paleo-Indians to establish a permanent American presence.

To investigate where the mysterious first Americans came from, experts have supplemented archaeological evidence with careful study of modern-day Native Americans. Although many millennia separate today's Native Americans from those ancient hunters, most

as 350 feet below its current level. The falling sea level exposed a land bridge connecting Asian Siberia and American Alaska. This land bridge, which scientists call **Beringia** (see page 7), opened a passageway hundreds of miles wide between the Eastern and Western Hemispheres.

Siberian hunters roamed Beringia for centuries in search of game animals. Grasses and small shrubs that covered Beringia supported herds of mammoths, bison, and numerous smaller animals. As the hunters ventured farther and farther east, they eventually became pioneers of human life in the Western Hemisphere. Their migrations probably had very little influence on their own lives, which continued more or less in the age-old ways they had learned from their Siberian ancestors. Although they did not know it, their migrations revolutionized the history of the world.

Archaeologists refer to these first migrants and their descendants for the next few millennia as **Paleo-Indians**. They speculate that these Siberian hunters traveled in small bands of no more than twenty-five people. How many

Clovis Point

This spear point excavated from a Clovis-era site along the Columbia River in what is now Washington state was crafted by Clovis people around 11,000 BP. It illustrates the shape, size, and technique of flaking — the chipping away of small fragments of stone to create the point — common to Clovis points throughout the hemisphere. Archaeologists believe that such commonalities in Clovis artifacts document a widely shared Clovis culture practiced for many human generations. Clovis hunters wedged the point into a wooden shaft, bound it with leather or twine, and then had a sharp-edged weapon for killing (and butchering) game animals. Washington State Historical Society.

scholars agree that telltale clues to the identity of the first Americans can be gleaned from dental, linguistic, and genetic evidence collected from their descendants who still live throughout the hemisphere.

Detailed scientific analyses of the teeth of thousands of ancient and modern Native Americans have identified distinctive dental shapes — such as incisors with a scooped-out inner surface — commonly found among ancient Siberians, ancient Americans, and modern Native Americans, but rare elsewhere. This dental evidence strongly supports the Asian origins and Beringian

migration route of the first Americans.

Linguistic analysis of more than a thousand modern Native American languages demonstrates that Native Americans throughout the hemisphere speak some form of Amerind, the consequence (presumably) of its arrival with the earliest wave of ancient migrants around 13,000 BP. This migration chronology and linguistic analysis remain controversial among experts, but they suggest that Clovis peoples spoke some ancient form of Amerind.

Genetic research into the mutation rate of DNA reveals that many modern Native Americans share

genetic characteristics commonly found among Asians. Estimates of the evolutionary time required to produce the subtle differences between Asian and Native American DNA suggest a migration from Asia as early as 25,000 BP or before. But like the other high-tech evidence, this genetic evidence is sharply disputed by experts.

Fascinating as the genetic, linguistic, and dental studies are, they are unlikely to win widespread support among experts until they can be corroborated by archaeological evidence that, so far, has not been found. Until then, specialists will continue to debate when the first Americans arrived and how they were related to subsequent generations of ancient Americans.

Thinking about Evidence

1. What evidence supports the hypothesis that the first Americans came from Asia? Do you find the evidence persuasive?

2. If pre-Clovis peoples were the first Americans, what evidence suggests when they arrived and what happened to them?

3. Can you imagine archaeological evidence that, if found, would conclusively identify the first Americans and when they arrived?

such bands arrived in North America before Beringia disappeared beneath the sea will never be known.

When the first migrants came is hotly debated by experts. They probably arrived sometime after 15,000 BP. Scattered and inconclusive evidence suggests that they may have arrived several thousand years earlier. (See "Historical Question," page 8.) Certainly, humans who came from Asia — whose ancestors had left Africa hundreds of thousands of years earlier — inhabited the Western Hemisphere by 13,500 BP.

Paleo-Indian Hunters

When humans first arrived in the Western Hemisphere, massive glaciers covered most of present-day Canada. A narrow corridor not entirely obstructed by ice ran along the eastern side of Canada's Rocky Mountains, and most archaeologists believe that Paleo-Indians probably migrated through the ice-free passageway in pursuit of game. They may have also traveled along the Pacific coast in small boats, hunting marine life and hopscotching from one desirable landing spot to another. At the southern edge of the glaciers, Paleo-Indians entered a hunters' paradise. North, Central, and South America teemed with wildlife that had never before confronted wily two-legged predators armed with razor-sharp spears. The abundance of game presumably made hunting relatively easy. Ample food permitted the Paleo-Indian population to grow. Within a thousand years or so, Paleo-Indians had migrated to the tip of South America and virtually everywhere else in the Western Hemisphere, as proved by discoveries of their spear points in numerous excavations.

Early Paleo-Indians used a distinctively shaped spearhead known as a **Clovis point**, named for the place in New Mexico where it was first excavated. Archaeologists' discovery of Clovis points throughout North and Central America in sites occupied between 13,500 BP and 13,000 BP provides evidence that these nomadic hunters shared a common ancestry and way of life. Paleo-Indians hunted mammoths and bison — judging from the artifacts and bones that

> **Some Paleo-Indians refrigerated killed mammoths by filling the intestines with stones and sinking the carcasses to the bottom of an icy lake.**

have survived from this era — but they probably also hunted smaller animals. Concentration on large animals, when possible, made sense because just one mammoth kill supplied hunters with meat for weeks or, if dried, for months. Some Paleo-Indians even refrigerated killed mammoths by filling the intestines with stones and sinking the carcasses to the bottom of an icy lake to be retrieved and used later. In addition to food, mammoth kills provided hides and bones for clothing, shelter, tools, and much more.

About 11,000 BP, Paleo-Indians confronted a major crisis. The mammoths and other large mammals they hunted became extinct. The extinction was gradual, stretching over several hundred years. Scientists are not completely certain why it occurred, although environmental change probably contributed to it. About this time, the earth's climate warmed, glaciers melted, and sea levels rose. Mammoths and other large mammals probably had difficulty adapting to the warmer climate. Many archaeologists also believe, however, that Paleo-Indians probably contributed to the extinctions in the Western Hemisphere by killing large animals more rapidly than they could reproduce. Although some experts dispute this overkill hypothesis, similar environmental changes had occurred for millions of years without triggering the large-mammal extinctions that followed the arrival of Paleo-Indian hunters. Whatever the causes, Paleo-Indians faced a radical change in the natural environment within just a few thousand years of their arrival in the Western Hemisphere — namely, the extinction of large mammals. After the extinction, Paleo-Indians literally inhabited a new world.

Paleo-Indians adapted to the drastic environmental change of the big-game extinction by making at least two important changes in their way of life. First, hunters began to prey more intensively on smaller animals. Second, Paleo-Indians devoted more energy to foraging — that is, to collecting wild plant foods such as roots, seeds, nuts, berries, and fruits. When Paleo-Indians made these changes, they replaced the apparent uniformity of the big-game-oriented Clovis culture with great cultural diversity adapted to the many natural environments throughout the hemisphere, ranging from icy tundra to steamy jungles.

These post-Clovis adaptations to local environments resulted in the astounding variety of Native American cultures that existed when Europeans arrived in AD 1492. By then, more than three hundred major tribes and hundreds of lesser groups inhabited North America alone.

Ancient Petroglyphs

These petroglyphs — drawings incised onto the surface of rocks — probably depict shamans, ancient American spiritual leaders and healers who claimed the ability to communicate with supernatural powers. Shamans may well have made the petroglyphs to help them cure sicknesses, attempt to control the weather, or assure success for hunters. Petroglyphs can be found throughout North America; often they portray animals, people, or geometric designs. The petroglyphs shown here are among thousands located in the Coso Mountains on the edge of the Mojave Desert in what is now eastern California, where ancient Americans etched them onto rocks for millennia. © David Muench.

Clovis Spear Straightener
Clovis hunters used this bone spear straightener about 11,000 BP at a campsite in Arizona, where archaeologists discovered it lying among the butchered remains of two mammoth carcasses and thirteen ancient bison. Similar objects often appear in ancient sites in Eurasia, but this is the only bone artifact yet discovered in a Clovis-era site in North America. Presumably Clovis hunters stuck their spear shafts through the opening and then grasped the handle of the straightener and moved it back and forth along the length of the shaft to remove imperfections and make the spear a more effective weapon. Arizona State Museum, University of Arizona.

Hundreds more lived in Central and South America. Hundreds of other ancient American cultures had disappeared or transformed themselves as their people constantly adapted to environmental change and other challenges.

REVIEW   How and why did humans migrate into North America after 15,000 BP?

▶ Archaic Hunters and Gatherers

Archaeologists use the term *Archaic* to describe the many different hunting and gathering cultures that descended from Paleo-Indians and the long period of time when those cultures dominated the history of ancient America — roughly from 10,000 BP to somewhere between 4000 BP and 3000 BP. The term describes the era in the history of ancient America that followed the Paleo-Indian big-game hunters and preceded the development of agriculture. It denotes a **hunter-gatherer** way of life that persisted in North America long after European colonization.

Like their Paleo-Indian ancestors, **Archaic Indians** hunted with spears, but they also took smaller game with traps, nets, and hooks. Unlike their Paleo-Indian predecessors, most Archaic peoples used a variety of stone tools to prepare food from wild plants. A characteristic Archaic artifact is a grinding stone used to pulverize seeds into edible form. Most Archaic Indians migrated from place to place to harvest plants and hunt animals. They usually did not establish permanent villages, although they often returned to the same river valley or fertile meadow year after year. In regions with especially rich resources — such as present-day California and the Pacific Northwest — they developed permanent settlements. Many groups became excellent basket makers in order to collect and store food they gathered from wild plants. Archaic peoples followed these practices in distinctive ways in the different environmental regions of North America (Map 1.2).

Great Plains Bison Hunters

After the extinction of large game animals, some hunters began to concentrate on bison in the huge herds that grazed the grassy, arid plains stretching hundreds of miles east of the Rocky Mountains. For almost a thousand years after the big-game extinctions, Archaic Indians hunted bison with Folsom points, named after a site near Folsom, New Mexico. In 1908, George McJunkin, an African American cowboy, discovered this site, which contained a deposit of large fossilized bones. In 1926, archaeologists excavated the site McJunkin had discovered and found evidence that proved conclusively for the first time that ancient Americans and giant bison — which were known to have been extinct for at least ten thousand years — were contemporaries. One Folsom point remained stuck between two ribs of a giant bison, where a Stone Age hunter had plunged it more than ten thousand years earlier.

Like their nomadic predecessors, Folsom hunters moved constantly to maintain contact with their prey. **Great Plains hunters** developed trapping techniques that made it easy to kill large numbers of animals. At the original Folsom site, careful study of the bones McJunkin found suggests that early one winter hunters drove bison into a narrow gulch and speared twenty-three of them. At other sites, Great Plains hunters stampeded bison herds over cliffs and then slaughtered the animals that plunged to their deaths.

Bows and arrows reached Great Plains hunters from the north about AD 500. They largely replaced spears, which had been the hunters' weapons of choice for millennia. Bows permitted

MAP ACTIVITY

Map 1.2   Native North American Cultures
Environmental conditions defined the boundaries of the broad zones of cultural similarity among ancient North Americans.

READING THE MAP: What crucial environmental features set the boundaries of each cultural region? (The topography indicated on Map 1.3, "Native North Americans about 1500," may be helpful.)

CONNECTIONS: How did environmental factors and variations affect the development of different groups of Native American cultures? Why do you think historians and archaeologists group cultures together by their regional positions?

hunters to wound animals from farther away, arrows made it possible to shoot repeatedly, and arrowheads were easier to make and therefore less costly to lose than the larger, heavier spear points. But these new weapons did not otherwise alter age-old techniques of bison hunting on the Great Plains. Although we often imagine ancient Great Plains bison hunters on horseback, in fact they hunted on foot, like their Paleo-Indian ancestors. Horses that had existed in North America millions of years earlier had long since become extinct. Horses did not return to the Great Plains until Europeans imported them in the decades after 1492, when Native American bison hunters acquired them and soon became expert riders.

Fishhooks

Ancient Americans crafted these fishhooks sometime between AD 900 and 1600 from abalone shells collected in the waters off coastal California. Fishermen attached a line to the nub shown at the top of three of the hooks, skewered bait onto the point of the hook, then pulled up when a fish nibbled, hoping to snag the lip of the unsuspecting fish. (The numbers on the hooks were added in modern times.) The hooks illustrate Pacific Coast cultures' exploitation of their rich marine environment. ©The Field Museum #A114464_32d.

Great Basin Cultures

Archaic peoples in the Great Basin between the Rocky Mountains and the Sierra Nevada inhabited a region of great environmental diversity. Some **Great Basin Indians** lived along the shores of large marshes and lakes that formed during rainy periods, eating fish they caught with bone hooks and nets. Other cultures survived in the foothills of mountains between the blistering heat on the desert floor and the cold, treeless mountain heights. Hunters killed deer, antelope, and sometimes bison, as well as smaller game such as rabbits, rodents, and snakes. These broadly defined zones of habitation changed constantly, depending largely on the amount of rain.

Despite the variety and occasional abundance of animals, Great Basin peoples relied on plants as their most important food source. Unlike meat and fish, plant food could be collected and stored for long periods to protect against shortages caused by the fickle rainfall. Many Great Basin peoples gathered piñon nuts as a dietary staple. By diversifying their food sources and migrating to favorable locations to collect and store them, Great Basin peoples adapted to the severe environmental challenges of the region and maintained their Archaic hunter-gatherer way of life for centuries after Europeans arrived in AD 1492.

Ancient California Peoples

Pacific Coast Cultures

The richness of the natural environment made present-day California the most densely settled area in all of ancient North America. The land and ocean offered such ample food that **California peoples** remained hunters and gatherers for hundreds of years after AD 1492. The diversity of California's environment also encouraged corresponding variety among native peoples. The mosaic of Archaic settlements in California included about five hundred separate tribes speaking some ninety languages, each with local dialects. No other region of comparable size in ancient North America exhibited such cultural variety.

The Chumash, one of the many California cultures, emerged in the region surrounding what is now Santa Barbara about 5000 BP. Comparatively plentiful food resources — especially acorns — permitted Chumash people to establish relatively permanent villages. Conflict, evidently caused by competition for valuable acorn-gathering territory, frequently broke out among the villages, as documented by Chumash skeletons that display signs of violent deaths. Although few other

> **The richness of the natural environment made present-day California the most densely settled area in all of ancient North America.**

Chumash Necklace
Long before the arrival of Europeans, ancient Chumash people in southern California made this elegant necklace of abalone shell. The carefully formed, polished, and assembled pieces of shell illustrate the artistry of the Chumash and their access to the rich and diverse marine life of the Pacific coast. Since living abalone cling stubbornly to submerged rocks along the coast, Chumash divers presumably pried abalone from their rocky perches to obtain their delicious flesh; then one or more Chumash artisans recycled the inedible shell to make this necklace. Its iridescent splendor demonstrates that Chumash people wore beautiful as well as useful adornments. Natural History Museum of Los Angeles County.

California cultures achieved the population density and village settlements of the Chumash, all shared the hunter-gatherer way of life and reliance on acorns as a major food source.

Another rich natural environment lay along the Pacific Northwest coast. Like the Chumash, **Northwest peoples** built more or less permanent villages. After about 5500 BP, they concentrated on catching whales and large quantities of salmon, halibut,

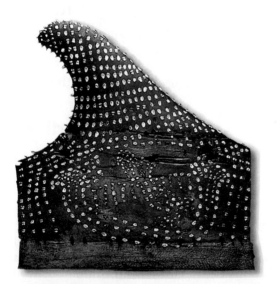

Ozette Whale Effigy
This carving of a whale fin decorated with hundreds of sea otter teeth was discovered along with thousands of other artifacts of daily life at Ozette, an ancient village on the tip of the Olympic Peninsula in present-day Washington that was inundated by a catastrophic mud slide about five hundred years ago. The fin illustrates the importance of whale hunting to the residents of Ozette, who set out in canoes, each carrying eight men armed with harpoons, to catch and kill animals weighing twenty to thirty tons each. Richard Alexander Cooke III.

and other fish, which they dried to last throughout the year. They also traded with people who lived hundreds of miles from the coast. Fishing freed Northwest peoples to develop sophisticated woodworking skills. They fashioned elaborate wood carvings that denoted wealth and status, as well as huge canoes for fishing, hunting, and conducting warfare against neighboring tribes. Much of the warfare among Archaic northwesterners grew out of attempts to defend or gain access to prime fishing sites.

Eastern Woodland Cultures

East of the Mississippi River, Archaic peoples adapted to a forest environment that included many local variants, such as the major river valleys of the Mississippi, Ohio, Tennessee, and Cumberland; the Great Lakes region; and the Atlantic coast (see Map 1.2). Throughout these diverse locales, Archaic peoples pursued similar survival strategies.

Woodland hunters stalked deer as their most important prey. Deer supplied **Woodland peoples** with food as well as hides and bones that they crafted into clothing, weapons, and many other tools. Like Archaic peoples elsewhere, Woodland Indians gathered edible plants, seeds, and nuts, especially hickory nuts, pecans, walnuts, and acorns. About 6000 BP, some Woodland groups established more or less permanent settlements of 25 to 150 people, usually near a river or lake that offered a wide variety of plant and animal resources. The existence of such settlements has permitted archaeologists to locate numerous Archaic burial sites that suggest Woodland people had a life expectancy of about eighteen years, a relatively short time to learn all the skills necessary to survive, reproduce, and adapt to change.

Around 4000 BP, Woodland cultures added two important features to their basic hunter-gatherer lifestyles: agriculture and pottery. Gourds and pumpkins that were first cultivated thousands of years earlier in Mexico spread north to Woodland peoples through trade and migration. Woodland peoples also began to cultivate local species such as sunflowers, as well as small quantities of tobacco, another import from South America. Corn, which had been grown by Mesoamerican and South American peoples since about 7000 BP, slowly traveled north with migrants and traders and eventually became a significant food crop among Eastern Woodland peoples around 2500 BP. Most likely, women learned how to plant, grow, and harvest these crops as an outgrowth of their work gathering edible wild plants. Cultivated crops added to the quantity, variety, and predictability of Woodland food sources, but they did not alter Woodland peoples' dependence on gathering wild plants, seeds, and nuts.

Like agriculture, pottery probably originated in Mexico. Traders and migrants most likely brought pottery-making skills northward along with Mesoamerican and South American seeds. Pots were more durable than baskets for cooking and the storage of food and water, but they were also much heavier and therefore were shunned by nomadic peoples. The permanent settlements of Woodland peoples made the heavy weight of pots much less important than their advantages compared to leaky and fragile baskets. While pottery and agriculture introduced changes in Woodland cultures, ancient Woodland Americans retained the other basic features of their Archaic hunter-gatherer lifestyle, which persisted in most areas to 1492 and beyond.

REVIEW   Why did Archaic Native Americans shift from big-game hunting to foraging and hunting smaller animals?

Mississippian Effigy Bowl
A Mississippian craftsman carved this effigy bowl from the mineral diorite within a century or two of AD 1200. Excavated from the Moundville site near the Black Warrior River in what is today central Alabama, the bowl was probably used in ceremonies to hold ritualistic liquids or herbs, rather than as a vessel for day-to-day drinking and eating. Depicting a crested wood duck, a figure commonly represented among the thousands of artifacts discovered at Moundville, the bowl illustrates the stunning artistry achieved by ancient Mississippians. Richard Alexander Cooke III.

► Agricultural Settlements and Chiefdoms

Among Eastern Woodland peoples and most other Archaic cultures, agriculture supplemented hunter-gatherer subsistence strategies but did not replace them. Reliance on wild animals and plants required most Archaic groups to remain small and mobile. But beginning about 4000 BP, distinctive southwestern cultures slowly began to depend on agriculture and to build permanent settlements. Later, around 2500 BP, Woodland peoples in the vast Mississippi valley began to construct burial mounds and other earthworks that suggest the existence of social and political hierarchies that archaeologists term *chiefdoms*. Although the hunter-gatherer lifestyle never entirely disappeared, the development of agricultural settlements and chiefdoms represented important innovations to the Archaic way of life.

Southwestern Cultures

Ancient Americans in present-day Arizona, New Mexico, and southern portions of Utah and Colorado developed cultures characterized by **agricultural settlements** and multiunit dwellings called pueblos. All southwestern peoples confronted the challenge of a dry climate and unpredictable fluctuations in rainfall that made the supply of wild plant food very unreliable. These ancient Americans probably adopted agriculture in response to this basic environmental uncertainty.

About 3500 BP, southwestern hunters and gatherers began to cultivate corn, their signature food crop. The demands of corn cultivation encouraged hunter-gatherers to restrict their migratory habits in order to tend the crop. A vital consideration was access to water. Southwestern Indians became irrigation experts, conserving water from streams, springs, and rainfall and distributing it to thirsty crops.

About AD 200, small farming settlements began to appear throughout southern New Mexico, marking the emergence of the **Mogollon culture**. Typically, a Mogollon settlement included a dozen pit houses, each made by digging out a rounded pit about fifteen feet in diameter and a foot or two deep and then erecting poles to support a roof of branches or dirt. Larger villages usually had one or two bigger pit houses that may have been the predecessors of the circular kivas, the ceremonial rooms that became a characteristic of nearly all southwestern settlements. About AD 900, Mogollon culture began to decline, for reasons that remain obscure. Its descendants included the Mimbres people in southwestern New Mexico, who crafted spectacular pottery adorned with human and animal designs. By about AD 1250, the Mimbres culture disappeared, for reasons unknown.

Around AD 500, while the Mogollon culture prevailed in New Mexico, other ancient people migrated from Mexico to southern Arizona and

VISUAL ACTIVITY

Ancient Agriculture

Dropping seeds into holes punched in cleared ground by a pointed stick known as a "dibble," this ancient American farmer sows a new crop while previously planted seeds — including the corn and beans immediately opposite him — bear fruit for harvest. Created by a sixteenth-century European artist, the drawing misrepresents who did the agricultural work in many ancient American cultures — namely, women rather than men. The Pierpont Morgan Library/Art Resource, NY.

READING THE IMAGE: In what ways has this ancient farmer modified and taken advantage of the natural environment?

CONNECTIONS: What were the advantages and disadvantages of agriculture compared to hunting and gathering?

Hohokam "Cigarettes"
Ancient Hohokam smokers in present-day Arizona stuffed these reeds (which probably grew near their irrigation canals) with shredded tobacco. They wrapped cotton thread around each reed to protect their fingers from heat while they inhaled the smoke of the burning tobacco. When hunting or tending their crops, Hohokam smokers probably found these "cigarettes" more convenient than their heavier and more cumbersome stone or ceramic pipes, which were better suited for sedentary occasions.
Jerry Jacka Photography.

established the distinctive **Hohokam culture**. Hohokam settlements used sophisticated grids of irrigation canals to plant and harvest crops twice a year. Hohokam settlements reflected the continuing influence of Mexican cultural practices that migrants brought with them as they traveled north. Hohokam people built sizable platform mounds and ball courts characteristic of many Mexican cultures. About AD 1400, Hohokam culture declined for reasons that remain a mystery, although the rising salinity of the soil brought about by centuries of irrigation probably caused declining crop yields and growing food shortages.

North of the Hohokam and Mogollon cultures, in a region that encompassed southern Utah and Colorado and northern Arizona and New Mexico, the **Anasazi culture** began to flourish about AD 100. The early Anasazi built pit houses on mesa tops and used irrigation much as their neighbors did to the south. Beginning around AD 1000 (again, it is not known why), some Anasazi began to move to large, multistory cliff dwellings whose spectacular ruins still exist at Mesa Verde, Colorado, and elsewhere. Other Anasazi communities—like the one whose impressive ruins can be visited at Chaco Canyon, New Mexico — erected huge stone-walled pueblos with enough rooms to house everyone in the settlement. (See "Visualizing History," page 18.) Anasazi pueblos and cliff dwellings typically included one or

> **Southwestern Indians became irrigation experts, conserving water from streams, springs, and rainfall and distributing it to thirsty crops.**

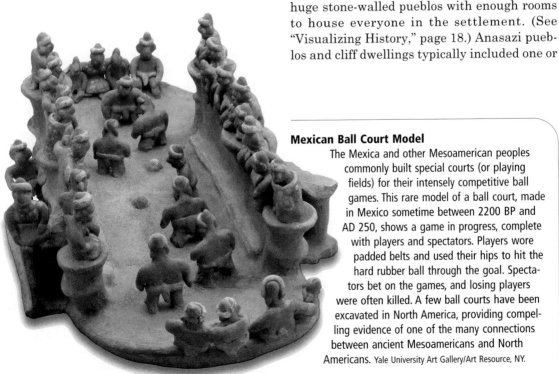

Mexican Ball Court Model
The Mexica and other Mesoamerican peoples commonly built special courts (or playing fields) for their intensely competitive ball games. This rare model of a ball court, made in Mexico sometime between 2200 BP and AD 250, shows a game in progress, complete with players and spectators. Players wore padded belts and used their hips to hit the hard rubber ball through the goal. Spectators bet on the games, and losing players were often killed. A few ball courts have been excavated in North America, providing compelling evidence of one of the many connections between ancient Mesoamericans and North Americans. Yale University Art Gallery/Art Resource, NY.

Daily Life in Chaco Canyon

Pueblo Bonito, Chaco Canyon, New Mexico

About AD 1000, Pueblo Bonito stood at the center of Chacoan culture, which ranged over 20,000 square miles in the arid region at the intersection of present-day Utah, Colorado, Arizona, and New Mexico. The largest of more than 3,600 Chacoan archaeological sites, Pueblo Bonito originally stood four or five stories tall and housed more than 600 rooms, including 35 kivas, the circular structures visible around the perimeter of the large plazas.

Chacoans covered each kiva with a roof, creating a darkened underground space for ceremonial rituals. Why might these spaces be built belowground and separated from the other rooms of the pueblo?

The exact nature of Chacoan ceremonies remains a mystery, but less mysterious are the routines of daily life that sustained the people at Pueblo Bonito for centuries. Imagine a woman setting out from the pueblo on a spring day to plant corn,

Sandal

the most important food crop. She might first strap on sandals, like the one shown here, woven from fibers of the yucca plant. What does the

more kivas used for secret ceremonies, restricted to men, that sought to communicate with the supernatural world. The alignment of Chaco buildings with solar and lunar events (such as the summer and winter solstices) suggests that Anasazi studied the sky carefully, probably because they believed supernatural celestial powers influenced their lives.

Drought began to plague the region about AD 1130, and it lasted for more than half a century, triggering the disappearance of the Anasazi culture. By AD 1200, the large Anasazi pueblos had been abandoned. The prolonged drought probably intensified conflict among pueblos and made it impossible to depend on the

techniques of irrigated agriculture that had worked for centuries. Some Anasazi migrated toward regions with more reliable rainfall and settled in Hopi, Zuñi, and Acoma pueblos that their descendants in Arizona and New Mexico have occupied ever since.

Woodland Burial Mounds and Chiefdoms

No other ancient Americans created dwellings similar to pueblos, but around 2500 BP, Woodland cultures throughout the vast watershed drained by the Mississippi River began to build burial mounds. The size of the mounds, the labor and

sandal suggest about the importance of the harvesting, processing, and weaving of yucca fibers?

To dig a hole for planting corn seeds, our imagined woman might use a digging stick like the one shown here, tipped by the horn of a mountain sheep, tightly bound with sinew to a sturdy cottonwood branch, and covered with animal hide to protect the binding. What does the digging stick suggest about the interdependence of hunting and agriculture in the daily lives of Chacoans?

Digging Stick

Once harvested and dried, corn needed to be ground in order to be cooked and eaten. By looking at the small flat stone (the *mano*) and the larger stone slab (the *metate*) shown here, can you imagine how our Chacoan woman used these tools? Some rooms at Pueblo Bonito

held numerous grinding stones like the ones shown here. What does such grouping suggest about the corn-grinding process?

To cook the cornmeal she had ground, our imagined woman would need to mix it with water. She might use a ceramic ladle like the one shown here — crafted and decorated by a pottery maker at Chaco — to dip some fresh water from a storage pot. To make a fire, she could use the Chacoan fire starter kit shown here. Can you visualize how the fire starter worked? After kindling a cooking fire, she could heat the cornmeal gruel in a ceramic pot. Once the mixture was cooked, she might use the ladle again to

Ladle

Mano and Metate

transfer servings into small bowls for eating. Why do you think the decoration at the end of the ladle's handle is blurred?

Chacoans flourished at Pueblo Bonito despite the arid climate and limited natural resources. In their daily lives, they sustained themselves by using their knowledge and skills to grow and cook corn and to craft vital items such as ceramics and footwear. Can you imagine each step in the creation of the artifacts shown here? Can you imagine the organization and scheduling of daily tasks required to make and use these basic items?

SOURCES: Pueblo Bonito, Chaco Canyon, New Mexico: Richard Alexander Cooke III; sandal, digging stick, mano and metate, fire starter kit, and ladle: Chaco Culture National Historic Park.

Fire Starter Kit

organization required to erect them, and differences in the artifacts buried with certain individuals suggest the existence of a social and political hierarchy that archaeologists term a **chiefdom**. Experts do not know the name of a single chief, nor do they know the organizational structure a chief headed. But the only way archaeologists can account for the complex and labor-intensive burial mounds and the artifacts found in them is to assume that one person — whom scholars term a *chief* — commanded the labor and obedience of very large numbers of other people, who made up the chief's chiefdom.

Between 2500 BP and 2100 BP, **Adena people** built hundreds of burial mounds radiat-

ing from central Ohio. In the mounds, the Adena usually accompanied burials with grave goods that included spear points and stone pipes as well as thin sheets of mica (a glasslike mineral) crafted into the shapes of birds, beasts, and human hands. Over the body and grave goods, Adena people piled dirt into a mound. Sometimes burial mounds were constructed all at once, but often they were built up slowly over many years.

About 2100 BP, Adena culture evolved into the more elaborate **Hopewell culture**, which lasted about five hundred years. Centered in Ohio, Hopewell culture extended throughout the enormous drainage of the Ohio and Mississippi rivers. Hopewell people built larger mounds than did their Adena predecessors and filled them with more magnificent grave goods. Burial was probably reserved for the most important members of Hopewell groups. Most people were cremated. Burial rituals appear to have brought many people together to honor the dead person and to help build the mound. Hopewell mounds were often one hundred feet in diameter and thirty feet high. Grave goods at Hopewell sites testify to the high quality of Hopewell crafts and to a thriving trade network that ranged from present-day Wyoming to Florida. Archaeologists believe that Hopewell chiefs probably played an important role in this sprawling interregional trade.

Hopewell culture declined about AD 400 for reasons that are obscure. Archaeologists speculate that bows and arrows, along with increasing reliance on agriculture, made small settlements more self-sufficient and therefore less dependent on the central authority of the Hopewell chiefs who were responsible for the burial mounds.

Four hundred years later, another mound-building culture flourished. The **Mississippian culture** emerged in the floodplains of the major southeastern river systems about AD 800 and lasted until about AD 1500. Major Mississippian sites, such as the one at Cahokia (see pages 3–4), included huge mounds with platforms on top for ceremonies and for the residences of great chiefs. Most likely, the ceremonial mounds and ritual

practices derived from Mexican cultural expressions that were brought north by traders and migrants. At Cahokia, skilled farmers supported the large population with ample crops of corn. In addition to mounds, Cahokians erected what archaeologists call woodhenges (after the famous Stonehenge in England) — long wooden poles set upright in the ground and carefully arranged in huge circles. Although the purpose of woodhenges is unknown, experts believe that Cahokians probably built them partly for celestial observations.

Cahokia and other Mississippian cultures dwindled by AD 1500. When Europeans arrived, most of the descendants of Mississippian cultures, like those of the Hopewell culture, lived in small dispersed villages supported by hunting and gathering, supplemented by agriculture. Clearly, the conditions that caused large chiefdoms to emerge — whatever they were — had changed, and chiefs no longer commanded the sweeping powers they had once enjoyed.

REVIEW   How did food-gathering strategies influence ancient cultures across North America?

▶ Native Americans in the 1490s

On the eve of European colonization in the 1490s, Native Americans lived throughout North and South America, but their total population is a subject of spirited debate among scholars. Some experts claim that Native Americans inhabiting what is now the United States and Canada numbered 18 million to 20 million, while others place the population at no more than 1 million. A prudent estimate is about 4 million, or about the same as the number of people living on the small island nation of England at that time. The vastness of the territory meant that the overall population density of North America (excluding Mesoamerica) was low, just 60 people per 100 square miles, compared to more than 8,000 in England. Native Americans were spread thin across the land because of their survival strategies of hunting, gathering, and agriculture, although variations in climate and natural resources meant that some regions were more populous than others (Figure 1.2).

Cahokia Tablet
This stone tablet excavated from the largest mound at Cahokia depicts a bird-man whose sweeping wings and facial features — especially the nose and mouth — resemble those of a bird. Crafted around AD 1100, the tablet probably played some role in rituals enacted on the mound by Cahokian people. Similar bird-like human forms have been found among other Mississippian cultures. Cahokia Mounds Historic Site.

Eastern and Great Plains Peoples

About one-third of native North Americans inhabited the enormous Woodland region east of the Mississippi River; their population density approximated the average for North America as a whole (excluding Mesoamerica). Eastern Woodland peoples clustered into three broad linguistic and cultural groups: Algonquian, Iroquoian, and Muskogean.

Algonquian tribes inhabited the Atlantic seaboard, the Great Lakes region, and much of the upper Midwest (Map 1.3). The relatively mild climate along the Atlantic permitted the coastal Algonquians to grow corn and other crops as well as to hunt and fish. Around the Great Lakes and in northern New England, however, cool summers and severe winters made agriculture impractical. Instead, the Abenaki, Penobscot, Chippewa, and other tribes concentrated on hunting and fishing, using canoes both for transportation and for gathering wild rice.

Inland from the Algonquian region, **Iroquoian** tribes occupied territories centered in Pennsylvania and upstate New York, as well as the hilly upland regions of the Carolinas and Georgia. Three features distinguished Iroquoian tribes from their neighbors. First, their success in cultivating corn and other crops allowed them to build permanent settlements, usually consisting of several bark-covered longhouses up to one hundred feet long and housing five to ten families. Second, Iroquoian societies adhered to matrilineal rules of descent. Property of all sorts belonged to women. Women headed family clans and even selected the chiefs (normally men) who governed the tribes. Third, for purposes of war and diplomacy, an Iroquoian confederation — including the Seneca, Onondaga, Mohawk, Oneida, and Cayuga tribes — formed

FIGURE 1.2   Native American Population in North America about 1492 (Estimated)
On the eve of the arrival of Europeans, Native Americans lived throughout North America, as their ancestors had for millennia (see Map 1.2, page 12). Population densities varied widely, depending in large part on the availability of natural resources, but the Pacific coast, where rich marine resources supported hunter-gatherers, had the highest concentration of people. The lowest population density was in the Arctic, where the vast expanse of land offered few resources. Overall, the population density of North America was less than 1 percent of the population density of England, which helps explain why European colonists tended to view North America as a comparatively empty wilderness.

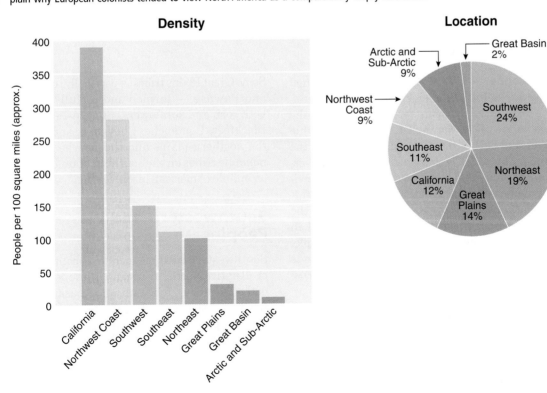

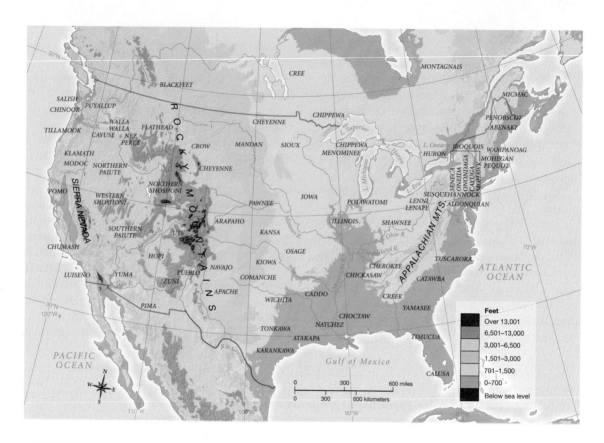

MAP 1.3

Native North Americans about 1500

Distinctive Native American peoples resided throughout the area that, centuries later, would become the United States. This map indicates the approximate location of some of the larger tribes about 1500. In the interest of legibility, many other peoples who inhabited North America at the time are omitted from the map.

the **League of Five Nations**, which remained powerful well into the eighteenth century.

Muskogean peoples spread throughout the woodlands of the Southeast, south of the Ohio River and east of the Mississippi. Including the Creek, Choctaw, Chickasaw, and Natchez tribes, Muskogeans inhabited a bountiful natural environment that provided abundant food from hunting, gathering, and agriculture. Remnants of the earlier Mississippian culture still existed in Muskogean religion. The Natchez, for example, worshipped the sun and built temple mounds modeled after those of their Mississippian ancestors, including Cahokia.

Great Plains peoples accounted for about one out of seven native North Americans. Inhabiting the huge region west of the Eastern Woodland people and east of the Rocky Mountains, many tribes had migrated to the Great Plains within the century or two before the 1490s, forced westward by Iroquoian and Algonquian tribes.

Some Great Plains tribes — especially the Mandan and Pawnee — farmed successfully, growing both corn and sunflowers. But the Teton Sioux, Blackfeet, Comanche, Cheyenne, and Crow on the northern plains and the Apache and other nomadic tribes on the southern plains depended on buffalo (American bison) for their subsistence.

Southwestern and Western Peoples

Southwestern cultures included about a quarter of all native North Americans. These descendants of the Mogollon, Hohokam, and Anasazi cultures lived in settled agricultural communities, many of them pueblos. They continued to grow corn, beans, and squash using methods they had refined for centuries.

However, their communities came under attack by a large number of warlike Athapascans who invaded the Southwest beginning around

AD 1300. The Athapascans — principally Apache and Navajo — were skillful warriors who preyed on the sedentary pueblo Indians, reaping the fruits of agriculture without the work of farming.

About a fifth of all native North Americans resided along the Pacific coast. In California, abundant acorns and nutritious marine life continued to support high population densities, but this abundance retarded the development of agriculture. Similar dependence on hunting and gathering persisted along the Northwest coast, where fishing reigned supreme. Salmon were so plentiful that at **The Dalles**, a prime fishing site on the Columbia River on the border of present-day Oregon and Washington, Northwest peoples caught millions of pounds of salmon every summer and traded their catch as far away as California and the Great Plains. Although important trading centers existed throughout North America, particularly in the Southwest, it is likely that The Dalles was the largest Native American trading center in ancient North America.

Cultural Similarities

While trading was common, all native North Americans in the 1490s still depended on hunting and gathering for a major portion of their food. Most of them also practiced agriculture. Some used agriculture to supplement hunting and gathering; for others, the balance was reversed. People throughout North America used bows, arrows, and other weapons for hunting and warfare. None of them employed writing, expressing themselves instead in many other ways: drawings sketched on stones, wood, and animal skins; patterns woven in baskets and textiles; designs painted on pottery, crafted into beadwork, or carved into effigies; and songs, dances, religious ceremonies, and burial rites.

These rich and varied cultural resources of native North Americans did not include features of life common in Europe during the 1490s. Native North Americans did not use wheels; sailing ships were unknown to them; they had no large domesticated animals such as horses, cows, or oxen; their use of metals was restricted to copper. However, the absence of these European conveniences mattered less to native North Americans than their own cultural adaptations to the natural environment local to each tribe and to the social environment among neighboring peoples. That great similarity — adaptation to natural and social environments — underlay all the cultural diversity among native North Americans.

It would be a mistake, however, to conclude that native North Americans lived in blissful harmony with nature and one another. Archaeological sites provide ample evidence of violent conflict. Skeletons, like those at Cahokia, bear the marks of wounds as well as of ritualistic human sacrifice. Religious, ethnic, economic, and familial conflicts must have occurred, but they remain in obscurity because they left few archaeological traces. In general, fear and anxiety must have been at least as common among native North Americans as feelings of peace and security.

Native North Americans not only adapted to the natural environment but also changed it in many ways. They built thousands of structures, from small dwellings to massive pueblos and enormous mounds, permanently altering the landscape. Their gathering techniques selected productive and nutritious varieties of plants, thereby shifting the balance of local plants toward useful varieties. The first stages of North American agriculture, for example, probably involved Native Americans gathering wild seeds and then sowing them in a meadow for later harvest. It is almost certain that fertile and hardy varieties of corn were developed this way, first in Mesoamerica and later in North America. To clear land for planting corn, native North Americans set fires that burned off thousands of acres of forest.

Native North Americans also used fires for hunting. Great Plains hunters often started fires to force buffalo together and make them easy to slaughter. Eastern Woodland, Southwest, and Pacific coast Indians also set fires to hunt deer and other valuable prey. Hunters crouched downwind from a brushy area while their companions set a fire upwind; as animals raced out of the burning underbrush, hunters killed them.

Throughout North America, Indians started fires along the edges of woods to burn off shrubby undergrowth and encroaching tree seedlings. These burns encouraged the growth of tender young plants that attracted deer and other game animals, bringing them within convenient range of hunters' weapons. The burns also encouraged the growth of sun-loving food plants that Indians

> **While trading was common, all native North Americans in the 1490s still depended on hunting and gathering for a major portion of their food.**

THE PROMISE OF TECHNOLOGY

Ancient American Weaving

The workbasket of a master weaver shown here illustrates the technology of ancient American textile production. Found in the Andes in a woman's grave dating from one thousand years ago, the workbasket contains tools for every stage of textile production. Weaving — like other activities such as cooking, hunting, and worship — depended above all on human knowledge passed from one person to another in cycle after cycle of teaching and learning. This cycle of teaching and learning was fragile. A weaver's knowledge could die with her if she had not taught it to somebody else. What kinds of human knowledge would have been required to make weavings with the contents of this workbasket? Museum of Fine Arts, Boston. Gift of Charles H. White, 02.680.

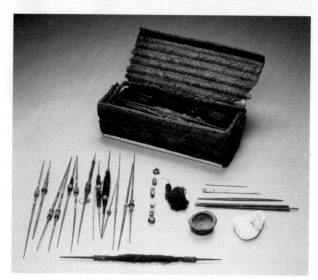

relished, such as blackberries, strawberries, and raspberries.

Because the fires set by native North Americans usually burned until they ran out of fuel or were extinguished by rain or wind, enormous regions of North America were burned over. In the long run, fires created and maintained light-dappled meadows for hunting and agriculture, cleared entangling underbrush from forests, and promoted a diverse and productive natural environment. Fires, like other activities of native North Americans, shaped the landscape of North America long before Europeans arrived in 1492.

REVIEW What cultural similarities were shared by the diverse peoples of the Western Hemisphere in the 1490s, and why?

▶ The Mexica: A Mesoamerican Culture

The vast majority of the 80 million people who lived in the Western Hemisphere in the 1490s inhabited Mesoamerica and South America, where the population approximately equaled that of Europe. Like their much less numerous counterparts north of the Rio Grande, these people lived in a natural environment of tremendous diversity. They too developed hundreds of cultures, far too numerous to catalog here. But among all these cultures, the **Mexica** stood out. (Europeans often called these people Aztecs, a name the Mexica did not use.) Their empire stretched from coast to coast across central Mexico, encompassing between 8 million and 25 million people (experts disagree about the total population). We know more about the Mexica than about any other Native American society of the time, principally because of their massive monuments and their Spanish conquerors' well-documented interest in subduing them (as discussed in chapter 2). Their significance in the history of the New World after 1492 dictates a brief discussion of their culture and society.

The Mexica began their rise to prominence about 1325, when small bands settled on a marshy island in Lake Texcoco, the site of the future city of Tenochtitlán, the capital of the Mexican empire. Resourceful, courageous, and cold-blooded warriors, the Mexica were often hired out as mercenaries for richer, more settled tribes.

By 1430, the Mexica succeeded in asserting their dominance over their former allies and leading their own military campaigns in an ever-widening arc of empire building. Despite pockets of resistance, by the 1490s the Mexica ruled an empire that covered more land than Spain and Portugal combined and contained almost three times as many people.

The empire exemplified the central values of Mexican society. The Mexica worshipped the

Mexican Human Sacrifice
This graphic portrayal of human sacrifice was drawn by a Mexican artist in the sixteenth century. It shows the typical routine of human sacrifice practiced by the Mexica for centuries before Europeans arrived. The victim climbed the temple steps and then was stretched over a stone pillar (notice the priest's helper holding the victim's legs) to make it easier for the priest to plunge a stone knife into the victim's chest, cut out the still-beating heart, and offer it to the blood-thirsty gods. The body of the previous victim has already been pushed down from the temple heights and is about to be dragged away. Scala/Art Resource, NY; Biblioteca Nazionale, Florence, Italy.

war god **Huitzilopochtli**. Warriors held the most exalted positions in the social hierarchy, even above the priests who performed the sacred ceremonies that won Huitzilopochtli's favor. In the almost constant battles necessary to defend and extend the empire, young Mexican men exhibited the courage and daring that would allow them to rise in the carefully graduated ranks of warriors. The Mexica considered capturing prisoners the ultimate act of bravery. Warriors usually turned over the captives to Mexican priests, who sacrificed them to Huitzilopochtli by cutting out their hearts. The Mexica believed that human sacrifice fed the sun's craving for blood, which kept the sun aflame and prevented the fatal descent of everlasting darkness and chaos.

The empire contributed far more to Mexican society than victims for sacrifice. At the most basic level, the empire functioned as a military and political system that collected **tribute** from subject peoples. The Mexica forced conquered tribes to pay tribute in goods, not money. Tribute redistributed to the Mexica as much as one-third of the goods produced by conquered tribes. It included everything from candidates for human sacrifice to textiles and basic food products such as corn and beans, as well as exotic luxury items such as gold, turquoise, and rare bird feathers.

Tribute reflected the fundamental relations of power and wealth that pervaded the Mexican empire. The relatively small nobility of Mexican warriors, supported by a still smaller priesthood, possessed the military and religious power to command the obedience of thousands of non-noble Mexicans and of millions of non-Mexicans in subjugated colonies. The Mexican elite exercised their power to obtain tribute and thereby to redistribute wealth from the conquered to the conquerors, from the commoners to the nobility, from the poor to the rich. This redistribution of wealth made possible the achievements of Mexican society that eventually amazed the Spaniards: the huge cities, fabulous temples, teeming markets, and luxuriant gardens, not to mention the storehouses stuffed with gold and other treasures.

On the whole, the Mexica did not interfere much with the internal government of conquered regions. Instead, they usually permitted the traditional ruling elite to stay in power — so long as they paid tribute. The conquered provinces received very little in return from the Mexica, except immunity from punitive raids. Subjugated communities felt exploited by the constant payment of tribute to the Mexica. By depending on military conquest and the constant collection of tribute, the Mexica failed to create among their subjects a belief that Mexican domination was, at some level, legitimate and equitable. The high

> By the 1490s, the Mexica ruled an empire that covered more land than Spain and Portugal combined and contained almost three times as many people.

Salado Ritual Figure
About AD 1350, this figure was carefully wrapped in a reed mat with other items and stored in a cave in a mountainous region of New Mexico by people of the Salado culture, descendants of the Mimbres, who had flourished three centuries earlier. The face of this figure is as close to a self-portrait of ancient Americans on the eve of their encounter with Europeans as we are ever likely to have. Adorned with vivid pigments, cotton string, bright feathers, and stones, the effigy testifies to the human complexity of all ancient Americans. Photography © 2000 The Art Institute of Chicago.

level of discontent among subject peoples constituted the soft, vulnerable underbelly of the Mexican empire, a fact that Spanish intruders exploited after AD 1492 to conquer the Mexica.

REVIEW   Why was tribute important in the Mexican empire?

▶ Conclusion: The World of Ancient Americans

Ancient Americans shaped the history of human beings in the New World for more than thirteen thousand years. They established continuous human habitation in the Western Hemisphere from the time the first big-game hunters crossed Beringia until 1492 and beyond. Much of their history remains irretrievably lost because they relied on oral rather than written communication. But much can be pieced together from artifacts they left behind at camps, kill sites, and ceremonial and residential centers such as Cahokia. Ancient Americans achieved their success through resourceful adaptation to the hemisphere's many and ever-changing natural environments. They also adapted to social and cultural changes caused by human beings — such as marriages, deaths, political struggles, and warfare — but the sparse evidence that has survived renders those adaptations almost entirely unknowable. Their creativity and artistry are unmistakably documented in their numerous artifacts. Those material objects sketch the only likenesses of ancient Americans we will ever have — blurred, shadowy images that are indisputably human but forever silent.

When European intruders began arriving in the Western Hemisphere in 1492, their attitudes about the promise of the New World were heavily influenced by the diverse peoples they encountered. Europeans coveted Native Americans' wealth, labor, and land, and Christian missionaries sought to save their souls. Likewise, Native Americans marveled at such European technological novelties as sailing ships, steel weapons, gunpowder, and horses, while often reserving judgment about Europeans' Christian religion.

In the four centuries following 1492, as the trickle of European strangers became a flood of newcomers from both Europe and Africa, Native Americans and settlers continued to encounter each other. Peaceful negotiations as well as violent conflicts over both land and trading rights resulted in chronic fear and mistrust. Yet even as the era of European colonization marked the beginning of the end of ancient America, the ideas, subsistence strategies, and cultural beliefs of native North Americans remained powerful among their descendants for generations and continue to persist to the present.

▶ Selected Bibliography

General Works

Robson Bonnichsen and Karen L. Turnmire, *Ice Age Peoples of North America* (1999).
Karen Olsen Bruhns and Karen R. Stothert, *Women in Ancient America* (1999).
Thomas D. Dillehay, *The Settlement of the Americas: A New Prehistory* (2000).
Brian Fagan, *Ancient North America* (2005).
Tim Flannery, *The Eternal Frontier: An Ecological History of North America and Its Peoples* (2001).
J. C. H. King, *First People, First Contacts: Native Peoples of North America* (1999).
Charles C. Mann, *1491: New Revelations of the Americas before Columbus* (2006).
Francis McManamon et al., eds., *Archaeology in America* (2008).
Steven Mithen, *After the Ice: A Global Human History, 20,000–5000 BC* (2003).
David Hurst Thomas, *Skull Wars: Kennewick Man, Archaeology, and the Battle for Native American Identity* (2000).
Nicholas Wade, *Before the Dawn: Recovering the Lost History of Our Ancestors* (2006).

Native American Cultures in Territory of Present-Day United States

Mary J. Adair, *Prehistoric Agriculture in the Central Plains* (1988).
Kenneth M. Ames and Herbert D. G. Maschner, *Peoples of the Northwest Coast: Their Archaeology and Prehistory* (1999).
Sally A. Kitt Chappell, *Cahokia: Mirror of the Cosmos* (2002).
Linda S. Cordell, *Archaeology of the Southwest* (2009).
Richard J. Dent Jr., *Chesapeake Prehistory: Old Traditions, New Directions* (1995).
E. James Dixon, *Bones, Boats, and Bison: Archeology and the First Colonization of Western North America* (1999).
Thomas E. Emerson et al., eds., *Late Woodland Societies: Tradition and Transformation across the Midcontinent* (2008).
Kendrick Frazier, *People of Chaco: A Canyon and Its Cultures* (1999).
George C. Frison, *Prehistoric Hunters of the High Plains* (2nd ed., 1991).

Sarah A. Kerr, *Beyond Chaco: Great Kiva Communities on the Mogollon Rim Frontier* (2001).
Steven A. LeBlanc, *Prehistoric Warfare in the American Southwest* (1999).
Stephen H. Lekson, *The Chaco Meridian: Centers of Political Power in the Ancient Southwest* (1999).
Jerald T. Milanich, *Archaeology of Precolumbian Florida* (1994).
Timothy R. Pauketat, *Cahokia: Ancient America's Greatest City on the Mississippi* (2009).
Jefferson Reid and Stephanie Whittlesley, *The Archaeology of Ancient Arizona* (1997).
Karl H. Schlesier, *Plains Indians, A.D. 500–1500: The Archaeological Past of Historic Groups* (1994).
Lynne Sebastian, *The Chaco Anasazi: Sociopolitical Evolution in the Prehistoric Southwest* (1992).
Lynda Shaffer, *Native Americans before 1492: The Moundbuilding Centers of the Eastern Woodlands* (1992).
Marvin T. Smith, *Coosa: The Rise and Fall of a Southeastern Mississippian Chiefdom* (2000).
Biloine Whiting Young and Melvin L. Fowler, *Cahokia: The Great Native American Metropolis* (1999).

The Mexica

David Carrasco, *City of Sacrifice: The Aztec Empire and the Role of Violence in Civilization* (1999).
Michael D. Coe and Rex Koontz, *Mexico: From the Olmecs to the Aztecs* (5th ed., 2002).
Susan Toby Evans, *Ancient Mexico and Central America: Archaeology and Culture History* (2008).
Eduardo Matos Moctezuma and Felipe Solis Olguin, *Aztecs* (2002).

▶ **FOR MORE BOOKS ABOUT TOPICS IN THIS CHAPTER,** see the Online Bibliography at **bedfordstmartins.com/roark.**

▶ **FOR ADDITIONAL PRIMARY SOURCES FROM THIS PERIOD,** see Michael Johnson, ed., *Reading the American Past,* Fifth Edition.

▶ **FOR WEB SITES, IMAGES, AND DOCUMENTS RELATED TO TOPICS AND PLACES IN THIS CHAPTER,** visit Make History at **bedfordstmartins.com/roark.**

Reviewing Chapter 1

KEY TERMS

Explain each term's significance

Archaeology and History
    artifacts (p. 5)
    archaeologists (p. 5)

The First Americans
    Pangaea (p. 6)
    continental drift (p. 6)
    Homo sapiens (p. 7)
    Beringia (p. 8)
    Paleo-Indians (p. 8)
    Clovis point (p. 10)

Archaic Hunters and Gatherers
    hunter-gatherer (p. 11)
    Archaic Indians (p. 11)
    Great Plains hunters (p. 11)
    Great Basin Indians (p. 13)
    California peoples (p. 13)
    Northwest peoples (p. 14)
    Woodland peoples (p. 14)

Agricultural Settlements and Chiefdoms
    agricultural settlements (p. 16)
    Mogollon culture (p. 16)
    Hohokam culture (p. 17)
    Anasazi culture (p. 17)
    chiefdom (p. 19)
    Adena people (p. 19)
    Hopewell culture (p. 19)
    Mississippian culture (p. 20)

Native Americans in the 1490s
    Algonquian (p. 21)
    Iroquoian (p. 21)
    League of Five Nations (p. 22)
    Muskogean (p. 22)
    The Dalles (p. 23)

The Mexica: A Mesoamerican Culture
    Mexica (p. 24)
    Huitzilopochtli (p. 25)
    tribute (p. 25)

REVIEW QUESTIONS

Use key terms and dates to support your answers.

1. Why do historians rely on the work of archaeologists to write the history of ancient America? (pp. 5–6)

2. How and why did humans migrate into North America after 15,000 BP? (pp. 6–11)

3. Why did Archaic Native Americans shift from big-game hunting to foraging and hunting smaller animals? (pp. 11–15)

4. How did food-gathering strategies influence ancient cultures across North America? (pp. 15–20)

5. What cultural similarities were shared by the diverse peoples of the Western Hemisphere in the 1490s, and why? (pp. 20–24)

6. Why was tribute important in the Mexican empire? (pp. 24–26)

MAKING CONNECTIONS

Draw on key terms, the timeline, and review questions.

1. Explain the different approaches historians and archaeologists bring to studying people in the past. How do the different kinds of evidence they draw upon shape their accounts of the human past? In your answer, cite specific examples from the history of ancient America.

2. Discuss ancient peoples' strategies for surviving in the varied climates of North America. How did their different approaches to survival contribute to the diversity of Native American cultures? What else might have contributed to the diversity?

3. For more than twelve thousand years, Native Americans both adapted to environmental change in North America and produced significant changes in the environments around them. Discuss specific examples of Native Americans' adaptation to environmental change and the changes they caused in the North American landscape.

4. Rich archaeological and manuscript sources have enabled historians to develop a detailed portrait of the Mexica on the eve of European contact. How did the Mexica establish and maintain their expansive empire?

Link events in this chapter to earlier events.

1. Did the history of ancient Americans make them unusually vulnerable to eventual conquest by European colonizers? Why or why not?

2. Do you think that ancient American history would have been significantly different if North and South America had never been disconnected from the Eurasian landmass? If so, how and why? If not, why not?

▶ **FOR PRACTICE QUIZZES AND OTHER STUDY TOOLS**, visit the Online Study Guide at bedfordstmartins.com/roark.

TIMELINE

NOTE: Major events are depicted below in chronological order, but the time scale between events varies from millennia to centuries.

(BP is an abbreviation used by archaeologists for "years before the present.")

ca. 400,000 BP	• Modern humans (*Homo sapiens*) evolve in Africa.
ca. 25,000–14,000 BP	• Wisconsin glaciation exposes Beringia, land bridge between Siberia and Alaska.
ca. 15,000 BP	• First humans arrive in North America.
ca. 13,500–13,000 BP	• Paleo-Indians in North and Central America use Clovis points to hunt big game.
ca. 11,000 BP	• Mammoths and many other big-game prey of Paleo-Indians become extinct.
ca. 10,000–3000 BP	• Archaic hunter-gatherer cultures dominate ancient America.
ca. 5000 BP	• Chumash culture emerges in southern California.
ca. 4000 BP	• Some Eastern Woodland peoples begin growing gourds and pumpkins and making pottery.
ca. 3500 BP	• Southwestern cultures begin corn cultivation.
ca. 2500 BP	• Eastern Woodland cultures start to build burial mounds, cultivate corn.
ca. 2500–2100 BP	• Adena culture develops in Ohio.
ca. 2100 BP–AD 400	• Hopewell culture emerges in Ohio and Mississippi valleys.
ca. AD 200–900	• Mogollon culture develops in New Mexico.
ca. AD 500	• Bows and arrows appear in North America south of Arctic.
ca. AD 500–1400	• Hohokam culture develops in Arizona.
ca. AD 800–1500	• Mississippian culture flourishes in Southeast.
ca. AD 1000–1200	• Anasazi peoples build cliff dwellings at Mesa Verde and pueblos at Chaco Canyon.
ca. AD 1325–1500	• Mexica conquer neighboring peoples and establish Mexican empire.
AD 1492	• Christopher Columbus arrives in New World, beginning European colonization.

**SPANISH
GOLD COIN**
This Spanish gold
coin celebrates the Spanish
monarchs Queen Isabella and King Ferdinand, who patronized
the voyages of Christopher Columbus that eventually
transformed Europeans' knowledge of the world. Minted
around 1500, before Spaniards captured the gold hoards of
Mexico and Peru, the coin illustrates the use of gold as the
premier form of currency in sixteenth-century Europe. Since gold
epitomized wealth and power, Spaniards spared no effort to
confiscate as much gold in the New World as possible and ship it
back to the Spanish monarchy. The map in the background
depicts a European view of Brazil in 1519.

2

Europeans Encounter the New World

1492–1600

TWO BABIES WERE BORN IN SOUTHERN EUROPE IN 1451, SEPARATED by about seven hundred miles and a chasm of social, economic, and political power. The baby girl, Isabella, was born in a king's castle in what is now Spain. The baby boy, Christopher, was born in the humble dwelling of a weaver near Genoa in what is now Italy. Forty-one years later, the lives and aspirations of these two people intersected in southern Spain and permanently changed the history of the world.

Isabella was named for her mother, the Portuguese second wife of King John II of Castile, whose monarchy encompassed the large central region of present-day Spain. She grew up amid the swirling countercurrents of dynastic rivalries and political conflict. Isabella's father died when she was three, and her half-brother, Henry, assumed the throne. Henry proved an ineffective ruler who made many enemies among the nobility and the clergy.

As a young girl, Isabella was educated by private tutors who were bishops in the Catholic Church, and her learning helped her become a strong, resolute woman. King Henry tried to control her and plotted to undermine her independence by arranging her marriage to one of several eligible sons of European monarchs. Isabella refused to accept Henry's choices and maneuvered to obtain Henry's consent that she would succeed him as monarch. She then selected Ferdinand, a man she had never met, to be her husband. A year younger than Isabella, Ferdinand was the king of Aragon, a region encompassing a triangular slice of northeastern Spain bordering France and the Mediterranean Sea. The couple married in 1469, and Isabella became queen when Henry died in 1474.

Queen Isabella and King Ferdinand fought to defeat other claimants to Isabella's throne, to unite the monarchies of Spain under their rule, to complete the long campaign known as the Reconquest to eliminate Muslim strongholds on the Iberian Peninsula, and to purify Christianity. In their intense decades-long campaign to defend Christianity, persecute Jews, and defeat Muslims, Isabella and Ferdinand traveled throughout their realm, staying

Spanish Tapestry
This detail from a lavish sixteenth-century tapestry depicts Columbus (kneeling) receiving a box of jewels from Queen Isabella (whose husband, King Ferdinand, stands slightly behind her) in appreciation for his voyages to the New World. These gifts and others signified the monarchs' elation about the immense promise of the lands and peoples that Columbus encountered. The exact nature of that promise did not become clear until after the deaths of both Columbus and Isabella, when Cortés invaded and eventually conquered Mexico between 1519 and 1521. © Julio Conoso/Corbis Sygma.

a month or two in one place after another, meeting local notables, hearing appeals and complaints, and impressing all with their regal splendor.

Tagging along in the royal cavalcade of advisers, servants, and assorted hangers-on that moved around Spain in 1485 was Christopher Columbus, a deeply religious man obsessed with obtaining support for his scheme to sail west across the Atlantic Ocean to reach China and Japan. An experienced sailor, Columbus had become convinced that it was possible to reach the riches of the East by sailing west. Columbus pitched his idea to the king of Portugal in 1484. The king's geography experts declared Columbus's proposal impossible: The globe was too big, the ocean between Europe and China was too wide, and no sailors or ships could possibly withstand such a long voyage.

Rejected in Portugal, Columbus made his way to the court of Isabella and Ferdinand in 1485 and joined their entourage until he finally won an audience with the monarchs in January 1486. They too rejected his plan. Doggedly, year after year Columbus kept trying to interest Isabella until finally she changed her mind. In mid-April 1492, hoping to expand the wealth and influence of her monarchy, she summoned Columbus and agreed to support his risky scheme.

Columbus hurriedly organized his expedition, and just before sunrise on August 3, 1492, three ships under his command caught the tide out of a harbor in southern Spain and sailed west. Barely two months later, in the predawn moonlight of October 12, 1492, he glimpsed an island on the western horizon. At daybreak, Columbus rowed ashore, and as the curious islanders crowded around, he claimed possession of the land for Isabella and Ferdinand.

Columbus's encounters with Isabella and those islanders in 1492 transformed the history of the world and unexpectedly made Spain the most important European power in the Western Hemisphere for more than a century. Long before 1492, other Europeans had restlessly expanded the limits of the world known to them, and their efforts helped make possible Columbus's voyage. But without Isabella's sponsorship, it is doubtful that Columbus could have made his voyage. With her support and his own unflagging determination, Columbus blazed a watery trail to a world that neither he nor anyone else in Europe knew existed. As Isabella, Ferdinand, and subsequent Spanish monarchs sought to reap the rewards of what they considered their emerging empire in the West, they created a distinctively Spanish colonial society that conquered and killed Native Americans, built new institutions, and extracted great wealth that enriched the Spanish monarchy and made Spain the envy of other Europeans.

► Europe in the Age of Exploration

Historically, the East — not the West — attracted Europeans. Around the year 1000, Norsemen ventured west across the North Atlantic and founded a small fishing village at L'Anse aux Meadows on the tip of Newfoundland that lasted only a decade or so. After the world's climate cooled, choking the North Atlantic with ice, the Norse left. Viking sagas memorialized the Norse "discovery," but it had virtually no other impact in the New World or in Europe. Instead, wealthy Europeans developed a taste for luxury goods from Asia and Africa, and merchants competed to satisfy that taste. As Europeans traded with the East and with one another, they acquired new information about the world they inhabited. A few people — sailors, merchants, and aristocrats — took the risks of exploring beyond the limits of the world known to Europeans. Those risks were genuine and could be deadly. But sometimes they paid off in new information, new opportunities, and eventually the discovery of a world entirely new to Europeans.

Mediterranean Trade and European Expansion

From the twelfth through the fifteenth centuries, spices, silk, carpets, ivory, gold, and other exotic goods traveled overland from Persia, Asia Minor, India, and Africa and then were funneled into continental Europe through Mediterranean trade routes (Map 2.1). Dominated primarily by the Italian cities of Venice, Genoa, and Pisa, this lucrative trade enriched Italian merchants and bankers, who fiercely defended their near monopoly of access to Eastern goods. The vitality of the Mediterranean trade offered few incentives

MAP 2.1

European Trade Routes and Portuguese Exploration in the Fifteenth Century
The strategic geographic position of Italian cities as a conduit for overland trade from Asia was slowly undermined during the fifteenth century by Portuguese explorers who hopscotched along the coast of Africa and eventually found a sea route that opened the rich trade of the East to Portuguese merchants.

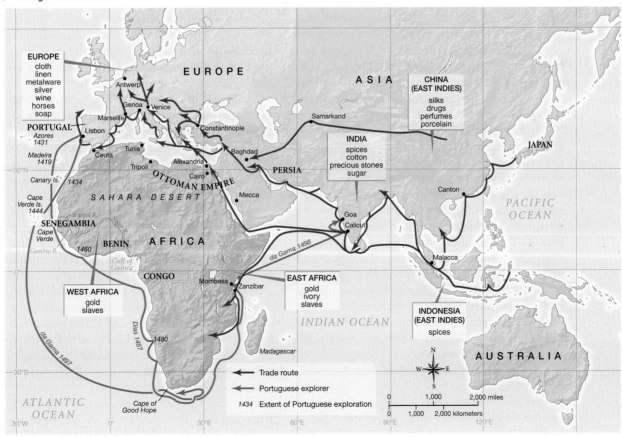

to look for alternatives. New routes to the East and the discovery of new lands were the stuff of fantasy.

Preconditions for turning fantasy into reality developed in fifteenth-century Europe. In the mid-fourteenth century, Europeans suffered a catastrophic epidemic of bubonic plague. The **Black Death**, as it was called, killed about a third of the European population. This devastating pestilence had major long-term consequences. By drastically reducing the population, it made Europe's limited supply of food more plentiful for survivors. Many survivors inherited property from plague victims, giving them new chances for advancement. The turmoil caused by the plague also prompted many peasants to move away from their homes and seek opportunities elsewhere.

Understandably, most Europeans perceived the world as a place of alarming risks where the delicate balance of health, harvests, and peace could quickly be tipped toward disaster by epidemics, famine, and violence. Most people protected themselves from the constant threat of calamity by worshipping the supernatural, by living amid kinfolk and friends, and by maintaining good relations with the rich and powerful. But the insecurity and uncertainty of fifteenth-century European life also encouraged a few people to take greater risks, such as embarking on dangerous sea voyages through uncharted waters to points unknown.

> Portugal devoted far more energy and wealth to the geographic exploration of the world between 1415 and 1460 than all other European countries combined.

In European societies, exploration promised fame and fortune to those who succeeded, whether they were kings or commoners. Monarchs such as Isabella who hoped to enlarge their realms and enrich their dynasties also had reasons to sponsor journeys of exploration. More territory meant more subjects who could pay more taxes, provide more soldiers, and participate in more commerce, magnifying the monarch's power and prestige. Voyages of exploration also could stabilize the monarch's regime by diverting unruly noblemen toward distant lands. Some explorers, such as Columbus, were commoners who hoped to be elevated to the aristocracy as a reward for their daring achievements.

Scientific and technological advances also helped set the stage for exploration. The invention of movable type by Johannes Gutenberg around 1450 in Germany made printing easier and cheaper, stimulating the diffusion of information, including news of discoveries, among literate Europeans; one such European was Isabella, who had an extensive personal library. By 1400, crucial navigational aids employed by maritime explorers such as Columbus were already available: compasses; hourglasses, which allowed for the calculation of elapsed time, useful in estimating speed; and the astrolabe and quadrant, which were devices for determining latitude. Many people throughout fifteenth-century Europe knew about these and other technological advances, but the Portuguese were the first to use them in a campaign to sail beyond the limits of the world known to Europeans.

A Century of Portuguese Exploration

With only 2 percent of the population of Christian Europe, Portugal devoted far more energy and wealth to the geographic exploration of the world between 1415 and 1460 than all other European countries combined. Facing the Atlantic on the Iberian Peninsula, the Portuguese lived on the fringes of the thriving Mediterranean trade. As a Christian kingdom, Portugal cooperated with Spain in the **Reconquest**, the centuries-long drive to expel the Muslims from the Iberian Peninsula. The religious zeal that propelled the Reconquest also justified expansion into what the Portuguese considered heathen lands. A key victory came in 1415 when Portuguese forces conquered Ceuta, the Muslim bastion at the mouth of the Strait of Gibraltar that had blocked Portugal's access to the Atlantic coast of Africa.

The most influential advocate of Portuguese exploration was **Prince Henry the Navigator**, son of the Portuguese king (and great-uncle of Queen Isabella of Spain). From 1415 until his death in 1460, Henry collected the latest information about sailing techniques and geography, supported new crusades against the Muslims, sought fresh sources of trade to fatten Portuguese pocketbooks, and pushed explorers to go farther still. Expeditions to Africa also promised to wrest wheat fields from their Moroccan owners and to obtain gold, the currency of European trade. Gold was scarce in Europe because the quickening pace of commerce increased the need for currency while purchases in the East drained gold away from Europeans.

Neither the Portuguese nor anybody else in Europe knew the immensity of Africa or the

Ivory Saltcellar

This exquisitely carved sixteenth-century ivory saltcellar combines African materials, craftsmanship, and imagery in an artifact for Portuguese tables. Designed to hold table salt in the central globe, the saltcellar portrays a victim about to be beheaded by the armed man who has already beheaded five others. To Portuguese eyes, the saltcellar dramatized African brutality and quietly suggested the superiority of Portuguese virtues and their beneficial influence in Africa. Archivio Fotografico del Museo Preistorico Etnografico L. Pigorini, Roma.

length or shape of its coastline, which, in reality, fronted the Atlantic for more than seven thousand miles — about five times the considerable distance from Genoa, Columbus's hometown, to Lisbon, the Portuguese capital. At first, Portuguese mariners cautiously hugged the west coast of Africa, seldom venturing beyond sight of land. By 1434, they had reached the northern edge of the Sahara Desert, where strong westerly currents swept them out to sea. They soon learned to ride those currents far away from the coast before catching favorable winds that turned them back toward land, a technique that allowed them to reach Cape Verde by 1444 (see Map 2.1).

To stow the supplies necessary for long periods at sea and to withstand the battering of waves in the open ocean, the Portuguese developed the caravel, a fast, sturdy ship that became explorers' vessel of choice. In caravels, Portuguese mariners sailed into and around the Gulf of Guinea and as far south as the Congo by 1480.

Fierce African resistance confined Portuguese expeditions to coastal trading posts, where they bartered successfully for gold, slaves, and ivory. Powerful African kingdoms welcomed Portuguese trading ships loaded with iron goods, weapons, textiles, and ornamental shells. Portuguese merchants learned that establishing relatively peaceful trading posts on the coast was far more profitable than attempting the violent conquest and colonization of inland regions. In the 1460s, the Portuguese used African slaves to develop sugar plantations on the Cape Verde Islands, inaugurating an association between enslaved Africans and plantation labor that would be transplanted to the New World in the centuries to come.

About 1480, Portuguese explorers, eager to bypass the Mediterranean merchants, began a conscious search for a sea route to Asia. In 1488, Bartolomeu Dias sailed around the Cape of Good Hope at the southern tip of Africa and hurried back to Lisbon with the exciting news that it appeared to be possible to sail on to India and China. In 1498, after ten years of careful preparation, Vasco da Gama commanded the first Portuguese fleet to sail to India. Portugal quickly capitalized on the commercial potential of da Gama's new sea route. By the early sixteenth century, the Portuguese controlled a far-flung commercial empire in India, Indonesia, and China (collectively referred to as the East Indies). Their new sea route to the East eliminated overland travel and allowed Portuguese merchants to charge much lower prices for the Eastern goods they imported and still make handsome profits.

Sixteenth-Century Pomander
This jewel-encrusted pomander was designed to be stuffed with aromatic spices brought to Europe through the Mediterranean trade routes dominated by Italians or through the Indian Ocean trade route around Africa dominated by the Portuguese. A wealthy European wore the pomander on a chain at the neck or waist and sniffed it to overcome noxious stenches common in daily life. Ordinary Europeans could not afford the pomander or the spices, and simply had to live with vile odors. The pomander illustrates the strong connection in the sixteenth century between fashion, luxury, and the spice trade. The Burghley House Collection, Stamford, England EWA008553.

Portugal's African explorations during the fifteenth century broke the monopoly of the old Mediterranean trade with the East, dramatically expanded the world known to Europeans, established a network of Portuguese outposts in Africa and Asia, and developed methods of sailing the high seas that Columbus employed on his revolutionary voyage west.

> **REVIEW** Why did European exploration expand dramatically in the fifteenth century?

▶ A Surprising New World in the Western Atlantic

In retrospect, the Portuguese seemed ideally qualified to venture across the Atlantic. They had pioneered the frontiers of seafaring, exploration, and geography for almost a century. However, Portuguese and most other experts believed that sailing west across the Atlantic to Asia was literally impossible. The European discovery of America required someone bold enough to believe that the experts were wrong and that the risks were surmountable. That person was **Christopher Columbus**. His explorations inaugurated a geographic revolution that forever altered Europeans' understanding of the world and its peoples, including themselves. Columbus's landfall in the Caribbean initiated a thriving exchange between the people, ideas, cultures, and institutions of the Old and New Worlds that continues to this day.

The Explorations of Columbus

Columbus went to sea when he was about fourteen, and he eventually made his way to Lisbon, where he married Felipa Moniz, whose father had been raised in the household of Prince Henry the Navigator. Through Felipa, Columbus gained access to explorers' maps and information about the tricky currents and winds encountered in sailing the Atlantic. Columbus himself ventured into the Atlantic frequently and at least twice sailed to the central coast of Africa.

Like other educated Europeans, Columbus believed that the earth was a sphere and that theoretically it was possible to reach the East Indies by sailing west. With flawed calculations, he estimated that Asia was only about 2,500 miles away, a shorter distance than Portuguese ships routinely sailed between Lisbon and the Congo. In fact, the shortest distance to Japan from Europe's jumping-off point was nearly 11,000 miles. Convinced by his erroneous calculations, Columbus became obsessed with a scheme to prove he was right.

In 1492, after years of unsuccessful lobbying in Portugal and Spain, plus overtures to England and France, Columbus finally won financing for his journey from the Spanish monarchs, **Queen Isabella and King Ferdinand**. They saw Columbus's venture as an inexpensive gamble: The potential loss was small, but the potential gain was huge. They gave Columbus a letter of introduction to China's Grand Khan, the ruler they hoped he would meet upon reaching the other side of the Atlantic.

After scarcely three months of frantic preparation, Columbus and his small fleet — the *Niña* and *Pinta*, both caravels, and the *Santa María*, a larger merchant vessel — headed west. Six weeks after leaving the Canary Islands, where he stopped for supplies, Columbus landed on a tiny Caribbean island about three hundred miles north of the eastern tip of Cuba.

Columbus claimed possession of the island for Isabella and Ferdinand and named it San Salvador, in honor of the Savior, Jesus Christ. He called the islanders "Indians," assuming that they inhabited the East Indies somewhere near Japan or China. The islanders called themselves **Tainos**, which in their language meant "good" or "noble." The Tainos inhabited most of the Caribbean islands Columbus visited on his first voyage, as had their ancestors for more than two centuries. An agricultural people, the Tainos grew cassava, corn, cotton, tobacco, and other crops. Instead of dressing in the finery Columbus had expected to find in the East Indies, the Tainos "all . . . go around as naked as their mothers bore them," Columbus wrote. Although Columbus concluded that the Tainos "had no religion," in reality they worshipped gods they called *zemis,* ancestral spirits who inhabited natural objects such as trees and stones. The Tainos mined a little gold, but they had no riches. "It seemed to me that they were a people very poor in everything," Columbus wrote.

What the Tainos thought about Columbus and his sailors we can only surmise, since they left no written documents. At first, Columbus got the impression that the Tainos believed the Spaniards came from heaven. But after six weeks of encounters, Columbus decided that "the people of these lands do not understand me nor do I, nor anyone else that I have with me, [understand] them. And many times I understand one thing said by these Indians . . . for another, its contrary." The confused communication between the Spaniards and the Tainos suggests how strange each group seemed to the other. Columbus's perceptions of the Tainos were shaped by European attitudes, ideas, and expectations, just as the Tainos' perceptions of the Europeans were no doubt colored by their own culture.

Columbus and his men understood that they had made a momentous discovery, but they found it frustrating. Although the Tainos proved friendly, they did not have the riches Columbus expected to find in the East. In mid-January 1493, he started back to Spain, where Queen Isabella and King Ferdinand were overjoyed by his news. With a voyage that had lasted barely eight months, Columbus appeared to have catapulted Spain from the position of an also-ran in the race for a sea route to Asia into that of a serious challenger to Portugal, whose explorers had not yet sailed to India or China. The Spanish monarchs elevated Columbus to the nobility and awarded him the title "Admiral of the Ocean Sea." The seven Tainos Columbus had brought to Spain were baptized as Christians, and King Ferdinand became their godfather.

Soon after Columbus returned to Spain, the Spanish monarchs rushed to obtain the pope's support for their claim to the new lands in the West. When the pope, a Spaniard, complied, the Portuguese feared that their own claims to recently discovered territories were in jeopardy. To protect their claims, the Portuguese and Spanish monarchs negotiated the **Treaty of Tordesillas** in 1494. The treaty drew an imaginary line eleven hundred miles west of the Canary Islands (Map 2.2). Land discovered west of the line (namely, the islands that Columbus discovered and any additional land that might be found) belonged to Spain; Portugal claimed land to the east (namely, its African and East Indian trading empire).

Isabella and Ferdinand moved quickly to realize the promise of their new claims. In the fall of 1493, they dispatched Columbus once again, this time with a fleet of seventeen ships and more than a thousand men who planned to locate the Asian mainland, find gold, and get rich. When Columbus returned to the island where he had left behind thirty-nine of his sailors (because of a shipwreck near the end of his first voyage), he received

Columbus's First Voyage to the New World, 1492–1493

Columbus called the islanders "Indians," assuming that they inhabited the East Indies somewhere near Japan or China.

Taino Zemi Basket
This basket is an example of the effigies Tainos made to represent zemis, or deities. The effigy illustrates the artistry of the basket maker, almost certainly a Taino woman. Crafted sometime between 1492 and about 1520, the effigy demonstrates that the Tainos readily incorporated goods obtained through contacts with Europeans into their own traditional beliefs and practices. The basket maker used African ivory and European mirrors as well as Native American fibers, dyes, and designs. © The Trustees of the British Museum.

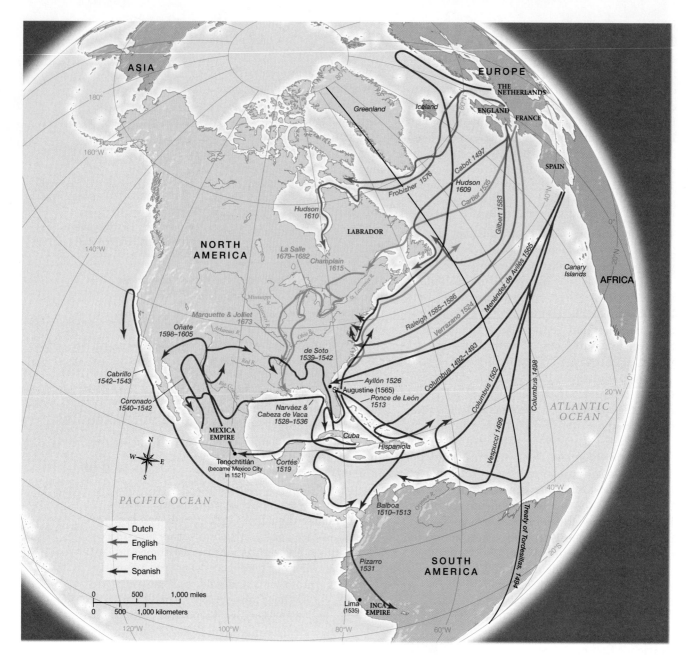

MAP ACTIVITY

Map 2.2   European Exploration in Sixteenth-Century America
This map illustrates the approximate routes of early European explorations of the New World.

READING THE MAP: Which countries were most actively exploring the New World? Which countries were exploring later than others?

CONNECTIONS: What were the motivations behind the explorations? What were the motivations for colonization?

disturbing news. In his absence, his sailors had terrorized the Tainos by kidnapping and sexually abusing their women. In retaliation, the Tainos had killed all the sailors. This small episode prefigured much of what was to happen in encounters between Native Americans and Europeans in the years ahead.

Before Columbus died in 1506, he returned to the New World two more times (in 1498 and 1502) without relinquishing his belief that the East Indies were there, someplace. Other explorers continued to search for a passage to the East or some other source of profit. Before long, however, prospects of beating the Portuguese to Asia began to dim along with the hope of finding vast hoards of gold. Nonetheless, Columbus's discoveries forced sixteenth-century Europeans to think about the world in new ways. It was possible to sail from Europe to the western rim of the Atlantic and return to Europe. Most important, Columbus's voyages proved that lands and peoples entirely unknown to Europeans lay across the Atlantic.

The Geographic Revolution and the Columbian Exchange

Within thirty years of Columbus's initial discovery, Europeans' understanding of world geography underwent a revolution. An elite of perhaps twenty thousand people with access to Europe's royal courts and trading centers learned the exciting news about global geography. But it took a generation of additional exploration before they could comprehend the larger contours of Columbus's discoveries.

European monarchs hurried to stake their claims to the newly discovered lands. In 1497, King Henry VII of England, who had spurned Columbus a decade earlier, sent John Cabot to look for a **Northwest Passage** to the Indies across the North Atlantic (see Map 2.2). Cabot reached the tip of Newfoundland, which he believed was part of Asia, and hurried back to England, where he assembled a small fleet and sailed west in 1498. But he was never heard from again.

Three thousand miles to the south, a Spanish expedition landed on the northern coast of South America in 1499 accompanied by Amerigo Vespucci, an Italian businessman. In 1500, Pedro Álvars Cabral commanded a Portuguese fleet bound for the Indian Ocean that accidentally made landfall on the east coast of Brazil as it looped westward into the Atlantic.

By 1500, European experts knew that several large chunks of land cluttered the western Atlantic. A few cartographers speculated that these chunks were connected to one another in a landmass that was not Asia. In 1507, Martin Waldseemüller, a German cartographer, published the first map that showed the New World separate from Asia; he named the land America, in honor of Amerigo Vespucci.

Two additional discoveries confirmed Waldseemüller's speculation. In 1513, Vasco Núñez de Balboa crossed the

Isthmus of Panama and reached the Pacific Ocean. Clearly, more water lay between the New World and Asia. **Ferdinand Magellan** discovered just how much water when he led an expedition to circumnavigate the globe in 1519. Sponsored by King Charles I of Spain, Magellan's voyage took him first to the New World, around the southern tip of South America, and into the Pacific late in November 1520. Crossing the Pacific took almost four months, decimating his crew with hunger and thirst. Magellan himself was killed by Philippine tribesmen. A remnant of his expedition continued on to the Indian Ocean and managed to transport a cargo of spices back to Spain in 1522.

In most ways, Magellan's voyage was a disaster. One ship and 18 men crawled back from an expedition that had begun with five ships and more than 250 men. But the geographic information it provided left no doubt that America was a continent separated from Asia by the enormous Pacific Ocean. Magellan's voyage made clear that it was possible to sail west to reach the East Indies, but that was a terrible way to go. After Magellan, most Europeans who sailed west set their sights on the New World, not on Asia.

Columbus's arrival in the Caribbean anchored the western end of what might be imagined as a sea bridge that spanned the Atlantic, connecting the Western Hemisphere to Europe. Somewhat like the Beringian land bridge traversed by the first Americans millennia earlier (see chapter 1), the new sea bridge reestablished a connection between the Eastern and Western Hemispheres. The Atlantic Ocean, which had previously isolated America from Europe, became an aquatic highway, thanks to sailing technology, intrepid seamen, and their European sponsors. This new sea bridge launched the **Columbian exchange**, a transatlantic trade of goods, people, and ideas that has continued ever since.

Maize Goddess

The arrival of Columbus in the New World started an ongoing transatlantic exchange of goods, people, and ideas. In 1493, Columbus told Isabella and Ferdinand about an amazingly productive New World plant he called *maize*, his version of the Taino word *mahiz*, which means "life-giver." This maize, or corn, goddess crafted in Peru about a thousand years before Columbus arrived in the New World suggests ancient Americans' worship of corn. Within a generation after 1493, corn had been carried across the Atlantic and was growing in Europe, the Middle East, Africa, India, and China. Bildarchiv Preussischer Kulturbesitz/Art Resource, NY.

Spaniards brought novelties to the New World that were commonplace in Europe, including Christianity, iron technology, sailing ships, firearms, wheeled vehicles, horses and other domesticated animals, and much else. Unknowingly, they also carried many Old World microorganisms that caused devastating epidemics of smallpox, measles, and other diseases that would kill the vast majority of Indians during the sixteenth century and continue to decimate survivors in later centuries. European diseases made the Columbian exchange catastrophic for Native Americans. In the long term, these diseases were decisive in transforming the dominant peoples of the New World from descendants of Asians, who had inhabited the hemisphere for millennia, to descendants of Europeans and Africans, the recent arrivals from the Old World.

Ancient American goods, people, and ideas made the return trip across the Atlantic. Europeans were introduced to New World foods such as corn and potatoes that became important staples in European diets, especially for poor people. Columbus's sailors became infected with syphilis in sexual encounters with New World women and unwittingly carried the deadly bacteria back to Europe. New World tobacco created a European fashion for smoking that ignited quickly and has yet to be extinguished. But for almost a generation after 1492, this Columbian exchange did not reward the Spaniards with the riches they yearned to find.

REVIEW How did Columbus's discoveries help revolutionize Europeans' understanding of global geography?

▶ Spanish Exploration and Conquest

During the sixteenth century, the New World helped Spain become the most powerful monarchy in both Europe and the Americas. Initially, Spanish expeditions reconnoitered the Caribbean, scouted stretches of the Atlantic coast, and established settlements on the large islands of Hispaniola, Puerto Rico, Jamaica, and Cuba. Spaniards enslaved Caribbean tribes and put them to work growing crops and mining gold. But the profits from these early ventures barely covered the costs of maintaining the settlers. After almost thirty years of exploration, the promise of Columbus's discovery seemed illusory.

In 1519, however, that promise was spectacularly fulfilled by Hernán Cortés's march into Mexico. By about 1545, Spanish conquests extended from northern Mexico to southern Chile, and New World riches filled Spanish treasure chests. Cortés's expedition served as the model for Spaniards' and other Europeans' expectations that the New World could yield bonanza profits for its conquerors. Meanwhile, forced labor and deadly epidemics meant that native populations plummeted.

The Conquest of Mexico

Hernán Cortés, an obscure nineteen-year-old Spaniard seeking adventure and the chance to make a name for himself, arrived in the New

Smallpox Victim in Hut
This sixteenth-century Mexican drawing shows a victim of smallpox lying in a hut made of branches. Spaniards brought smallpox to Mexico where it sickened and killed millions. A highly contagious and often fatal viral infection, smallpox spread like wildfire among native Americans in the New World who, unlike most Europeans, had no previous exposure to the virus and therefore had developed no immunity to it. Smallpox and other European microbes decimated native Americans, greatly disfiguring and demoralizing many of those who survived. At the time, nearly everybody recognized the horrors of smallpox, but nobody knew how to prevent or cure it. Arxiu Mas.

World in 1504. Throughout his twenties, he fought in the conquest of Cuba and elsewhere in the Caribbean. In 1519, the governor of Cuba authorized Cortés to organize an expedition of about six hundred men and eleven ships to investigate rumors of a fabulously wealthy kingdom somewhere in the interior of the mainland.

A charismatic and confident man, Cortés could not speak any Native American language. Landing first on the Yucatán peninsula with his ragtag army, he had the good fortune to receive from a local chief of the Tobasco people the gift of a young girl named **Malinali**. She spoke several native languages, including Mayan and Nahuatl, the language of the **Mexica**, the most powerful people in what is now Mexico and Central America (see chapter 1). Malinali had acquired her linguistic skills painfully. Born into a family of Mexican nobility, she learned Nahuatl as a child. After her father died and her mother remarried, her stepfather sold her as a slave to Mayan-speaking Indians, who subsequently gave her to the Tobascans. Malinali, whom the Spaniards called Marina, soon learned Spanish and became Cortés's interpreter. She also became one of Cortés's several mistresses and bore him a son. (Several years later, after Cortés's wife arrived in New Spain, Cortés cast Marina aside, and she married one of his soldiers.) Malinali was the Spaniards' essential conduit of communication with the Indians. "Without her help," wrote one of the Spaniards who accompanied Cortés, "we would not have understood the language of New Spain and Mexico." Malinali allowed Cortés to talk and fight with Indians along the Gulf coast of Mexico as he tried to discover the location of the fabled kingdom. By the time Marina died, the people among whom she had grown up — who had taught her languages, enslaved her, and given her to Cortés — had been conquered by the Spaniards with her help.

In **Tenochtitlán**, the capital of the Mexican empire, the emperor **Montezuma** heard about some strange creatures sighted along the coast. (Montezuma and his people are often called Aztecs, but they called themselves Mexica.) He feared that the

strangers were led by the god Quetzalcoatl, who was returning to Tenochtitlán to fulfill a prophecy of the Mexican religion. Marina had told Cortés about Quetzalcoatl, and when Montezuma's messengers arrived, Cortés donned the regalia they had brought, almost certain proof to the Mexica that he was indeed the god they feared. The Spaniards astounded the messengers by blasting their cannons and displaying their swords.

The messengers hurried back to Montezuma with their amazing news. The emperor sent representatives to bring the strangers large quantities of food and perhaps postpone their dreaded arrival in the capital. Before the Mexican messengers served food to the Spaniards, they sacrificed several human hostages and soaked the food in their blood. This fare disgusted the Spaniards and might have been enough to turn them back to Cuba. But along with the food, the Mexica also brought the Spaniards another gift, a "disk in the shape of a sun, as big as a cartwheel and made of very fine gold," as one of the Mexica recalled. Here was conclusive evidence that the rumors of fabulous riches heard by Cortés had some basis in fact.

In August 1519, Cortés marched inland to find Montezuma. Leading about 350 men armed with swords, lances, and muskets and supported by ten cannons, four smaller guns, and sixteen horses, Cortés had to live off the land, establishing peaceful relations with indigenous tribes when he could and killing them when he thought it necessary. On November 8, 1519, Cortés reached Tenochtitlán, where Montezuma welcomed him. After presenting Cortés with gifts, Montezuma ushered the Spaniards to the royal palace and showered them with lavish hospitality. The Spaniards were stunned by the magnificence that surrounded them. One of Cortés's soldiers recalled that "it all seemed like an enchanted vision . . . [or] a dream." Quickly, Cortés took Montezuma hostage and held him under house arrest, hoping to make him a puppet through whom the Spaniards could rule the Mexican empire. This uneasy peace existed for several months until one of Cortés's men led a brutal massacre of many Mexican nobles, causing the people of

Cortés's Invasion of Tenochtitlán, 1519–1521

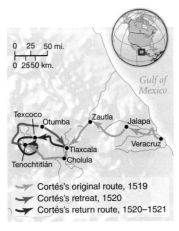

0 25   50 mi.

0 25 50 km.

Gulf of Mexico

Texcoco
Otumba   Zautla   Jalapa
Tlaxcala   Veracruz
Tenochtitlán   Cholula

➤ Cortés's original route, 1519
➤ Cortés's retreat, 1520
➤ Cortés's return route, 1520–1521

Cortés Arrives in Tenochtitlán
In this portrayal of Cortés and his army arriving in the Mexican capital, Malinali stands at the front of the procession, serving as the Spaniards' translator and intermediary with Montezuma (not pictured). Painted by a Mexican artist after the conquest, the work contrasts Cortés — dressed as a Spanish gentleman, respectfully doffing his hat to Montezuma — with his soldiers, who are armed and ready for battle. The painting displays the choices confronted by the Mexica: accept the pacific overtures of Cortés or face the Spanish soldiers' powerful weapons. Why were the Indians who carried the Spaniards' supplies important? Bibliothèque Nationale de France.

Tenochtitlán to revolt. Montezuma was killed (whether by his own people or Spaniards is not certain), and the Mexica mounted a ferocious assault on the Spaniards. On June 30, 1520, Cortés and about a hundred other Spaniards fought their way out of Tenochtitlán and retreated about one hundred miles to Tlaxcala, a stronghold of bitter enemies of the Mexica. The friendly Tlaxcalans — who had long resented Mexican power — allowed Cortés to regroup, obtain reinforcements, and plan a strategy to conquer Tenochtitlán.

In the spring of 1521, Cortés and tens of thousands of Indian allies laid siege to the Mexican capital. With a relentless, scorched-earth strategy, Cortés finally defeated the last Mexican defenders on August 13, 1521. The great capital of the Mexican empire "looked as if it had been ploughed up," one of Cortés's soldiers remembered.

How did a few hundred Spaniards so far away from home defeat millions of Indians fighting on their home turf? For one thing, the Spaniards had superior military technology that partially offset the Mexicans' numerical advantages. (See "Visualizing History," page 44.) They fought with weapons of iron and steel against the Mexicans' stone, wood, and copper. The muscles of Mexican warriors could not match the endurance of cannons and muskets fueled by gunpowder.

European viruses proved to be even more powerful weapons. Smallpox arrived in Mexico with Cortés, and in the ensuing epidemic thousands of Mexicans died and many others became too sick to fight. After Cortés evacuated Tenochtitlán, a plague — probably another smallpox outbreak — decimated the Mexican capital, "striking everywhere in the city and killing a vast number of our people," as one Mexican recalled. The sickness spread back along the network of trade and tribute feeding Tenochtitlán, weakening the entire Mexican empire and causing many to fear that their gods had abandoned them. "Cut us loose," one Mexican pleaded, "because the gods have died."

The Spaniards' concept of war also favored them. Mexicans tended to consider war a way to impose their tribute system on conquered people and to take captives for sacrifice. They believed that the high cost of continuing to fight would cause their adversaries to surrender and pay tribute. While Mexicans sought surrender, Spaniards sought total victory. As one Mexican described a Spanish attack, soldiers "stabbed everyone with iron lances and . . . iron swords. They stuck some in the belly, and then their entrails came spilling out. They split open the heads of some, . . . their skulls were cut up into little bits. Some they hit on the shoulders; their bodies broke open and ripped." To Spaniards, war meant destroying their enemy's ability to fight.

Politics proved decisive in Cortés's victory over the Mexicans. Cortés shrewdly exploited the tensions between the Mexica and the people they ruled in their empire (see chapter 1). Cortés reinforced his small army with thousands of Indian allies who were eager to seek revenge against the Mexica. Cortés's Indian allies fought alongside the Spaniards and provided a fairly secure base from which to maneuver against the Mexican stronghold of Tenochtitlán. Hundreds of thousands of other Indians aided Cortés by failing to come to the Mexicans' defense. In the end, the political tensions created by the Mexican empire proved to be its crippling weakness.

Incan Gold Figure and Spanish Gold Ingot
Before conquest by the Spaniards, craftsmen in Mexico, Peru, and elsewhere in Central and South America fashioned spectacular objects from gold — like this Incan pre-conquest figure — for leaders who sought to display their wealth, status, and — probably — their supernatural power. Spaniards had no interest in the artistry or ceremonial meanings of such artifacts and routinely melted them down into ingots of gold to be shipped back to Spain, like the one shown here. This ingot was excavated in Mexico City in 1982, more than 450 years after 1521, when it was probably dropped by one of Cortés's soldiers.
Figure: Bildarchiv Preussischer Kulturbesitz/Art Resource, NY; ingot: Museo Nacional de Antropologia, conaculta-inah, 10-220012.

The Search for Other Mexicos

Lured by their insatiable appetite for gold, Spanish **conquistadors** (soldiers who fought in conquests) quickly fanned out from Tenochtitlán in search of other sources of treasure. The most spectacular prize fell to **Francisco Pizarro**, who conquered the **Incan empire** in Peru. The Incas controlled a vast, complex region that contained more than nine million people and stretched along the western coast of South America for more than two thousand miles. In 1532, Pizarro and his army of fewer than two hundred men captured the Incan emperor Atahualpa and held him hostage. As ransom, the Incas gave Pizarro the largest treasure yet produced by the conquests: gold and silver equivalent to half a century's worth of precious-metal production in Europe. With the ransom safely in their hands, the Spaniards murdered Atahualpa. The Incan treasure proved that at least one other Mexico did indeed exist, and it spurred the search for others.

Juan Ponce de León had sailed along the Florida coast in 1513. Encouraged by Cortés's success, he went back to Florida in 1521 to find riches, only to be killed in battle with Calusa Indians. A few years later, Lucas Vázquez de Ayllón explored the Atlantic coast north of Florida to present-day South Carolina. In 1526, he established a small settlement on the Georgia coast that he named San Miguel de Gualdape, the first Spanish attempt to establish a foothold in what is now the United States. This settlement was soon swept away by sickness and hostile Indians. Pánfilo de Narváez surveyed the Gulf coast from Florida to Texas in 1528, but his expedition ended disastrously with a shipwreck near present-day Galveston, Texas.

In 1539, Hernando de Soto, a seasoned conquistador who had taken part in the conquest of Peru, set out with nine ships and more than six hundred men to find another Peru in North America. Landing in Florida, de Soto literally slashed his way through much of southeastern North America for three years, searching for the rich, majestic civilizations he believed were there. After the brutal slaughter of many Native Americans and much hardship, de Soto died of a fever in 1542. His men buried him in the Mississippi River and turned back to Mexico, disappointed.

Tales of the fabulous wealth of the mythical Seven Cities of Cíbola also lured Francisco Vásquez de Coronado to search the Southwest and Great Plains of North America. In 1540, Coronado left northern Mexico with more than three hundred Spaniards, a thousand Indians, and a priest who claimed to know the way to what he called "the greatest and best of the discoveries." Cíbola turned out to be a small Zuñi pueblo of about a hundred families. When the Zuñi shot arrows at the Spaniards, Coronado attacked the pueblo and routed the defenders after a hard battle. Convinced that the rich cities must lie somewhere over the horizon, Coronado kept moving all the way to central Kansas before deciding in 1542 that the rumors he had pursued were just that.

The same year Coronado abandoned his search for Cíbola, Juan Rodríguez Cabrillo's maritime expedition sought to find wealth along the coast of California. Cabrillo died on Santa Catalina Island, offshore from present-day Los Angeles, but his men sailed on to Oregon, where a ferocious storm forced them to turn back toward Mexico.

These probes into North America by de Soto, Coronado, and Cabrillo persuaded other Spaniards that although enormous territories stretched northward, their inhabitants had little to loot

Weapons of Conquest

For centuries, Spanish soldiers and Mexican warriors wielded weapons that had proven to be effective in their respective military cultures. In Spain, royal soldiers completed the centuries-long Reconquest in 1492, driving out Muslims and affirming Christian rule in the Iberian Peninsula. In ancient Mesoamerica, the Mexica had asserted their dominance among the many regional tribes and established an empire that covered much of present-day Mexico (see chapter 1). When the Spanish conquistadors traveled to the New World during the sixteenth century, the battles of conquest revealed the deadly limitations of weaponry that the Mexica had used to build their mighty empire.

The Mexica fought with offensive weapons similar to the wooden club shown here. Razor-sharp fragments of obsidian, a glasslike min-

Mexican Warriors Battle Spanish Conquistadors

eral, studded the edges of the club, allowing Mexican warriors, like the three shown here, to deliver lacerating, even lethal, blows against an enemy at close range. The Mexica and their enemies tried to defend themselves by deflecting these weapons of wood and stone with shields made of hides, wood, and feathers, as shown here. Why do you think Mexican warriors had such elaborate and colorful shields and

Mexican War Club

Mexican Warrior's Shield

or exploit. After a generation of vigorous exploration, the Spaniards concluded that there was only one Mexico and one Peru.

Spanish Outposts in Florida and New Mexico

Disappointed by the explorers' failure to discover riches in North America, the Spanish monarchy insisted that a few settlements be established in Florida and New Mexico to give a token of reality to its territorial claims. Settlements in Florida would have the additional benefit of protecting Spanish ships from pirates and privateers who lurked along the southeastern coast, waiting for the Spanish treasure fleet sailing toward Spain.

In 1565, the Spanish king sent Pedro Menéndez de Avilés to create settlements along the Atlantic coast of North America. In early September,

Menéndez founded **St. Augustine** in Florida, the first permanent European settlement within what became the United States. By 1600, St. Augustine had a population of about five hundred, the only remaining Spanish beachhead on North America's vast Atlantic shoreline.

More than sixteen hundred miles west of St. Augustine, the Spaniards founded another outpost in 1598. Juan de Oñate led an expedition of about five hundred people to settle northern Mexico, now called New Mexico, and claim the booty rumored to exist there. Oñate had impeccable credentials for both conquest and mining. His father helped to discover the bonanza silver mines of Zacatecas in central Mexico, and his wife was Isabel Tolosa Cortés Montezuma — the granddaughter of Cortés and the great-granddaughter of Montezuma.

After a two-month journey from Mexico, Oñate and his companions reached pueblos near

Spanish Battle Sword

battle dress? Why might Mexican warriors have considered bright designs made with feathers useful for offense or defense?

In Europe, Spaniards had gone to battle for centuries with offensive weapons made of steel, like the sword shown here. This sword is inscribed with Latin mottoes that read on one side, "Turn away these troubles from us," and on the other side, "With God we achieve lofty goals but nothing by ourselves." Why might these inscriptions have been meaningful to a Spanish soldier who slashed and stabbed enemies with this sword?

On the battlefields of sixteenth-century Europe, Spanish soldiers defended themselves against the steel weapons of their enemies with steel shields and body armor, as shown here. In Mexico, the wood and stone weapons of Mexican warriors tended to bounce off the Spaniards' shields and armor, in effect disarming Mexicans' major offensive weap-

onry. Likewise, Spaniards' sword blows, which might have clanked off a European enemy's steel shield, slashed through a Mexican warrior's shield of hide and feathers, destroying this basic form of defense.

Like the Mexican club, the steel sword was effective only at close range; the sword shown here, for example, is three feet long. (The effective range of a modern military rifle is nearly a mile.) What does the relatively short effective range of the Spanish sword and the Mexican club suggest about combat during the conquest? What does each

weapon's design suggest about the fighter's ultimate goal in combat?

Horses were unknown in Mexico until Spaniards imported them. What offensive and defensive advantages did horses provide for mounted Spanish soldiers when in combat against Mexican foot soldiers? Did horses have any disadvantages for Spaniards or any advantages for the Mexica?

While the Mexica wounded and killed many Spaniards, in the end Spaniards prevailed and conquered Mexico. Although Spaniards' superior weaponry contributed to their success, can you imagine tactics that the Mexica might have used to delay, subvert, or even defeat Spanish conquest?

SOURCE: Mexican warriors and Spanish conquistadors: Biblioteca Nacional, Madrid; Spanish shield: The Royal Armory, Madrid; Spanish sword: The Metropolitan Museum of Art, Purchase, The Lauder Foundation Gift, 1984. Photograph © The Metropolitan Museum of Art Accession Number 1984.73; Mexican shield: Museum fur Volkerkunde Vienna; Mexican war club: Image # 7864 American Museum of Natural History.

Spanish Shield

present-day Albuquerque and Santa Fe. He solemnly convened the pueblos' leaders and received their oath of loyalty to the Spanish king and the Christian God. Oñate sent out scouting parties to find the legendary treasures of the region and to locate the ocean, which he believed must be nearby. Meanwhile, many of his soldiers planned to mutiny, and relations with the Indians deteriorated. When Indians in the Acoma pueblo revolted against the Spaniards, Oñate ruthlessly suppressed the uprising, killing eight hundred men, women, and children. Although Oñate's response to the **Acoma pueblo revolt** reconfirmed the Spaniards' military superiority, he did not bring peace or stability to the region. After another pueblo revolt occurred in 1599, many of Oñate's settlers returned to Mexico, leaving New Mexico as a small, dusty assertion of Spanish claims to the North American Southwest.

New Spain in the Sixteenth Century

For all practical purposes, Spain was the dominant European power in the Western Hemisphere during the sixteenth century (Map 2.3, page 47). Portugal claimed the giant territory of Brazil under the Tordesillas treaty but was far more concerned with exploiting its hard-won trade with the East Indies than with colonizing the New World. England and France were absorbed by domestic and diplomatic concerns in Europe and largely lost interest in America until late in the century. In the decades after 1519, the Spaniards created the distinctive colonial society of **New Spain**, which showed other Europeans how the New World could be made to serve the purposes of the Old.

The Spanish monarchy gave the conquistadors permission to explore and plunder what they

Connections between Spanish Christianity and Mexican Traditional Religions
Spanish missionaries struggled to eradicate all forms of Mexicans' traditional religion. The painting portrays a Catholic priest instructing two Mexican children while another priest shelters a group of children and wields a cross to protect them from the diabolical creatures seeking to tempt them to embrace evil. Even Mexicans who converted to Christianity continued to express their spirituality in traditional ways. The sixteenth-century chalice cover shown here, designed to cover the cup that contains wine for Christian communion — is made of traditional Mexican feather work and features a whirlpool design emblematic of a major Mexican goddess.
Painting: Collection Revillagigedo Historia/Archivos General de la Nacion, Palacio Nacional; chalice cover: Werner Forman/Art Resource, NY.

found. (See "Documenting the American Promise," page 48.) The crown took one-fifth, called the "royal fifth," of any loot confiscated and allowed the conquerors to divide the rest. In the end, most conquistadors received very little after the plunder was divided among leaders such as Cortés and his favorite officers. To compensate his disappointed battle-hardened soldiers, Cortés gave them towns the Spaniards had subdued.

The distribution of conquered towns institutionalized the system of **encomienda**, which empowered the conquistadors to rule the Indians and the lands in and around their towns. The concept of encomienda was familiar to Spaniards, who had used it to govern regions recaptured from Muslims during the Reconquest. Encomienda transferred to the Spanish *encomendero* (the man who "owned" the town) the tribute that the town had previously paid to the Mexican empire. In theory, encomienda involved a reciprocal relationship between the encomendero and "his" Indians. In return for the tribute and labor of the Indians, the encomendero was supposed to be responsible for their material well-being, to guarantee order and justice in the town, and to encourage the Indians to convert to Christianity.

Catholic missionaries labored earnestly to convert the Indians. They fervently believed that God expected them to save the Indians' souls by convincing them to abandon their old sinful beliefs and to embrace the one true Christian faith. (See "Seeking the American Promise," page 50.) But after baptizing tens of thousands of Indians, the

missionaries learned that many Indians continued to worship their own gods. Most priests came to believe that the Indians were lesser beings inherently incapable of fully understanding Christianity.

In practice, encomenderos were far more interested in what the Indians could do for them than in what they or the missionaries could do for the Indians. Encomenderos subjected the Indians to chronic overwork, mistreatment, and abuse. According to one Spaniard, the Indians' behavior justified the encomenderos' cruelty: "Everything [the Indians] do is slowly done and by compulsion. They are malicious, lying, [and] thievish." Economically, however, encomienda recognized a fundamental reality of New Spain: The most important treasure the Spaniards could plunder from the New World was not gold but uncompensated Indian labor.

The practice of coerced labor in New Spain grew directly out of the Spaniards' assumption that they were superior to the Indians. As one missionary put it, the Indians "are incapable of learning. . . . [They] are more stupid than asses and refuse to improve in anything." Therefore, most Spaniards assumed, Indians' labor should be organized by and for their conquerors. Spaniards seldom hesitated to use violence to punish and intimidate recalcitrant Indians.

Encomienda engendered two groups of influential critics. A few of the missionaries were horrified at the brutal mistreatment of the Indians. The cruelty of the encomenderos made it difficult for priests to persuade the Indians

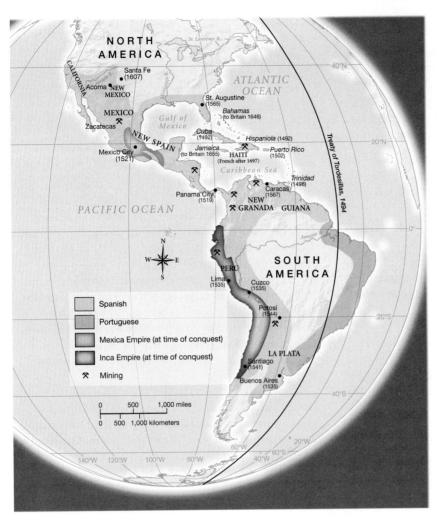

MAP ACTIVITY

Map 2.3 Sixteenth-Century European Colonies in the New World

Spanish control spread throughout Central and South America during the sixteenth century, with the important exception of Portuguese Brazil. North America, though claimed by Spain under the Treaty of Tordesillas, remained peripheral to Spain's New World empire.

READING THE MAP: Track Spain's efforts at colonization by date. How did political holdings, the physical layout of the land, and natural resources influence where the Spaniards directed their energies?

CONNECTIONS: What was the purpose of the Treaty of Tordesillas? How might the location of silver and gold mines have affected Spain's desire to assert its claims over regions still held by Portugal after 1494, and Spain's interest in California, New Mexico, and Florida?

Zuñi Defend Pueblo against Coronado

This sixteenth-century drawing by a Mexican artist shows Zuñi bowmen fighting back against the arrows of Coronado's men and the entreaties of Christian missionaries. Intended to document the support some Mexican Indians gave to Spanish efforts to extend the conquest into North America, the drawing depicts the Zuñi defender at the bottom of the pueblo aiming his arrow at a Mexican missionary armed only with religious weaponry: a crucifix, a rosary, and a book (presumably the Bible). Hunterian Museum Library, University of Glasgow. Glasgow University Library, Department of Special Collections.

Justifying Conquest

The immense riches Spain reaped from its New World empire came largely at the expense of Native Americans. A few individual Spaniards raised their voices against the brutal exploitation of the Indians. Their criticisms prompted the Spanish monarchy to formulate an official justification of conquest that, in effect, blamed the Indians for resisting Spanish dominion.

DOCUMENT 1
Montecino's 1511 Sermon

In 1511, a Dominican friar named Antón Montecino delivered a blistering sermon that astonished the Spaniards gathered in the church in Santo Domingo, headquarters of the Spanish Caribbean.

Your greed for gold is blind. Your pride, your lust, your anger, your envy, your sloth, all blind. . . . You are in mortal sin. And you are heading for damnation. . . . For you are destroying an innocent people. For they are God's people, these innocents, whom you destroyed. By what right do you make them die? Mining gold for you in your mines or working for you in your fields, by what right do you unleash enslaving wars upon them? They have lived in peace in this land before you came, in peace in their own homes. They did nothing to harm you to cause you to slaughter them wholesale. . . .

Are you not under God's command to love them as you love yourselves?

Are you out of your souls, out of your minds? Yes. And that will bring you to damnation.

SOURCE: Zvi Dor-Ner, *Columbus and the Age of Discovery* (New York: William Morrow, 1991), 220–21.

DOCUMENT 2
The Requerimiento

Montecino returned to Spain to bring the Indians' plight to the king's attention. In 1512 and 1513, King Ferdinand met with philosophers, theologians, and other advisers and concluded that the holy duty to spread the Christian faith justified conquest. To buttress this claim, the king had his advisers prepare the Requerimiento.

According to the Requerimiento, Indians who failed to welcome Spanish conquest and all its blessings deserved to die. Conquistadors were commanded to read the Requerimiento to the Indians before any act of conquest. Beginning in 1514, they routinely did so, speaking in Spanish while other Spaniards brandishing unsheathed swords stood nearby.

On the part of the King . . . [and] queen of [Spain], subduers of the barbarous nations, we their servants notify and make known to you, as best we can, that the Lord our God, living and eternal, created the heaven and the earth, and one man and one woman, of whom you and we, and all the men of the world, were and are descendants. . . .

God our lord gave charge to one man called St. Peter, that he should be lord and superior to all the men in the world, that all should obey him, and that he should be the head of the whole human race, wherever men should live . . . and he gave him the world for his kingdom and jurisdiction.

And he commanded him to place his seat in Rome, as the spot most fitting to rule the world from. . . . This man was called Pope, as if to say, Admirable Great Father and Governor of men. The men who lived in that time obeyed that St. Peter and took him for lord, king, and superior of the universe. So also they have regarded the others who after him have been elected to the pontificate, and so has

of the tender mercies of the Spaniards' God. "What will [the Indians] think about the God of the Christians," Friar Bartolomé de Las Casas asked, when they see their friends "with their heads split, their hands amputated, their intestines torn open? . . . Would they want to come to Christ's sheepfold after their homes had been destroyed, their children imprisoned, their wives raped, their cities devastated, their maidens deflowered, and their provinces laid waste?" Las Casas and other outspoken missionaries softened few hearts among the encomenderos, but they did win some sympathy for the Indians from the Spanish monarchy and royal bureaucracy. The Spanish monarchy moved to abolish encomienda in an effort to replace swashbuckling

it been continued even till now, and will continue till the end of the world.

One of these pontiffs, who succeeded that St. Peter as lord of the world . . . made donation of these islands and mainland to the aforesaid king and queen [of Spain] and to their successors. . . .

So their highnesses are kings and lords of these islands and mainland by virtue of this donation; and . . . almost all those to whom this has been notified, have received and served their highnesses, as lords and kings, in the way that subjects ought to do, with good will, without any resistance, immediately, without delay, when they were informed of the aforesaid facts. And also they received and obeyed the priests whom their highnesses sent to preach to them and to teach them our holy faith; and all these, of their own free will, without any reward or condition have become Christians, and are so, and their highnesses have joyfully and graciously received them, and they have also commanded them to be treated as their subjects and vassals; and you too are held and obliged to do the same. Wherefore, as best we can, we ask and require that you consider what we have said to you, and that you take the time that shall be necessary to understand and deliberate upon it, and that you acknowledge the Church as the ruler and superior of the whole world, and the high priest called Pope, and in his name the king and queen [of Spain] our lords, in his place, as superiors and lords and kings of these islands and this mainland by virtue of the said donation, and that you consent and permit that these religious fathers declare and preach to you. . . .

If you do so . . . we . . . shall receive you in all love and charity, and shall leave you your wives and your children and your lands free without servitude, that you may do with them and with yourselves freely what you like and think best, and they shall not compel you to turn to Christians unless you yourselves, when informed of the truth, should wish to be converted to our holy Catholic faith. . . . And besides this, their highnesses award you many privileges and exemptions and will grant you many benefits.

But if you do not do this or if you maliciously delay in doing it, I certify to you that with the help of God we shall forcefully enter into your country and shall make war against you in all ways and manners that we can, and shall subject you to the yoke and obedience of the Church and of their highnesses; we shall take you and your wives and your children and shall make slaves of them, and as such shall sell and dispose of them as their highnesses may command; and we shall take away your goods and shall do to you all the harm and damage that we can, as to vassals who do not obey and refuse to receive their lord and resist and contradict him; and we protest that the deaths and losses which shall accrue from this are your fault, and not that of their highnesses, or ours, or of these soldiers who come with us.

The Indians who heard the Requerimiento could not understand Spanish, of course. No native documents survive to record the Indians' thoughts upon hearing the Spaniards' official justification for conquest, even when it was translated into a language they recognized. But one conquistador reported that when the Requerimiento was translated for two chiefs in Colombia, they responded that if the pope gave the king so much territory that belonged to other people, "the Pope must have been drunk."

SOURCE: Adapted from A. Helps and M. Oppenheim, eds., *The Spanish Conquest in America and Its Relation to the History of Slavery and to the Government of the Colonies*, 4 vols. (London and New York, 1900–1904), 1:264–67.

Questions for Analysis and Debate

1. How did the Requerimiento address the criticisms of Montecino? According to the Requerimiento, why was conquest justified? What was the source of the Indians' resistance to conquest?

2. What arguments might a critic like Montecino have used to respond to the Requerimiento's justification of conquest? What arguments might the Mexican leader Montezuma have made against those of the Requerimiento?

3. Was the Requerimiento a faithful expression or a cynical violation of the Spaniards' Christian faith?

old conquistadors with royal bureaucrats as the rulers of New Spain.

In 1549, a reform called the ***repartimiento*** began to replace encomienda. It limited the labor an encomendero could command from his Indians to forty-five days per year from each adult male. The repartimiento, however, did not challenge the principle of forced labor, nor did it prevent encomenderos from continuing to cheat, mistreat, and overwork their Indians. Many Indians were put to work in silver mines, which required large capital investments and large groups of laborers. Silver mining was grueling and dangerous for the workers, but very profitable for the Spaniards who supervised them: During

Spreading Christianity in New Spain

Spanish officials aspired to accompany the military and political conquest of the New World with spiritual conquest. With royal support, priests flocked to New Spain to harvest the millions of souls unexpectedly disclosed by the voyages of Columbus. In 1529, a young priest named Bernardino de Sahagún sailed to New Spain, where he spent the remaining sixty-one years of his life seeking to realize the promise of spreading Christianity to people who had never heard of it.

Sahagún believed that preaching the gospel in the New World was a heaven-sent opportunity to revitalize global Christianity. In Asia, he wrote, "there are nothing but Turks and Moors"; in Africa, "there are no longer any Christians"; in Germany, "there are nothing but heretics"; and in Europe, "in most places there is no obedience to the Church." Now, Sahagún wrote, "Our Lord [ordained] the Spanish people to traverse the Ocean Sea to make discoveries in the West" and to "bring into the embrace of the Church that multitude of peoples, kingdoms, and nations." In pursuit of his goal to rescue Christianity by converting the New World Indians, Sahagún compiled the most important collection of information in existence about the lives and beliefs of sixteenth-century Mexicans.

Sahagún and other Spaniards considered Christianity the one true faith. When Cortés and his men marched into Mexico a decade before Sahagún arrived, they went out of their way to destroy effigies of Mexican gods and to replace them with crosses, the icons of Christianity. "It was necessary," Sahagún wrote, "to destroy the idolatrous things, and all the idolatrous buildings, and even the customs of the [Mexicans] . . . that were intertwined with idolatrous rites and accompanied by idolatrous ceremonies."

What Sahagún considered idolatry was rooted in individual Mexicans' belief in what he called their own "innumerable insanities and gods without number." Sahagún and other priests set out to persuade the Indians to reject belief in traditional deities and to have faith instead in the divinity of Jesus Christ and in the Catholic Church as Christ's representative on earth.

At first, the conversion campaign seemed amazingly successful. One priest claimed that more than nine million Mexicans had been baptized by 1539. But after a few years, Sahagún and other priests realized that many Indians simply "took [Jesus Christ] as yet another god . . . without . . . relinquishing their ancient gods." Adopting some of the outward rituals of Christianity while maintaining belief in what Spaniards considered pagan idols was a "twisted perversity," Sahagún wrote, one that caused the New World church "to be founded on falsehood."

Unlike many other Spaniards, Sahagún believed that in order to purge Mexicans' idolatries, church leaders needed to become familiar with Mexicans' traditional religious ideas. To diagnose what he called the Mexicans' "spiritual illnesses," Sahagún set out to record everything he could learn about the Indians' beliefs.

As a first step, Sahagún learned Nahuatl, the Mexicans' unwritten language. Next, he and other priests started schools to teach Latin and eventually Spanish to young Indian students, usually drawn from elite families. These "trilinguals," as Sahagún called them, could translate religious texts into Nahuatl, which the priests could use in their missionary efforts.

the entire sixteenth century, precious-metal exports from New Spain to Spain were worth twenty-five times more than the next most important export, leather hides (Figure 2.1).

For the Spaniards, life in New Spain after the conquests was relatively easy. Although the riches they won fell far short of their expectations, encomienda gave them a comfortable, leisurely life that was the envy of many Spaniards back in Europe. As one colonist wrote to his brother in Spain, "Don't hesitate [to come]. . . . This land [New Spain] is as good as ours [in Spain], for God has given us more here than there, and we shall be better off." During the

century after 1492, about 225,000 Spaniards settled in the colonies. Virtually all of them were poor young men of common (non-noble) lineage who came directly from Spain. Laborers and artisans made up the largest proportion, but soldiers and sailors were also numerous. Throughout the sixteenth century, men vastly outnumbered women, although the proportion of women grew from about one in twenty before 1519 to nearly one in three by the 1580s.

The gender and number of Spanish settlers shaped two fundamental features of the society of New Spain. First, Europeans never made up more than 1 or 2 percent of the total population.

Beginning in 1558, Sahagún used his trilinguals to undertake a systematic investigation of every facet of Mexican life. Sahagún and his assistants interviewed Mexican elders, asking them not only about gods and religious ceremonies but also about farming, family life, education, poetry, songs, and even their conquest by the Spaniards. Sahagún developed great admiration for both the Mexicans and their language. "They are quick to learn," he wrote. "There is no art for which they do not have the talent to learn and use it." In fact, Sahagún declared, the Mexicans "are held to be barbarians and a people of little worth, yet in truth, in matters of culture, they are a step ahead of many nations that presume to be civilized."

For years, Sahagún edited and organized this massive treasure trove of information about Mexican life and beliefs, all in the hope that it would ultimately help priests make converts to Christianity. When church officials heard about Sahagún's great work, they obtained a royal order in 1577 to collect all copies and send them immediately to Spain for destruction. The Spanish monarchy and most church officials wanted to stamp out the Mexicans' beliefs, not preserve them. Sahagún dutifully sent his volumes to Spain, but he was still working on a final copy, which he later gave to a priest friend, who saved it, and it survives to this day. Unbeknownst to him, Sahagún's

Montezuma Receiving Tribute
This drawing from Sahagún's Florentine Codex portrays Montezuma (seated at left) receiving a rich array of featherwork, ritualistic costumes, textiles, battle shields, and other luxuries from one of his subjects. Made by a Mexican artist in the mid-sixteenth century, the drawing adapts preconquest symbols to illustrate the enormous power and respect that Montezuma commanded. By the time the drawing was made, Montezuma had been dead for about forty years, and the Spaniards, not Montezuma's descendants, collected tribute (mostly in the form of labor) from the Indians. Bridgeman Art Library Ltd.

masterwork preserved for posterity an unrivaled account of the hearts and souls of sixteenth-century Mexicans in their own words.

Questions for Consideration

1. In what ways did Sahagún's work contribute to the conquest of Mexico?

2. What ideas about the Mexicans did Sahagún hold in common with the Spanish monarchy, royal officials, and other Catholic missionaries? To what extent did his ideas conflict with those held by other Spaniards?

3. What did Sahagún believe about the global significance of his missionary work? How might his "trilinguals" and Mexican informants have interpreted his efforts?

Although Spaniards ruled New Spain, the population was almost wholly Indian. Second, the shortage of Spanish women meant that Spanish men frequently married Indian women or used them as concubines. For the most part, the relatively few women from Spain married Spanish men, contributing to a tiny elite defined by European origins.

The small number of Spaniards, the masses of Indians, and the frequency of intermarriage created a steep social hierarchy defined by perceptions of national origin and race. Natives of Spain — *peninsulares* (people born on the Iberian Peninsula) — enjoyed the highest social status in New Spain. Below them but still within the white elite were *creoles*, the children born in the New World to Spanish men and women. Together, peninsulares and creoles made up barely 1 or 2 percent of the population. Below them on the social pyramid was a larger group of *mestizos*, the offspring of Spanish men and Indian women, who accounted for 4 or 5 percent of the population. So many of the mestizos were born out of wedlock that the term *mestizo* (after the Spanish word for "mixed") became almost synonymous with *bastard* during the sixteenth century. Some mestizos worked as artisans and labor overseers and lived well, and a few rose

Español con India, Mestizo.

Mestizo con Española, Castizo.

Castizo con Española, Español.

Español con Mora, Mulato.

5

Mulato con Española, Morisco.

6

Morisco con Española, Chino.

7

Chino con India, Salta atras.

Salta atras con Mulata, Lobo.

VISUAL ACTIVITY

Mixed Races

The residents of New Spain maintained a lively interest in each person's racial lineage. These eighteenth-century paintings illustrate forms of racial mixture common in the sixteenth century. In the first painting, a Spanish man and an Indian woman have a mestizo son; in the fourth, a Spanish man and a woman of African descent have a mulatto son; in the fifth, a Spanish woman and a mulatto man have a *morisco* daughter. The many racial permutations led the residents of New Spain to develop an elaborate vocabulary of ancestry. The child of a morisco and a Spaniard was a *chino*; the child of a chino and an Indian was a *salta abas*; the child of a salta abas and a mulatto was a *lobo*; and so on. Can you detect hints of some of the meanings of racial categories in the clothing depicted in these paintings? Bob Schalkwijk/INAH.

READING THE IMAGE: : What do these paintings reveal about social status in New Spain?

CONNECTIONS: How do the paintings of mixed-race families illustrate the power the Spaniards exercised in their New World colonies? What were some other aspects of colonial society that demonstrated Spanish domination?

pronounced pattern in the European colonies of the New World: a society stratified sharply by social origin and race. All Europeans of whatever social origin considered themselves superior to Native Americans; in New Spain, they were a dominant minority in both power and status.

The Toll of Spanish Conquest and Colonization

By 1560, the major centers of Indian civilization had been conquered, their leaders overthrown, their religion held in contempt, and their people forced to work for the Spaniards. Profound demoralization pervaded Indian society. As a Mexican poet wrote:

> Nothing but flowers and songs of sorrow are left in Mexico . . .
>
> where once we saw warriors and wise men. . . .
>
> We are crushed to the ground; we lie in ruins. There is nothing but grief and suffering in Mexico.

into the ranks of the elite, especially if their Indian ancestry was not obvious from their skin color. Most mestizos, however, were lumped with the Indians, the enormous bottom slab of the social pyramid.

The society of New Spain established the precedent for what would become a

Adding to the culture shock of conquest and colonization was the deadly toll of European

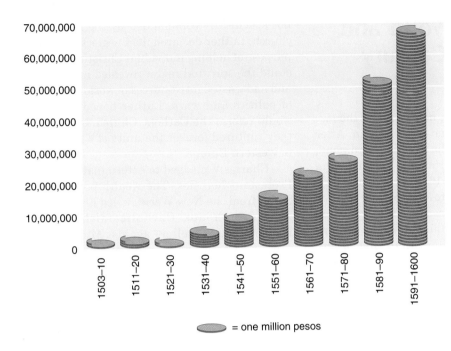

FIGURE 2.1 New World Gold and Silver Imported into Spain during the Sixteenth Century, in Pesos
Spain imported more gold than silver during the first three decades of the sixteenth century, but the total value of this treasure was quickly eclipsed during the 1530s and 1540s, when rich silver mines were developed. Silver accounted for most of the enormous growth in Spain's precious-metal imports from the New World.

diseases. As conquest spread, the Indians succumbed to virulent epidemics of measles, smallpox, and respiratory illnesses. They had no immunity to these diseases because they had not been exposed to them before the arrival of Europeans. The isolation of the Western Hemisphere before 1492 had protected ancient Americans from the contagious diseases that had raged throughout Eurasia for millennia. The new post-1492 sea bridge eliminated that isolation, and by 1570 the Indian population of New Spain had fallen about 90 percent from what it was when Columbus arrived. The destruction of the Indians was a catastrophe unequaled in human history. A Mayan Indian recalled that when sickness struck his village, "great was the stench of the dead. . . . The dogs and vultures devoured the bodies. The mortality was terrible." For most Indians, New Spain was a graveyard.

For the Spaniards, Indian deaths meant that the most valuable resource of New Spain — Indian labor — dwindled rapidly. By the last quarter of the sixteenth century, Spanish colonists felt the pinch of a labor shortage. To help supply laborers, the colonists began to import African slaves. Some Africans had come to Mexico with the conquistadors. One Mexican recalled that among Cortés's men were "some black-skinned one[s] with kink[y] hair." In the years before 1550, while Indian labor was still adequate, only 15,000 slaves were imported from Africa. Even after Indian labor began to decline, the

relatively high cost of African slaves kept imports low, totaling approximately 36,000 from 1550 to the end of the century. During the sixteenth century, New Spain continued to rely primarily on a shrinking number of Indians.

REVIEW How did New Spain's distinctive colonial population shape its economy and society?

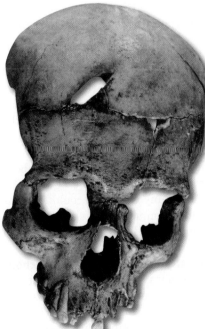

A Sign of Conquest
This skull of an Indian man in his fifties was excavated from the site of a Native American village in southwestern Georgia visited by de Soto's expedition in 1540. The skull shows that the man suffered a fatal sword wound above his right eye. Combined with slashed and severed arm and leg bones from the same site, the skull demonstrates the brutality de Soto employed against indigenous peoples on his journey through the Southeast. No native weapons could have inflicted the wounds left on this skull and the other bones. Private Collection.

▶ The New World and Sixteenth-Century Europe

The riches of New Spain helped make the sixteenth century the Golden Age of Spain. After the deaths of Queen Isabella and King Ferdinand, their sixteen-year-old grandson became King Charles I of Spain in 1516. Three years later, just as Cortés ventured into Mexico, King Charles used judicious bribes to secure his selection as Holy Roman Emperor Charles V. His empire encompassed more territory than that of any other European monarch. He used the wealth of New Spain to protect the sprawling empire and promote his interests in the fierce dynastic battles of sixteenth-century Europe. He also sought to defend orthodox Christianity from the insurgent heresy of the Protestant Reformation. The power of the Spanish monarchy spread the clear message throughout sixteenth-century Europe that a New World empire could bankroll Old World ambitions.

The Protestant Reformation and the Spanish Response

In 1517, **Martin Luther**, an obscure Catholic priest in central Germany, initiated the **Protestant Reformation** by publicizing his criticisms of the Catholic Church. Luther's ideas won the sympathy of many Catholics, but they were considered extremely dangerous by church officials and monarchs such as Charles V who believed that just as the church spoke for God, they ruled for God.

Luther preached a doctrine known as "justification by faith": Individual Christians could obtain salvation and life everlasting only by having faith that God would save them. Giving monetary offerings to the church, following the orders of priests, or participating in church rituals would not bring believers closer to heaven. Also, the only true source of information about God's will was the Bible, not the church. By reading the Bible, any Christian could learn as much about God's commandments as any priest. Indeed, Luther called for a "priesthood of all believers."

In effect, Luther charged that the Catholic Church was in many respects fraudulent. He insisted that priests were unnecessary for salvation and that they encouraged Christians to violate God's will by promoting religious practices not specifically commanded by the Bible. The church, Luther declared, had neglected its true purpose of helping individual Christians understand the spiritual realm revealed in the Bible and had wasted its resources in worldly conflicts of politics and wars. Luther hoped his ideas would reform the Catholic Church, but instead they ruptured forever the unity of Christianity in western Europe.

Charles V pledged to exterminate Luther's Protestant heresies. The wealth pouring into Spain from the New World fueled his efforts to defend orthodox Catholic faith against Protestants, as well as against Muslims and Jews in eastern Europe and against any nation bold or foolhardy enough to contest Spain's supremacy. As the wealthiest and most powerful monarch in Europe, Charles V, followed by his son and successor Philip II, assumed responsibility for upholding the existing order of sixteenth-century Europe.

American wealth, particularly Mexican silver, fueled Spanish ambitions and made the Spanish monarchy rich and powerful among the states of Europe. But Charles V's and Philip II's expenses for constant warfare far outstripped the revenues arriving from New Spain. To help meet military expenditures, both kings raised taxes in Spain more than fivefold during the sixteenth century. Since the nobility, the wealthiest Spaniards by far, were exempt from taxation, the burdensome new taxes fell mostly on poor peasants. The monarchy's ambitions impoverished the vast majority of Spain's population and brought the nation to the brink of bankruptcy. When taxes failed to produce enough revenue to fight its wars, the monarchy borrowed heavily from European bankers. By the end of the sixteenth century, interest payments on royal debts swallowed two-thirds of the crown's annual revenues. In retrospect, the riches from New Spain proved a short-term blessing but a long-term curse.

Most Spaniards, however, looked upon New Spain as a glorious national achievement that displayed Spain's superiority over Native Americans and over other Europeans. As they surveyed their many accomplishments in the New World, they saw clear signs of progress. They had added enormously to their knowledge and wealth. They had built mines, cities, Catholic churches, and even universities on the other side of the Atlantic. These military, religious, and economic achievements gave them great pride and confidence that their European rivals often considered swaggering arrogance.

Europe and the Spanish Example

The lessons of sixteenth-century Spain were not lost on Spain's European rivals. Spain proudly displayed the fruits of its New World conquests. In 1520, for example, the German artist Albrecht Dürer wrote in his diary that he "marveled over the subtle ingenuity of the men in these distant lands" who created "things which were brought to the King . . . [such as] a sun entirely of gold, a whole fathom [six feet] broad." But the most exciting news about "the men in these distant lands" was that they could serve the interests of Europeans, as Spain had shown. With a few notable exceptions, Europeans saw the New World as a place for the expansion of European influence, a place where, as one Spaniard wrote, Europeans could "give to those strange lands the form of our own."

France and England tried to follow Spain's example. Both nations warred with Spain in Europe, preyed on Spanish treasure fleets, and ventured to the New World, where they too hoped to find an undiscovered passageway to the East Indies or another Mexico or Peru.

In 1524, France sent Giovanni da Verrazano to scout the Atlantic coast of North America from North Carolina to Canada, looking for a Northwest Passage (see Map 2.2). Eleven years later, France probed farther north with Jacques Cartier's voyage up the St. Lawrence River. Encouraged, Cartier returned to the region with a group of settlers in 1541, but the colony they established — like the search for a Northwest Passage — came to nothing.

English attempts to follow Spain's lead were slower but equally ill-fated. Not until 1576, almost eighty years after John Cabot's voyages, did the

Algonquian Ceremonial Dance
When English artist John White visited the coast of present-day North Carolina in 1585 as part of Raleigh's expedition, he painted this watercolor of an Algonquian ceremonial dance. This and White's other portraits are the only surviving likenesses of sixteenth-century North American Indians that were drawn from direct observation. White's portrait captures the individuality of the Indians while depicting a ceremony that must have appeared bizarre and alien to a sixteenth-century Englishman. The significance of this ceremonial dance is still a mystery, although the portrait's obvious signs of order, organization, and collective understanding show that the dancing Indians knew its purpose. Copyright Trustees of the British Museum/Bridgeman Art Library.

English again try to find a Northwest Passage. This time Martin Frobisher sailed into the frigid waters of northern Canada (see Map 2.2). His sponsor was the Cathay Company, which hoped to open trade with China. Like many other explorers, Frobisher was mesmerized by the Spanish example and was sure he had found gold. But the tons of "ore" he hauled back to England proved worthless, the Cathay Company collapsed, and English interests shifted southward to the giant region on the northern margins of New Spain.

Roanoke Settlement, 1585–1590

English explorers' attempts to establish North American settlements were no more fruitful than their search for a northern route to China. Sir Humphrey Gilbert led expeditions in 1578 and 1583 that made feeble efforts to found colonies in Newfoundland until Gilbert vanished at sea. Sir Walter Raleigh organized an expedition in 1585 to settle Roanoke Island off the coast of present-day North Carolina. The first group of explorers left no colonists on the island, but two years later Raleigh sent a contingent of more than one hundred settlers to **Roanoke** under John White's leadership. White went back to England for supplies, and when he returned to Roanoke in 1590, the colonists had disappeared, leaving only the word *Croatoan* (whose meaning is unknown) carved in a tree. The Roanoke colonists most likely died from a combination of natural causes and unfriendly Indians. By the end of the century, England had failed to secure a New World beachhead.

> **REVIEW**   How did Spain's conquests in the New World shape Spanish influence in Europe?

▶ Conclusion: The Promise of the New World for Europeans

The sixteenth century in the New World belonged to the Spaniards who employed Columbus and to the Indians who greeted him as he stepped ashore. The Portuguese, whose voyages to Africa and Asia set the stage for Columbus's voyages, won the important consolation prize of Brazil, but Spain hit the jackpot. Isabella of Spain helped initiate the Columbian exchange between the New World and the Old, which massively benefited first Spain and later other Europeans and which continues to this day. The exchange also subjected Native Americans to the ravages of European diseases and Spanish conquest. Spanish explorers, conquistadors, and colonists forced the Indians to serve the interests of Spanish settlers and the Spanish monarchy. The exchange illustrated one of the most important lessons of the sixteenth century: After millions of years, the Atlantic no longer was an impermeable barrier separating the Eastern and Western Hemispheres. After the voyages of Columbus, European sailing ships regularly bridged the Atlantic and carried people, products, diseases, and ideas from one shore to the other.

No European monarch could forget the seductive lesson taught by Spain's example: The New World could vastly enrich the Old. Spain remained a New World power for almost four centuries, and its language, religion, culture, and institutions left a permanent imprint. By the end of the sixteenth century, however, other European monarchies had begun to contest Spain's dominion in Europe and to make forays into the northern fringes of Spain's New World preserve. To reap the benefits the Spaniards enjoyed from their New World domain, the others had to learn a difficult lesson: how to deviate from Spain's example. That discovery lay ahead.

While England's rulers eyed the huge North American hinterland of New Spain for possible exploitation, they realized that it lacked the two main attractions of Mexico and Peru: incredible material wealth and large populations of Indians to use as workers. In the absence of gold and silver booty and plentiful native labor in North America, England would need to find some way to attract colonizers to a region that — compared to New Spain — did not appear very promising. During the next century, England's leaders overcame these dilemmas by developing a distinctive colonial model, one that encouraged land-hungry settlers from England and Europe to engage in agriculture and that depended on other sources of unfree labor: indentured servants from Europe and slaves from Africa.

► Selected Bibliography

General Works

J. H. Elliott, *Empires of the Atlantic World: Britain and Spain in America, 1491–1830* (2006).

Jonathan Locke Hart, *Representing the New World: The English and French Uses of the Example of Spain* (2001).

Jonathan Locke Hart, *Columbus, Shakespeare, and the Interpretation of the New World* (2003).

John L. Kessell, *Spain in the Southwest: A Narrative History of Colonial New Mexico, Arizona, Texas, and California* (2002).

Kenneth F. Kiple and Stephen V. Beck, eds., *Biological Consequences of European Expansion, 1450–1800* (1997).

Diarmaid MacCulloch, *Christianity: The First Three Thousand Years* (2009).

William D. Phillips and Carla Rahn Phillips, *The Worlds of Christopher Columbus* (1992).

David J. Weber, *The Spanish Frontier in North America* (2009).

Explorers and Empires

James Horn, *A Kingdom Strange: The Brief and Tragic History of the Lost Colony of Roanoke* (2010).

Henry Arthur Francis Kamen, *Empire: How Spain Became a World Power, 1492–1763* (2004).

Karen Ordahl Kupperman, *Roanoke: The Abandoned Colony* (2nd ed., 2007).

Francesc Relaño, *The Shaping of Africa: Cosmographic Discourse and Cartographic Science in Late Medieval and Early Modern Europe* (2002).

A. J. R. Russell-Wood, *The Portuguese Empire, 1415–1808: A World on the Move* (1998).

Hugh Thomas, *Rivers of Gold: The Rise of the Spanish Empire from Columbus to Magellan* (2004).

Europeans Encounter the New World

Ricardo Alegria and Jose Arrom, *Taino: Pre-Columbian Art and Culture from the Caribbean* (1998).

Rebecca Catz, *Christopher Columbus and the Portuguese, 1476–1498* (1993).

Noble David Cook, *Born to Die: Disease and New World Conquest, 1492–1650* (1998).

Valerie J. Flint, *The Imaginative Landscape of Christopher Columbus* (1992).

Anthony Pagden, *Lords of All the World: Ideologies of Empire in Spain, Britain, and France, 1500–1800* (1995).

Irving Rouse, *The Tainos: Rise and Decline of the People Who Greeted Columbus* (1992).

Conquest and New Spain

Herman L. Bennett, *Africans in Colonial Mexico: Absolutism, Christianity, and Afro-Creole Consciousness, 1570–1640* (2003).

Louise M. Burkhart, *The Slippery Earth: Nahua-Christian Moral Dialogue in Sixteenth-Century Mexico* (1989).

David Ewing Duncan, *Hernando de Soto: A Savage Quest in the Americas* (1995).

Richard Flint and Shirley Cushing Flint, *The Coronado Expedition* (2003).

Serge Gruzinski, *The Conquest of Mexico: The Incorporation of Indian Societies into the Western World, Sixteenth–Eighteenth Centuries* (1993).

Ramón A. Gutiérrez, *When Jesus Came, the Corn Mothers Went Away: Marriage, Sexuality, and Power in New Mexico, 1500–1846* (1991).

Robert H. Jackson, *Race, Caste, and Status: Indians in Colonial Spanish America* (1999).

John L. Kessell, *Pueblos, Spaniards, and the Kingdom of New Mexico* (2010).

Andrew L. Knaut, *The Pueblo Revolt of 1680: Conquest and Resistance in Seventeenth-Century New Mexico* (1995).

Miguel León-Portilla, *Bernardino de Sahagún: First Anthropologist* (2002).

James Lockhart, *The Nahuas after Conquest: A Social and Cultural History of the Indians of Central Mexico, Sixteenth through Eighteenth Centuries* (1992).

Jerald T. Milanich, *Laboring in the Fields of the Lord: Spanish Missions and Southwestern Indians* (1999).

Stuart B. Schwartz, *All Can Be Saved: Religious Tolerance and Salvation in the Iberian Atlantic World* (2009).

Charles A. Truxillo, *By the Sword and the Cross: The Historical Evolution of the Catholic World Monarchy in Spain and the New World, 1492–1825* (2001).

Stephanie Gail Wood, *Transcending Conquest: Nahua Views of Spanish Colonial Mexico* (2003).

► **FOR MORE BOOKS ABOUT TOPICS IN THIS CHAPTER,** see the Online Bibliography at **bedfordstmartins.com/roark.**

► **FOR ADDITIONAL PRIMARY SOURCES FROM THIS PERIOD,** see in Michael Johnson, ed., *Reading the American Past*, Fifth Edition.

► **FOR WEB SITES, IMAGES, AND DOCUMENTS RELATED TO TOPICS AND PLACES IN THIS CHAPTER,** visit Make History at **bedfordstmartins.com/roark.**

Reviewing Chapter 2

REVIEW QUESTIONS

Use key terms and dates to support your answers.

1. Why did European exploration expand dramatically in the fifteenth century? (pp. 33–36)

2. How did Columbus's discoveries help revolutionize Europeans' understanding of world geography? (pp. 36–40)

3. How did New Spain's distinctive colonial population shape its economy and society? (pp. 40–53)

4. How did Spain's conquests in the New World shape Spanish influence in Europe? (pp. 54–56)

MAKING CONNECTIONS

Draw on key terms, the timeline, and review questions.

1. The Columbian exchange exposed people on both sides of the Atlantic to surprising new people and goods. It also produced dramatic demographic and political transformations in the Old World and the New. How did the Columbian exchange lead to redistributions of power and population? Discuss these changes, being sure to cite examples from both contexts.

2. Despite inferior numbers, the Spaniards were able to conquer the Mexica and maintain control of the colonial hierarchy that followed. Why did the Spanish conquest of the Mexica succeed, and how did the Spaniards govern the conquered territory to maintain their dominance?

3. Spanish conquest in North America brought new peoples into constant contact. How did the Spaniards' and Indians' perceptions of each other shape their interactions? In your answer, cite specific examples and consider how perceptions changed over time.

4. How did the astonishing wealth generated for the Spanish crown by its conquest of the New World influence European colonial exploration throughout the sixteenth century? In your answer, discuss ways it both encouraged and limited interest in exploration.

LINKING TO THE PAST

Link events in this chapter to earlier events.

1. How did the legacy of ancient Americans influence their descendants' initial encounters and subsequent economic, social, and military relations with Europeans in the sixteenth century? (See chapter 1.)

2. Before the arrival of Europeans, Native Americans in the New World had no knowledge of Christianity, just as Europeans had no knowledge of Native American religions. To what extent did contrasting religious beliefs and assumptions influence relations among Europeans and Native Americans in the New World in the sixteenth century? (See chapter 1.)

▶ **FOR PRACTICE QUIZZES AND OTHER STUDY TOOLS,** visit the Online Study Guide at **bedfordstmartins.com/roark.**

TIMELINE 1480–1599

1480	• Portuguese ships reach Congo.
1488	• Bartolomeu Dias rounds Cape of Good Hope.
1492	• Christopher Columbus lands on Caribbean island that he names San Salvador.
1493	• Columbus makes second voyage to New World.
1494	• Portugal and Spain negotiate Treaty of Tordesillas.
1497	• John Cabot searches for Northwest Passage.
1498	• Vasco da Gama sails to India.
1513	• Vasco Núñez de Balboa crosses Isthmus of Panama.
1517	• Protestant Reformation begins in Germany.
1519	• Hernán Cortés leads expedition to find wealth in Mexico. • Ferdinand Magellan sets out to sail around the world.
1520	• Mexica in Tenochtitlán revolt against Spaniards.
1521	• Cortés conquers Mexica at Tenochtitlán.
1532	• Francisco Pizarro begins conquest of Peru.
1535	• Jacques Cartier explores St. Lawrence River.
1539	• Hernando de Soto explores southeastern North America.
1540	• Francisco Vásquez de Coronado starts to explore Southwest and Great Plains.
1542	• Juan Rodríguez Cabrillo explores California coast.
1549	• Repartimiento reforms begin to replace encomienda.
1565	• St. Augustine, Florida, settled.
1576	• Martin Frobisher explores northern Canadian waters.
1587	• English settle Roanoke Island.
1598	• Juan de Oñate explores New Mexico.
1599	• Acoma pueblos revolt against Oñate.

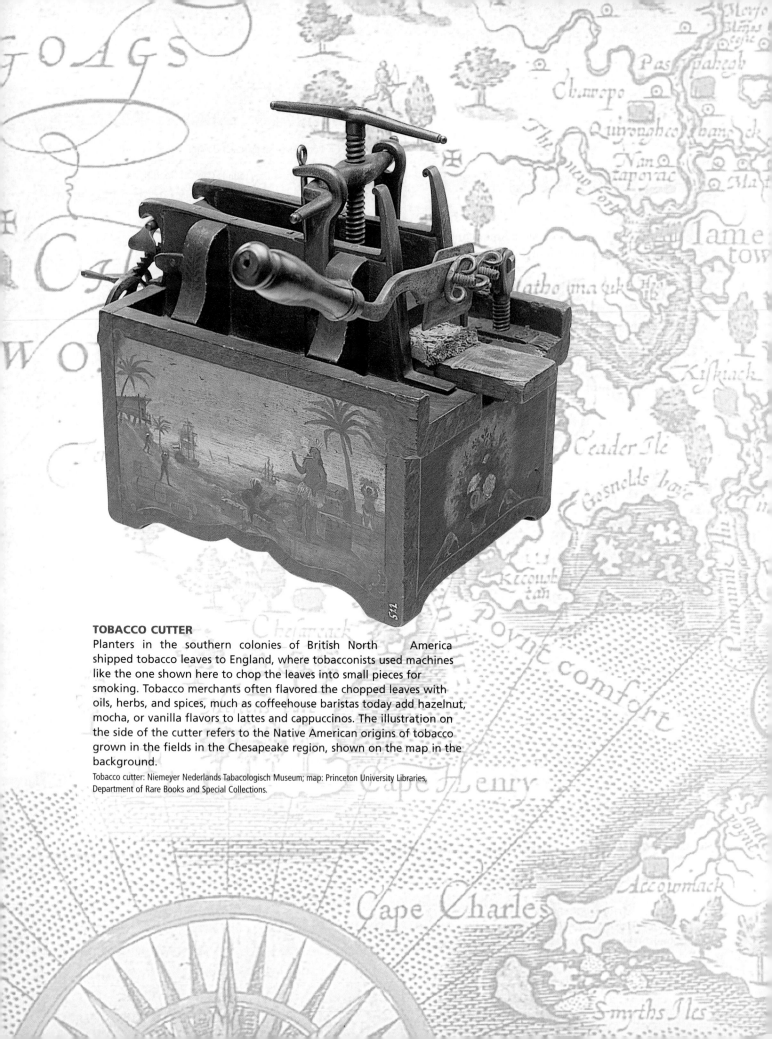

TOBACCO CUTTER

Planters in the southern colonies of British North America shipped tobacco leaves to England, where tobacconists used machines like the one shown here to chop the leaves into small pieces for smoking. Tobacco merchants often flavored the chopped leaves with oils, herbs, and spices, much as coffeehouse baristas today add hazelnut, mocha, or vanilla flavors to lattes and cappuccinos. The illustration on the side of the cutter refers to the Native American origins of tobacco grown in the fields in the Chesapeake region, shown on the map in the background.

Tobacco cutter: Niemeyer Nederlands Tabacologisch Museum; map: Princeton University Libraries, Department of Rare Books and Special Collections.

The Southern Colonies in the Seventeenth Century 1601–1700

IN DECEMBER 1607, BARELY SIX MONTHS AFTER ARRIVING AT Jamestown with the first English colonists, Captain John Smith was captured by warriors of Powhatan, the supreme chief of about fourteen thousand Algonquian Indians who inhabited the coastal plain of present-day Virginia, near Chesapeake Bay. According to Smith, Powhatan "feasted him after their best barbarous manner." Then, Smith recalled, "two great stones were brought before Powhatan: then as many [Indians] as could layd hands on [Smith], dragged him to [the stones], and thereon laid his head, and being ready with their clubs, to beate out his braines." At that moment, Pocahontas, Powhatan's eleven-year-old daughter, rushed forward and "got [Smith's] head in her armes, and laid her owne upon his to save him from death." Pocahontas, Smith wrote, "hazarded the beating out of her owne braines to save mine, and . . . so prevailed with her father, that I was safely conducted [back] to James towne."

This romantic story of an Indian maiden rescuing a white soldier and saving Jamestown — and ultimately English colonization of North America — has been enshrined in the writing of American history since 1624, when Smith published his *Generall Historie of Virginia*. Historians believe that this episode happened more or less as Smith described it. But Smith did not understand why Pocahontas acted as she did.

Most likely, when Pocahontas intervened to save Smith, she was a knowing participant in an Algonquian ceremony that expressed Powhatan's supremacy and his ritualistic adoption of Smith as a subordinate chief, or *werowance*. What Smith interpreted as Pocahontas's saving him from certain death was instead a ceremonial enactment of Powhatan's willingness to incorporate Smith and the white strangers at Jamestown into Powhatan's empire. Powhatan routinely attached his sons and daughters to subordinate tribes as an expression of his protection and his dominance. By appearing to save Smith, Pocahontas was probably acting out Smith's new status as an adopted member of Powhatan's extended family.

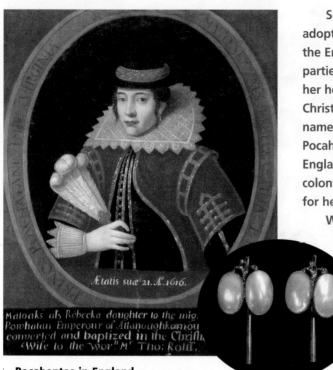

Ætatis suæ 21. Aᵒ. 1616.

Matoaks als Rebecka daughter to the mig. Powhatan Emperour of Attanoughkomouk converted and baptized in the Christi. Wife to the worᵗʰ Mʳ Thoː Rolff.

Pocahontas in England
Shortly after Pocahontas and her husband, John Rolfe, arrived in England in 1616, she posed for this portrait dressed in English clothing, possibly including the earrings shown here, suitable for a princess. The portrait captures the dual novelty of England for Pocahontas and of Pocahontas for the English. Ornate, courtly clothing probably signified to English observers that Pocahontas was royalty and to Pocahontas that the English were accepting her as befitted the "Emperour" Powhatan's daughter. The mutability of Pocahontas's identity is displayed in the identification of her as "Matoaks" or "Rebecka." Painting: National Portrait Gallery, Smithsonian Institution/Art Resource, NY; earrings: Courtesy of Preservation Virginia.

Smith returned to England about two years after the adoption ritual. In Virginia, relations between Powhatan and the English colonists deteriorated into bloody raids by both parties. In 1613, the colonists captured Pocahontas and held her hostage at Jamestown. Within a year, she converted to Christianity and married one of the colonists, a widower named John Rolfe. After giving birth to a son named Thomas, Pocahontas, her husband, and the new baby sailed for England in the spring of 1616. There, promoters of the Virginia colony dressed her as a proper Englishwoman and arranged for her to go to a ball attended by the king and queen.

When John Smith heard that Pocahontas was in London, he went to see her. According to Smith, Pocahontas said, "You did promise Powhatan what was yours should bee his, and he the like to you; you called him father, being in his land a stranger, and by the same reason so must I doe you." It seems likely that Pocahontas believed that her incorporation into English society was a counterpart of the adoption ritual Powhatan had staged for John Smith in Virginia back in 1607.

Pocahontas died in England in 1617. Her son, Thomas, ultimately returned to Virginia, and by the time of the American Revolution his descendants numbered in the hundreds. But the world Thomas Rolfe and his descendants inhabited was shaped by a reversal of the power ritualized when his mother "saved" John Smith. By the end of the seventeenth century, Native Americans no longer dominated the newcomers who had arrived in the Chesapeake with John Smith.

During the seventeenth century, English colonists learned how to deviate from the example of New Spain (see chapter 2) by growing tobacco, a crop Native Americans had cultivated in small quantities for centuries. The new settlers grew enormous quantities of tobacco and exported most of it to England. Instead of incorporating Powhatan's people into their new society, the settlers encroached on Indian land and built new societies on the foundation of tobacco agriculture and transatlantic trade.

Producing large crop surpluses for export required hard labor and people who were willing — or could be forced — to do it. While New Spain took advantage of Native American labor, for the most part the Native Americans in British North America refused to be conscripted into the English colonists' fields. Instead, the settlers depended on the labor of family members, indentured servants, and, by the last third of the seventeenth century, African slaves.

By the end of the century, the southern colonies had become sharply different both from the world dominated by Powhatan when the Jamestown settlers first arrived and from contemporary English society. In ways unimaginable to Powhatan, Pocahontas, and John Smith, the colonists paid homage to the international market and the English monarch by working mightily to make a good living growing crops for sale to the Old World.

▶ An English Colony on Chesapeake Bay

When James I became king of England in 1603, he looked toward North America as a possible location for English colonies that could be as profitable as New Spain. In 1606, he granted the Virginia Company more than six million acres in North America in hopes of establishing the English equivalent of Spain's New World empire. Enthusiastic reports from the Roanoke voyages twenty years earlier (see chapter 2) claimed that in Virginia "the earth bringeth foorth all things in aboundance . . . without toile or labour."

Even if these reports were exaggerated, investors reasoned, perhaps some valuable exotic crop could be grown profitably. Maybe rich lodes of gold and silver awaited discovery, as they had in New Spain. Or maybe quick and easy profits could be grabbed in an occasional raid on the gold and silver stashed in the holds of Spanish ships that cruised up the Atlantic coast on their way to Spain. Such hopes failed to address the difficulties of adapting English desires and expectations to the New World already inhabited by Native Americans. The Jamestown settlement struggled to survive for nearly two decades, until the royal government replaced the private Virginia Company, which never earned a penny for its investors.

The Fragile Jamestown Settlement

Although Spain claimed all of North America under the 1494 Treaty of Tordesillas (see chapter 2),

VISUAL ACTIVITY

Secotan Village
This engraving, published in 1612, was copied from an original drawing John White made in 1585 when he visited the village of Secotan on the coast of North Carolina. The drawing provides a schematic view of daily life in the village, which may have resembled one of Powhatan's settlements. White noted on the original that the fire burning behind the line of crouching men was "the place of solemne prayer." The large building in the lower left was a tomb where the bodies of important leaders were kept. Dwellings lined a central space where men and women ate. Corn is growing in the fields along the right side of the village. The engraver included hunters shooting deer at the upper left. Hunting was probably never so convenient — no such hunters or deer appear in White's original drawing. This drawing conveys the message that Secotan was orderly, settled, religious, harmonious, and peaceful (notice the absence of fortifications), and very different from English villages.
Princeton University Libraries, Department of Rare Books and Special Collections.

READING THE IMAGE: What does this image say about Indian life in Secotan?
CONNECTIONS: How did Indian society differ from the English tobacco society that emerged later?

King James believed that England could encroach on the outskirts of Spain's New World empire. In 1588, England had successfully defended itself from the Spanish Armada, a large fleet of warships sent to invade England and bring it under Spanish rule. Now, the king hoped to flex England's muscles overseas and build new colonies in areas of North America that Spain could not defend. In effect, his land grant to the **Virginia Company**, a joint-stock company, was a royal license to poach on both Spanish claims and Powhatan's chiefdom.

English merchants had pooled their capital and shared risks for many years by using joint-stock companies for trading voyages to Europe, Asia, and Africa. The London investors of the Virginia Company, however, had larger ambitions: They hoped to found an empire that would strengthen England both overseas and at home. Richard Hakluyt, a strong proponent of colonization, claimed that a colony would provide work for swarms of poor "valiant youths rusting and hurtfull by lack of employment" in England. Colonists could buy English goods and supply products that England now had to import from other nations. More trade and more jobs would benefit many people in England, but the Virginia Company investors risked their capital because they fervently hoped to reap quick profits from the new colony.

In December 1606, the ships *Susan Constant*, *Discovery*, and *Godspeed* carried 144 Englishmen toward Virginia. They arrived at the mouth of Chesapeake Bay on April 26, 1607. That night while the colonists rested onshore, one of them later recalled, a band of Indians "creeping upon all foure, from the Hills like Beares, with their Bowes in their mouthes," attacked and dangerously wounded two men. The attack by **Algonquian Indians** gave the colonists an early warning that the North American wilderness was not quite the paradise described by the Virginia Company's publications in England. A few weeks later, they went ashore on a small peninsula in the midst of the territory ruled by **Powhatan**. With the memory of their first night in America fresh in their minds, they quickly built a fort, the first building in the settlement they named **Jamestown**.

The Jamestown fort showed the colonists' awareness that they needed to protect themselves from Indians and Spaniards. Spain planned to wipe out Jamestown when the time was ripe, but that time never came. Powhatan's people defended Virginia as their own. For weeks, the settlers and Powhatan's warriors skirmished repeatedly. English muskets and cannons repelled Indian attacks on Jamestown, but the Indians' superior numbers and knowledge of the Virginia wilderness made it risky for the settlers to venture far beyond the peninsula.

The settlers soon confronted dangerous, invisible threats: disease and starvation. Salt water and freshwater mixed in the swampy marshlands surrounding Jamestown, creating an ecological zone that allowed waterborne diseases to thrive, especially since the colonists' sanitation precautions were haphazard. During the summer, many of the Englishmen lay "night and day groaning in every corner of the Fort most pittiful to heare," wrote George Percy, one of the settlers. By September, fifty colonists had died. The colonists increased their misery by bickering among themselves, leaving crops unplanted and food supplies shrinking. "For the most part [the settlers] died of meere famine," Percy wrote; "there were never Englishmen left in a forreigne Countrey in such miserie as wee were in this new discovered Virginia."

Chief Powhatan

In 1612, John Smith published a map of early Virginia that included this drawing of Powhatan, surrounded by some of his many wives, smoking a pipe, and adorned with a feathered headdress. The illustration was almost certainly made by an English artist who had never been to Virginia or seen Powhatan but who tried to imagine the scene as described by John Smith. Princeton University Libraries, Department of Rare Books and Special Collections.

Powhatan's people came to the rescue of the weakened and demoralized Englishmen. Early in September 1607, they began to bring corn to the colony for barter. Accustomed to eating food derived from wheat, English people considered corn the food "of the barbarous Indians which know no better . . . a more convenient food for swine than for man." The famished colonists soon overcame their prejudice against corn. Jamestown leader **Captain John Smith** recalled that the settlers were so hungry that "they would have sould their soules" for half a basket of Powhatan's corn. Indians' corn acquired by both trade and plunder managed to keep 38 of the original settlers alive until a fresh supply of food and 120 more colonists arrived from England in January 1608.

It is difficult to exaggerate the fragility of the early Jamestown settlement. One colonist lamented that "this place [is] a meere plantacion of sorrowes and Cropp of trobles, having been plentifull in nothing but want and wanting nothing but plenty." During the "starving time" winter of 1609–10, food became so short that one or two famished settlers resorted to eating their recently deceased neighbors. When a new group of colonists arrived in 1610, they found only 60 of the 500 previous settlers still alive. The Virginia Company sent hundreds of new settlers to Jamestown each year, each of them eager to find the paradise promised by the company. But most settlers went instead to early graves.

Cooperation and Conflict between Natives and Newcomers

Powhatan's people stayed in contact with the English settlers but maintained their distance. The Virginia Company boasted that the settlers bought from the Indians "the pearles of earth [corn] and [sold] to them the pearles of heaven [Christianity]." In fact, few Indians converted to Christianity, and the English devoted scant effort to proselytizing. Marriage between Indian women and English men also was rare, despite the acute shortage of English women in Virginia in the early years. Few settlers other than John Smith bothered to learn the Indians' language.

Powhatan's people regarded the English with suspicion, for good reason. Although the settlers often made friendly overtures to the Indians, they did not hesitate to use their guns and swords to enforce English notions of proper Indian behavior. More than once, the Indians refused to trade their corn to the settlers, evidently hoping to starve them out. Each time, the English broke the boycott by attacking the uncooperative Indians, pillaging their villages, and confiscating their corn.

The Indians retaliated against English violence, but for fifteen years they did not organize an all-out assault on the European intruders, probably for several reasons. Although Christianity held few attractions for the Indians, the power of the settlers' God impressed them. One chief told John Smith that "he did believe that our [English] God as much exceeded theirs as our guns did their bows and arrows." Powhatan probably concluded that these powerful strangers would make better allies than enemies. As allies, the English strengthened Powhatan's dominance over the tribes in the region.

They also traded with his people, usually exchanging European goods for corn. Native Virginians had some copper weapons and tools before the English arrived, but they quickly recognized the superiority of the intruders' iron and steel knives, axes, and pots, and they traded eagerly to obtain them. The trade that supplied the Indians with European conveniences provided the English settlers with a necessity: food.

But why were the settlers unable to feed themselves for more than a decade? First, as the staggering death rate suggests, many settlers were too sick to be productive members of the colony. Second, very few farmers came to Virginia in the early years. Instead, most of the newcomers were gentlemen and their servants. In John Smith's words, these men "never did know what a day's work was." The proportion of gentlemen in Virginia in the early years was six times greater than in England, a reflection of the Virginia Company's urgent need for investors and settlers. John Smith declared repeatedly that in Virginia "there is no country to pillage [as in New Spain]. . . . All you can expect from [Virginia] must be by labor." For years, however, colonists clung to English notions that gentlemen should not work with their hands and that tradesmen should work only in trades for which they had been trained. These ideas made more sense in labor-rich England than in labor-poor Virginia. In the meantime, the colonists depended on the Indians' corn for food.

> "This place [is] a meere plantacion of sorrowes and Cropp of trobles, having been plentifull in nothing but want and wanting nothing but plenty."
> — A Jamestown colonist

Becaufe many doe defire to know the manner of their Language, I haue inferted thefe few words.

Ka katorawincs yowo. What call you this.
Nemarough, a man.
Crenepo, a woman.
Marowancheffo, a boy.
Yehawkans, Houfes.
Matchcores, Skins, or garments.
Mockafins, Shooes.
Tuffan, Beds. *Pokatawer,* Fire.
Attawp, A bow. *Attonce,* Arrowes.
Monacookes, Swords.
Aumoubhowgh, A Target.
Pawcuffacks, Gunnes.
Tomahacks, Axes.
Tockahacks, Pickaxes.
Pamefacks, Kniues.
Accowprets, Sheares.
Pawpecones, Pipes. *Mattaffin,* Copper
Vffawaffin, Iron, Braffe, Silver, or any white mettall. *Muffes,* Woods.
Attaffkuff, Leaues, weeds, or graffe.
Chepfin, Land. *Shacquohocan.* A ftone.
Wepenter, A cookold.
Suckahanna, Water. *Noughmaff,* Fifh.
Copotone, Sturgeon.
Weghfhaughes, Flefh.
Sawwehone, Bloud.
Netoppew, Friends.
Marrapough, Enemies.
Maskapow, the worft of the enemies.
Mawchick chammay, The beft of friends
Cafacunnakack, peya quagh acquintan uttafantafough, In how many daies will there come hither any more Englifh Ships.
  Their Numbers.
Necut, 1. *Ningh,* 2. *Nuff,* 3. *Yowgh,* 4.
Paranske, 5. *Comotinch,* 6. *Toppawoff,* 7
Nuffwafh, 8. *Kekatawgh,* 9. *Kaskeke* 10
They count no more but by tennes as followeth.
Cafe, how many.
Ninghfapooeksku, 20.
Nuffapooeksku, 30.

Yowghapooeksku, 40.
Parankeftafsapoockfku, 50.
Comatincktafsapoockfku, 60.
Nuffwafhtafsapoockfku, 70.
Kekataughtafsapoockfku, 90.
Necuttoughtyfimough, 100.
Necuttwevnquaough, 1000.
Rawcofowghs, Dayes.
Kefkowghes, Sunnes:
Toppquough. Nights.
Nepawwefhowghs, Moones.
Pawpaxfoughes, Yeares.
Pummahumps, Starres.
Ofies, Heavens.
Okees, Gods.
Quiyougheofoughs, Pettie Gods, and their affinities.
Righcomoughes, Deaths.
Kekughes, Liues.
Mowchick woyawgh tawgh noeragh kaquere mecher, I am very hungry? what fhall I eate?
Tawnor nehiegh Powhatan, Where dwels Powhatan.
Mache, nehiegh yourowgh, Orapaks. Now he dwelsa great way hence at Orapaks.
Vittapitchewayne anpechitchs nehawper Werowacomoco, You lie, he ftaid ever at Werowacomoco.
Kator nehiegh mattagh neer vttapitchewayne, Truely he is there I doe not lie.
Spaughtynere keragh werowance mawmarinough kekatê wawgh peyaquaugh. Run you then to the King Mawmarynough and bid him come hither.
Vtteke, e peya weyack wighwhip, Get you gone, & come againe quickly.
Kekaten Pokahontas patiaquagh niugh tanks manotyens neer mowchick rawrenock audowgh, Bid Pokahontas bring hither two little Baskets, and I will giue her white Beads to make her a Chaine. *FINIS.*

John Smith's Dictionary of Powhatan's Language
In 1612, John Smith published this list of the English equivalents of words used by Powhatan's people, almost the only record of the coastal Algonquian language that exists. Smith probably compiled the list by pointing and listening carefully. Can you find any of Powhatan's words that made their way into common English usage? Princeton University Libraries, Department of Rare Books and Special Collections.

The persistence of the Virginia colony created difficulties for Powhatan's chiefdom. Steady contact between natives and newcomers spread European diseases among the Indians, who suffered deadly epidemics in 1608 and between 1617 and 1619. The settlers' insatiable appetite for corn introduced other tensions within Powhatan's villages.

To produce enough corn for their own survival and for trade with the English required the Indians to spend more time and effort growing crops. Since Native American women did most of the agricultural work, their burden increased along with the cultural significance of their chief crop. The corn surplus grown by Indian women was bartered for desirable English goods such as iron pots, which replaced the baskets and ceramic jugs Native Americans had used for millennia. Growing enough corn to feed the English altered age-old patterns of village life. But from the Indians' viewpoint, the most important fact about the always-hungry English colonists was that they were not going away.

Powhatan died in 1618, and his brother **Opechancanough** replaced him as supreme chief. In 1622, Opechancanough organized an all-out assault on the English settlers. As an English colonist observed, "When the day appointed for the massacre arrived [March 22], a number of savages visited many of our people in their dwellings, and while partaking with them of their meal[,] the savages, at a given signal, drew their weapons and fell upon us murdering and killing everybody they could reach[,] sparing neither women nor children, as well inside as outside the dwellings." In all, the Indians killed 347 colonists, nearly a third of the English population. But the attack failed to dislodge the colonists. Instead, in the years to come the settlers unleashed a murderous campaign of Indian extermination that pushed the Indians beyond the small circumference of white settlement. Before 1622, the settlers knew that the Indians, though dangerous, were necessary to keep the colony alive. In the years after 1622, most colonists considered the Indians their perpetual enemies.

From Private Company to Royal Government

In the immediate aftermath of the 1622 uprising, the survivors became discouraged and demoralized because, as one explained, the "massacre

Advertisement for Jamestown Settlers
Virginia imported thousands of indentured servants to labor in the tobacco fields, but the colony also advertised in 1631 for settlers like those pictured here. The notice features men and women equally, although men heavily outnumbered women in the Chesapeake region. How would the English experiences of the individuals portrayed in the advertisement have been useful in Virginia? Why would such individuals have wanted to leave England and go to Virginia? If indentured servants had been pictured, how might they have differed in appearance from these people?
Harvard Map Collection, Pusey Library, Harvard University.

killed all our Countrie . . . [and] burst the heart of all the rest." The disaster prompted a royal investigation of affairs in Virginia. The investigators discovered that the appalling mortality among the colonists was caused more by disease and mismanagement than by Indian raids. In 1624, King James revoked the charter of the Virginia Company and made Virginia a **royal colony**, subject to the direction of the royal government rather than to the company's private investors, an arrangement that lasted until 1776.

The king now appointed the governor of Virginia and his council, but most other features of local government established under the Virginia Company remained intact. In 1619, for example, the company had inaugurated the **House of Burgesses**, an assembly of representatives (called burgesses) elected by the colony's inhabitants. (Historians do not know exactly which settlers were considered inhabitants and were thus qualified to vote.) Under the new royal government, laws passed by the burgesses had to be approved by the king's bureaucrats in England rather than by the company. Otherwise, the House of Burgesses continued as before, acquiring distinction as the oldest representative legislative assembly in the English colonies. Under the new royal government, all free adult men in Virginia could vote for the House of Burgesses, giving it a far broader and more representative constituency than the English House of Commons had.

The demise of the Virginia Company marked the end of the first phase of colonization of the Chesapeake region. From the first 105 adventurers in 1607, the population had grown to about 1,200 by 1624. Despite mortality rates higher than during the worst epidemics in London, new settlers still came. Their arrival and King James's willingness to take over the struggling colony reflected a fundamental change in Virginia. After years of fruitless experimentation, it was becoming clear that English settlers could make a fortune in Virginia by growing tobacco.

> **REVIEW** Why did Powhatan behave as he did toward the English colonists?

▶ A Tobacco Society

Tobacco grew wild in the New World, and Native Americans used it for thousands of years before Europeans arrived. Columbus observed Indians smoking tobacco on his first voyage to the New World. Many other sixteenth-century European explorers noticed the Indians' habit of "drinking smoke." During the sixteenth century, Spanish colonists in the New World sent tobacco to Europe, where it was an expensive luxury used sparingly by a few. During the next century,

English colonists in North America sent so much tobacco to European markets that it became an affordable indulgence used often by many people. (See "Beyond America's Borders," page 70.)

By 1700, nearly 100,000 colonists lived in the Chesapeake region, encompassing Virginia, Maryland, and northern North Carolina (Map 3.1). They exported more than 35 million pounds of tobacco, a fivefold increase in per capita production since 1620. Clearly, Chesapeake colonists mastered the demands of tobacco agriculture, and the "Stinkinge Weede" (a seventeenth-century Marylander's term for tobacco) also mastered the colonists. Settlers lived by the rhythms of tobacco agriculture, and their endless need for labor attracted droves of English indentured servants to work in tobacco fields.

Tobacco Agriculture

Initially, the Virginia Company had no plans to grow and sell tobacco. "As for tobacco," John Smith wrote, "we never then dreamt of it." **John Rolfe** — future husband of **Pocahontas** — planted West Indian tobacco seeds in 1612 and learned that they flourished in Virginia. By 1617, the colonists had grown enough tobacco to send the first commercial shipment to England, where it sold for a high price. After that, Virginia transformed itself from a colony of rather aimless adventurers who had difficulty growing enough corn to feed themselves to a society of dedicated planters who grew as much tobacco as possible.

A demanding crop, tobacco required close attention and a great deal of hand labor year-round. Primitive tools and methods made this intensive cycle of labor taxing. Like the Indians, the colonists "cleared" fields by cutting a ring of bark from each tree (a procedure known as "girdling"), thereby killing the tree. Girdling brought sunlight to clearings but left fields studded with tree stumps, making the use of plows impractical. Instead, colonists used heavy hoes to till their tobacco

Tobacco Plantation

This print illustrates the processing of tobacco on a seventeenth-century plantation. Workers cut the mature plants and put the leaves in piles to wilt (left foreground). After the leaves dried somewhat, they were suspended from poles in a drying barn (right foreground), where they were seasoned before being packed in casks for shipping. The print suggests the labor demands of tobacco by showing twenty-two individuals, all but two of them actively at work with the crop. The couple in the left foreground may be on their way to work, but it is more likely that they are overseeing the labor of their servants or employees. From "About Tobacco," Lehman Brothers.

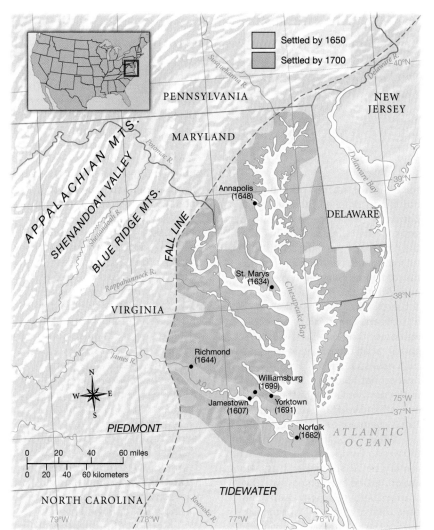

MAP ACTIVITY

Map 3.1 Chesapeake Colonies in the Seventeenth Century

This map illustrates the intimate association between land and water in the settlement of the Chesapeake in the seventeenth century. The fall line indicates the limit of navigable water, where rapids and falls prevented travel farther upstream. Although Delaware had excellent access to navigable water, it was claimed and defended by the Dutch colony at New Amsterdam (discussed in chapter 4) rather than by the English settlements in Virginia and Maryland shown on this map.

READING THE MAP: Using the notations on the map, create a chronology of the establishment of towns and settlements. What physical features correspond to the earliest habitation by English settlers?

CONNECTIONS: Why was access to navigable water so important? Given the settlers' need for defense against native tribes, what explains the distance between settlements?

---

fields. To plant, a visitor observed, they "just make holes [with a stick] into which they drop the seeds," much as the Indians did. Growing tobacco with such methods left little time for idleness, but the colonists enjoyed the fruits of their labor. "Everyone smokes while working or idling," one traveler reported, including "men, women, girls, and boys, from the age of seven years."

The English settlers worked hard because their labor promised greater rewards in the Chesapeake region than in England. One colonist proclaimed that "the dirt of this Province affords as great a profit to the general Inhabitant, as the Gold of Peru doth to . . . the Spaniard." Although he exaggerated, it was true that a hired man could expect to earn two or three times more in Virginia's tobacco fields than in England. Better still, in Virginia land was so abundant

that it was extremely cheap compared with land in England.

By the mid-seventeenth century, common laborers could buy a hundred acres for less than their annual wages — an impossibility in England. New settlers who paid their own transportation to the Chesapeake received a grant of fifty acres of free land (termed a **headright**). The Virginia Company granted headrights to encourage settlement, and the royal government continued them for the same reason.

A Servant Labor System

Headrights, cheap land, and high wages gave poor English folk powerful incentives to immigrate to the New World. Yet many potential immigrants could not scrape together the money to pay for a trip across the Atlantic. Their poverty

American Tobacco and European Consumers

English colonies in the Chesapeake were "wholly built upon smoke," King Charles I observed during the second quarter of the seventeenth century. The king's shrewd observation highlighted the fundamental reason the seventeenth-century Chesapeake colonies prospered by growing ever-larger crops of tobacco: namely, because people on the eastern side of the Atlantic were willing to buy ever-greater quantities of tobacco to smoke — and to sniff, chew, drink, and even use for enemas. Europeans' desire for tobacco was the only reason it had commercial value. Without this demand, the history of both the English North American colonies and the rest of the world would have been very different.

Still, some Europeans hated tobacco, most notably England's King James I (who preceded Charles I). In *A Counterblaste to Tobacco*, a pamphlet published in 1611, James declared that smoking was "A custome lothsome to the eye, hatefull to the Nose, harmefull to the braine, dangerous to the Lungs, and in the blacke stinking fume thereof, neerest resembling the horrible . . . smoke of the pit that is bottomelesse." He reviled the "filthy smoke," the "stinking Suffumigation," the "spitting," the "lust," the "shameful imbecilitie," and the "sin" of tobacco. James's fulminations acknowledged that "the generall use of Tobacco" was "daily practiced . . . by all sorts and complexions of people." He noted, "The publike use [of tobacco], at all times, and in all places, hath now so farre prevailed that a man cannot heartily welcome his friend now, but straight they must bee in hand with Tobacco." Clearly, James championed a lost cause.

When the Spaniards first brought tobacco to Europe during the sixteenth century, physicians praised it as a wonder drug. One proclaimed that "this precious herb is so general a human need [that it is] not only for the sick but for the healthy." Such strong recommendations from learned men were reinforced by everyday experiences of commoners. Sailors returning from the New World "suck in as much smoke as they can," one Spaniard observed,

"[and] in this way they say that their hunger and thirst are allayed, their strength is restored and their spirits are refreshed; [and] . . . their brains are lulled by a joyous intoxication." That joyous intoxication — "a bewitching quality," King James called it — made tobacco irresistible to most Europeans.

At the beginning of the seventeenth century, tobacco was scarce and therefore expensive. In 1603, for example, England imported only about 25,000 pounds of tobacco, all from New Spain. By 1700, England imported nearly 40 million pounds of tobacco, almost all from the Chesapeake colonies. The huge increase in the tobacco supply caused prices to plummet. A quantity of tobacco that sold for a dollar in 1600 cost less than two and a half cents by 1700.

The low prices made possible by bumper crops harvested by planters in the Chesapeake transformed tobacco consumption in England and elsewhere in Europe. Annual per capita tobacco use in England grew more than 200-fold during the seventeenth century, from less than a fifth of an ounce in the 1620s to 2.3 pounds by 1700. American tobacco became the first colonial product of mass consumption by Europeans, blazing a trail followed by New World sugar, coffee, and chocolate.

Tobacco altered European culture. It spawned new industries, new habits, and new forms of social life. Smoking was the most common form of tobacco consumption in the seven-

and the colonists' crying need for labor formed the basic context for the creation of a servant labor system.

About 80 percent of the immigrants to the Chesapeake during the seventeenth century came as **indentured servants**. Instead of a slave society, the seventeenth-century Chesapeake region was fundamentally a society of white servants and ex-servants.

Relatively few African slaves were brought to the Chesapeake in the first half century after settlement. The first known Africans arrived in Virginia in 1619 aboard the *White Lion*, an English privateer that had seized

them from a Portuguese slave ship bound for South America. The "20. And odd Negroes," as John Rolfe called them, were slaves captured in Angola in west-central Africa. Virginia officials acquired them by giving the privateer captain supplies in exchange. A few more slaves trickled into the Chesapeake region during the next several decades. Until the 1670s, however, only a small number of slaves labored in Chesapeake tobacco fields. (Large numbers of slaves came in the eighteenth century, as chapter 5 explains.) Men and women of African descent occasionally became indentured servants, served out their terms of servitude, and

teenth century, and smokers needed far more than tobacco to light up. They needed pipes; they needed boxes or tins to hold their tobacco and a container to hold the embers they used to light the tobacco, or a flint and steel to strike sparks; they needed pipe cleaners; they needed spittoons if they were smoking in a respectable place that disapproved of spitting on the floor. European merchants and manufacturers supplied all these needs, along with the tobacco itself, which had to be graded, chopped, flavored, packaged, stored, advertised, and sold. Men and women smoked in taverns, in smoking clubs, around dinner tables, and in bed.

The somewhat cumbersome paraphernalia of smoking caused many tobacco users to shift to snuff, which became common in the eighteenth century. Snuff use eliminated smoke, fire, and spitting, replacing them with the more refined gesture of taking a pinch of powdered, flavored tobacco from a snuffbox and sniffing it into one or both nostrils, which produced a fashionable sneeze followed by a genteel wipe with a dainty handkerchief. One snuff taker explained the health benefits of such a sneeze: "by its gently pricking and stimulating the membranes, [snuff] causes Sneezing or Contractions, whereby the Glands like so many squeezed Sponges, dismiss their Seriosities and Filth."

Whether consumed by sniffing, by smoking, or in other ways, tobacco profoundly changed European habits,

Smoking Club
In Europe, tobacco smokers congregated in clubs to enjoy the intoxicating weed. This seventeenth-century print satirizes smokers' gatherings of fashionable men, women, and children who indulged their taste for tobacco. Emblems of the tobacco trade adorn the wall; pipes, spittoons, and other smoking implements are close at hand; and the dog cleans up after those who cannot hold their smoke. Koninklijke Bibliotheek, The Hague.

economies, and societies. And its popularity turned the Chesapeake colonies into invaluable assets for England.

America in a Global Context

1. Why did European demand for tobacco grow so dramatically during the seventeenth century?

2. How did Europeans use tobacco, and why? Why did some people object to tobacco use?

3. What were the consequences of the transatlantic tobacco market both in the Chesapeake and in Europe?

became free. A few slaves purchased their way out of bondage and lived as free people, even owning land and using the local courts to resolve disputes, much as freed white servants did. These people were exceptions, however. Almost all people of African descent were slaves and remained enslaved for life.

A small number of Native Americans also became servants. But the overwhelming majority of indentured servants were white immigrants from England. To buy passage aboard a ship bound for the Chesapeake, an English immigrant had to come up with about £5, roughly a year's wages for an English servant or laborer. Earning

wages at all was difficult in England since job opportunities were shrinking. Many country landowners needed fewer farmhands because they shifted from growing crops to raising sheep in newly enclosed fields.

Unemployed people drifted into seaports such as Bristol, Liverpool, and London, where they learned about the plentiful jobs in North America. Unable to pay for their trip across the Atlantic, poor immigrants agreed to a contract called an indenture, which functioned as a form of credit. By signing an indenture, an immigrant borrowed the cost of transportation to the Chesapeake from a merchant or ship captain in

Bristol Docks
This painting of the docks in Bristol, England, portrays a scene common at ports throughout the seventeenth-century Atlantic world. Workers unload colonial commodities shipped to Bristol while merchants meet in small groups to make deals to sell the colonial goods and reload the ships with English exports, including indentured servants. Tobacco flooded into Bristol in the seventeenth century while Bristol merchants also became active in the African slave trade, trading British goods on the west African coast for slaves, who were then taken to the New World to be sold to eager sugar and tobacco planters. © Bristol City Museum and Art Gallery/UK Bridgeman Art Library.

England. To repay this loan, the indentured person agreed to work as a servant for four to seven years in North America.

Once the indentured person arrived in the colonies, the merchant or ship captain sold his right to the immigrant's labor to a local tobacco planter. To obtain the servant's labor, the planter paid about twice the cost of transportation and agreed to provide the servant with food and shelter during the term of the indenture. When the indenture expired, the planter owed the former servant "freedom dues," usually a few barrels of corn and a suit of clothes.

Ideally, indentures allowed poor immigrants to trade their most valuable assets — their freedom and their ability to work — for a trip to the New World and a period of servitude followed by freedom in a land of opportunity. Planters reaped more immediate benefits. Servants meant more hands to grow more tobacco. A planter expected a servant to grow enough tobacco in one year to cover the price the planter paid for the indenture. Servants' labor during the remaining three to six years of the indenture promised a handsome profit for the planter. No wonder one Virginian declared, "Our principall wealth . . . consisteth in servants." But roughly half of all servants became sick and died before serving out their indentures, reducing planters' gains. Planters still profited, however, since they received a headright of fifty acres of land from the colonial government for every newly purchased servant.

About three out of four servants were young men between the ages of fifteen and twenty-five when they arrived in the Chesapeake. Typically, they shared the desperation of sixteen-year-old

Francis Haires, who indentured himself for seven years because, according to his contract, "his father and mother and All friends [are] dead and he [is] a miserable wandering boy." Like Francis, most servants had no special training or skills, although the majority had some experience with agricultural work. "Hunger and fear of prisons bring to us onely such servants as have been brought up to no Art or Trade," one Virginia planter complained. A skilled craftsman could obtain a shorter indenture, but few risked coming to the colonies since their prospects were better in England.

Women were almost as rare as skilled craftsmen in the Chesapeake and more ardently desired. In the early days of the tobacco boom, the Virginia Company shipped young single women servants to the colony as prospective wives for male settlers willing to pay "120 weight [pounds] of the best leaf tobacco for each of them," in effect getting both a wife and a servant. The company reasoned that, as one official wrote in 1622, "the plantation can never flourish till families be planted, and the respect of wives and children fix the people on the soil." The company's efforts as a marriage broker proved no more successful than its other ventures. Women remained a small minority of the Chesapeake population until late in the seventeenth century.

The servant labor system perpetuated the gender imbalance. Although female servants cost about the same as males and generally served for the same length of time, only about one servant in four was a woman. Planters preferred male servants, as one explained, because they were "the mor[e] excellent and yousefull Cretuers," especially for field work. Although many servant women hoed and harvested tobacco fields, most also did household chores such as cooking, washing, cleaning, gardening, and milking.

The Rigors of Servitude

Servants — whether men or women, whites or blacks, English or African — tended to work together and socialize together. During the first half century of settlement, racial intermingling occurred, although the small number of blacks made it infrequent. Courts punished sexual relations between blacks and whites, but the court cases show that sexual desire readily crossed the color line. In general, the commonalities of servitude caused servants — regardless of their race and gender — to consider themselves apart from free people, whose ranks they longed to join eventually.

Servant life was harsh by the standards of seventeenth-century England and even by the frontier standards of the Chesapeake. Unlike servants in England, Chesapeake servants had no control over who purchased their labor — and thus them — for the period of their indenture. They were "sold here upp and downe like horses," one observer reported. Before their indentures expired, many servants were bought and sold several times. A Virginia servant protested in 1623 that his master "hath sold me for £150 sterling like a damnd slave." But tobacco planters' need for labor muffled complaints about treating servants as property.

For servants, the promise of indentured servitude that loomed large in their decision to leave England and immigrate to the Chesapeake often withered when they confronted the rigors of labor in the tobacco fields. James Revel, an eighteen-year-old thief punished by being indentured to a Virginia tobacco planter, declared he was a "slave" sent to hoe "tobacco plants all day" from dawn to dark. Severe laws aimed to keep servants in their place. Punishments for petty crimes stretched servitude far beyond the original terms of indenture. Richard Higby, for example, received six extra years of servitude for killing three hogs. After midcentury, the Virginia legislature added three or more years to the indentures of most servants by requiring them to serve until they were twenty-four years old.

Women servants were subject to special restrictions and risks. They were prohibited from marrying until their servitude had expired. A servant woman, the law assumed, could not serve two masters at the same time: one who owned her indentured labor and another who was her husband. However, the predominance of men in the Chesapeake population inevitably pressured women to engage in sexual relations. (See "Seeking the American Promise," page 74.) About a third of immigrant women were pregnant when they married. Pregnancy and childbirth sapped a woman's strength, and a new child diverted her attention, reducing her usefulness as a servant. As a rule, if a woman servant gave birth to a child, she had to serve two extra years and pay a fine. However, for some servant women, premarital pregnancy was a path out of servitude: The father of an unborn child sometimes purchased the indenture of the servant mother-to-be and then freed and married her.

> "The plantation can never flourish till families be planted, and the respect of wives and children fix the people on the soil."
> — An official of the Virginia Company

The Gamble of Indentured Servitude

Anne Orthwood sailed out of her native Bristol, England, in September 1662, shortly after her twenty-third birthday. Her mother, Mary, had moved there in 1640 to escape the humiliation of giving birth to Anne out of wedlock, and in Bristol she had a second daughter, also illegitimate. Mary never married. Anne and her sister grew up with the stigma of being bastards, a shameful and degraded status at a time when the vast majority of children were born to married couples.

Bristol was a thriving seaport, second only to London in its overseas trade, but poor unmarried women — especially those like Mary, with two illegitimate daughters — had little hope to share in the city's commercial prosperity. Instead, they usually worked at menial jobs such as domestic servant or washerwoman. The continual arrival and departure of ships, sailors, merchants, passengers, and cargoes of all kinds from throughout the Atlantic world made Bristol a hub of information and gossip that Anne could not have avoided. She probably heard that in Virginia jobs were plentiful and workers were few. Hundreds of

people sailed from Bristol to Virginia every year, five hundred in 1662 alone, most of them poor young men who agreed to become indentured servants. Anne probably also heard about the shortage of women in Virginia, along with the tantalizing news that, as one promoter declared, if women "come of an honest stock and have a good repute, they may pick and chuse their Husbands out of the better sort of people." The promise of both work and matrimony proved irresistible to Anne, especially compared to the gloomy prospect of staying in Bristol. In August 1662, Anne signed an indenture to a ship's surgeon who agreed to pay her way to Virginia in exchange for her consent to work for four years as a servant.

Anne arrived in Virginia late in the fall of 1662, and the surgeon quickly sold her indenture — and thus her — to William Kendall, a wealthy planter and prominent official on Virginia's Eastern Shore. Kendall himself had come to Virginia as a servant in 1650, but unlike Anne, he was from a respectable family and had received a valuable education as a merchant's clerk. When he became free in

1654, he prospered, thanks in large part to his good fortune in marriage. Kendall married a wealthy widow in Virginia, and after she died, he married another wealthy widow, helping him amass more than 25,000 acres of land. When Anne joined Kendall's household, some twenty people lived there, including seven or eight servants, two slaves, a free black man, and numerous relatives, among them a nephew, John Kendall.

Like Anne, John Kendall had recently arrived in Virginia from England, was in his early twenties, and was unmarried. We can't know if Anne thought John was one of the "better sort of people" she might marry, but it appears that she and John felt a mutual attraction. William Kendall had no intention of allowing his nephew to get mixed up with a lowly servant woman, and a bastard at that. His own experience confirmed that marrying upward was the path to prosperity in Virginia. About eight months after Anne became his servant, William Kendall decided to separate her and John by selling Anne's indenture — and thus her — to a tenant farmer named Jacob Bishop, who lived several miles away.

As young people will, Anne and John found a way to get together. Anne accompanied Bishop when he went to conduct legal business at court, held at a local tavern, as was customary at the time. While there, on Saturday night and Sunday,

Harsh punishments reflected four fundamental realities of the servant labor system. First, planters' hunger for labor caused them to demand as much labor as they could get from their servants, including devising legal ways to extend the period of servitude. Second, servants hoped to survive their servitude and use their freedom to obtain land and start a family. Third, servants' hopes frequently conflicted with planters' demands. Since servants saw themselves as free people in a temporary status of servitude, they often made grudging, halfhearted workers. Finally, planters put up with this contentious arrangement because the alternatives were less desirable.

Planters could not easily hire free men and women because land was readily available and free people preferred to work for themselves on

their own land. Nor could planters depend on much labor from family members. The preponderance of men in the population meant that families were few, were started late, and thus had few children. And, until the 1680s and 1690s, slaves were expensive and hard to come by. Before then, masters who wanted to expand their labor force and grow more tobacco had few alternatives to buying indentured servants.

Cultivating Land and Faith

Villages and small towns dotted the rural landscape of seventeenth-century England, but in the Chesapeake towns were few and far between. Instead, tobacco farms occupied small clearings surrounded by hundreds of acres of wilderness.

English Servants
This collective portrait of English servants painted by William Hogarth in the mid-eighteenth century features three young women who perhaps somewhat resembled indentured servant Anne Orthwood, who had immigrated to Virginia nearly a century earlier. No likeness of Orthwood exists. Unlike Orthwood, most servants who came to the Chesapeake during the seventeenth century were young boys, like the boy depicted here at top center. Tate Gallery, London/Art Resource, NY.

November 28 and 29, 1663, she met John Kendall, and they had sex. "Three tymes She thought hee had to doe with her," Anne later testified, "but twice She was Certaine."

John impregnated Anne. We don't know if Anne hoped that John would buy her indenture, free her, and marry her, but she probably did. She refused to say who was responsible for her condition; her silence suggests that she hoped John Kendall would step forward and rescue her. But he didn't. She finally identified John as the father when a midwife quizzed her during the rigors of giv-ing birth to twin boys. One baby died shortly after birth, as did Anne. Her other son, whom she named Jasper, was indentured as an infant to a Virginia planter and, after twenty-two years of servitude, became a free man. John Kendall never acknowl-edged Jasper as his son, but he did follow his uncle William's advice and marry a wealthy widow.

Like so many other Virginia colo-nists, Anne found an early grave rather than the work, marriage, and respectability she craved. She gam-bled her freedom for the promise of a better life in Virginia, and she lost.

Other former servants gambled and won, grandly like William Kendall or modestly like Anne's son Jasper.

Questions for Consideration

1. How did family relationships and popular assumptions about them influence Anne Orthwood? How did they influence John Kendall?

2. How did Anne Orthwood's experiences reflect the risks and opportunities confronted by other female and male servants?

Tobacco was such a labor-intensive crop that one field worker could tend only about two acres of the plants in a year (an acre is slightly smaller than a football field), plus a few more acres for food crops. A successful farmer needed a great deal more land, however, because tobacco quickly exhausted the fertility of the soil. Since each farmer cultivated only 5 or 10 percent of his land at any one time, a "settled" area comprised swatches of cultivated land sur-rounded by forest. Arrangements for marketing tobacco also con-tributed to the dispersion of settle-ments. Tobacco planters sought land that fronted a navigable river in order to minimize the work of transporting the heavy barrels of tobacco onto ships. A settled region thus resembled a lacework of farms stitched around waterways.

Most Chesapeake colonists were nominally Protestants. Attendance at Sunday services and conformity to the doctrines of the Church of England were required of all English men and women. Few clergymen migrated to the Chesapeake, however, and too few of those who did were models of righ-teousness and piety. Certainly,

Settlement Patterns along the James River

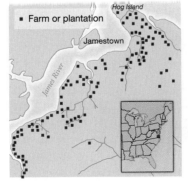

some colonists took their religion seriously. Church courts punished fornicators, censured blasphemers, and served notice on parishioners who spent Sundays "goeing a fishing." But on the whole, religion did not awaken the zeal of Chesapeake settlers, certainly not as it did the zeal of New England settlers in these same years (as discussed in chapter 4). What quickened the pulse of most Chesapeake folk was a close horse race, a bloody cockfight, or — most of all — an exceptionally fine tobacco crop. The religion of the Chesapeake colonists was Anglican, but their faith lay in the turbulent, competitive, high-stakes gamble of survival as tobacco planters.

The situation was similar in the Catholic colony of Maryland. In 1632, England's King Charles I granted his Catholic friend **Lord**

Jamestown Church Tower

This modern-day photograph shows the remains of the tower of the Anglican church that colonists constructed in Jamestown beginning in 1639. Nearby is the foundation of an older church, built in 1617, that also served as the site of the first meeting of the Virginia general assembly or House of Burgesses, the first representative legislative body in British North America. The churches illustrate the importance Virginia's leaders attached to maintaining the central British institution of worship and spiritual order in the fledgling colony.

Courtesy of Preservation Virginia.

Baltimore about six and a half million acres in the northern Chesapeake region. In return, the king specified that Lord Baltimore pay him the token rent of "two Indian arrowheads" a year. Lord Baltimore intended to create a refuge for Catholics, who suffered severe discrimination in England. He fitted out two ships, the *Ark* and the *Dove*; gathered about 150 settlers; and sent them to the new colony, where they arrived on March 25, 1634. However, Maryland failed to live up to Baltimore's hopes. The colony's population grew very slowly for twenty years, and most settlers were Protestants rather than Catholics. The religious turmoil of the Puritan Revolution in England (discussed in chapter 4) spilled across the Atlantic, creating conflict between Maryland's few Catholics—most of them wealthy and prominent — and the Protestant majority, most of them neither wealthy nor prominent. During the 1660s, Maryland began to attract settlers, mostly Protestants, as readily as Virginia. Although Catholics and the Catholic faith continued to exert influence in Maryland, the colony's society, economy, politics, and culture became nearly indistinguishable from Virginia's. Both colonies shared a devotion to tobacco, the true faith of the Chesapeake.

REVIEW Why did the vast majority of European immigrants to the Chesapeake come as indentured servants?

► Hierarchy and Inequality in the Chesapeake

The system of indentured servitude sharpened inequality in Chesapeake society by the mid-seventeenth century, propelling social and political polarization that culminated in 1676 with Bacon's Rebellion. The rebellion prompted reforms that stabilized relations between elite planters and their lesser neighbors and paved the way for a social hierarchy that muted differences of landholding and wealth and amplified racial differences. (See "Historical Question," page 78.) Amid this social and political evolution, one thing did not change: Chesapeake colonists' dedication to growing tobacco.

Social and Economic Polarization

The first half of the seventeenth century in the Chesapeake was the era of the **yeoman** — a farmer who owned a small plot of land sufficient to support a family and tilled largely by servants and a few family members. A small number of elite planters had larger estates and commanded ten or more servants. But for the first several decades, few men lived long enough to accumulate fortunes sufficient to set them much apart from their neighbors. On the whole, a rough frontier equality characterized free families in the Chesapeake until about 1650.

Until midcentury, the principal division in Chesapeake society was less between rich and poor planters than between free farmers and unfree servants. Although these two groups contrasted sharply in their legal and economic status, their daily lives had many similarities. Servants looked forward to the time when their indentures would expire and they would become free and eventually own land.

Three major developments splintered the equality during the third quarter of the century. First, as planters grew more and more tobacco, the ample supply depressed tobacco prices in European markets. Cheap tobacco reduced planters' profits and made saving enough to become landowners more difficult for freed servants. Second, because the mortality rate in the Chesapeake colonies declined, more and more servants survived their indentures, and landless freemen became more numerous and grew more discontented. Third, declining mortality also encouraged the formation of a planter elite. By living longer, the most successful planters compounded their success. The wealthiest planters also began to buy slaves as well as to serve as merchants, marketing crops for their less successful neighbors, importing English goods for sale, and extending credit to hard-pressed customers.

By the 1670s, the society of the Chesapeake had become polarized. Landowners — the planter elite and the more numerous yeoman planters — clustered around one pole. Landless colonists, mainly freed servants, gathered at the other. Each group eyed the other with suspicion and mistrust. For the most part, planters saw landless freemen as a dangerous rabble rather than as fellow colonists with legitimate grievances.

Governor William Berkeley feared the political threat to the governing elite posed by "six parts in seven [of Virginia colonists who] . . . are poor, indebted, discontented, and armed."

Government Policies and Political Conflict

In general, government and politics strengthened the distinctions in Chesapeake society. The most vital distinction separated servants and masters, and the colonial government enforced it with an iron fist. Poor men such as William Tyler complained that "nether the Governor nor Counsell could or would doe any poore men right, but that they would shew favor to great men and wronge the poore." Most Chesapeake colonists, like most Europeans, assumed that "great men" should bear the responsibilities of government. Until 1670, all freemen could vote, and they routinely elected prosperous planters to the legislature. No former servant served in either the governor's council or the House of Burgesses after 1640. Yet Tyler and other poor Virginians believed that the "great men" used their government offices to promote their selfish personal interests rather than governing impartially.

As discontent mounted among the poor during the 1660s and 1670s, colonial officials tried to keep political power in safe hands. Beginning in 1661, for example, Governor William Berkeley did not call an election for the House of Burgesses for fifteen years. In 1670, the House of Burgesses outlawed voting by poor men, permitting only men who headed households and were landowners to vote.

The king also began to tighten the royal government's control of trade and to collect substantial revenue from the Chesapeake. A series of English laws funneled the colonial trade exclusively into the hands of English merchants and shippers. The **Navigation Acts** of 1650 and 1651 specified that colonial goods had to be transported in English ships with predominantly English crews. A 1660 act required colonial products to be sent only to English ports, and a 1663 law stipulated further that all goods sent to the colonies must pass through English ports and be carried on English ships manned by English sailors. Taken together, these navigation acts reflected the English government's mercantilist assumptions about the colonies: What was good for England should determine colonial policy.

Why Did English Colonists Consider Themselves Superior to Indians and Africans?

Were seeds of the racial prejudice that has been such a powerful force in American history planted in the seventeenth-century Chesapeake? To answer that question, historians have paid close attention to the language colonists used to describe Indians, Africans, and themselves.

In the mid-1500s, the English adopted the words *Indian* and *Negro* from Spanish, where they had come to mean, respectively, an aboriginal inhabitant of the New World and a black person of African ancestry. Both terms were generic, homogenizing an enormous diversity of tribal affiliations, languages, and cultures. Neither term originated with the people to whom it referred. The New England minister Roger Williams, who published a book on Indian languages in 1643, reported, "They have often asked mee, why we call them Indians," a poignant question that reveals the European origins of the term, dating back to Columbus.

After *Indians*, the word the settlers used most frequently to describe Native Americans was *savages*. The Indians were savages in the colonists' eyes because they lacked the traits of

English civilization. As one Englishman put it in 1625, the natives of Virginia were "so bad a people, having little of humanitie but shape, ignorant of Civilitie, of Arts, of Religion; more brutish than the beasts they hunt, more wild and unmanly than that unmanned wild countrey, which they range rather than inhabite; captivated also to Satans tyranny in foolish pieties, mad impieties, wicked idlenesse, busie and bloudy wickednesse." Some English colonists counterbalanced this harsh indictment with admiration for certain features of Indian behavior. They praised Indians' calm dignity and poise, their tender love and care for family members, and their simple, independent way of life in apparent harmony with nature.

Color was not a feature of the Indians' savagery. During the seventeenth century, colonists never referred to Indians as "red." Instead, they saw Indians' skin color as tawny or tanned, the "Sun's livery," as one settler wrote. To the English, tanned skin denoted a member of the working class who spent his or her days toiling under the sun; pale skin was the fashion. Many settlers held the

view that Indians were innately white like the English but in other ways woefully un-English.

Despite their savagery in English eyes, Indians controlled two things colonists desperately wanted: land and peace. Early in the seventeenth century, when English settlements were small and weak, peace with the Indians was a higher priority than land. In this period, English comments on Indian savagery noted the obvious differences between settlers and Indians, but the colonists' need for peace kept them attuned to ways to coexist with the Indians. By the middle of the seventeenth century, as colonial settlements grew and the desire for land increased, violent conflict with Indians erupted repeatedly. The violence convinced settlers that the only way to achieve both land and peace was to eliminate the Indians, by either killing them or pushing them far away from colonial settlements. English assumptions of their superiority to savage Indians provided justification and a gloss of respectability to the colonists' violent and relentless grab of Indian land.

The colonists identified Africans quite differently. Their most common term for Africans was *Negroes*, but the other was not *savage* or *heathen* but *black*. What struck English colonists most forcefully about Africans was not their un-English ways but their un-English skin color.

Black was not a neutral color to the colonists. According to the *Oxford English Dictionary* (which catalogs the changing meaning of words), *black* meant to the English people who settled the Chesapeake "deeply stained with dirt; soiled, dirty, foul . . . having dark or deadly purposes, malignant; pertaining to or involving death, deadly; baneful, disastrous, sinister . . .

Assumptions about **mercantilism** also underlay the import duty on tobacco inaugurated by the Navigation Act of 1660. The law assessed an import tax of two pence on every pound of colonial tobacco brought into England, about the price a Chesapeake tobacco farmer received. The tax

gave the king a major financial interest in the size of the tobacco crop. During the 1660s, these tobacco import taxes yielded about a quarter of all English customs revenues, an impressive sign of the growing importance of the Chesapeake colonies in England's Atlantic empire.

European Attitudes toward Africans
This lavish portrait of two seventeenth-century aristocratic ladies illustrates common European attitudes toward Africans. Both ladies appear completely at ease with the black servant boy. One casually drapes her arm over his shoulder; the other daintily plucks fruit from the bowl he holds. While the two ladies gaze confidently at the viewer, the boy stares at the black lapdog, whose color and protruding eyes he shares, along with an ornamental collar. The portrait suggests that the ladies consider the African boy akin to the dog — an exotic pet vastly inferior to them but safely domesticated and fit to be a plaything or accessory. Réunion des Musées Nationaux/Art Resource, NY.

foul, iniquitous, atrocious, horrible, wicked." Black was the opposite of white, which connoted purity, beauty, and goodness — attributes the colonists identified with themselves. By the middle of the seventeenth century, the colonists referred to themselves not only as English but also as free, hinting that they believed that people who were not English were not free. After about 1680, colonists often referred to themselves as white, acknowledging the color of free people. By the end of the seventeenth century, blacks were triply cursed in English eyes: un-English, un-white, and un-free.

Virginians did not legally define slavery as permanent, lifelong, inherited bondage until 1660. The sparse surviving evidence demonstrates, however, that colonists practiced slavery from the start. The debasements of slavery strengthened the colonists' prejudice toward blacks, while racial prejudices buttressed slavery.

Colonists' attitudes toward Indians and Africans exaggerated and hardened English notions about social hierarchy, about superiority and inferiority. Colonists' convictions of their own superiority to Indians and Africans justified, they believed, their exploitation of Indians' land and Africans' labor.

Those justifications planted the seeds of pernicious racial prejudices that flourished in America for centuries.

Thinking about Beliefs and Attitudes

1. How did the words colonists used to describe Indians and Africans indicate their beliefs?

2. To what extent did colonists' ideas about themselves shape their attitudes toward Indians and Africans?

3. What were the consequences of English colonists' belief in their own superiority?

Bacon's Rebellion

Colonists, like residents of European monarchies, accepted class divisions and inequality as long as they believed that government officials ruled for the general good. When rulers violated that precept, ordinary people felt justified in rebelling.

In 1676, **Bacon's Rebellion** erupted as a dispute over Virginia's Indian policy. Before it was over, the rebellion convulsed Chesapeake politics and society, leaving in its wake death, destruction, and a legacy of hostility between the great planters and their poorer neighbors.

Governor William Berkeley
This portrait illustrates the distance that separated Governor Berkeley and the other Chesapeake grandees from poor planters, landless freemen, servants, and slaves. Berkeley's clothing suited the genteel homes of Jamestown, not the rustic dwellings of lesser Virginians. His haughty, satisfied demeanor suggests his lack of sympathy for poor Virginians, who, he was certain, deserved their lot. National Gallery of Art, Washington, D.C., USA/SuperStock.

Opechancanough, the Algonquian chief who had led the Indian uprising of 1622 in Virginia, mounted another surprise attack in 1644 and killed about five hundred Virginia colonists in two days. During the next two years of bitter fighting, the colonists eventually gained the upper hand, capturing and murdering the old chief. The treaty that concluded the war established policies toward the Indians that the government tried to maintain for the next thirty years. The Indians relinquished all claims to land already settled by the English. Wilderness land beyond the fringe of English settlement was supposed to be reserved exclusively for Indian use. The colonial government hoped to minimize contact between settlers and Indians and thereby maintain the peace.

> **"See what spounges have suckt up the Publique Treasure."**
> — NATHANIEL BACON

If the Chesapeake population had not grown, the policy might have worked. But the number of land-hungry colonists, especially poor, recently freed servants, continued to multiply. In their quest for land, they pushed beyond the treaty limits of English settlement and encroached steadily on Indian land. During the 1660s and 1670s, violence between colonists and Indians repeatedly flared along the advancing frontier. The government, headquartered in the tidewater region near the coast, far from the danger of Indian raids, took steps to calm the disputes and reestablish the peace. Frontier settlers thirsted for revenge against what their leader, Nathaniel Bacon, termed "the protected and Darling Indians." Bacon proclaimed his "Design not only to ruine and extirpate all Indians in Generall but all Manner of Trade and Commerce with them." Indians were not the only enemies Bacon and his men singled out. Bacon also urged the colonists to "see what spounges have suckt up the Publique Treasure." He charged that **grandees**, or elite planters, operated the government for their private gain, a charge that made sense to many colonists. In fact, officeholders had profited enough to buy slaves to replace their servants; by the 1660s, they owned about 70 percent of all the colony's slaves. Bacon crystallized the grievances of the small planters and poor farmers against both the Indians and the colonial rulers in Jamestown.

Hoping to maintain the fragile peace on the frontier in 1676, Governor Berkeley pronounced Bacon a rebel, threatened to punish him for treason, and called for new elections of burgesses who, Berkeley believed, would endorse his get-tough policy. To Berkeley's surprise, the elections backfired. Almost all the old burgesses were voted out of office, and they were replaced by local leaders, including Bacon. The legislature was now in the hands of minor grandees who, like Bacon, chafed at the rule of the elite planters.

In June 1676, the new legislature passed a series of reform measures known as Bacon's Laws. Among other changes, the laws gave local settlers a voice in setting tax levies, forbade officeholders from demanding bribes or other extra fees for carrying out their duties, placed limits on holding multiple offices, and restored the vote to all freemen. Under pressure, Berkeley pardoned Bacon and authorized his campaign of Indian warfare. But elite planters soon convinced Berkeley that Bacon and his men were a greater threat than Indians.

When Bacon learned that Berkeley had once again branded him a traitor, he declared war against Berkeley and the other grandees. For three months, Bacon's forces fought the Indians, sacked the grandees' plantations, and attacked

Jamestown. Berkeley's loyalists retaliated by plundering the homes of Bacon's supporters. The fighting continued until late October, when Bacon unexpectedly died, most likely from dysentery, and several English ships arrived to bolster Berkeley's strength. With the rebellion crushed, Berkeley hanged several of Bacon's allies and destroyed farms that belonged to Bacon's supporters.

The rebellion did nothing to dislodge the grandees from their positions of power. If anything, it strengthened them. When the king learned of the turmoil in the Chesapeake and its devastating effect on tobacco exports and customs duties, he ordered an investigation. Royal officials replaced Berkeley with a governor more attentive to the king's interests, nullified Bacon's Laws, and instituted an export tax on every hogshead (large barrel) of tobacco as a way of paying the expenses of government without having to obtain the consent of the tightfisted House of Burgesses.

In the aftermath of Bacon's Rebellion, tensions between great planters and small farmers gradually lessened. Bacon's Rebellion showed, a governor of Virginia said, that it was necessary "to steer between . . . either an Indian or a civil war." The ruling elite concluded that it was safer for the colonists to fight the Indians than to fight each other, and the government made little effort to restrict settlers' encroachment on Indian land. Tax cuts also were welcomed by all freemen. The export duty on tobacco imposed by the king allowed the colonial government to reduce taxes by 75 percent between 1660 and 1700. In the long run, however, the most important contribution to political stability was the declining importance of the servant labor system. During the 1680s and 1690s, fewer servants arrived in the Chesapeake, partly because of improving economic conditions in England. Accordingly, the number of poor, newly freed servants also declined, reducing the size of the lowest stratum of free society. In 1700, as many as one-third of the free colonists still worked as tenants on land owned by others, but the social and political distance between them and the great planters did not seem as important as it had been in 1660. The main reason was that by 1700 the Chesapeake was in the midst of transitioning to a slave labor system that minimized the differences between poor farmers and rich planters and magnified the differences between whites and blacks.

REVIEW Why did Chesapeake colonial society become increasingly polarized between 1650 and 1670?

▶ Toward a Slave Labor System

Although forced native labor was already a common practice under New Spain's system of *repartimiento* (see chapter 2), repeated Indian uprisings in the Spanish colonies of New Mexico and Florida kept them marginal and unprofitable. English colonists, who had been unsuccessful in conscripting Indian labor, looked to another source of workers used by the Spaniards and Portuguese: enslaved Africans. On this foundation, European colonizers built African **slavery** into the most important form of coerced labor in the New World.

During the seventeenth century, English colonies in the West Indies followed the Spanish and Portuguese examples and developed sugar plantations with slave labor. In the English North American colonies, however, a slave labor system did not emerge until the last quarter of the seventeenth century. During the 1670s, settlers from Barbados brought slavery to the new English mainland colony of Carolina, where the imprint of the West Indies remained strong for decades. In Chesapeake tobacco fields at about the same time, slave labor began to replace servant labor, marking the transition toward a society of freedom for whites and slavery for Africans.

Religion and Revolt in the Spanish Borderland

While English colonies in the Chesapeake grew and prospered with the tobacco trade, the northern outposts of the Spanish empire in New Mexico and Florida stagnated. Spanish officials seriously considered eliminating both settlements because their costs greatly exceeded their benefits. Only about fifteen hundred Spaniards lived in Florida, and roughly twice as many inhabited New Mexico, yet both colonies required regular deliveries of goods and large subsidies because their populations proved unable to sustain themselves. One royal governor complained that "no [Spaniard] comes . . . to plow and sow [crops], but only to eat and loaf."

Instead of attracting settlers and growing crops for export, New Mexico and Florida appealed to Spanish missionaries seeking to convert Indians to Christianity. In both colonies, Indians outnumbered Spaniards ten or twenty to one. Royal officials hoped that the missionaries' efforts would pacify the Indians and be a relatively cheap way to preserve Spanish footholds in North America.

Sugar Plantation
This portrait of a Brazilian sugar plantation shows the house of the Brazilian owners, attended by numerous slaves. Cartloads of sugarcane are being hauled to the mill, which is powered by a waterwheel (far right), where the cane will be squeezed between rollers to extract the sugary juice. The juice will then be distilled over a fire tended by the slaves (at the left end of the mill) until it has the desired consistency and purity. Notice that all of the working people are of African descent, and probably all of them are slaves. How does the artist differentiate slaves from their owners?
Courtesy of the John Carter Brown Library at Brown University.

The missionaries baptized thousands of Indians in Spanish North America during the seventeenth century, but they also planted the seeds of Indian uprisings against Spanish rule.

Dozens of missionaries came to Florida and New Mexico, as one announced, to free the Indians "from the miserable slavery of the demon and from the obscure darkness of their idolatry." The missionaries followed royal instructions that Indians should be taught "to live in a civilized manner, clothed and wearing shoes . . . [and] given the use of . . . bread, linen, horses, cattle, tools, and weapons, and all the rest that Spain has had." Stirrups adorned with Christian crosses on soldiers' saddles proclaimed the faith behind the Spaniards' swords, and vice versa. In effect, the missionaries sought to convert the Indians not just into Christians but also into surrogate Spaniards.

The missionaries supervised the building of scores of Catholic churches across Florida and New Mexico. Adopting practices common elsewhere in New Spain, they forced the Indians both to construct these churches and to pay tribute in the form of food, blankets, and other goods. Although the missionaries congratulated themselves on the many Indians they converted, their coercive methods subverted their goals. A missionary reported that an Indian in New Mexico asked him, "If we [missionaries] who are Christians caused so much harm and violence [to Indians], why should they become Christians?"

The Indians retaliated repeatedly against Spanish exploitation, but the Spaniards sup-

pressed the violent uprisings by taking advantage of the disunity among the Indians, much as Cortés did in the conquest of Mexico (see chapter 2). In 1680, however, the native leader **Popé** organized

Spanish Stirrup
This seventeenth-century stirrup used by Spaniards on the northern frontier of New Spain illustrates the use of elaborate ornamentation and display to convey a sense of Spanish power. It is no accident that the stirrup is in the shape of a Christian cross, a vivid symbol of the Spaniards' belief in the divine source of their authority. © George H. H. Huey.

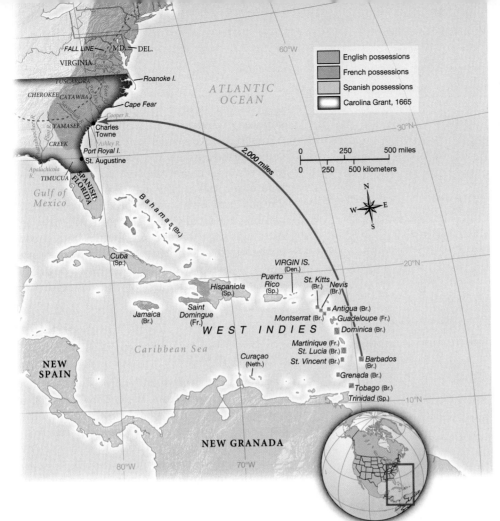

MAP ACTIVITY

Map 3.2 The West Indies and Carolina in the Seventeenth Century

Although Carolina was geographically close to the Chesapeake colonies, it was culturally closer to the West Indies in the seventeenth century because its early settlers — both blacks and whites — came from Barbados. South Carolina maintained strong ties to the West Indies for more than a century, long after the arrival of many later settlers from England, Ireland, France, and elsewhere.

READING THE MAP: Locate English colonies in America and English holdings in the Caribbean. Which European country controlled most of the mainland bordering the Caribbean? Where was the closest mainland English territory?
CONNECTIONS: Why were colonists in Carolina so interested in Barbados? What goods did they export? Describe the relationship between Carolina and Barbados in 1700.

---

the **Pueblo Revolt**, ordering his followers, as one recounted, to "break up and burn the images of the holy Christ, the Virgin Mary, and the other saints, the crosses, and everything pertaining to Christianity." During the revolt, Indians desecrated churches, killed two-thirds of the Spanish missionaries, and drove the Spaniards out of New Mexico to present-day El Paso, Texas. The Spaniards managed to return to New Mexico by the end of the seventeenth century, but only by curtailing the missionaries and reducing labor exploitation. Florida Indians never mounted a unified attack on Spanish rule, but they too organized sporadic uprisings and resisted conversion, causing a Spanish official to report by the end of the seventeenth century that "the law of God and the preaching of the Holy Gospel have now ceased."

The West Indies: Sugar and Slavery

The most profitable part of the English New World empire in the seventeenth century lay in the Caribbean (Map 3.2). The tiny island of **Barbados**, colonized in the 1630s, was the jewel of the English West Indies. During the 1640s, Barbadian planters began to grow sugarcane with such success that a colonial official proclaimed Barbados "the most flourishing Island in all those American parts, and I verily believe in all the world for the production of sugar." Sugar commanded high prices in England, and planters rushed to grow as much as they could. By midcentury, annual sugar exports from the English Caribbean totaled about 150,000 pounds; by 1700, exports reached nearly 50 million pounds.

Sugar transformed Barbados and other West Indian islands. Poor farmers could not afford the expensive machinery that extracted and refined sugarcane juice, but planters with enough capital to grow sugar got rich. By 1680, the wealthiest Barbadian sugar planters were, on average, four times richer than tobacco grandees in the Chesapeake. The sugar grandees differed from their Chesapeake counterparts in another crucial

> "Barbados is grown the most flourishing Island in all those American parts, and I verily believe in all the world for the production of sugar."
> — A colonial official of Barbados

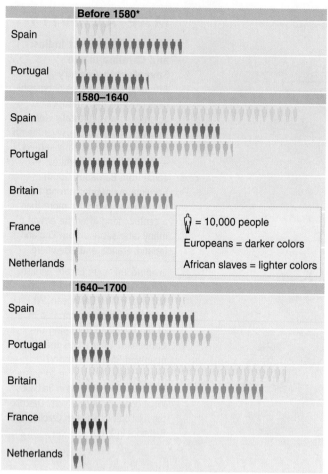

*Note: Before 1580, migration from Britain, France, and the Netherlands was negligible.

Figure 3.1 GLOBAL COMPARISON: Migration to the New World from Europe and Africa, 1492–1700

Before 1640, Spain and Portugal sent four out of five European migrants to the New World, virtually all of them bound for New Spain or Brazil. But from 1640 to 1700, nearly as many migrants came from England as from all other European nations combined, a measure of the growing significance of England's colonies. From 1492 to 1700, more enslaved Africans than Europeans arrived in the New World. What might explain the shifts in the destinations of enslaved Africans? Were those shifts comparable to shifts among European immigrants?

For slaves, work on a sugar plantation was a life sentence to brutal, unremitting labor. Slaves suffered high death rates. Since slave men out-numbered slave women two to one, few slaves could form families and have children. These grim realities meant that in Barbados and else-where in the West Indies, the slave population did not grow by natural reproduction. Instead, planters continually purchased enslaved Africans. Although sugar plantations did not gain a foot-hold in North America in the seventeenth century, the West Indies nonetheless exerted a powerful influence on the development of slavery in the mainland colonies.

Carolina: A West Indian Frontier

The early settlers of what became South Carolina were immigrants from Barbados. In 1663, a Barbadian planter named John Colleton and a group of seven other men obtained a charter from England's King Charles II to establish a colony south of the Chesapeake and north of the Spanish territories in Florida. The men, known as "pro-prietors," hoped to siphon settlers from Barbados and other colonies and encourage them to develop a profitable export crop comparable to West Indian sugar and Chesapeake tobacco. The proprietors enlisted the English philosopher John Locke to help draft the *Fundamental Constitutions of Carolina*, which provided for religious liberty and political rights for small property holders while envisioning a landed aristocracy supported by bound laborers and slaves. Following the Chesapeake example, the proprietors also offered headrights of up to 150 acres of land for each settler, a provision that eventually undermined the *Constitutions'* goal of a titled aristocracy. In 1670, the proprietors established the colony's first permanent English settlement, Charles Towne, later spelled Charleston (see Map 3.2).

As the proprietors had planned, most of the early settlers were from Barbados. In fact, Carolina was the only seventeenth-century English colony to be settled principally by colonists from other colonies rather than from England. The Barbadian immigrants brought their slaves with them. More than a fourth of the early settlers were slaves, and as the colony continued to attract settlers from Barbados, the black population multiplied. By 1700, slaves made up about half the popula-tion of Carolina. The new colony's close associa-tion with Barbados caused English officials to refer routinely to "Carolina in ye West Indies."

way: The average sugar baron in Barbados owned 115 slaves in 1680.

African slaves planted, cultivated, and har-vested the sugarcane that made West Indian planters wealthy. Beginning in the 1640s, Barbadian planters purchased thousands of slaves to work their plantations, and the African pop-ulation on the island mushroomed. During the 1650s, when blacks made up only 3 percent of the Chesapeake population, they had already become the majority in Barbados. By 1700, slaves constituted more than three-fourths of the island's population (Figure 3.1).

The Carolinians experimented unsuccessfully to match their semitropical climate with profitable export crops of tobacco, cotton, indigo, and olives. In the mid-1690s, colonists identified a hardy strain of rice and took advantage of the knowledge of rice cultivation among their many African slaves to build rice plantations. Settlers also sold livestock and timber to the West Indies, as well as another "natural resource": They captured and enslaved several thousand local Indians and sold them to Caribbean planters. Both economically and socially, seventeenth-century Carolina was a frontier outpost of the West Indian sugar economy.

Slave Labor Emerges in the Chesapeake

By 1700, more than eight out of ten people in the southern colonies of English North America lived in the Chesapeake. Until the 1670s, almost all Chesapeake colonists were white people from England. By 1700, however, one out of eight people in the region was a black person from Africa. A few black people had lived in the Chesapeake since the 1620s, but the black population grew fivefold between 1670 and 1700 as hundreds of tobacco planters made the transition from servant to slave labor. Only relatively prosperous planters could afford to buy slaves, concentrating slave ownership among the elite.

Planters saw several advantages to purchasing slaves rather than servants. Although slaves cost three to five times more than servants, slaves never became free. Because the mortality rate had declined by the 1680s, planters could reasonably expect a slave to live longer than a servant's period of indenture. Slaves also promised to be a perpetual labor force, since children of slave mothers inherited the status of slavery. And unlike servants, they could be controlled politically. Bacon's Rebellion had demonstrated how disruptive former servants could be when their expectations were not met. A slave labor system promised to avoid the political problems caused by the servant labor system. Slavery kept discontented laborers in permanent servitude, and their color was a badge of their bondage.

The slave labor system polarized Chesapeake society along lines of race and status: All slaves were black, and nearly all blacks were slaves; almost all free people were white, and all whites were free or only temporarily bound in indentured servitude. Unlike Barbados, however, the Chesapeake retained a vast white majority. Among whites, huge differences of wealth and

status still existed. By 1700, more than three-quarters of white families had neither servants nor slaves. Nonetheless, poor white farmers enjoyed the privileges of free status. They could own property, get married, have families, and bequeath their property and their freedom to their descendants; they could move when and where they wanted; they could associate freely with other people; they could serve on juries, vote, and hold political office; and they could work, loaf, and sleep as they chose. These privileges of freedom — none of them possessed by slaves — made lesser white folk feel they had a genuine stake in the existence of slavery, even if they did not own a single slave. By emphasizing the privileges of freedom shared by all white people, the slave labor system reduced the ten-

Tobacco Wrapper
This wrapper labeled a container of tobacco from the English colonies sold at Reighly's shop in Essex. The wrapper was much like a brand, promising consumers consistency in quality and taste. The wrapper features two black slaves enjoying a pipe of the leaves they presumably helped grow. It also illustrates tobacco growing in a field and harvested leaves ready to be packed into a barrel, ferried to the ships waiting off-shore, and transported to Reighly's and other tobacconists in England. Reighly's owners didn't worry that depicting slaves would alienate their customers. The Granger Collection, New York.

sions between poor folk and grandees that had plagued the Chesapeake region in the 1670s.

In contrast to slaves in Barbados, most slaves in the seventeenth-century Chesapeake colonies had frequent and close contact with white people. Slaves and white servants performed the same tasks on tobacco plantations, often working side by side in the fields. Slaves took advantage of every opportunity to slip away from white supervision and seek out the company of other slaves. Planters often feared that slaves would turn such seemingly innocent social pleasures to political ends, either to run away or to conspire to strike against their masters. Slaves often did run away, but they were usually captured or returned after a brief absence. Despite planters' nightmares, slave insurrections did not occur.

Although slavery resolved the political unrest caused by the servant labor system, it created new political problems. By 1700, the bedrock political issue in the southern colonies was keeping slaves in their place, at the end of a hoe. The slave labor system in the southern colonies stood roughly midway between the sugar plantations and black majority of Barbados to the south and the small farms and homogeneous villages that developed in seventeenth-century New England to the north (as discussed in chapter 4).

> **REVIEW** Why had slave labor largely displaced indentured servant labor by 1700 in Chesapeake tobacco production?

► Conclusion: The Growth of English Colonies Based on Export Crops and Slave Labor

By 1700, the colonies of Virginia, Maryland, and Carolina were firmly established. The staple crops they grew for export provided a livelihood for many, a fortune for a few, and valuable revenues for shippers, merchants, and the English monarchy. Their societies differed markedly from English society in most respects, yet the colonists considered themselves English people who happened to live in North America. They claimed the same rights and privileges as English men and women, while they denied those rights and privileges to Native Americans and African slaves.

The English colonies also differed from the example of New Spain. Settlers and servants flocked to English colonies, in contrast to Spaniards who trickled into New Spain. Few English missionaries sought to convert Indians to Protestant Christianity, unlike the numerous Catholic missionaries in the Spanish settlements in New Mexico and Florida. Large quantities of gold and silver never materialized in English North America. English colonists never adopted the system of encomienda (see chapter 2) because the Indians in these areas were too few and too hostile and their communities too small and decentralized compared with those of the Mexica. Yet some forms of coerced labor and racial distinction that developed in New Spain had North American counterparts, as English colonists employed servants and slaves and defined themselves as superior to Indians and Africans.

By 1700, the remnants of Powhatan's people still survived. As English settlement pushed north, west, and south of Chesapeake Bay, the Indians faced the new colonial world that Powhatan and Pocahontas had encountered when John Smith and the first colonists had arrived at Jamestown. By 1700, the many descendants of Pocahontas's son, Thomas, as well as other colonists and Native Americans, understood that the English had come to stay.

Economically, the southern colonies developed during the seventeenth century from the struggling Jamestown settlement that could not feed itself into a major source of profits for English merchants, shippers, and the king. The European fashion for tobacco provided livelihoods for numerous white families and riches for elite planters. But after 1700, enslaved Africans were conscripted in growing numbers to grow tobacco in the Chesapeake and rice in Carolina. The slave society that dominated the eighteenth-century southern colonies was firmly rooted in the developments of the seventeenth century.

A desire for land, a hope for profit, and a dream for security motivated southern white colonists. Realizing these aspirations involved great risks, considerable suffering, and frequent disappointment, as well as seizing Indian lands and coercing labor from servants and slaves. By 1700, despite huge disparities in individual colonists' success in achieving their goals, tens of thousands of white colonists who were immigrants or descendants of immigrants now considered the southern colonies their home, shaping the history of the region and of the nation as a whole for centuries to come.

► Selected Bibliography

Chesapeake Society

Kathleen Brown, *Good Wives, Nasty Wenches, and Anxious Patriarchs: Gender, Race, and Power in Colonial Virginia* (1996).

Lois Green Carr et al., *Robert Cole's World: Agriculture and Society in Early Maryland* (1991).

Alison Games, *The Web of Empire: English Cosmopolitans in the Age of Expansion, 1560–1660* (2009).

April Hatfield, *Atlantic Virginia: Intercolonial Relations in the Seventeenth Century* (2003).

Karen Ordahl Kupperman, *The Jamestown Project* (2010).

Peter C. Mancall, *The Atlantic World and Virginia, 1550–1624* (2007).

Peter C. Mancall, *Hakluyt's Promise: An Elizabethan's Obsession for an English America* (2010).

Debra Meyers, *Common Whores, Vertuous Women, and Loveing Wives: Free Will Christian Women in Colonial Maryland* (2003).

Marcy Norton, *Sacred Gifts, Profane Pleasures: A History of Tobacco and Chocolate in the Atlantic World* (2010).

Steve Sarson, *British America, 1500–1800: Creating Colonies, Imagining an Empire* (2005).

Terry L. Snyder, *Brabbling Women: Disorderly Speech and the Law in Early Virginia* (2003).

Christopher L. Tomlins, *Freedom Bound: Law, Labor, and Civic Identity in Colonizing English America, 1580–1865* (2010).

Lorena S. Walsh, *Motives of Honor, Pleasure, and Profit: Plantation Management in the Colonial Chesapeake, 1607–1763* (2010).

Indians

Alan Gallay, *The Indian Slave Trade: The Rise of the English Empire in the American South, 1670–1717* (2002).

Ramón A. Gutiérrez, *When Jesus Came, the Corn Mothers Went Away: Marriage, Sexuality, and Power in New Mexico, 1500–1846* (1991).

Pekka Hämäläinen, *The Comanche Empire* (2009).

Karen Ordahl Kupperman, *Indians and English: Facing Off in Early America* (2000).

Helen C. Rountree, *Pocahontas, Powhatan, Opechancanough: Three Indian Lives Changed by Jamestown* (2005).

Jayme A. Sokolow, *The Great Encounter: Native Peoples and European Settlers in the Americas, 1492–1800* (2003).

Margaret Holmes Williamson, *Powhatan Lords of Life and Death: Command and Consent in Seventeenth-Century Virginia* (2003).

Slavery and Indentured Servitude

Susan Dwyer Amussen, *Caribbean Exchanges: Slavery and the Transformation of English Society, 1640–1700* (2007).

Ira Berlin, *The Making of African America: The Four Great Migrations* (2010).

James F. Brooks, *Captives and Cousins: Slavery, Kinship, and Community in the Southwest Borderlands* (2002).

Tim Hashaw, *The Birth of Black America: The First African Americans and the Pursuit of Freedom at Jamestown* (2007).

Linda M. Heywood and John K. Thornton, *Central Africans, Atlantic Creoles, and the Foundation of the Americas* (2007).

Russell R. Menard, *Migrants, Servants, and Slaves: Unfree Labor in Colonial British America* (2001).

Jerald T. Milanich, *Laboring in the Fields of the Lord: Spanish Missions and Southeastern Indians* (1999).

Edmund S. Morgan, *American Slavery, American Freedom: The Ordeal of Colonial Virginia* (1975).

Jennifer L. Morgan, *Laboring Women: Reproduction and Gender in New World Slavery* (2004).

John Ruston Pagan, *Anne Orthwood's Bastard: Sex and Law in Early Virginia* (2003).

Carolina Society and the West Indies

Cara Anzilotti, *In the Affairs of the World: Women, Patriarchy, and Power in Colonial South Carolina* (2002).

S. Max Edelson, *Plantation Enterprise in Colonial South Carolina* (2006).

Kirsten Fischer, *Suspect Relations: Sex, Race, and Resistance in Colonial North Carolina* (2002).

Michael Jarvis, *In the Eye of All Trade: Bermuda, Bermudians, and the Maritime Atlantic World, 1680–1783* (2010).

Russell K. Menard, *Sweet Negotiations: Sugar, Slavery, and Plantation Agriculture in Early Barbados* (2006).

► **FOR MORE BOOKS ABOUT TOPICS IN THIS CHAPTER,** see the Online Bibliography at **bedfordstmartins.com/roark.**

► **FOR ADDITIONAL PRIMARY SOURCES FROM THIS PERIOD,** see Michael Johnson, ed., *Reading the American Past,* Fifth Edition.

► **FOR WEB SITES, IMAGES, AND DOCUMENTS RELATED TO TOPICS AND PLACES IN THIS CHAPTER,** visit Make History at **bedfordstmartins.com/roark.**

Reviewing Chapter 3

KEY TERMS

Explain each term's significance

An English Colony on Chesapeake Bay
Virginia Company (p. 64)
Algonquian Indians (p. 64)
Powhatan (p. 64)
Jamestown (p. 64)
Captain John Smith (p. 65)
Opechancanough (p. 66)
royal colony (p. 67)
House of Burgesses (p. 67)

A Tobacco Society
tobacco (p. 68)
John Rolfe (p. 68)
Pocahontas (p. 68)
headright (p. 69)
indentured servants (p. 70)
Lord Baltimore (p. 76)

Hierarchy and Inequality in the Chesapeake
yeoman (p. 77)
Governor William Berkeley (p. 77)
Navigation Acts (p. 77)
mercantilism (p. 78)
Bacon's Rebellion (p. 79)
grandees (p. 80)

Toward a Slave Labor System
slavery (p. 81)
Popé (p. 82)
Pueblo Revolt (p. 83)
Barbados (p. 83)

REVIEW QUESTIONS

Use key terms and dates to support your answers.

1. Why did Powhatan behave as he did toward the English colonists? (pp. 63–68)

2. Why did the vast majority of European immigrants to the Chesapeake come as indentured servants? (pp. 68–76)

3. Why did Chesapeake colonial society become increasingly polarized between 1650 and 1670? (pp. 76–81)

4. Why had slave labor largely displaced indentured servant labor by 1700 in Chesapeake tobacco production? (pp. 81–86)

MAKING CONNECTIONS

Draw on key terms, the timeline, and review questions.

1. Given the vulnerability of the Jamestown settlement in its first two decades, why did its sponsors and settlers not abandon it? In your answer, discuss the challenges the settlement faced and the benefits different participants in England and the New World hoped to derive from their efforts.

2. Tobacco dominated European settlement in the Chesapeake during the seventeenth century. How did tobacco agriculture shape the region's development? In your answer, be sure to address the demographic and geographic features of the colony.

3. Bacon's Rebellion highlighted significant tensions within Chesapeake society. What provoked the rebellion, and what did it accomplish? In your answer, be sure to consider causes and results in the colonies and in England.

4. In addition to making crucial contributions to the economic success of seventeenth-century English colonies, Native Americans and enslaved Africans influenced colonial politics. Describe how European colonists' relations with these populations contributed to political friction and harmony within the colony.

LINKING TO THE PAST

Link events in this chapter to earlier events.

1. How did England's colonization efforts in the Chesapeake and Carolina during the seventeenth century compare with Spain's conquest and colonization of Mexico? (See chapter 2.)

2. How did the development of the transatlantic tobacco trade exemplify the Columbian exchange? (See chapter 2.)

▶ **FOR PRACTICE QUIZZES AND OTHER STUDY TOOLS,** visit the Online Study Guide at bedfordstmartins.com/roark.

TIMELINE 1606–1680

1606	• Virginia Company receives royal charter.
1607	• English colonists found Jamestown settlement; Pocahontas "rescues" John Smith.
1607–1610	• Starvation plagues Jamestown.
1612	• John Rolfe begins to plant tobacco in Virginia.
1617	• First commercial tobacco shipment leaves Virginia for England. • Pocahontas dies in England.
1618	• Powhatan dies; Opechancanough becomes chief of the Algonquians.
1619	• First Africans arrive in Virginia. • House of Burgesses begins to meet in Virginia.
1622	• Opechancanough leads first Indian uprising against Virginia colonists.
1624	• Virginia becomes royal colony.
1630s	• Barbados colonized by English.
1632	• King Charles I grants Lord Baltimore land for colony of Maryland.
1634	• Colonists begin to arrive in Maryland.
1640s	• Barbados colonists begin to grow sugarcane with labor of African slaves.
1644	• Opechancanough leads second Indian uprising against Virginia colonists.
1660	• Navigation Act imposes mercantilist requirement that colonial products to be shipped only to English ports. • Virginia law defines slavery as inherited, lifelong servitude.
1663	• Royal charter granted for Carolina colony.
1670	• Charles Towne, South Carolina, founded.
1670–1700	• Slave labor system emerges in Carolina and Chesapeake colonies.
1676	• Bacon's Rebellion.
1680	• Pueblo Revolt.

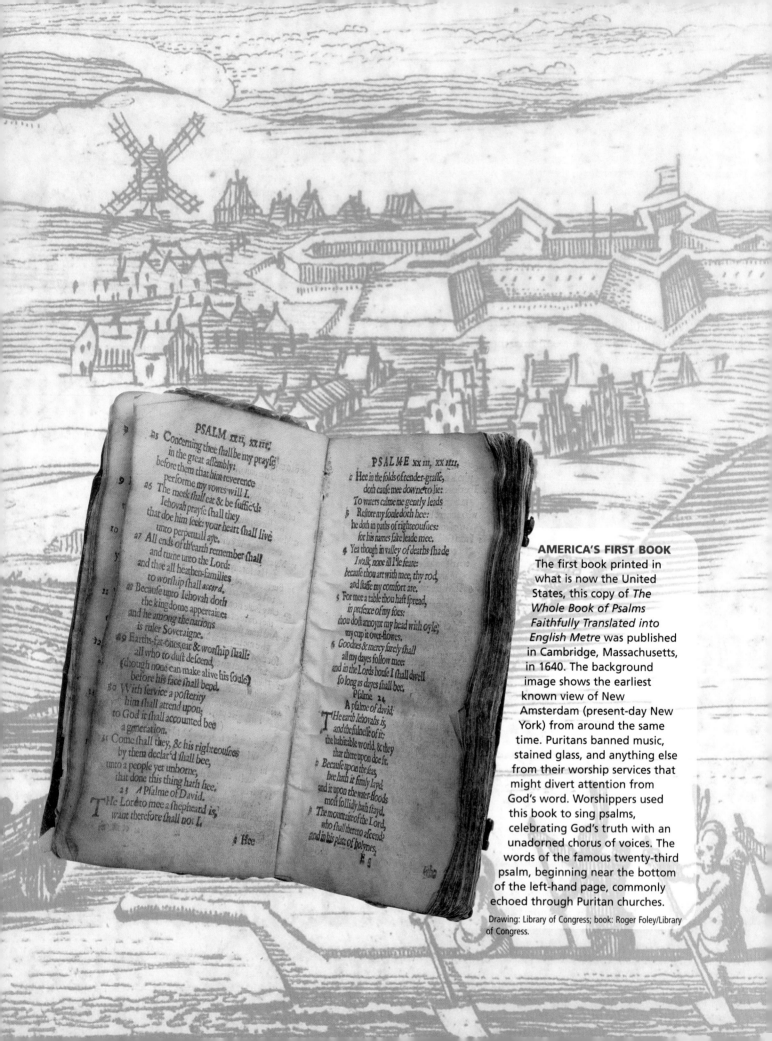

AMERICA'S FIRST BOOK
The first book printed in what is now the United States, this copy of *The Whole Book of Psalms Faithfully Translated into English Metre* was published in Cambridge, Massachusetts, in 1640. The background image shows the earliest known view of New Amsterdam (present-day New York) from around the same time. Puritans banned music, stained glass, and anything else from their worship services that might divert attention from God's word. Worshippers used this book to sing psalms, celebrating God's truth with an unadorned chorus of voices. The words of the famous twenty-third psalm, beginning near the bottom of the left-hand page, commonly echoed through Puritan churches.

Drawing: Library of Congress; book: Roger Foley/Library of Congress.

4

The Northern Colonies in the Seventeenth Century 1601–1700

ROGER WILLIAMS AND HIS WIFE, MARY, ARRIVED IN MASSACHUSETTS in February 1631. Educated at Cambridge University, the twenty-eight-year-old Williams was "a godly [Puritan] minister," noted Governor John Winthrop. But when Winthrop's Boston church asked Williams to become its minister, he refused because the church had not openly rejected the corrupt Church of England. New England's premier Puritan church was not pure enough for Roger Williams.

Williams and his wife moved to Plymouth colony for two years. While there, he spent a great deal of time among the Narragansett Indians. "My soul's desire was to do the natives good," he said. Williams believed that "Nature knows no difference between Europeans and [Native] Americans in blood, birth, [or] bodies . . . God having made of one blood all mankind." He sought to learn about the Indians' language, religion, and culture without trying to convert them to Christianity, insisting that all human beings—Christians and non-Christians alike—should live according to their consciences as revealed to them by God.

Believing that English claims were legally, morally, and spiritually invalid, Williams condemned English colonists for their "sin of unjust usurpation" of Indian land. In contrast, Massachusetts officials defended colonists' settlement on Indian land. If land "lies common, and hath never been replenished or subdued, [it] is free to any that possess or improve it," Governor Winthrop explained. Besides, he said, "if we leave [the Indians] sufficient [land] for their use, we may lawfully take the rest, there being more than enough for them and us."

In 1633, Williams became minister of the church in Salem, Massachusetts, where church members believed, like other New England Puritans, that churches and governments should enforce both godly belief and behavior according to biblical rules. They claimed that "the Word of God is . . . clear." In contrast, Williams believed that the Bible shrouded the Word of God in "mist and fog." Williams contended that devout and pious Christians could and did differ about what the Bible said and what God expected. That observation led him to denounce the emerging New England order as impure, ungodly, and tyrannical.

Williams disagreed with the New England government's requirement that everyone attend church services. He argued that forcing non-Christians to attend church was akin to requiring "a dead child to suck the breast, or a dead man [to] feast." This "False Worshipping" only promoted "spiritual drunkenness and whoredom." He believed that to regulate religious behavior would be "spiritual rape"; that governments should tolerate all religious beliefs because only God knows the Truth; that no person and no religion can understand God with absolute certainty. "I commend that man," Williams wrote, "whether Jew, or Turk, or Papist, or whoever, that steers no otherwise than his conscience dares." In Williams's view, toleration of religious belief and liberty of conscience were the only paths to religious purity and political harmony.

New England's leaders denounced Williams's arguments and banished him for his "extreme and dangerous" opinions. In January 1636, he escaped from an attempt to ship him back to England and fled south to Narragansett Bay, wandering for "fourteen weeks in a bitter winter season," Williams later wrote, "not knowing what bed or bread did mean." In the spring, he and his followers purchased land from the Narragansetts and established the colony of Rhode Island, which enshrined "Liberty of Conscience" as a fundamental ideal and became a refuge for other dissenters. Although New England's leaders expelled Williams from their holy commonwealth, his dissenting ideas arose from orthodox Puritan doctrines, which inspired him to draw his own conclusions and stick to them.

During the seventeenth century, New England's Puritan zeal cooled, and the promise of a holy New England faded. Late in the century, the new "middle" colonies of New York, New Jersey, and Pennsylvania were founded, featuring greater religious and ethnic diversity than New England. Religion remained important throughout all the colonies, but it competed with the growing faith that a better life required less focus on salvation and more attention to worldly concerns of family, work, and trade.

Throughout the English mainland colonies, settlements encroached on Indian land, causing violent conflict to flare up repeatedly. Political conflict also arose among colonists, particularly in response to major political upheavals in England. By the end of the seventeenth century, the English monarchy exerted greater control over North America and the rest of its Atlantic empire, but the products, people, and ideas that pulsed between England and the colonies energized both.

New England

This 1677 map highlights the importance of water in the New England settlements. Why do you think roads and trails linking settlements are not shown? Rhode Island, haven for Roger Williams and other religious dissenters, is located on the left side, just below the center. The small numbers on the map indicate Indian attacks during King Philip's War.

© Massachusetts Historical Society, Boston, MA, USA/The Bridgeman Art Library.

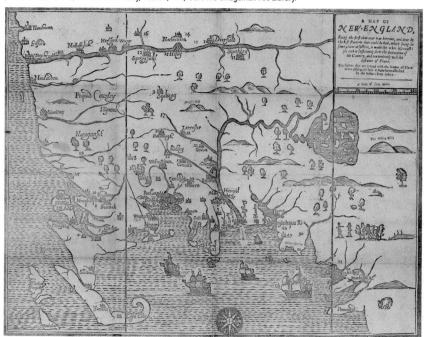

▶ Puritans and the Settlement of New England

Puritans who emigrated to North America aspired to escape the turmoil and persecution they suffered in England, a long-term consequence of the English Reformation. They also sought to build a new, orderly, Puritan version of England. Puritans established the first small settlement in New England in 1620, followed a few years later by additional settlements by the Massachusetts Bay Company. Allowed self-government through royal charter, these Puritans were in a unique position to direct the new colonies according to their faith. Their faith shaped the colonies they established in almost every way. Although many New England colonists were not Puritans, Puritanism remained a paramount influence in New England's religion, politics, and community life during the seventeenth century.

Puritan Origins: The English Reformation

The religious roots of the Puritans who founded New England reached back to the Protestant Reformation, which arose in Germany in 1517 (see chapter 2). The Reformation spread quickly to other countries, but the English church initially remained within the Catholic fold and continued its allegiance to the pope in Rome. Henry VIII, who reigned from 1509 to 1547, saw that the Reformation offered him an opportunity to break with Rome and take control of the church in England. In 1534, Henry formally initiated the **English Reformation**. At his insistence, Parliament passed the Act of Supremacy, which outlawed the Catholic Church and proclaimed the king "the only supreme head on earth of the Church of England." Henry seized the vast properties of the Catholic Church in England as well as the privilege of appointing bishops and others in the church hierarchy.

In the short run, the English Reformation allowed Henry VIII to achieve his political goal of controlling the church. In the long run, however, the Reformation brought to England the political and religious turmoil that Henry had hoped to avoid. Henry himself sought no more than a halfway Reformation. Protestant doctrines held no attraction for him; in almost all matters of religious belief and practice, he

Queen Elizabeth
This sixteenth-century portrait of Queen Elizabeth celebrates English victory over the Spanish Armada in 1588 (shown in the panels on either side of Elizabeth's head) that resulted in England's empire reaching North America (notice her right hand covering North America on the globe). Shortly before the battle, Elizabeth rallied the English people with a famous speech, declaring that, "I have the body of a weak and feeble woman; but I have the heart and stomach of a king — and of a King of England too." In a sense, this portrait depicts a queen with the virtues of a king.
© Bettmann/Corbis.

remained an orthodox Catholic. Many English Catholics wanted to revoke the English Reformation; they hoped to return the Church of England to the pope and to restore Catholic doctrines and ceremonies. But many other English people insisted on a genuine, thoroughgoing Reformation; these people came to be called **Puritans**.

During the sixteenth century, Puritanism was less an organized movement than a set of ideas and religious principles that appealed strongly to many dissenting members of the Church of England. They sought to eliminate what they considered the offensive features of Catholicism that remained in the religious doctrines and practices of the Church of England. For example, they demanded that the church hierarchy be abolished and that ordinary Christians be given greater control over religious life. They wanted to do away with the rituals of Catholic worship and instead emphasize an individual's relationship with God developed through Bible study, prayer, and introspection. Although there were many varieties and degrees of Puritanism, all Puritans

English Monarchy and the Protestant Reformation

1509–1547	Henry VIII	Leads the English Reformation, outlawing the Catholic Church in England and establishing the English monarch as supreme head of the Church of England.
1547–1553	Edward VI	Moves religious reform in a Protestant direction.
1553–1558	Mary I	Outlaws Protestantism and strives to reestablish the Catholic Church in England.
1558–1603	Elizabeth I	Tries to position the Church of England between extremes of Catholicism and Protestantism.
1603–1625	James I	Authorizes a new, Protestant translation of the Bible but is unsympathetic to Puritan reformers.
1625–1649	Charles I	Continues move away from Puritan reformers. Beheaded during the Puritan Revolution.
1642		Puritan Revolution (English Civil War) begins.
1644–1660	Oliver Cromwell	Leads Puritan side to victory in the English Civil War. Parliament proclaims England a Puritan republic (1649) and declares Cromwell the nation's "Lord Protector" (1653).
1660–1685	Charles II	Restored to the monarchy by Parliament and attempts to enforce religious toleration of Catholics and Protestant dissenters from the Church of England.
1685–1688	James II	Ousted by Parliament for pro-Catholic policies and replaced by his Protestant son-in-law, William, and his daughter (William's wife) in the "Glorious Revolution" (1688).
1689–1694	William III and Mary II	Reassert Protestant influence in England and its empire.

shared a desire to make the English church thoroughly Protestant.

The fate of Protestantism waxed and waned under the monarchs who succeeded Henry VIII. When Henry died in 1547, the advisers of the new king, Edward VI — the nine-year-old son of Henry and his third wife, Jane Seymour — initiated religious reforms that moved in a Protestant direction. The tide of reform reversed in 1553 when Edward died and was succeeded by Mary I, the daughter of Henry and Catherine of Aragon, his first wife. Mary was a steadfast Catholic, and shortly after becoming queen, she married Philip II of Spain, Europe's most powerful guardian of Catholicism. Mary attempted to restore the pre-Reformation Catholic Church. She outlawed Protestantism in England and persecuted those who refused to conform, sentencing almost three hundred to burn at the stake.

The tide turned again in 1558 when Mary died and was succeeded by Elizabeth I, the daughter of Henry and his second wife, Anne Boleyn. During her long reign, Elizabeth reaffirmed the English Reformation and tried to position the English church between the extremes of Catholicism and Puritanism. Like her father, she was less concerned with theology than with politics. Above all, she desired a church that would strengthen the monarchy and the nation.

By the time Elizabeth died in 1603, many people in England looked on Protestantism as a defining feature of national identity.

When Elizabeth's successor, James I, became king, English Puritans petitioned for further reform of the Church of England. James authorized a new translation of the Bible, known ever since as the King James version. However, neither James I nor his son Charles I, who became king in 1625, was receptive to the ideas of Puritan reformers. James and Charles moved the Church of England away from Puritanism. They enforced conformity to the Church of England and punished dissenters, both ordinary Christians and ministers. In 1629, Charles I dissolved Parliament — where Puritans were well represented — and initiated aggressive anti-Puritan policies. Many Puritans despaired about continuing to defend their faith in England and began to make plans to emigrate. Some left for Europe, others for the West Indies. The largest number set out for America.

The Pilgrims and Plymouth Colony

One of the first Protestant groups to emigrate, later known as **Pilgrims**, espoused an unorthodox view known as separatism. These **Separatists** sought to withdraw — or separate — from the Church of England, which they considered hopelessly corrupt. In 1608, they moved to Holland; by 1620, they realized that they could not live and worship there as they had hoped. **William Bradford**, a leader of the group, recalled that "many of their children, by . . . the great licentiousness of youth in [Holland], and the manifold temptations of the place, were drawn away by evil examples." Bradford and other Separatists believed that America promised to better protect their children's piety and preserve their community. Separatists obtained permission to settle in the extensive territory granted to the Virginia Company (see chapter 3). To finance their journey, they formed a joint-stock company with English investors. The investors provided the capital; the Separatists provided their labor and lives and received a share of the profits for seven years. In August 1620, the Pilgrim families boarded the *Mayflower*, and after eleven weeks at sea all but one of the 102 immigrants arrived at the outermost tip of Cape Cod, in present-day Massachusetts.

The Pilgrims realized immediately that they had landed far north of the Virginia grants and had no legal authority to settle in the area. To provide order and security as well as a claim to legitimacy, they drew up the **Mayflower Compact** on the day they arrived. They pledged to "covenant and combine ourselves together into a civil Body Politick, for our better Ordering and Preservation." The signers (all men) agreed to enact and obey necessary and just laws.

The Pilgrims settled at Plymouth and elected William Bradford their governor. That first winter, which they spent aboard their ship, "was most sad and lamentable," Bradford wrote later. "In two or three months' time half of [our] company died . . . being the depth of winter, and wanting houses and other comforts [and] being infected with scurvy and other diseases."

In the spring, Indians rescued the floundering Plymouth settlement. First Samoset and then Squanto befriended the settlers. Samoset had learned English from previous contacts with sailors and fishermen who had visited the coast to dry fish and make repairs years before the Plymouth settlers arrived. Squanto had been kidnapped by an English trader in 1614 and taken as a slave to Spain, where he escaped to London. There he learned English and finally made his way back home. Samoset arranged for the Pilgrims to meet and establish good relations with Massasoit, the chief of the **Wampanoag Indians**, whose territory included Plymouth. Squanto, Bradford recalled, "was a special instrument sent of God for their [the Pilgrims'] good. . . . He directed them how to set their corn, where to take fish, and to procure other commodities, and was also their pilot to bring them to unknown places." With the Indians' guidance, the Pilgrims managed to harvest enough food to guarantee their survival through the coming winter, an occasion they celebrated in the fall of 1621 with a feast of thanksgiving attended by Massasoit and other Wampanoags.

Still, the Plymouth colony remained precarious. Only seven dwellings were erected that first year, and a new group of threadbare, sickly settlers arrived in November 1621, requiring the colony to adopt stringent food rationing. The colonists quarreled with their London investors, who became frustrated when Plymouth failed to produce the expected profits.

Yet the Pilgrims persisted, living simply and coexisting in relative peace with the Indians. They paid the Wampanoags when settlers gradually encroached on Indian land. By 1630, Plymouth had become a small permanent settlement, but it failed to attract many other English Puritans.

> "In two or three months' time half of [our] company died . . . being the depth of winter, and wanting houses and other comforts [and] being infected with scurvy and other diseases."
> — Governor
> **WILLIAM BRADFORD**

The Founding of Massachusetts Bay Colony

In 1629, shortly before Charles I dissolved Parliament, a group of Puritan merchants and country gentlemen obtained a royal charter for the **Massachusetts Bay Company**. The charter provided the usual privileges granted to joint-stock companies, including land for colonization that spanned present-day Massachusetts, New Hampshire, Vermont, Maine, and upstate New York. In addition, a unique provision of the charter permitted the government of the Massachusetts Bay Company to be located in the colony rather than in England. This provision allowed Puritans to exchange their status as a harassed minority in England for self-government in Massachusetts.

To lead the emigrants, the stockholders of the Massachusetts Bay Company elected **John Winthrop**, a prosperous lawyer and landowner, to serve as governor. In March 1630, eleven ships crammed with seven hundred passengers sailed

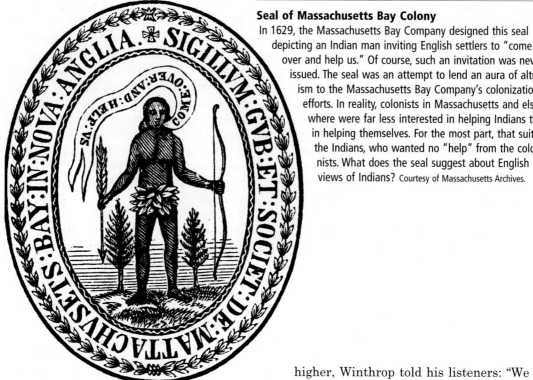

Seal of Massachusetts Bay Colony
In 1629, the Massachusetts Bay Company designed this seal depicting an Indian man inviting English settlers to "come over and help us." Of course, such an invitation was never issued. The seal was an attempt to lend an aura of altruism to the Massachusetts Bay Company's colonization efforts. In reality, colonists in Massachusetts and elsewhere were far less interested in helping Indians than in helping themselves. For the most part, that suited the Indians, who wanted no "help" from the colonists. What does the seal suggest about English views of Indians? Courtesy of Massachusetts Archives.

for Massachusetts; six more ships and another five hundred emigrants followed a few months later. Winthrop's fleet arrived in Massachusetts Bay in early June. Unlike the Separatists, Winthrop's Puritans aspired to reform the corrupt Church of England (rather than separate from it) by setting an example of godliness in the New World. Winthrop and a small group chose to settle on the peninsula that became Boston, and other settlers clustered at promising locations nearby (Map 4.1).

In a sermon to his companions aboard the *Arbella* while they were still at sea — probably the most famous sermon in American history — Winthrop proclaimed the cosmic significance of their journey. The Puritans had "entered into a covenant" with God to "work out our salvation under the power and purity of his holy ordinances," Winthrop declared. This sanctified agreement with God meant that the Puritans had to make "extraordinary" efforts to "bring into familiar and constant practice" religious principles that most people in England merely preached. To achieve their pious goals, the Puritans had to subordinate their individual interests to the common good. "We must be knit together in this work as one man," Winthrop preached. "We must delight in each other, make others' conditions our own, rejoice together, mourn together, labor and suffer together." The stakes could not be

higher, Winthrop told his listeners: "We must consider that we shall be as a city upon a hill. The eyes of all people are upon us."

That belief shaped seventeenth-century New England as profoundly as tobacco shaped the Chesapeake. Winthrop's vision of a city on a hill fired the Puritans' fierce determination to keep their covenant and live according to God's laws, unlike the backsliders and compromisers who accommodated to the Church of England. Their resolve to adhere strictly to God's plan charged nearly every feature of life in seventeenth-century New England with a distinctive, high-voltage piety.

The new colonists, as Winthrop's son John wrote later, had "all things to do, as in the beginning of the world." Unlike the early Chesapeake settlers, the first Massachusetts Bay colonists encountered few Indians because the local population had been almost entirely exterminated by an epidemic probably caused by contact with Europeans more than a decade earlier. Still, as in the Chesapeake, the colonists fell victim to deadly ailments. More than two hundred settlers died during the first year, including one of Winthrop's sons and eleven of his servants. But Winthrop maintained a confidence that proved infectious. He wrote to his wife, "I like so well to be heer as I do not repent my comminge. . . . I would not have altered my course, though I had forseene all these Afflictions." And each year from 1630 to 1640, ship after ship followed in the wake of Winthrop's fleet. In all, more than

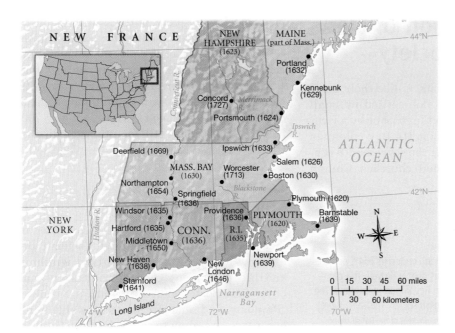

MAP ACTIVITY

Map 4.1 New England Colonies in the Seventeenth Century
New Englanders spread across the landscape town by town during the seventeenth century. (For the sake of legibility, only a few of the more important towns are shown on the map.)

READING THE MAP: Using the dates on the map, create a chronology of the establishment of towns in New England. What physical features correspond to the earliest habitation by English settlers?
CONNECTIONS: Why were towns so much more a feature of seventeenth-century New England than of the Chesapeake (see also chapter 3)? How did Puritan dissent influence the settlement of New England colonies?

twenty thousand new settlers came, their eyes focused on the Puritans' city on a hill.

Often, when the Church of England cracked down on a Puritan minister in England, he and many of his followers moved together to New England. Smaller groups of English Puritans moved to the Chesapeake, Barbados, and elsewhere in the New World, including New Amsterdam (present-day New York). By 1640, New England had one of the highest ratios of preachers to population in all of Christendom. Several ministers sought to carry the message of Christianity to the Indians in order to replace what missionary John Eliot termed the Indians' "unfixed, confused, and ungoverned . . . life, uncivilized and unsubdued to labor and order." They established "praying towns" to encourage Indians to leave their communities and adopt English ways. A few Indians moved to these towns and converted to Christianity, but for the most part the colonists focused less on saving Indians' souls than on saving their own.

The occupations of New England immigrants reflected the social origins of English Puritans. On the whole, the immigrants came from the middle ranks of English society. The vast majority were either farmers or tradesmen, including carpenters, tailors, and textile workers. Indentured servants, whose numbers dominated the Chesapeake settlers, accounted for only about a fifth of those headed for New England. Most New England immigrants paid their way to Massachusetts, even though the journey often took their life savings. They were encouraged by the promise of bounty in New England reported in Winthrop's letter to his son: "Here is as good land as I have seen there [in England]. . . . Here can be no want of anything to those who bring means to raise [it] out of the earth and sea."

In contrast to Chesapeake newcomers, New England immigrants usually arrived as families. In fact, more Puritans came with family members than did any other group of immigrants in all of American history. A ship that left Weymouth, England, in 1635, for example, carried 106 passengers, all but eight of them part of a family unit. Unlike immigrants to the Chesapeake, women and children made up a solid majority in New England.

As Winthrop reminded the first settlers in his *Arbella* sermon, each family was a "little commonwealth" that mirrored the hierarchy among all God's creatures. Just as humankind was subordinate to God, so young people were subordinate to their elders, children to their parents, and wives to their husbands. The immigrants' family ties reinforced their religious beliefs with universally understood notions of hierarchy and mutual dependence. Whereas immigrants to the Chesapeake were disciplined mostly by the coercions of servitude and the caprices of the tobacco market, immigrants to New England entered a social order defined by the interlocking institutions of family, church, and community.

REVIEW Why did the Puritans immigrate to North America?

▶ The Evolution of New England Society

The New England colonists, unlike their counterparts in the Chesapeake, settled in small towns, usually located on the coast or by a river (see Map 4.1). Massachusetts Bay colonists founded 133 towns during the seventeenth century, each with one or more churches. Church members' fervent piety, buttressed by the institutions of local government, enforced remarkable religious and social conformity in the small New England settlements. During the century, tensions within the Puritan faith and changes in New England communities splintered religious orthodoxy and weakened Puritan zeal. By 1700, however, Puritanism still maintained a distinctive influence in New England.

Church, Covenant, and Conformity

Puritans believed that the church consisted of men and women who had entered a solemn covenant with one another and with God. Winthrop and three other men signed the original covenant of the first Boston church in 1630, agreeing to "Promisse, and bind our selves, to walke in all our wayes according to the Rule of the Gospell, and in all sincere Conformity to His holy Ordinaunces." Each new member of the covenant had to persuade existing members that she or he had fully experienced conversion. By 1635, the Boston church had added more than 250 names to the four original subscribers to the covenant.

Puritans embraced a distinctive version of Protestantism derived from **Calvinism**, the doctrines of John Calvin, a sixteenth-century Swiss Protestant theologian. Calvin insisted that Christians strictly discipline their behavior to conform to God's commandments announced in the Bible. Like Calvin, Puritans believed in **predestination** — the idea that the all-powerful God, before the creation of the world, decided which few human souls would receive eternal life. Only God knows the identity of these fortunate predestined individuals — the "elect" or "saints." Nothing a person did in his or her lifetime could alter God's inscrutable choice or provide assurance that the person was predestined for salvation with the elect or damned to hell with the doomed multitude. The gloomy inevitability and exclusivity of predestination contrasted sharply with Catholic doctrines that all human beings could potentially be granted eternal life by God, acting through the Catholic Church.

Despite the looming uncertainty about God's choice of the elect, Puritans believed that if a person lived a rigorously godly life — constantly winning the daily battle against sinful temptations — his or her behavior was likely to be a hint, a visible sign, that he or she was one of God's chosen few. Puritans thought that "sainthood" would become visible in individuals'

Sabbath Breakers

These seventeenth-century prints show some of the punishments Sabbath breakers might suffer from man and God. In the upper illustration, a person who gathered sticks on the Sabbath is stoned to death as Puritans believed the Bible commanded. In the lower print, women who broke the Sabbath by preparing flax for spinning suffer God's retribution when they are burned to death. Some New Englanders thought the Sabbath started at sunset on Saturday evening; others believed it began about 3:00 p.m. on Saturday. Given the extreme punishments for Sabbath breaking, New Englanders needed to tread carefully between Saturday afternoon and Monday morning. *Divine Examples of God's Severe Judgements upon Sabbath-Breakers* (London, 1671).

behavior, especially if they were privileged to know God's Word as revealed in the Bible.

The connection between sainthood and saintly behavior, however, was far from certain. Some members of the elect, Puritans believed, had not heard God's Word as revealed in the Bible, and therefore their behavior did not necessarily signal their sainthood. One reason Puritans required all town residents to attend church services was to enlighten anyone who was ignorant of God's Truth. The slippery relationship between saintly behavior, observable by anybody, and God's predestined election, invisible and unknowable to anyone, caused Puritans to worry constantly that individuals who acted like saints were fooling themselves and others. Nevertheless, Puritans thought that **visible saints** — persons who passed their demanding tests of conversion and church membership — probably, though not certainly, were among God's elect.

Members of Puritan churches ardently hoped that God had chosen them to receive eternal life and tried to demonstrate saintly behavior. Their covenant bound them to help one another attain salvation and to discipline the entire community by saintly standards. Church members kept an eye on the behavior of everybody in town. Infractions of morality, order, or propriety were reported to Puritan elders, who summoned the wayward to a church inquiry. By overseeing every aspect of life, the visible saints enforced a remarkable degree of righteous conformity in Puritan communities. Total conformity, however, was never achieved. Ardent Puritans differed among themselves; non-Puritans shirked orthodox rules. Every community contained dissenters and recalcitrants, such as the Roxbury servant who declared that "if hell were ten times hotter, [I] would rather be there than [I] would serve [my] master."

Despite the central importance of religion, churches played no direct role in the civil government of New England communities. Puritans did not want to mimic the Church of England, which they considered a puppet of the king rather than an independent body that served the Lord. They were determined to insulate New England churches from the contaminating influence of the civil state and its merely human laws.

Seats of Power

New England Great Chair

The two chairs shown here highlight important contrasts between the dominant ideas of New England Puritans and those of Old World rulers. While neither chair is typical of furniture owned by ordinary people, both chairs illustrate designs that appealed to leaders in their respective societies.

The elaborately carved European throne chair belonged to an unknown wealthy person and dates from the late sixteenth century. The more simple New England great chair belonged to Michael Metcalf, a teacher and community leader in seventeenth-century Dedham, Massachusetts.

The magnificent carvings on the throne chair feature at least seven human images; abundant likenesses of fruit, foliage, textiles, and architecture; and two dramatic rams' heads. What do these images convey about the wood carver who made them? What might the chair suggest about the person who sat in it? To what degree could the throne chair be viewed as an example of the handiwork of God rather than human handiwork?

The carving on Metcalf's great chair lacks the ornate artistry of that on the throne chair. How does the less skillful carving suggest the colonial origins of the great chair? Under the seat, which lifts up to reveal an enclosed compartment, Metcalf stored books, presumably including a Bible. Why would a space for book storage be important for a New Englander like Metcalf? Why do you think the throne chair lacks an obvious place for books?

Although ministers were the most highly respected figures in New England towns, they were prohibited from holding government office.

Puritans had no qualms, however, about their religious beliefs influencing New England governments. As much as possible, the Puritans tried to bring public life into conformity with their view of God's law. For example, fines were issued for Sabbath-breaking activities such as working, traveling, playing a flute, smoking a pipe, and visiting neighbors.

Puritans mandated other purifications of what they considered corrupt English practices. (See "Visualizing History," above.) They refused to celebrate Christmas or Easter because the Bible did not mention either one. They outlawed religious wedding ceremonies; couples were married by a magistrate in a civil ceremony (the first wedding in Massachusetts performed by a minister occurred in 1686). They prohibited elaborate clothing and finery such as lace trim and short sleeves — "whereby the nakedness of the arm may be discovered." They banned cards, dice, shuffleboard, and other games of chance, as well as music and dancing. The distinguished minister Increase Mather insisted that "Mixt or Promiscuous Dancing . . . of Men and Women" could not be tolerated since "the unchaste Touches and Gesticulations used by Dancers have a palpable tendency to that which is evil." On special occasions, Puritans proclaimed days of fasting and humiliation, which, as one preacher boasted, amounted to "so many Sabbaths more."

Government by Puritans for Puritanism

It is only a slight exaggeration to say that seventeenth-century New England was governed by Puritans for Puritanism. The charter of the Massachusetts Bay Company empowered the company's stockholders, known as freemen, to meet as a body known as the General Court and make the laws needed to govern the company's affairs. The colonists transformed this arrangement for running a joint-stock company into a structure for governing

The space between the arms and seat of the great chair is solid wood, designed to block cold drafts and keep Metcalf relatively warm while he sat in the chair and read. What does the open space under the arms of the throne chair suggest about the clothing of the person who sat in it?

The carved wings that decorate the top of the back of Metcalf's chair symbolized the soul of a human being. The wings, combined with Metcalf's initials, the date 1652, and the large diamond, make the carving on the back of the great chair notably similar to the carving on New England gravestones. What might such symbolism have suggested to the carver and to Metcalf? How did the tombstone-like reference to human mortality relate to Puritanism? Does the throne chair also evoke mortality?

Imagine Metcalf sitting in his great chair and looking at the

European Throne Chair

throne chair. What might he have said about it and the ideas it represents? Likewise, imagine the owner of the throne chair sitting in it and observing the great chair. What might that person have said about the ideas represented by the great chair?

Neither the throne chair nor the great chair displays the Christian symbol of the cross or any other obvious sign of Christianity. What do you think accounts for that absence?

If the great chair hints at the importance of serious Bible study and unflinching introspection in Puritan New England, what major ideas in sixteenth-century Europe are suggested by the throne chair?

SOURCE: New England great chair: Dedham Historical Society/photo by Forrest Frasier; European throne chair: courtesy of Huntington Antiques Ltd., Gloucestershire, England.

the colony. Hoping to ensure that godly men would decide government policies, the General Court expanded the number of freemen in 1631 to include all male church members. Only freemen had the right to vote for governor, deputy governor, and other colonial officials. As new settlers were recognized as freemen, the size of the General Court grew too large to meet conveniently. So in 1634, the freemen in each town agreed to send two deputies to the General Court to act as the colony's legislative assembly. All other men were classified as "inhabitants," and they had the right to vote, hold office, and participate fully in town government.

A "town meeting," composed of a town's inhabitants and freemen, chose the selectmen and other officials who administered local affairs. New England town meetings routinely practiced a level of popular participation in political life that was unprecedented elsewhere in the world during the seventeenth century. Almost every adult man could speak out in town meetings and fortify his voice with a vote. However, all women — even church members — were prohibited from voting, and towns did not permit "contrary-minded" men to become or remain inhabitants. Although town meeting participants

wrangled from time to time, widespread political participation tended to reinforce conformity to Puritan ideals.

One of the most important functions of New England government was land distribution. Settlers who wanted to establish a new town entered a covenant and petitioned the General Court for a grant of land. The court granted town sites to suitably pious petitioners but did not allow settlement until the Indians who inhabited a grant agreed to relinquish their claim to the land, usually in exchange for manufactured goods. For instance, William Pynchon purchased the site of Springfield, Massachusetts, from the Agawam Indians for "eighteen fathams [arm's lengths] of Wampum [strings of shell beads used in trade], eighteen coates, 18 hatchets, 18 hoes, [and] 18 knives."

Having obtained their grant, town founders apportioned land among themselves and any newcomers they permitted to join them. Normally, each family received a house lot large enough for an adjacent garden as well as one or more strips of agricultural land on the perimeter of the town. Although there was a considerable difference between the largest and smallest family plots, most clustered in the middle range — roughly

Old Ship Meeting House
Built in Hingham, Massachusetts, in 1681, this meeting house is one of the oldest surviving buildings used for church services in English North America. The unadorned walls and windows reflect the austere religious aesthetic of New England Puritanism. The family pews mark boundaries of kinship and piety visible to all. The elevated pulpit signals the superiority of God's word as preached by the minister. The open space in front of the pulpit suggests worshippers' unblocked access to biblical truth.
Old Ship Church, Hingham, MA, photo by Steve Dunwell.

fifty to one hundred acres — resulting in a more nearly equal distribution of land in New England than in the Chesapeake.

The physical layout of New England towns encouraged settlers to look inward toward their neighbors, multiplying the opportunities for godly vigilance. Most people considered the forest that lay just beyond every settler's house an alien environment that was interrupted here and there by those oases of civilization, the towns. Footpaths connecting one town to another were so rudimentary that even John Winthrop once got lost within half a mile of his house and spent a sleepless night in the forest, circling the light of his small campfire and singing psalms.

The Splintering of Puritanism

Almost from the beginning, John Winthrop and other leaders had difficulty enforcing their views of Puritan orthodoxy. In England, persecution as a dissenting minority had unified Puritan voices in opposition to the Church of England. In New England, the promise of a godly society and the Puritans' emphasis on individual Bible study led New Englanders toward different visions of godliness. Puritan leaders, however, interpreted dissent as an error caused either by a misguided believer or by the malevolent power of Satan. Whatever the cause, errors could not be tolerated. As one Puritan minister proclaimed, "The Scripture saith . . . there is no Truth but one."

Shortly after banishing **Roger Williams** (see pages 91–92), Winthrop confronted another dissenter, this time a devout Puritan woman steeped in Scripture and absorbed by religious questions: **Anne Hutchinson**. The mother of fourteen children, Hutchinson served her neighbors as a midwife. After she settled into her new home in Boston in 1634, women gathered there to hear her weekly lectures on recent sermons. As one listener observed, she was a "Woman that Preaches better Gospell then any of your blackcoates . . . [from] the Ninneversity." As the months passed, Hutchinson began to lecture twice a week, and crowds of sixty to eighty women and men assembled to listen to her.

Hutchinson expounded on the sermons of John Cotton, her favorite minister. Cotton stressed what he termed the "covenant of grace" — the idea that individuals could be saved only by God's grace in choosing them to be members of the elect. Cotton contrasted this familiar Puritan doctrine with the covenant of works, the erroneous belief that a person's behavior — one's works — could win God's favor and ultimately earn a person salvation. Belief in the covenant of works and in the possibility of salvation for all was known as **Arminianism**. Cotton's sermons strongly hinted that many Puritans, including ministers, embraced Arminianism, which claimed — falsely, Cotton declared — that human beings could influence God's will. Anne Hutchinson agreed with Cotton. Her lectures emphasized her opinion that many of the colony's leaders affirmed the Arminian covenant of works. Like Cotton, she preached that only God's covenant of grace led to salvation.

The meetings at Hutchinson's house alarmed her nearest neighbor, Governor John Winthrop, who believed that she was subverting the good order of the colony. In 1637, Winthrop had formal charges brought against Hutchinson and denounced her lectures as "not tolerable nor comely in the sight of God nor fitting for your sex." He told her, "You have stept out of your place, you have rather bine a Husband than a Wife and a preacher than a Hearer; and a Magistrate than a Subject."

In court, Winthrop interrogated Hutchinson, fishing for a heresy he could pin on her. Winthrop and other Puritan elders referred to Hutchinson and her followers as **antinomians**, people who believed that Christians could be saved by faith alone and did not need to act in accordance with God's law as set forth in the Bible and as interpreted by the colony's leaders. Hutchinson nimbly defended herself against the accusation of antinomianism. Yes, she acknowledged, she believed that men and women were saved by faith alone; but no, she did not deny the need to obey God's law. "The Lord hath let me see which was the clear ministry and which the wrong," she said. Finally, Winthrop had cornered her. How could she tell which ministry was which? "By an immediate revelation," she replied, "by the voice of [God's] own spirit to my soul." Winthrop spotted in this statement the heresy of prophecy, the view that God revealed his will directly to a believer instead of exclusively through the Bible, as every right-minded Puritan knew.

In 1638, the Boston church formally excommunicated Hutchinson. The minister decreed, "I doe cast you out and . . . deliver you up to Satan that you may learne no more to blaspheme[,] to seduce and to lye. . . . I command you . . . as a Leper to withdraw your selfe out of the Congregation." Banished, Hutchinson and her family moved first to Roger Williams's Rhode Island and then to present-day New York, where she and most of her family were killed by Indians.

The strains within Puritanism exemplified by Anne Hutchinson and Roger Williams caused communities to splinter repeatedly during the seventeenth century. **Thomas Hooker**, a prominent minister, clashed with Winthrop and other leaders over the composition of the church. Hooker argued that men and women who lived godly lives should be admitted to church membership even if they had not experienced conversion. This issue, like most others in New England,

had both religious and political dimensions, for only church members could vote in Massachusetts. In 1636, Hooker led an exodus of more than eight hundred colonists from Massachusetts to the Connecticut River valley, where they founded Hartford and neighboring towns. In 1639, the towns adopted the Fundamental Orders of Connecticut, a quasi-constitution that could be altered by the vote of freemen, who did not have to be church members, though nearly all of them were.

Other Puritan churches divided and subdivided throughout the seventeenth century as acrimony developed over doctrine and church government. Sometimes churches split over the appointment of a controversial minister. Sometimes families who had a long walk to the meetinghouse simply decided to form their own church nearer their homes. These schisms arose from ambiguities and tensions within Puritan belief. As the colonies matured, other tensions developed as well.

Religious Controversies and Economic Changes

A revolutionary transformation in the fortunes of Puritans in England had profound consequences in New England. Disputes between King Charles I and Parliament, which was dominated by Puritans, escalated in 1642 to civil war in England, a conflict known as the **Puritan Revolution**. Parliamentary forces led by the staunch Puritan Oliver Cromwell were victorious, executing Charles I in 1649 and proclaiming England a Puritan republic. From 1649 to 1660, England's rulers were not monarchs who suppressed Puritanism but believers who championed it. In a half century, English Puritans had risen from a harassed group of religious dissenters to a dominant power in English government.

When the Puritan Revolution began, the stream of immigrants to New England dwindled to a trickle, creating hard times for the colonists. They could no longer consider themselves a city on a hill setting a godly example for humankind. Puritans in England, not New England, were reforming English society. Furthermore, when immigrant ships became rare, the colonists faced sky-high prices for scarce English goods and few customers for their own colonial products. As they searched to find new products and markets, they established the enduring patterns of New England's economy.

New England's rocky soil and short growing season ruled out cultivating the southern colonies' crops of tobacco and rice that found ready markets in Atlantic ports. Exports that New Englanders could not get from the soil they took instead from the forest and the sea. During the first decade of settlement, colonists traded with the Indians for animal pelts, which were in demand in Europe. By the 1640s, furbearing animals had become scarce unless traders ventured far beyond the frontiers of English settlement. Trees from the seemingly limitless forests of New England proved a longer-lasting resource. Masts for ships and staves for barrels of Spanish wine and West Indian sugar were crafted from New England timber.

The most important New England export was fish. During the turmoil of the Puritan Revolution, English ships withdrew from the rich North Atlantic fishing grounds, and New England fishermen quickly took their place. Dried, salted codfish found markets in southern Europe and the West Indies. The fish trade also stimulated colonial shipbuilding and trained generations of fishermen, sailors, and merchants, creating a commercial network that endured for more than a century. But this export econ-

omy remained peripheral to most New England colonists. Their lives revolved around their farms, their churches, and their families.

Although immigration came to a standstill in the 1640s, the population continued to boom, doubling every twenty years. In New England, almost everyone married, and women often had eight or nine children. Long, cold winters minimized the presence of warm-weather ailments such as malaria and yellow fever in the northern colonies, so the mortality rate was lower than in the South. The descendants of the immigrants of the 1630s multiplied, boosting the New England population to roughly equal that of the southern colonies (Figure 4.1).

During the second half of the seventeenth century, under the pressures of steady population growth and integration into the Atlantic economy, the red-hot piety of the founders cooled. After 1640, the population grew faster than church membership. All residents attended sermons on pain of fines and punishment, but many could not find seats in the meetinghouses. Boston's churches in 1650 could house only about a third of the city's residents. By the 1680s, women were the majority of church members throughout New England. In some towns, only 15 percent of the adult men were members. A growing fraction of New Englanders, especially men, embraced what one historian has termed "horse-shed Christianity": They attended sermons but loitered outside near the horse shed, gossiping about the weather, fishing, their crops, or the scandalous behavior of neighbors. This slackening of piety led the Puritan minister Michael Wigglesworth to ask, in verse:

> How is it that
>   I find In stead of holiness Carnality;
> In stead of heavenly frames an Earthly mind,
>   For burning zeal luke-warm Indifferency,
> For flaming love, key-cold Dead-heartedness. . . .
> Whence cometh it, that Pride, and Luxurie
>   Debate, Deceit, Contention and Strife,
> False-dealing, Covetousness, Hypocrisie
>   (With such Crimes) amongst them are so rife,
> That one of them doth over-reach another?
>   And that an honest man can hardly
>   Trust his Brother?

Most alarming to Puritan leaders, many of the children of the visible saints of Winthrop's generation failed to experience conversion and attain full church membership. Puritans tended

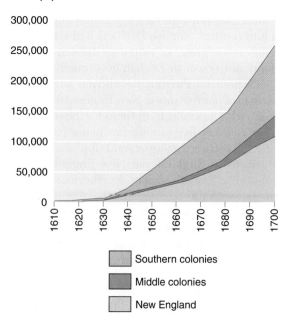

FIGURE 4.1 Population of the English North American Colonies in the Seventeenth Century The colonial population grew at a steadily accelerating rate during the seventeenth century. New England and the southern colonies each accounted for about half the total colonial population until after 1680, when growth in Pennsylvania and New York contributed to a surge in the population of the middle colonies.

to assume that sainthood was inherited — that the children of visible saints were probably also among the elect. Acting on this premise, churches permitted saints to baptize their infant sons and daughters, symbolically cleansing them of their contamination with original sin. As these children grew up during the 1640s and 1650s, however, they seldom experienced the inward transformation that signaled conversion and qualification for church membership. The problem of declining church membership and the watering-down of Puritan orthodoxy became urgent during the 1650s when the children of saints, who had grown to adulthood in New England but had not experienced conversion, began to have children themselves. Their sons and daughters — the grandchildren of the founders of the colony — could not receive the protection that baptism afforded against the terrors of death because their parents had not experienced conversion.

Puritan churches debated what to do. To allow anyone, even the child of a saint, to become a church member without conversion was an unthinkable retreat from fundamental Puritan doctrine. In 1662, a synod of Massachusetts ministers reached a compromise known as the **Halfway Covenant**. Unconverted children of saints would be permitted to become "halfway" church members. Like regular church members, they could baptize their infants. But unlike full church members, they could not participate in communion or have the voting privileges of church membership. The Halfway Covenant generated a controversy that sputtered through Puritan churches for the remainder of the century. With the Halfway Covenant, Puritan churches came to terms with the lukewarm piety that had replaced the founders' burning zeal.

Nonetheless, New England communities continued to enforce piety with holy rigor. Beginning in 1656, small bands of **Quakers** — members of the Society of Friends, as they called themselves — began to arrive in Massachusetts. Many of their beliefs were at odds with orthodox Puritanism. Quakers believed that God spoke directly to each individual through an "inner light" and that individuals needed neither a preacher nor the Bible to discover God's Word. Maintaining that all human beings were equal in God's eyes, Quakers refused to conform to mere temporal powers such as laws and governments unless God requested otherwise. For example, Quakers refused to observe the Sabbath because, they insisted, God had not set aside any special day for worship, expecting believers to worship faithfully every day. Women often took a leading role in Quaker meetings, in contrast to Puritan congregations, where women usually outnumbered men but remained subordinate.

New England communities treated Quakers with ruthless severity. Some Quakers were branded on the face "with a red-hot iron with [an] H. for heresie." When Quakers refused to leave Massachusetts, Boston officials hanged four of them between 1659 and 1661.

New Englanders' partial success in realizing the promise of a godly society ultimately undermined the intense appeal of Puritanism. In the pious Puritan communities of New England, leaders tried to eliminate sin. In the process, they diminished the sense of utter

David, Joanna, and Abigail Mason
In this 1670 painting, which depicts the children of Bostonians Joanna and Anthony Mason, the artist lavished attention on the young subjects' elaborate clothing and adornments: fashionable slashed sleeves, fancy lace, silver-studded shoes, necklaces for the girls, and a silver-headed cane for the boy. The painting hints that the children themselves were adornments—young sprouts of the Mason lineage, which could afford such finery. Unified by trappings of wealth and sober self-importance, rather than by signs of warm affection, innocent smiles, and familial solidarity, the portrait expresses the growing respect for wealth and its worldly rewards in seventeenth-century New England.
Fine Arts Museums of San Francisco. Gift of Mr. and Mrs. John D. Rockefeller III.

Hunting Witches in Salem, Massachusetts

In the summer of 1692, many people in and around Salem, Massachusetts, accused dozens of their neighbors and kinfolk of being witches. Officials convened a special court to hear the testimony of the accusers and to examine the accused. In the end, nineteen convicted witches were hanged, and more than 150 accused witches crammed the jails before the trials were called off, in part because some people began to have doubts about whether the accused witches were truly guilty.

DOCUMENT 1
Cotton Mather, *Wonders of the Invisible World*, 1692

Cotton Mather, one of the most prominent Puritan ministers at the time, supported the trials and encouraged the witch-hunt, which he believed purged New England of the malicious handiwork of the devil. Mather summarized evidence of Satan's diabolical presence to explain and justify the need for the witch-hunt.

That the Devil, is *Come down unto us with great Wrath,* we find, we feel, we now deplore. . . . The *Devil,* Exhibiting himself ordinarily as a small *Black man,* has decoy'd a fearful Knot of Proud, Froward, Ignorant, Envious, and Malicious Creatures, to Lift themselves in his Horrid Service, by Entering their Names in a Book by him Tendered unto them. These *Witches* . . . have met in Hellish *Randezvouzes,* wherein . . . they have had their Diabolical Sacraments, imitating the *Baptism* and the *Supper* of our Lord. In these Hellish Meetings, these Monsters have associated themselves to do no less a Thing than, *To Destroy the Kingdom of our Lord Jesus Christ, in these parts of the World.* . . . These wicked Spectres, or *Devils,* . . . Seize poor people about the Country with Various and bloody *Torments.* . . . The People thus Afflicted, are miserably Scratched and Bitten, so that the Marks are most *Visible* to all the World, but the causes utterly *Invisible;* and the same *Invisible* Furies, do most *Visibly* stick *Pins* into the Bodies of the Afflicted, and *Scald* them, & hideously Distort, and Disjoint all their members. . . . Yea, they sometimes drag the poor People out of their Chambers, and Carry them over *Trees* and *Hills,* for diverse Miles together. A large part of the Persons tortured by these Diabolical *Spectres,* are horribly Tempted by them . . . to sign the *Devils Laws,* in a Spectral *Book* laid before them. . . .

SOURCE: Cotton Mather, *The Wonders of the Invisible World* (Boston, 1692), 48–50.

DOCUMENT 2
Witnesses against Accused Witch Susanna Martin, 1692

Neighbors lined up to give testimony that, in their minds, proved that the accused were witches. Like many other accused people, Susanna Martin pleaded not guilty to witchcraft. The court, persuaded by the testimony of witnesses like the following, sentenced her to death, and she was executed on July 19, 1692.

Bernard Peache testify'd, That being in Bed on a Lordsday Night, he heard a scrabbling at the Window, whereat he then saw, *Susanna Martin* come in, and jump down upon the Floor. She took hold of this Deponents Feet, and drawing his Body up into an Heap, she lay upon him, near Two Hours; in all which time he could neither speak nor stirr. At length, when he could begin to move, he laid hold on her Hand, and pulling it up to his mouth, he bit three of her Fingers, as he judged, unto the Bone. Whereupon she went from the Chamber, down the Stairs, out at the Door. . . .

John Kembal . . . Being desirous to furnish himself with a Dog, he applied himself to buy one of this Martin. . . . But she not letting him have his Choice [Kembal went to another neighbor to get a puppy]. Within a few days after, [when] this *Kembal* . . . came below the Meeting-House, there appeared unto him, a little thing like a *Puppy,* of a Darkish Colour; and it shot Backwards and forwards between his Leggs. He had the Courage to use all possible Endeavors of Cutting it, with his Axe; but he could not Hit it; the Puppy gave a jump from him, and went, as to him, it seem'd into the Ground. Going a little further, there appeared unto him a Black Puppy, somewhat bigger than the first; but Black as Cole. Its motions were quicker than those of his Ax; it Flew at his Belly and away; then at his Throat, also over his Shoulder. . . . His heart now began to fail him, and he thought the Dog would have Tore his Throat out. But he recovered himself, and called upon God in his Distress; and Naming the Name of JESUS CHRIST, it Vanished away at once. . . . [The next day, Susanna Martin told other people that he had been frightened by puppies, although] Kembal [said he] had mentioned the Matter to no Creature Living.

Joseph Ring . . . has been strangely carried about by *Demons,* from one *Witch-Meeting* to another, for near two years together; and for one Quarter of this Time, they have made him, and kept him Dumb, tho he is now again able to speak. . . . Afterwards . . . this poor man would be visited with unknown shapes . . . which would force him away with them, unto unknown Places, where he saw meetings, Feastings, Dancings. . . . When he was brought into these Hellish meetings, one of the First things they still did unto him, was to give him a knock on the Back, whereupon he was ever as if Bound with chains, uncapable of Stirring out of the place, till they should Release him. . . . There often came to him a man, who presented him a Book, whereto he would have him set his Hand; promising to him, that he should then have even what he would; and presenting him with all the delectable Things, persons, and places that he could imagine. But he refusing to subscribe, the business would end with dreadful Shapes, Noises and Screechings, which almost scared him out of his witts. . . . This man did now affirm, that he saw the Prisoner [Susanna Martin], at several of those Hellish Randezvouzes. Note, This Woman was one of the most Impudent, Scurrilous, wicked creatures in the world & she did now throughout her whole Trial, discover herself to be such an one. Yet when she was asked what she had to say for her self, her Cheef Plea was, *That she had Led a most virtuous and Holy Life.*

SOURCE: Cotton Mather, *The Wonders of the Invisible World* (Boston, 1692), 115–26.

DOCUMENT 3
Robert Calef, *More Wonders of the Invisible World*, 1700

A few New Englanders spoke out against the witch-hunt as the persecution of innocent people. Robert Calef, a Boston merchant, wrote a scathing criticism of the witch trials and their supporters, such as Cotton Mather. Printers in New England refused to publish Calef's book, which was eventually published in London.

And now to sum up all in a few words, we have seen a biggotted zeal, stirring up a blind, and most bloody rage, not against enemies, or irreligious, profligate persons—but . . . against as virtuous and religious as any they have left behind them in this country, which have suffered as evil doers . . . and this by the testimony of vile varlets, as not only were known before, but have been further apparent since, by their manifest lives, whoredoms, incest &c. The accusations of these, from their spectral sight, being the chief evidence against those that suffered; in which accusations they were upheld by both magistrats and ministers, so long as they apprehended themselves in no danger. And then, tho' they could defend neither the doctrine nor the practice, yet none of them have in such a publick manner as the case requires, testified against either; tho', at the same time they could not but be sensible what a stain and lasting infamy they have brought upon the whole country, to the indangering of the future welfare not only of this but of other places, induced by their example . . . occasioning the great dishonour and blasphemy of the name of God, scandalizing the Heathen, hardening of enemies; and as a natural effect thereof, to the great increase of Atheism.

SOURCE: Robert Calef, *More Wonders of the Invisible World* (London, 1700), unpaginated "Epistle to the Reader."

Questions for Analysis and Debate

1. According to Cotton Mather, why was the devil dangerous? How did the devil operate in New England? What was the significance of Mather's emphasis that invisible "Furies" could inflict visible injuries?

2. What persuaded witnesses against Susanna Martin that she was a witch? How might a critic such as Robert Calef have responded to the testimony of these witnesses? How might Cotton Mather and these witnesses have explained Martin's claim that she led "a most virtuous and Holy Life"?

3. What do these documents suggest about the status of Christianity in New England in the late seventeenth century? Why did Mather and the witch-hunters believe that the devil was such a threat, when Calef believed that the witch-hunters themselves were the greater danger?

Storage Chest
This painted storage chest made in Hadley, Massachusetts, reflects late-seventeenth-century New Englanders' delight in color and ornament, in contrast to the plain and simple styles favored by their early-seventeenth-century predecessors. The initials "SW" likely refer to the first owner of the chest, probably the daughter of a proud father who had the chest made for SW's upcoming marriage. SW would have used the chest to store textiles, another indication that by the late seventeenth century, prosperous New England families owned more than they required for daily use and needed a place to store the surplus. Pocumtuck Valley Memorial Association Memorial Hall Museum.

human depravity that was the wellspring of Puritanism. By 1700, New Englanders did not doubt that human beings sinned, but they were more concerned with the sins of others than with their own.

Witch trials held in Salem, Massachusetts, signaled the erosion of religious confidence and assurance. From the beginning of English settlement in the New World, more than 95 percent of all legal accusations of witchcraft occurred in New England, a hint of the Puritans' preoccupation with sin and evil. The most notorious witchcraft trials took place in Salem in 1692, when witnesses accused more than one hundred people of witchcraft, a capital crime. (See "Documenting the American Promise," page 106.) Bewitched young girls shrieked in pain, their limbs twisted into strange contortions, as they pointed out the witches who tortured them. According to the trial court record, the bewitched girls declared that "the shape of [one accused witch] did oftentimes very grievously pinch them, choke them, bite them, and afflict them; urging them to write their names in a book" — the devil's book. Most of the accused witches were older women, and virtually all of them were well known to their accusers. The Salem court hanged nineteen accused witches and pressed one to death, signaling enduring belief in the supernatural origins of evil and gnawing doubt about the strength of Puritan New Englanders' faith. Why else, after all, had so many New Englanders succumbed to what their accusers and the judges believed were the temptations of Satan?

REVIEW Why did Massachusetts Puritans adopt the Halfway Covenant?

Witches Show Their Love for Satan
Mocking pious Christians' humble obeisance to God, witches willingly debased themselves by standing in line to kneel and kiss Satan's buttocks — or so it was popularly believed. This seventeenth-century print portrays Satan with clawlike hands and feet, the tail of a rodent, the wings of a bat, and the head of a lustful ram attached to the torso of a man. Notice that women predominate among the witches eager to express their devotion to Satan and to do his bidding. UCSF Library/Center for Knowledge Management.

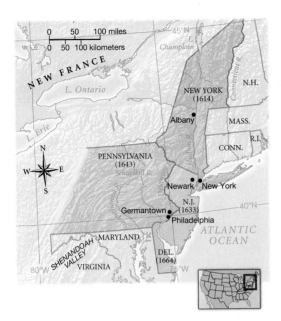

MAP 4.2
Middle Colonies in the Seventeenth Century
For the most part, the middle colonies in the seventeenth century were inhabited by settlers who clustered along the Hudson and Delaware rivers. The vast geographic extent of the colonies shown in this map reflects land grants authorized in England. Most of this area was inhabited by Native Americans rather than settled by colonists.

▶ The Founding of the Middle Colonies

South of New England and north of the Chesapeake, a group of middle colonies were founded in the last third of the seventeenth century. Before the 1670s, few Europeans settled in the region. For the first two-thirds of the seventeenth century, the most important European outpost in the area was the relatively small Dutch colony of New Netherland. By 1700, however, the English monarchy had seized New Netherland, renamed it New York, and encouraged the creation of a Quaker colony in Pennsylvania led by William Penn. Unlike the New England colonies, the middle colonies of New York, New Jersey, and Pennsylvania originated as land grants by the English monarch to one or more proprietors, who then possessed both the land and the extensive, almost monarchical, powers of government (Map 4.2). These middle colonies attracted settlers of more diverse European origins and religious faiths than were found in New England.

From New Netherland to New York

In 1609, the Dutch East India Company dispatched Henry Hudson to search for a Northwest Passage to the Orient. Hudson sailed along the Atlantic coast and ventured up the large river that now bears his name until it dwindled to a stream that obviously did not lead to China. A decade later, the Dutch government granted the West India Company — a group of Dutch merchants and shippers — exclusive rights to trade with the Western Hemisphere. In 1626, Peter Minuit, the resident director of the company, purchased Manhattan Island from the Manhate Indians for trade goods worth the equivalent of a dozen beaver pelts. New Amsterdam, the small settlement established at the southern tip of Manhattan Island, became the principal trading center in **New Netherland** and the colony's headquarters.

Unlike the English colonies, New Netherland did not attract many European immigrants. Like New England and the Chesapeake colonies, New Netherland never realized its sponsors' dreams of great profits. The company tried to stimulate immigration by granting patroonships — allotments of eighteen miles of land along the Hudson River — to wealthy stockholders who would bring fifty families to the colony and settle them as serflike tenants on their huge domains. Only one patroonship succeeded; the others failed to attract settlers, and the company eventually recovered much of the land.

Though few in number, New Netherlanders were remarkably diverse, especially compared with the homogeneous English settlers to the north and south. Religious dissenters and immigrants from Holland, Sweden, France, Germany, and elsewhere made their way to the colony. A minister of the Dutch Reformed Church complained to his superiors in Holland that several groups of Jews had recently arrived, adding to the religious mixture of "Papists, Mennonites and Lutherans among the Dutch [and] many Puritans . . . and many other atheists . . . who conceal themselves under the name of Christians."

The West India Company struggled to govern the motley colonists. Peter Stuyvesant, governor from 1647 to 1664, tried to enforce conformity to the Dutch Reformed Church, but the company declared that "the consciences of men should be free and unshackled," making a virtue

> **"In souls there is no sex."**
> — Quaker saying about the religious equality of men and women

New Amsterdam

The settlement on Manhattan Island — complete with a windmill — appears in the background of this 1673 Dutch portrait of New Amsterdam. In the foreground, the Dutch artist placed native inhabitants of the mainland, drawing them to resemble Africans rather than Lenni Lenape (Delaware) Indians. The artist probably had never seen Indians and depended on well-known artistic conventions about the appearance of Africans to create his Native Americans. The portrait contrasts orderly, efficient, business-like New Amsterdam with the exotic natural environment of America, to which the native woman on the left clings. © Collection of the New-York Historical Society.

of New Netherland necessity. The company never permitted the colony's settlers to form a representative government. Instead, the company appointed government officials who established policies, including taxes, that many colonists deeply resented.

In 1664, New Netherland became New York. Charles II, who became king of England in 1660 when Parliament restored the monarchy, gave his brother James, the Duke of York, an enormous grant of land that included New Netherland. Of course, the Dutch colony did not belong to the king of England, but that legal technicality did not deter the king or his brother. The duke quickly organized a small fleet of warships, which

appeared off Manhattan Island in late summer 1664, and demanded that Stuyvesant surrender. With little choice, he did.

As the new proprietor of the colony, the Duke of York exercised almost the same unlimited authority over the colony as had the West India Company. The duke never set foot in New York, but his governors struggled to impose order on the unruly colonists. Like the Dutch, the duke permitted "all persons of what Religion soever, quietly to inhabit . . . provided they give no disturbance to the publique peace, nor doe molest or disquiet others in the free exercise of their religion." This policy of religious toleration was less an affirmation of liberty of conscience than a recognition

William Penn

This portrait was drawn about a decade after the founding of Pennsylvania. At a time when extravagant clothing and a fancy wig proclaimed that the wearer was important, Penn is portrayed informally, lacking even a coat, his natural hair neat but undressed — all a reflection of his Quaker faith. Penn's full face and double chin show that his faith did not make him a stranger to the pleasures of the table. No hollow-cheeked ascetic or wild-eyed enthusiast, Penn appears sober and observant. The portrait captures the calm determination — anchored in faith — that inspired Penn's hopes for his new colony. Historical Society of Pennsylvania.

Unlike most Quakers, William Penn came from an eminent family. His father had served both Cromwell and Charles II and had been knighted. Born in 1644, the younger Penn trained for a military career, but the ideas of dissenters from the reestablished Church of England appealed to him, and he became a devout Quaker. By 1680, he had published fifty books and pamphlets and spoken at countless public meetings, although he had not won official toleration for Quakers in England.

The Quakers' concept of an open, generous God who made his love equally available to all people manifested itself in behavior that continually brought them into conflict with the English government. Quaker leaders were ordinary men and women, not specially trained preachers. Quakers allowed women to assume positions of religious leadership. "In souls there is no sex," they said. Since all people were equal in the spiritual realm, Quakers considered social hierarchy false and evil. They called everyone "friend" and shook hands instead of curtsying or removing their hats — even when meeting the king. These customs enraged many non-Quakers and provoked innumerable beatings and worse. Penn was jailed four times for such offenses, once for nine months.

Despite his many run-ins with the government, Penn remained on good terms with Charles II. Partly to rid England of the troublesome Quakers, in 1681 Charles made Penn the proprietor of a new colony of some 45,000 square miles called Pennsylvania.

Toleration and Diversity in Pennsylvania

Quakers flocked to Pennsylvania in numbers exceeded only by the great Puritan migration to New England fifty years earlier. Between 1682 and 1685, nearly eight thousand immigrants arrived, most of them from England, Ireland, and Wales. They represented a cross section of the artisans, farmers, and laborers who predominated among English Quakers. Quaker missionaries also encouraged immigrants from the European continent, and many came, giving Pennsylvania greater ethnic diversity than any other English colony except New York. The Quaker colony prospered, and the capital city, Philadelphia, soon rivaled New York as a center of commerce. By 1700, the city's five thousand inhabitants participated in a thriving trade exporting flour and other food products to the West Indies and

of the reality of the most heterogeneous colony in seventeenth-century North America.

New Jersey and Pennsylvania

The creation of New York led indirectly to the founding of two other middle colonies, New Jersey and Pennsylvania (see Map 4.2). In 1664, the Duke of York subdivided his grant and gave the portion between the Hudson and Delaware rivers to two of his friends. The proprietors of this new colony, New Jersey, quarreled and called in a prominent English Quaker, **William Penn**, to arbitrate their dispute. Penn eventually worked out a settlement that continued New Jersey's proprietary government. In the process, Penn became intensely interested in what he termed a "holy experiment" of establishing a genuinely Quaker colony in America.

importing English textiles and manufactured goods.

Penn was determined to live in peace with the Indians who inhabited the region. His Indian policy expressed his Quaker ideals and contrasted sharply with the hostile policies of the other English colonies. As he explained to the chief of the Lenni Lenape (Delaware) Indians, "God has written his law in our hearts, by which we are taught and commanded to love and help and do good to one another . . . [and] I desire to enjoy [Pennsylvania lands] with your love and consent." Penn instructed his agents to obtain the Indians' consent by purchasing their land, respecting their claims, and dealing with them fairly.

Penn declared that the first principle of government was that every settler would "enjoy the free possession of his or her faith and exercise of worship towards God." Accordingly, Pennsylvania tolerated Protestant sects of all kinds as well as Roman Catholicism. All voters and officeholders had to be Christians, but the government did not compel settlers to attend religious services, as in Massachusetts, or to pay taxes to maintain a state-supported church, as in Virginia.

Despite its toleration and diversity, Pennsylvania was as much a Quaker colony as New England was a stronghold of Puritanism. Penn had no hesitation about using civil government to enforce religious morality. One of the colony's first laws provided severe punishment for "all such offenses against God, as swearing, cursing, lying, profane talking, drunkenness, drinking of healths, [and] obscene words . . . which excite the people to rudeness, cruelty, looseness, and irreligion."

As proprietor, Penn had extensive powers subject only to review by the king. He appointed a governor, who maintained the proprietor's power to veto any laws passed by the colonial council, which was elected by property owners who possessed at least one hundred acres of land or who paid taxes. The council had the power to originate laws and administer all the affairs of government. A popularly elected assembly served as a check on the council; its members had the authority to reject or approve laws framed by the council.

Penn stressed that the exact form of government mattered less than the men who served in it. In Penn's eyes, "good men" staffed Pennsylvania's government because Quakers dominated elective and appointive offices. Quakers, of course, differed among themselves. Members of the assembly struggled to win the right to debate and amend laws, especially tax laws. They finally won the battle in 1701 when a new Charter of Privileges gave the proprietor the power to appoint the council and in turn stripped the council of all its former powers and gave them to the assembly, which became the only single-house legislature in all the English colonies.

REVIEW How did Quaker ideals shape the colony of Pennsylvania?

▶ The Colonies and the English Empire

Proprietary grants to faraway lands were a cheap way for the king to reward friends. As the colonies grew, however, the grants became more valuable. After 1660, the king took initiatives to channel colonial trade through English hands and to consolidate royal authority over colonial governments. Occasioned by such economic and political considerations and triggered by King Philip's War between colonists and Native Americans, these initiatives defined the basic relationship between the colonies and England that endured until the American Revolution (Map 4.3).

Royal Regulation of Colonial Trade

English economic policies toward the colonies were designed to yield customs revenues for the monarchy and profitable business for English merchants and shippers. Also, the policies were intended to divert the colonies' trade from England's enemies, especially the Dutch and the French.

The Navigation Acts of 1650, 1651, 1660, and 1663 (see chapter 3) set forth two fundamental rules governing colonial trade. First, goods shipped to and from the colonies had to be transported in English ships using primarily English crews. Second, the Navigation Acts listed ("enumerated," in the language of the time) colonial products that could be shipped only to England or to other English colonies. While these regulations prevented Chesapeake planters from shipping their tobacco directly to the European continent, they interfered less with the commerce of New England and the middle colonies, whose principal exports — fish, lumber, and flour — were not enumerated and could legally be sent directly to their most important markets in the West Indies.

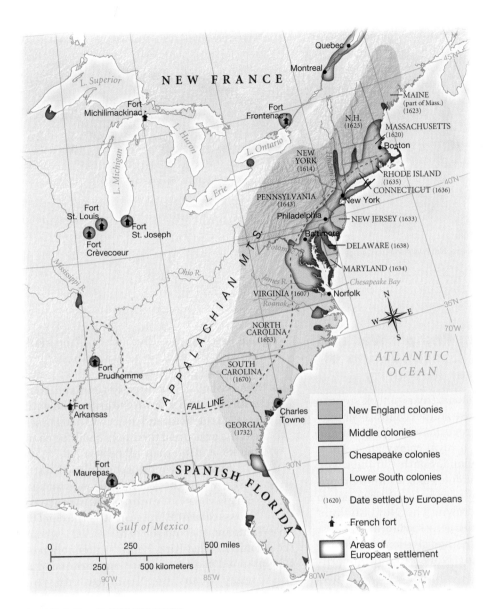

MAP ACTIVITY

Map 4.3 American Colonies at the End of the Seventeenth Century

By the end of the seventeenth century, settlers inhabited a narrow band of land that stretched more or less continuously from Boston to Norfolk, with pockets of settlement farther south. The colonies' claims to enormous tracts of land to the west were contested by Native Americans as well as by France and Spain.

READING THE MAP: What geographic feature acted as the western boundary for colonial territorial claims? Which colonies were the most settled and which the least?

CONNECTIONS: The map divides the colonies into four regions. Can you think of an alternative organization? On what criteria would it be based?

By the end of the seventeenth century, colonial commerce was defined by regulations that subjected merchants and shippers to royal supervision and gave them access to markets throughout the English empire. In addition, colonial commerce received protection from the English navy. By 1700, colonial goods (including those from the West Indies) accounted for one-fifth of all English imports and for two-thirds of all goods re-exported from England to the European continent. In turn, the colonies absorbed more than one-tenth of English exports. The commercial regulations gave economic value to England's proprietorship of the American colonies.

Beaver

North American beaver, shown here in a drawing from New France, became avidly hunted and trapped during the seventeenth century. Beaver populations in Europe, especially in Russia, had become badly depleted from overtrapping, although the demand for beaver pelts remained strong, providing an eager market for North American fur traders. Merchants and manufacturers prized beaver pelts because the fur could be shaved from the skin and felted — that is pressed together into a dense mat that was soft, warm, somewhat water repellent, and useful for making hats, like the one shown here. Drawing: Gilcrease Museum, Tulsa, Oklahoma; hat: Private collection. Image courtesy of Pilgrim Hall Museum, Plymouth, Massachusetts.

> **"[It was a] solemn sight to see so many Christians lying in their blood . . . like a company of sheep torn by wolves. All of them stripped naked by a company of hell-hounds, roaring, singing, ranting and insulting."**
>
> — MARY ROWLANDSON, describing an Indian attack

King Philip's War and the Consolidation of Royal Authority

The monarchy also took steps to exercise greater control over colonial governments. Virginia had been a royal colony since 1624; Maryland, South Carolina, and the middle colonies were proprietary colonies with close ties to the crown. The New England colonies possessed royal charters, but they had developed their own distinctively Puritan governments. Charles II, whose father, Charles I, had been executed by Puritans in England, took a particular interest in harnessing the New England colonies more firmly to the English empire. The occasion was a royal investigation following **King Philip's War**.

A series of skirmishes in the Connecticut River valley between 1636 and 1637 culminated in the Pequot War when colonists massacred hundreds of Pequot Indians. In the decades that followed, New Englanders established relatively peaceful relations with the more potent Wampanoags, but they steadily encroached on Indian land. In 1642, a native leader urged warring tribes to band together against the English. "We [must]

be one as they [the English] are," he said; "otherwise we shall be gone shortly, for our fathers had plenty of deer and skins . . . but these English having gotten our land, they with scythes cut down the grass, and with axes fell the trees, and their cows and horses eat the grass, and their hogs spoil our clam banks, and we shall all be starved."

Such grievances accumulated until 1675, when the Wampanoags attacked English settlements in western Massachusetts. Metacomet — the chief of the Wampanoags (and son of Massasoit), whom the colonists called King Philip — probably neither planned the attacks nor masterminded a conspiracy with the Nipmucs and the Narragansetts, as the colonists feared. But when militias from Massachusetts and other New England colonies counterattacked all three tribes, a deadly sequence of battles killed more than a thousand colonists and thousands more Indians.

The Indians destroyed thirteen English settlements and partially burned another half dozen. Mary Rowlandson, a minister's wife in Lancaster, Massachusetts, who was captured by Indians after her relatives were killed and wounded, recalled later that it was a "solemn sight to see so many Christians lying in their blood . . . like a company of sheep torn by wolves. All of them stripped naked by a company of hell-hounds, roaring, singing, ranting and insulting, as if they would have torn our very hearts out."

King Philip's War, 1675

MASSACHUSETTS
Boston
Plymouth
NIPMUCK
NARRAGANSETT
POCASSET
WAMPANOAG
Hartford
PEQUOT
NAUSET
CONNECTICUT
SAKONNET
MOHEGAN
New Haven
RHODE ISLAND

• Indian settlement
● English settlement attacked

**Wampanoag
War Club**

This seventeenth-century war club was
used to kill King Philip, according to the Anglican missionary who obtained it from Indians early in the eighteenth
century. Although the missionary's tale is probably a legend, the club is certainly a seventeenth-century Wampanoag weapon that might well have been used in King Philip's War. The heavy ball carved into the head of the club
could deliver a disabling, even fatal, blow. Unlike a bow
and arrow, the club needed to be wielded at very close
range. For this reason, it was most useful against a
wounded or utterly unaware enemy. Courtesy of the Fruitlands
Museums, Harvard, Massachusetts.

By the spring of 1676, Indian warriors ranged
freely within seventeen miles of Boston. The
colonists finally defeated the Indians, principally
with a scorched-earth policy of burning their
food supplies. But King Philip's War left the
New England colonists with a large war debt,
a devastated frontier, and an enduring hatred
of Indians. "A Swarm of Flies, they may arise,
a Nation to Annoy," a colonial officer wrote in
justification of destroying the Indians, "Yea Rats
and Mice, or Swarms of Lice a Nation may
destroy." And in 1676, an agent of the king
arrived to investigate whether New England
was abiding by English laws.

Not surprisingly, the king's agent found all
sorts of deviations from English rules, and the
monarchy decided to govern New England more
directly. In 1684, an English court revoked the
Massachusetts charter, the foundation of the
distinctive Puritan government. Two years later,
royal officials incorporated Massachusetts and
the other colonies north of Maryland into the
Dominion of New England. To govern the dominion, the English sent Sir **Edmund Andros** to
Boston. Some New England merchants cooperated with Andros, but most colonists were offended
by his flagrant disregard of such Puritan tradi-

tions as keeping the Sabbath. Worst of all, the
Dominion of New England invalidated all land
titles, confronting every landowner in New
England with the horrifying prospect of losing
his or her land.

Events in England, however, permitted
Massachusetts colonists to overthrow Andros
and retain title to their property. When Charles
II died in 1685, he was succeeded by his brother
James II, a zealous Catholic. James's aggressive
campaign to appoint Catholics to government
posts engendered such unrest that in 1688 a
group of Protestant noblemen in Parliament
invited the Dutch ruler William III of Orange,
James's son-in-law, to claim the English throne.

When William III landed in England at the
head of a large army, James fled to France, and
William III and his wife, Mary II (James's daughter), became co-rulers in the relatively bloodless
"Glorious Revolution," reasserting Protestant
influence in England and its empire. Rumors of
the revolution raced across the Atlantic and
emboldened colonial uprisings against royal
authority in Massachusetts, New York, and
Maryland.

In Boston in 1689, rebels tossed Andros and
other English officials in jail, destroyed the
Dominion of New England, and reestablished the
former charter government. New Yorkers followed
the Massachusetts example. Under the leadership
of Jacob Leisler, rebels seized the royal governor
in 1689 and ruled the colony for more than a year.
That same year in Maryland, the Protestant
Association, led by John Coode, overthrew the
colony's pro-Catholic government, fearing it would
not recognize the new Protestant king.

John Sheldon's Snowshoes
John Sheldon, a resident of Deerfield, Massachusetts — first settled
by colonists in 1669 — wore these snowshoes to rescue more than
one hundred colonists taken hostage by the French and their Indian allies during
the Deerfield Raid of 1704. The design of snowshoes, which colonists in 1666
called "a Rackett tyed to each foote," was adopted from the Native Americans, who had used them for centuries. Pocumtuck Valley Memorial Association Memorial Hall Museum.

New France and the Indians: The English Colonies' Northern Borderlands

North of New England, French explorers, traders, and missionaries carved out a distinctive North American colony that contrasted, competed, and periodically fought with the English colonies to the south.

The explorer Jacques Cartier sailed into the St. Lawrence River in 1535 and claimed the region for France. Cartier's attempts to found a permanent colony failed, but French ships followed in his wake and began to trade with Native Americans for wild animal pelts. By the time King Louis XIV made New France a royal colony in 1663, the fur trade had become the colony's economic foundation.

The French monarchy hoped to channel the fur trade through French hands into the broader European market and to compete against rival Dutch traders, whose headquarters at Albany (in what is now New York) funneled North American furs down the Hudson River to markets in the Netherlands. The crown also hoped the fur trade would allow the creation of a North American colony on the cheap.

The fur trade required little investment other than the construction and staffing of trading outposts at Quebec, Montreal, and elsewhere. In exchange for textiles and various metal trade goods, the Iroquois, Huron, Ottawa, Ojibwa, and other Native Americans did the arduous, time-consuming, and labor-intensive work of tracking, trapping, and skinning the animals and transporting the pelts — usually by canoe — to French traders. Unlike the English colonies, which attracted numerous settlers to engage in agriculture and produce food as well as valuable export crops, New France needed only a few colonists to keep the trading posts open and to maintain friendly relations with their Indian suppliers. By 1660, English colonists in North America outnumbered their French counterparts by more than twenty to one.

After England seized control of New York in 1664, English fur traders replaced the Dutch at Albany and eagerly competed to divert the northern fur trade away from New France. By then, the Iroquois — strategically located between the supply of furs to the north and west, New France to the east, and New York to the south — had become middlemen, collecting pelts from Huron, Ottawa, and other Indians and swapping them with French or English traders, depending on who offered the better deal. Able to mobilize scores of fierce warriors to threaten European traders as well as their Indian suppliers, the Iroquois managed to play the French and English off against each other and to maintain a near choke hold on the supply of furs.

Native Americans preferred English trade goods, which tended to be of higher quality and less expensive than those available at French outposts, but New France cultivated better relationships with the Indians. When English colonists had the required military strength, they seldom hesitated to kill Indians, especially those who occupied land the colonists craved. The small number of colonists in New France never had as much military power as the English colonists; hence, they sought to stay on relatively peaceful and friendly terms with the Indians. French men commonly married or cohabited with Indian women, an outgrowth of both the shortage of French women among the colonists and the acceptance of such couplings, compared with the strong taboo prevalent in the English colonies.

But these rebel governments did not last. When King William III's governor of New York arrived in 1691, he executed Leisler for treason. Coode's men ruled Maryland until the new royal governor arrived in 1692 and ended both Coode's rebellion and Lord Baltimore's proprietary government. In Massachusetts, John Winthrop's city on a hill became another royal colony in 1691. The new charter said that the governor of the colony would be appointed by the king rather than elected by the colonists' representatives. But perhaps the most unsettling change was the new qualification for voting. Possession of property replaced church membership as a prerequisite for voting in colony-wide elections. Wealth

Jesuit missionaries led the spiritual colonization of New France. Zealous enemies of what they considered Protestant heresies and stout defenders of Catholicism, the Jesuits fanned out to Indian villages throughout New France, determined to convert the Native Americans and to preserve the colony as a Catholic stronghold. Unwittingly, the missionaries also spread European diseases among the Native Americans, repeatedly causing deadly epidemics. Above all, the missionaries worked hand in hand with the fur traders and royal officials to make New France a low-cost Catholic colony on the thinly defended borders of the predominantly Protestant English colonies.

To extend the boundaries of New France far to the west and south, almost encircling the English colonies along the Atlantic coast, royal officials in 1673 sponsored a voyage by the explorer Louis Jolliet and the priest Jacques Marquette to explore the vast interior of the North American continent by canoeing down the Mississippi River to what is now Arkansas. Jolliet and Marquette made grandiose claims to the Mississippi valley, but in reality these claims amounted to little more than a colored patch on European maps. The dominant military power in New France remained the Iroquois, not the French.

England and France clashed repeatedly in North America over the fur trade and in a colonial extension of their rivalry at home. European conflict between France and England spread to North America during King William's War (1689–1697), when the colonists and their Indian allies carried out numerous deadly raids, marking the contested boundary between New France and the English colonies as a bloody zone controlled by none of its claimants or inhabitants.

Indians in New France
Native Americans used canoes as the most efficient form of transportation on waterways throughout North America. Heavy bundles of animal pelts, for example, were carried long distances from a remote trapping region to a fur trading post in canoes. This seventeenth-century drawing from New France illustrates Native Americans' "very amazing" skills in handling a canoe, in this case by standing up while netting and spearing fish. The figure on the right appears to be playing a flute, perhaps to attract fish. Why do you think the artist was so fascinated with the fishermen's tattoos and body paint? Gilcrease Museum, Tulsa, Oklahoma.

America in a Global Context

1. In what ways did New France reflect the colonial objectives of the French monarchy?

2. How did New France differ from the English colonies in seventeenth-century North America?

3. How did European rivalries influence the encounters of Indians with French and English colonists?

replaced God's grace as the defining characteristic of Massachusetts citizenship.

Much as colonists chafed under increasing royal control, they still valued English protection from hostile neighbors. Colonists worried that the Catholic colony of New France menaced frontier regions by encouraging Indian raids and by competing for the lucrative fur trade. (See "Beyond America's Borders," page 116.) Although French leaders tried to buttress the military strength of New France during the last third of the seventeenth century to block the expansion of the English colonies, most of the military efforts mustered by New France focused on defending against attacks by the powerful Iroquois. However, when the English colonies were distracted by the

Glorious Revolution, French forces from the fur-trading regions along the Great Lakes and in Canada attacked villages in New England and New York. Known as King William's War, the conflict with the French was a colonial outgrowth of William's war against France in Europe. The war dragged on until 1697 and ended inconclusively in both Europe and the colonies. But it made clear to many colonists that along with English royal government came a welcome measure of military security.

> **REVIEW** Why did the Glorious Revolution in England lead to uprisings in the American colonies?

▶ Conclusion: An English Model of Colonization in North America

By 1700, the northern English colonies of North America had developed along lines quite different from the example set by their southern counterparts. Emigrants came with their families and created settlements unlike the scattered plantations and largely male environment of early Virginia. Puritans in New England built towns and governments around their churches and placed worship of God, not tobacco, at the center of their society. They depended chiefly on the labor of family members rather than on that of servants and slaves.

The convictions of Puritanism that motivated John Winthrop and others to reinvent England in the colonies became muted, however, as New England matured and dissenters such as Roger Williams multiplied. Catholics, Quakers, Anglicans (members of the Church of England), Jews, and others settled in the middle and southern colonies, creating considerable religious toleration, especially in Pennsylvania and New York. At the same time, northern colonists, like their southern counterparts, developed an ever-increasing need for land that inevitably led to bloody conflict with the Indians who were displaced.

During the next century, the English colonial world would undergo surprising new developments built on the achievements of the seventeenth century. Immigrants from Scotland, Ireland, and Germany streamed into North America, and unprecedented numbers of African slaves poured into the southern colonies. On average, white colonists attained a relatively comfortable standard of living, especially compared with most people in England and continental Europe. While religion remained important, the intensity of religious concern that characterized the seventeenth century waned during the eighteenth century. Colonists worried more about prosperity than about providence, and their societies grew increasingly secular, worldly, and diverse.

▶ Selected Bibliography

General Works

Virginia DeJohn Anderson, *Creatures of Empire: How Domestic Animals Transformed Early America* (2004).
Colin G. Calloway, *New Worlds for All: Indians, Europeans, and the Remaking of Early America* (1998).
Eric Jay Dolin, *Fur, Fortune, and Empire: The Epic History of the Fur Trade in America* (2010).
David D. Hall, *Worlds of Wonder, Days of Judgment: Popular Religious Belief in Early New England* (1989).
Diarmaid MacCulloch, *The Reformation* (2005).
Peter Moogk, *La Nouvelle France: The Making of French Canada—A Cultural History* (2000).
Carla Gardina Pestana, *The English Atlantic in the Age of Revolution, 1640–1661* (2004).
James Pritchard, *In Search of Empire: The French in the Americas, 1670–1730* (2007).

Native Americans

Russell Bourne, *Gods of War, Gods of Peace: How the Meeting of Native and Colonial Religions Shaped Early America* (2002).
Roger M. Carpenter, *The Renewed, the Destroyed, and the Remade: The Three Thought Worlds of the Huron and the Iroquois, 1609–1675* (2004).
Richard W. Cogley, *John Eliot's Mission to the Indians before King Philip's War* (1999).
Jill Lepore, *The Name of War: King Philip's War and the Origins of American Identity* (1998).
Daniel R. Mandell, *King Philip's War: Colonial Expansion, Native Resistance, and the End of Indian Sovereignty* (2010).
Donna Merwick, *The Shame and the Sorrow: Dutch-Amerindian Encounters in New Netherland* (2006).
Michael Leroy Oberg, *Dominion and Civility: English Imperialism and Native America, 1585–1685* (1999).
Ann Marie Plane, *Colonial Intimacies: Indian Marriages in Early New England* (2000).

New England

Louise A. Breen, *Transgressing the Bounds: Subversive Enterprises among the Puritan Elite in Massachusetts, 1630–1692* (2001).

Nick Bunker, *Making Haste from Babylon: The Mayflower Pilgrims and Their World* (2010).

James F. Cooper Jr., *Tenacious of Their Liberties: The Congregationalists in Colonial Massachusetts* (1999).

Cornelia Hughes Dayton, *Women before the Bar: Gender, Law, and Society in Connecticut, 1639–1789* (1995).

Lisa M. Gordis, *Opening Scriptures: Bible Reading and Interpretive Authority in Puritan New England* (2003).

Jane Kamensky, *Governing the Tongue: The Politics of Speech in Early New England* (1997).

Eve LaPlante, *American Jezebel: The Uncommon Life of Anne Hutchinson, the Woman Who Defied the Puritans* (2005).

Mary Beth Norton, *In the Devil's Snare: The Salem Witchcraft Crisis of 1692* (2002).

Mark A. Peterson, *The Price of Redemption: The Spiritual Economy of Puritan New England* (1998).

Nathaniel Philbrick, *Mayflower: A Story of Courage, Community, and War* (2006).

Michael P. Winship, *Making Heretics: Militant Protestantism and Free Grace in Massachusetts, 1636–1641* (2002).

Middle Colonies

Ned C. Landsman, *Crossroads of Empire: The Middle Colonies in British North America* (2010).

Peter C. Mancall, *Fatal Journey: The Final Expedition of Henry Hudson* (2009).

Cathy Matson, *Merchants and Empire: Trading in Colonial New York* (1998).

David E. Narrett, *Inheritance and Family Life in Colonial New York City* (1992).

Russell Shorto, *The Island at the Center of the World: The Epic Story of Dutch Manhattan and the Forgotten Colony That Shaped America* (2004).

Allen Tully, *Forming American Politics: Ideals, Interests, and Institutions in Colonial New York and Pennsylvania* (1994).

▶ FOR MORE BOOKS ABOUT TOPICS IN THIS CHAPTER, see the Online Bibliography at **bedfordstmartins.com/roark**.

▶ FOR ADDITIONAL PRIMARY SOURCES FROM THIS PERIOD, see Michael Johnson, ed., *Reading the American Past*, Fifth Edition.

▶ FOR WEB SITES, IMAGES, AND DOCUMENTS RELATED TO TOPICS AND PLACES IN THIS CHAPTER, visit Make History at **bedfordstmartins.com/roark**.

Reviewing Chapter 4

KEY TERMS

Explain each term's significance.

Puritans and the Settlement of New England
- English Reformation (p. 93)
- Puritans (p. 93)
- Pilgrims (p. 94)
- Separatists (p. 94)
- William Bradford (p. 95)
- Mayflower Compact (p. 95)
- Wampanoag Indians (p. 95)
- Massachusetts Bay Company (p. 95)
- John Winthrop (p. 95)

The Evolution of New England Society
- Calvinism (p. 98)
- predestination (p. 98)
- visible saints (p. 99)
- Roger Williams (p. 102)
- Anne Hutchinson (p. 102)
- Arminianism (p. 102)
- antinomians (p. 103)
- Thomas Hooker (p. 103)
- Puritan Revolution (p. 103)
- Halfway Covenant (p. 105)
- Quakers (p. 105)

The Founding of the Middle Colonies
- New Netherland (p. 109)
- William Penn (p. 111)

The Colonies and the English Empire
- King Philip's War (p. 114)
- Dominion of New England (p. 115)
- Edmund Andros (p. 115)

REVIEW QUESTIONS

Use key terms and dates to support your answers.

1. Why did the Puritans immigrate to North America? (pp. 93–97)

2. Why did Massachusetts Puritans adopt the Halfway Covenant? (pp. 98–108)

3. How did Quaker ideals shape the colony of Pennsylvania? (pp. 109–112)

4. Why did the Glorious Revolution in England lead to uprisings in the American colonies? (pp. 112–118)

MAKING CONNECTIONS

Draw on key terms, the timeline, and review questions.

1. How did the religious dissenters who flooded into the northern colonies address the question of religious dissent in their new homes? Comparing two colonies, discuss their different approaches and the implications of those approaches for colonial development.

2. In his sermon aboard the *Arbella*, John Winthrop spoke of the Massachusetts Bay Colony as "a city upon a hill." What did he mean? How did this expectation influence life in New England during the seventeenth century? In your answer, be sure to consider the relationship between religious and political life in the colony.

3. Religious conflict and political turmoil battered England in the seventeenth century. How did political developments in England affect life in the colonies? In your answer, consider the establishment of the colonies and the crown's attempts to exercise authority over them.

4. To what extent did the New England and middle colonies become more alike during the seventeenth century? To what extent did they remain distinctive? In your answer, consider religions, economies, systems of governance, and patterns of settlement in the colonies.

LINKING TO THE PAST

Link events in this chapter to earlier events.

1. How did the communal goals of New England settlers compare with the aspirations of the tobacco and rice planters of the southern colonies? (See chapter 3.)

2. To what degree did religious intolerance shape events in the New World colonies of Spain, France, and England? (See chapters 2 and 3.)

▶ FOR PRACTICE QUIZZES AND OTHER STUDY TOOLS, visit the Online Study Guide at bedfordstmartins.com/roark.

TIMELINE 1534–1692

1534	• King Henry VIII breaks with Roman Catholic Church; English Reformation begins.
1609	• Henry Hudson searches for Northwest Passage.
1620	• Plymouth colony founded.
1626	• Manhattan Island purchased; New Amsterdam founded.
1629	• Massachusetts Bay Company receives royal charter.
1630	• John Winthrop leads Puritan settlers to Massachusetts Bay.
1636	• Rhode Island colony established. • Connecticut colony founded.
1636–1637	• Pequot War.
1638	• Anne Hutchinson excommunicated.
1642	• Puritan Revolution inflames England.
1649	• English Puritans win civil war and execute Charles I.
1656	• Quakers arrive in Massachusetts and are persecuted there.
1660	• Monarchy restored in England; Charles II becomes king.
1662	• Many Puritan congregations adopt Halfway Covenant.
1664	• English seize Dutch colony, rename it New York. • Colony of New Jersey created.
1675–1676	• King Philip's War.
1681	• William Penn receives charter for colony of Pennsylvania.
1686	• Dominion of New England created.
1688	• England's Glorious Revolution; William III and Mary II become new rulers.
1689–1697	• King William's War.
1692	• Salem witch trials.

TEXTILE SAMPLE BOOK
This bulging collection of
cloth samples assembled by a
textile manufacturer in Norwich,
England, allowed colonial merchants to choose
combinations of colors, designs, textures, weights,
and fibers (such as wool, cotton, or linen) that they believed
their customers would purchase. The book illustrates the astonishing
variety of textiles the Norwich manufacturer could readily produce and ship
throughout the Atlantic world. The book also depicts the bewildering and
somewhat intoxicating range of choices available to British North American
consumers. The background image, of Charleston harbor in South Carolina,
portrays the bustling Atlantic commerce of the eighteenth century.

Background: Colonial Williamsburg Foundation; book: NWHCM: 1966.658 Despatch book by Ives and Basely,
1792, from the collections of Norfolk Museums and Archaeology Service.

5

Colonial America in the Eighteenth Century 1701–1770

THE BROTHERS AMBOE ROBIN JOHN AND LITTLE EPHRAIM ROBIN JOHN and their cousin Ancona Robin John lived during the 1750s and 1760s in Old Calabar on the Bight of Biafra in West Africa. The Robin Johns were part of a slave-trading dynasty headed by their kinsman Grandy King George, one of the most powerful leaders of the Efik people. Grandy King George owned hundreds of slaves whom he employed to capture and trade for still more slaves in the African interior. He sold these captives to captains of European slave ships seeking to fill their holds with human cargo for the transatlantic voyage to the sugar, tobacco, and rice fields in the New World. Old Calabar was a major contributor to the massive flow of more than 1.2 million slaves from the Bight of Biafra to the New World during the eighteenth century.

Grandy King George nearly monopolized the Old Calabar slave trade during the 1760s, allowing him to live in luxury, surrounded by fine British trade goods. British slave ship captains and Grandy King George's African rivals resented his choke hold on the supply of slaves and in 1767 conspired to trap the king and the Robin Johns, seize hundreds of their slaves, and destroy the king's monopoly. In the bloody melee, Grandy King George managed to escape, but other members of his family were less fortunate. Amboe Robin John was beheaded by the leader of the African attackers. Little Ephraim and Ancona Robin John were enslaved, packed aboard the ship Duke of York with more than 330 other slaves, and transported across the Atlantic to the West Indies.

Unlike most slaves, the Robin Johns understood, spoke, and even wrote English, an essential skill they had learned as slave traders in Old Calabar. A French physician bought the Robin Johns and, according to Ancona, "treated [them] . . . upon ye whole not badly." After seven months, the Robin Johns escaped from their owner and boarded a ship "determined to get home," Little Ephraim wrote. But the ship captain took them to Virginia instead and sold them as slaves to a merchant who traded between the

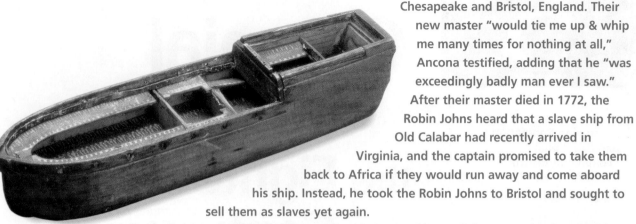

Model of a Slave Ship
Jammed into the holds of slave ships, enslaved Africans made the dreaded Middle Passage to the New World. The model of a slave ship shown here was used in parliamentary debates by anti-slavery leaders in Britain to demonstrate the inhumanity of shipping people as if they were cargo. The model does not show another typical feature of slave ships: weapons. Slaves vastly outnumbered the crews aboard the ships, and crew members justifiably feared slave uprisings. Wilberforce House, Hull City Museums and Art Galleries, UK/Bridgeman Art Library.

Chesapeake and Bristol, England. Their new master "would tie me up & whip me many times for nothing at all," Ancona testified, adding that he "was exceedingly badly man ever I saw." After their master died in 1772, the Robin Johns heard that a slave ship from Old Calabar had recently arrived in Virginia, and the captain promised to take them back to Africa if they would run away and come aboard his ship. Instead, he took the Robin Johns to Bristol and sought to sell them as slaves yet again.

While imprisoned "in this Deplorable condition" on a ship in Bristol harbor, the Robin Johns managed to smuggle letters to a Bristol slave trader they had known and dealt with in Old Calabar. With help from him and other English sympathizers, the Robin Johns appeared before Lord Mansfield, the chief justice of England, and appealed for their freedom on the grounds that they were unjustly enslaved because they "were free people . . . [who] had not done anything to forfeit our liberty." After complex negotiations, they won legal recognition of their freedom.

As free Africans in Bristol, the Robin Johns converted to Christianity under the ministry of the famous Methodists John and Charles Wesley, but they longed to return to Africa. In 1774, they left Bristol as free men on a slave ship bound for Old Calabar, where they resumed their careers as slave traders.

The Robin Johns' unrelenting quest to escape enslavement and redeem their freedom was shared but not realized by millions of Africans who were victims of slave traders such as Grandy King George and numberless merchants, ship captains, and colonists. In contrast, tens of thousands of Europeans voluntarily crossed the Atlantic to seek opportunities in North America — often by agreeing to several years of contractual servitude. Both groups illustrate the undertow of violence and deceit beneath the surface of the eighteenth-century Atlantic commerce linking Britain, Africa, the West Indies, and British North America. In the flux and uncertainty of the eighteenth-century world, many, like the Robin Johns, turned to the consolations of religious faith as a source of meaning and hope in an often cruel and unforgiving society.

The flood of free and unfree migrants crossing the Atlantic contributed to unprecedented population growth in eighteenth-century British North America. In contrast, Spanish and French colonies in North America remained thinly populated outposts of European empires interested principally in maintaining a toehold in the vast continent. While the New England, middle, and southern colonies retained regional distinctions, commercial, cultural, and political trends built unifying experiences and assumptions among British North American colonists.

▶ A Growing Population and Expanding Economy in British North America

The most important fact about eighteenth-century British America is its phenomenal population growth: In 1700, colonists numbered about 250,000; by 1770, they tallied well over 2 million. An index of the emerging significance of colonial North America is that in 1700, there were nineteen people in England for every American colonist; by 1770, there were only three. The eightfold growth of the colonial population signaled the maturation of a distinctive colonial society. That society was by no means homogeneous. Colonists of different ethnic groups, races, and religions lived in varied environments under thirteen different colonial governments, all of them part of the British empire.

In general, the growth and diversity of the eighteenth-century colonial population derived from two sources: immigration and **natural increase** (growth through reproduction). Natural increase contributed about three-fourths of the population growth, immigration about one-fourth. Immigration shifted the ethnic and racial balance among the colonists, making them by 1770 less English and less white than ever before. Fewer than 10 percent of eighteenth-century immigrants came from England; about 36 percent were Scots-Irish, mostly from northern Ireland; 33 percent arrived from Africa, almost all of them slaves; nearly 15 percent had left the many German-language principalities (the nation of Germany did not exist until 1871); and almost 10 percent came from Scotland. In 1670, more than 9 out of 10 colonists were of English ancestry, and only 1 out of 25 was of African ancestry. By 1770, only about half of the colonists were of English descent, while more than 20 percent descended from Africans. Thus, by 1770, the people of the colonies had a distinctive colonial — rather than English — profile (Map 5.1).

The booming population of the colonies hints at a second major feature of eighteenth-century colonial society: an expanding economy. In 1700, after almost a century of settlement, nearly all the colonists lived within fifty miles of the Atlantic coast. The nearly limitless wilderness stretching westward made land relatively cheap compared with its price in the Old World. The abundance of land in the colonies made labor precious, and the colonists always needed more. The insatiable demand for labor was the fundamental economic environment that sustained the mushrooming

"Dummy Board" of Phyllis, a New England Slave
This life-size portrait of a slave woman named Phyllis, a mulatto who worked as a domestic servant for her owner, Elizabeth Hunt Wendell, was painted sometime before 1753. Known as a "dummy board," it was propped against a wall or placed in a doorway or window to suggest that the residence was occupied and to discourage thieves. Phyllis's dress and demeanor suggest that she was capable, orderly, and efficient. She illustrates the integration of the mundane tasks of housekeeping with the shifting currents of transatlantic commerce. Although tens of thousands of slaves were brought from Africa to British North America during the eighteenth century, Phyllis was probably not one of them. Instead, she was most likely born in the colonies of mixed black and white parentage. Courtesy of Historic New England.

CHAPTER 5 • COLONIAL AMERICA IN THE EIGHTEENTH CENTURY / 1701–1770

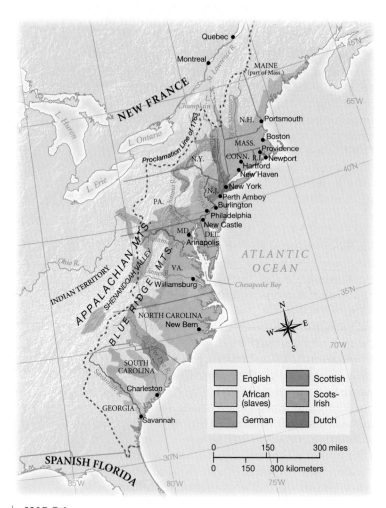

MAP 5.1

Europeans and Africans in the Eighteenth Century

This map illustrates regions where Africans and certain immigrant groups clustered. It is important to avoid misreading the map. Predominantly English and German regions, for example, also contained colonists from other places. Likewise, regions where African slaves resided in large numbers also included many whites, slave masters among them. The map suggests the diversity of eighteenth-century colonial society.

population. Economic historians estimate that free colonists (those who were not indentured servants or slaves) had a higher standard of living than the majority of people elsewhere in the Atlantic world. The unique achievement of the eighteenth-century colonial economy was this modest economic welfare of the vast bulk of the free population.

> **REVIEW** How did the North American colonies achieve the remarkable population growth of the eighteenth century?

▶ New England: From Puritan Settlers to Yankee Traders

The New England population grew sixfold during the eighteenth century but lagged behind the growth in the other colonies. Most immigrants chose other destinations because of New England's relatively densely settled land and because Puritan orthodoxy made these colonies comparatively inhospitable to those of other faiths and those indifferent to religion. As the population grew, many settlers in search of farmland dispersed from towns, and Puritan communities lost much of their cohesion. Nonetheless, networks of economic exchange laced New Englanders to their neighbors, to Boston merchants, and to the broad currents of Atlantic commerce. In many ways, trade became a faith that competed strongly with the traditions of Puritanism.

Natural Increase and Land Distribution

The New England population grew mostly by natural increase, much as it had during the seventeenth century. Nearly every adult woman married. Most married women had children — often many children, thanks to the relatively low mortality rate in New England. The perils of childbirth gave wives a shorter life expectancy than husbands, but wives often lived to have six, seven, or eight babies. Anne Franklin and her husband, Josiah, a soap and candle maker in Boston, had seven children. Four months after Anne died, Josiah married his second wife, Abiah, and the couple had ten more children, including their son Benjamin, who became one of the most prominent colonial leaders of the eighteenth century. Like many other New Englanders, Benjamin Franklin felt hemmed in by family pressures and lack of opportunity and left the region when he was seventeen years old "to assert my freedom," as he put it, first in New York and then in Philadelphia.

The growing New England population pressed against a limited amount of land. Compared to colonies farther south, New England had less land for the expansion of settlement (see Map 5.1). Moreover, as the northernmost group of British colonies, New England had contested northern and western frontiers. Powerful Native Americans, especially the Iroquois and Mahican tribes, jealously guarded their territory. The French (and Catholic) colony of New France also menaced the British (and mostly Protestant) New England colonies when provoked by colonial or European disputes. (See chapter 4, "Beyond America's Borders," page 116.)

During the seventeenth century, New England towns parceled out land to individual families. In most cases, the original settlers practiced **partible inheritance** — that is, they subdivided land more or less equally among sons. By the eighteenth century, the original land allotments had to be further subdivided to accommodate grandsons and great-grandsons, and many plots of land became too small to support a family. Sons who could not hope to inherit sufficient land to farm had to move away from the town where they were born.

During the eighteenth century, colonial governments in New England abandoned the seventeenth-century policy of granting land to towns. Needing revenue, the governments of both Connecticut and Massachusetts sold land directly to individuals, including speculators. Now money, rather than membership in a community bound by a church covenant, determined whether a person could obtain land. The new land policy eroded the seventeenth-century pattern of settlement. As colonists spread north and west, they tended to settle on individual farms rather than in the towns and villages that characterized the seventeenth century. New Englanders still depended on their relatives and neighbors, but far more than in the seventeenth century, they regulated their behavior in newly settled areas by their own individual choices.

Farms, Fish, and Atlantic Trade

A New England farm was a place to get by, not to get rich. New England farmers grew food for their families, but their fields did not produce huge marketable surpluses. Instead of one big crop, a farmer grew many small ones. If farmers had extra, they sold to or traded with neighbors. Poor roads made travel difficult, time-consuming, and expensive, especially with bulky and heavy agricultural goods. The one major agricultural product the New England colonies exported — livestock — walked to market on its own legs. By 1770, New Englanders had only one-fourth as much wealth per capita as free colonists in the southern colonies.

As consumers, New England farmers participated in a diversified commercial economy that linked remote farms to markets throughout the Atlantic world. Merchants large and small stocked imported goods — British textiles, ceramics, and metal goods; Chinese tea; West Indian sugar; and Chesapeake tobacco. Farmers' needs supported local shoemakers, tailors, wheelwrights, and carpenters. Larger towns, especially Boston, housed skilled tradesmen such as cabinetmakers, silversmiths, and printers. Shipbuilders tended to do better than other artisans because they served the most dynamic sector of the New England economy. Many New Englanders made their fortunes at sea, as they had since the seventeenth century.

Fish accounted for more than a third of New England's eighteenth-century exports; livestock and timber made up another third. The West Indies absorbed two-thirds of all New England's exports. Slaves on Caribbean sugar plantations ate dried, salted codfish caught by New England fishermen, filled barrels crafted from New England timber with molasses and refined sugar, and loaded those barrels aboard ships bound ultimately for Europeans with a sweet tooth. Almost all of the rest of New England's exports went to Britain and continental Europe (Map 5.2). This **Atlantic commerce** benefited the entire New England economy, providing jobs for laborers and tradesmen as well as for ship captains, clerks, merchants, and sailors. (See "Seeking the American Promise," page 130.)

Merchants dominated Atlantic commerce. The largest and most successful New England merchants lived in Boston at the hub of trade between local folk and the international market. Merchants not only bought and sold goods but also owned and insured the ships that carried the merchandise throughout the Atlantic world. Shrewd, diligent, and lucky merchants could make fortunes. The magnificence of a wealthy Boston merchant's home stunned John Adams, a thrifty Massachusetts lawyer who became a leader during the American Revolution and ultimately the second president of the United States. To Adams, the merchant's house seemed fit "for a noble Man, a Prince." Such luxurious Boston homes contrasted with the modest dwellings of Adams and other New Englanders, an indication of the polarization of wealth that developed in Boston and other seaports during the eighteenth century.

By 1770, the richest 5 percent of Bostonians owned about half the city's wealth; the poorest two-thirds of the population owned less than one-tenth. While the rich got richer and

> "We in New England know nothing of poverty and want, we have no idea of the thing, how much better do our poor people live than 7/8 of the people on this much famed island."
> — A Connecticut traveler, writing from England

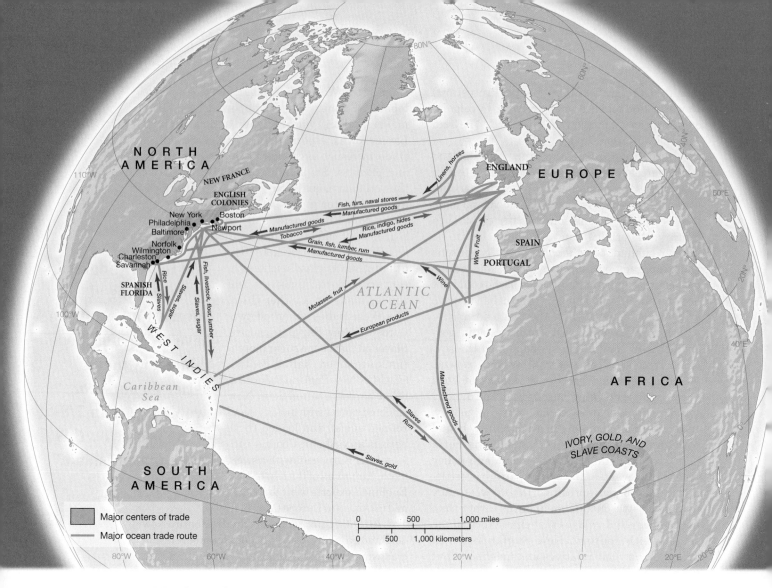

MAP ACTIVITY

MAP 5.2 Atlantic Trade in the Eighteenth Century

This map illustrates the economic outlook of the colonies in the eighteenth century — east toward the Atlantic world rather than west toward the interior of North America. The long distances involved in the Atlantic trade and the uncertainties of ocean travel suggest the difficulties Britain experienced governing the colonies and regulating colonial commerce.

READING THE MAP: What were the major Atlantic markets for trade coming out of Europe? What goods did the British colonies import and export?

CONNECTIONS: In what ways did the flow of raw materials from the colonies affect British industry? How did British colonial trade policies influence the Atlantic trade?

everybody else had a smaller share of the total wealth, the incidence of genuine poverty did not change much. About 5 percent of New Englanders qualified for poor relief throughout the eighteenth century. Overall, colonists were better off than most people in England. A Connecticut traveler wrote from England in 1764, "We in New England know nothing of poverty and want, we have no idea of the thing, how much better do our poor people live than 7/8 of the people on this much famed island."

The contrast with English poverty had meaning because the overwhelming majority of New Englanders traced their ancestry to England. New England was more homogeneously English than any other colonial region. People of African ancestry (almost all of them slaves) numbered more than fifteen thousand by 1770, but they barely diversified the region's 97 percent white majority. In the Narragansett region of Rhode Island, large landowners imported numerous slaves to raise livestock. But most New Englanders had little use for slaves on their family farms. Instead, slaves were concentrated in towns, especially Boston, where most of them worked as domestic servants and laborers.

Boston Common in Needlework
Hannah Otis embroidered this exquisite needlework portrait of Boston Common in 1750, when she was eighteen years old. From the perspective of the twenty-first century, the scene gives few hints of city life. Otis populated the cityscape with more animals than people and more plants than paving stones. The large house (center right) belonged to the Hancock family. John Hancock, who later signed the Declaration of Independence, is shown on horseback in the foreground. Eighteenth-century Bostonians owned slaves, as Otis shows. What features of this portrait would suggest a city to an eighteenth-century viewer? Photograph © 2012 Museum of Fine Arts, Boston.

By 1770, the population, wealth, and commercial activity of New England differed from what they had been in 1700. Ministers still enjoyed high status, but Yankee traders had replaced Puritan saints as the symbolic New Englanders. Atlantic commerce competed with religious convictions in ordering New Englanders' daily lives.

> **REVIEW**   Why did settlement patterns in New England change from the seventeenth to the eighteenth century?

► The Middle Colonies: Immigrants, Wheat, and Work

In 1700, almost twice as many people lived in New England as in the middle colonies of Pennsylvania, New York, New Jersey, and Delaware. But by 1770, the population of the middle colonies had multiplied tenfold — mainly from an influx of German, Irish, Scottish, and other immigrants — and nearly equaled the population of New England. Immigrants made the middle colonies a uniquely diverse society. By 1800, barely one-third of Pennsylvanians and

less than half the total population of the middle colonies traced their ancestry to England. New settlers, whether free or in servitude, poured into the middle colonies because they perceived unparalleled opportunities. However, the increasing number of slaves arriving in bondage had little hope of sharing in such rewards.

German and Scots-Irish Immigrants

Germans made up the largest contingent of migrants from the European continent to the middle colonies. By 1770, about 85,000 Germans had arrived in the colonies. Their fellow colonists often referred to them as **Pennsylvania Dutch**, an English corruption of *Deutsch*, the word the immigrants used to describe themselves.

Most German immigrants came from what is now southwestern Germany, where, one observer noted, peasants were "not as well off as cattle elsewhere." Devastating French invasions of Germany during Queen Anne's War (1702–1713) made bad conditions worse and triggered the first large-scale migration. German immigrants included numerous artisans and a few merchants, but the great majority were farmers and laborers. Economically, they represented "middling folk," neither the poorest (who could not afford the trip) nor the better-off (who did not want to leave).

A Sailor's Life in the Eighteenth-Century Atlantic World

Although most eighteenth-century North American colonists made their living on farms, tens of thousands manned the vessels that ferried people, animals, commodities, consumer goods, ideas, and microorganisms from port to port throughout the Atlantic world. Built almost entirely from wood and fiber, ships were the most complex machines in the eighteenth century. Seamen needed to learn how to handle the intricacies of a vessel's working parts quickly, smoothly, and reliably. The ship, the cargo, and their own lives depended on their knowledge and dexterity. They had to endure hard physical labor for weeks or months on end in a cramped space packed with cargo and crew. Sailors followed "one of the hardest and dangerousest callings," one old salt declared.

Despite the certainty of strenuous work and spartan accommodations, young men like Ashley Bowen made their way to wharves in small ports such as Marblehead, Massachusetts — Bowen's hometown — or large commercial centers such as Boston, Philadelphia, New York, and Charleston. There they boarded vessels and launched a life of seafaring, seeking the promise of a future wafting on the surface of the deep rather than rooted below the surface of the soil.

Born in 1728, Bowen grew up in Marblehead, one of the most important fishing ports in North America. Like other boys who lived in or near ports, Bowen probably watched ships come and go; heard tales of adventure, disaster, and intrigue; and learned from neighbors and pals how to maneuver small, shallow-draft boats within sight of land. Young girls sometimes learned to handle a small boat, but they almost never worked as sailors aboard Atlantic vessels. When Bowen was only eleven years old, he sailed as a ship's boy aboard a vessel captained by the father of a friend to pick up a load of tar bound for Bristol, England. The ship then loaded a cargo of coal in Wales and carried it to Boston, where Bowen, now twelve, arrived with a yearlong seafaring education under his belt.

Most commonly, young men first went to sea when they were fifteen to eighteen years old. Like Bowen, they were single, living with their parents, and casting about for work. They usually sailed with friends, neighbors, or kinfolk, and they sought an education in the ways of the sea. Also like Bowen, they aspired to earn some wages, to rise in the ranks eventually from seaman to mate and possibly to master (the common term for captain), to save enough to marry and support a family, and after twenty years or so to retire from the rigors of the seafaring life with a "competency" — that is, enough money to live modestly.

It typically took about four years at sea to become a fully competent seaman. Shortly after Bowen returned from his first voyage, his father apprenticed him to a sea captain for seven years. In return for a hefty payment, the captain agreed to tutor young Bowen in the art of seafaring, which ideally promised to ease his path to become a captain himself. In reality, the captain employed him as a cabin boy, taught him little except to obey, and beat him for trivial mistakes, causing Bowen to run away after four years of servitude.

Now seventeen years old, Bowen had already sailed to dozens of ports in North America, the West Indies, the British Isles, and Europe. For the next eighteen years, he shipped out as a common seaman on scores of vessels carrying nearly every kind of cargo afloat on the Atlantic. He sailed mostly aboard merchant freighters, but he also worked on whalers, fishing boats, privateers, and warships. He survived sickness, imprisonment, foul weather, accidents, and innumerable close calls. But when he retired

---

By the 1720s, Germans who had established themselves in the colonies wrote back to their friends and relatives, as one reported, "of the civil and religious liberties [and] privileges, and of all the goodness I have heard and seen." Such letters prompted still more Germans to pull up stakes and embark for America, to exchange the miserable certainties of their lives in Europe for the uncertain attractions of life in the middle colonies.

Similar motives propelled the **Scots-Irish**, who considerably outnumbered German immigrants. The "Scots-Irish" actually hailed from northern Ireland, Scotland, and northern England. Like the Germans, the Scots-Irish were Protestants, but with a difference. Most German immigrants worshipped in Lutheran or German Reformed churches; many others belonged to dissenting sects such as the Mennonites, Moravians, and Amish, whose adherents sought relief from persecution they had suffered in Europe for their refusal to bear arms and to swear oaths, practices they shared with the Quakers. In contrast, the Scots-Irish tended to be militant Presbyterians who seldom hesitated to bear arms or swear oaths. Like

from seafaring at age thirty-five, he still had not managed to attain command. In twenty-four years at sea, he had worked as either a common seaman or a mate. For whatever reason, when most shipowners eyed Bowen, they did not see a man they would trust to command their vessels.

Like Bowen, about three out of ten seamen spent their entire seafaring lives as seamen or mates, earning five dollars or so a month in wages, roughly comparable to the wages of farm laborers. Another three out of ten seamen died at sea, many by drowning or as a result of injuries or, most commonly, from tropical diseases usually picked up in the West Indies. Bowen lived to the age of eighty-five, working as a rigger, crafting nautical fittings for sailing vessels. When Bowen, like thousands of other seafarers, looked at the world, his gaze did not turn west toward the farms and forests of the interior but rather turned east, toward the promise of the Atlantic deep beyond.

Questions for Consideration

1. What attracted Ashley Bowen to a seafaring life? How successful was he?

2. How did Bowen's experiences as a seaman compare to those of farmers in the colonies?

3. How might Bowen's outlook on the world compare to that of the vast majority of colonists who seldom or never went to sea?

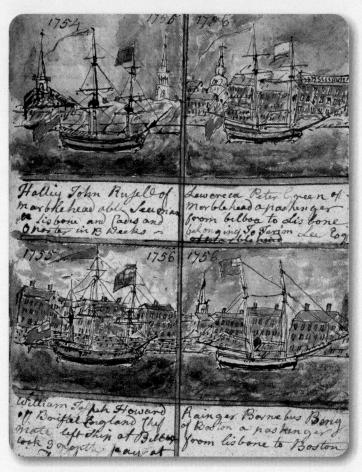

Ashley Bowen's Journal

Ashley Bowen painted these watercolors of ships he sailed aboard in 1754, 1755, and 1756. Befitting an experienced seaman, he paid attention to the distinctive rigging and flags of each vessel, and he kept notes about the vessels' owners, masters, mates, passengers, and destinations. As the focus of Bowen's fascination, the vessels dwarf the buildings of Marblehead, Massachusetts, in the background. To Bowen, each ship had distinctive features. Can you spot the differences that caught his eye? Why might such differences be important to Bowen? Photo courtesy of The Marblehead Historical Society, Marblehead, MA.

German settlers, however, Scots-Irish immigrants were clannish, residing when they could among relatives or neighbors from the old country.

In the eighteenth century, wave after wave of Scots-Irish immigrants arrived, culminating in a flood of immigration in the years just before the American Revolution. Deteriorating economic conditions in northern Ireland, Scotland, and England pushed many toward America. Most of the immigrants were farm laborers or tenant farmers fleeing droughts, crop failures, high food prices, or rising rents. They came, they told inquisitive British officials, because of "poverty," the "tyranny of landlords," and their desire to "do better in America."

Both Scots-Irish and Germans probably heard the common saying "Pennsylvania is heaven for farmers [and] paradise for artisans," but they almost certainly did not fully understand the risks of their decision to leave their native lands. Ship captains, aware of the hunger for labor in the colonies, eagerly signed up the penniless German emigrants as **redemptioners**, a variant of indentured servants. A captain would agree to provide transportation to Philadelphia, where redemptioners would obtain the money to pay for their passage by borrowing it from a friend or relative who was already in the colonies or, as most did, by selling themselves as servants.

Many redemptioners traveled in family groups, unlike impoverished Scots-Irish emigrants, who usually traveled alone and paid for their passage by contracting as indentured servants before they sailed to the colonies.

Redemptioners and indentured servants were packed aboard ships "as closely as herring," one migrant observed. Seasickness compounded by exhaustion, poverty, poor food, bad water, inadequate sanitation, and tight quarters encouraged the spread of disease. On the sixteen immigrant ships arriving in Philadelphia in 1738, more than half the passengers died en route. When one ship finally approached land, a traveler wrote, "everyone crawls from below to the deck . . . and people cry for joy, pray, and sing praises and thanks to God." Unfortunately, their troubles were far from over. Redemptioners and indentured servants had to stay on board until somebody came to purchase their labor. Unlike indentured servants, redemptioners negotiated independently with their purchasers about their period of servitude. Typically, a healthy adult redemptioner agreed to four years of labor. Indentured servants commonly served five, six, or seven years.

"God Gives All Things to Industry": Urban and Rural Labor

An indentured servant in 1743 wrote that Pennsylvania was "the best poor Man's Country in the World." Although the servant reported that "the Condition of bought Servants is very hard" and masters often failed to live up to their promise to provide decent food and clothing, opportunity abounded in the middle colonies because there was more work to be done than workers to do it.

Most servants toiled in Philadelphia, New York City, or one of the smaller towns or villages. Artisans, small manufacturers, and shopkeepers prized the labor of male servants. Female servants made valuable additions to households, where nearly all of them cleaned, washed, cooked, or minded children. From the masters' viewpoint, servants were a bargain. A master could purchase five or six years of a servant's labor for approximately the wages a common laborer would earn in four months. Wageworkers could walk away from their jobs when they pleased, and they did so often enough to be troublesome for employers. Servants, however, could not walk away; they were legally bound to work for their masters until their terms expired.

Since a slave cost at least three times as much as a servant, only affluent colonists could afford the long-term investment in slave labor. Like many other prosperous urban residents, Benjamin Franklin purchased a few slaves after he became wealthy. But most farmers in the middle colonies used family labor, not slaves. Wheat, the most widely grown crop, did not require more labor than farmers could typically muster from relatives, neighbors, and a hired hand or two. Consequently, although people of African ancestry (almost all slaves) increased to more than thirty thousand in the middle colonies by 1770, they accounted for only about 7 percent of the total population and much less outside the cities.

Most slaves came to the middle colonies and New England after a stopover in the West Indies, as the Robin Johns did. Very few came directly from Africa. Enough slaves arrived to prompt colonial assemblies to pass laws that punished slaves much more severely than servants for the same transgressions. "For the least trespass," an indentured servant reported, slaves "undergo the severest Punishment." And slaves — unlike servants — could not charge masters with violating the terms of their contracts. A master's commands, not a written contract, set the terms of a slave's bondage. Small numbers of slaves managed to obtain their freedom, though few of them as dramatically as the Robin Johns. But free African Americans did not escape whites' firm convictions about black inferiority and white supremacy.

Whites' racism and blacks' lowly social status made African Americans scapegoats for European Americans' suspicions and anxieties. In 1741, when arson and several unexplained thefts plagued New York City, officials suspected a murderous slave conspiracy and executed thirty-one slaves. On the basis of little evidence other than the slaves' "insolence" (refusal to conform fully to whites' expectations of servile behavior), city authorities burned thirteen slaves at the stake and hanged eighteen others. Although slaves were certifiably impoverished, they were not among the poor for whom the middle colonies were reputed to be the best country in the world.

Immigrants swarmed to the middle colonies because of the availability of land. The Penn family (see chapter 4) encouraged immigration to bring in potential buyers for their enormous tracts of land in Pennsylvania. From the beginning, Pennsylvania followed a policy of negotiating with Indian tribes to purchase additional land. This policy reduced the violent frontier clashes more common elsewhere in the colonies.

Yet even the Penn family did not shrink from occasionally testing its agreement with Indians. In a dispute with tribes on the northern Delaware River in 1737, the Penns pulled out a document showing that local Indians had granted the colonists land that stretched as far as a man could walk in a day and a half. Under the terms of this infamous "Walking Purchase," the Penns sent out three runners, one of whom raced more than sixty miles in the time limit and doubled the size of the Penns' claim.

Few colonists drifted beyond the northern boundaries of Pennsylvania. Owners of the huge estates in New York's Hudson valley preferred to rent rather than sell their land, and therefore they attracted fewer immigrants. The **Iroquois Indians** dominated the lucrative fur trade of the St. Lawrence valley and eastern Great Lakes, and they vigorously defended their territory from colonial encroachment. Few settlers chose to risk having their scalps lifted by Iroquois warriors in northern New York when they could settle instead in the comparatively safe environs of Pennsylvania.

The price of farmland depended on soil quality, access to water, distance from a market town, and extent of improvements. One hundred acres of improved land that had been cleared, plowed, fenced, and ditched, and perhaps had a house and barn built on it, cost three or four times more than the same acreage of uncleared, unimproved land. Since the cheapest land always lay at the margin of settlement, would-be farmers tended to migrate to promising areas just beyond

already improved farms. By midcentury, settlement had reached the eastern slopes of the Appalachian Mountains, and newcomers spilled south down the fertile valley of the Shenandoah River into western Virginia and the Carolinas. Thousands of settlers migrated from the middle colonies through this back door to the South. Abraham Lincoln's great-grandfather, John Lincoln — whose own grandfather, Mordecai, had migrated from England to Puritan Massachusetts in the 1630s — moved his family in the 1760s from Pennsylvania down the Shenandoah Valley into Virginia, where the future president's grandfather, also named Abraham, raised his family, including the future president's father, Thomas Lincoln.

Patterns of Settlement, 1700–1770

Farmers like the Lincolns made the middle colonies the breadbasket of North America. They planted a wide variety of crops to feed their families, but they grew wheat in abundance. Flour milling was the number one industry and flour the number one export, constituting nearly three-fourths of all exports from the middle colonies. Pennsylvania flour fed residents in other colonies, in southern Europe, and, above all, in the West Indies (see Map 5.2). For farmers, the

Marten Van Bergen Farm
This detail from a rare 1730s painting depicts the home of Marten and Catarina Van Bergen, prosperous Dutch colonists in New York's Hudson valley. The full-size painting, commissioned by the Van Bergens to hang over their fireplace mantel, is a panorama portraying the farm as a peaceable, small-scale kingdom governed by the couple and populated by their seven children, their slaves and indentured servants, and neighboring Native Americans. Rather than a place of fields and crops, which are absent from the painting, the farm is the locus of a happy, orderly family revolving around Marten and Catarina and the warm hearth just behind them. Copyright © New York State Historical Association, Cooperstown, NY.

VISUAL ACTIVITY

Bethlehem, Pennsylvania

This view of the small community of Bethlehem, Pennsylvania, in 1757 dramatizes the profound transformation of the natural landscape wrought in the eighteenth century by highly motivated human labor. Founded by Moravian immigrants in 1740, Bethlehem must have appeared at first like the dense woods on the upper left horizon. In less than twenty years, precisely laid-out orchards and fields replaced forests and glades. By carefully penning their livestock (lower center right) and fencing their fields (lower left), farmers safeguarded their livelihoods from the risks and disorders of untamed nature. Individual farmsteads (lower center) and impressive multistory brick town buildings (upper center) integrated the bounty of the land with the delights of community life. Few eighteenth-century communities were as orderly as Bethlehem, but many effected a comparable transformation of the environment. Print Collection, Miriam and Ira D. Wallack Division of Art, Prints and Photographs, The New York Public Library. Astor, Lenox, and Tilden Foundations.

READING THE IMAGE: What does this painting indicate about the colonists' priorities?

CONNECTIONS: Why might Pennsylvanians have been so concerned about maintaining order?

grain market in the Atlantic world proved risky but profitable. Grain prices rose steadily after 1720. By 1770, a bushel of wheat was worth twice as much (adjusted for inflation) as it had been fifty years earlier.

The standard of living in rural Pennsylvania was probably higher than in any other agricultural region of the eighteenth-century world. The comparatively widespread prosperity of all the middle colonies permitted residents to indulge in a half-century shopping spree for British imports.

The middle colonies' per capita consumption of imported goods from Britain more than doubled between 1720 and 1770, far outstripping the per capita consumption of British goods in New England and the southern colonies.

Philadelphia stood at the crossroads of trade in wheat exports and British imports. By 1776, Philadelphia had a larger population than any other city in the entire British empire except London. Merchants occupied the top stratum of Philadelphia society. In a city where only 2 percent of the residents owned enough property to qualify to vote, merchants built grand homes and dominated local government. Many of Philadelphia's wealthiest merchants were Quakers. Quaker traits of industry, thrift, honesty, and sobriety encouraged the accumulation of wealth. A colonist complained that a Quaker "prays for his neighbors on First Days [the Sabbath] and then preys on him the other six."

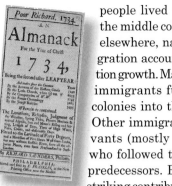

The lower ranks of merchants included aspiring tradesmen such as **Benjamin Franklin**. In 1728, Franklin opened a small shop, run mostly by his wife, Deborah, that sold a little of everything: cheese, codfish, coffee, goose feathers, soap, and occasionally a slave. In 1733, Benjamin Franklin began to publish *Poor Richard's Almanack*, which preached the likelihood of long-term rewards for tireless labor and quickly became Franklin's most profitable product.

The popularity of *Poor Richard's Almanack* suggests that many Pennsylvanians thought less about the pearly gates than about their pocketbooks. Poor Richard's advice that "God gives all Things to Industry" might be considered the motto for the middle colonies. The promise of a worldly payoff made work a secular faith. Poor Richard advised, "Work as if you were to live 100 years, Pray as if you were to die Tomorrow."

William Penn's Quaker utopia became a center of worldly affluence whose most famous citizen, Franklin, was neither a Quaker nor a utopian. Quakers remained influential, but Franklin spoke for most colonists with his aphorisms of work, discipline, and thrift that echoed Quaker rules for outward behavior. Franklin's maxims did not look to the Quaker's divine inner light for guidance. Instead, they celebrated the spark of ambition and the promise of gain.

REVIEW   Why did immigrants flood into Pennsylvania during the eighteenth century?

▶ The Southern Colonies: Land of Slavery

Between 1700 and 1770, the population of the southern colonies of Virginia, Maryland, North Carolina, South Carolina, and Georgia grew almost ninefold. By 1770, about twice as many people lived in the South as in either the middle colonies or New England. As elsewhere, natural increase and immigration accounted for the rapid population growth. Many Scots-Irish and German immigrants funneled from the middle colonies into the southern backcountry. Other immigrants were indentured servants (mostly English and Scots-Irish) who followed their seventeenth-century predecessors. But slaves made the most striking contribution to the booming southern colonies, transforming the racial composition of the population. Slavery became the defining characteristic of the southern colonies during the eighteenth century, shaping the region's economy, society, and politics.

The Atlantic Slave Trade and the Growth of Slavery

The number of southerners of African ancestry (nearly all of them slaves) rocketed from just over 20,000 in 1700 to well over 400,000 in 1770. The black population increased nearly three times faster than the South's briskly growing white population. Consequently, the proportion of southerners of African ancestry grew from 20 percent in 1700 to 40 percent in 1770.

Southern colonists clustered into two distinct geographic and agricultural zones. The colonies in the upper South, surrounding the Chesapeake Bay, specialized in growing tobacco, as they had since the early seventeenth century. Throughout the eighteenth century, nine out of ten southern whites and eight out of ten southern blacks lived in the Chesapeake region. The upper South retained a white majority during the eighteenth century.

In the lower South, a much smaller cluster of colonists inhabited the coastal region and specialized in the production of rice and indigo (a plant used to make blue dye). Lower South colonists made up only 5 percent of the total population of the southern colonies in 1700 but inched upward to 15 percent by 1770. South Carolina was the sole British colony along the southern Atlantic coast until 1732. (North Carolina, founded in 1711, was largely an extension of the Chesapeake region.) Georgia was founded in 1732 as a refuge for poor people from England. Georgia's leaders banned slaves from 1735 to 1750, but few settlers arrived until after 1750, when the prohibition on slavery was lifted and slaves flooded in. In South Carolina, in contrast to Georgia and every other British mainland

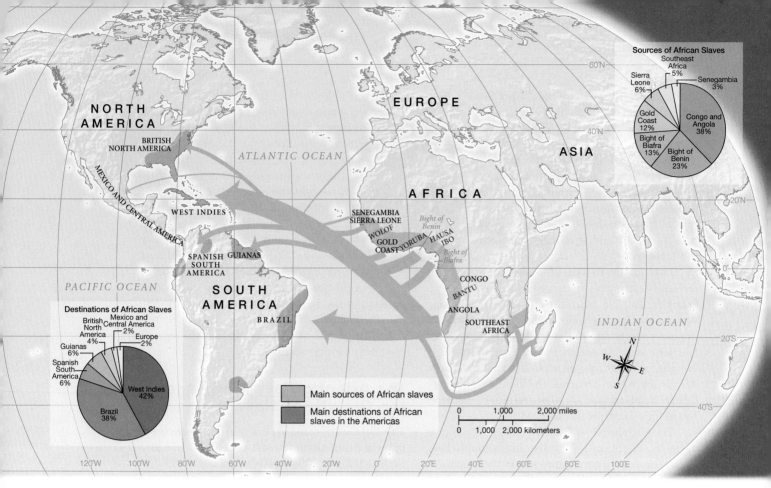

Sources of African Slaves

- Southeast Africa 5%
- Senegambia 3%
- Sierra Leone 6%
- Congo and Angola 38%
- Gold Coast 12%
- Bight of Biafra 13%
- Bight of Benin 23%

Destinations of African Slaves

- Mexico and Central America 2%
- Europe 2%
- British North America 4%
- Guianas 6%
- Spanish South America 6%
- West Indies 42%
- Brazil 38%

Main sources of African slaves

Main destinations of African slaves in the Americas

0   1,000   2,000 miles
0 1,000 2,000 kilometers

MAP ACTIVITY

Map 5.3   The Atlantic Slave Trade

Although the Atlantic slave trade lasted from about 1450 to 1870, it peaked during the eighteenth century, when more than six million African slaves were imported to the New World. Only a small fraction of these slaves were taken to British North America. Most went to sugar plantations in Brazil and the Caribbean.

READING THE MAP: Where in Africa did most slaves originate? Approximately how far was the trip from the busiest ports of origin to the two most common New World destinations?

CONNECTIONS: Why were so many more African slaves sent to the West Indies and Brazil than to British North America?

colony, slaves outnumbered whites almost two to one; in some low-country districts, the ratio of blacks to whites exceeded ten to one.

The enormous growth in the South's slave population occurred through natural increase

TABLE 5.1	SLAVE IMPORTS, 1451–1870
Estimated Slave Imports to the Western Hemisphere	
1451–1600	275,000
1601–1700	1,341,000
1701–1810	6,100,000
1811–1870	1,900,000

and the flourishing Atlantic slave trade (Table 5.1 and Map 5.3). Slave ships brought almost 300,000 Africans to British North America between 1619 and 1780. Of these Africans, 95 percent arrived in the South and 96 percent arrived during the eighteenth century. Unlike indentured servants and redemptioners, these Africans did not choose to come to the colonies. Like the Robin Johns, most of them had been born into free families in villages located within a few hundred miles of the West African coast.

Although they shared African origins, they came from many different African cultures, including Akan, Angolan, Asante, Bambara, Gambian, Igbo, and Mandinga, among others. They spoke different languages, worshipped different deities, observed different rules of kinship, grew different crops, and recognized different rulers. The most

Olaudah Equiano
Painted more than a decade after he had bought his freedom, this portrait evokes Equiano's successful acculturation to eighteenth-century English customs. His clothing and hairstyle reflect the fashions of a respectable young Englishman. In his *Interesting Narrative*, Equiano wrote that he "looked upon [the English] . . . as men superior to us [Africans], and therefore I had the stronger desire to resemble them, to imbibe their spirit and imitate their manners." Yet Equiano did not forsake his African roots. He honored his dual identity by campaigning against slavery. His *Narrative* was one of the most important and powerful antislavery documents of the time. Library of Congress.

important experience they had in common was enslavement.

Captured in war, kidnapped, or sold into slavery by other Africans, they were brought to the coast, sold to African traders like the Robin Johns who assembled slaves for resale, and sold again to European or colonial slave traders or ship captains, who packed two hundred to three hundred or more aboard ships that carried them on the **Middle Passage** across the Atlantic and then sold them yet again to colonial slave merchants or southern planters.

Olaudah Equiano published an account of his enslavement that hints at the stories that might have been told by the millions of other Africans swept up in the slave trade. Equiano wrote that he was born in 1745 in the interior of what is now Nigeria. "I had never heard of white men or Europeans, nor of the sea," he recalled. One day when he was eleven years old, he was kidnapped by Africans, who sold him to other Africans, who in turn eventually sold him to a slave ship on the coast. Equiano feared that he was "going to be killed" and "eaten by those white men with horrible looks, red faces, and loose hair." Once the ship set sail, many of the slaves, crowded together in suffocating heat fouled by filth of all descriptions, died from sickness. "The shrieks of the women and the groans of the dying rendered the whole a scene of horror almost inconceivable," Equiano recalled. Most of the slaves on the ship were sold in Barbados,

but Equiano and other leftovers were shipped off to Virginia, where he "saw few or none of our native Africans and not one soul who could talk to me." Equiano felt isolated and "exceedingly miserable" because he "had no person to speak to that I could understand." Finally, the captain of a tobacco ship bound for England purchased Equiano, and he traveled as a slave between North America, England, and the West Indies for ten years until he succeeded in buying his freedom in 1766.

Only about 15 percent of the slaves brought into the southern colonies came aboard ships from the West Indies, as Equiano and the Robin Johns did. All the other slaves brought into the southern colonies came directly from Africa, and almost all the ships that brought them (roughly 90 percent) belonged to British merchants. Most of the slaves on board were young adults, with men usually outnumbering women two to one. Children under the age of fourteen, like Equiano, typically accounted for no more than 10 to 15 percent of a cargo.

Mortality during the Middle Passage varied considerably from ship to ship. On average, about 15 percent of the slaves died, but sometimes half or more perished. The average mortality among the white crew of slave ships was often nearly as bad. In general, the longer the voyage lasted, the more people died. Recent studies suggest that many slaves succumbed not only to virulent epidemic diseases such as smallpox and dysentery but also to acute dehydration caused by fluid loss from perspiration, vomiting, and diarrhea combined with a severe shortage of drinking water.

Normally, an individual planter purchased at any one time a relatively small number of newly arrived Africans, or **new Negroes**, as they were called. New Negroes were often profoundly depressed, demoralized, and disoriented. Planters

The African Slave Trade
The African slave trade existed to satisfy the New World's demand for labor and Europe's voracious appetite for New World products such as sugar, tobacco, and rice. African men, women, and children, like those pictured in this early-eighteenth-century engraving of a family residence in Sierra Leone, were kidnapped or captured in wars — typically by other Africans — and enslaved. Uprooted from their homes and kin, they were usually taken to coastal enclaves where African traders and European ship captains negotiated prices, made deals, and often branded the newly enslaved people. The collaboration between Europeans and their African trading partners is evident in the seventeenth-century Benin bronze box in the shape of a royal palace in Nigeria. The palace is guarded by two massive predatory birds and two Portuguese soldiers. Benin bronze box: Bildarchiv Preussischer Kulturbesitz/Art Resource, NY; engraving: Courtesy, Earl Gregg Swen Library, College of William and Mary, Williamsburg, Virginia.

expected their other slaves — either those born into slavery in the colonies (often called **country-born** or **creole slaves**) or Africans who had arrived earlier — to help new Negroes become accustomed to their strange new surroundings. Planters' preferences for slaves from specific regions of Africa aided slaves' acculturation (or seasoning, as it was called) to the routines of bondage in the southern colonies. Chesapeake planters preferred slaves from Senegambia, the Gold Coast, or — like Equiano and the Robin Johns — the Bight of Biafra, which combined accounted for 40 percent of all Africans imported to the Chesapeake. South Carolina planters favored slaves from the central African Congo and Angola regions, the origin of about 40 percent of the African slaves they imported (see Map 5.3). Although slaves within each of these regions spoke many different languages, enough linguistic and cultural similarities existed that they could usually communicate with other Africans from the same region.

Seasoning acclimated new Africans to the physical as well as the cultural environment of the southern colonies. Slaves who had just endured the Middle Passage were poorly nourished, weak, and sick. In this vulnerable state, they encountered the alien diseases of North America without having developed a biological arsenal of acquired immunities. As many as 10 to 15 percent of newly arrived Africans, sometimes more, died during their first year in the southern colonies. Nonetheless, the large number of newly enslaved Africans made the influence of African culture in the South stronger in the eighteenth century than ever before — or since.

While newly enslaved Africans poured into the southern colonies, slave mothers bore children, which caused the slave population in the South to grow rapidly. Slave owners encouraged these births. Thomas Jefferson explained, "I consider the labor of a breeding [slave] woman as no object, that a [slave] child raised every 2 years is of more profit than the crop of the best laboring [slave] man." Although slave mothers loved and nurtured their children, the mortality rate among slave children was high, and the ever-present risk of being separated by sale brought grief to many slave families. Nonetheless, the growing number of slave babies set the southern colonies apart from other New World slave societies, where mortality rates were so high that deaths exceeded births. The high rate of natural increase in the southern colonies meant that by the 1740s the majority of southern slaves were country-born.

Slave Labor and African American Culture

Southern planters expected slaves to work from sunup to sundown and beyond. George Washington wrote that his slaves should "be at their work as soon as it is light, work til it is dark, and be diligent while they are at it." The conflict between the masters' desire for maximum labor and the slaves' reluctance to do more than necessary made the threat of physical punishment a constant for eighteenth-century slaves. Masters preferred black slaves to white indentured servants, not just because slaves served for life but also because colonial laws did not limit the force masters could use against slaves. As a traveler observed in 1740, "A new negro . . . [will] let a hundred men show him how to hoe, or drive a wheelbarrow; he'll still take the one by the bottom and the other by the wheel and . . . often die before [he] can be conquered." Slaves resisted their masters' demands, the traveler noted, because of their "greatness of soul" — their stubborn unwillingness to conform to their masters' definition of them as merely slaves.

Some slaves escalated their acts of resistance to direct physical confrontation with the master, the mistress, or an overseer. But a hoe raised in anger, a punch in the face, or a desperate swipe with a knife led to swift and predictable retaliation by whites. Throughout the southern colonies, the balance of physical power rested securely in the hands of whites.

Rebellion occurred, however, at Stono, South Carolina, in 1739. Before dawn on a September Sunday, a group of about twenty slaves attacked a country store, killed the two storekeepers, and confiscated the store's guns, ammunition, and powder. Enticing other slaves to join, the group plundered and burned more than half a dozen plantations and killed more than twenty white men, women, and children. A mounted force of whites quickly suppressed the rebellion. They placed the rebels' heads atop mileposts along the road, grim reminders of the consequences of rebellion. The **Stono rebellion** illustrated that eighteenth-century slaves had no chance of overturning slavery and very little chance of defending themselves in any bold strike for freedom. After the rebellion, South Carolina legislators enacted repressive laws designed to guarantee that whites would always have the upper hand. No other similar uprisings occurred during the colonial period.

Slaves maneuvered constantly to protect themselves and to gain a measure of autonomy within the boundaries of slavery. In Chesapeake tobacco fields, most slaves were subject to close supervision by whites. In the lower South, the **task system** gave slaves some control over the pace of their work and some discretion in the use of the rest of their time. A "task" was typically defined as a certain area of ground to be cultivated or a specific job to be completed. A slave who completed the assigned task might use the remainder of the day, if any, to work in a garden, fish, hunt, spin, weave, sew, or cook. When masters sought to boost productivity by increasing tasks, slaves did what they could to defend their customary work assignments.

Eighteenth-century slaves also planted the roots of African American lineages that branch out to the present. Slaves valued family ties, and, as in West African societies, kinship structured slaves' relations with one another. Slave parents often gave a child the name of a grandparent,

> "My [slaves] should be at their work as soon as it is light, work til it is dark, and be diligent while they are at it."
> — GEORGE WASHINGTON

Colonial Slave Drum
An African in Virginia made this drum sometime around the beginning of the eighteenth century. The drum combines deerskin and cedarwood from North America with African workmanship and designs. During rare moments of respite from their work, slaves played drums to accompany dances learned in Africa. They also drummed out messages from plantation to plantation. Whites knew that slaves used drums for communication, but they could not decipher the meanings of the rhythms and sounds. Fearful that drums signaled rebellious uprisings, whites outlawed drumming but could not eliminate it. Most likely, the messages sent included lamentations about the drummers' lives of bondage.
© The Trustees of the British Museum.

minister claimed in 1757 that "to live in Virginia without slaves is morally impossible." The southern colonies supplied 90 percent of all North American exports to Britain. Rice exports from the lower South exploded from less than half a million pounds in 1700 to eighty million pounds in 1770, nearly all of it grown by slaves. Exports of indigo also boomed. Together, rice and indigo made up three-fourths of lower South exports, nearly two-thirds of them going to Britain and most of the rest to the West Indies, where sugar-growing slaves ate slave-grown rice.

Tobacco was by far the most important export from British North America; by 1770, it represented almost one-third of all colonial exports and three-fourths of all Chesapeake exports. Under the provisions of the Navigation Acts (see chapter 4), nearly all of it went to Britain, where the monarchy collected a lucrative tax on each pound. British merchants then reexported more than 80 percent of the tobacco to the European continent, pocketing a nice markup for their troubles.

These products of slave labor made the southern colonies by far the richest in North America. The per capita wealth of free whites in the South was four times greater than that in New England and three times that in the middle colonies. At the top of the wealth pyramid stood the rice grandees of the lower South and the tobacco gentry of the Chesapeake. These elite families commonly resided on large estates in handsome mansions adorned by luxurious gardens, all maintained and supported by slaves. The extravagant lifestyle of one gentry family astonished a young tutor from New Jersey, who noted that during the winter months the family kept twenty-eight large fires roaring, requiring six oxen to haul four heavy cartloads of slave-cut firewood to the house every day. In contrast, yeoman families — who supported themselves on small plots of land with family labor — cut their own firewood and usually warmed themselves around just one fire.

The vast differences in wealth among white southerners engendered envy and occasional tension between rich and poor, but remarkably little open hostility. In private, the planter elite spoke disparagingly of humble whites, but in public the planters acknowledged their lesser neighbors as equals, at least in belonging to the superior — in their minds — white race. Looking upward, white yeomen and tenants (who owned neither land nor slaves) sensed the gentry's condescension and veiled contempt. But they also appreciated the gentry for granting favors,

aunt, or uncle. In West Africa, kinship identified a person's place among living relatives and linked the person to ancestors in the past and to descendants in the future. Newly imported African slaves usually arrived alone, like Equiano, without kin. Often slaves who had traversed the Middle Passage on the same ship adopted one another as "brothers" and "sisters." Likewise, as new Negroes were seasoned and incorporated into existing slave communities, established families often adopted them as fictive kin.

When possible, slaves expressed many other features of their West African origins in their lives on New World plantations. They gave their children traditional dolls and African names such as Cudjo or Quash, Minda or Fuladi. They grew food crops they had known in Africa, such as yams and okra. They constructed huts with mud walls and thatched roofs similar to African residences. They fashioned banjos, drums, and other musical instruments, held dances, and observed funeral rites that echoed African practices. In these and many other ways, slaves drew upon their African heritages as much as the oppressive circumstances of slavery permitted.

Tobacco, Rice, and Prosperity

Slaves' labor bestowed prosperity on their masters, British merchants, and the monarchy. Slavery was so important and valuable that one

upholding white supremacy, and keeping slaves in their place. Although racial slavery made a few whites much richer than others, it also gave those who did not get rich a powerful reason to feel similar (in race) to those who were so different (in wealth).

The slaveholding gentry dominated the politics and economy of the southern colonies. In Virginia, only adult white men who owned at least one hundred acres of unimproved land or twenty-five acres of land with a house could vote. This property-holding requirement prevented about 40 percent of white men in Virginia from voting for representatives to the House of Burgesses. In South Carolina, the property requirement was only fifty acres of land, and therefore most adult white men qualified to vote. In both colonies, voters elected members of the gentry to serve in the colonial legislature. The gentry passed elected political offices from generation to generation, almost as if they were hereditary. Politically, the gentry built a self-perpetuating oligarchy — rule by the elite few — with the votes of their many humble neighbors.

The gentry also set the cultural standard in the southern colonies. They entertained lavishly, gambled regularly, and attended Anglican (Church of England) services more for social than for religious reasons. Above all, they cultivated the leisurely pursuit of happiness. They did not condone idleness, however. Their many pleasures and responsibilities as plantation owners kept them busy. Thomas Jefferson, a phenomenally productive member of the gentry, recalled that his earliest childhood memory was of being carried on a pillow by a family slave — a powerful image of the slave hands supporting the gentry's leisure and achievement.

REVIEW How did slavery influence the society and economy of the southern colonies?

Eliza Lucas Pinckney's Gown
When Eliza Lucas was sixteen years old in 1738, she took over day to day management of her father's rice plantations when he was called to duty in the British army. Highly educated, independent, and energetic, Lucas relished her duties and introduced numerous innovations on the plantations, including the cultivation of indigo — which became a major export crop in South Carolina — and silkworms. She married Charles Pinckney, a wealthy rice planter, in 1744 and continued her interest in agricultural innovation while raising four children. The gown shown here was made for her out of silk produced on her plantation and sent to England to be dyed and woven.
Smithsonian Institution, Washington, D.C.

► Unifying Experiences

The societies of New England, the middle colonies, and the southern colonies became more sharply differentiated during the eighteenth century, but colonists throughout British North America also shared unifying experiences that eluded settlers in the Spanish and French colonies. The first was economic. All three British colonial regions had their economic roots in agriculture. Colonists sold their distinctive products in markets that, in turn, offered a more or less uniform array of goods to consumers throughout British North America. Another unifying experience was a decline in the importance of religion. Some settlers called for a revival of religious intensity, but most people focused less on religion and more on the affairs of the world than they had in the seventeenth century. Also, white inhabitants throughout British North America became aware that they shared a distinctive identity as *British* colonists. Thirteen different governments presided over these North American colonies, but all of them answered to the British monarchy. British policies governed not only trade but also military and diplomatic relations with the Indians, French, and Spanish arrayed along colonial borderlands. Royal officials who expected loyalty from the colonists often had difficulty obtaining obedience. The British colonists asserted their prerogatives as British subjects to defend their special colonial interests.

Commerce and Consumption

Eighteenth-century commerce whetted colonists' appetites to consume. Colonial products spurred the development of mass markets throughout the Atlantic world (Figure 5.1). Huge increases in the supply of colonial tobacco and sugar brought the price of these small luxuries within the reach of most free whites. Colonial goods brought into focus an important lesson of eighteenth-century commerce: Ordinary people, not just the wealthy elite, would buy the things that they desired in addition to what they absolutely needed. Even news, formerly restricted mostly to a few people through face-to-face conversations or private letters, became an object of public consumption through the innovation of newspapers and the rise in literacy among whites. With the appropriate stimulus, market demand seemed unlimited.

The Atlantic commerce that took colonial goods to markets in Britain brought objects of consumer desire back to the colonies. British merchants and manufacturers recognized that colonists made excellent customers, and the Navigation Acts gave British exporters privileged access to the colonial market. By midcentury, export-oriented industries in Britain were growing ten times faster than firms attuned to the home market. Most British exports went to the vast European market, where potential customers outnumbered those in the colonies by more than one hundred to one.

But as European competition stiffened, colonial markets became increasingly important. British exports to North America multiplied eightfold between 1700 and 1770, outpacing the rate of population growth after midcentury. When the colonists' eagerness to consume exceeded their ability to pay, British exporters willingly extended credit, and colonial debts soared. Imported mirrors, silver plates, spices, bed and table linens, clocks, tea services, wigs, books, and more infiltrated parlors, kitchens, and bedrooms throughout the colonies. Despite the many differences among the colonists, the consumption of British exports built a certain material uniformity across region, religion, class, and status. Buying and using British exports made the colonists look and feel more British even though they lived at the edge of a wilderness an ocean away from Britain.

The dazzling variety of imported consumer goods also presented women and men with a novel array of choices. In many respects, the choices might appear trivial: whether to buy knives and forks, teacups, a mirror, or a clock. But such small choices confronted eighteenth-century consumers with a big question: What do you want? As colonial consumers defined and expressed their desires with greater frequency during the eighteenth century, they became accustomed to thinking of themselves as individuals who had the power to make decisions that influenced the quality of their lives — attitudes of significance in the hierarchical world of eighteenth-century British North America.

Religion, Enlightenment, and Revival

Eighteenth-century colonists could choose from almost as many religions as consumer goods. Virtually all of the bewildering variety of religious denominations represented some form of Christianity, almost all of them Protestant. Slaves made up the largest group of non-Christians. A few slaves converted to Christianity in Africa or after they arrived in North America, but most continued to embrace elements of indigenous African religions. Roman Catholics concentrated in Maryland as they had since the seventeenth century, but even there they were far outnumbered by Protestants.

The varieties of Protestant faith and practice ranged across a broad spectrum. The middle colonies and the southern backcountry included militant Baptists and Presbyterians. Huguenots

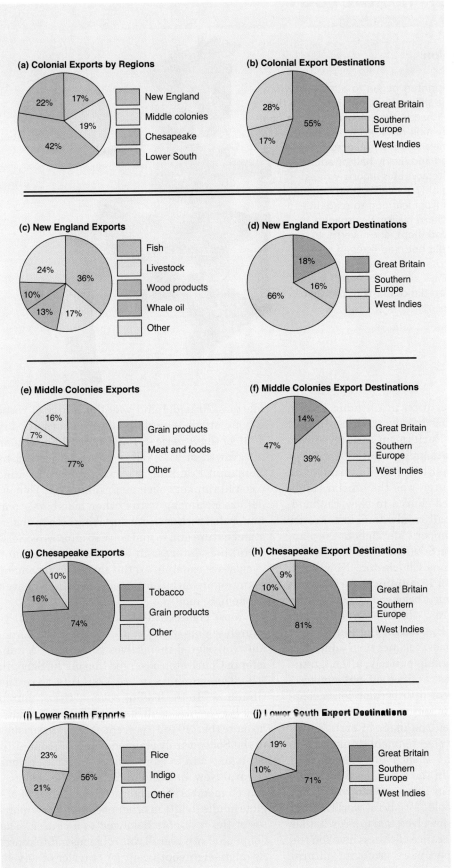

(a) Colonial Exports by Regions

- 17% New England
- 19% Middle colonies
- 42% Chesapeake
- 22% Lower South

(b) Colonial Export Destinations

- 55% Great Britain
- 17% Southern Europe
- 28% West Indies

(c) New England Exports

- 36% Fish
- 17% Livestock
- 13% Wood products
- 10% Whale oil
- 24% Other

(d) New England Export Destinations

- 18% Great Britain
- 16% Southern Europe
- 66% West Indies

(e) Middle Colonies Exports

- 77% Grain products
- 7% Meat and foods
- 16% Other

(f) Middle Colonies Export Destinations

- 14% Great Britain
- 39% Southern Europe
- 47% West Indies

(g) Chesapeake Exports

- 74% Tobacco
- 16% Grain products
- 10% Other

(h) Chesapeake Export Destinations

- 81% Great Britain
- 10% Southern Europe
- 9% West Indies

(i) Lower South Exports

- 56% Rice
- 21% Indigo
- 23% Other

(j) Lower South Export Destinations

- 71% Great Britain
- 10% Southern Europe
- 19% West Indies

FIGURE 5.1   Colonial Exports, 1768–1772
These pie charts provide an overview of the colonial export economy in the 1760s. The first two show that almost two-thirds of colonial exports came from the South and that the majority of the colonies' exports went to Great Britain. The remaining charts illustrate the distinctive patterns of exports in each colonial region. What do these patterns reveal about regional variations in Britain's North American colonies? What do they suggest about Britain's economic interest in the colonies?

THE PROMISE OF TECHNOLOGY

Newspapers and Public Opinion

In the eighteenth century, colonial printers began to publish newspapers on printing presses like the one shown here. By 1740, more than a dozen newspapers were being published in the colonies, and the number continued to increase. Relatively high rates of literacy gave them a large audience. In the northern colonies, readers included well over half of adult men and nearly half of adult women. In the southern colonies, literacy rates among whites were slightly lower but still considerably above those in England. Since whites tried to prevent slaves from learning to read, literacy rates remained low among southern blacks. Newspapers were often read aloud in homes, workshops, and taverns. In these public places, people who could not read listened to the controversial ideas and partisan accusations that caused information to spread beyond official channels and to help form public opinion. What sources of information did colonists have other than newspapers? Newport Historical Society.

who had fled persecution in Catholic France peopled congregations in several cities. In New England, old-style Puritanism splintered into strands of Congregationalism that differed over fine points of theological doctrine. The Congregational Church was the official established church in New England, and all residents paid taxes for its support. Throughout the plantation South and in urban centers such as Charleston, New York, and Philadelphia, prominent colonists belonged to the Anglican Church, which received tax support in the South. But dissenting faiths grew everywhere, and in most colonies their adherents won the right to worship publicly, although the established churches retained official support.

> ### "The Taverns have more Visitants than the Churches."
> — A Charleston minister

Many educated colonists became deists, looking for God's plan in nature more than in the Bible. **Deism** shared the ideas of eighteenth-century European Enlightenment thinkers, who tended to agree that science and reason could disclose God's laws in the natural order. In the colonies as well as in Europe, **Enlightenment** ideas encouraged people to study the world around them, to think for themselves, and to ask whether the disorderly appearance of things masked the principles of a deeper, more profound natural order. From New England towns to southern drawing rooms, individuals met to discuss such

matters. Philadelphia was the center of these conversations, especially after the formation in 1769 of the American Philosophical Society, an outgrowth of an earlier group organized by Benjamin Franklin, who was a deist. Leading colonial thinkers such as Franklin and Thomas Jefferson, among many other members, communicated with each other seeking both to understand nature and to find ways to improve society. Franklin's interest in electricity, stoves, and eyeglasses exemplified the shift of focus among many eighteenth-century colonists from heaven to the here and now.

Most eighteenth-century colonists went to church seldom or not at all, although they probably considered themselves Christians. A minister in Charleston observed that on the Sabbath "the Taverns have more Visitants than the Churches." In the leading colonial cities, church members were a small minority of eligible adults, no more than 10 to 15 percent. Anglican parishes in the South rarely claimed more than one-fifth of eligible adults as members. In some regions of rural New England and the middle colonies, church membership embraced two-thirds of eligible adults, while in other areas only one-quarter of the residents belonged to a church. The dominant faith overall was religious indifference. As a late-eighteenth-century traveler observed, "Religious indifference is imperceptibly disseminated from one end of the continent to the other."

The spread of religious indifference, of deism, of denominational rivalry, and of comfortable backsliding profoundly concerned many Christians. A few despaired that, as one wrote, "religion . . . lay a-dying and ready to expire its last breath of life." To combat what one preacher called the "dead formality" of church services, some ministers set out to convert nonbelievers and to revive the piety of the faithful with a new style of preaching that appealed more to the heart than to the head. Historians have termed this wave of revivals the **Great Awakening**. In Massachusetts during the mid-1730s, the fiery Puritan minister **Jonathan Edwards** reaped a harvest of souls by reemphasizing traditional Puritan doctrines of humanity's utter depravity and God's vengeful omnipotence. The title of Edwards's most famous sermon, "Sinners in the Hands of an Angry God," conveys the flavor of his message. In Pennsylvania and New Jersey, William Tennent led revivals that dramatized spiritual rebirth with accounts of God's miraculous powers, such as raising Tennent's son from the dead.

The most famous revivalist in the eighteenth-century Atlantic world was **George Whitefield**. An Anglican, Whitefield preached well-worn messages of sin and salvation to large audiences in England using his spellbinding, unforgettable voice. Whitefield visited the North American colonies seven times, staying for more than three years during the mid-1740s and attracting tens of thousands to his sermons, including Benjamin Franklin and Olaudah Equiano. Whitefield's preaching transported many in his audience to emotion-choked states of religious ecstasy. About one revival he

George Whitefield

An anonymous artist portrayed George Whitefield preaching, emphasizing the power of his sermons to transport his audience to a revived awareness of divine spirituality. Light from above gleams off his forehead. His crossed eyes and faraway gaze suggest that he spoke in a semihypnotic trance. Notice the absence of a Bible on the pulpit. Rather than elaborating on God's Word as revealed in Scripture, Whitefield speaks from his own inner awareness. The woman below his hands appears transfixed. Her eyes and Whitefield's do not meet, yet the artist's use of light suggests that she and Whitefield see the same core of holy Truth. National Portrait Gallery, London.

wrote, "The bitter cries and groans were enough to pierce the hardest heart. Some of the people were as pale as death; others were wringing their hands; others lying on the ground; others sinking into the arms of their friends; and most lifting their eyes to heaven, and crying to God for mercy."

Whitefield's successful revivals spawned many lesser imitations. Itinerant preachers, many of them poorly educated, toured the colonial backcountry after midcentury, echoing Whitefield's medium and message as best they could. Bathsheba Kingsley, a member of Jonathan Edwards's flock, preached the revival message informally — as did an unprecedented number of other women throughout the colonies — causing her congregation to brand her a "brawling woman" who had "gone quite out of her place."

The revivals awakened and refreshed the spiritual energies of thousands of colonists struggling with the uncertainties and anxieties of eighteenth-century America. The conversions at revivals did not substantially boost the total number of church members, however. After the revivalists moved on, the routines and pressures of everyday existence reasserted their primacy in the lives of many converts. But the revivals communicated the important message that every soul mattered, that men and women could choose to be saved, that individuals had the power to make a decision for everlasting life or death. Colonial revivals expressed in religious terms many of the same democratic and egalitarian values expressed in economic terms by colonists' patterns of consumption. One colonist noted the analogy by referring to itinerant revivalists as "Pedlars in divinity." Like consumption, revivals contributed to a set of common experiences that bridged colonial divides of faith, region, class, and status.

Trade and Conflict in the North American Borderlands

British power defended the diverse inhabitants of its colonies from Indian, French, and Spanish enemies on their borders — as well as from foreign powers abroad. Each colony organized a militia, and privateers sailed from every port to prey on foreign ships. But the British navy and army bore ultimate responsibility for colonial defense (Figure 5.2). Royal officials warily eyed the small North American settlements of New France and New Spain for signs of threats to the colonies.

Alone, neither New France nor New Spain jeopardized British North America, but with Indian allies they could become a potent force that kept colonists on their guard (Map 5.4). Native Americans' impulse to defend their territory from colonial incursions competed with their desire for trade, which tugged them toward the settlers. As a colonial official observed in 1761, "A modern Indian cannot subsist without Europeans. . . . [The European goods that were] only conveniency at first [have] now become necessity." To obtain such necessities as guns, ammunition, clothing, sewing utensils, and much more that was manufactured largely by the British, Indians trapped beavers, deer, and other furbearing animals throughout the interior.

British, French, Spanish, and Dutch officials monitored the fur trade to prevent their competitors from deflecting the flow of furs toward their own markets. Indians took advantage of this competition to improve their own prospects, playing one trader and empire off another. The Iroquois, for example, promised the French exclusive access to the furs and territory of the Great Lakes region and at the same time made the

FIGURE 5.2   GLOBAL COMPARISON: Large Warships in European Navies, 1660–1760
The large warships in England's navy usually outnumbered those of rival nations from 1660 to 1760. During the eighteenth century, the British fleet grew dramatically, while the fleets of rival nations declined. The British monarchy paid the enormous cost of building, manning, and maintaining the largest European navy because defending commerce and communication with its far-flung colonies was fundamental to the integrity of its empire. Although Britain's North American colonies benefited from defense by the most powerful navy in the Atlantic, colonists constantly worried about surprise attacks by other nations when British warships were someplace else. What might account for the changing numbers of warships between 1660 and 1760?

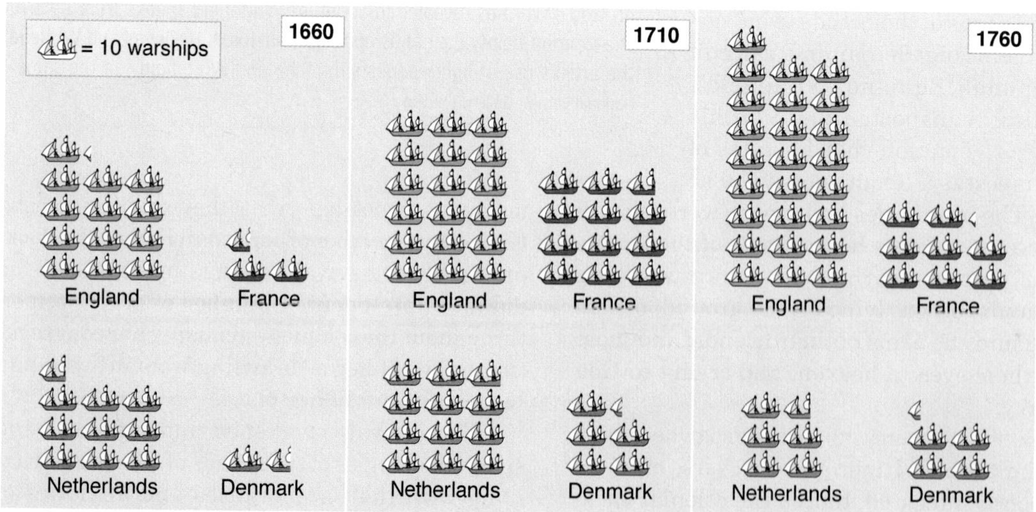

Note: Comparable data does not exist for Spain.

same pledge of exclusive rights to the British. Indian tribes and confederacies also competed among themselves for favored trading rights with one colony or another, a competition colonists encouraged.

The shifting alliances and complex dynamics of the fur trade struck a fragile balance along the frontier. The threat of violence from all sides was ever present, and the threat became reality often enough for all parties to be prepared for the worst. In the **Yamasee War of 1715**, Yamasee and Creek Indians — with French encouragement — mounted a coordinated attack against colonial settlements in South Carolina and inflicted heavy casualties. The Cherokee Indians, traditional enemies of the Creeks, refused to join the attack. Instead, they protected their access to British trade goods by allying with the colonists and turning the tide of battle, thus triggering a murderous rampage of revenge by the colonists against the Creek and Yamasee tribes.

Relations between Indians and colonists differed from colony to colony and from year to year. But the British colonists' nagging perceptions of menace on the frontier kept them continually hoping for help from the British to keep the Indians at bay and to maintain the essential flow of trade. In 1754, the British colonists' endemic competition with the French flared into the Seven Years' War (also known as the French and Indian War), which would inflame the frontier for years (as discussed in chapter 6). Before the 1760s, neither the British colonists nor the British themselves developed a coherent policy toward the Indians. But both agreed that Indians made deadly enemies, profitable trading partners, and powerful allies. As a result, the British and their colonists kept an eye on both the French and Spanish empires and relations with the Indians.

The Spanish, in turn, were keeping an eye on the Pacific coast, where Russian hunters in search of seals and sea otters threatened to become a permanent presence on New Spain's northern frontier. To block Russian access to present-day California, officials in New Spain mounted a campaign to build forts (called **presidios**) and missions there. In 1769, an expedition headed by a military man, **Gaspar de Portolá**, and a Catholic priest, **Junípero Serra**, traveled north from Mexico to present-day San Diego, where they founded the first California mission, San Diego de Alcalá. They soon journeyed all the way to Monterey, which became the capital of Spanish California. There Portolá established a presidio in 1770 "to defend us from attacks by the Russians," he wrote. The same year, Serra founded Mission

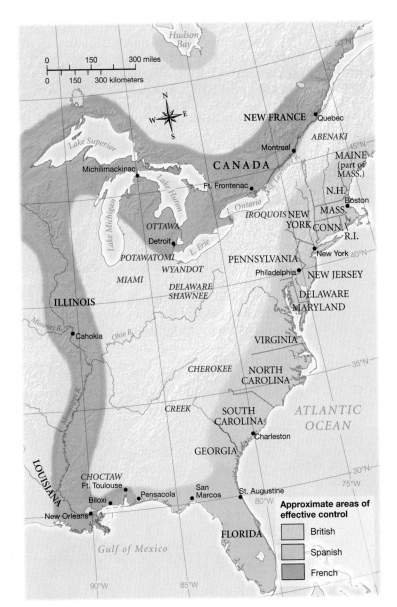

MAP 5.4

Zones of Empire in Eastern North America

The British zone, extending west from the Atlantic coast, was much more densely settled than the zones under French, Spanish, and Indian control. The comparatively large number of British colonists made them more secure than the relatively few colonists in the vast regions claimed by France and Spain or the settlers living among the many Indian peoples in the huge area between the Mississippi River and the Appalachian Mountains. Yet the British colonists were not powerful enough to dominate the French, Spaniards, or Indians. Instead, they had to guard against attacks by powerful Indian groups allied with the French or Spaniards.

San Carlos Borroméo de Carmelo in Monterey to convert the Indians and recruit them to work to support the soldiers and other Spaniards in the presidio. By 1772, Serra had founded other missions along the path from San Diego to Monterey.

One Spanish soldier praised the work of the missionaries, writing that "with flattery and presents [the missionaries] attract the savage Indians and persuade them to adhere to life in society and to receive instruction for a knowledge of the Catholic faith, the cultivation of the land, and the arts necessary for making the instruments most needed for farming." Yet for the Indians, the Spaniards' California missions had horrendous consequences, as they had elsewhere in the Spanish borderlands. European diseases decimated Indian populations, Spanish soldiers raped Indian women, and missionaries beat Indians and subjected them to near slavery. Indian uprisings against the Spaniards occurred repeatedly (see "Documenting the American Promise," page 150), but the presidios and missions endured as feeble projections of the Spanish empire along the Pacific coast.

Spanish Missions in California

Colonial Politics in the British Empire

The plurality of peoples, faiths, and communities that characterized the North American colonies arose from the somewhat haphazard policies of the eighteenth-century British empire. Since the Puritan Revolution of the mid-seventeenth century, British monarchs had valued the colonies' contributions to trade and encouraged their growth and development. Unlike Spain and France — whose policies of excluding Protestants and foreigners kept the

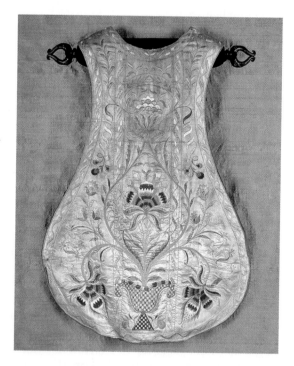

Mission Carmel

This eighteenth-century drawing portrays a reception for a Spanish visitor at Mission Carmel in what is now Carmel, California. Lines of mission Indians dressed in robes flank the entrance to the chapel where a priest and his assistants await the visitor. During worship, priests wore lavishly decorated chasubles, like the one shown here from Mission Santa Clara. The intricate and colorful embroidery signified the magnificence of divine authority, embodied in the priests — God's representatives on earth — and their Spanish sponsors. The reception ritual dramatized the strict hierarchy that governed relations among Spanish missionaries, ruling officials, and the subordinate Indians. Reception: University of California at Berkeley, Bancroft Library; chasuble: de Saisset Museum, Santa Clara University.

Ambush of Spanish Expedition

In May 1720, the New Mexico governor sent forty-three Spanish soldiers and sixty Pueblo Indians to expel French intruders from New Spain's northern borderlands. In August, when the expedition reached present-day Nebraska, the French and their Indian allies attacked, killing thirty-three Spaniards and twelve Pueblos. Shortly afterward, an artist — whether Indian or Spanish is unknown — recorded the ambush in this hide painting. The priest in the center of the painting shown here is Father Juan Minguez, the first priest assigned to Albuquerque; he was killed in the ambush. The Indian directly in front of him is Joseph Naranjo, leader of the Spaniards' Pueblo allies, who also was killed.

Courtesy of the Museum of New Mexico, Neg. No. 149804.

population of their North American colonial territories tiny — Britain kept the door to its colonies open to anyone, and tens of thousands of non-British immigrants settled in the North American colonies and raised families.

The open door did not extend to trade, however, as the seventeenth-century Navigation Acts restricted colonial trade to British ships and traders. These policies evolved because they served the interests of the monarchy and of influential groups in Britain and the colonies. The policies also gave the colonists a common framework of political expectations and experiences.

British attempts to exercise political power in their colonial governments met with success so long as British officials were on or very near the sea. Colonists acknowledged — although they did not always readily comply with — British authority to collect customs duties, inspect cargoes, and enforce trade regulations. But when royal officials tried to wield their authority in the internal affairs of the colonies on land, they invariably encountered colonial resistance. A governor appointed by the king in each of the nine royal colonies (Rhode Island and Connecticut selected their own governors) or by the proprietors in Maryland and Pennsylvania

headed the government of each colony. The British envisioned colonial governors as mini-monarchs able to exert influence in the colonies much as the king did in Britain. But colonial governors were not kings, and the colonies were not Britain.

Eighty percent of colonial governors had been born in England, not in the colonies. Some governors stayed in England, close to the source of royal patronage, and delegated the grubby details of colonial affairs to subordinates. Even the best-intentioned colonial governors had difficulty developing relations of trust and respect with influential colonists because their terms of office averaged just five years and could be terminated at any time. Colonial governors controlled few patronage positions to secure political friendships in the colonies. Officials who administered the colonial customs service, for example, received their appointments through patronage networks centered in England rather than from colonial governors. Obedient and loyal to their superiors in Britain, colonial governors fought incessantly with the colonists' assemblies. They battled over governors' vetoes of colonial legislation, removal of colonial judges, creation of new courts, dismissal of the representative assemblies, and other local issues.

Spanish Priests Report on California Missions

Catholic missionaries sent regular reports to their superiors in Mexico City, New Spain's capital city. The reports described what the missionaries considered their successes in converting pagan Indians — whom they called gentiles — as well as the difficulties caused by the behavior of both Spaniards and Indians.

DOCUMENT 1
Father Luís Jayme Describes Conditions at Mission San Diego de Alcalá, 1772

Father Luís Jayme, a Franciscan missionary, reported on the deplorable behavior of some of the Spanish soldiers at Mission San Diego de Alcalá, who frequently raped Indian women, causing many Indians to resist the efforts of the missionaries.

With reference to the Indians, I wish to say that great progress [in converting Indians] would be made if there was anything to eat and the soldiers would set a good example. We cannot give them anything to eat because what Don Pedro [the governor] has given is not enough to last half a year for the Indians from the Californias who are here. Thus little progress will be made under present conditions. As for the example set by the soldiers, no doubt some of them are good exemplars and deserve to be treated accordingly, but very many of them deserve to be hanged on account of the continuous outrages which they are committing in seizing and raping the women. There is not a single mission where all the gentiles have not been scandalized, and even on the roads, so I have been told. Surely, as the gentiles themselves state, they [the soldiers] are committing a thousand evils, particularly of a sexual nature. . . .

At one of these Indian villages near this mission of San Diego, which said village is very large, and which is on the road to Monterey, the gentiles therein many times have been on the point of coming here to kill us all, and the reason for this is that some soldiers went there and raped their women, and other soldiers who were carrying the mail to Monterey turned their animals into their fields and they ate up their crops. Three other Indian villages . . . [near] here have reported the same thing to me several times. For this reason on several occasions when . . . I have gone to see these Indian villages, as soon as they saw us they fled from their villages and fled to the woods or other remote places. . . . They do this so that the soldiers will not rape their women as they have already done so many times in the past.

No wonder the Indians here were bad when the mission was first founded. To begin with, they did not know why [the Spaniards] had come, unless they wanted to take their lands away from them. Now they all want to be Christians because they know that there is a God who created the heavens and earth and all things, that there is a Hell and Glory, that they have souls, etc., but when the mission was first founded . . . they thought they were like animals, and . . . they were very loath to pray, and they did not want to be Christians at all. . . . [Now] they all know the natural law, which, so I am informed, they have observed as well or better than many Christians elsewhere. They do not have idols; they do not go on drinking sprees; they do not marry relatives; and they have but one wife. The married men sleep with their wives only. . . . Some of the first adults whom we baptized, when we pointed out to them that it was wrong to have sexual intercourse with a woman to whom they were not married, told me that they already knew that, and that among them it was

---

Some governors developed a working relationship with the colonists' assemblies. But during the eighteenth century, the assemblies gained the upper hand.

Since British policies did not clearly define the colonists' legal powers, colonial assemblies seized the opportunity to make their own rules.

Gradually, the assemblies established a strong tradition of representative government analogous, in their eyes, to the British Parliament. Voters often returned the same representatives to the assemblies year after year, building continuity in power and leadership that far exceeded that of the governor.

considered to be very bad, and so they do not do so at all. "The soldiers," they told me, "are Christians and, although they know that God will punish them in Hell, do so, having sexual intercourse with our wives." "We," they said, "although we did not know that God would punish us for that in Hell, considered it to be very bad, and we did not do it, and even less now that we know that God will punish us if we do so." When I heard this, I burst into tears to see how these gentiles were setting an example for us Christians.

SOURCE: Maynard Geiger, trans. and ed., *The Letter of Luís Jayme, O.F.M.: San Diego, October 17, 1772* (Los Angeles, 1970), 38–42.

DOCUMENT 2
Father Junípero Serra Describes the Indian Revolt at Mission San Diego de Alcalá, 1775

Father Junípero Serra, the founder of many of the California missions, reported to his superiors in Mexico City that an Indian uprising had destroyed Mission San Diego de Alcalá. He recommended rebuilding and urged officials to provide additional soldiers to defend the missions, but not to punish the rebellious Indians.

As we are in the vale of tears, not all the news I have to relate can be pleasant. And so I make no excuses for announcing . . . the tragic news that I have just received of the total destruction of the San Diego Mission, and of the death of the senior of its two religious ministers, called Father Luís Jayme, at the hand of the rebellious gentiles and of the Christian neophytes [Indians who lived in the mission]. All this happened, November 5th, about one or two o'clock at night. The gentiles came together from forty rancherías [settlements], according to information given me, and set fire to the church, after sacking it. They then went to the storehouse, the house where the Fathers lived, the soldiers' barracks, and all the rest of the buildings. They killed a carpenter . . . and a blacksmith. . . . They wounded with their arrows the four soldiers, who alone were on guard at the . . . mission. . . .

And now, after the Father has been killed, the Mission burned, its many and valuable furnishings destroyed, together with the sacred vessels, its paintings, its baptis-

mal, marriage, and funeral records, and all the furnishings for the sacristy, the house, and the farm implements — now the forces [of soldiers] of both presidios [nearby] come together to set things right. . . . What happened was that before they set about reestablishing the Mission, they wanted to . . . lay hands on the guilty ones who were responsible for the burning of the Mission, and the death of the Fathers, and chastise them. The harassed Indians rebelled anew and became more enraged. . . . And so the soldiers there are gathered together in their presidios, and the Indians in their state of heathenism. . . .

While the missionary is alive, let the soldiers guard him, and watch over him, like the pupils of God's very eyes. That is as it should be. . . . But after the missionary has been killed, what can be gained by campaigns [against the rebellious Indians]? Some will say to frighten them and prevent them from killing others. What I say is that, in order to prevent them from killing others, keep better guard over them than they did over the one who has been killed; and, as to the murderer, let him live, in order that he should be saved — which is the very purpose of our coming here, and the reason which justifies it.

SOURCE: Antonine Tibesar, O.F.M., ed., *The Writings of Junípero Serra* (Washington, D.C., 1956), 2:401–7. Reprinted by permission of the American Academy of Franciscan History.

Questions for Analysis and Debate

1. In what ways did Jayme and Serra agree about the motivations of Indians in and around Mission San Diego de Alcalá? In what ways did they disagree? How would Serra's recommendations for rebuilding the mission have addressed the problems identified by Jayme that caused the revolt?

2. How did the goals and activities of the Spanish soldiers compare with those of the Catholic missionaries?

3. How did the religious convictions of Jayme and Serra influence their reports? What might Spanish soldiers or Indians have said about these events? What might they have said about missionaries like Jayme and Serra?

By 1720, colonial assemblies had won the power to initiate legislation, including tax laws and authorizations to spend public funds. Although all laws passed by the assemblies (except in Maryland, Rhode Island, and Connecticut) had to be approved by the governor and then by the Board of Trade in Britain, the difficulties in communication about complex subjects over long distances effectively ratified the assemblies' decisions. Years often passed before colonial laws were repealed by British authorities, and in the meantime the assemblies' laws prevailed.

The heated political struggles between royal governors and colonial assemblies that occurred throughout the eighteenth century taught colonists a common set of political lessons. They learned to employ traditionally British ideas of representative government to defend their own colonial interests. More important, they learned that power in the British colonies rarely belonged to the British government.

REVIEW   What experiences tended to unify the colonists in British North America during the eighteenth century?

► Conclusion: The Dual Identity of British North American Colonists

During the eighteenth century, a society that was both distinctively colonial and distinctively British emerged in British North America. Tens of thousands of immigrants and slaves gave the colonies an unmistakably colonial complexion and contributed to the colonies' growing population and expanding economy. People of different ethnicities and faiths sought their fortunes in the colonies, where land was cheap, labor was dear, and — as Benjamin Franklin preached — work promised to be rewarding. Indentured servants and redemptioners risked temporary periods of bondage for the potential reward of better opportunities in the colonies than on the Atlantic's eastern shore. Slaves arrived in unprecedented numbers and endured lifelong servitude, which they neither chose nor desired but from which their masters greatly benefited.

None of the European colonies could claim complete dominance of North America. The desire to expand and defend their current claims meant that the English, French, and Spanish colonies were drawn into regular conflict with one another, as well as with the Indians upon whose land they encroached. In varying degrees, all sought control of the Native Americans and their land, their military power, their trade, and even their souls. Spanish missionaries and soldiers sought to convert Indians on the West Coast and exploit their labor; French alliances with Indian tribes posed a formidable barrier to westward expansion of the British empire.

Yet despite their attempts to tame their New World holdings, Spanish and French

colonists did not develop societies that began to rival the European empires that sponsored and supported them. They did not participate in the cultural, economic, social, and religious changes experienced by their counterparts in British North America, nor did they share in the emerging political identity of the British colonists.

Identifiably colonial products from New England, the middle colonies, and the southern colonies flowed to the West Indies and across the Atlantic. Back came unquestionably British consumer goods along with fashions in ideas, faith, and politics. The bonds of the British empire required colonists to think of themselves as British subjects and, at the same time, encouraged them to consider their status as colonists. By 1750, British colonists in North America could not imagine that their distinctively dual identity — as British and as colonists — would soon become a source of intense conflict. But by 1776, colonists in British North America had to choose whether they were British or American.

Selected Bibliography

General Works

Ira Berlin, *Generations of Captivity: A History of African-American Slaves* (2003).
Holly Brewer, *By Birth or Consent: Children, Law, and the Anglo-American Revolution in Authority* (2005).
Jan de Vries, *The Industrious Revolution: Consumer Behavior and the Household Economy, 1650 to the Present* (2008).
Eric Jay Dolin, *Fur, Fortune, and Empire: The Epic History of the Fur Trade in America* (2010).
Kathleen DuVal, *The Native Ground: Indians and Colonists in the Heart of the Continent* (2006).
Julie Flavell, *When London Was Capital of America* (2010).
Patrick Griffin, *The People with No Name: Ireland's Ulster Scots, America's Scots Irish, and the Creation of a British Atlantic World, 1689–1764* (2001).
David Hancock, *Oceans of Wine: Madeira and the Emergence of American Trade and Taste* (2009).
Brendan McConville, *The King's Three Faces: The Rise and Fall of Royal America, 1688–1776* (2007).
Nancy Shoemaker, *A Strange Likeness: Becoming Red and White in Eighteenth-Century North America* (2005).
Peter Silver, *Our Savage Neighbors: How Indian War Transformed Early America* (2008).

New England

Richard Aquila, *The Iroquois Restoration: Iroquois Diplomacy on the Colonial Frontier, 1701–1754* (1997).

Elaine Forman Crane, *Ebb Tide in New England: Women, Seaports, and Social Change, 1630–1800* (1998).

Phyllis Whitman Hunter, *Purchasing Identity in the Atlantic World: Massachusetts Merchants, 1670–1780* (2001).

George M. Marsden, *Jonathan Edwards: A Life* (2003).

Lisa Norling, *Captain Ahab Had a Wife: New England Women and the Whale Fishery, 1720–1870* (2000).

Daniel Vickers, *Young Men and the Sea: Yankee Seafarers in the Age of Sail* (2005).

Middle Colonies

Katherine Carté Engel, *Religion and Profit: Moravians in Early America* (2009).

Leslie M. Harris, *In the Shadow of Slavery: African Americans in New York City, 1626–1863* (2003).

Eric Hinderaker, *Elusive Empires: Constructing Colonialism in the Ohio Valley, 1673–1800* (1997).

Jill Lepore, *New York Burning: Liberty, Slavery, and Conspiracy in Eighteenth-Century Manhattan* (2005).

James H. Merrell, *Into the American Woods: Negotiators on the Pennsylvania Frontier* (1999).

Jane T. Merritt, *At the Crossroads: Indians and Empires on a Mid-Atlantic Frontier, 1700–1763* (2003).

Donna Merwick, *The Shame and the Sorrow: Dutch-Amerindian Encounters in New Netherland* (2006).

Simon P. Newman, *Embodied History: The Lives of the Poor in Early Philadelphia* (2003).

David Waldstreicher, *Runaway America: Benjamin Franklin, Slavery, and the American Revolution* (2004).

Southern Colonies

Vincent Carretta, *Equiano the African: Biography of a Self-Made Man* (2005).

Steven W. Hackel, *Children of Coyote, Missionaries of Saint Francis: Indian-Spanish Relations in Colonial California, 1769–1850* (2005).

Robert H. Jackson, *Missions and the Frontiers of Spanish America* (2005).

Catherine Kerrison, *Claiming the Pen: Women and Intellectual Life in the Early American South* (2006).

Philip D. Morgan, *Slave Counterpoint: Black Culture in the Eighteenth-Century Chesapeake and Low Country* (1998).

Robert Olwell, *Masters, Slaves, and Subjects: The Culture of Power in the South Carolina Low Country, 1740–1790* (1998).

Jon F. Sensbach, *Rebecca's Revival: Creating Black Christianity in the Atlantic World* (2005).

Randy Sparks, *The Two Princes of Calabar: An Eighteenth-Century Atlantic Odyssey* (2004).

David J. Weber, *Bárbaros: Spaniards and Their Savages in the Age of Enlightenment* (2005).

Bradford J. Wood, *This Remote Part of the World: Regional Formation in Lower Cape Fear, North Carolina, 1725–1775* (2004).

▶ **FOR MORE BOOKS ABOUT TOPICS IN THIS CHAPTER,** see the Online Bibliography at **bedfordstmartins.com/roark.**

▶ **FOR ADDITIONAL PRIMARY SOURCES FROM THIS PERIOD,** see Michael Johnson, ed., *Reading the American Past,* Fifth Edition.

▶ **FOR WEB SITES, IMAGES, AND DOCUMENTS RELATED TO TOPICS AND PLACES IN THIS CHAPTER,** visit Make History at **bedfordstmartins.com/roark.**

Reviewing Chapter 5

KEY TERMS

Explain each term's significance.

A Growing Population and Expanding Economy in British North America
    natural increase (p. 125)

New England: From Puritan Settlers to Yankee Traders
    partible inheritance (p. 127)
    Atlantic commerce (p. 127)

The Middle Colonies: Immigrants, Wheat, and Work
    Pennsylvania Dutch (p. 129)
    Scots-Irish (p. 130)
    redemptioners (p. 131)
    Iroquois Indians (p. 133)
    Benjamin Franklin (p. 135)

The Southern Colonies: Land of Slavery
    Middle Passage (p. 137)
    Olaudah Equiano (p. 137)
    new Negroes (p. 137)
    country-born or creole slaves (p. 138)
    Stono rebellion (p. 139)
    task system (p. 139)

Unifying Experiences
    deism (p. 144)
    Enlightenment (p. 144)
    Great Awakening (p. 145)
    Jonathan Edwards (p. 145)
    George Whitefield (p. 145)
    Yamasee War of 1715 (p. 147)
    presidios (p. 147)
    Gaspar de Portolá (p. 147)
    Junípero Serra (p. 147)

REVIEW QUESTIONS

Use key terms and dates to support your answer.

1. How did the North American colonies achieve the remarkable population growth of the eighteenth century? (pp. 125–126)

2. Why did settlement patterns in New England change from the seventeenth to the eighteenth century? (pp. 126–129)

3. Why did immigrants flood into Pennsylvania during the eighteenth century? (pp. 129–135)

4. How did slavery influence the society and economy of the southern colonies? (pp. 135–141)

5. What experiences tended to unify the colonists in British North America during the eighteenth century? (pp. 141–152)

MAKING CONNECTIONS

Draw on key terms, the timeline, and review questions.

1. Colonial products such as tobacco and sugar transformed consumption patterns on both sides of the Atlantic in the eighteenth century. How did consumption influence the relationship between the American colonies and Britain? In your answer, consider how it might have strengthened and weakened connections.

2. Why did the importance of religion decline throughout the colonies from the seventeenth to the eighteenth century? How did American colonists respond to these changes?

3. How did different colonies attempt to manage relations with the Indians? How did the Indians attempt to manage relationships with the Europeans? In your answer, consider disputes over territory and trade.

4. Varied immigration patterns contributed to important differences among the British colonies. Compare and contrast patterns of immigration to the middle and southern colonies. Who came, and how did they get there? How did they shape the economic, cultural, and political character of each colony?

LINKING TO THE PAST

Link events in this chapter to earlier events.

1. How did the British North American colonies in 1750 differ politically and economically from those in 1650? Were there important continuities? (See chapters 3 and 4.)

2. Is there persuasive evidence that colonists' outlook on the world shifted from the seventeenth to the eighteenth century? Why or why not? (See chapters 3 and 4.)

▶ FOR PRACTICE QUIZZES AND OTHER STUDY TOOLS, visit the Online Study Guide at bedfordstmartins.com/roark.

TIMELINE 1702–1775

1711– 1713	• Queen Anne's War triggers German migration to North America.
1711	• North Carolina founded.
1715	• Yamasee War.
1730s	• Jonathan Edwards promotes Great Awakening.
1732	• Georgia founded.
1733	• Benjamin Franklin begins to publish *Poor Richard's Almanack*.
1739	• Stono rebellion.
1740s	• George Whitefield preaches religious revival in North America. • Majority of southern slaves are country-born.
1745	• Olaudah Equiano born.
1750s	• Colonists begin to move down Shenandoah Valley.
1754	• Seven Years' War begins.
1769	• American Philosophical Society founded. • First California mission, San Diego de Alcalá, established.
1770	• Mission and presidio established at Monterey, California. • British North American colonists number more than two million.
1775	• Indians destroy San Diego mission.

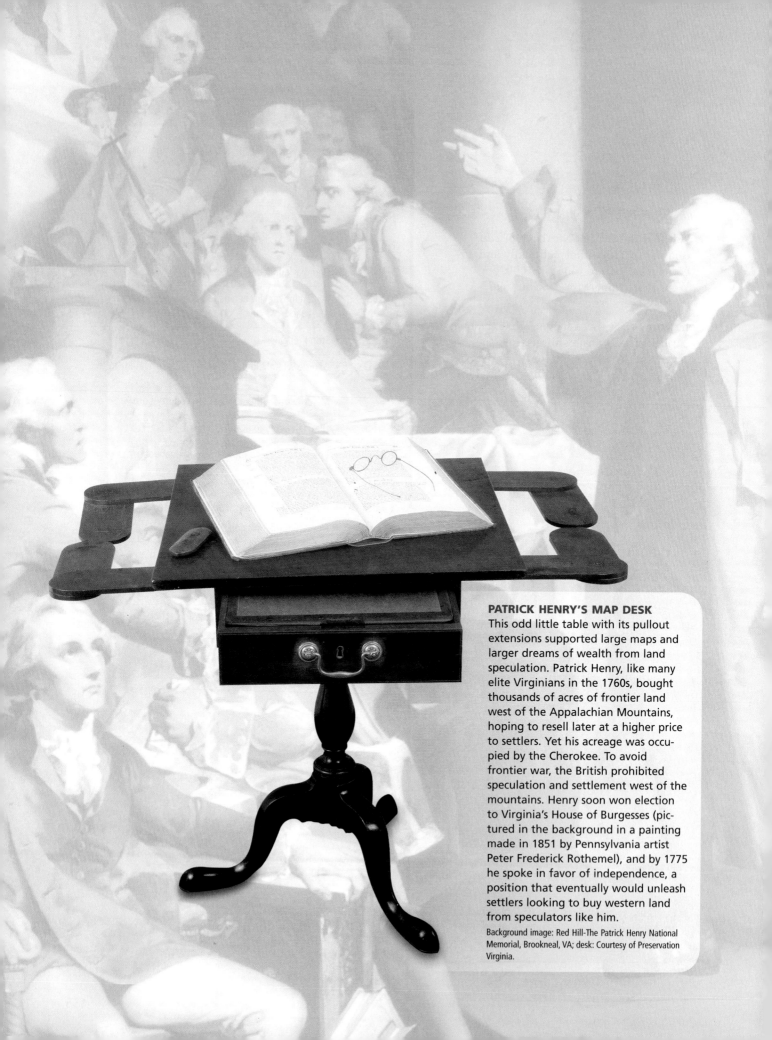

PATRICK HENRY'S MAP DESK

This odd little table with its pullout extensions supported large maps and larger dreams of wealth from land speculation. Patrick Henry, like many elite Virginians in the 1760s, bought thousands of acres of frontier land west of the Appalachian Mountains, hoping to resell later at a higher price to settlers. Yet his acreage was occupied by the Cherokee. To avoid frontier war, the British prohibited speculation and settlement west of the mountains. Henry soon won election to Virginia's House of Burgesses (pictured in the background in a painting made in 1851 by Pennsylvania artist Peter Frederick Rothemel), and by 1775 he spoke in favor of independence, a position that eventually would unleash settlers looking to buy western land from speculators like him.

Background image: Red Hill-The Patrick Henry National Memorial, Brookneal, VA; desk: Courtesy of Preservation Virginia.

6

The British Empire and the Colonial Crisis
1754–1775

IN 1771, THOMAS HUTCHINSON BECAME THE ROYAL GOVERNOR OF the colony of Massachusetts. Unlike most royal governors, who were British aristocrats sent over by the king for short tours of duty, Hutchinson was a fifth-generation American. A Harvard-educated member of the Massachusetts elite, from a family of successful merchants, he had served two decades in the Massachusetts general assembly. In 1758, Thomas Hutchinson was appointed lieutenant governor, and in 1760 he also became chief justice of the colony's highest court. He lived in the finest mansion in Boston. Wealth, power, and influence were his in abundance. He was proud of his connection to the British empire and loyal to his king.

Hutchinson had the misfortune to be a loyal colonial leader during the two very tumultuous decades leading up to the American Revolution. He worked hard to keep the British and colonists aligned in interests, even promoting a plan to unify the colonies with a limited government (the Albany Plan of Union) to deal with Indian policy. His plan of union ultimately failed, however, and a major war — the Seven Years' War — ensued, pitting the British and colonists against the French and their Indian allies in the backcountry of the American colonies. When the war ended and the British government began to think about taxing colonists to pay for it, Hutchinson had no doubt that the new British taxation policies were legitimate — unwise, perhaps, but legitimate.

Not everyone in Boston shared his opinion. Fervent, enthusiastic crowds protested against a succession of British taxation policies enacted after 1763 — the Sugar Act, the Stamp Act, the Townshend duties, the Tea Act, all landmark events on the road to the American Revolution. But Hutchinson maintained his steadfast loyalty to Britain. His love of order and tradition inclined him to unconditional support of the British empire, and by nature he was a measured and cautious man. "My temper does not incline to enthusiasm," he once wrote.

Privately, he lamented the stupidity of the British acts that provoked trouble, but his sense of duty required him to defend the king's policies, however misguided. Quickly, he became an inspiring villain to the emerging

Thomas Hutchinson
The only formal portrait of Thomas Hutchinson still in existence shows an assured young man in ruffles. Decades of turmoil in Boston failed to puncture his self-confidence. Doubtless he sat for other portraits, as did all the Boston leaders in the 1760s to 1780s, but no other likeness has survived. One portrait of him hung in his summer house outside Boston; a revolutionary crowd mutilated it and stabbed out the eyes. In 1775, Hutchinson fled to Britain, the country he regarded as his cultural home, only to realize how very American he was. Courtesy of the Massachusetts Historical Society.

revolutionary movement. Governor Hutchinson came to personify all that was wrong with British and colonial relations. The man not inclined to enthusiasm unleashed popular enthusiasm all around him. He never appreciated that irony.

In another irony, Thomas Hutchinson was actually one of the first Americans to recognize the difficulties of maintaining full rights and privileges for colonists so far from their supreme government, the king and Parliament in Britain. In 1769, when British troops occupied Boston in an effort to provide civil order, he wrote privately to a friend in England, "There must be an abridgement of what are called English liberties. . . . I doubt whether it is possible to project a system of government in which a colony three thousand miles distant from the parent state shall enjoy all the liberty of the parent state." What he could not imagine was the possibility of giving up the parent state and creating an independent government closer to home.

Thomas Hutchinson was a loyalist; in the 1750s, most English-speaking colonists were affectionately loyal to Britain. But the Seven Years' War, which Britain and its colonies fought together as allies, shook that affection, and imperial policies in the decade following the war shattered it completely. Over the course of 1763 to 1773, Americans insistently raised serious questions about Britain's governance of its colonies. Many came to believe what Thomas Hutchinson could never accept — that a tyrannical Britain had embarked on a course to enslave the colonists by depriving them of their traditional English liberties.

The opposite of liberty was slavery, a condition of nonfreedom and coercion. Political rhetoric about liberty, tyranny, and slavery heated up the emotions of white colonists during the many crises of the 1760s and 1770s. But this rhetoric turned out to be a two-edged sword. The call for an end to tyrannical slavery meant one thing when sounded by Boston merchants whose commercial shipping rights had been revoked, but the same call meant something quite different in 1775 when sounded by black Americans locked in the bondage of slavery.

► The Seven Years' War, 1754–1763

For the first half of the eighteenth century, Britain was at war intermittently with France or Spain. Often the colonists in America experienced reverberations from these conflicts, most acutely along the frontier of New France in northern New England.

In the 1750s, international tensions returned, this time sparked by conflicts over contested land in America's Ohio Valley. The land, variously claimed by Virginians, Pennsylvanians, and the French, was actually inhabited by more than a dozen Indian tribes. The result was the costly **Seven Years' War** (its British name), known in the colonies as the French and Indian War, in which Americans and the British shared the hardships of battle and finally the glory of victory. Before it ended in 1763, fighting had extended through Europe, into the Caribbean, and even to India. The immense costs of the war — in money, death, and desire for revenge by losers and even winners — laid the groundwork for the imperial crisis of the 1760s between the British and Americans.

French-British Rivalry in the Ohio Country

For several decades, French traders had cultivated alliances with the Indian tribes in the Ohio Country, a frontier region they regarded as part of New France (Map 6.1). Cementing their relationships with gifts, the French established a profitable exchange of manufactured goods for beaver furs. But in the 1740s, Pennsylvania traders began to infringe on the territory. Adding to the tensions, a group of enterprising Virginians, including the brothers Lawrence and Augustine Washington, formed the **Ohio Company** in 1747 and advanced into French-claimed territory. Their goal was to secure wilderness tracts to be resold later on to the exploding Anglo-American population seeking fresh land.

French soldiers began building a series of military forts to secure their trade routes and to create a western barrier to American population expansion.

In response, the royal governor of Virginia, Robert Dinwiddie, also a shareholder in the Ohio Company, dispatched a messenger in 1753 to warn the French that they were trespassing on Virginia land. For this dangerous mission, he chose the twenty-one-year-old George Washington, half-brother of the Ohio Company leaders, who did not disappoint. Washington returned with crucial intelligence confirming French military intentions.

Impressed, Dinwiddie appointed the youth to lead a small military expedition west to assert and, if need be, defend Virginia's claim. Imperial officials in London, concerned about the French fortifications, had authorized the governor "to repell force by force," only if the French attacked first. By early 1754, the French had built Fort Duquesne at the forks of the Ohio River; Washington's delicate assignment was to chase the French away without actually being the aggressor.

In the spring of 1754, Washington set out with 160 Virginians and a small contingent of Mingo Indians, who were also concerned about the French military presence in the Ohio Country. The first battle of what would become known as the French and Indian War occurred early one May morning when the Mingo chief Tanaghrisson led a detachment of Washington's soldiers to a small French encampment in the woods. Who fired first was later a matter of dispute, but fourteen Frenchmen (and no Virginians) were wounded. While Washington, lacking a translator, struggled to communicate with the injured French commander, Tanaghrisson and his men intervened to kill and then scalp the wounded soldiers, including the commander, probably with the aim of inflaming hostilities between the French and the colonists.

This sudden massacre violated Washington's instructions to avoid being the aggressor and raised the stakes considerably. Fearing retaliation, Washington ordered his men to fortify their position, resulting in the makeshift "Fort Necessity." Reinforcements amounting to several hundred more Virginians arrived, but the Mingos, sensing disaster and displeased by Washington's style of command, fled. (Tanaghrisson later said, "The Colonel was a good-natured man, but had no experience; he took upon him to

Ohio River Valley, 1753

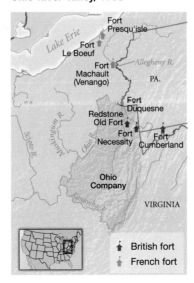

Fort Presqu'isle
Fort Le Boeuf
Lake Erie
Fort Machault (Venango)
Allegheny R.
PA.
Fort Duquesne
Redstone Old Fort
Fort Necessity
Fort Cumberland
Ohio Company
VIRGINIA
Monongahela R.
Scioto R.
Ohio R.
Kanawha R.

↑ British fort
↑ French fort

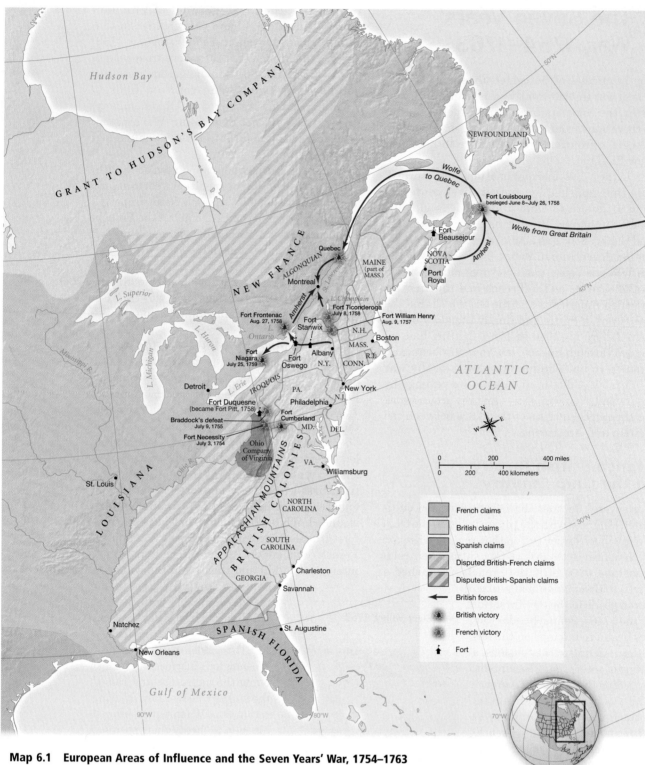

Map 6.1   European Areas of Influence and the Seven Years' War, 1754–1763
In the mid-eighteenth century, France, Britain, and Spain claimed vast areas of North America, many of them already inhabited by various Indian peoples. The early flash points of the Seven Years' War were in regions of disputed claims where the French had allied with powerful native groups — the Iroquois and the Algonquian tribes — to put pressure on the westward-moving British and Americans.

command the Indians as his slaves, [and] would by no means take advice from the Indians.") In early July, more than six hundred French soldiers aided by one hundred Shawnee and Delaware warriors attacked Fort Necessity, killing or wounding a third of Washington's men. The message was clear: The French would not depart from the disputed territory.

The Albany Congress

Even as Virginians, Frenchmen, and Indians fought and died in the Ohio Country, British imperial leaders hoped to prevent a larger war. One obvious strategy was to strengthen frayed British alliances with once friendly Indian tribes. Since 1692, Mohawks and New York merchants in the fur trade had participated in an alliance called the Covenant Chain, but lately the Mohawks felt neglected by British officials and left open to victimization by unsavory land speculators and Albany fur traders. British authorities in London directed the governor to convene a colonial conference to repair trade relations and secure the Indians' help — or at least their neutrality — against the looming French threat.

More than just New Yorkers and Mohawks were called to the Albany meeting, held in June and July 1754. Seven colonies sent a total of twenty-four delegates, making this an unprecedented pan-colony gathering. All six constituent tribes of the Iroquois Confederacy, of which the Mohawks were the easternmost tribe, also attended. The Mohawk chief Hendrick, a gray-haired man with long-term friendships with English and Dutch colonists, gave a powerful and widely cited speech at the congress, asserting that the recent neglect would inevitably reorient Indian trade relations to the French. "Look at the French, they are men; they are fortifying every where; but we are ashamed to say it; you are like women, bare and open, without any fortifications." Hendrick urged the assembled colonists to prepare for defense against the French. (See "Visualizing History," page 162.)

Two delegates at the congress seized the occasion to push for yet more ambitious plans. Benjamin Franklin of Pennsylvania and Thomas Hutchinson of Massachusetts, both rising political stars, coauthored the **Albany Plan of Union**, a proposal for a unified but limited government to formulate Indian policy and coordinate colonial

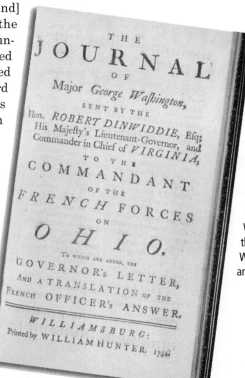

Washington's Journal, 1754
After George Washington's first mission to contact the French, he submitted to Governor Dinwiddie a report of about seven thousand words (the equivalent of a twenty-five-page paper), written in two days. He coolly narrated scenes of personal danger: traveling in deep snow, falling off a raft into an icy river, and being shot at by a lone Indian. Dinwiddie published Washington's report to inform Virginians and British leaders about the French threat in the West. With its republication in London, the pamphlet brought renown to Washington as a young man of resolute and rugged courage. Huntington Library.

military forces. Key features included a president-general, appointed by the crown, and a grand council representing the colonies, meeting annually to consider questions of war, peace, and trade with the Indians. The writers of the Albany Plan humbly reaffirmed Parliament's authority; this was no bid for enlarged autonomy of the colonies. Hutchinson and Franklin easily persuaded the conference delegates to take the plan back to their respective assemblies.

To Franklin's surprise, not a single colony approved the Albany Plan. The Massachusetts assembly feared it was "a Design of gaining power over the Colonies," especially the power of taxation. Others objected that it would be impossible to agree on unified policies toward scores of quite different Indian tribes. The British government never backed the Albany Plan either; instead, it appointed two superintendents of Indian affairs, one for the northern and another for the southern colonies, each with exclusive powers to negotiate treaties, trade, and land sales with all tribes.

The Indians at the Albany Congress were not impressed with the Albany Plan either. The Covenant Chain alliance with the Mohawk tribe was reaffirmed, but the other nations left without pledging to help the British battle the French. At this very early point in the Seven Years' War,

Cultural Cross-Dressing in Eighteenth-Century Portraits

Chief Hendrick

John Caldwell

the Iroquois figured that the French military presence around the Great Lakes would discourage the westward push of American colonists and therefore better serve their interests.

The War and Its Consequences

By 1755, George Washington's frontier skirmish had turned into a major mobilization of British and American troops against the French. At first, the British expected a quick victory on three fronts. General Edward Braddock, recently arrived from England, marched his army toward Fort Duquesne in western Pennsylvania. Farther north, British troops moved toward Fort Niagara, critically located between Lakes Erie and Ontario. And William Johnson, a New Yorker recently

appointed superintendent of northern Indian affairs, led forces north toward Lake Champlain, intending to defend the border against the French in Canada (see Map 6.1). Unfortunately for the British, the French were prepared to fight and had cemented respectful alliances with many Indian tribes throughout the region.

Braddock's march west was the first of a series of disasters for the British. Accompanied by George Washington and his Virginia soldiers, Braddock led 2,000 troops into the backcountry in July 1755. Although Indian guidance and support amounted to a mere 8 Oneida warriors, Braddock expected an easy victory with his big artillery and overwhelming numbers. One day short of reaching Fort Duquesne, in heavy woods where their cannons were useless, the British

Having one's individual likeness rendered in paint was a mark of distinction in the eighteenth century. The subjects of portraiture were typically the wealthy, who had the means to pay an artist's fee, or, less often, nonwealthy but noteworthy people with public name recognition. Rarer still were portraits that presented such sitters dressed in clothes from other cultures. Here, Chief Hendrick Peters Theyanoguin, spokesman for the Mohawk Indians at the 1754 Albany Congress, appears in fine British clothing in a 1755 engraving, while John Caldwell, a titled young Irishman and an officer in the British army, sports colorful Indian dress in a painting made in Britain in 1780.

Soon after the Albany Congress, Hendrick traveled to Philadelphia, where an elite men's club paid for a professional portrait, likely the basis for the engraving shown here. Within the year, the sixty-three-year-old Hendrick was dead, killed at Lake George in the first northern battle in the Seven Years' War. His passing sparked great public mourning. Two taverns and three sailing vessels in Philadelphia were named in his honor. In London, this engraving was published in the *Gentleman's Magazine*, and hand-colored prints were sold in British and American bookshops.

Hendrick's gold-braided coat, ruffled shirt, and three-cornered hat are all signs of a well-dressed English gentleman. Why might he have chosen this outfit for the portrait painted in Philadelphia? What statement might it have made to London purchasers about Hendrick's political allegiance? Based on this portrait, was Hendrick some kind of cultural broker? What marks his Indianness in the engraving? Is there any visual evidence indicating that this London engraving is based on the actual portrait of Hendrick posing in person, as opposed to its being a picture of a generic Indian made up from the artist's imagination? Consider, for example, the facial tattoos — a starburst over his ear, the two lines under the eye — and the long scar on his left cheek. Do they suggest a generic Indian or a particular man?

Ensign John Caldwell, born into an aristocratic family in 1756, was stationed during the Revolutionary War (see chapter 7) at Fort Detroit, a British garrison that provided aid to eastern Great Lakes tribes battling Americans. The Ojibwas of that region bestowed a high honor on Caldwell by giving him an Indian name in a ceremony, and it was likely that he then acquired the clothing and accessories shown in this portrait. Notice the headdress, breechcloth, beaded pouch, knife and sheath, tomahawk, wampum belt, red leggings and garters (showing an expanse of thigh, immodest by British standards), and fringed moccasins. What might have been the purpose of Caldwell's posing for a portrait in this garb? Was he trying to channel the power of Indian men, doubtless seen as exotic by British viewers of the painting? Did Caldwell "go native"? Or was this his way to display manly courage?

Although we cannot generalize from two images, we can place the portraits in the context of their time and draw some conclusions about what their purposes were. Hendrick's portrait was created in 1755 and was publicly disseminated to memorialize the leader of one of the few tribes loyal to Britain during the Seven Years' War. The taverns and sailing ships named for him further mark his celebrated status. Caldwell's portrait was a private possession, commissioned after the Revolutionary War when much of Britain's North American land claims had fallen to the colonies. What attitude do you think Hendrick and Caldwell intended to convey regarding the other's culture? How might each have reacted to the other's portrait?

SOURCE: Chief Hendrick: Courtesy of the John Carter Brown Library at Brown University; John Caldwell: The Board of Trustees of the National Museums & Galleries on Merseyside (King's Regiment Collection).

were ambushed by 250 French soldiers joined by 640 Indian warriors, including Ottawas, Ojibwas, Potawatomis, Shawnees, and Delawares. Surviving soldiers reported that they never saw more than a half dozen Indians at a time, so hidden were they in the woods. But the soldiers could hear them. One soldier wrote weeks later that "the yell of the Indians is fresh on my ear, and the terrific sound will haunt me until the hour of my dissolution." The disciplined British troops stood their ground, making them easy targets. In the bloody Battle of the Monongahela, named for a nearby river, nearly a thousand on the British side were killed or wounded. Washington was unhurt, though two horses in succession were shot out from under him. General Braddock was killed.

Braddock's defeat stunned British leaders. For the next two years, they stumbled badly, deploying inadequate numbers of troops. Colonial assemblies, unwilling to be forced to shoulder the costs of war, held back from contributing provincial troops. What finally turned the war around was the rise to power in 1757 of **William Pitt**, Britain's prime minister, a man ready to commit massive resources to fight France and its ally Spain worldwide. Pitt treated the assemblies as allies, not subordinates, and paid them to raise and equip provincial soldiers, an intensification of manpower that led at last to the capture of Forts Duquesne, Niagara, and Ticonderoga, followed by victories over the French cities of Quebec and finally Montreal, all from 1758 to 1760.

By 1761, the war subsided in America but expanded globally, with battles in the Caribbean, Austria, Prussia, and India. The British captured the French sugar islands Martinique and Guadeloupe and then invaded Spanish Cuba with an army of some four thousand provincial soldiers from New York and New England. By the end of 1762, France and Spain capitulated, and the **Treaty of Paris** was signed in 1763.

The triumph was sweet but short-lived. In the complex peace negotiations, Britain gained control of Canada, eliminating the French threat from the north. British and American title to the eastern half of North America, precisely what Britain had claimed before the war, was confirmed. France transferred all its territory west of the Mississippi River, including New Orleans, to Spain as compensation for Spain's assistance during the war. France retained Martinique and Guadeloupe, while Cuba, where two thousand Americans had died of injury or disease in the invasion, was restored to Spain (Map 6.2).

In the aftermath of the war, Britain and the colonies, having worked as allies to defeat the French, began to eye each other warily. The British credited their mighty army for their victory and criticized the colonists for inadequate support. William Pitt was convinced that colonial smuggling — beaver pelts from French fur traders and illegal molasses in the French Caribbean — "principally, if not alone, enabled France to sustain and protract this long and expensive war." American traders, grumbled British leaders, were really traitors.

Colonists read the lessons of the war differently. American soldiers had turned out in force, they claimed, but had been relegated to grunt work by arrogant British commanders and subjected to unexpectedly harsh military discipline, ranging from frequent floggings (stealing a shirt brought a thousand lashes) to executions, the punishment for desertion. One Massachusetts army doctor avoided attending the punishments: "I saw not the men whiped, for altho' there is almost every Day more or less whiped or Piqueted [forced to stand on a sharpened stake], I've never had the curiosity to see 'm, the Shrieks and Crys" being more than he could bear.

Further, the British army did not always wage frontier warfare so brilliantly. Benjamin Franklin heard General Braddock brag that "these savages may, indeed, be a formidable enemy to your raw American militia, but upon the king's regular and disciplined troops, sir, it is impossible they should make any impression." Braddock's crushing defeat "gave us Americans," Franklin wrote, "the first suspicion that our exalted ideas of the prowess of British regulars had not been well founded."

MAP ACTIVITY

Map 6.2 Europe Redraws the Map of North America, 1763

In the peace treaty of 1763, France ceded to Britain its interior territory from Quebec to New Orleans, retaining fishing rights in the far north and several sugar islands in the Caribbean. France transferred to Spain its claim to extensive territory west of the Mississippi River.

READING THE MAP: Who actually lived on and controlled the lands ceded by France? In what sense, if any, did Britain or Spain own these large territories?
CONNECTIONS: What was the goal of the Proclamation of 1763? (See page 166.) Could it ever have worked?

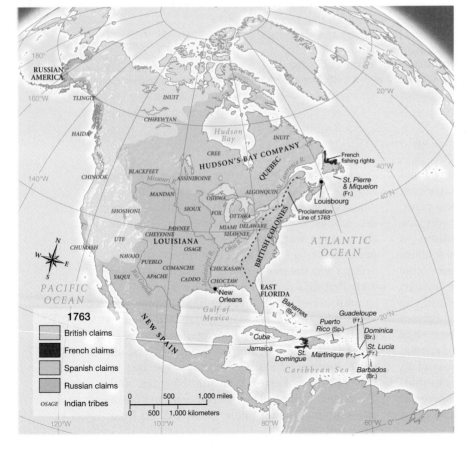

Perhaps most important, the enormous expense of the Seven Years' War caused by Pitt's no-holds-barred military strategy cast a huge shadow over the victory. And the costs continued to mount, because British leaders decided in 1762 to maintain a force of ten thousand soldiers in North America to guard against potential hostilities with Indians or French Canadians. By 1763, Britain's national debt, double what it had been when Pitt took office, posed a formidable challenge to the next decade of leadership in Britain.

Pontiac's Rebellion and the Proclamation of 1763

One glaring omission marred the Treaty of Paris: The major powers at the treaty table failed to include the Indians. Minavavana, an Ojibwa chief of the Great Lakes region, put it succinctly to an English trader: "Englishman, although you have conquered the French, you have not yet conquered us! We are not your slaves. These lakes, these woods and mountains were left to us by our ancestors. They are our inheritance; and we will part with them to none." Furthermore, Minavavana pointedly noted, "your king has never sent us any presents, nor entered into any treaty with us, wherefore he and we are still at war."

Minavavana's complaint about the absence of British presents was significant. To Indians, gifts cemented social relationships, symbolizing honor and establishing obligation. Over many decades, the French had mastered the subtleties of gift exchange, distributing textiles and hats and receiving calumets (ceremonial pipes) in return. British military leaders, new to the practice, often discarded the calumets as trivial trinkets, thereby insulting the givers. From the British view, a generous gift might signify tribute (thus demeaning the giver), or it might be positioned as a bribe. "It is not my intention ever to attempt to gain the friendship of Indians by presents," Major General Jeffery Amherst declared. The Indian view was the opposite: Generous givers expressed dominance and protection, not subordination, in the ceremonial practices of giving.

Despite Minavavana's confident words, Indians north of the Ohio River had plenty of cause for concern. Old French trading posts all over the Northwest were beefed up by the British into military bases. Fort Duquesne, renamed Fort Pitt to honor the victorious British prime minister, was fortified with new walls sixty feet thick at their base, ten at the top, announcing that this was no fur trading post. Americans settlers were beginning to cluster around Fort Pitt's protective sphere, further alarming the local Indians.

A religious revival among the Indians magnified feelings of antagonism toward the British. A Delaware prophet named Neolin reported a vision in which the Master of Life chastised Indians: "Whence comes it that ye permit the Whites upon your lands? Can ye not live without them?" Neolin urged a return to traditional ways, and his preaching spread quickly, gaining credence as the British bungled diplomacy and American settlers continued to penetrate western lands.

> "Englishman, although you have conquered the French, you have not yet conquered us! We are not your slaves."
> — Ojibwa chief MINAVAVANA

The Seven Years' War

1692–1750s	English and Iroquois create and affirm the Covenant Chain alliance in western New York.
1700–1740s	French settlers enjoy exclusive trade with Indians in Ohio Valley.
1747	Ohio Company receives land grant from British king.
1753	Mohawk chief Hendrick accuses English of breaking Covenant Chain.
	French soldiers advance from Canada into Ohio Country.
	George Washington delivers message telling French they are trespassing.
1754	French build Fort Duquesne.
	Washington returns to Ohio Country with troops and Mingo allies.
	May. Washington, guided by Mingo chief Tanaghrisson, attacks French.
	June–July. Albany Congress convenes.
	July. French and Indian soldiers defeat Washington at Fort Necessity.
1755	British authorities appoint two superintendents of Indian affairs.
	July. Braddock defeated at Monongahela.
1756	William Pitt becomes British prime minister.
1758	British capture Fort Duquesne.
1759	British capture Forts Niagara and Ticonderoga.
1760	British capture Montreal.
1762	British capture Cuba.
1763	Treaty of Paris signed.

166 CHAPTER 6 • THE BRITISH EMPIRE AND THE COLONIAL CRISIS / 1754–1775

Sir Jeffery Amherst in 1765
After five years in America, commander-in-chief Jeffery Amherst returned to England and basked in the glory of his military successes against the French in Canada, which had brought him knighthood. Britain's leading artist, Joshua Reynolds, painted him in a clunky, medieval suit of knight's armor—certainly not what he wore in the wilds along the St. Lawrence River, pictured behind him. Amherst's face expresses self-assured amusement, yet his arms strike a pensive and even feminine pose. An acquaintance wrote of Amherst that "his manners were grave, formal, and cold." Mead Art Museum, Amherst College, Amherst, Massachusetts.

In 1763, a renewal of commitment to Indian ways and the formation of tribal alliances led to open warfare, which the British called **Pontiac's Rebellion**, after the chief of the Ottawas. (The coordinated uprising was actually the work of many men.) In mid-May, Ottawa, Potawatomi, and Huron warriors attacked Fort Detroit. Six more attacks on forts followed within weeks, and frontier settlements were also raided by nearly a dozen tribes from western New York, the Ohio Valley, and the Great Lakes region. By the fall, Indians had captured every fort west of Detroit. More than four hundred British soldiers were dead and another two thousand colonists killed or taken captive.

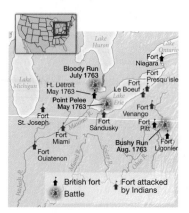

Pontiac's Uprising, 1763

Not all of the attacks were instigated by Indians. The worst of a number of violent aggressions by Americans occurred in late 1763, when some fifty Pennsylvania vigilantes known as the Paxton Boys descended on a peaceful village of Conestoga Indians — friendly Indians, living not far from Philadelphia — and murdered and scalped twenty of them. The vigilantes, now numbering five hundred and out to make war on all Indians, marched on Philadelphia to try to capture and murder some Christian Indians held in protective custody there. British troops prevented that, but the Paxton Boys escaped punishment for their murderous attack on the Conestoga village.

In early 1764, the uprising faded. The Indians were short on ammunition, and the British were tired and broke. The British government recalled the imperious general Amherst, blaming him for mishandling the conflict, and his own soldiers toasted his departure. A new military leader, Thomas Gage, took command and began distributing gifts profusely among the Indians.

To minimize the violence, the British government issued the **Proclamation of 1763**, forbidding colonists to settle west of the Appalachian Mountains. More than just naming a boundary, the Proclamation offered assurances that Indian territory would be respected. It limited trade with Indians to traders licensed by colonial governors, and it forbade private sales of Indian land. But the Proclamation's language also took care not to identify western lands as belonging to the Indians. Instead, it spoke of lands that "are reserved to [Indians], as their Hunting Grounds."

Other parts of the Proclamation of 1763 referred to American and even French colonists in Canada as "our loving subjects," entitled to English rights and privileges. In contrast, the Indians were clearly rejected as British subjects and instead were described more vaguely as those "who live under our protection" and as "Tribes of Indians with whom We are connected." Of course, the British were not really well connected with any Indians, nor did they wish connections to form among the tribes. As William Johnson, the superintendent of northern Indian affairs, advised in 1764, "It will be expedient to treat with each nation separately . . . for could they arrive at a perfect union, they must prove very dangerous Neighbours."

The 1763 boundary was yet a further provocation to many Americans, and most especially to land speculators (like Virginia's Patrick Henry or the men of the Ohio Company) who had already staked claims to huge tracts of land west of the Appalachians and who had no desire to lose profitable resale opportunities. The boundary also proved impossible to enforce, despite the large British military presence. Surging population growth had already sent many hundreds of settlers, many of them squatters, west of the Appalachians.

By 1774, continuous hostilities and periodic bloodshed escalated into a conflict named Lord Dunmore's War, after Virginia's royal governor. In this short but deadly war, Virginia soldiers traversed the Appalachian Mountains to attack Mingo and Shawnee peoples south of the Ohio River, thereby establishing speculators' land claims in western Virginia and Kentucky. But they left the frontier aflame with such ethnic antagonism that would-be settlers were left fearful, uncertain about their future, and increasingly wary of British claims to be a protective mother country.

> **REVIEW** How did the Seven Years' War erode relations between colonists and British authorities?

▶ The Sugar and Stamp Acts, 1763–1765

In 1760, **George III**, twenty-two years old, became king of England. Timid and insecure, George struggled to gain his footing in his new job. He rotated through a succession of leaders, searching for a prime minister he could trust. A half dozen ministers in seven years took turns dealing with one basic, underlying British reality: A huge war debt needed to be serviced, and the colonists, as British subjects, should help pay it off. To many Americans, however, that proposition seemed in deep violation of what they perceived to be their rights and liberties as British subjects, and it created resentment that eventually erupted in large-scale street protests. The first provocative revenue acts were the work of Sir George Grenville, prime minister from 1763 to 1765.

Silver Medal to Present to Indians
After Pontiac's uprising ended, the British aimed to conciliate the Indians by distributing gifts. This silver medal of 1766 shows King George III on the front and a cozy depiction of an Indian and a Briton smoking a peace pipe on the back. The Latin words announce George's name, title, and kingly dominions.
Imagine a conversation between an Indian chief and an English translator who tried to explain what the slogan HAPPY WHILE UNITED might mean. The scene of two men with friendly body language illustrates HAPPY and UNITED. The WHILE, conveying a sense of temporariness and contingency, might have been trickier to explain. Why? The American Numismatic Society.

Grenville's Sugar Act

To find revenue, George Grenville scrutinized the customs service, which monitored the shipping trade and collected all import and export duties. Grenville found that the salaries of customs officers cost the government four times what was collected in revenue. The shortfall was due in part to bribery and smuggling, so Grenville began to insist on rigorous attention to paperwork and a strict accounting of collected duties.

The hardest duty to enforce was the one imposed by the Molasses Act of 1733 — a stiff tax of six pence per gallon on any molasses imported to British colonies from non-British sources. The purpose of the tax was to discourage trade with French Caribbean islands and to redirect the molasses trade to British sugar islands, but it did not work. French molasses remained cheap and abundant because French planters on Martinique and Guadeloupe had no use for it. A by-product of sugar production, molasses was a key ingredient in rum, a drink the French scorned. Rum-loving Americans were eager to buy French molasses, and for decades American importers lined the pockets of customs officials in order to avoid paying the tariffs.

Grenville's inspired solution was the **Revenue Act** of 1764, popularly dubbed the **Sugar Act**. It lowered the duty on French molasses to three pence, making it more attractive for shippers to obey the law, and at the same time raised penalties for smuggling. The act appeared to be in the tradition of navigation acts meant to regulate trade (see chapter 4), but Grenville's actual intent was to raise revenue. He was using an established form of law for new ends and accomplishing his goal by the novel means of lowering a duty.

The Sugar Act toughened enforcement policies. From now on, all British naval crews could act as impromptu customs officers, boarding suspicious ships and seizing cargoes found to be in violation. Smugglers caught without proper paperwork would be prosecuted, not in a local court with a friendly jury but in a vice-admiralty court located in Nova Scotia, where a single judge presided. The implication was that justice would be sure and severe.

Grenville's hopes for the Sugar Act did not materialize. The small decrease in duty did not offset the attractions of smuggling, while the increased vigilance in enforcement led to several ugly confrontations in port cities. Reaction to the Sugar Act foreshadowed questions about Britain's right to tax Americans, but in 1764 objections to the act came principally from the small numbers of Americans engaged in the shipping trades.

From the British point of view, the Sugar Act seemed to be a reasonable effort to administer the colonies. To American shippers, however, the Sugar Act was not just about regulating trade. The British supervision appeared to be a disturbing intrusion into the long-held colonial practice of self-taxation by elected colonial assemblies. Benjamin Franklin, Pennsylvania's lobbyist in London, warned that "two distinct Jurisdictions or Powers of Taxing cannot well subsist together in the same country."

The Stamp Act

By his second year in office, Grenville had made almost no dent in the national debt. So in February 1765, he escalated his revenue program with the **Stamp Act**, precipitating a major conflict between Britain and the colonies over Parliament's right to tax. The Stamp Act imposed a tax on all paper

A Philadelphia Tavern Scene
This trade card advertises the pleasures that await customers at Isaac Jones's tavern on Front Street—smoking and drinking. These men are likely drinking rum, a favorite colonial beverage frequently imbibed in taverns in sociable groups. The Sugar Act of 1763 put into question the supply of West Indies molasses, politicizing an essential ingredient in rum. Library Company of Philadelphia.

used for official documents — newspapers, pamphlets, court documents, licenses, wills, ships' cargo lists — and required an affixed stamp as proof that the tax had been paid. Unlike the Sugar Act, which regulated trade, the Stamp Act was designed plainly and simply to raise money. It affected nearly everyone who used any taxed paper but, most of all, users of official documents in the business and legal communities.

Grenville was no fool. Anticipating that the stamp tax would be unpopular—Thomas Hutchinson had forewarned him — he delegated the administration of the act to Americans, to avoid taxpayer hostility toward British enforcers. In each colony, local stamp distributors would be hired at a handsome salary of 8 percent of the revenue collected.

English tradition held that taxes were a gift of the people to their monarch, granted by the people's representatives. This view of taxes as a freely given gift preserved an essential concept of English political theory: the idea that citizens have the liberty to enjoy and use their property without fear of confiscation. The king could not demand money; only the House of Commons could grant it. Grenville agreed with the notion of taxation by consent, but he argued that the colonists were already "virtually" represented in Parliament. The House of Commons, he insisted, represented all British subjects, wherever they were.

Colonial leaders emphatically rejected this view, arguing that **virtual representation** could not withstand the stretch across the Atlantic. Colonists willingly paid local and provincial taxes, levied by their town, county, or colonial assemblies. Typically, such annual taxes were based on property valuation, with an emphasis on income-generating property, such as numbers of cultivated acres and of livestock. The taxes paid for government administrative expenses and for shared necessities like local roads, schools, and poor relief. In contrast, the stamp tax was a clear departure as a fee-per-document tax, levied by a distant Parliament on unwilling colonies.

Resistance Strategies and Crowd Politics

News of the Stamp Act arrived in the colonies in April 1765, seven months before it was to take effect. There was time, therefore, to object. Governors were unlikely to challenge the law, for most of them owed their office to the king. Instead, the colonial assemblies took the lead; eight of them held discussions on the Stamp Act.

Virginia's assembly, the House of Burgesses, was the first. At the end of its May session, after two-thirds of the members had left, **Patrick Henry**, a young political newcomer, presented a series of resolutions on the Stamp Act that were debated and passed, one by one. They became known as the **Virginia Resolves**. Henry's resolutions inched the assembly toward radical opposition to the Stamp Act. The first three stated the obvious: that Virginians were British citizens, that they enjoyed the same rights and privileges as Britons, and that self-taxation was one of those rights. The fourth resolution noted that Virginians had always taxed themselves, through their representatives in the House of Burgesses. The fifth took a radical leap by pushing the other four unexceptional statements to one logical conclusion — that the Virginia assembly alone had the right to tax Virginians.

Two more fiery resolutions were debated as Henry pressed the logic of his case to the extreme. The sixth resolution denied legitimacy to any tax law originating outside Virginia, and the seventh boldly called anyone who disagreed with these propositions an enemy of Virginia. This was too much for the other representatives. They voted down resolutions six and seven and later rescinded their vote on number five as well.

Their caution hardly mattered, however, because newspapers in other colonies printed all seven Virginia Resolves, creating the impression that a daring first challenge to the Stamp Act had occurred. Consequently, other assemblies were willing to consider even more radical questions, such as this: By what authority could Parliament legislate for the colonies without also taxing them? No one disagreed, in 1765, that Parliament had legislative power over the colonists, who were, after all, British subjects. Several assemblies advanced the argument that there was a distinction between *external* taxes, imposed to regulate trade, and *internal* taxes, such as a stamp tax or a property tax, which could only be self-imposed.

Reaction to the Stamp Act ran far deeper than political debate in assemblies. Every person whose livelihood required official paper had to decide whether to comply with the act. There were only three options: boycotting, which was within the law but impractical because of the reliance on paper; defying the law and using unstamped paper; or preventing distribution of the stamps at the source before the law took effect, thus ensuring universal noncompliance.

Newspapers Protest the Stamp Act
The Stamp Act affected newspapers more than any other business. From New Hampshire to South Carolina, papers issued in late October 1765 featured black mourning lines and funereal symbols to forecast the imminent death of the press. The *Pennsylvania Journal*'s first page was designed as a tombstone complete with skull and cross-bones. A New Hampshire editor dramatically declared, "I must Die, or Submit to that which is worse than Death, Be Stamped, and lose my Freedom." All colonial newspapers resumed publication within a week or two, defiantly operating without stamped paper and with a jubilant sense of the power of the press. Library of Congress.

The first organized resistance to the Stamp Act began in Boston in August 1765 under the direction of town leaders, chief among them **Samuel Adams**, John Hancock, and Ebenezer Mackintosh. The first two, both Harvard graduates, were town officers. Adams, in his forties, had shrewd political instincts and a gift for organizing. Hancock, though not yet thirty, had recently inherited his uncle's shipping business and was one of the wealthiest men in Massachusetts. Mackintosh, the same age as Hancock, was a shoemaker and highly experienced street activist. (See "Seeking the American Promise," page 172.) Many other artisans, tradesmen, printers, tavern keepers, dockworkers, and sailors — the middling and lower orders — mobilized in resistance to the Stamp Act, taking the name "**Sons of Liberty**."

The plan hatched in Boston called for a large street demonstration highlighting a mock execution designed to convince Andrew Oliver, the designated stamp distributor, to resign. On August 14, 1765, a crowd of two thousand to three thousand demonstrators, led by Mackintosh, hung an effigy of Oliver in a tree and then paraded it around town before finally beheading and burning it. In hopes of calming tensions, the royal governor Francis Bernard took no action. The flesh-and-blood Oliver stayed in hiding; the next day he resigned his office in a well-publicized announcement. The Sons of Liberty were elated.

The demonstration provided lessons for everyone. Oliver learned that stamp distributors would be very unpopular people. Governor Bernard, with no police force to call on, learned the limitations of his power to govern. The demonstration's leaders learned that street action was effective. And hundreds of ordinary men not only learned what the Stamp Act was all about but also gained pride in their ability to have a decisive impact on politics.

Twelve days later, a second crowd action showed how well these lessons had been learned. On August 26, a crowd visited the houses of three detested customs and court officials, breaking windows and raiding wine cellars. A fourth target was the finest dwelling in Massachusetts, owned by the stiff-necked lieutenant governor and chief justice **Thomas Hutchinson**. Rumors abounded that Hutchinson had urged Grenville to adopt the Stamp Act. Although he had actually done the opposite, Hutchinson refused to set the record straight, saying curtly, "I am not obliged to give an answer to all the questions that may be put me by every lawless person." The crowd attacked his house, and by daybreak only the exterior walls were standing. Governor Bernard gave orders to call out the militia, but he was told that many militiamen were among the crowd.

The destruction of Hutchinson's house brought a temporary halt to protest activities in Boston. The town meeting issued a statement of sympathy for Hutchinson, but a large reward for the arrest and conviction of rioters failed to produce a single lead. Hutchinson assumed that Mackintosh had led the attack, under orders issued by Samuel Adams, but Adams denied involvement and professed shock at the "truly mobbish Nature" of the violence.

Essentially, the opponents of the Stamp Act in Boston had triumphed; no one replaced Oliver as distributor. When the act took effect on November 1, ships without stamped permits continued to clear the harbor. Since he could not bring the lawbreakers to court, Hutchinson, ever principled, felt obliged to resign his office as chief justice. He remained lieutenant governor, however, and within five years he became the royal governor.

Liberty and Property

Boston's crowd actions of August sparked similar eruptions by groups calling themselves Sons of Liberty in nearly fifty towns throughout the

Symbolic Death to Stamp Agents
Crowds of protesters in many American towns staged threatening demonstrations designed to make any stamp distributor think twice about selling the hated stamps. In this contemporary cartoon, a dummy wearing a hat and waistcoat is being led to destruction. One protester carries a hangman's gallows, another a large bundle of sticks to burn the dummy after it is hanged. Do you think the cartoonist was in sympathy with the demonstrators? Why or why not? Granger Collection.

colonies, and stamp distributors everywhere hastened to resign. A crowd forced one Connecticut distributor to throw his hat and powdered wig in the air while shouting a cheer for "Liberty and property!" This man fared better than another Connecticut stamp agent who was nearly buried alive by Sons of Liberty. Only when the thuds of dirt sounded on his coffin did he have a sudden change of heart, shouting out his resignation to the crowd above. Luckily, he was heard. In Charleston, South Carolina, the stamp distributor resigned after crowds burned effigies and chanted "Liberty! Liberty!" The royal governor of Virginia glumly assessed the situation in a letter to British authorities: "The flame is spread through all the continent, and one colony supports another in their disobedience to superior powers."

Some colonial leaders, disturbed by the riots, sought a more moderate challenge to parliamentary authority. In October 1765, twenty-seven delegates representing nine colonial assemblies met in New York City as the **Stamp Act Congress**. For two weeks, the men hammered out a petition about taxation addressed to the king and Parliament. Their statement closely resembled the first five Virginia Resolves, claiming that taxes were "free gifts of the people," which only the people's representatives could give. They dismissed virtual representation: "The people of these colonies are not, and from their local circumstances, cannot be represented in the House of Commons." At the same time, the delegates carefully affirmed their subordination to Parliament and monarch in deferential language. Nevertheless, the Stamp Act Congress, by the mere fact of its meeting, advanced a radical potential — the notion of intercolonial political action.

The rallying cry of "Liberty and property" made perfect sense to many white Americans of all social ranks, who feared that the Stamp Act threatened their traditional right to liberty as British subjects. The liberty in question was the right to be taxed only by representative government. "Liberty and property" came from a trinity of concepts — "life, liberty, property" — that

> **"The flame is spread through all the continent, and one colony supports another in their disobedience to superior powers."**
> — The royal governor of Virginia

Pursuing Liberty, Protesting Tyranny

In August 1765, a little-known Boston shoemaker gained sudden prominence as the leader of crowd actions opposing the Stamp Act. Ebenezer Mackintosh boldly encouraged thousands of ordinary men in Massachusetts to assert a claim to liberty against what they identified as British tyranny. Mackintosh's story offers a glimpse into the political thinking of the man in the street during the decade of pre-Revolutionary turmoil. By 1776, this quest for liberty would be a defining feature of the fledgling United States.

Born in poverty in 1737, Ebenezer Mackintosh lacked family resources to ease his way in the world. His ancestors arrived in the Puritan migration of the 1630s; a century later, his family was quite poor. Ebenezer's father, an orphan, struggled against bad fortune. He owned no land and lacked a trade; he married and buried wives at least three times. The best he could do for young Ebenezer was to apprentice him to a shoemaker. During the Seven Years' War, Ebenezer joined the army to secure a signing bonus. He saw brief action and returned to Boston in 1758 to resume shoemaking. He was twenty-one.

A major fire in Boston in 1760 marked a dramatic change in direction for Mackintosh. In the aftermath of the fire, the city looked to young, able-bodied men to reinvigorate its volunteer fire companies and picked Ebenezer to join a select firemen's association in the city's South End. Fighting fires demonstrated one's sense of civic duty and manly responsibility. Fire clubs also generated fraternal sociability, with firemen regularly meeting in taverns over pitchers of beer, cementing the team spirit so critical to successful firefighting. Mackintosh proved to be a leader of men in times of emergency; he soon became head of the South End gang, which staged a mock battle once a year against the rival North End gang. In this traditional street festival, Mackintosh gained direct experience managing rowdy crowds.

Expertise in fire and crowd control paved the way for Mackintosh's transition from community leader to community activist in 1765. Stamp Act protests erupted twice in August of that year. In the first event, Mackintosh presided over the mock hanging of a dummy representing Andrew Oliver, the stamp distributor, at a century-old elm tree known as the Liberty Tree. The shoemaker led several thousand protesters in a march on the new stamp office, which was pulled down and burned. Twelve days later, a smaller but far more destructive demonstration almost certainly led by Mackintosh demolished the mansion of Governor Thomas Hutchinson. Hutchinson ordered Mackintosh arrested, but no witnesses cared to identify him. Hours later, the sheriff — a member of Mackintosh's fire company — released him, predicting worse trouble if he was kept in jail.

The shoemaker continued to lead large demonstrations in November and December, forcing Andrew Oliver to repudiate his stamp distributor duties. Ordinary people like Mackintosh exerted a new authority and confidence, commanding their social betters to do their bidding.

In 1766, the Stamp Act was repealed, and Mackintosh went back to shoemaking. He married Elizabeth Maverick and had two children by 1769. Perhaps he took a break from activism; no record links him to protest activities when British troops came to town in 1769–1770, nor was his presence recorded at the Boston Massacre in March 1770. In 1773, he was apparently back at it, bragging later in life that he helped throw tea into Boston harbor.

A well-publicized rumor spread in 1774 that a ship en route from London carried official orders to arrest four rebellious subjects, most notably Samuel Adams and Mackintosh. Adams stayed put, but Mackintosh, still lacking resources and at a low moment in life — his young wife had recently died — decided that flight was his best option. Carrying his two young children and his meager belongings, he walked 150 miles to a village in northern New Hampshire, where he set up shop as a shoemaker. He served locally and briefly as a soldier in the Revolution and then remarried and fathered four more children.

An especially telling clue to Mackintosh's idealization of liberty appears in the unusual name he gave his son born in 1769: Paschal Paoli Mackintosh, named in honor of Pasquale Paoli of Corsica, an anti-monarchical freedom fighter who battled Italian foes and who won approving coverage in American newspapers in 1767–1769. (In those years, some

had come to be regarded as the birthright of freeborn British subjects since at least the seventeenth century. A powerful tradition of British political thought invested representative government with the duty to protect individual lives, liberties, and property against potential abuse by royal authority. Up to 1765, Americans had consented to accept Parliament as a body that represented them. But now, in this matter of taxation via stamps, Parliament seemed a distant body that had failed to protect Americans' liberty and property against royal authority.

Alarmed, some Americans began to speak and write about a plot by British leaders to enslave them. A Maryland writer warned that if the colonies lost "the right of exemption from all taxes without their consent," that loss would "deprive them of every privilege distinguishing

Mackintosh the Fireman

Mackintosh's signature demonstrates his facility with a pen. The woodcut depicts advanced firefighting techniques in Boston in the 1760s. Underground water mains made from bored-out wooden logs brought pond water to Boston's center. Firemen punched a hole in the log to tap the water, moving it via hose and bucket brigade. (A fireplug resealed the hole.) Teams of vigorous men pumped the water with sufficient force to spray it on the fire. Demolition to halt the spread of fires was also essential work. Mackintosh's fire-control skills transferred easily to anti–Stamp Act actions, whether burning effigies and small buildings or pulling down Hutchinson's house. Signature: Publications of the Colonial Society of Massachusetts; fire engine: Granger Collection.

scores of babies throughout the colonies were named Paschal.) Mackintosh enjoyed his brief moment of fame, and he lived to see liberty defined and enshrined in the foundational documents of the United States. Although his life ended in 1816 in obscurity, as it had begun, Mackintosh's activism in 1765 helped ensure that the thousands of people he mobilized learned a new political language of rights and liberties — a language that still resonates loudly today.

Questions for Consideration

1. Why would a twenty-eight-year-old shoemaker of low social status get upset about Britain's passage of the Stamp Act?

2. How likely was it that Mackintosh's wife, Elizabeth Maverick Mackintosh, participated in any of the crowd actions led by her husband?

3. What was at stake for Mackintosh in the American Revolution? What did he gain? What stayed the same?

freemen from slaves." In Virginia, a group of planters headed by Richard Henry Lee issued a document called the Westmoreland Resolves, claiming that the Stamp Act was an attempt "to reduce the people of this country to a state of abject and detestable slavery." The opposite meanings of *liberty* and *slavery* were utterly clear to white Americans, but they stopped short of applying similar logic to the half million black Americans they held in bondage. Many blacks, however, could see the contradiction. When a crowd of Charleston blacks paraded with shouts of "Liberty!" just a few months after white Sons of Liberty had done the same, the town militia turned out to break up the demonstration.

Politicians and merchants in Britain reacted with distress to the American demonstrations and petitions. Merchants particularly feared trade disruptions and pressured Parliament to repeal the Stamp Act. By late 1765, yet another new minister, the Marquess of Rockingham, headed the king's cabinet and sought a way to repeal the act without losing face. The solution came in March 1766: The Stamp Act was repealed, but with the repeal came the **Declaratory Act**, which asserted Parliament's right to legislate for the colonies "in all cases whatsoever." Perhaps the stamp tax had been inexpedient, but the power to tax — one prime case of a legislative power — was stoutly upheld. As yet, the Sugar Act lowered the molasses tax, and the Stamp Act was a complete bust; very little tax revenue had been extracted from the colonies.

> **REVIEW**   Why did the Sugar Act and the Stamp Act draw fierce opposition from colonists?

▶ The Townshend Acts and Economic Retaliation, 1767–1770

Rockingham did not last long as prime minister. By the summer of 1766, George III had persuaded William Pitt to resume that position. Pitt appointed Charles Townshend to be chancellor of the exchequer, the chief financial minister. Facing both the old war debt and the cost of the British troops in America, not successfully shifted to the Americans, Townshend turned again to taxation. But his knowledge of the changing political climate in the colonies was limited, and his plan to raise revenue touched off coordinated boycotts of British goods in 1768 and 1769. Even women were politicized as self-styled "Daughters of Liberty." Boston led the uproar, causing the British to send peacekeeping soldiers to assist the royal governor. The stage was thus set for the first fatalities in the brewing revolution.

The Townshend Duties

Townshend proposed new taxes in the old form of a navigation act. Officially called the Revenue Act of 1767, it established new duties on tea, glass, lead, paper, and painters' colors imported into the colonies, to be paid by the importer but passed on to consumers in the retail price. A

year before, the duty on French molasses had been reduced from three pence to one pence per gallon, and finally the Sugar Act was pulling in a tidy revenue of about £45,000 annually. Townshend naively assumed that external taxes on transatlantic trade would be acceptable to Americans.

The **Townshend duties** were not especially burdensome, but the principle they embodied — taxation through trade duties — looked different to the colonists in the wake of the Stamp Act crisis. Although Americans once distinguished between external and internal taxes, accepting external duties as a means to direct the flow of trade, that distinction was wiped out by an external tax meant only to raise money. John Dickinson, a Philadelphia lawyer, articulated this view in a series of articles titled *Letters from a Farmer in Pennsylvania*, widely circulated in late 1767. "We are taxed without our consent. . . . We are therefore — SLAVES," Dickinson wrote, calling for "a total denial of the power of Parliament to lay upon these colonies any 'tax' whatever."

A controversial provision of the Townshend duties directed that some of the revenue generated would pay the salaries of royal governors. Before 1767, local assemblies set the salaries of their own officials, giving them significant influence over crown-appointed officeholders. Through his new provision, Townshend aimed to strengthen the governors' position as well as to curb what he perceived to be the growing independence of the assemblies.

The New York assembly, for example, seemed particularly defiant. It refused to enforce Parliament's Quartering Act of 1765, which directed the colonies to shelter and supply British regiments still based in America. This was effectively a tax levied without consent, the assembly argued, because it required New Yorkers to pay money by order of Parliament. In response, Townshend pushed through the New York Suspending Act, which declared all the assembly's acts null and void until it met its obligations to the army. Both measures — the new compensation model for royal governors and the suspension of the governance functions of the New York assembly — struck a chill throughout the colonies. Many wondered whether legislative government was at all secure.

Massachusetts again took the lead in protesting the Townshend duties. Samuel Adams, now an elected member of the provincial assembly, argued that any form of parliamentary taxation was unjust because Americans were not represented in Parliament. Further, he argued that the new way to pay governors' salaries subverted the proper relationship between the people and their rulers. The assembly circulated a letter with Adams's arguments to other colonial assemblies for their endorsement. As with the Stamp Act Congress of 1765, colonial assemblies were starting to coordinate their protests.

In response to Adams's letter, Lord Hillsborough, the new man in charge of colonial affairs in Britain, instructed Massachusetts governor Bernard to dissolve the assembly if it refused to repudiate the letter. The assembly refused, by a vote of 92 to 17, and Bernard carried out his instruction. In the summer of 1768, Boston was in an uproar.

Nonconsumption and the Daughters of Liberty

The Boston town meeting led the way with **nonconsumption agreements** calling for a boycott of all British-made goods. Dozens of other towns passed similar resolutions in 1767 and 1768. For example, prohibited purchases in the town of New Haven, Connecticut, included carriages, furniture, hats, clothing, lace, clocks, and textiles. The idea was to encourage home manufacture and to hurt trade, causing London merchants to pressure Parliament for repeal of the duties.

Nonconsumption agreements were very hard to enforce. With the Stamp Act, there was one hated item, a stamp, and a limited number of official distributors. In contrast, an agreement to boycott all British goods required serious personal sacrifice. Some merchants were wary because it hurt their pocketbooks, and a few continued to import in readiness for the end of nonconsumption (or to sell on the side to people choosing to ignore the boycotts). In Boston, such merchants found themselves blacklisted in newspapers and broadsides.

A more direct blow to trade came from nonimportation agreements, but getting merchants to agree to these proved more difficult, because of fears that merchants in other colonies might continue to import goods and make handsome profits. Not until late 1768 could Boston merchants agree to suspend trade through a nonimportation agreement lasting one year starting January 1, 1769. Sixty signed the agreement. New York merchants soon followed suit, as did Philadelphia and Charleston merchants in 1769.

Doing without British products, whether luxury goods, tea, or textiles, no doubt was a hardship. But it also presented an opportunity,

Edenton Tea Ladies
American women in many communities renounced British apparel and tea during the early 1770s. Women in Edenton, North Carolina, publicized their pledge and drew hostile fire in the form of a British cartoon. The cartoon's message is that brazen women who meddled in politics would undermine their femininity. Neglected babies, urinating dogs, wanton sexuality, and mean-looking women would be some of the dire consequences, according to the artist. The cartoon works as humor for the British because of the gender reversals it predicts and because of the insult it directs at American men. Library of Congress.

for many of the British products specified in nonconsumption agreements were household goods traditionally under the control of the "ladies." By 1769, male leaders in the patriot cause clearly understood that women's cooperation in nonconsumption and home manufacture was beneficial to their cause. The Townshend duties thus provided an unparalleled opportunity for encouraging female patriotism. During the Stamp Act crisis, Sons of Liberty took to the streets in protest. During the difficulties of 1768 and 1769, the concept of **Daughters of Liberty** emerged to give shape to a new idea — that women might play a role in public affairs. Any woman could express affiliation with the colonial protest through conspicuous boycotts of British-made goods. In Boston, more than three hundred women signed a petition to abstain from tea, "sickness excepted," in order to "save this abused Country from Ruin and Slavery." A nine-year-old girl visiting the royal governor's house in New Jersey took the tea she was offered, curtsied, and tossed the beverage out a nearby window.

> **A nine-year-old girl visiting the royal governor's house in New Jersey took the tea she was offered, curtsied, and tossed the beverage out a nearby window.**

Homespun cloth became a prominent symbol of patriotism. A young Boston girl learning to spin called herself "a daughter of liberty," noting that "I chuse to wear as much of our own manufactory as pocible." In the boycott period of 1768 to 1770, newspapers reported on spinning matches, or bees, in some sixty New England towns, in which women came together in public to make yarn. Nearly always, the bee was held at the local minister's house, and the yarn produced was charitably handed over to him for distribution to the poor. Newspaper accounts variously called the spinners "Daughters of Liberty" or "Daughters of Industry."

This surge of public spinning was related to the politics of the boycott, which infused traditional women's work with new political purpose. But the women spinners were not equivalents of the Sons of Liberty. The Sons marched in streets, burned effigies, threatened hated officials, and celebrated anniversaries of their successes with raucous drinking in taverns. The Daughters manifested their patriotism quietly, in ways marked by piety, industry, and charity. The difference was due in part to cultural ideals of gender, which prized masculine self-assertion and feminine selflessness. It also was due to class. The Sons were a cross-class alliance, with leaders from the middling orders reliant on men and boys of the lower ranks to fuel their crowds. The Daughters dusting off spinning wheels and shelving their teapots were genteel ladies accustomed to buying British goods. The difference between the Sons and the Daughters also speaks to two views of how best to challenge authority: violent threats and street actions, or the self-disciplined, self-sacrificing boycott of goods?

On the whole, the anti-British boycotts were a success. Imports fell by more than 40 percent; British merchants felt the pinch and let Parliament know it. In Boston, the Hutchinson family — whose fortune rested on British trade — also endured losses, but even more alarming to the lieutenant governor, Boston seemed overrun with anti-British sentiment. The Sons of Liberty staged rollicking annual celebrations of the Stamp Act riot, and both Hutchinson and Governor Bernard concluded that British troops were necessary to restore order.

Military Occupation and "Massacre" in Boston

In the fall of 1768, Britain sent three thousand uniformed troops to occupy Boston. The soldiers drilled conspicuously on the town Common, played loud music on the Sabbath, and in general grated on the nerves of Bostonians. Although the situation was frequently   tense, no

Spinning Wheel
This wheel, used for spinning flax into linen thread, is likely the type used in the politicized 1768–1769 spinning bees in which Daughters of Liberty proclaimed their boycott of British textiles. The spinning Daughters of Liberty were praised for their virtuous industry. Responding to such praise, one young woman complained about her male counterparts: "Alas! We hear nothing of their working matches, nothing of their concern for the honor of their King or for the safety or liberties of their country." Instead, the news was of "nocturnal Carousals and Exploits; of their drinking, gaming & whoring matches; and how they disturb the quiet of honest people." Smithsonian Institution, Washington, D.C.

"Perspective View of the Boston Commons, October 1, 1768"
The first regiment of British soldiers arrived in Boston on October 1, sent to maintain law and order. Christian Remick, amateur artist, captured that first moment of uneasy contact. Locals stroll on the Boston Commons—families, dogs, romancing couples—eyeing the soldiers at their tented encampment. The redcoated soldiers, no doubt glad to be on land after their journey at sea, drill with their weapons. Even in this crude rendering, the bayonets on their guns stand out. Mather Byles, a local minister and wit, remarked that the Bostonians had wished for a "redress of grievances, which grievances had returned red-dressed." Photograph courtesy of the Concord Museum, Concord, MA.

major troubles occurred that winter and through most of 1769. But as January 1, 1770, approached, marking the end of the nonimportation agreement, it was clear that some merchants—such as Thomas Hutchinson's two sons, both importers — were ready to break the boycott.

Trouble began in January, when a crowd defaced the door of the Hutchinson brothers' shop with "Hillsborough paint," a potent mixture of human excrement and urine. In February, a crowd surrounded the house of customs official Ebenezer Richardson, who panicked and fired a musket, accidentally killing a young boy passing on the street. The Sons of Liberty mounted a massive funeral procession to mark this first instance of violent death in the struggle with Britain.

For the next week, tension gripped Boston. The climax came on Monday evening, March 5, 1770, when a crowd taunted eight British soldiers

guarding the customs house. Onlookers threw snowballs and rocks and dared the soldiers to fire; finally one did. After a short pause, someone yelled "Fire!" and the other soldiers shot into the crowd, hitting eleven men, killing five of them.

The **Boston Massacre**, as the event quickly became called, was over in minutes. In the immediate aftermath, Hutchinson (now acting governor after Bernard's recall to Britain) showed courage in addressing the crowd from the balcony of the statehouse. He quickly removed the regiments to an island in the harbor to prevent further bloodshed, and he jailed Captain Thomas Preston and his eight soldiers for their own protection, promising they would be held for trial.

The Sons of Liberty staged elaborate martyrs' funerals for the five victims. Significantly, the one nonwhite victim shared equally in the public's

VISUAL ACTIVITY

The Bloody Massacre Perpetrated in King Street, Boston, on March 5, 1770
This mass-produced engraving by Paul Revere sold for sixpence per copy. In this patriot version of events, the soldiers are posed as a firing squad, shooting under orders at an unarmed and bewigged crowd. Actually, the shots were chaotic, and the five fatalities were all from the lower orders of youth and laborers, not the sort to wear wigs. Among them was Crispus Attucks, a dockworker of African and Indian ethnicity, but Revere shows only whites among the wounded and dead.
Anne S. K. Brown Military Collection, Providence, RI.

READING THE IMAGE: How does this picture attempt to sway its viewers' sympathies?
CONNECTIONS: Does this picture accurately represent the events of the Boston Massacre? What might account for its biases?

veneration. Crispus Attucks, a sailor and rope maker in his forties, was the son of an African man and a Natick Indian woman. A slave in his youth, he was at the time of his death a free laborer at the Boston docks. Attucks was one of the first American partisans to die in the revolutionary struggle with Britain, and certainly the first African American.

The trial of the eight soldiers came in the fall of 1770. They were defended by two young Boston attorneys, Samuel Adams's cousin John Adams and Josiah Quincy. Because Adams and Quincy had direct ties to the leadership of the Sons of Liberty, their decision to defend the British soldiers at first seems odd. But Adams was deeply committed to the idea that even unpopular defendants deserved a fair trial. Samuel Adams respected his cousin's decision to take the case, for there was a tactical benefit as well. It showed that the Boston leadership was not lawless but could be seen as defenders of British liberty and law.

The five-day trial resulted in acquittal for Preston and for all but two of the soldiers, who were convicted of manslaughter, branded on the thumbs, and released. Nothing materialized in the trial to indicate a conspiracy or concerted plan to provoke trouble by either the British or the Sons of Liberty. To this day, the question of responsibility for the Boston Massacre remains obscure.

REVIEW   Why did British authorities send troops to occupy Boston in the fall of 1768?

▶ The Destruction of the Tea and the Coercive Acts, 1770–1774

In the same week as the Boston Massacre, yet another new British prime minister, Frederick North, acknowledged the harmful impact of the boycott on trade and recommended repeal of the Townshend duties. A skillful politician, Lord North took office in 1770 and kept it for twelve years; at last King George had stability at the helm. Seeking peace with the colonies and prosperity for British merchants, North persuaded Parliament to remove all the duties except the tax on tea, kept as a symbol of Parliament's power.

The renewal of trade and the return of co-operation between Britain and the colonies gave men like Thomas Hutchinson hope that the worst of the crisis was behind them. For nearly two years, peace seemed possible, but tense incidents in 1772, followed by a renewed struggle over the tea tax in 1773, precipitated a full-scale crisis in the summer and fall of 1774.

The Calm before the Storm

Repeal of the Townshend duties brought an end to nonimportation. Trade boomed in 1770 and 1771, driven by pent-up demand. Moreover, the leaders of the popular movement seemed to be losing their power. Samuel Adams, for example, ran for a minor local office and lost to a conservative merchant. Then in 1772, several incidents again brought the conflict with Britain into sharp focus. One was the burning of the *Gaspée*, a Royal Navy ship pursuing suspected smugglers near Rhode Island. A British investigating commission failed to arrest anyone but announced that it would send suspects, if any were found, to Britain for trial on charges of high treason. This ruling seemed to fly in the face of the traditional English right to trial by a jury of one's peers.

When news of the *Gaspée* investigation spread, it was greeted with disbelief in other colonies. Patrick Henry, Thomas Jefferson, and Richard Henry Lee in the Virginia House of Burgesses proposed that a network of standing committees be established to link the colonies and pass along alarming news. By mid-1773, every colonial assembly except Pennsylvania's had a "committee of correspondence."

Another British action in 1772 further spread the communications network. Lord North proposed to pay the salaries of superior court justices out of the tea revenue, similar to Townshend's plan for paying royal governors. The Boston town meeting, fearful that judges would now be improperly influenced by their new paymasters, established a committee of correspondence and urged all Massachusetts towns to do likewise. The first message, circulated in December 1772, attacked the salary policy for judges as the latest proof of a sinister British conspiracy to undermine traditional liberties: first taxation without consent, followed by military occupation, a massacre, and now a plot to subvert the justice system. By spring 1773, more than half the towns in Massachusetts had set up **committees of correspondence**, providing local forums for debate.

These committees politicized ordinary townspeople, sparking a revolutionary language of rights and constitutional duties. They also bypassed the official flow of power and information through the colony's royal government.

The final incident shattering the relative calm of the early 1770s was the **Tea Act of 1773**. Americans had resumed buying the taxed British tea, but they were also smuggling large quantities of Dutch tea, cutting into the sales of Britain's East India Company. So Lord North proposed legislation giving favored status to the East India Company, allowing it to sell tea directly to a few selected merchants in four colonial cities, cutting out British middlemen. The appointed agents would resell the tea, collecting the three pence tax that had its origins in the Townshend duty on tea of 1767. The reduced shipping costs would lower the final price of the East India tea below that of smuggled Dutch tea, thus motivating Americans to obey the law.

Tea in Boston Harbor

In the fall of 1773, news of the Tea Act reached the colonies. Parliamentary legislation to make tea inexpensive struck many colonists as an insidious plot to trick Americans into buying the dutied tea. The real goal, some argued, was the increased revenue that would pay the salaries of royal governors and judges. The Tea Act was thus a painful reminder of Parliament's claim to the power to tax and legislate for the colonies.

But how to resist the Tea Act? Nonimportation was not viable, because the tea trade was too lucrative to expect merchants to give it up willingly. Consumer boycotts seemed ineffective, because it was impossible to distinguish between dutied tea (the object of the boycott) and smuggled tea (illegal but politically clean) once it was in the teapot. The appointment of official tea agents, parallel to the Stamp Act distributors, suggested one solution. In Charleston, Philadelphia, and New York, revived Sons of Liberty pressured tea agents to resign. Without agents, governors yielded, and tea cargoes either landed duty-free or were sent home.

Governor Hutchinson, however, would not bend any rules. Three ships bearing tea arrived in Boston in November 1773. The ships cleared customs, and the crews, sensing the town's extreme tension, unloaded all cargo except the tea. The captains wished to leave Boston with their tea on board, but because the ships had already cleared customs, Hutchinson would not grant them passage without paying the tea duty.

Tossing the Tea
This colored English engraving shows Boston men in Indian disguise dumping tea chests into the harbor. A large crowd on the shore cheers them on. The red rowboat stacked with chests suggests that the raiders were stealing as well as destroying the tea. This event was not dubbed the "Tea Party" until the 1830s, when a later generation celebrated the illegal destruction of the tea and made heroes out of the few surviving participants, by then well into their eighties. The bottle at right was a souvenir item of the 1830s, with tea leaves said to have been salvaged from that fateful night.
Engraving: Library of Congress; bottle: © Massachusetts Historical Society/The Bridgeman Art Library.

To add to the difficulties, another long-standing law imposed a time limit on ships in the harbor. After twenty days, the required duty had to be paid, or local authorities would confiscate the cargo.

For the full twenty days, pressure built in Boston. Daily mass meetings energized citizens from Boston and surrounding towns, alerted by the committees of correspondence. On the final day, December 16, when for a final time Hutchinson refused clearance for the ships, a large crowd gathered at Old South Church to debate a course of action. No official plan was agreed on at that meeting, but immediately following it, 100 to 150 men, disguised as Indians, boarded the ships and dumped thousands of pounds of tea into the harbor while a crowd of 2,000 watched. In admiration, John Adams wrote: "This Destruction of the Tea is so bold, so daring, so firm, intrepid and inflexible, and it must have so important Consequences."

The Coercive Acts

Lord North's response was swift and stern: He persuaded Parliament to issue the **Coercive Acts**, four laws meant to punish Massachusetts for destroying the tea. In America, those laws, along with a fifth one, the Quebec Act, were soon known as the **Intolerable Acts**.

The first act, the Boston Port Act, closed Boston harbor to all shipping as of June 1, 1774, until the destroyed tea was paid for. Britain's objective was to halt the commercial life of the city.

The second act, called the Massachusetts Government Act, greatly altered the colony's charter, underscoring Parliament's claim to supremacy over Massachusetts. The royal governor's powers were augmented, and the governor's council became an appointive, rather than elective, body. Further, the governor could now appoint all judges, sheriffs, and officers of the court. No town meeting beyond the annual spring election of town selectmen could be held without the governor's approval, and every agenda item required prior approval. Every Massachusetts town was affected.

The third Coercive Act, the Impartial Administration of Justice Act, stipulated that any royal official accused of a capital crime — for example, Captain Preston and his soldiers at the Boston Massacre — would be tried in a court in Britain. It did not matter that Preston had received a fair trial in Boston. What this act ominously suggested was that down the road, more Captain Prestons and soldiers might be firing into unruly crowds.

The fourth act amended the 1765 Quartering Act and permitted military commanders to lodge soldiers wherever necessary, even in private households. In a related move, Lord North appointed General **Thomas Gage**, commander of the Royal Army in New York, as governor of Massachusetts. Thomas Hutchinson was out, relieved at long last of his duties. Military rule, including soldiers, returned once more to Boston.

The fifth act, the Quebec Act, had nothing to do with the four Coercive Acts, but it fed American fears. It confirmed the continuation of French civil law and government form, as well as Catholicism, for Quebec — an affront to Protestant New Englanders who had recently been denied their own representative government. The act also gave Quebec control of disputed land (and the lucrative fur trade) throughout the Ohio Valley, land also claimed by Virginia, Pennsylvania, and a number of Indian tribes.

The five Intolerable Acts spread alarm in all the colonies. If Britain could squelch Massachusetts — change its charter, suspend local government, inaugurate military rule, and on top of that give Ohio to Catholic Quebec — what liberties were secure? Fearful royal governors in a half dozen colonies dismissed the sitting assemblies, adding to the sense of urgency. A few of the assemblies defiantly continued to meet in new locations. Through the committees of correspondence, colonial leaders arranged to convene in Philadelphia in September 1774 to respond to the crisis.

Beyond Boston: Rural New England

Well before the delegates assembled in Philadelphia, all of New England had arrived at the brink of open insurrection. With a British general occupying the Massachusetts governorship and some three thousand troops controlling Boston, the revolutionary momentum shifted from urban radicals to rural farmers who protested

Hutchinson the Traitor Faces Death
This hideous engraving enlivened the cover of an almanac published in Boston in December 1773, during the high drama over tea. It shows Thomas Hutchinson with the devil behind him holding up a list of his many crimes and a skeleton representing death about to spear him. The caption below the picture read: "The wicked Statesman, or the Traitor to his Country, at the Hour of DEATH." On page 2, readers of this anti-Hutchinson diatribe were invited to think about "the Horrors that Man must endure, who owes his Greatness to his Country's Ruin." The color here is probably a later addition. Granger Collection.

the Massachusetts Government Act in dozens of spontaneous, dramatic showdowns. To get around the prohibition on new meetings, some towns refused to adjourn their last authorized town meeting. More defiant towns just ignored the law. Gage's call for elections for a new provincial assembly under his control sparked elections for a competing unauthorized assembly.

In all Massachusetts counties except one, crowds of thousands of armed men converged to prevent the opening of county courts run by crown-appointed jurists. No judges were physically harmed, but they were forced to resign and made to doff their judicial wigs or run a humiliating gantlet. In Suffolk County, the courts met in troop-filled Boston, making mass intimidation of judges impossible. One by one, however, the citizen jurors called to serve in court refused. By August 1774, farmers and artisans all over Massachusetts had effectively taken full control of their local institutions.

Unfettered by the crown, ordinary citizens throughout New England began serious planning for the showdown everyone assumed would come. Town militias stockpiled gunpowder "in case of invasion." Militia officers repudiated their official chain of command to the governor and stepped up drills of their units. Town after town withheld its tax money from the royal governor and diverted it to military supplies. Governor Gage felt under heavy threat, but he could do little. He beefed up fortifications around Boston and in general rattled his sword loudly, praying for reinforcements from Britain.

At this point in the struggle, confrontations did not lead to bloodshed. But one incident, the Powder Alarm, nearly provoked violence and showed how close New England farmers were to armed insurrection. On September 1, 1774, Gage sent troops to capture a supply of gunpowder just outside Boston. In the surprise and scramble of the attack, false news spread that the troops had fired on men defending the powder, killing six. Within twenty-four hours, several thousand armed men from Massachusetts, New Hampshire, and Connecticut streamed on foot to Boston to avenge the first blood spilled. At this moment, ordinary men became insurgents, willing to kill or be killed in the face of the British clampdown. Once the error was corrected and the crisis defused, the men returned home peaceably. But Gage could no longer doubt the speed, numbers, and deadly determination of the rebellious subjects.

> "We ask only for peace, liberty and security. We wish no diminution of royal prerogatives, we demand no new rights."
> — The First Continental Congress

All this had occurred without orchestration by Boston radicals, Gage reported. But British leaders found it hard to believe, as one put it, that "a tumultuous Rabble, without any Appearance of general Concert, or without any Head to advise, or Leader to conduct" could pull off such effective resistance. Repeatedly in the years to come, the British would seriously underestimate their opponents.

The First Continental Congress

Every colony except Georgia sent delegates to Philadelphia in September 1774 to discuss the looming crisis in what was later called the First Continental Congress. The gathering included notables such as Samuel Adams and John Adams from Massachusetts and George Washington and Patrick Henry from Virginia. A few colonies purposely sent men who opposed provoking Britain, such as Pennsylvania's Joseph Galloway, to keep the congress from becoming too radical.

Delegates sought to articulate their liberties as British subjects and the powers Parliament held over them, and they debated possible responses to the Coercive Acts. Some wanted a total ban on trade with Britain to force repeal, while others, especially southerners dependent on tobacco and rice exports, opposed halting trade. Samuel Adams and Patrick Henry were eager for a ringing denunciation of all parliamentary control. The conservative Joseph Galloway proposed a plan (quickly defeated) to create a secondary parliament in America to assist the British Parliament in ruling the colonies.

The congress met for seven weeks and produced a declaration of rights couched in traditional language: "We ask only for peace, liberty and security. We wish no diminution of royal prerogatives, we demand no new rights." But from Britain's point of view, the rights assumed already to exist were radical. Chief among them was the claim that Americans were not represented in Parliament and so each colonial government had the sole right to govern and tax its own people. The one slight concession to Britain was a carefully worded agreement that the colonists would "cheerfully consent" to trade regulations for the larger good of the empire, so long as trade regulation was not a covert means of raising revenue.

To put pressure on Britain, the delegates agreed to a staggered and limited boycott of trade: imports prohibited this year, exports the following, and rice totally exempted (to keep South Carolinians happy). To enforce the boycott, they called for a Continental Association, with chapters in each town variously called committees of public safety or of inspection, to monitor all commerce and punish suspected violators of the boycott (sometimes with a bucket of tar and a bag of feathers). Its work done in under two months, the congress disbanded in late October, with agreement to reconvene the following May.

The committees of public safety, the committees of correspondence, the regrouped colonial assemblies, and the Continental Congress were all political bodies functioning defiantly without any constitutional authority. British officials did not recognize them as legitimate, but many Americans who supported the patriot cause instantly accepted them. A key reason for the stability of such unauthorized governing bodies was that they were composed of many of the same men who had held elective office before.

Britain's severe reaction to Boston's destruction of the tea finally succeeded in making many colonists from New Hampshire to Georgia realize that the problems of British rule went far beyond questions of nonconsensual taxation. The Coercive Acts infringed on liberty and denied self-government; they could not be ignored. With one colony already subordinated to military rule and a British army at the ready in Boston, the threat of a general war was on the doorstep.

REVIEW   Why did Parliament pass the Coercive Acts in 1774?

▶ Domestic Insurrections, 1774–1775

Before the Second Continental Congress could meet, violence and bloodshed came to Massachusetts. Fearing the threat of domestic insurrection, General (and Governor) Thomas Gage requested more troops from Britain and prepared to subdue rebellion. On the other side, New England farmers prepared to defend their homes against an intrusive power they feared was bent on enslaving them. To the south, a different and inverted version of the same story began to unfold, as thousands of enslaved black men and women seized an unprecedented opportunity to mount a different kind of insurrection — against planter-patriots who looked over their shoulders uneasily whenever they called out for liberty from the British.

The British Retreat from Concord, April 19, 1775
Two young self-trained artists hustled to Concord and Lexington some ten days after the clash that touched off the American Revolution. After interviewing witnesses, 18-year-old Ralph Earle sketched scenes and 21-year-old Amos Doolittle, a silversmith, transferred them to copper engraving plates for mass production. This scene depicts British soldiers streaming toward Boston and under ambush by American insurgents firing from behind a stone wall. The British set fire to several houses suspected of harboring snipers. Doolittle's set of four engravings went on sale in December 1775.
Miriam and Ira D. Wallach Division of Art, Prints and Photographs, The New York Public Library. Astor, Lenox and Tilden Foundations.

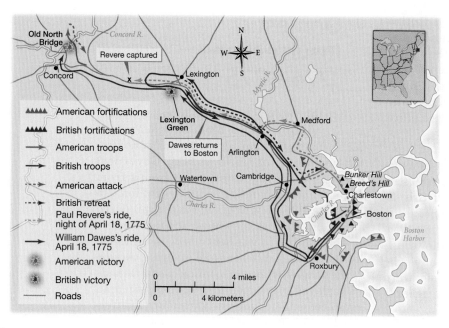

MAP ACTIVITY

MAP 6.3 Lexington and Concord, April 1775
When British soldiers left Boston to raid a suspected arms supply in Concord, Paul Revere and William Dawes set out to warn the patriots. Revere went by boat from Boston to Charlestown and then by horse through Medford to Lexington. Dawes casually passed British sentries guarding the narrow land route out of Boston and then rode his horse at full speed to Lexington. Once there, Revere and Dawes urged Samuel Adams and John Hancock, guests in a Lexington home, to flee to avoid capture. The two couriers then went on to Concord to warn residents of the impending attack.

READING THE MAP: How did Dawes's route differ from Revere's? What kinds of terrain and potential dangers did each man face during his ride, according to the map?
CONNECTIONS: Why send two men on the same mission? Why not send four or more?

Lexington and Concord

During the winter of 1774–75, Americans pressed on with boycotts. Optimists hoped to effect a repeal of the Coercive Acts; pessimists stockpiled arms and ammunition. In Massachusetts, militia units known as minutemen prepared to respond at a minute's notice to any threat from the British troops in Boston.

> **"A phrenzy of revenge seems to have seized all ranks of people."**
> — THOMAS JEFFERSON, on the Battles of Lexington and Concord

Thomas Gage soon realized how desperate the British position was. The people, Gage wrote to Lord North, were "numerous, worked up to a fury, and not a Boston rabble but the freeholders and farmers of the country." Gage requested twenty thousand reinforcements. He also strongly advised repeal of the Coercive Acts, but leaders in Britain could not admit failure. Instead, in mid-April 1775, they ordered Gage to arrest the troublemakers immediately, before the Americans got better organized.

Gage quickly planned a surprise attack on a suspected ammunition storage site at Concord, a village eighteen miles west of Boston (Map 6.3). Near midnight on April 18, 1775, more than fifteen hundred British soldiers moved west across the Charles River. Boston silversmith Paul Revere and William Dawes, a tanner, learned of the attack by a prearranged signal, two lanterns hung in a church belfry, and they raced ahead to alert the minutemen. When the British arrived at **Lexington**, a village five miles east of **Concord**, they were met by some seventy armed men assembled on the village green. The British commander barked out, "Lay down your arms, you damned rebels, and disperse." The militiamen hesitated and began to comply, turning to leave the green, but then someone — nobody knows who — fired. In the next two minutes, more firing left eight Americans dead and ten wounded.

The British units continued their march to Concord, any pretense of surprise gone. Three companies of minutemen nervously occupied the town center but offered no challenge to the British, who searched in vain for the ammunition. Finally, at Old North Bridge in Concord, British troops and three hundred to four hundred local minutemen exchanged shots, killing two Americans and three British soldiers.

By now, both sides were very apprehensive. The British failed to find the expected arms, and the Americans failed to stop their raid. As the British returned to Boston, militia units from the countryside converged on the Concord road and ambushed them, bringing the bloodiest fighting of the day. In the end, 273 British soldiers were wounded or dead; the toll for the Americans stood at about 95. It was April 19, 1775, and the war had begun.

Rebelling against Slavery

News of the battles of Lexington and Concord spread rapidly. Within eight days, Virginians had heard of the fighting, and, as Thomas Jefferson reflected, "a phrenzy of revenge seems to have

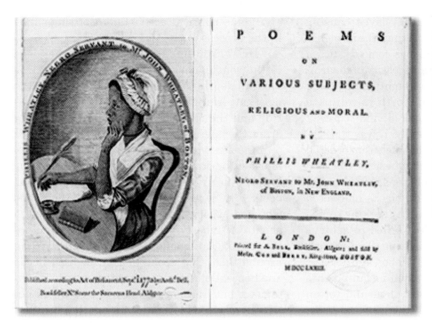

Phillis Wheatley's Title Page
Phillis, born in Africa, became the slave of John Wheatley at age seven. Remarkably gifted in English, she wrote poetry and could read the Bible with ease by age sixteen. Her master took her to London in 1773, where this book of poems was published, gaining her great literary notice. The Wheatleys freed Phillis, who then married a free black man; two of their three children died in infancy, and her husband deserted her. Poetry alone could not support her, and she found work in a boardinghouse. By the end of 1784, Phillis and her remaining child had died. Library of Congress.

seized all ranks of people." The royal governor of Virginia, **Lord Dunmore**, removed a large quantity of gunpowder from the Williamsburg powder house and put it on a ship in the dead of night, out of reach of any frenzied Virginians. Next, he threatened to arm slaves, if necessary, to ward off attacks by colonists.

This was an effective threat; Dunmore understood full well how to produce panic among planters. In November 1775, he issued an official proclamation promising freedom to defecting able-bodied slaves who would fight for the British. Although Dunmore wanted to scare the planters, he had no intention of liberating all the slaves or starting a real slave rebellion. Female, young, and elderly slaves were not welcome to flee, and many were sent back to face irate masters. Astute blacks noticed that Dunmore neglected to free his own slaves. A Virginia barber named Caesar declared that "he did not know any one foolish enough to believe him [Dunmore], for if he intended to do so, he ought first to set his own free." By December 1775, around fifteen hundred slaves in Virginia had fled to Lord Dunmore, who armed them and called them his "Ethiopian Regiment." Camp diseases quickly set in: dysentery, typhoid fever, and smallpox. When Dunmore sailed for England in mid-1776, he took just three hundred black survivors with him. But the association of freedom with the British authorities had been established, and throughout the war thousands more southern slaves made bold to run away as soon as they heard the British army was approaching.

In the northern colonies as well, slaves clearly recognized the evolving political struggle with Britain as an ideal moment to bid for freedom. A twenty-one-year-old Boston domestic slave employed biting sarcasm in a 1774 newspaper essay to call attention to the hypocrisy of local slave owners: "How well the Cry for Liberty, and the reverse Disposition for exercise of oppressive Power over others agree, — I humbly think it does not require the Penetration of a Philosopher to Determine." This extraordinary young woman, **Phillis Wheatley**, had already gained international recognition through a book of poems endorsed by Governor Thomas Hutchinson and Boston merchant John Hancock and published in London in 1773. Possibly neither man fully appreciated the irony of his endorsement, however, for Wheatley's poems spoke of "Fair Freedom" as the "Goddess long desir'd" by Africans enslaved in America. At the urging of his wife, Wheatley's master freed the young poet in 1775.

Wheatley's poetic ideas about freedom found concrete expression among other discontented groups. Some slaves in Boston petitioned Thomas Gage, promising to fight for the British if he would liberate them. Gage turned them down. In Ulster County, New York, along the Hudson River, two blacks were overheard discussing gunpowder, and thus a plot unraveled that involved at least twenty slaves in four villages discovered to have ammunition stashed away.

In Maryland, soon after the news of the Lexington battle arrived, blacks exhibited impatience with their status as slaves, causing one Maryland planter to report that "the insolence of the Negroes in this county is come to such a height, that we are under a necessity of disarming them. . . . We took about eighty guns, some bayonets, swords, etc." In North Carolina, a planned uprising was uncovered, and scores of slaves were arrested. Ironically, it was the revolutionary committee of public safety that ordered the whippings to punish this quest for liberty.

By 1783, when the Revolutionary War ended, as many as twenty thousand blacks had voted against slavery with their feet by seeking refuge with the British army. Most failed to achieve the liberation they were seeking. The British generally used them for menial labor, and disease, especially smallpox, devastated encampments of runaways. But some eight thousand to ten thousand persisted through the war and later, under the protection of the British army, left America to start new lives of freedom in Canada's Nova Scotia or Africa's Sierra Leone.

> **REVIEW**   How did enslaved people in the colonies react to the stirrings of revolution?

▶ Conclusion: The Long Road to Revolution

In the aftermath of the Seven Years' War, Britain and its American colonies were victorious, but almost none of the warring parties came away satisfied. France lost vast amounts of North American land claims, and Indian land rights were increasingly violated or ignored. As for the victors, Britain's huge war debt and subsequent revenue-generating policies distressed Americans and set the stage for the imperial crisis of the 1760s and 1770s. The years 1763 to 1775 brought repeated attempts by the British government to subordinate the colonies into contributing partners in the larger scheme of empire.

American resistance to British policies grew slowly but steadily. In 1765, loyalist Thomas Hutchinson shared with patriot Samuel Adams the belief that it was exceedingly unwise for Britain to assert a right to taxation because Parliament did not adequately represent Americans. By temperament and office, Hutchinson was obliged to uphold British policy. Adams, in contrast, protested the policy

and made political activists out of thousands in the process.

By 1775, events propelled many Americans to the conclusion that a concerted effort was afoot to deprive them of all their liberties, the most important of which were the right to self-rule and the right to live free of an occupying army. Prepared to die for those liberties, hundreds of minutemen converged on Concord. April 19 marked the start of their rebellion.

Another rebellion under way in 1775 was doomed to be short-circuited. Black Americans who had experienced actual slavery listened to shouts of "Liberty!" from white crowds and appropriated the language of revolution swirling around them that spoke to their deepest needs and hopes. Defiance of authority was indeed contagious, but freedom for black slaves would not be fully granted in America for nearly a century.

In 1765, patriot leaders had wanted a correction, a restoration of the ancient liberty of self-taxation, but events over the next decade convinced many that a return to the old ways was impossible. Challenging Parliament's right to tax had led, step-by-step, to challenging Parliament's right to legislate over the colonies in any matter. By 1774, many in New England were willing to shoulder guns and risk death to free the colonies from Parliament's rule. Yet even after the battles of Lexington and Concord, a war with Britain seemed far from inevitable to colonists outside New England. In the months ahead, American colonial leaders pursued peaceful as well as military solutions to the question of who actually had authority over them. By the end of 1775, however, reconciliation with the crown would be unattainable.

▶ Selected Bibliography

General Works

Edward Countryman, *The American Revolution* (2003).

Merrill Jensen, *The Founding of a Nation: A History of the American Revolution, 1763–1776* (2004).

Robert Middlekauff, *The Glorious Cause: The American Revolution, 1763–1789* (2005).

Gordon Wood, *The Radicalism of the American Revolution* (1993).

Alfred F. Young, *Liberty Tree: Ordinary People and the American Revolution* (2006).

Native Americans and the Seven Years' War

Fred Anderson, *Crucible of War: The Seven Years' War and the Fate of Empire in British North America, 1754–1766* (2001).

Colin G. Calloway, *The Scratch of a Pen: 1763 and the Transformation of America* (2007).

Gregory Evans Dowd, *War under Heaven: Pontiac, the Indian Nations, and the British Empire* (2004).

Eric Hinderaker, *The Two Hendricks: Unraveling a Mohawk Mystery* (2010).

James H. Merrell, *Into the American Woods: Negotiators on the Pennsylvania Frontier* (2000).

Timothy J. Shannon, *Indians and Colonists at the Crossroads of Empire: The Albany Congress of 1754* (2002).

Peter Silver, *Our Savage Neighbors: How Indian War Transformed Early America* (2009).

Richard White, *The Middle Ground: Indians, Empires, and Republics in the Great Lakes Region, 1650–1815* (1991).

The Revolutionary Crisis of the 1760s and 1770s

Richard Archer, *As If an Enemy's Country: The British Occupation of Boston and the Origins of Revolution* (2010).

Bernard Bailyn, *The Ordeal of Thomas Hutchinson* (1976).

Carol Berkin, *Revolutionary Mothers: Women in the Struggle for America's Independence* (2006).

T. H. Breen, *American Insurgents, American Patriots: The Revolution of the People* (2010).

Benjamin L. Carp, *Defiance of the Patriots: The Boston Tea Party and the Making of America* (2010).

John E. Ferling, *The First of Men: A Life of George Washington* (1988).

David Hackett Fischer, *Paul Revere's Ride* (1995).

Robert A. Gross, *The Minutemen and Their World* (2001).

Joan Gundersen, *To Be Useful to the World: Women in Revolutionary America, 1740–1790* (1996).

Woody Holton, *Forced Founders: Indians, Debtors, Slaves, and the Making of the American Revolution in Virginia* (1999).

Pauline Maier, *From Resistance to Revolution: Colonial Radicals and the Development of American Opposition to Britain, 1765–1776* (1992).

Edmund S. and Helen M. Morgan, *The Stamp Act Crisis: Prologue to Revolution* (1995).

Gary B. Nash, *The Unknown American Revolution: The Unruly Birth of Democracy and the Struggle to Create America* (2006).

Mary Beth Norton, *Liberty's Daughters: The Revolutionary Experience of American Women, 1750–1800* (1996).

Ray Raphael, *The First American Revolution: Before Lexington and Concord* (2002).

Alfred F. Young, *The Shoemaker and the Tea Party: Memory and the American Revolution* (2000).

Slavery

Ira Berlin, *Many Thousands Gone: The First Two Centuries of Slavery in North America* (2000).

Douglas R. Egerton, *Death or Liberty: African Americans and Revolutionary America* (2009).

Sylvia Frey, *Water from the Rock: Black Resistance in a Revolutionary Age* (1991).

Sidney Kaplan and Emma Nogrady Kaplan, *The Black Presence in the Era of the American Revolution* (1989).

Philip Morgan, *Slave Counterpoint* (1998).

▶ FOR MORE BOOKS ABOUT TOPICS IN THIS CHAPTER, see the Online Bibliography at **bedfordstmartins.com/roark**.

▶ FOR ADDITIONAL PRIMARY SOURCES FROM THIS PERIOD, see Michael Johnson, ed., *Reading the American Past*, Fifth Edition.

▶ FOR WEB SITES, IMAGES, AND DOCUMENTS RELATED TO TOPICS AND PLACES IN THIS CHAPTER, visit Make History at **bedfordstmartins.com/roark**.

Reviewing Chapter 6

KEY TERMS

Explain each term's significance.

The Seven Years' War, 1754–1763
- Seven Years' War (p. 159)
- Ohio Company (p. 159)
- Albany Plan of Union (p. 161)
- William Pitt (p. 163)
- Treaty of Paris, 1763 (p. 164)
- Pontiac's Rebellion (p. 166)
- Proclamation of 1763 (p. 166)

The Sugar and Stamp Acts, 1763–1765
- George III (p. 167)
- Sugar (Revenue) Act (p. 167)
- Stamp Act (p. 168)
- virtual representation (p. 169)
- Patrick Henry (p. 169)
- Virginia Resolves (p. 169)
- Samuel Adams (p. 170)
- Sons of Liberty (p. 170)
- Thomas Hutchinson (p. 170)
- Stamp Act Congress (p. 171)
- Declaratory Act (p. 174)

The Townshend Acts and Economic Retaliation, 1767–1770
- Townshend duties (p. 174)
- nonconsumption agreements (p. 175)
- Daughters of Liberty (p. 175)
- Boston Massacre (p. 177)

The Destruction of the Tea and the Coercive Acts, 1770–1774
- committees of correspondence (p. 179)
- Tea Act of 1773 (p. 179)
- Coercive (Intolerable) Acts (p. 180)
- Thomas Gage (p. 181)
- First Continental Congress (p. 182)

Domestic Insurrections, 1774–1775
- Lexington and Concord (p. 184)
- Lord Dunmore (p. 185)
- Phillis Wheatley (p. 185)

REVIEW QUESTIONS

Use key terms and dates to support your answer.

1. How did the Seven Years' War erode relations between colonists and British authorities? (pp. 159–167)

2. Why did the Sugar Act and the Stamp Act draw fierce opposition from colonists? (pp. 167–174)

3. Why did British authorities send troops to occupy Boston in the fall of 1768? (pp. 174–178)

4. Why did Parliament pass the Coercive Acts in 1774? (pp. 178–183)

5. How did enslaved people in the colonies react to the stirrings of revolution? (pp. 183–186)

MAKING CONNECTIONS

Draw on key terms, the timeline, and review questions.

1. In the mid-eighteenth century, how did Native Americans influence relations between European nations? Between Britain and the colonies?

2. What other grievances, besides taxation, led colonists by 1775 to openly rebel against Britain?

3. How did the colonists organize to oppose British power so effectively? In your answer, discuss the role of communication in facilitating the colonial resistance, being sure to cite specific examples.

LINKING TO THE PAST

Link events in this chapter to earlier events.

1. In Bacon's Rebellion in Virginia in 1676, backcountry farmers protested the rule of a royal governor who did not seem to have the economic interests of many Virginians at heart. Compare the administration of Sir William Berkeley of Virginia with that of Thomas Hutchinson of Massachusetts in the 1760s. Are there more differences than similarities? (See chapter 3.)

2. How does the growing ethnic and religious diversity of the mid-eighteenth-century colonies help explain the evolution of anti-British feeling that would culminate in insurrection in 1775? (See chapter 5.)

▶ FOR PRACTICE QUIZZES AND OTHER STUDY TOOLS, visit the Online Study Guide at bedfordstmartins.com/roark.

TIMELINE 1754–1775

1754	• Seven Years' War begins in North America.
	• Albany Congress proposes Plan of Union (never implemented).
1755	• Braddock defeated in western Pennsylvania.
1757	• William Pitt fully commits Britain to war effort.
1760	• Montreal falls to British.
	• George III becomes British king.
1763	• Treaty of Paris ends Seven Years' War.
	• Pontiac's Rebellion.
	• Proclamation of 1763.
	• Paxton Boys massacre friendly Indians in Pennsylvania.
1764	• Parliament enacts Sugar (Revenue) Act.
1765	• Parliament enacts Stamp Act.
	• Virginia Resolves challenge Stamp Act.
	• Sons of Liberty stage dozens of crowd actions.
	• Stamp Act Congress meets.
1766	• Parliament repeals Stamp Act and passes Declaratory Act.
1767	• Parliament enacts Townshend duties.
1768	• British station troops in Boston.
1768–1769	• Merchants sign nonimportation agreements.
1770	• Boston Massacre.
	• Parliament repeals Townshend duties.
1772	• British navy ship *Gaspée* burned.
1773	• Parliament passes Tea Act.
	• Dumping of tea in Boston harbor.
1774	• Parliament passes Coercive (Intolerable) Acts.
	• Powder Alarm shows colonists' readiness to engage in battle with British.
	• First Continental Congress meets, Continental Association formed.
1775	• Battles of Lexington and Concord.
	• Lord Dunmore promises freedom to defecting slaves.

CONTINENTAL ARMY UNIFORM

This uniform belonged to Colonel Peter Gansevoort, commander of Fort Stanwix in the Mohawk Valley of New York. In a cost-saving move, color-coded shoulder ribbons indicated military title; as Gansevoort rose in the ranks he changed ribbons, not coats. Young Gansevoort won fame and several promotions for successfully defending Fort Stanwix against a siege by British and Indians. Yet a related battle diminished the joy of his victory. Hundreds of neighboring militiamen hurrying to aid Gansevoort met ambush and slaughter by loyalists and Indians (pictured in the background in an artistic interpretation from the 1850s) in a battle called Oriskany.

Background: Library of Congress; uniform: National Museum of American History, Smithsonian Institution, Washington, D.C.

7

The War for America
1775–1783

ROBERT SHURTLIFF OF MASSACHUSETTS WAS A LATECOMER TO THE
American Revolution, enlisting in the Continental army months after the
last decisive battle at Yorktown had been fought. The army needed fresh
recruits as a holding action against the large British force still occupying
New York City. Both sides were waiting for the peace treaty to be finalized
in Paris — a process that would take nearly two years.

To secure those new recruits in a country exhausted by eight years of
war, some towns offered cash bounties of $50 in silver. Beardless boys who
had been children when the first shots were fired at Lexington now
stepped forward, Shurtliff among them. Reportedly eighteen, the youth
was single, poor, and at loose ends. With a muscular physique and a ready
proficiency with a musket, Shurtliff won assignment to the army's elite light
infantry unit, part of Washington's army of 10,000 men stationed along the
Hudson River, north of New York City.

That is, 10,000 men and 1 woman. "Robert Shurtliff" was actually
Deborah Sampson, age twenty-three, from Middleborough, Massachusetts.
For seventeen months, Sampson masqueraded as a man, marching through
woods, skirmishing with the enemy, and enduring the boredom of camp.
Understating her age enabled her to blend in with the beardless boys, as
did her competence as a soldier. With privacy at a minimum, she faced constant risk of discovery. Soldiers slept six to a tent, "spooning" their bodies
together for warmth. Somehow, Sampson managed to escape detection
Although many thousands of women served the army as cooks, laundresses, and caregivers, they were never placed in combat. Not only was
Sampson defrauding the military, but she was also violating a legal prohibition on cross-dressing. Why did she run this risk?

A hard-luck childhood had left Sampson both impoverished and unusually plucky. When she was five, her father deserted the family, forcing
her mother to place the children in foster care. Deborah trained to be a
servant in a succession of families. Along the way, she learned to plow a
field and to read and write, uncommon skills for a female servant. Freed
from servitude at age eighteen, she earned a living as a weaver and then

191

as a teacher, low-wage jobs but also ones without supervising bosses. Marriage would have been her normal next step, but either lack of inclination or a wartime shortage of men kept her single and "masterless," rare for an eighteenth-century woman. But like most single females, she was also poor; the $50 bounty enticed her to enlist.

Sampson's true sex was finally discovered by a physician when she was hospitalized for a fever. She was discharged immediately, but her fine service record kept her superiors from prosecuting her for cross-dressing. What eventually made Sampson famous was not her war service alone — there were several other instances of women who wielded weapons in various battles — but her success in selling her story to the public. In 1797, now a middle-aged mother of three, she told her life story (a blend of fact and fiction) in a short book. During 1802–1803, she reenacted her wartime masquerade on a speaking tour of New England and New York. Once again, she was crossing gender boundaries, since women who were not actresses normally did not speak from public stages.

Except for her disguised sex, Sampson's Revolutionary War experience was similar to that of most Americans. Disruptions affected everyone's life, whether in military service or on the home front. Wartime shortages caused women and children to take up traditionally male labor. Soldiers fought for ideas, but they also fought to earn money. Hardship was widely endured. And Sampson's quest for personal independence — a freedom from the constraints of being female — was echoed in the general quest for political independence that many Americans identified as a major goal of the war.

Political independence was not everyone's primary goal at first. For more than a year after fighting began, the Continental Congress in Philadelphia resisted declaring America's independence. Some delegates cautiously hoped for reconciliation with Britain. The congress raised an army, financed it, and sought alliances with foreign countries — all while exploring diplomatic channels for peace.

Once King George III rejected all peace overtures, Americans loudly declared their independence, and the war moved into high gear. In part a classic war with professional armies and textbook battles, the Revolutionary War was also a civil war and at times a brutal guerrilla war between committed rebels and loyalists. It also had complex ethnic dimensions, pitting Indian tribes allied with the British against others allied with the Americans. And it provided an unprecedented opportunity for enslaved African Americans to win their freedom, either by joining the British, who openly encouraged slaves to desert their masters, or by joining the Continental army and state militias, fighting alongside white Americans.

Deborah Sampson

In the mid-1790s, Deborah Sampson sat for this small portrait painted by Massachusetts folk artist Joseph Stone. An engraved copy of it illustrated *The Female Review*, a short book about Sampson's unusual military career and life published in 1797. Sampson, by then a wife and mother, displays femininity in this picture. Note her long curly hair, the necklace, and the stylish gown with a low, lace-trimmed neckline filled in (for modesty's sake) with a white neckerchief. Sampson the soldier had used a cloth band to compress her breasts; Sampson the matron wore a satin band to define her bustline. Rhode Island Historical Society.

▶ The Second Continental Congress

On May 10, 1775, nearly one month after the fighting at Lexington and Concord, the **Second Continental Congress** assembled in Philadelphia. The congress immediately set to work on two crucial but contradictory tasks: to raise and supply an army and to explore reconciliation with Britain. To do the former, they needed soldiers and a commander, they needed money, and they needed to work out a declaration of war. To do the latter, they needed diplomacy to approach the king. But the king was not receptive, and by 1776, as the war progressed and hopes of reconciliation faded, delegates at the congress began to ponder the treasonous act of declaring independence — said by some to be plain common sense.

Assuming Political and Military Authority

Like members of the First Continental Congress (see chapter 6), the delegates to the second were well-established figures in their home colonies, but they still had to learn to know and trust one another. They did not always agree. The Adams cousins John and Samuel defined the radical end of the spectrum, favoring independence. **John Dickinson** of Pennsylvania, no longer the eager revolutionary who had dashed off *Letters from a Farmer* in 1767, was now a moderate, seeking reconciliation with Britain. Benjamin Franklin, fresh off a ship from an eleven-year residence in London, was feared by some to be a British spy. Mutual suspicions flourished easily when the undertaking was so dangerous, opinions were so varied, and a misstep could spell disaster.

Most of the delegates were not yet prepared to break with Britain. Some felt that government without a king was unworkable, while others feared it might be suicidal to lose Britain's protection against its traditional enemies, France and Spain. Colonies that traded actively with Britain feared undermining their economies. Probably the vast majority of ordinary Americans were unable to envision independence. From the Stamp Act of 1765 to the Coercive Acts of 1774 (see chapter 6), the constitutional struggle with Britain had focused on the issue of parliamentary power, but almost no one had questioned the legitimacy of the monarchy.

The few men at the Continental Congress who did think that independence was desirable were, not surprisingly, from Massachusetts. Their colony had been stripped of civil government under the Coercive Acts, their capital was occupied by the British, and their blood had been shed at Lexington and Concord. Even so, those men knew that it was premature to push for a break with Britain. John Adams wrote his wife, Abigail, in June 1775: "America is a great, unwieldy body. Its progress must be slow. It is like a large fleet sailing under convoy. The fleetest sailors must wait for the dullest and slowest."

Yet swift action was needed, for the Massachusetts countryside was under threat of further attack. Even the hesitant moderates in the congress agreed that a military buildup was necessary. Around the country, militia units from New York to Georgia collected arms and trained on village greens in anticipation. On June 14, the congress voted to create the **Continental army**, choosing a Virginian, not a New Englander, as commander in chief. The appointment of **George Washington** sent the clear message that there was widespread commitment to war beyond New England.

Next the congress drew up a document titled "A Declaration on the Causes and Necessity of Taking Up Arms," which rehearsed familiar arguments about the tyranny of Parliament and the need to defend English liberties. This declaration was first drafted by a young Virginia planter, **Thomas Jefferson**, a radical on the question of independence. The moderate John Dickinson, fearing that the declaration would offend Britain, was allowed to rewrite it. However, he left intact much of Jefferson's highly charged language about choosing "to die freemen rather than to live slaves." Even a man as reluctant about independence as Dickinson acknowledged the necessity of military defense against an invading army.

To pay for the military buildup, the congress authorized a currency issue of $2 million. The Continental dollars were merely paper; they were not backed by gold or silver. The delegates somewhat naively expected that the currency would be accepted as valuable on trust as it spread in the population through the hands of soldiers, farmers, munitions suppliers, and beyond.

In just two months, the Second Continental Congress had created an army, declared war, and issued its own currency. It had taken on the major functions of a legitimate government, both

THE PROMISE OF TECHNOLOGY

Muskets and Rifles

Muskets were the weapon of choice in the Revolutionary War. Formal combat involved successive ranks (rows) of soldiers in precise formation firing row

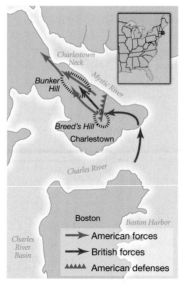

by row in unison at an enemy within a 50-yard range. The massed fire made up for the notoriously inaccurate aim of each musket. Long-barreled rifles, used to hunt game in frontier regions, offered much greater accuracy because of spiral grooves inside the barrel. Grooved (rifled) barrels imparted spin to the ball, which in turn stabilized and lengthened its flight, enabling expert marksmen to hit small targets at 150 to 200 yards. Yet rifles took twice as long to load and fire, and the longer barrels made them unwieldy for soldiers on the march. Not for another half century would there be machine-tooled, mass-produced firearms like the Colt revolver and the Remington rifle. These new repeat-fire weapons were cheaper, more accurate, and far more deadly in the hands of an individual shooter. What might happen if a close-standing rank of musketeers fired their weapons individually instead of in unison? York County Historical Society.

military and financial, without any legal basis for its authority, for it had not yet declared independence from the authority of the king.

Pursuing Both War and Peace

Three days after the congress established the army, one of the bloodiest battles of the Revolution occurred. The British commander in Boston, Thomas Gage, had recently received troop reinforcements, including three talented generals (William Howe, John Burgoyne, and Henry Clinton), and new instructions to attack the Massachusetts rebels. But before Gage could take the offensive, the Americans fortified the hilly terrain of Charlestown, a peninsula just north of Boston, on the night of June 16, 1775.

The British generals could have closed off the peninsula to box in the Americans. But General **William Howe** insisted on a bold frontal assault, sending 2,500 soldiers across the water and up the hill in an intimidating but potentially costly attack. The American troops, 1,400 strong, turned them back twice with deadly short-range fire.

On the third assault, the British took the hill, mainly because the American ammuni-

Battle of Bunker Hill, 1775

(map showing Charlestown Neck, Bunker Hill, Breed's Hill, Charlestown, Mystic River, Charles River, Boston, Boston Harbor, Charles River Basin)

→ American forces
→ British forces
▲▲▲ American defenses

tion supply gave out, and the defenders quickly retreated. The **battle of Bunker Hill** was thus a British victory, but an expensive one. The dead numbered 226 on the British side, with more than 800 wounded; the Americans suffered 140 dead, 271 wounded, and 30 captured. As General Clinton later remarked, "It was a dear bought victory; another such would have ruined us."

Unwilling to risk more raids into the countryside, Howe retreated to Boston instead of pursuing the fleeing Americans. If the British had had any grasp of the basic instability of the American units around Boston, they might have decisively defeated the Continental army in its infancy. Instead, they lingered in Boston, abandoning it without a fight nine months later.

Howe used the time in Boston to inoculate his army against smallpox because a new epidemic of the deadly disease was spreading in port cities along the Atlantic. Inoculation worked by producing a mild but real (and therefore risky) case of smallpox, followed by lifelong immunity. Howe's instinct was right: During the American Revolution, some 130,000 people on the American continent, most of them Indians, died of smallpox. When hundreds of Bostonians began to contract the disease, Howe ordered them to leave town, causing American

An Exact View of the Late Battle at Charlestown, June 17th 1775
This dramatic panorama is the earliest visual representation of the battle of Bunker Hill. On sale to the public six weeks after the battle, the engraving shows Charlestown in flames (center back) and British and American soldiers in fixed formation firing muskets at each other. The Americans, to the left, are dug in along the crest of the hill; British casualties have begun to litter the field of battle. Created by noted cartographer Bernard Romans, this illustration likely decorated many a patriot's wall. Technically, the British won the battle by taking the hill. Is that the story told by this picture? Colonial Williamsburg Foundation.

leaders to fear that the British intended to spread smallpox into the countryside as a "weapon of defense."

A week after Bunker Hill, when General Washington arrived to take charge of the new Continental army, he found enthusiastic but undisciplined troops. Sanitation was an unknown concept, with inadequate latrines fouling the campground. The amazed general attributed the disarray to the New England custom of letting militia units elect their own officers, which he felt undermined deference. Washington spotted a militia captain, a barber in civilian life, shaving an ordinary soldier, and he moved quickly to impose more hierarchy and authority. "Be easy," he advised his newly appointed officers, "but not too familiar, lest you subject yourself to a want of that respect, which is necessary to support a proper command."

While military plans moved forward, the Second Continental Congress pursued its contradictory objective: reconciliation with Britain.

Delegates from the middle colonies (Pennsylvania, Delaware, and New York), whose merchants depended on trade with Britain, urged that channels for negotiation remain open. In July 1775, congressional moderates led by John Dickinson engineered an appeal to the king called the **Olive Branch Petition**. The petition affirmed loyalty to the monarchy and strategically blamed all the troubles on the king's ministers and on Parliament. It proposed that the American colonial assemblies be recognized as individual parliaments under the umbrella of the monarchy. But **King George III** rejected the Olive Branch Petition and heatedly condemned the Americans as traitors. Reconciliation was now out of the question.

Thomas Paine, Abigail Adams, and the Case for Independence

Pressure for independence started to mount in January 1776, when a pamphlet titled *Common Sense* appeared in Philadelphia. **Thomas Paine,**

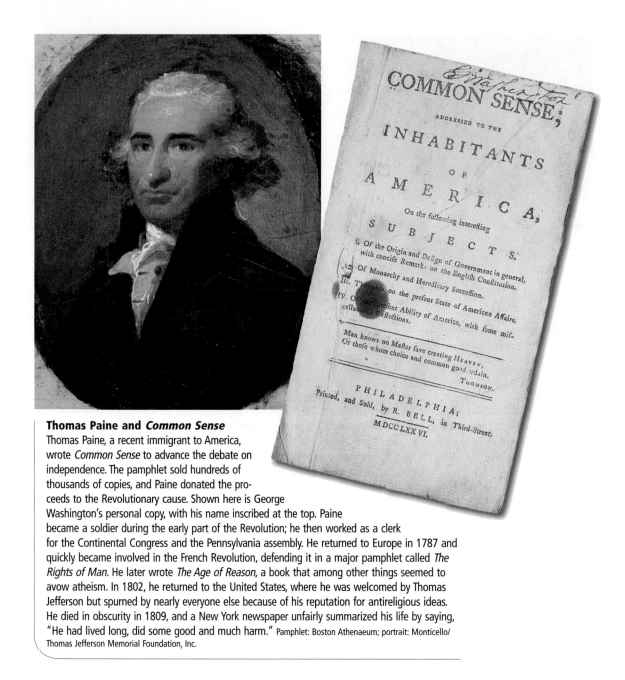

Thomas Paine and *Common Sense*

Thomas Paine, a recent immigrant to America, wrote *Common Sense* to advance the debate on independence. The pamphlet sold hundreds of thousands of copies, and Paine donated the proceeds to the Revolutionary cause. Shown here is George Washington's personal copy, with his name inscribed at the top. Paine became a soldier during the early part of the Revolution; he then worked as a clerk for the Continental Congress and the Pennsylvania assembly. He returned to Europe in 1787 and quickly became involved in the French Revolution, defending it in a major pamphlet called *The Rights of Man*. He later wrote *The Age of Reason*, a book that among other things seemed to avow atheism. In 1802, he returned to the United States, where he was welcomed by Thomas Jefferson but spurned by nearly everyone else because of his reputation for antireligious ideas. He died in obscurity in 1809, and a New York newspaper unfairly summarized his life by saying, "He had lived long, did some good and much harm." Pamphlet: Boston Athenaeum; portrait: Monticello/ Thomas Jefferson Memorial Foundation, Inc.

its author, was an English artisan and coffeehouse intellectual who had befriended Benjamin Franklin in London. He came to America in the fall of 1774 with letters of introduction from Franklin to several Philadelphia printers, one of whom hired him. He soon met delegates from the Second Continental Congress, and, with their encouragement, he wrote *Common Sense* to lay out a lively and compelling case for complete independence.

In simple yet forceful language, Paine elaborated on the absurdities of the British monarchy. Why should one man, by accident of birth, claim extensive power over others? he asked. A king might be foolish or wicked. "One of the strongest natural proofs of the folly of hereditary right in kings," Paine wrote, "is that nature disapproves it; otherwise she would not so frequently turn it into ridicule by giving mankind *an ass for a lion*." Calling the British king an ass broke through the automatic deference most Americans still had for the monarchy. To replace monarchy, Paine advocated republican government based on the consent of the people. Rulers, according to Paine, were only representatives of the people, and the best form of government relied on frequent elections to achieve the most direct democracy possible.

Paine's pamphlet sold more than 150,000 copies in a matter of weeks. Newspapers reprinted it; men read it aloud in taverns and coffeehouses; John Adams sent a copy to his wife, Abigail, who passed it around to neighbors in Braintree, Massachusetts. New Englanders desired independence, but other colonies, under no immediate threat of violence, remained cautious.

Abigail Adams was impatient not only for independence but also for other legal changes that would revolutionize the new country. In a series of astute letters to her husband, she outlined obstacles and gave advice. She worried that southern slave owners might shrink from a war in the name of liberty: "I have sometimes been ready to think that the passion for Liberty cannot be Equally strong in the Breasts of those who have been accustomed to deprive their fellow Creatures of theirs." And in March 1776, she expressed her hope that women's legal status would improve under the new government: "In the new Code of Laws which I suppose it will be necessary for you to make I desire you would Remember the Ladies, and be more generous and favourable to them than your ancestors." Her chief concern was husbands' legal dominion over wives: "Do not put such unlimited power into the hands of the Husbands," she advised. "Remember all Men would be tyrants if they could." Abigail Adams anticipated a more radical end to tyranny than did Thomas Paine.

The Continental Congress was, in fact, not rewriting family law; that task was left to individual states in the 1780s. John Adams dismissed his wife's concerns. But to a male politician, Adams privately rehearsed the reasons why women (and men who were free blacks, or young, or propertyless) should remain excluded from political participation. Even though he concluded that nothing should change, at least Abigail's letter had forced him to ponder the exclusion, something few men — or women — did in 1776. Urgent talk of political independence was as radical as most could imagine.

The Declaration of Independence

In addition to Paine's *Common Sense*, another factor hastening independence was the prospect of an alliance with France, Britain's archrival. France was willing to provide military supplies and naval power only if assured that the Americans would separate from Britain. News that the British were negotiating to hire German mercenary soldiers further solidified support for independence. By May 1776, all but four colonies were agitating for a declaration. The

holdouts were Pennsylvania, Maryland, New York, and South Carolina, the latter two containing large loyalist populations. An exasperated Virginian wrote to his friend in the congress, "For God's sake, why do you dawdle in the Congress so strangely? Why do you not at once declare yourself a separate independent state?" In early June, the Virginia delegation introduced a resolution calling for independence. The moderates still commanded enough support to postpone a vote on the measure until July. In the meantime, the congress appointed a committee, with Thomas Jefferson and others, to draft a longer document setting out the case for independence.

On July 2, after intense politicking, all but one state voted for independence; New York abstained. The congress then turned to the document drafted by Jefferson and his committee. Jefferson began with a preamble that articulated philosophical principles about natural rights, equality, the right of revolution, and the consent of the governed as the only true basis for government. He then listed more than two dozen specific grievances against King George. The congress merely glanced at the philosophical principles, as though ideas about natural rights and the consent of the governed were accepted as "self-evident truths," just as the document claimed. The truly radical phrase declaring the natural equality of "all men" was likewise passed over without comment.

> "Do not put such unlimited power into the hands of the Husbands. Remember all Men would be tyrants if they could."
> — ABIGAIL ADAMS

For two days, the congress wrangled over the list of grievances, especially the issue of slavery. Jefferson had included an impassioned statement blaming the king for slavery, which delegates from Georgia and South Carolina struck out. They had no intention of denouncing their labor system as an evil practice. But the congress let stand another of Jefferson's fervent grievances, blaming the king for mobilizing "the merciless Indian Savages" into bloody frontier warfare, a reference to Pontiac's Rebellion (see chapter 6).

On July 4, the amendments to Jefferson's text were complete, and the congress formally adopted the **Declaration of Independence**. (See appendix I, page A-1.) The New York delegation switched from abstention to endorsement on July 15, making the vote on independence unanimous. In early August, the delegates gathered to sign the official parchment copy.

Jefferson's Laptop Writing Desk
On a stagecoach ride from Virginia to Philadelphia in May 1776, thirty-three-year-old Thomas Jefferson sketched a design for a portable laptop writing desk. On arrival, he hired a Philadelphia cabinetmaker to produce it in mahogany. The adjustable book rest (notice the notches) could also open up to create a large writing surface. Pens, quills, ink, and paper were stored below. Jefferson used this desk to pen rough drafts of the Declaration of Independence. Near the end of his life, he gave the desk to his granddaughter's husband, expressing the hope that it might become esteemed for its connection to the Declaration. National Museum of American History, Smithsonian Institution, Washington, D.C.

Four men, including John Dickinson, declined to sign; several others "signed with regret . . . and with many doubts," according to John Adams. The document was then printed, widely distributed, and read aloud in celebrations everywhere.

Printed copies did not include the signers' names, for they had committed treason, a crime punishable by death. On the day of signing, they indulged in gallows humor. When Benjamin Franklin paused before signing to look over the document, John Hancock of Massachusetts teased him, "Come, come, sir. We must be unanimous. No pulling different ways. We must all hang together." Franklin replied, "Indeed we must all hang together. Otherwise we shall most assuredly hang separately."

> **REVIEW**   Why were many Americans initially reluctant to pursue independence from Britain?

▶ The First Year of War, 1775–1776

Both sides approached the war for America with uneasiness. The Americans, with inexperienced militias, were opposing the mightiest military power in the world. Also, their country was not unified; many people remained loyal to Britain. The British faced serious obstacles as well. Their disdain for the fighting abilities of the Americans required reassessment in light of the Bunker Hill battle. The logistics of supplying an army with food across three thousand miles of water were daunting. And since the British goal was to regain allegiance, not to destroy and conquer, the army was often constrained in its actions. These patterns—undertrained American troops and British troops strangely unwilling to press their advantage—played out repeatedly in the first year of war.

The American Military Forces

Americans claimed that the initial months of war were purely defensive, triggered by the British invasion. But the war also quickly became a rebellion, an overthrowing of long-established authority. As both defenders and rebels, many Americans were highly motivated to fight, and the potential manpower that could be mobilized was, in theory, very great.

Local defense in the colonies had long rested with a militia composed of all able-bodied men over age sixteen. Militias, however, were best suited for local and limited engagements, responding to conflict with Indians or slave rebellions. Such events were relatively infrequent, and the traditional militia training day in most communities had evolved into a holiday of drinking, marching, and shooting practice.

In forming the Continental army, the congress first set enlistment at one year, which proved to be too optimistic. Incentives produced longer commitments: a $20 bonus for three years of service, a hundred acres of land for enlistment for the duration of the war. For this inducement to be effective, of course, recruits had to believe that the Americans would win. Over the course of the war, some 230,000 men enlisted, about one-quarter of the white male adult population. (See Figure 7.1, page 200.)

Women also served in the Continental army, cooking, washing, and nursing the wounded. The British army established a ratio of one woman to every ten men; in the Continental army, the ratio was set at one woman to fifteen men. Close to 20,000 "camp followers," as they were called, served during the war, many of them wives of men in service. Some 12,000 children also tagged along, and babies were born in the camps. Some women helped during battles, supplying drinking water or ammunition to soldiers. One soldier recalled a woman at the battle of Monmouth whose petticoats were shot off by a cannonball that whizzed between her outstretched legs.

Flute-playing African American
This eighteenth-century portrait was displayed for many years in the State Department in Washington D.C., with artist and sitter unrecorded. One compelling hypothesis suggests it is Barzillai Lew, a talented musician from Groton, Massachusetts. As a boy, Lew served as a fifer in the Seven Years' War, and in 1775 he again was a fifer in the Revolutionary War through three enlistments, seeing action at Bunker Hill and Fort Ticonderoga. Fife and drum music supplied rhythm and mood for military marches, so this was an essential job in the army. Lew lived until 1822; many of his 13 children were also musicians.
Courtesy of Mae Theresa Bonitto; photograph courtesy of the *Boston Globe*.

"Looking at it with apparent unconcern," he wrote of the gutsy woman, "she observed that it was lucky it did not pass a little higher, for in that case it might have carried away something else."

Black Americans at first were excluded from the Continental army by slave owner George Washington's orders. But as manpower needs abruptly increased, the Continental Congress permitted free blacks and even slaves to enlist, compensating their masters up to $400 for each man released. In Rhode Island and Connecticut, black Continental soldiers served in segregated units with white officers. While some of these men were involuntary substitutes sent by their owners, others were clearly inspired by ideals of freedom in a war against tyranny. For example, twenty-three Rhode Island blacks gave "Liberty,"

"Freedom," and "Freeman" as their surnames at the time of enlistment, expressing the hope that successful wartime service would bring them actual freedom and liberty. About 5,000 black men served in the Revolutionary War on the rebel side, nearly all from the northern states.

Military service helped politicize Americans during the early stages of the war. In early 1776, independence was a risky, potentially treasonous idea. But as the war heated up and recruiters demanded commitment, some Americans discovered that apathy had its dangers as well. Anyone who refused to serve ran the risk of being called a traitor to the cause. Military service became a prime way of demonstrating political allegiance.

The American army was at times raw and inexperienced, and often woefully undermanned. It never had the precision and discipline of European professional armies. But it was never as bad as the British continually assumed. The British would learn that it was a serious mistake to underrate the enemy.

The British Strategy

The American strategy was straightforward — to repulse and defeat an invading army. The British strategy was not as clear. Britain wanted to put down a rebellion and restore monarchical power in the colonies, but the question was how to accomplish this. A decisive defeat of the Continental army was essential but not sufficient to end the rebellion, for the British would still have to contend with an armed and motivated insurgent population. Furthermore, there was no single political nerve center whose capture would spell certain victory. The Continental Congress moved from place to place, staying just out of reach of the British. During the course of the war, the British captured and occupied every major port city, but that brought no serious loss to the Americans, 95 percent of whom lived in the countryside.

King George had told Parliament at the outset that once his army subdued the rebels, "I shall be ready to receive the misled with tenderness and mercy" as soon as "the unhappy and deluded multitude . . . shall become sensible of their error." While this was calmingly deceptive talk appropriate to the start of war, it did underscore the real tension in the British position. Britain's delicate task was to restore the old governments, not to destroy an enemy country. Hence, the British generals were at first reluctant to ravage the countryside, confiscate food, or burn villages. There were thirteen distinct political entities to

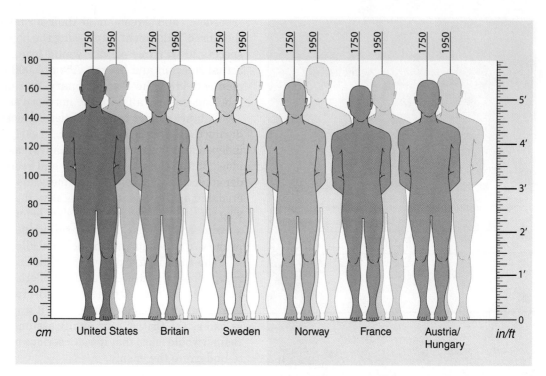

FIGURE 7.1   GLOBAL COMPARISON: How Tall Were Eighteenth-Century Men on Average?
Although individuals within a population vary in height for genetic reasons, variations between populations are generally due to differences in the basic standard of living. A key factor is inadequate nutrition, which typically stunts childhood growth and leads to shorter adults. Military enlistment records provide large data sets on male height, allowing historians to gain insight into comparative standards of living. This figure shows that American men during the Revolution were on average 8 centimeters (cm) or about 3 inches taller than British and European men, indicating an abundance of food and fewer endemic diseases than in Europe. American soldiers exhibited modest but distinct regional differences, with southerners an average of 1.3 cm taller than New Englanders. A much wider spread occurred in Britain, where officers from the gentry were a full 15 cm taller on average than soldiers recruited from the working class. What might account for these differences?

capture, pacify, and then restore to the crown, and they stretched in a long line from New Hampshire to Georgia. Clearly, a large land army was required for the job. Without the willingness to seize food from the locals, the British needed hundreds of supply ships — hence their desire to capture the ports. The British strategy also assumed that many Americans remained loyal to the king and would come to their aid.

The overall British plan was a divide-and-conquer approach, focusing first on New York, the state judged to have the greatest number of loyal subjects. New York offered a geographic advantage as well: Control of the Hudson River would allow the British to isolate the rebellious New Englanders. British armies could descend from Canada and move up from New York City along the Hudson River into western Massachusetts. Squeezed between a naval blockade on the eastern coast and army raids in the west, Massachusetts could be driven to surrender. New Jersey and

Pennsylvania would fall in line, the British thought, because of loyalist strength. Virginia was a problem, like Massachusetts, but the British were confident that the Carolinas would help them isolate and subdue Virginia.

Quebec, New York, and New Jersey

In late 1775, an American expedition was launched to capture the cities of Montreal and Quebec before British reinforcements could arrive (Map 7.1). This offensive was a clear sign that the war was not purely a reaction to the invasion of Massachusetts. A force of New York Continentals commanded by General Richard Montgomery took Montreal easily in September 1775 and then advanced on Quebec. Meanwhile, a second contingent of Continentals led by Colonel Benedict Arnold moved north through Maine to Quebec, a punishing trek through freezing rain with woefully

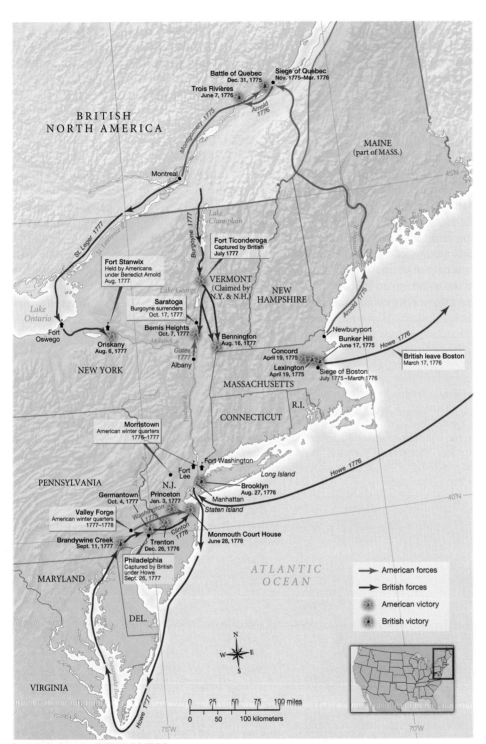

MAP ACTIVITY

Map 7.1   The War in the North, 1775–1778

After the early battles in Massachusetts in 1775, rebel forces invaded Canada but failed to capture Quebec. A large British army landed in New York in August 1776, turning New Jersey into a continual battle site in 1777 and 1778. Burgoyne arrived from England to secure Canada and attempted to pinch off New England along the Hudson River, but he was stopped at Saratoga in 1777 in the key battle of the early war.

READING THE MAP: Which general's troops traveled the farthest in each of these years: 1775, 1776, and 1777? How did the availability of water routes affect British and American strategy?

CONNECTIONS: Why did the French wait until early 1778 to join American forces against the British? What did France hope to gain from participating in the war?

inadequate supplies. Arnold showed heroic determination, but close to half of his men either died or turned back during the march. Arnold and Montgomery jointly attacked Quebec in December but failed to take the city. Worse yet, they encountered smallpox, which killed more men than had the battle for Quebec.

The main action of the first year of the war came not in Canada, however, but in New York, crucial to British strategy. In August 1776, some 45,000 British troops (including 8,000 German mercenaries, called **Hessians**) under the command of General Howe landed south of New York City. General Washington had anticipated this move and had relocated his army of 20,000 south from Massachusetts. The **battle of Long Island**, in late August 1776, pitted the well-trained British "redcoats" (slang referring to their red uniforms) against a very green Continental army. Howe attacked,

inflicting many casualties (1,500 dead and wounded, with another 1,000 taken prisoner). A British general crowed, "If a good bleeding can bring those Bible-faced Yankees to their senses, the fever of independency should soon abate." Howe failed to press forward, however, perhaps remembering the costly victory of Bunker Hill, and Washington evacuated his troops to Manhattan Island in the dead of a foggy night. Knowing it would be hard to hold Manhattan, he withdrew farther north to two forts on either side of the Hudson River, allowing the British command to set up headquarters in the wealthy island city. For two months, the armies engaged in limited skirmishing, but in November Howe finally captured Fort Washington and Fort Lee, taking another 3,000 prisoners.

Washington retreated quickly across New Jersey into Pennsylvania. Again Howe

Triumphal Entry of Royal Troops in New York, 1776
An artist in Germany portrayed British troops marching into New York City in September 1776, in rank and file as far as the eye can see. It looks like a peaceful take-over, with Americans watching quietly from windows and street corners. The picture shows a European-looking city, with blocks of far more substantial buildings than New York actually had. Clearly this artist was not familiar with the real New York. Just days before the British marched in, several hundred wooden buildings went up in smoke from a fire set by a disgruntled American woman. Museum of the City of New York, The J. Clarence Davies Collection.

Der Einzug der Königlichen Völker in Neu Yorck.   L'Entré triumphale de Troupes royales a Nouvelle Yorck.

unaccountably failed to press his advantage. Had he attacked Washington's army at Philadelphia, he could have taken the city. Instead, he parked his German troops in winter quarters along the Delaware River. Perhaps he knew that many of the Continental soldiers' enlistment periods ended on December 31, making him confident that the Americans would not attack him. He was wrong.

On December 25, in an icy rain, Washington stealthily moved his army across the Delaware River and at dawn made a quick capture of the unsuspecting German soldiers. This impressive victory lifted the sagging morale of the patriot side. For the next two weeks, Washington remained on the offensive, capturing supplies in a clever attack on British units at Princeton. Soon he was safe in Morristown, in northern New Jersey, where he settled his army for the winter. Washington finally had time to administer mass smallpox inoculations and see his men through the abbreviated course of the disease.

All in all, in the first year of declared war, the rebellious Americans had a few proud moments but also many worries. The inexperienced Continental army had barely hung on in the New York campaign. Washington had shown exceptional daring and admirable restraint, but what really saved the Americans was the repeated reluctance of the British to follow through militarily when they had the advantage.

REVIEW Why did the British initially exercise restraint in their efforts to defeat the rebellious colonies?

▶ The Home Front

Battlefields alone did not determine the outcome of the war. Struggles on the home front were equally important. In 1776, each community contained small numbers of highly committed people on both sides and far larger numbers who were uncertain about whether independence was worth a war. Both persuasion and force were used to gain the allegiance of the many neutrals. Revolutionaries who took control of local government often used it to punish loyalists and intimidate neutrals, while loyalists worked to reestablish British authority. A major factor pushing neutrals to side with the revolution was the British treatment of prisoners of war. Adding to the turbulence of the times was a very shaky wartime economy. The creative financing of the fledgling government brought hardships as well

as opportunities, forcing Americans to confront new manifestations of virtue and corruption.

Patriotism at the Local Level

Committees of correspondence, of public safety, and of inspection dominated the political landscape in patriot communities. These committees took on more than customary local governance; they enforced boycotts, picked army draftees, and policed suspected traitors. They sometimes invaded homes to search for contraband goods such as British tea or textiles.

Loyalists were dismayed by the increasing show of power by patriots. A man in Westchester, New York, described his response to intrusions by committees: "Choose your committee or suffer it to be chosen by a half dozen fools in your neighborhood — open your doors to them — let them examine your tea-cannisters and molasses-jugs, and your wives' and daughters' petty coats — bow and cringe and tremble and quake — fall down and worship our sovereign lord the mob.... Should any pragmatical committee-gentleman come to my house and give himself airs, I shall show him the door." Oppressive or not, the local committees were rarely challenged. Their persuasive powers convinced many middle-of-the-road citizens that neutrality was not a comfortable option.

Another group new to political life — white women — increasingly demonstrated a capacity for patriotism as wartime hardships dramatically altered their work routines. Many wives whose husbands were away on military or political service took on masculine duties. Their competence to tend farms and make business decisions encouraged some to assert competence in politics as well. Abigail Adams managed the family farm in Massachusetts while John Adams was away for several years engaged in politics, in which Abigail took a keen interest. Eliza Wilkinson managed a South Carolina plantation and talked revolutionary politics with women friends. "None were greater politicians than the several knots of ladies who met together," she remarked, alert to the unusual turn female conversations had taken. "We commenced perfect statesmen."

Women from prominent Philadelphia families took more direct action, forming the **Ladies Association** in 1780 to collect money for Continental soldiers. A published broadside, "The Sentiments

"If a good bleeding can bring those Bible-faced Yankees to their senses, the fever of independency should soon abate."
— A British general

Abigail Adams

Abigail Smith Adams was twenty-two when she sat for this pastel portrait in 1766. A wife for two years and a mother for one year, Adams exhibits a steady, intelligent gaze. Pearls and a lace collar anchor her femininity, while her facial expression projects a confidence and maturity not often credited to young women of the 1760s. A decade later, she was running the family's Massachusetts farm while her husband, John, attended the Continental Congress in Philadelphia. Her frequent letters gave him the benefit of her sage advice on politics and the war. Courtesy of the Massachusetts Historical Society.

of an American Woman," defended their female patriotism. "The time is arrived to display the same sentiments which animated us at the beginning of the Revolution, when we renounced the use of teas [and] when our republican and laborious hands spun the flax."

The Loyalists

Around one-fifth of the American population remained loyal to the crown in 1776, and probably another two-fifths tried to stay neutral. With proper cultivation, this large base might have sustained the British empire in America. In general, **loyalists** of the elite classes often had strong cultural and economic ties to England; they thought that social stability depended on a government anchored by monarchy and aristocracy, and they feared democratic tyranny.

Patriots seemed to them to be unscrupulous, violent, self-interested men who simply wanted power for themselves. There were many non-elite loyalists as well, with diverse and often highly local reasons for opposing the revolutionary leaders of their region.

The most visible loyalists (called **Tories** by their enemies) were royal officials, not only governors such as Thomas Hutchinson of Massachusetts but also local judges and customs officers. Wealthy merchants gravitated toward loyalism to maintain the trade protections of navigation acts and the British navy. Conservative urban lawyers admired the stability of British law and order. Among the ordinary colonists, some chose loyalism simply to oppose traditional adversaries. Backcountry Carolina farmers leaned loyalist out of resentment of the power of the lowlands gentry, generally of patriot persuasion. Tenant farmers of the Hudson River valley in New York, who harbored decades of grievances against rich landlords now active in the Continental Congress, also tended to side with the British. And, of course, southern slaves had their own resentments against the white slave-owning class and looked to Britain in hope of freedom.

Many Indian tribes hoped to remain neutral at the war's start, seeing the conflict as a civil war between the English and Americans. Eventually, however, most were drawn in, many taking the British side. The powerful Iroquois Confederacy divided: The Mohawk, Cayuga, Seneca, and Onondaga peoples lined up with the British; the Oneida and Tuscarora tribes aided Americans. One young Mohawk leader, **Thayendanegea** (known also by his English name, **Joseph Brant**), traveled to England in 1775 to complain to King George about land-hungry American settlers. "It is very hard when we have let the King's subjects have so much of our lands for so little value," he wrote; "they should want to cheat us in this manner of the small spots we have left for our women and children to live on." Brant pledged Indian support for the king in exchange for protection from encroaching settlers. In the Ohio Country, parts of the Shawnee and Delaware tribes started out pro-American but shifted to the British side by 1779 in the face of repeated betrayals by American settlers and soldiers.

Pockets of loyalism thus existed everywhere — in the middle colonies, in the backcountry of the southern colonies, and out beyond the Appalachian Mountains in Indian country (Map 7.2). Even New England towns at the heart of the turmoil, such as Concord, Massachusetts, had a small

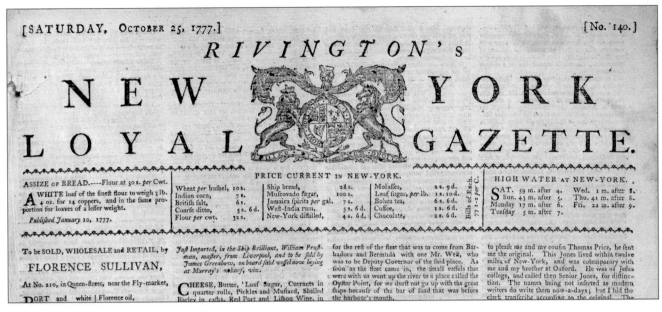

Rivington's New-York Loyal Gazette
Not all newspaper editors supported the Revolution. James Rivington of New York City heaped abuse on Washington and others, and earned a reputation for mean-spirited polemics. In return, rioters hanged him in effigy, broke up his press, and burned down his house. When New York became British headquarters, Rivington curried favor with the British command. Yet it appears now that long-standing rumors about his duplicity are likely true: by 1781, evidence suggests he was indeed passing codes to George Washington about British military plans. Courtesy, American Antiquarian Society.

and increasingly silenced core of loyalists who refused to countenance armed revolution. On occasion, husbands and wives, fathers and sons disagreed completely on the war. (See "Documenting the American Promise," page 206.)

Loyalists were most vocal between 1774 and 1776, when the possibility of a full-scale rebellion against Britain was still uncertain. They challenged the emerging patriot side in pamphlets and newspapers. In 1776 in New York City, 547 loyalists signed and circulated a broadside titled "A Declaration of Dependence" in rebuttal to the congress's July 4 declaration, denouncing the "most unnatural, unprovoked Rebellion that ever disgraced the annals of Time."

Who Is a Traitor?

In June 1775, the Second Continental Congress declared all loyalists to be traitors. Over the next year, state laws defined as treason acts such as provisioning the British army, saying anything that undermined patriot morale, and discouraging men from enlisting in the Continental army. Punishments ranged from house arrest and suspension of voting privileges to confiscation of property and deportation. Sometimes self-appointed committees of Tory-hunters bypassed the judicial niceties and terrorized loyalists, raiding their houses or tarring and feathering them.

Were wives of loyalists also traitors? When loyalist families fled the country, their property was typically confiscated. But if the wife stayed, courts usually allowed her to keep one-third of the property, the amount due her if widowed, and confiscated the rest, so long as she was known to be "a steady and true and faithful friend to the American states," in the case of one Connecticut woman. This legal position supported a wife's autonomy to choose political sides, if she stayed in the United States. Yet what about a wife who favored the patriot side but was obligated by her fleeing loyalist husband to join him? After the Revolution, descendants of refugee loyalists filed several lawsuits to regain property that had entered the family through the mother's inheritance. In one well-publicized Massachusetts case in 1805, the outcome confirmed the traditional view of women as political blank slates. The American son of loyalist refugee Anna Martin recovered her

> "They call me a brainless Tory, but tell me . . . which is better — to be ruled by one tyrant three thousand miles away, or by three thousand tyrants not a mile away?"
> — Boston loyalist MATHER BYLES

Families Divide over the Revolution

Generalizing about rebels versus loyalists is a complex historical task. Sometimes categorizing by class, race, and geographic descriptors helps explain the split. But beyond economic interests or cultural politics, sometimes the loyalist-patriot divide cut across families — and cut deeply. These documents reveal men and women pitted against loved ones over wartime allegiance.

DOCUMENT 1
A Loyalist Wife Writes to Her Patriot Husband, 1778

Mary Gould Almy, a wife and mother, lived in Newport, Rhode Island, an island town occupied by the British army in 1778. She was a Quaker and a loyalist, in contrast to her Anglican husband, Benjamin Almy, who joined the Continental army. Mary wrote to Benjamin in September 1778, sending him her account of the monthlong siege of the town by the French fleet and American troops.

September 02, 1778. Once more, my dear Mr. Almy, I am permitted to write you. . . . I am to give you an account of what passes during the siege; but first let me tell you, it will be done with spirit, for my dislike to the nation that you call your friends, is the same as when you knew me, knowing there is no confidence to be placed in them. . . .

[The 1st day]: At nine in the morning a signal was made for a fleet in sight; at ten o'clock was discovered the number to be eleven large ships . . . the French fleet. . . . With a distressed heart, I endeavor to comfort my poor children by saying, that they would not come in till morning, and then began to secure my papers and plate in the ground.

[The 9th day]: Heavens! what a scene of wretchedness before this once happy and flourishing island. . . . Neither sleep to my eyes, nor slumber to my eyelids, this night; but judge you, what preparation could I make, had I been endowed with as much presence of mind as ever woman was; six children hanging around me, the little girls crying out, "Mamma, will they kill us?" The boys endeavor to put on an air of manliness, and strive to assist, but slip up to the girls, in a whisper, "Who do you think will hurt you? Ain't your papa coming with them?" Indeed this cut me to the soul.

[The 18th day]: Still carting, still fortifying; your people encroaching nearer, throwing up new works every night. . . . And really, Mr. Almy, my curiosity was so great, as to wish to behold the entrenchment that I supposed you were behind; . . . different agitations as by turns took hold upon me. Wishing most ardently to call home my wanderer, at the same time, filled with resentment against those he calls his friends.

[The 24th day]: They kept up a smart firing till two o'clock, and then they began to bury the dead and bring in the wounded. . . . The horrors of that day will never be quite out of my remembrance. I quitted company and hid myself to mourn in silence, for the wickedness of my country. Never was a heart more differently agitated than mine. Some of my good friends in the front of the battle here; and Heaven only knows how many of the other side. . . . At last I shut myself from the family, to implore Heaven to protect you, and keep you from imprisonment and death.

SOURCE: *Mrs. Almy's Journal: Siege of Newport, R.I., August 1778* (Newport, RI: Newport Historical Publishing Company, 1881), 19–31. Reprinted with permission. Available online in select college libraries in the electronic database: *North American Women's Letters and Diaries*, Alexander Street Press.

DOCUMENT 2
Patriot Benjamin Franklin and Loyalist Son William Correspond, 1784

Benjamin Franklin, a keen advocate of the Revolution, had a son who stayed loyal to the crown. William was Benjamin's illegitimate son, resulting from a youthful indiscretion. He was raised in the Franklin family and accompanied Benjamin to England in 1757 for four years' service as Pennsylvania's colonial agent. Thanks to his father, William acquired connections at court, and in 1762, at the age of thirty-one, he was appointed royal governor of New Jersey, a post he held until 1776. When the war began, he was declared a traitor to the patriot cause and placed under house arrest. Father and son did not communicate for the next nine years, even when William was confined in a Connecticut prison for eight months. During this time, Benjamin took charge of William's oldest son, an illegitimate child born before William's legal marriage. After the war, William moved to England, and in 1784 he wrote to his father, then in Paris, asking for a meeting of reconciliation. He did not apologize for his loyalism.

Dear and honored Father,

Ever since the termination of the unhappy contest between Great Britain and America, I have been anxious to write to you. . . . There are narrow illiberal Minds in all Parties. In that which I took, and on whose Account I have so much suffered, there have not been wanting some who have insinuated that my Conduct has been founded on Collusion with you, that one of us might succeed whichever Party should prevail. . . . The Falsity of such Insinuation in our Case you well know, and I am happy that I can with Confidence appeal not only to you but to my God, that I have uniformly acted from a strong Sense of what I conceived my Duty to my King, and Regard to my Country, required. If I have been mistaken, I cannot help it. It is an Error of Judgment what the maturest Reflection I am capable of cannot rectify; and I verily believe were the same Circumstances to occur again Tomorrow, my Conduct would be exactly similar to what it was heretofore.

The father replied:
Dear Son,

I . . . am glad to find that you desire to revive the affectionate Intercourse, that formerly existed between us. It will be very agreeable to me; indeed nothing has ever hurt me so much and affected me with such keen Sensations, as to find myself deserted in my old age by my only Son; and not only deserted, but to find him taking up Arms against me, in a Cause, wherein my good Fame, Fortune and Life were all at Stake. You conceived, you say, that your Duty to your King and regard for your Country requir'd this. I ought not to blame you for differing in Sentiment with me in Public Affairs. We are Men, all subject to errors. Our opinions are not in our own Power; they are form'd and govern'd much by Circumstances, that are often as inexplicable as they are irresistible. Your Situation was such that few would have censured your remaining Neuter, *tho' there are Natural Duties which preceded political ones, and cannot be extinguish'd by them.*

This is a disagreeable Subject. I drop it. And we will endeavor, as you propose mutually to forget what has happened relating to it, as well as we can. I send your Son over to pay his Duty to you. . . . He is greatly esteem'd and belov'd in this Country, and will make his Way anywhere. . . . Wishing you Health, and more happiness than it seems you have lately experienced, I remain your affectionate father, B. Franklin

SOURCE: Courtesy of the American Philosophical Society, www .amphilsoc.org.

DOCUMENT 3
Two Oneida Brothers Confront Their Different Allegiances, 1779

Mary Jemison was captured as a girl during the Seven Years' War and adopted into the Seneca tribe of western

New York, where she remained for life. When she was eighty, her narrative was taken down and published. In this story from her narrative, she relates how some Oneida warriors siding with the British captured two Indians guiding General Sullivan's 1779 campaign of terror in central New York. One of the captors recognized his own brother.

Envy and revenge glared in the features of the conquering savage, as he advanced to his brother (the prisoner) in all the haughtiness of Indian pride, heightened by a sense of power, and addressed him in the following manner:

"Brother, you have merited death! The hatchet or the war-club shall finish your career! When I begged of you to follow me in the fortunes of war, you was deaf to my cries — you spurned my entreaties!

"Brother! You have merited death and shall have your deserts! When the rebels raised their hatchets to fight their good master, you sharpened your knife, you brightened your rifle and led on our foes to the fields of our fathers! You have merited death and shall die by our hands! When those rebels had drove us from the fields of our fathers to seek out new homes, it was you who could dare to step forth as their pilot, and conduct them even to the doors of our wigwams, to butcher our children and put us to death! No crime can be greater! But though you have merited death and shall die on this spot, my hands shall not be stained in the blood of a brother! *Who will strike?*"

Little Beard, who was standing by, as soon as the speech was ended, struck the prisoner on the head with his tomahawk, and dispatched him at once.

SOURCE: James E. Seaver, *A Narrative of the Life of Mrs. Mary Jemison, who was taken by the Indians, in the year 1755, when only about twelve years of age, and has continued to reside amongst them to the present time* (1824), chapter VII, Project Gutenberg, www.gutenberg.org/ebooks/6960 (accessed June 28, 2011).

Questions for Analysis and Debate

1. Why was Mary Almy "cut . . . to the soul" by the remarks of her sons? She was frightened for her husband's safety. Was she also angry with him? Why or why not?

2. What did Benjamin Franklin mean by the emphasized words *"Natural Duties"*? Do you think Franklin really believed that his son was entitled to his own political opinions on the Revolutionary War? What factors help explain why William remained loyal to the crown?

3. Why did the Oneida warrior believe that his brother merited death?

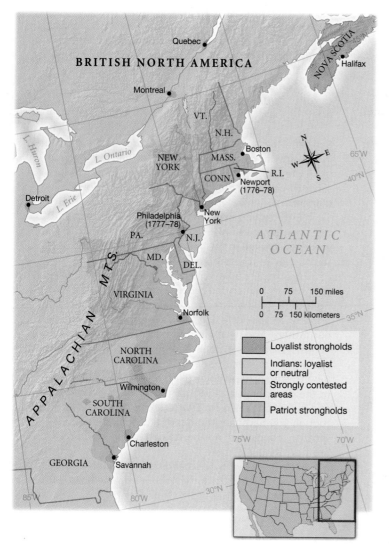

MAP ACTIVITY

Map 7.2 Loyalist Strength and Rebel Support

The exact number of loyalists can never be known. No one could have made an accurate count at the time, and political allegiance often shifted with the wind. This map shows the regions of loyalist strength on which the British relied — most significantly, the lower Hudson valley and the Carolina Piedmont.

READING THE MAP: Which forces were stronger, those loyal to Britain or those rebelling? (Consider the size of their respective areas, centers of population, and vital port locations.) What areas were contested? If the contested areas ultimately had sided with the British, how would the balance of power have changed?

CONNECTIONS: Who was more likely to be a loyalist and why? How many loyalists left the United States? Where did they go?

dowry property on the grounds that she had no independent will to be a loyalist.

Tarring and feathering, property confiscation, deportation, terrorism — to the loyalists, such denials of liberty of conscience and of freedom to own private property proved that democratic tyranny was more to be feared than the monarchical variety. A Boston loyalist named Mather Byles aptly expressed this point: "They call me a brainless Tory, but tell me . . . which is better — to be ruled by one tyrant three thousand miles away, or by three thousand tyrants not a mile away?" Byles was soon sentenced to deportation.

Throughout the war, probably 7,000 to 8,000 loyalists fled to England, and 28,000 found haven in Canada. British strategy depended on using loyalists to hold occupied territory, but for many loyalists, that was impossible without British protection. In New Jersey, for example, 3,000 Jerseyites

felt protected (or scared) enough by the occupying British army in 1776 to swear an oath of allegiance to the king. But then General Howe drew back to New York City, leaving them to the mercy of local patriot committees that pressured for new loyalty oaths to the Continental Congress. Despite the staunch backing of loyalists in 1776, the British could not build a winning strategy on their support.

Prisoners of War

The poor treatment of loyalists as traitors by the revolutionaries was more than matched by the horrendous treatment of American prisoners of war by the British. Such captives were a predictable by-product of war, and George Washington fully expected the British to provide humane treatment, as was customary among European military powers. Among these civilities were

A British Prison Ship
A carefully executed cutaway drawing of an unnamed ship by an unnamed artist shows scores of American POWs below decks being guarded by redcoats. The degree of crowding and of care—note the infirmary on the middle level to the right of the gangplank—is represented as more humane than was actually the case. The artist added these words in French on the border of the paper, "My God, Have you forgotten me?" Museum of the City of New York, Gift of Mrs. Edith Gregor Halpert.

provision of food, clothing, blankets, and laundry, all paid for by the captives' own government, and the possibility of release via prisoner exchanges. These customs recognized that captured soldiers were not common criminals subject to punishing incarceration. But British leaders refused to see the captives as foot soldiers employed by a sovereign nation. In their eyes, the captured Americans were traitors — and therefore worse than common criminals.

The British crowded their initial 4,000 prisoners on two dozen vessels anchored in the river between Manhattan and Brooklyn. The largest of these was the half-century-old HMS *Jersey*, stripped of its masts and guns. Built to house a crew of 400, the *Jersey*'s hull was packed with more than 1,100 prisoners of war. Survivors described the dark, stinking space belowdecks where more than half a dozen men died daily, wasted and parched from extreme thirst. Food and sanitation facilities were inadequate. A twenty-year-old captive seaman described his first view of the hold: "Here was a motley crew, covered with rags and filth; visages pallid with disease, emaciated with hunger and anxiety, and retaining hardly a trace of their original appearance. Here were men . . . now shriveled by a scanty and unwholesome diet, ghastly with inhaling an impure atmosphere, exposed to contagion and disease, and surrounded with the horrors of sickness and death."

The Continental Congress sent food and funds to supply rations to the prisoners, but only a fraction of the provisions reached the men; most of the supplies were diverted to British use. Washington fumed at General Howe and threatened severe treatment of British prisoners, but Howe remained uncooperative.

Treating the captives as criminals potentially triggered the Anglo-American right of habeas corpus, a central feature of English law since the thirteenth century, which guaranteed every prisoner the right to challenge his detention before a judge and to learn the charges against him. To remove that possibility, Parliament voted in early 1777 to suspend habeas corpus specifically for "persons taken in the act of high treason" in any of the colonies.

Despite the treatment of his own men, Washington insisted that captured British soldiers be treated humanely. From the initial group of Hessians taken on Christmas of 1776 to the several thousands more captured in American victories by 1778, America's prisoners of war were gathered in rural encampments that shifted location from Massachusetts to Virginia and points in between. Guarded by local townsmen, the captives typically could cultivate small gardens, move about freely during the day, and even hire themselves out to farmers suffering wartime labor shortages. Officers with money could purchase comfortable lodging with private families and mixed socially with Americans. Officers enjoyed the freedom to travel locally; many were even allowed to keep their guns as they waited for prisoner exchanges to release them.

As the war dragged on, such exchanges were negotiated out of necessity, when the British were desperate to regain valued officers. American officers benefited from these limited exchanges, but for ordinary soldiers and seamen, death — or the rare escape — was their fate. More than 15,000 men endured captivity in the prison ships during the war, and two-thirds of them died, a larger number than those who died in battle (estimated to be around 5,000). News of the horrors of the British death ships increased the revolutionaries' resolve and convinced some neutrals of the necessity of the war.

Financial Instability and Corruption

Wars cost money — for arms and ammunition, for food and uniforms, for soldiers' pay, for provisions for prisoners. The Continental Congress printed money, but its value quickly deteriorated

because the congress held no reserves of gold or silver to back the currency. In practice, it was worth only what buyers and sellers agreed it was worth. When the dollar eventually bottomed out at one-fortieth of its face value, a loaf of bread that once sold for two and a half cents then sold for a dollar. States, too, were printing paper money to pay for wartime expenses, further complicating the economy.

As the currency depreciated, the congress turned to other means to procure supplies and labor. One method was to borrow hard money (gold or silver coins) from wealthy men in exchange for certificates of debt (public securities) promising repayment with interest. The certificates of debt were similar to present-day government bonds. To pay soldiers, the congress issued land grant certificates, written promises of acreage usually located in frontier areas such as central Maine or eastern Ohio. Both the public securities

and the land grant certificates quickly became forms of negotiable currency. A soldier with no cash, for example, could sell his land grant certificate to get food for his family. These certificates soon depreciated, too.

Depreciating currency inevitably led to rising prices, as sellers compensated for the falling value of the money. The wartime economy of the late 1770s, with its unreliable currency and price inflation, was extremely demoralizing to Americans everywhere. In 1778, in an effort to impose stability, local committees of public safety began to fix prices on essential goods such as flour. Inevitably, some turned this unstable situation to their advantage. Money that fell fast in value needed to be spent quickly; being in debt was suddenly advantageous because the debt could be repaid in devalued currency. A brisk black market sprang up in prohibited luxury imports, such as tea, sugar, textiles, and wines, even though these items came from Britain. A New Hampshire delegate to the Continental Congress denounced the violation of the homespun association agreements of just a few years before: "We are a crooked and perverse generation, longing for the fineries and follies of those Egyptian task masters from whom we have so lately freed ourselves."

REVIEW   How did the patriots promote support for their cause in the colonies?

▶ The Campaigns of 1777–1779: The North and West

In early 1777, the Continental army faced bleak choices. General Washington had skillfully avoided defeat, but the minor victories in New Jersey lent only faint optimism to the American side. Meanwhile, British troops moved south from Quebec, aiming to isolate New England from the rest of the colonies by taking control of the Hudson River. Their presence drew the Continental army up into central New York, polarizing Indian tribes of the Iroquois nation and turning the Mohawk Valley into a bloody war zone. By 1779, tribes in western New York and in Indian country in the Ohio Valley were fully involved in the Revolutionary War. Most sided with the British and against the Americans. The Americans had some success in this period, such as the victory at Saratoga, but the involvement of Indians and the continuing strength of the British forced the American government to look to France for help.

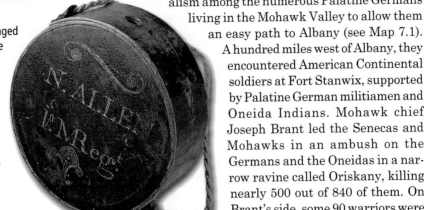

A Soldier's Canteen
This wooden canteen belonged to Noah Allen, whose name and regiment number are carved into the side. Allen was from the Sixth Continental Regiment from Massachusetts. Almost no piece of equipment surpassed the soldier's canteen in importance. The water it carried came from streams, lakes, and, when available, wells.
Fort Ticonderoga Museum.

Burgoyne's Army and the Battle of Saratoga

In 1777, British general **John Burgoyne** assumed command of an army of 7,800 soldiers in Canada and began the northern squeeze on the Hudson River valley. His goal was to capture Albany, near the intersection of the Hudson and Mohawk rivers (see Map 7.1). Accompanied by 1,000 "camp followers" (cooks, laundresses, and musicians) and some 400 Indian warriors, Burgoyne's army did not travel light. In addition to food and supplies for 9,200 people, the army carried food for the 400 horses hauling heavy artillery. Burgoyne also carted thirty trunks of personal belongings and fine wines.

In July, Burgoyne captured Fort Ticonderoga with ease. American troops stationed there spotted the approaching British and abandoned the fort without a fight. The British continued to move south, but the large army moved slowly on primitive roads through dense forests. Burgoyne lost a month hacking his way south; meanwhile, his supply lines back to Canada were severely stretched. Soldiers sent out to forage for food were beaten back by local militia units.

The logical second step in isolating New England should have been to advance troops up the Hudson from New York City to meet Burgoyne. American surveillance indicated that General Howe in Manhattan was readying his men for a major move in August 1777. But Howe surprised everyone by sailing south to attack Philadelphia.

To reinforce Burgoyne, British and Hessian troops stationed at Montreal traveled south and then east along the Mohawk River, joined there by Mohawks and Senecas of the Iroquois Confederacy. The British were counting on loy-

alism among the numerous Palatine Germans living in the Mohawk Valley to allow them an easy path to Albany (see Map 7.1). A hundred miles west of Albany, they encountered American Continental soldiers at Fort Stanwix, supported by Palatine German militiamen and Oneida Indians. Mohawk chief Joseph Brant led the Senecas and Mohawks in an ambush on the Germans and the Oneidas in a narrow ravine called Oriskany, killing nearly 500 out of 840 of them. On Brant's side, some 90 warriors were killed. Meanwhile, Continental defenders of Fort Stanwix forced their British and Indian attackers to retreat (see Map 7.1). The **Oriskany** and **Fort Stanwix** battles were very deadly; they were also complexly multiethnic, pitting Indians against Indians, German Americans (the Palatines) against German mercenaries, New York patriots against New York loyalists, and English Americans against British soldiers.

The British retreat at Fort Stanwix deprived General Burgoyne of the additional troops he expected. Camped at a small village called Saratoga, he was isolated, with food supplies dwindling and men deserting. His adversary at Albany, General Horatio Gates, began moving his army toward Saratoga. Burgoyne decided to attack first because every day his soldiers weakened. The British prevailed, but at the great cost of 600 dead or wounded redcoats. Three weeks later, an American attack on Burgoyne's forces at Saratoga cost the British another 600 men and most of their cannons. General Burgoyne finally surrendered to the American forces on October 17, 1777.

Americans on the side of the rebellion were jubilant. After the battle of Saratoga, the first decisive victory for the Continental army, a popular dance called "General Burgoyne's Surrender" swept through the country, and bookies in the major cities set odds at five to one that the war would be won in six months.

General Howe, meanwhile, had succeeded in occupying Philadelphia in September 1777. Figuring that the Saratoga loss was balanced by the capture of

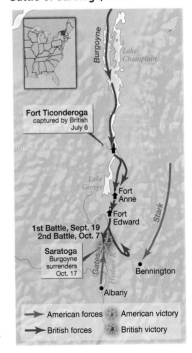

Battle of Saratoga, 1777

Fort Ticonderoga
captured by British
July 6

Burgoyne

Lake Champlain

Lake George

Fort Anne

Fort Edward

Stark

1st Battle, Sept. 19
2nd Battle, Oct. 7

Saratoga
Burgoyne surrenders
Oct. 17

Gates

Hudson R.

Bennington

Albany

→ American forces   ⚔ American victory
→ British forces   ⚔ British victory

Philadelphia, the British government proposed a negotiated settlement — not including independence — to end the war. The American side refused.

Patriot optimism was not well founded. Spirits ran high, but supplies of arms and food ran precariously low. Washington moved his troops into winter quarters at Valley Forge, just west of Philadelphia. Quartered in drafty huts, the men lacked blankets, boots, stockings, and food. Some 2,000 men at Valley Forge died of disease; another 2,000 deserted over the bitter six-month encampment.

> **"The people at home are destroying the Army by their conduct much faster than Howe and all his army can possibly do by fighting us."**
> — A Continental army officer

Washington blamed the citizenry for lack of support; indeed, evidence of corruption and profiteering was abundant. Army suppliers too often provided defective food, clothing, and gunpowder. One shipment of bedding arrived with blankets one-quarter their customary size. Food supplies arrived rotten. As one Continental officer said, "The people at home are destroying the Army by their conduct much faster than Howe and all his army can possibly do by fighting us."

The War in the West: Indian Country

Burgoyne's defeat in the fall of 1777 and Washington's long stay at Valley Forge up to June 1778 might suggest that the war paused for a time, and it did on the Atlantic coast. But in the interior western areas — the Mohawk Valley, the Ohio Valley, and Kentucky — the war of Indians against the American pro-independence side heated up. For native tribes, the struggle was not about taxation, representation, or monarchical rule; it was about independence, freedom, and land.

The ambush and slaughter at Oriskany in August 1777 marked the beginning of three years of terror for the inhabitants of the Mohawk Valley. Loyalists and Indians engaged in many raids on farms throughout 1778, capturing or killing the residents. In retaliation, American militiamen destroyed Joseph Brant's home village, Onanquaga. Although they failed to capture any warriors, they killed several children in hiding. A month later, Brant's warriors attacked the town of Cherry Valley, killing 16 soldiers and 32 civilians and taking 71 people captive.

Death of Jane McCrea
In 1804, artist John Vanderlyn memorialized the martyr legend of Jane McCrea. McCrea, daughter of an American patriot family, was in love with a loyalist in Burgoyne's Army. In July 1777 she eloped to join her fiancé, guided by Indians sent by the British to escort her. But she was killed on the short journey—either shot in the crossfire of battle, as the British claimed, or murdered by Indians allied with the British, in the patriots' version. American general Horatio Gates used the story of the vulnerable, innocent maiden dressed in alluring wedding clothes as propaganda to inspire his soldiers' drive for victory at Saratoga. Wadsworth Atheneum Museum of Art, Hartford/Art Resource, NY.

The following summer, General Washington authorized a campaign to wreak "total destruction and devastation" on all the Iroquoian villages of central New York. Some 4,500 troops commanded by General John Sullivan implemented a deliberate campaign of terror in the fall of 1779. Forty Indian towns met with total obliteration; the soldiers looted and torched the dwellings and then burned cornfields and orchards. In a few towns, women and children were slaughtered, but in most, the inhabitants managed to escape, fleeing to the British at Fort Niagara. Thousands of Indian refugees, sick and starving, camped around the fort in one of the most miserable winters on record.

Much farther to the west, beyond Fort Pitt in the Ohio Valley, another complex story of alliances and betrayals between American mili-

tiamen and Indians unfolded. Some 150,000 native people lived between the Appalachian Mountains and the Mississippi River, and by 1779 neutrality was no longer an option. Most sided with the British, who maintained a garrison at Fort Detroit, but a portion of the Shawnee and Delaware tribes at first sought peace with the Americans. In mid-1778, the Delaware chief White Eyes negotiated a treaty at Fort Pitt, pledging Indian support for the Americans in exchange for supplies and trade goods. But escalating violence undermined the agreement. That fall, when American soldiers killed two friendly Shawnee chiefs, Cornstalk and Red Hawk, the Continental Congress hastened to apologize, as did the governors of Pennsylvania and Virginia, but the soldiers who stood trial for the murders

MAP 7.3

The Indian War in the West, 1777–1782

The American Revolution involved many Indian tribes, most of them supporting the British. Iroquois Indians, with British aid, attacked American towns in New York's Mohawk Valley throughout 1778. In 1779, the Continental army destroyed forty Iroquois villages in central New York. Shawnee and Delaware Indians to the west of Fort Pitt tangled with American militia units in 1779, while tribes supported by the British at Fort Detroit conducted raids on Kentucky settlers, who hit back with raids of their own. Sporadic fighting continued in the West through 1782, ending with Indian attacks on Hannastown, Pennsylvania, and Fort Henry on the Ohio River.

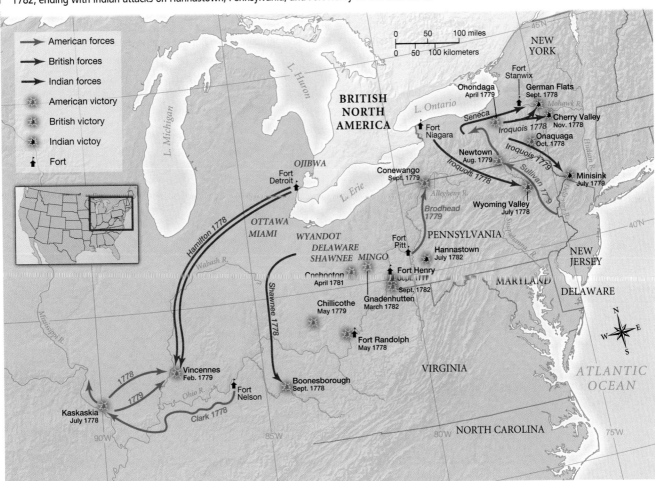

were acquitted. Two months later, White Eyes, nominally an ally of and an informant for the Americans, died under mysterious circumstances. He was almost certainly murdered by militiamen, who repeatedly had trouble honoring distinctions between allied and enemy Indians.

West of North Carolina (today's Tennessee), the frontier war zone of the South, militias attacked Cherokee settlements in 1779, destroying thirty-six villages and burning fields and livestock. Indian raiders from north of the Ohio River, in alliance with the British, repeatedly attacked white settlements such as Boonesborough (in present-day Kentucky) (Map 7.3). In retali-

ation, a young Virginian, George Rogers Clark, led Kentucky militiamen into what is now Illinois, attacking and taking the British fort at Kaskaskia. Clark's men wore native clothing — hunting shirts and breechcloths — but their dress was not a sign of solidarity with the Indians. When they attacked British-held Fort Vincennes in 1779, Clark's troops tomahawked Indian captives and threw their still-live bodies into the river in a gory spectacle witnessed by the redcoats. "To excel them in barbarity is the only way to make war upon Indians," Clark announced. And, he might have added, it was an effective way to terrorize British soldiers as well.

VISUAL ACTIVITY

"The Balance of Power," 1780

This cartoon was published in England soon after Spain and the Netherlands declared an alliance with France to support the war in America. On the left, Britannia, a female figure representing Great Britain, cannot be moved by all the lightweights on the right-hand side of the scale. France wears a ruffled shirt, Spain has a feather in his hat, and a Dutch boy has just hopped on, saying, "I'll do anything for Money." The forlorn Indian maiden, the standard icon representing America in the eighteenth century, sits on the scale, head in hand, wailing, "My Ingratitude is Justly punished." The poem printed below the cartoon predicts, "The Americans too will with Britons Unite." This fanciful prediction was punctured nine months after it appeared, when the British surrendered to the Americans and the French at Yorktown in 1781.

Print Collection, Miriam and Ira D. Wallach Division of Art, Prints, and Photographs, The New York Public Library. Astor, Lenox, and Tilden Foundations.

READING THE IMAGE: What does this cartoon reveal about British perceptions of the American Revolution?
CONNECTIONS: How did British attitudes toward the colonies contribute to the British defeat in the war?

By 1780, very few Indians remained neutral. Violent raids by Americans drove Indians into the arms of the British at Detroit and Niagara, or into the arms of the Spaniards, who still held much of the land west of the Mississippi River. Said one officer on the Sullivan campaign, "Their nests are destroyed but the birds are still on the wing." For those who stayed near their native lands, chaos and confusion prevailed. Rare as it was, Indian support for the American side occasionally emerged out of a strategic sense that the Americans were unstoppable in their westward pressure and that it was better to work out an alliance than to lose in a war. But American treatment of even friendly Indians showed that there was no winning strategy for them.

The French Alliance

On their own, the Americans could not have defeated Britain, especially as pressure from hostile Indians increased. Essential help arrived as a result of the victory at Saratoga, which convinced the French to enter the war; a formal alliance was signed in February 1778. France recognized the United States as an independent nation and promised full military and commercial support. Most crucial was the French navy, which could challenge British supplies and troops at sea and aid the Americans in taking and holding prisoners of war.

Well before 1778, however, the French had been covertly providing cannons, muskets, gunpowder, and highly trained military advisers to the Americans. Monarchical France was understandably cautious about endorsing a democratic revolution attacking kingship. Instead, the main attraction of an alliance was the opportunity it provided to defeat archrival Britain. A victory would also open pathways to trade and perhaps result in France's acquiring the coveted British West Indies. Even an American defeat would not be a disaster for France if the war lasted many years and drained Britain of men and money.

French support materialized slowly. The navy arrived off the Virginia coast in July 1778 but then sailed south to the West Indies to defend the French sugar-producing islands. French help would prove indispensable to the American victory, but the alliance's first months brought no dramatic victories, and some Americans grumbled that the partnership would prove worthless.

REVIEW Why did the Americans need assistance from the French to ensure victory?

▶ The Southern Strategy and the End of the War

When France joined the war, some British officials wondered whether the fight was worth continuing. A troop commander, arguing for an immediate negotiated settlement, shrewdly observed that "we are far from an anticipated peace, because the bitterness of the rebels is too widespread, and in regions where we are masters the rebellious spirit is still in them. The land is too large, and there are too many people. The more land we win, the weaker our army gets in the field." The commander of the British navy argued for abandoning the war, and even Lord North, the prime minister, agreed. But the king was determined to crush the rebellion, and he encouraged a new strategy for victory focusing on the southern colonies, thought to be more persuadably loyalist. He had little idea of the depth of anger that would produce deadly guerrilla warfare between loyalists and patriots. The king's plan was brilliant but desperate, and ultimately unsuccessful.

Georgia and South Carolina

The new strategy called for British forces to abandon New England and focus on the South, with its large slave population thought to be ready to run to the king's forces. Such desertions, the British assumed, would disrupt the economy and unnerve rebellious white slave owners. Banking on loyalism among the nonslaveholding whites of Georgia and the Carolinas, the British hoped to build a safe foothold that would allow them to recapture the southern colonies one by one, moving north to the more problematic middle colonies and saving prickly New England for last.

Georgia, the first target, fell at the end of December 1778 (Map 7.4). A small army of British soldiers occupied Savannah and Augusta, and a new royal governor and loyalist assembly were quickly installed. Taking Georgia was easy because the bulk of the Continental army was in New York and New Jersey, keeping an eye on General **Henry Clinton**, Howe's replacement as commander in chief, and the French were still in the West Indies. The British in Georgia quickly organized twenty loyal militia units, and 1,400 Georgians swore an oath of allegiance to the king. So far, the southern strategy looked as if it might work.

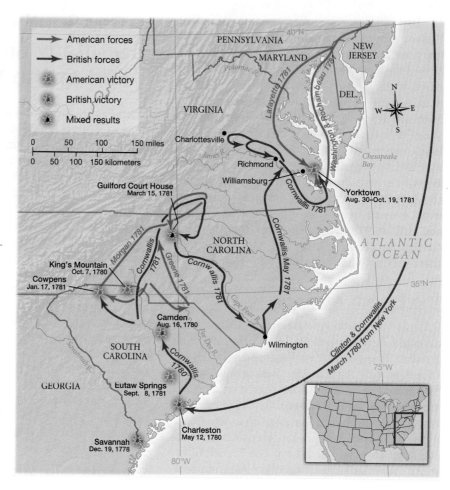

MAP 7.4

The War in the South, 1780–1781
After taking Charleston in May 1780, the British advanced into South Carolina and the foothills of North Carolina, leaving a bloody civil war in their wake. When the American general Horatio Gates and his men fled from the humiliating battle of Camden, Gates was replaced by General Nathanael Greene and General Daniel Morgan, who pulled off major victories at King's Mountain and Cowpens. The British general Cornwallis then moved north and invaded Virginia, but he was bottled up and finally overpowered at Yorktown in the fall of 1781.

Next came South Carolina. The Continental army put ten regiments into the port city of Charleston to defend it from attack by British troops shipped south from New York under the command of General Clinton. For five weeks in early 1780, the British laid siege to the city and took it in May 1780, in the process capturing 3,300 American soldiers, a tremendous loss for the patriots. Again, the king's new strategy seemed to be on target.

From Charleston, Clinton announced that slaves owned by rebel masters were welcome to seek refuge with his army. Several thousand responded by escaping to the coastal city. Untrained in formal warfare, they were of more immediate use to the British as knowledgeable guides to the surrounding countryside and as laborers in service to the army, building defensive earthworks and fortifications. Escaped slaves with boat piloting skills were particularly valuable to the British as they navigated the inland river systems of the southern colonies.

Clinton returned to New York, leaving the task of pacifying the rest of South Carolina to General **Charles Cornwallis** and 4,000 troops.

A bold commander, Lord Cornwallis quickly chased out the remaining Continentals and established military rule of South Carolina by midsummer. He purged rebels from government office and disarmed rebel militias. One officer under Cornwallis, Colonel Banastre Tarleton, plundered food and supplies from large plantations, using insurgent blacks to terrify wealthy whites. As in Georgia, pardons were offered to Carolinians willing to prove their loyalty by taking up arms for the British.

By August 1780, American troops arrived from the North to strike back at Cornwallis. General Gates, the hero of Saratoga, led 3,000 troops, half of them experienced Continental soldiers and others newly recruited militiamen, into battle against Cornwallis at Camden, South Carolina, on August 16 (see Map 7.4). Right from the battle's start, militia units panicked; one unit managed to return fire, but others threw down unfired muskets and fled. The remaining Continentals, seriously outnumbered, faced heavy fire and soon gave up. When regiment leaders tried to regroup the next day, only 700 soldiers showed up; the rest were dead, wounded, captured,

Battle of Cowpens
British Colonel Banastre Tarleton, widely reviled as "the Butcher" for killing surrendering Americans, attacked American troops in a South Carolina cow field sealed off by a river in January 1781. In one hour Tarleton had decisively lost. Six decades later, American painter William T. Ranney memorialized a legendary event in which Lt. Col. William Washington (second cousin to George, pictured on a white horse) taunted "Where now is the boasting Tarleton?" causing Tarleton's aide (black horse) to hoist his sword. A timely shot by a youthful African American (name unknown) saved Washington's life. By the 1840s, art patrons evidently preferred to remember slaves as loyal to patriot masters. Collection of the State of South Carolina/Picture Resource Consultants & Archives.

or still in flight. The **battle of Camden** was a devastating defeat, the worst of the entire war, and prospects seemed very grim for the Americans.

Treason and Guerrilla Warfare

Britain's southern strategy succeeded in 1780 in part because of information about American troop movements secretly conveyed by an American traitor: **Benedict Arnold**. The hero of several American battles, Arnold was a brilliant military talent but also a deeply insecure man who never felt he got his due in either honor or financial reward. Sometime in 1779, he opened secret negotiations with General Clinton in New York, trading information for money and hinting that he could deliver far more of value. When General Washington made him commander of

A Shaming Ritual Targeting the Great Traitor
In late September 1780, Philadelphians staged a ritual humiliation of Benedict Arnold, represented by an effigy with two faces and a mask, to manifest his duplicity. Behind him stands the devil, prodding him with a pitchfork and shaking a bag of coins near his ear, reminding all that Arnold sold out for money. While two fife players and a drummer keep the beat, soldiers and onlookers proceed to a bonfire, where the effigy was burned to ashes. Library of Congress.

West Point, a new fort on the Hudson River sixty miles north of New York City, Arnold's plan crystallized. West Point controlled the Hudson; its easy capture by the British might well have meant victory in the war.

Arnold's plot to sell a West Point victory to the British was foiled in the fall of 1780 when Americans captured the man carrying plans of the fort's defense from Arnold to Clinton. News of Arnold's treason created shock waves. Arnold represented all of the patriots' worst fears about themselves: greedy self-interest, like that of the war profiteers; the unprincipled abandonment of war aims, like that of turncoat southern Tories; panic, like that of the terrified soldiers at Camden. But instead of symbolizing all that was troubling about the American side of the war, Arnold's treachery was publicly denounced in a kind of displacement of the anxieties of the moment. Vilifying Arnold allowed Americans to stake out a wide distance between themselves and dastardly conduct. It inspired a renewal of patriotism at a particularly low moment.

Bitterness over Gates's defeat at Camden and Arnold's treason revitalized rebel support in western South Carolina, an area that Cornwallis thought was pacified and loyal. The backcountry of the South soon became the site of guerrilla warfare. In hit-and-run attacks, both sides burned and ravaged not only opponents' property but also the property of anyone claiming to be neutral. Loyalist militia units organized by the British were met by fierce rebel militia units whose members figured they had little to lose. In South Carolina, some 6,000 men became active partisan fighters, and they entered into at least twenty-six engagements with loyalist units. Some were classic battles, but on other occasions the fighters were more like bandits than soldiers. Guerrilla warfare soon spread to Georgia and North Carolina. Both sides committed atrocities and plundered property, clear deviations from standard military practice.

The British southern strategy depended on sufficient loyalist strength to hold reconquered

> "We had used them to good advantage, and set them free, and now, with fear and trembling, they had to face the reward of their cruel masters."
>
> — A Hessian officer, speaking of slaves expelled from the British army

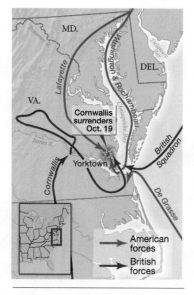

Cornwallis surrenders Oct. 19

Yorktown

→ American forces
→ British forces

Siege of Yorktown, 1781

territory as Cornwallis's army moved north. The backcountry civil war proved this assumption false. The Americans won few major battles in the South, but they ultimately succeeded by harassing the British forces and preventing them from foraging for food. In the fall of 1780, Cornwallis moved the war into North Carolina not because he thought South Carolina was secure—it was not—but because the North Carolinians were supplying the South Carolina rebels with arms and men (see Map 7.4). Then came word that 1,400 frontier riflemen had massacred loyalist troops at King's Mountain in western South Carolina, and the news sent Cornwallis hurrying back. The British were stretched too thin to hold even two of their onetime colonies.

Surrender at Yorktown

By early 1781, the war was going very badly for the British. Their defeat at King's Mountain was quickly followed by a second major defeat at the battle of Cowpens in South Carolina in January 1781. Cornwallis retreated to North Carolina and thence to Virginia, where he captured Williamsburg in June. A raiding party under Colonel Tarleton proceeded to Charlottesville, the seat of government, capturing members of the Virginia assembly but not Governor Thomas Jefferson, who escaped the soldiers by a mere ten minutes. (The slaves at Monticello, Jefferson's home, stood their ground and saved his house from plundering, but more than a dozen at two other plantations he owned sought refuge with the British.) These minor victories allowed Cornwallis to imagine he was succeeding in Virginia. His army, now swelled by some 4,000 escaped slaves, moved toward Yorktown, near Chesapeake Bay. As the general waited for backup troops by ship from British headquarters in New York City, smallpox and typhus began to set in among the black recruits.

At this juncture, the French-American alliance came into play. French regiments commanded by the Comte de Rochambeau had joined General Washington in Newport, Rhode Island, in mid-1780, and in early 1781 warships under the Comte de Grasse had sailed from France to the West Indies. Washington, Rochambeau, and de

Lafayette at Yorktown, with James
The French nobleman Lafayette came to the United States in 1777 to volunteer his services, and in 1781 he went to Virginia to fight Cornwallis. At the siege of Yorktown, Lafayette's borrowed slave James infiltrated the British command by pretending to be an escaped slave. James fed the British misinformation and brought crucial intelligence back to Lafayette. French artist Jean Baptiste Le Paon painted the two men in 1783 without ever having seen James, who appears as a mere ornament to the heroic white general. James obtained his freedom in 1786 after Lafayette wrote a letter on his behalf to the Virginia assembly. Art Gallery, Williams Center, Lafayette College.

Grasse now fixed their attention on Chesapeake Bay. The French fleet got there ahead of the British troop ships from New York; a five-day naval battle left the French navy in clear control of the Virginia coast. This proved to be the decisive factor in ending the war, because the French ships prevented any rescue of Cornwallis's army.

On land, General Cornwallis and his 7,500 troops faced a combined French and American army of 16,000. For twelve days, the Americans and French bombarded the British fortifications at Yorktown; Cornwallis ran low on food and ammunition. He also began to expel the black recruits, some of them sick and dying. A Hessian officer serving under Cornwallis later criticized this British action as disgraceful: "We had used them to good advantage, and set them free, and now, with fear and trembling, they had to face the reward of their cruel masters." Many never made it back to their masters but died in the no-man's-land between the two armies, causing an American observer to record that "an immense number of Negroes have died in the most miserable manner in York." The twelve-day siege brought Cornwallis to the realization that neither victory nor escape was possible. He surrendered on October 19, 1781.

What began as a promising southern strategy in 1778 had turned into a discouraging defeat by 1781. British attacks in the South had energized American resistance, as did the timely exposure of Benedict Arnold's treason. The arrival of the French fleet sealed the fate of Cornwallis at the **battle of Yorktown**, and major military operations came to a halt.

The Losers and the Winners

The surrender at Yorktown spelled the end for the British, but two more years of skirmishes ensued. Frontier areas in Kentucky, Ohio, and Illinois still blazed with battles pitting Americans against various Indian tribes. The British army remained in control of three coastal cities — Savannah, Charleston, and New York — and in response, an augmented Continental army stayed at the ready, north of New York City. Occasional clashes occurred, like the ones in which light infantryman Deborah Sampson saw action, while cross-dressing as a male soldier. Skirmishes continued around Savannah and Charleston as well, involving white loyalists teamed up with runaway black insurgents.

European Nations and the Peace of Paris, 1783

News of the decisive British defeat at Yorktown in late 1781 caused Britain's prime minister, Lord North, to stagger as though wounded and exclaim, "Oh, God, it is all over!" But in truth, it was far from over. A full year elapsed before the elements of a formal peace treaty could be worked out, and an additional year passed before the treaty was signed and Britain finally ended its occupation of New York City. The delay occurred in part because several European countries besides Britain had stakes in the war that had nothing to do with the chief American goal of political independence.

France had entered the war mainly to thwart and damage Britain. Certainly the French monarchy had no real sympathy for a democratic revolution in the British colonies. Indeed, for months before the victory at Yorktown, French leaders conferred covertly with the British about a plan to divide the colonies among the key European powers, with Britain to retain New York City and the rice and tobacco colonies of the South, while France and Spain would carve up the rest.

The stubbornness of Britain's George III prevented such a deal.

Even after receiving news of the defeat at Yorktown, the delusional king still imagined he could retain all thirteen rebellious colonies. After a series of antiwar votes in Parliament and the resignation of Lord North, George III briefly considered abdicating his throne. Instead, he replaced North with a new minister, Lord Shelburne, who approached the peace talks with the view that independence for America was still up for debate.

Spain's interest in the war stemmed from a secret alliance with France in 1779. The Spanish king wanted to oust the British from Gibraltar, a tiny three-square-mile territory dominated by a massive rock and situated at the southern end of the Iberian Peninsula. From this strategic location, Britain controlled the passage between the Atlantic and the Mediterranean, disrupting Spanish trade. Spain launched a siege that lasted more than three years and tied up scores of British ships and thousands of troops, military assets that were thus not available for the war in America. Another important interest for Spain was control of navigation rights on the Mississippi River. Since 1763, Spain had held the lands west

of the river, and it hoped to gain the eastern bank — and thus fully control all navigation of that major river — as a prize for its contribution to defeating Britain.

At various times, Russia, Austria, and even Poland had agents in Paris offering to mediate peace talks in order to adjust the balance of power in Europe. None of these countries viewed American independence as a priority. Only Holland offered formal diplomatic recognition of the new country, an act of faith quickly followed up by a sizable loan of money to the new government. No other country was so supportive.

The Continental Congress entrusted three Americans of great distinction to handle the treaty negotiations. Benjamin Franklin, John Adams, and John Jay considered independence as the precondition for the talks to begin, so they were taken aback when the British negotiator showed up with credentials that pointedly addressed them as "the Commissioners of the Colonies." A month later, updated credentials referenced the three as representatives "of the Thirteen United States of America," a far more satisfactory acknowledgment of their new standing. In September 1782, peace talks began in earnest. Shelburne conceded on independence and set his goal as the maintenance of favored trading status with the new country. He saw, perhaps more clearly than did his king, that although Britain's political dominance over its colonies had now ended, economic dominance might nicely replace it.

The congress also instructed its three diplomats to consult France at

The **Treaty of Paris**, also called the Peace of Paris, was two years in the making. (See "Beyond America's Borders," above.) Commissioners from America and Britain worked out the ten articles of peace, while a side treaty including Britain, France, Spain, and the Netherlands sealed related deals. The first article went to the heart of the matter: "His Britannic Majesty acknowledges the said United States to be free Sovereign and independent States." Other articles set the western boundary of the new country at the Mississippi River and guaranteed that creditors on both sides could collect debts owed them in sterling money, a provision especially important to British merchants. Britain agreed to withdraw its troops quickly, but more than a decade later this promise still had not been fully kept. A last-minute addition to the article about the British withdrawal prohibited the British from "carrying away any Negroes or other property of the American inhabitants." The treaty was signed on September 3, 1783.

The General P—s, or Peace.

Say what they will, I call this an honourable P—.

I call this a free and Independent P—.

Such English we confess your exceeding good nature, tho' we have wrangled you out of America you freely make P—, with us.

"The P - ss of Paris"
A British broadside of 1783 offers a cheeky affront to the Peace of Paris and the diplomats who negotiated it. The Indian declares "I call this a Free and Independent P-ss" while the Frenchman on the far right gloats that "tho' we have wrangled you out of America, you freely make P-ss with us." Britain, Spain, and France all participated in the Peace, but the Indians did not. Why do you think the artist included an Indian figure? What is the point of view of this cartoon?

Library of Congress.

every step of the negotiation with Britain, a condition insisted upon by the French minister to the United States. But Jay and Adams had deep suspicions of the motives of the French foreign minister, the Count of Vergennes. They feared, with justice, that Vergennes planned on placing their nation's western boundary some distance east of the Mississippi River, to meet the demands of Spain. So the Americans sidestepped their instructions and negotiated with Britain in secret, producing an acceptable draft treaty in just a few weeks.

By January 1783, France, Britain, and Spain had produced their own treaties, involving deals with lands in India, Africa, and the Mediterranean, and in September of that year all the treaties were officially approved and signed. Franklin wrote to a friend in Massachusetts, "We are now Friends with England and with all Mankind. May we never see another War! for in my Opinion, there never was a good War, or a bad Peace."

America in a Global Context

1. Why would the monarchies of France and Spain spend vast sums to help the rebellious American colonies in their fight against Britain?

2. A 1976 book about the Treaty of Paris is titled *The Virgin Diplomats*. Does anyone in this story fit that title? Why or why not?

3. On what grounds might the United States claim all land east of the Mississippi River?

News of the treaty signing was cause for celebration among most Americans, but not among the thousands of self-liberated blacks who had joined the British under promise of freedom. Boston King, a refugee from a South Carolina plantation, now huddled with his family at New York under protection of the British. He later wrote how the treaty's article prohibiting the British from evacuating any slaves "filled us with inexpressible anguish and terror." King and others pressed the British commander in

New York, Sir Guy Carleton, to honor pre-treaty British promises. Luckily, Carleton responded favorably. For all refugees able to state that they had been with the British for more than a year, he issued certificates of freedom — and hence they were no longer "property" to be returned. More than 4,000 blacks sailed out of New York for Nova Scotia, Boston King among them. As Carleton coolly explained to a protesting George Washington, "the Negroes in question . . . I found free when I arrived at New York, I had therefore no right, as I thought, to prevent their going to any part of the world they thought proper." British commanders in Savannah and Charleston followed Carleton's lead and aided the exit of perhaps 10,000 blacks from the United States.

The emancipation of slaves had never been a war goal of the British; destabilizing patriot planters and gaining manpower were their initial reasons for promises of freedom. Had the British won the war, they might well have reenslaved insurgent blacks to restore the profitable plantation economy of the South. For their part, blacks viewed British army camps as sites of refuge (not figuring on the devastations of epidemic diseases and food shortages) and had no reason to revere the British monarchy. In fact, some runaways had headed for Indian country instead.

The Treaty of Paris had nothing to say about the Indian participants in the Revolutionary War. Like the treaty ending the Seven Years' War, the 1783 treaty failed to recognize the Indians as players in the conflict. As one American told the Shawnee people, "Your Fathers the English have made Peace with us for themselves, but forgot you their Children, who Fought with them, and neglected you like Bastards." Indian lands were assigned to the victors as though they were uninhabited. Some Indian refugees fled west into present-day Missouri and Arkansas, and others, such as Joseph Brant's Mohawks, relocated to Canada. But significant numbers remained within the new United States, occupying their traditional homelands in areas west and north of the Ohio River. For them, the Treaty of Paris brought no peace at all; their longer war against the Americans would extend at least until 1795 and for some until 1813. Their ally, Britain, conceded defeat, but the Indians did not.

With the treaty finally signed, the British began their evacuation of New York, Charleston, and Savannah, a process complicated by the sheer numbers involved — soldiers, fearful loyalists, and runaway slaves by the thousands. In New York City, more than 27,000 soldiers and 30,000 loyalists sailed on hundreds of ships for England in the late fall of 1783. In a final act of mischief, on the November day when the last ships left, the losing side raised the British flag at the southern tip of Manhattan, cut away the ropes used to hoist it, and greased the flagpole.

REVIEW   Why did the British southern strategy ultimately fail?

▶ Conclusion: Why the British Lost

The British began the war for America convinced that they could not lose. They had the best-trained army and navy in the world; they were familiar with the landscape from the Seven Years' War; they had the willing warrior-power of most of the native tribes of the backcountry; and they easily captured every port city of consequence in America. A majority of colonists were either neutral or loyal to the crown. Why, then, did the British lose?

Beginning in 1775 and 1776, British royal officials fled the colonies, thereby abdicating civil power, which they never really regained. The Americans created their own government structures, from the Continental Congress to local committees and militias. Staffed by many who before 1775 had been the political elites, these new government agencies had remarkably little trouble establishing their authority to rule. The basic British goal — to turn back the clock to imperial rule — receded into impossibility as the war dragged on.

Another ongoing problem facing the British was the uncertainty of supplies. Unwilling to ravage the countryside until late in the war, the army depended on a steady stream of supply ships from home. Insecurity about food helps explain their reluctance to pursue the Continental army aggressively. And although any plan to repacify the colonies required the cooperation of the loyalists and neutrals, the British repeatedly failed to support them, leaving them to the mercy of vengeful rebels.

Finally, French aid looms large in any explanation of the British defeat. Even before the formal alliance, French artillery and ammunition proved vital to the Continental army. After 1780, the French army brought a new infusion of troops to a war-weary America, and the French navy made the Yorktown victory possible.

The war for America had lasted just over six years, from Lexington to Yorktown; negotiations and the evacuation took two more. It profoundly disrupted the lives of Americans everywhere. More than a war for independence from Britain, it required people to think about politics and the legitimacy of authority. The precise disagreement with Britain about representation and political participation had profound implications for the kinds of governance the Americans would adopt, both in the moment of emergency and later when states began to write their constitutions. The rhetoric employed to justify the revolution against Britain put the words *liberty*, *tyranny*, *slavery*, *independence*, and *equality* into common usage. These words carried far deeper meanings than a mere complaint over taxation without representation, meanings not lost on unfree groups — slaves, servants, wives — excluded from politics by their dependent status. In the decades to come, the Revolution unleashed a dynamic of equality and liberty that was largely unintended and unwanted by many of the political leaders of 1776. A half century later, the language of the Declaration of Independence would emerge as a potent force offering legitimacy to antislavery and woman's rights groups.

► Selected Bibliography

General Works

Carol Berkin, *Revolutionary Mothers: Women in the Struggle for America's Independence* (2005).
Edward Countryman, *The American Revolution* (1985).
John Fering, *Almost a Miracle: The American Victory in the War of Independence* (2009).
Piers Mackesy, *The War for America, 1775–1783* (1964).
Gary B. Nash, *The Unknown American Revolution: The Unruly Birth of Democracy and the Struggle to Create America* (2005).
Jack Rakove, *Revolutionaries: A New History of the Invention of America* (2010).
Ray Raphael, *A People's History of the American Revolution: How Common People Shaped the Fight for Independence* (2001).
Charles Royster, *A Revolutionary People at War: The Continental Army and American Character, 1775–1783* (1996).
Gordon S. Wood, *The Radicalism of the American Revolution* (1992).

The Wartime Confederation and Its Leaders

Ron Chernow, *George Washington: A Life* (2010).
Joseph J. Ellis, *His Excellency: George Washington* (2004).
John E. Ferling, *Setting the World Ablaze: Washington, Adams, Jefferson, and the American Revolution* (2000).
Eric Foner, *Tom Paine and Revolutionary America* (1976).
Edith Gelles, *Portia: The World of Abigail Adams* (1992).
Woody Holton, *Abigail Adams* (2010).
Pauline Maier, *American Scripture: Making the Declaration of Independence* (1997).
Jackson Turner Main, *The Sovereign States, 1775–1783* (1973).
Jack N. Rakove, *The Beginnings of National Politics: An Interpretive History of the Continental Congress* (1979).

Campaigns, Battles, and Soldiers

Wayne K. Bodle, *The Valley Forge Winter: Civilians and Soldiers in War* (2004).
W. Jeffrey Bolster, *Black Jacks: African American Seamen in the Age of Sail* (1998).
Edwin G. Burrows, *The Prisoners of New York* (2008).
Colin G. Calloway, *The American Revolution in Indian Country: Crisis and Diversity in Native American Communities* (1995).
E. Wayne Carp, *To Starve the Army at Pleasure: Continental Army Administration and American Political Culture, 1775–1783* (1984).
David Hackett Fischer, *Washington's Crossing* (2004).
Joseph R. Fischer, *A Well-Executed Failure: The Sullivan Campaign against the Iroquois, July–September 1779* (1997).
Sylvia Frey, *The British Soldier in America: A Social History of Military Life in the Revolutionary Period* (1965).
Robert Gross, *The Minutemen and Their World* (1976).
Sidney Kaplan and Emma Nogrady Kaplan, *The Black Presence in the Era of the American Revolution* (1989).
Richard M. Ketchum, *Saratoga: Turning Point of America's Revolutionary War* (1997).
John Komlos, ed., *Stature, Living Standards, and Economic Development: Essays in Anthropometric History* (1994).
David G. Martin, *The Philadelphia Campaign: June 1777–1778* (2003).
James Kirby Martin, *Benedict Arnold, Revolutionary Hero: An American Warrior Reconsidered* (1997).
Holly A. Mayer, *Belonging to the Army: Camp Followers and Community during the American Revolution* (1996).
David McCullough, *1776* (2005).
Alfred F. Young, *Masquerade: The Life and Times of Deborah Sampson, Continental Soldier* (2004).

► FOR MORE BOOKS ABOUT TOPICS IN THIS CHAPTER, see the Online Bibliography at **bedfordstmartins.com/roark.**

► FOR ADDITIONAL PRIMARY SOURCES FROM THIS PERIOD, see Michael Johnson, ed., *Reading the American Past*, Fifth Edition.

► FOR WEB SITES, IMAGES, AND DOCUMENTS RELATED TO TOPICS AND PLACES IN THIS CHAPTER, visit Make History at **bedfordstmartins.com/roark.**

Reviewing Chapter 7

KEY TERMS

Explain each term's significance.

The Second Continental Congress

Second Continental Congress (p. 193)
John Dickinson (p. 193)
Continental army (p. 193)
George Washington (p. 193)
Thomas Jefferson (p. 193)
William Howe (p. 194)
battle of Bunker Hill (p. 194)
Olive Branch Petition (p. 195)
King George III (p. 195)
Common Sense (p. 195)
Thomas Paine (p. 195)
Abigail Adams (p. 197)
Declaration of Independence (p. 197)

The First Year of War, 1775–1776

Hessians (p. 202)
battle of Long Island (p. 202)

The Home Front

Ladies Association (p. 203)
loyalists (Tories) (p. 204)
Joseph Brant (Thayendanegea) (p. 204)

The Campaigns of 1777–1779: The North and West

John Burgoyne (p. 211)
battle of Oriskany (p. 211)
battle of Fort Stanwix (p. 211)
battle of Saratoga (p. 211)

The Southern Strategy and the End of the War

Henry Clinton (p. 215)
Charles Cornwallis (p. 216)
battle of Camden (p. 217)
Benedict Arnold (p. 217)
battle of Yorktown (p. 219)
Treaty of Paris, 1783 (p. 220)

REVIEW QUESTIONS

Use key terms and dates to support your answer.

1. Why were many Americans reluctant to pursue independence from Britain? (pp. 193–198)

2. Why did the British initially exercise restraint in their efforts to defeat the rebellious colonies? (pp. 198–203)

3. How did the patriots promote support for their cause in the colonies? (pp. 203–210)

4. Why did the Americans need assistance from the French to ensure victory? (pp. 210–215)

5. Why did the British southern strategy ultimately fail? (pp. 215–222)

MAKING CONNECTIONS

Draw on key terms, the timeline, and review questions.

1. Even before the colonies had committed to independence, they faced the likelihood of serious military conflict. How did they mobilize for war? In your answer, discuss specific challenges they faced, noting the unintended consequences of their solutions.

2. Congress's adoption of the Declaration of Independence confirmed a decisive shift in the conflict between the colonies and Britain. Why did the colonies make this decisive break in 1776? In your answer, discuss some of the arguments for and against independence.

3. The question of whether the colonists would be loyal to the new government or to the old king was pivotal during the Revolutionary War. Discuss the importance of loyalty in the outcome of the conflict. In your answer, consider both military and political strategy.

4. American colonists and British soldiers were not the only participants in the Revolutionary War. How did Native Americans shape the conflict? What role did African Americans play? What benefits did these two groups hope to gain? Did they succeed?

LINKING TO THE PAST

Link events in this chapter to earlier events.

1. Most Indian tribes joined with the French and opposed the British in the Seven Years' War; yet in the American Revolution, most tribes sided with the British and opposed the Americans. What accounts for this apparent shift in alliances? (See chapter 6.)

2. Consider the leading roles of Massachusetts and Virginia in the coming of the American Revolution. With such very different origins and such very different economic, demographic, and religious histories, how could these two so readily join in partnership in the break from British rule? (See chapters 3, 4, and 5.)

TIMELINE 1775–1783

1775
- Second Continental Congress convenes; creates Continental army.
- British win battle of Bunker Hill.
- King George III rejects Olive Branch Petition.
- Americans lose battle of Quebec.

1776
- *Common Sense* published.
- British evacuate Boston.
- **July 4** Congress adopts Declaration of Independence.
- British take Manhattan.

1777
- British Parliament suspends habeas corpus for rebels.
- British take Fort Ticonderoga.
- Ambush at Oriskany; Americans hold Fort Stanwix.
- British occupy Philadelphia.
- British surrender at Saratoga.

1777–78
- Continental army endures winter at Valley Forge.

1778
- France enters war on American side.
- American militiamen destroy Mohawk chief Joseph Brant's village.
- White Eyes negotiates treaty with Americans; later mysteriously dies.
- British take Savannah, Georgia.

1779
- Militias attack Cherokee settlements in far western North Carolina.
- Americans destroy forty Iroquois villages in New York.
- Americans take Forts Kaskaskia and Vincennes.

1780
- Philadelphia Ladies Association raises money for soldiers.
- British take Charleston, South Carolina.
- French army arrives in Newport, Rhode Island.
- British win battle of Camden.
- Benedict Arnold exposed as traitor.
- Americans win battle of King's Mountain.

1781
- British forces invade Virginia.
- French fleet blockades Chesapeake Bay.
- Cornwallis surrenders at Yorktown; concedes British defeat.

1783
- Treaty of Paris ends war; United States gains all land east of Mississippi River.

A CHAIR FOR THE NEW NATION
George Washington sat in this splendid and unique mahogany chair, topped by a gold-painted sun, for three hot months in the summer of 1787. He was presiding over a convention of fifty-five delegates engaged in the difficult work of hammering out the new Constitution of the United States, pictured here in the background. On the day the delegates finished writing, Benjamin Franklin sagely observed that he had often stared at the sun on the chair, unable to tell if it was morning or evening: "But now at length I have the happiness to know that it is a rising and not a setting Sun."

Background: National Archives; chair: Independence National Historic Park.

8

Building a Republic

1775–1789

JAMES MADISON GRADUATED FROM PRINCETON COLLEGE IN NEW Jersey in 1771, not knowing what to do next with his life. Certainly, the twenty-year-old had an easy fallback position. As the firstborn son of a wealthy plantation owner, he could return to the foothills of Virginia and wait to inherit substantial land and many slaves. But Madison was an intensely studious young man, uninterested in farming. Five years at boarding school had given him fluency in Greek, Latin, French, and mathematics; and three years at Princeton had acquainted him with the great thinkers, both ancient and modern. Driven by a thirst for learning, young Madison hung around Princeton for six months after graduation.

In 1772, he returned home, still adrift. He tried studying law, but his unimpressive oratorical talents discouraged him. Instead, he swapped reading lists and ideas about political theory by letter with a Princeton classmate, prolonging his student life. While Madison struggled for direction, the powerful winds before the storm of the American Revolution swirled through the colonies. In May 1774, Madison traveled north to deliver his brother to boarding school and was in Philadelphia when the startling news broke that Britain had closed the port of Boston in retaliation for the destruction of the tea. Turbulent protests over the Coercive Acts turned him into a committed revolutionary.

Back in Virginia, Madison joined his father on the newly formed committee of public safety. For a few days in early 1775, the twenty-four-year-old took up musket practice in a burst of enthusiasm for war, but it was quickly plain that his greater contribution lay in the science of politics. In the spring of 1776, he gained election to the Virginia Convention, a Revolutionary assembly replacing the defunct royal government. The convention's main task was to hammer out a state constitution with innovations such as frequent elections and limited executive power. Shy, self-effacing, and still learning the ropes, Madison mostly stayed on the sidelines, but Virginia's elder statesmen noted the young man's logical, thoughtful contributions. When his county failed to return him to the assembly in the next election, he was appointed to the governor's council, where he spent two years gaining experience in a wartime government.

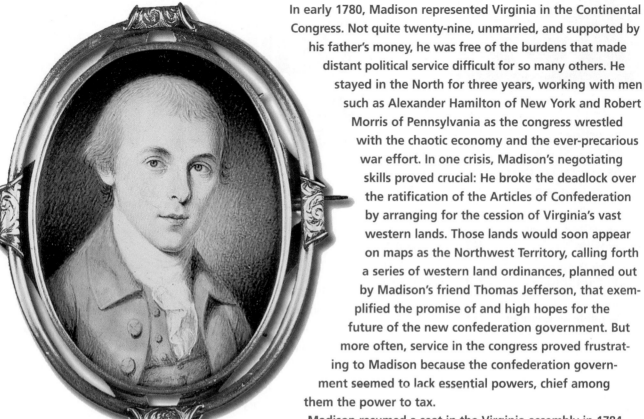

**James Madison,
by Charles Willson Peale**

Philadelphia artist Charles Willson Peale painted this miniature portrait of Madison in 1783, along with a matching miniature of Madison's fiancée, Kitty Floyd, the sixteen-year-old daughter of a New York delegate to the Continental Congress. Madison's portrait was mounted in a brooch (note the pin sticking out on the right) so that his lady love might wear it on her person, but Floyd returned the miniature to Madison when she broke off the engagement. Eleven years later, Madison tried romance again when New York congressman Aaron Burr introduced him to a young Virginia widow named Dolley Payne Todd. Madison was forty-three, and Todd was twenty-six; they married four months after meeting. Library of Congress.

In early 1780, Madison represented Virginia in the Continental Congress. Not quite twenty-nine, unmarried, and supported by his father's money, he was free of the burdens that made distant political service difficult for so many others. He stayed in the North for three years, working with men such as Alexander Hamilton of New York and Robert Morris of Pennsylvania as the congress wrestled with the chaotic economy and the ever-precarious war effort. In one crisis, Madison's negotiating skills proved crucial: He broke the deadlock over the ratification of the Articles of Confederation by arranging for the cession of Virginia's vast western lands. Those lands would soon appear on maps as the Northwest Territory, calling forth a series of western land ordinances, planned out by Madison's friend Thomas Jefferson, that exemplified the promise of and high hopes for the future of the new confederation government. But more often, service in the congress proved frustrating to Madison because the confederation government seemed to lack essential powers, chief among them the power to tax.

Madison resumed a seat in the Virginia assembly in 1784. But he did not retreat to a local point of view as so many other state politicians of the decade did. The economic hardships created by heavy state taxation programs — which in Massachusetts led to a full-fledged rebellion against state government — spurred Madison to pursue means to strengthen the government shared by the thirteen new states. In this, he was in the minority: To many Americans, it was not clear that the Articles of Confederation needed major revamping.

Madison thought the Articles did need overhauling. He worked hard to organize an all-state convention in Philadelphia in May 1787, where he took the lead in steering the delegates to a complete rewrite of the structure of the national government, investing it with considerably greater powers. True to form, Madison spent the months before the convention in feverish study of the great thinkers he had read in college, seeking the best way to constitute a government on republican principles. His lifelong passion for scholarly study, seasoned by a dozen years of energetic political experience, paid off handsomely. The United States Constitution was the result.

By the end of the 1780s, James Madison had had his finger in every kind of political pie on the local, state, confederation, and finally national level. He had transformed himself from a directionless and solitary youth into one of the leading political thinkers of the Revolutionary period. His personal history over the 1780s was deeply entwined with the path of the emerging United States.

▶ The Articles of Confederation

From 1775 to 1781, the Continental Congress met in Philadelphia and other cities without any formal constitutional basis. It took time to work out a plan of government that embodied Revolutionary principles. With monarchy gone, where would sovereignty lie? What would be the nature of representation? Who would hold the power of taxation? The resulting plan, called the **Articles of Confederation**, proved to be surprisingly difficult to implement, mainly because the thirteen states disagreed over boundaries in the land to the west of the states. Once the Articles were ratified and the active phase of the war had drawn to a close, the congress faded in importance compared with politics in the individual states.

Congress and Confederation

After the Declaration of Independence had been signed and circulated, the Continental Congress set a committee in motion to draft a document that would specify what powers the congress had and by what authority it existed. There was widespread agreement on key central governmental powers: pursuing war and peace, conducting foreign relations, regulating trade, and running a postal service. Yet the congress's attention was still mainly on the war, and so it took a year of tinkering before its members reached agreement on the Articles of Confederation in November 1777. The Articles defined the union as a loose confederation of states, characterized as "a firm league of friendship" existing mainly to foster a common defense. The structure of the government paralleled that of the existing Continental Congress. There was no national executive (that is, no president) and no national judiciary. Term limits of three years ensured rotation in congres-

sional offices. State delegations could vary in size from two to seven, and each delegation cast a single vote. Routine decisions in the congress required a simple majority of seven states; for momentous decisions, such as declaring war, nine states needed to agree. To approve or amend the Articles required the unanimous consent both of the thirteen state delegations and of the thirteen state legislatures — giving any state an unrealistic and eventually crippling veto power. Most crucially, the Articles gave the national government no power of direct taxation.

Taxation was a necessity, since all governments require money and governments pursuing wars need even more. The congress issued bonds to finance most of the war's hefty and immediate costs (for supplies and manpower); the bonds were held in part by French and Dutch bankers but also by large numbers of middling to wealthy Americans. (Bondholders considered bonds with 6 percent interest an attractive investment, especially when they could be purchased with depreciating Continental dollars that were accepted at face value.) The congress also anticipated new peacetime expenses in addition to the large war debt and the expanding interest owed to bondholders. Trade regulation required a paid force of customs officers; a postal system required postmen, horses and wagons, and well-maintained postal roads; the western lands required surveyors; and Indian diplomacy (or war) added further large costs. Article 8 of the confederation document declared that taxes were needed to support "the common defence or general welfare" of the country, yet the congress also had to be sensitive to the rhetoric of the Revolution, which denounced heavy taxation by a distant and nonrepresentative power.

The congress hoped to solve this delicate problem with a two-step procedure. The congress would **requisition** (that is, request) money to be paid into the common treasury, and each state legislature would then levy taxes within

Revolutionary War Flag from New Hampshire
In June 1777, the Continental Congress decreed specifications for the new American flag. Thirteen red and white stripes lay adjacent to a blue corner embellished with thirteen white stars "representing a new Constellation," a powerful metaphor that anchored the fragile union of the thirteen states in the vast and timeless expanse of the heavens. Flag designers experimented with the arrangement of the stars—in a circle or a square, in rows, or, in this case of a flag made in New Hampshire, in staggered rows. Early American flags were strictly military banners; not for another half century would they become ever-present symbols of nonmilitary patriotism. American Antiques, David A. Schorsch — Eileen M. Smiles.

its borders to pay the requisition. The Articles specified that state contributions were to be assessed in proportion to the property value of the state's land; thus, large and populous states paid more than did small or sparsely populated states. Requiring that the actual tax bill be passed by the state legislatures preserved the Revolution's principle of taxation only by direct representation. However, no mechanism compelled states to pay.

The lack of centralized authority in the confederation government was exactly what many state leaders wanted in the late 1770s. A league of states with rotating personnel, no executive branch, no power of direct taxation, and a requirement of unanimity for any major change seemed to be a good way to keep government in check. Yet there were problems, and the first was the requirement that every state ratify the Articles of Confederation. This mandatory unanimity stalled the acceptance of the Articles for four additional years, until 1781.

The Problem of Western Lands

The most serious disagreement over the Articles of Confederation involved the absence of any plan for the lands to the west of the thirteen original states. This absence was deliberate; an earlier draft of the Articles gave the congress the power to set state boundaries and to administer the sales of the western lands. But states with large land claims objected. A few states — Virginia and Connecticut, for example — had old colonial charters that located their western boundaries at the Mississippi River, and they insisted that their claims be recognized. Six more states also had plausible legal claims to extensive territories (Map 8.1). Five states lacked such land claims entirely, and they preferred that the congress preserve all the western lands as a national domain that would eventually be sold off to settlers and constitute new states, administered by the congress. Financial motives loomed large, for, as one Rhode Island delegate put it, "the western world opens an amazing prospect as a national fund; it is equal to our debt."

The eight land-claiming states were ready to sign the Articles of Confederation in 1777, since it protected their interests. Three states without claims — Rhode Island, Pennsylvania, and New Jersey — eventually capitulated and

> "The western world opens an amazing prospect as a national fund; it is equal to our debt."
>
> A Rhode Island delegate

signed, "not from a Conviction of the Equality and Justness of it," said a New Jersey delegate, "but merely from an absolute Necessity there was of complying to save the Continent." But Delaware and Maryland continued to hold out, insisting on a national domain policy. In 1779, the disputants finally compromised: Any land a state volunteered to relinquish would become the national domain. When James Madison and Thomas Jefferson ceded Virginia's huge land claim in 1781, the Articles of Confederation were at last unanimously approved. (See appendix I, page A-1.)

The western lands issue demonstrated that powerful interests divided the thirteen new states. The apparent unity of purpose inspired by fighting the war against Britain papered over sizable cracks in the new confederation.

Running the New Government

No fanfare greeted the long-awaited inauguration of the new government in 1781. The congress continued to sputter along, its problems far from solved by the signing of the Articles. Lack of a quorum often hampered day-to-day activities. The Articles required representation from seven states to conduct business and a minimum of two men from each state's delegation. But some days, fewer than fourteen men in total showed up. State legislatures were slow to select delegates, and many politicians preferred to devote their energies to state governments, especially when the congress seemed deadlocked or, worse, irrelevant. Some had difficulty learning the art of formal debate. A Pennsylvanian reflected that "I find there is a great deal of difference between sporting a sentiment in a letter, or over a glass of wine upon politics, and discharging properly the duties of a senator."

It also did not help that the congress had no permanent home. During the war, when the British army threatened Philadelphia, the congress relocated to small Pennsylvania towns such as Lancaster and York and then to Baltimore. After hostilities ceased, the congress moved from Trenton to Princeton to Annapolis to New York City. Many delegates were reluctant to travel far from home, especially if they had wives and children. Consequently, some of the most committed delegates were young bachelors, such as James Madison, and men in their fifties and sixties whose families were grown, such as Samuel Adams.

To address the difficulties of an inefficient congress, executive departments of war, finance,

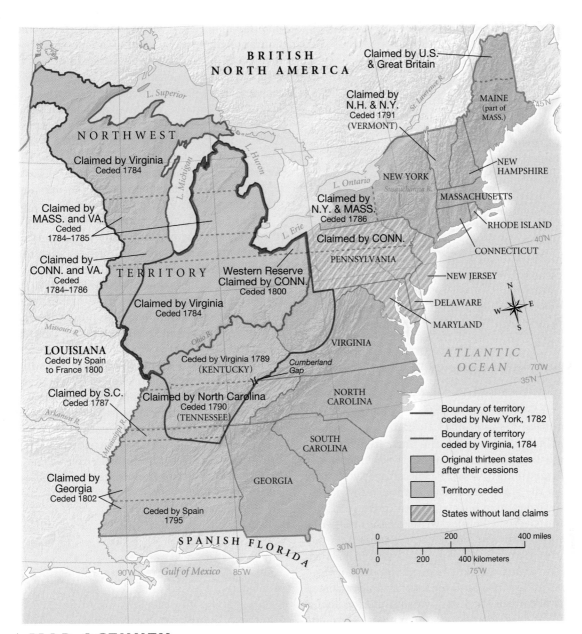

MAP ACTIVITY

Map 8.1   Cession of Western Lands, 1782–1802

The thirteen new states found it hard to ratify the Articles of Confederation without settling their conflicting land claims in the West, an area larger than the original states and occupied by Indian tribes. The five states objecting to the Articles' silence over western lands policy were Maryland, Delaware, New Jersey, Rhode Island, and Pennsylvania.

READING THE MAP: Which state had the largest claims on western territory?

CONNECTIONS: In what context did the first dispute regarding western lands arise? How was it resolved? Does the map suggest a reason why Pennsylvania, a large state, joined the four much smaller states on this issue?

and foreign affairs were created in 1781 to handle purely administrative functions. When the department heads were ambitious — as was Robert Morris, a wealthy Philadelphia merchant who served as superintendent of finance — they could exercise considerable executive power. The Articles of Confederation had deliberately refrained from setting up an executive branch, but a modest one was being invented by necessity.

REVIEW   Why was the confederation government's authority so limited?

▶ The Sovereign States

In the first decade of independence, the states were sovereign and all-powerful. Only a few functions, such as declaring war and peace, had been transferred to the confederation government. As Americans discarded their British identity, they thought of themselves instead as Virginians or New Yorkers or Rhode Islanders. Familiar and close to home, state governments claimed the allegiance of citizens and became the arena in which the Revolution's innovations would first be tried. States defined who was a voter, and they also defined who would be free. Squaring slavery with Revolutionary ideals became a front-burner issue everywhere; northern states had more success ending this inconsistency than did southern states, where slavery was deeply entrenched in the economy.

The State Constitutions

In May 1776, the congress recommended that all states draw up constitutions based on "the authority of the people." By 1778, all had done so. Having been denied the unwritten rights of Englishmen, Americans wanted written contracts that guaranteed basic principles. A shared feature of all the state constitutions was the conviction that government ultimately rests on the consent of the governed. Political writers in the late 1770s embraced the concept of **republicanism** as the underpinning of the new governments. Republicanism meant more than popular elections and representative institutions. For some, republicanism invoked a way of thinking about who leaders should be: autonomous, virtuous citizens who placed civic values above private interests. For others, it suggested direct democracy, with nothing standing in the way of the will of the people. For all, it meant government that promoted the people's welfare.

Widespread agreement about the virtues of republicanism went hand in hand with the idea that republics could succeed only in relatively small units, so that the people could make sure their interests were being served. Nearly every state continued the colonial practice of a two-chamber assembly but greatly augmented the powers of the lower house. Two states, Pennsylvania and Georgia, abolished the more elite upper house altogether, and most states severely limited the term and powers of the governor. Instead, real power resided with the lower houses, constituted to be responsive to popular majorities, with annual elections and guaranteed rotation in office. If a representative displeased his constituents, he could be out of office in a matter of months. James Madison learned about such political turnover when he lost reelection to the Virginia assembly in 1777. Ever shy, he attributed the loss to his reluctance to socialize at taverns and glad-hand his constituents in the traditional Virginia style. His series of increasingly significant political posts from 1778 to 1787 all came as a result of appointment, not popular election.

Six of the state constitutions included **bills of rights** — lists of basic individual liberties that government could not abridge. Virginia passed the first bill of rights in June 1776, and many of the other states borrowed from it. Its language resembles the Declaration of Independence, which Thomas Jefferson was drafting that month in Philadelphia. The Virginia bill of rights states: "That all men are by nature equally free and independent, and have certain inherent rights, of which, when they enter into a state of society, they cannot by any compact deprive or divest their posterity; namely, the enjoyment of life and liberty, with the means of acquiring and possessing property, and pursuing and obtaining happiness and safety." Along with these inherent rights went more specific rights to freedom of speech, freedom of the press, and trial by jury.

Who Are "the People"?

When the Continental Congress called for state constitutions based on "the authority of the people," and when the Virginia bill of rights granted "all men" certain rights, who was meant by "the people"? Who exactly were the citizens of this new country, and how far would the principle of democratic government extend? Different people answered these questions differently, but in the 1770s certain limits to political participation were widely agreed upon.

One limit was defined by property. In nearly every state, candidates for the highest offices had to meet substantial property qualifications. In Maryland, candidates for governor had to be worth the large sum of £5,000, while voters had to own fifty acres of land or £30. In the most democratic state, Pennsylvania, voters and candidates simply needed to be property tax payers, large or small. Only property owners were presumed to possess the necessary independence of mind to make wise political choices. Are not propertyless men, asked John Adams, "too little acquainted with public affairs to form a right judgment, and too dependent upon other men to have a will of their own?" Property qualifications probably disfranchised from one-quarter to one-half of adult white males in all the states. Not all of them took their nonvoter status quietly. One Maryland man challenged the £30 rule: "Every poor man has a life, a personal liberty, and a right to his earnings; and is in danger of being injured by government in a variety of ways." Why restrict such a man from voting? Others noted that propertyless men were fighting and dying in the Revolutionary War; surely they had legitimate political concerns. Finally, a few radical voices challenged the notion that wealth was correlated with good citizenship; maybe the opposite was true. But ideas like this were outside the mainstream. The writers of the new constitutions, themselves men of property, viewed the right to own and preserve property as a central principle of the Revolution.

Another exclusion from voting — women — was so ingrained that few stopped to question it. Yet the logic of allowing propertied females to vote did occur to a handful of well-placed women. Abigail Adams wrote to her husband, John, in 1782, "Even in the freest countrys our property is subject to the controul and disposal of our partners, to whom the Laws have given a sovereign Authority. Deprived of a voice in Legislation, obliged to submit to those Laws which are imposed upon us, is it not sufficient to make us indifferent to the publick Welfare?" A wealthy Virginia widow named Hannah Corbin wrote to her brother, congressional delegate Richard Henry Lee, to complain of her taxation without the corresponding representation. Her letter no longer exists, but Lee wrote in his reply that women would be "out of character . . . to press into those tumultuous assemblies of men where the business of choosing representatives is conducted."

Only three states specified that voters had to be male, so powerful was the unspoken assumption that only men could vote. Still, in one state, small numbers of women began to turn out at the polls in the 1780s. New Jersey's constitution of 1776 enfranchised all free inhabitants worth more than £50, language that in theory opened the door to free blacks as well as unmarried women who met the property requirement. (Married women owned no property, for by law their husbands held title to everything.) Little fanfare accompanied this radical shift, and some historians have inferred that the inclusion of unmarried women and blacks was an oversight. Yet other parts of the suffrage clause pertaining to residency and property were extensively debated when the clause was put in the state constitution, and no objections were raised at that time to its gender- and race-free language. Thus other historians have concluded that the law was intentionally inclusive. In 1790, a revised election law used the words *he or she* in reference to voters, making woman suffrage explicit. As one New Jersey legislator declared, "Our Constitution gives this right to maids or widows *black* or *white*." However, that legislator was complaining, not bragging, so his words do not mean that egalitarian suffrage was an accepted fact.

A Possible Voter in Essex County, New Jersey

Mrs. Elizabeth Alexander Stevens was married to John Stevens, a New Jersey delegate to the Continental Congress in 1783. Widowed in 1792, she would have then been eligible to vote in state elections according to New Jersey's unique enfranchisement of property-holding women. Essex County, where Elizabeth Stevens lived, was said to be the place where female suffrage was exercised most actively. This portrait, done around 1793–1794, represents the most likely face of that rare bird, the eighteenth-century female voter. The widow Stevens died in 1799, before suffrage was redefined to be the exclusive right of males. New Jersey Historical Society.

In 1790, only about 1,000 free black adults of both sexes lived in New Jersey, a state with a population of 184,000. The number of unmarried adult white women was probably also small and comprised mainly widows. In view of the property requirement, the voter blocs enfranchised under this law were minuscule. Still, this highly unusual situation lasted until 1807, when a new state law specifically disfranchised both blacks and women. Henceforth, independence of mind, that essential precondition of voting, was redefined to be sex- and race-specific.

In the 1780s, voting everywhere was class-specific because of property restrictions. John Adams urged the framers of the Massachusetts constitution not even to discuss the scope of suffrage but simply to adopt the traditional colonial property qualifications. If suffrage is brought up for debate, he warned, "there will be no end of it. New claims will arise; women will demand a vote; lads from twelve to twenty-one will think their rights not enough attended to; and every man who has not a farthing, will demand an equal voice with any other."

Equality and Slavery

Restrictions on political participation did not mean that propertyless people enjoyed no civil rights and liberties. The various state bills of rights applied to all individuals who were free; unfree people were another matter.

The author of the Virginia bill of rights was George Mason, a planter who owned 118 slaves. When he wrote that "all men are by nature equally free and independent," he meant that white Americans were the equals of the British and could not be denied the liberties of British citizens. Other Virginia legislators, worried about misinterpretations, added the phrase specifying that rights belonged only to people who had entered civil society. As one wrote, with relief, "Slaves, not being constituent members of our society, could never pretend to any benefit from such a maxim." One month later, the Declaration of Independence

> **"Slaves, not being constituent members of our society, could never pretend to any benefit from such a maxim."**
> — A Virginia legislator

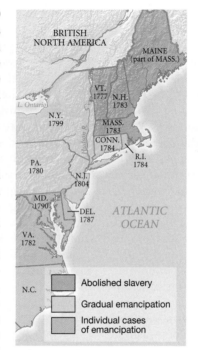

Legal Changes to Slavery, 1777–1804

used essentially the same phrase about equality, this time without the modifying clause about entering society. Two state constitutions, for Pennsylvania and Massachusetts, also picked it up. In Massachusetts, one town suggested rewording the draft constitution to read "All men, whites and blacks, are born free and equal." The suggestion was not implemented.

Slowly, the Revolutionary ideals about natural equality and liberty began to erode the institution of slavery. Often, enslaved blacks led the challenge. In 1777, several Massachusetts slaves petitioned for their "natural & unalienable right to that freedom which the great Parent of the Universe hath bestowed equally on all mankind." They modestly asked for freedom for their children at age twenty-one and were turned down. In 1779, similar petitions in Connecticut and New Hampshire met with no success. Seven Massachusetts free men, including the mariner brothers Paul and John Cuffe, refused to pay taxes for three years on the grounds that they could not vote and so were not represented. The Cuffe brothers landed in jail in 1780 for tax evasion, but their petition to the Massachusetts legislature spurred the extension of suffrage to taxpaying free blacks in 1783.

Another way to bring the issue before lawmakers was to sue in court. In 1781, a woman called **Elizabeth Freeman** (Mum Bett) was the first to win freedom in a Massachusetts court, basing her case on the just-passed state constitution that declared "all men are born free and equal." (See "Seeking the American Promise," page 236.) Another Massachusetts slave, Quok Walker, charged his master with assault and battery, arguing that he was a freeman under that same constitutional phrase. Walker won and was set free, a decision confirmed in an appeal to the state's superior court in 1783. Several similar cases followed, and by 1789 slavery had been effectively abolished by a series of judicial decisions in Massachusetts.

Pennsylvania's legislature enacted a **gradual emancipation** law in 1780, providing that infants born to a slave mother on or after March 1, 1780, would be freed at age twenty-eight. Not until 1847 did Pennsylvania fully abolish slavery, but slaves did not wait for such slow implementation.

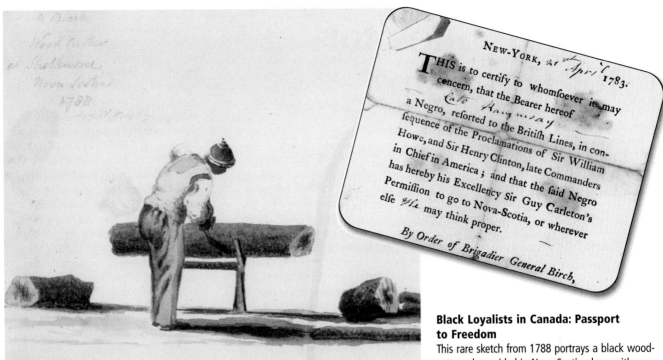

Black Loyalists in Canada: Passport to Freedom

This rare sketch from 1788 portrays a black wood-cutter who resided in Nova Scotia along with three thousand other black loyalists who had escaped to northeastern Canada between 1783 and 1785. The inset is a passport issued by the British high command to Cato Rammsay, permitting him to leave New York in 1783. Very few of the Nova Scotia refugees were able to acquire land, and after 1786 the British authorities stopped provisioning them. Most, like the man pictured here, were forced to become servants or day laborers for whites. Low wages created dissatisfaction, and racial tensions mounted. In 1791–1792, nearly a third of the black refugees in Nova Scotia left for Sierra Leone in West Africa, where British officials promised them land and opportunities for self-rule. Sketch: William Booth, National Archives of Canada C-401621; passport: Nova Scotia Archives & Records Management.

Untold numbers in Pennsylvania simply ran away and asserted their freedom. One estimate holds that more than half of young slave men in Philadelphia joined the ranks of free blacks, and by 1790, free blacks outnumbered slaves in Pennsylvania two to one.

Rhode Island and Connecticut adopted gradual emancipation laws in 1784. In 1785, New York expanded the terms under which individual owners could free slaves, but only in 1799 did the state adopt a gradual emancipation law; New Jersey followed suit in 1804. These were the two northern states with the largest number of slaves: New York in 1800 with 20,000, New Jersey with more than 12,000. In contrast, slaves in Pennsylvania numbered just 1,700. Gradual emancipation illustrates the tension between radical and conservative implications of republican ideology. Republican government protected people's liberties and property, yet slaves were both people and property. Gradual emancipation attempted to balance the civil rights of blacks and the property rights of their owners by delaying the promise of freedom.

South of Pennsylvania, in Delaware, Maryland, and Virginia, where slavery was critical to the economy, emancipation bills were rejected. All three states, however, eased legal restrictions and allowed individual acts of emancipation for adult slaves below the age of forty-five under new manumission laws passed in 1782 (Virginia),

1787 (Delaware), and 1790 (Maryland). By 1790, close to 10,000 newly freed Virginia slaves had formed local free black communities complete with schools and churches.

In the deep South — the Carolinas and Georgia — freedom for slaves was unthinkable among whites. Yet several thousand slaves had defected to the British during the war, and between 3,000 and 4,000 shipped out of Savannah and Charleston, destined for freedom. Adding northern blacks evacuated from New York City in 1783, the probable total of emancipated blacks who left the United States was between 8,000 and 10,000. Some went to Canada, some to England, and some to Sierra Leone on the west coast of Africa. Many hundreds took refuge with the Seminole and Creek Indians, becoming permanent members of their communities in Spanish Florida and western Georgia.

Although all these instances of emancipation were gradual, small, and certainly incomplete,

A Slave Sues for Her Freedom

The stirring language about liberty, equality, and freedom that inspired American revolutionaries in the 1770s was written into many state constitutions in the 1780s. Yet unfree people, held as property, had little recourse to challenge their status.

Massachusetts law presented an unusual opportunity because it recognized slaves as persons with legal standing to bring lawsuits against whites. Less than 2 percent of the state's population consisted of slaves, who numbered well under four thousand and lived mainly in the coastal cities. Before 1780, some thirty Massachusetts slaves had sued for their freedom, but their cases had turned on particular circumstances, such as an owner's unfulfilled promise to emancipate or a dispute over a slave's parentage. In 1780, a new Massachusetts state constitution boldly declared that "all men are born free and equal," opening the door to lawsuits based on a broad right to freedom. The first to bring suit under the new constitution was Bett, a thirty-year-old slave living in the western Massachusetts town of Sheffield.

Born of African parents in the early 1740s, Bett and her sister Lizzie grew up as slaves in Claverack, New York, in the wealthy Dutch American family of Pieter Hogeboom. When Hogeboom died in 1758, Bett and Lizzie were transported twenty-four miles east into Massachusetts, where Hogeboom's daughter Hannah lived with her husband, Colonel John Ashley. A town tax list of 1771 shows that Colonel Ashley, the richest man in Sheffield and a respected leader in the patriot cause, owned five slaves. He was known as a kind and gentle man, but as one account suggests, his wife was "a shrew untamable" and "the most despotic of mistresses." One day, Hannah Ashley became enraged with Lizzie and heaved a hot kitchen shovel at her. Bett interceded to protect her sister, sustaining a burn on her arm that left a lifelong scar.

On another occasion, in 1773, Bett was, in her own words, "keepin' still and mindin' things" while she served refreshments to a dozen white men gathered at her master's house to draw up a protest petition against the British. Colonel Ashley took the lead in drafting a set of resolutions, the first of which read, "Resolved, That mankind in a state of nature are equal, free, and independent of each other, and have a right to the undisturbed enjoyment of their lives, their liberty and property." Bett well noted the import of their discussion.

In the fall of 1780, Bett overheard conversations at the Ashleys' house about the new Massachusetts state constitution. Bett pondered the words proclaiming equality and reasonably concluded that they applied to her. She sought out a young lawyer named Theodore Sedgwick, who had been present at the petition meeting in 1773. Sedgwick, Sheffield's representative in the new Massachusetts legislature, filed a writ in April 1781 requesting the recovery of unlawfully held property — in this case, the human property of Bett and a second plaintiff owned by Ashley, a man identified only as Brom, "a Negro man" and a "labourer." Ashley contested the writ, and the case, officially called *Brom and Bett v. J. Ashley, Esq.*, went to court.

When the case went to trial, a jury agreed that Bett and Brom were entitled to freedom and ordered Ashley to pay each plaintiff thirty shillings in damages as well as all the court costs. The brief court records do not reveal the legal arguments presented, but Sedgwick descendants later boasted that Theodore Sedgwick invoked the Massachusetts constitution to argue that slavery could not exist in the state.

Bett chose a new name to go with her new status: Elizabeth Freeman. She left Colonel Ashley's employ and became a paid housekeeper in the Sedgwick family, rais-

their symbolic importance was enormous. Every state from Pennsylvania north acknowledged that slavery was fundamentally inconsistent with Revolutionary ideology. On some level, white southerners also understood this, but their inability to imagine a free biracial society prevented them from taking action. George Washington owned 390 slaves and freed not one of them in the 1780s, even when his friend the French general Lafayette urged him to do so as a model for others. In his will, written in 1799, Washington provided for the eventual freedom of his slaves — but only after his wife, Martha, died. She freed them one year later, preferring loss of income to the uneasy situation of her life being the only barrier to her slaves' freedom.

Emancipation in the 1780s, limited as it was, shows that the phrase of the Declaration of Independence — "all men are created equal" — was beginning to acquire real force as a basic principle. Yet a geographic pattern was taking shape: From the 1780s on, the North was associated with freedom and the South with slavery, with profound consequences for the next two centuries of American history.

REVIEW How did states determine who would be allowed to vote?

ing the children when their mother became incapacitated by mental illness. "Her spirit spurned slavery," a Sedgwick daughter wrote, offering this quotation from Bett as evidence: "Anytime, anytime while I was a slave, if one minute's freedom had been offered to me, and I had been told I must die at the end of that minute, I would have taken it — just to stand one minute on God's earth a free woman — I would."

The Sedgwicks were especially grateful to Freeman for her commanding presence of mind during Shays's Rebellion in 1786 (see page 244). Because Sedgwick represented the legal elite of the county, he was the target of hostile crowd action. Freeman was home alone when insurgents, searching for Sedgwick and for valuables to plunder, demanded entry. Unable to prevent their entry, Freeman let the dissidents in but followed the men around with a large shovel and threatened to flatten anyone who damaged any property. When Freeman died in 1829, she was buried in the Sedgwick family plot, with a gravestone inscription supplied by the Sedgwicks that ended "Good mother, farewell."

Freeman's lawsuit of 1781 inspired others to sue, and in a case in 1783 the judge of the Massachusetts Supreme Court declared that "slavery is in my judgment as effectively abolished as it can be by the granting of rights and privileges" in the state constitution. It took several more legal challenges and additional time for that news to trickle out, but the erosion of slavery in Massachusetts gradually picked up speed as blacks demanded manumission or wages for work, or simply walked away from their masters. In 1790, the federal census listed 5,369 "other free persons" (that is, nonwhites) in the state and not a single slave.

Questions for Consideration

1. What events encouraged the slave Bett to take her master to court to sue for freedom?

Elizabeth Freeman

Solo portraits of African American women in the early Republic are incredibly rare. This 1811 watercolor of "Mum Bett" was painted by Susan Ridley Sedgwick, wife of one of the Sedgwick sons, indicating the importance of Freeman to the family. A Sedgwick son later wrote: "If there could be a practical refutation of the imagined superiority of our race to hers, the life and character of this woman would afford that refutation. . . . She had nothing of the submissive or subdued character, which succumbs to superior force. . . . She had, when occasion required it, an air of command which conferred a degree of dignity." Massachusetts Historical Society.

2. How would you characterize Mum Bett's status in the Sedgwick household? Was she merely a hired servant, or something more?

3. Compare Elizabeth Freeman's desire to pass from slavery to freedom with the claim of white revolutionaries who sought freedom in order to escape being "enslaved" by Britain.

▶ The Confederation's Problems

In 1783, the confederation government faced three interrelated concerns: paying down the large war debt, making formal peace with the Indians, and dealing with western settlement. The federal debt remained a vexing problem, since the Articles of Confederation lacked the power to enforce its tax requisitions. Making matters worse, the debt suddenly escalated in 1783 when army officers threatened to stage a coup to secure pensions. Western lands suggested a promising source of income to reduce the federal debt, but competing land claims made it difficult for states to use the proceeds of land sales to retire state debts. The Indian inhabitants of those same lands had different ideas, of course.

From 1784 to 1786, the congress struggled mightily with these three issues. Some leaders were gripped by a sense of crisis, fearing that the Articles of Confederation were too weak. Others defended the Articles as the best guarantee of liberty because real governance occurred at the state level, closer to the people. A major outbreak of civil disorder in western Massachusetts quickly crystallized the debate and propelled the critics of the Articles into decisive and far-reaching action.

The War Debt and the Newburgh Conspiracy

For nearly two years, the Continental army camped at Newburgh, a town just north of the British-occupied city of New York, awaiting news of a finalized peace treaty that would send the British army home. The soldiers at Newburgh were bored, restless, and upset about the confederation government's wobbly financial standing. Military payrolls were far in arrears, and an earlier promise of generous pensions (half pay for life), made to all officers in 1780 in a desperate effort to retain them, seemed increasingly unlikely to be honored. In December 1782, officers petitioned the congress for immediate back pay for their men so that when peace arrived, no one would go home penniless. The petition carried an unspecified threat: "The uneasiness of the soldiers, for want of pay, is great and dangerous; any further experiments on their patience may have fatal effects."

> **"The uneasiness of the soldiers, for want of pay, is great and dangerous; any further experiments on their patience may have fatal effects."**
> — Officers' petition to the congress

Instead of rejecting the petition outright for lack of money, several members of the congress saw an opportunity to make an especially forceful case to the states for the necessity of taxation. One of these was **Robert Morris**, a Philadelphia merchant with a gift for financial dealings, who was the government's superintendent of finance. Morris single-handedly kept the books and wheedled loans from European bankers, using his own substantial fortune as collateral. He knew better than anyone how insolvent the United States was. In 1781 and later in 1786, Morris led an effort to amend the Articles to allow the government to collect a 5 percent **impost** (an import tax), yet each time it failed by one vote. The dissenters, Rhode Island and New York, collected state import duties at their bustling ports, so it was in their interest to block a national impost. Both states acknowledged the seriousness of the confederation's taxation problem — just not at the same time. The failure of the impost vote showed how unworkable the amendment provision of the Articles was. In this context, the petition from the army officers offered a new opening to pressure the states for the power to tax.

The result was a plot called the **Newburgh Conspiracy**, the country's first and only instance of a threatened military coup. Morris and several other congressmen offered encouragement to officers to act as if the army would march on the congress to demand its pay. No actual coup was envisioned; both sides simply wanted a more powerful central government to arise from the threat. Yet the risks were great, for not everyone would understand that this was a ruse. What if the soldiers, incited by their grievances, could not be held in check? One congressman was confident that the risk was worth taking. He wrote privately (and guardedly) about the officers' petition: "I am glad to see things in their present train. It must terminate in giving to Government that power without which Government is just a name."

General George Washington, sympathetic to the plight of unpaid soldiers and officers, had approved the initial petition. But the plotters, knowing of his reputation for integrity, did not inform him of their collusion with congressional leaders. In March 1783, when the general learned of these developments, he delivered an emotional speech to a meeting of five hundred officers, reminding them in stirring language of honor, heroism, and sacrifice. He urged them to put their faith in the congress, and he denounced the plotters as "subversive of all order and discipline." In essence, Washington asserted the key principle that civilian government takes precedence over the military. His audience was left speechless and tearful, and the plot was immediately defused.

In the midst of the crisis, congressman Robert Morris put forward his own threat, to resign. He complained that a government that could incur debts with no assured way to pay them, including the debts owed the soldiers, was unworkable: "I will never be the Minister of Injustice." Morris was not universally admired, for just a few years earlier he had left the congress amid accusations that he had unfairly profited from public service. But his threat to quit now, at this crucial juncture, sent shock waves around the country. Morris continued to work to find money to pay the soldiers, as did Washington. In the end, a trickle of money from a few states was too little and too late, coming after the army began to disband. For its part, the congress voted to endorse a plan to *commute*, or transform, the lifetime pension promised the officers into a lump-sum payment of full pay for five years. But no lump sum of money was available. Instead, the officers were issued "commutation certificates," promising future payment with interest, which quickly depreciated like other forms of public debt in the 1780s.

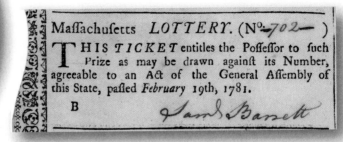

Massachusetts *LOTTERY.* (N°.702—)

THIS *TICKET* entitles the Possessor to such Prize as may be drawn against its Number, agreeable to an Act of the General Assembly of this State, passed *February* 19th, 1781.

B   *Saml Barrett*

In 1783, the soldiers' pay issue added some $5 million to the rising public debt, forcing the congress to press for larger requisitions from the states. The confederation, however, had one new source of enormous untapped wealth: the extensive western territories, attractive to the fast-growing white population but currently inhabited by Indians.

The Treaty of Fort Stanwix

Although the Indians were excluded from the 1783 Treaty of Paris, the confederation government now recognized the need to formalize treaties that would end ongoing hostilities between Indians and settlers and secure land cessions. The congress was particularly concerned with the land inhabited by the **Iroquois Confederacy**, a league of six tribes, but now claimed by the states of New York and Massachusetts based on their colonial charters (see Map 8.1). The Massachusetts charter was older by four decades, but New York felt entitled because the disputed land bordered its territory. The tension between the two states was such that it struck a southern delegate as "the seeds of dissension which I think will not end without a civil war."

At issue was the revenue stream that land sales would generate. The congress summoned the Iroquois to a meeting in October 1784 at Fort Stanwix, on the upper reaches of the Mohawk River. The Articles of Confederation gave the congress (as opposed to individual states) the right to manage diplomacy, war, and "all affairs with the Indians, not members of any of the States." Although Massachusetts accepted the confederation's authority, New York's governor seized on the ambiguous language in the Articles, claiming

that the Iroquois were in fact "members" of his state and that New York had sole rights to negotiate. He called his own meeting with the Iroquois at Fort Stanwix in September. Suspecting that New York might be superseded by the congress, the most important chiefs declined to come and instead sent deputies without authority to negotiate. The Mohawk leader Joseph Brant shrewdly identified the problem of divided authority that afflicted the confederation government: "Here lies some Difficulty in our Minds, that there should be two separate bodies to manage these Affairs." No deal was struck with New York.

Three weeks later, U.S. commissioners opened proceedings at Fort Stanwix with the Seneca chief Cornplanter and Captain Aaron Hill, a Mohawk leader, accompanied by six hundred Indians from the six tribes. The U.S. commissioners arrived with a security detail of one hundred New Jersey militiamen.

The Americans demanded a return of prisoners of war; recognition of the confederation's authority to negotiate, rather than that of individual states; and an all-important cession of a strip of land from Fort Niagara due south, which established U.S.-held territory adjacent to the border with Canada. This crucial change enclosed the Iroquois land within the United States and made it impossible for the Indians to claim to be *between* the United States and Canada. When the tribal leaders balked, one of the commissioners sternly replied, "You are mistaken in supposing that, having been excluded from the treaty between the United States and the King of England, you are become a free and independent nation and may make what terms you please. It is not so. You are a subdued people."

Cornplanter

Cornplanter, whose Indian name was Kaintwakon ("what one plants"), headed the Seneca delegation at Fort Stanwix in 1784. Raised fully Indian, he was the son of a Dutch fur trader and a highborn Seneca woman of the Wolf Clan. Evidently, the Dutch trader did not stick around for long, as Cornplanter never learned either Dutch or English. But during the Revolution, when his father faced capture by Indians, Cornplanter recognized him by his name and released him. The Seneca chief sat for this formal portrait in full finery in the 1790s; he died in 1836, at about age ninety. © Collection of the New-York Historical Society.

In the end, the treaty was signed, gifts were given, and six high-level Indian hostages were kept at the fort awaiting the release of the American prisoners taken during the Revolutionary War, mostly women and children. In addition, a significant side deal sealed the release of much of the Seneca tribe's claim to the Ohio Valley to the United States. This move was a major surprise and aggravation to the Delaware, Mingo, and Shawnee Indians who lived there. In the months to come, tribes not at the meeting tried to disavow the **Treaty of Fort Stanwix** as a document signed under coercion by virtual hostages. But the confederation government ignored those complaints and made plans to survey and develop the Ohio Territory.

New York's governor astutely figured that the congress's power to implement the treaty terms was limited. The confederation's financial coffers were nearly empty, and its leadership was stretched. So New York quietly began surveying and then selling the very land it had failed to secure by individual treaty with the Iroquois. As that fact became generally known, it pointed up the weakness of the confederation government. One Connecticut leader wondered, "What is to defend us from the ambition and rapacity of New York, when she has spread over that vast territory, which she claims and holds? Do we not already see in her the seeds of an over-bearing ambition?"

Land Ordinances and the Northwest Territory

The congress ignored western New York and turned instead to the Ohio Valley to make good on the promise of western expansion. Delegate Thomas Jefferson, charged with drafting a policy, proposed dividing the territory north of the Ohio River and east of the Mississippi — called the **Northwest Territory** — into nine new states with evenly spaced east-west boundaries and townships ten miles square. He at first advocated giving the land to settlers, rather than selling it, arguing that future property taxes on the improved land would be payment enough. Jefferson's aim was to encourage rapid and democratic settlement, to build a nation of freeholders (as opposed to renters), and to discourage land speculation. Jefferson also insisted on representative governments in the new states; they would not become colonies of the older states. Finally, Jefferson's draft prohibited slavery in the nine new states.

The congress adopted parts of Jefferson's plan in the Ordinance of 1784: the rectangular grid, the nine states, and the guarantee of self-government and eventual statehood. What the congress found too radical was the proposal to give away the land; the national domain was the confederation's only source of independent wealth. The slavery prohibition also failed, by a vote of seven to six states.

A year later, the congress revised the legislation with procedures for mapping and selling the land. The Ordinance of 1785 called for three to five states, divided into townships six miles square, further divided into thirty-six sections of 640 acres, each section enough for four family farms (Map 8.2). Property was thus reduced to easily mappable squares. Land would be sold by public auction at a minimum price of one dollar an acre, with highly desirable land bid up for more. Two further restrictions applied: The minimum purchase was 640

Treaty of Fort Stanwix, 1784

acres, and payment had to be in hard money or in certificates of debt from Revolutionary days. This effectively meant that the land's first owners would be prosperous speculators. The grid of invariant squares further enhanced speculation, allowing buyers and sellers to operate without ever setting foot on the acreage. The commodification of land had been taken to a new level.

Speculators usually held the land for resale rather than inhabiting it. Thus they avoided direct contact with the most serious obstacle to settlement: the dozens of Indian tribes that claimed the land as their own. The treaty signed at Fort Stanwix in 1784 was followed in 1785 by the Treaty of Fort McIntosh, which similarly coerced partial cessions of land from the Delaware, Wyandot, Chippewa, and Ottawa tribes. Finally, in 1786, a united Indian meeting near Detroit issued an ultimatum: No cession would be valid without the unanimous consent of the tribes. The Indians advised the United States to "prevent your surveyors and other people from coming upon our side of the Ohio river." For two more decades, violent Indian wars in Ohio and Indiana would continue to impede white settlement (see chapter 9).

In 1787, a third land act, called the **Northwest Ordinance**, set forth a three-stage process by which settled territories would advance to statehood. First, the congress would appoint officials for a sparsely populated territory who would adopt a legal code and appoint local magistrates to administer justice. When the free male population of voting age and landowning status (fifty acres) reached 5,000, the territory could elect its own legislature and send a nonvoting delegate to the congress. When the population of voting citizens reached 60,000, the territory could write a state constitution and apply for full admission to the Union. At all three territorial stages, the inhabitants were subject to taxation to support the Union, in the same manner as were the original states.

The Northwest Ordinance of 1787 was perhaps the most important legislation passed by the confederation government. It ensured that the new United States, so recently released from colonial dependency, would not itself become a colonial power—at least not with respect to white citizens. The mechanism it established allowed for the successful and orderly expansion of the United States across the continent in the next century.

MAP 8.2   The Northwest Territory and Ordinance of 1785

Surveyors ventured into the eastern edge of the Northwest Territory in the 1780s and produced this first plat map (at right), showing the 6-mile square townships neatly laid out. Each township was subdivided into one-mile squares each containing sixteen 40-acre farms. Jefferson got his straight lines and right angles after all; compare this map to his on page 242.

Plat Map © TNGenNet Inc. 2002.

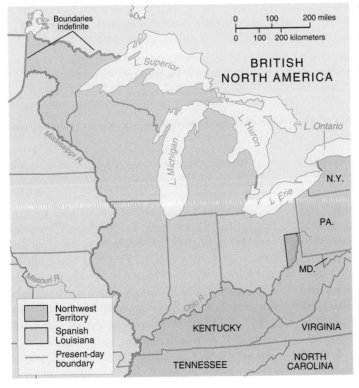

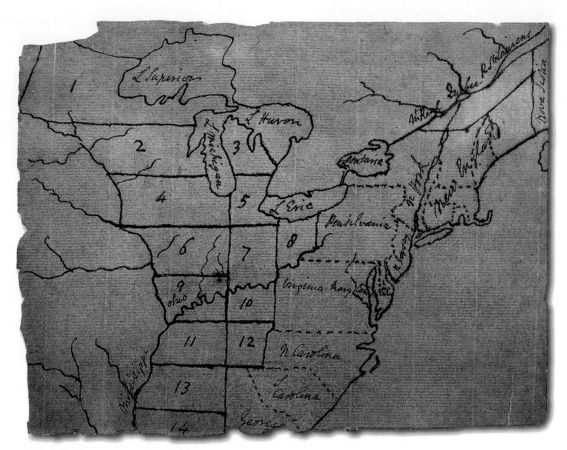

VISUAL ACTIVITY

Jefferson's Map of the Northwest Territory

Thomas Jefferson sketched out borders for nine new states in his initial plan for the Northwest Territory in 1784 and additional anticipated states below the Ohio River. Straight lines and right angles held a strong appeal for him. But such regularity ignored inconvenient geographic features such as rivers and even more inconvenient political facts such as Indian territorial claims, most unlikely to be ceded by treaty in orderly blocks. Jefferson also submitted a list of distinctive names for the states. Number 9, for example, was Polypotamia, "land of many rivers" in Greek. Other proposed names were Sylvania, Michigania, Assenisipia, and Metropotamia. William L. Clements Library.

READING THE IMAGE: What does this map indicate about Jefferson's vision of the Northwest Territory?

CONNECTIONS: What were the problems with Jefferson's design for the division of the territory? Why did the congress alter it in the land ordinances of 1784, 1785, and 1787?

Nonwhites were not forgotten or neglected in the 1787 ordinance. The brief document acknowledged the Indian presence in the Northwest Territory and promised that "the utmost good faith shall always be observed towards the Indians; their lands and property shall never be taken from them without their consent; and, in their property, rights, and liberty, they shall never be invaded or disturbed, unless in just and lawful wars authorized by Congress." The 1787 ordinance further pledged that "laws founded in justice and humanity, shall from time to time be made for preventing wrongs being done to them, and for preserving peace and friendship

with them." Such promises were full of noble intentions, but they were not generally honored in the decades to come.

Jefferson's original and remarkable suggestion to prohibit slavery in the Northwest Territory resurfaced in the 1787 ordinance, passing this time without any debate. Probably the addition of a fugitive slave provision in the act set southern congressmen at ease: Escaped slaves caught north of the Ohio River would be returned south. Also, abundant territory south of the Ohio remained available for the spread of slavery. The ordinance thus acknowledged and supported slavery even as it barred it from one region. Still,

View of a Farm Near Detroit, 1789
In French, Detroit means "the narrows," in this case the narrow river connecting Lake Huron and Lake Erie. Detroit was founded in 1701 by the French as a fur-trading and defensive fort; the British took it over in 1763. In 1783, it became part of the Northwest Territory, but the British failed to vacate until the Jay Treaty of 1795 forced them out. This water-color scene was painted in 1789 on a piece of silk by Anne Powell, a loyalist refugee from Boston whose family fled to Canada and then Detroit. Royal Ontario Museum.

the prohibition of slavery in the Northwest Territory perpetuated the dynamic of gradual emancipation in the North. North-South sectionalism based on slavery was slowly taking shape.

The Requisition of 1785 and Shays's Rebellion, 1786–1787

Without an impost amendment and with public land sales projected but not yet realized, the confederation turned again to the states in the 1780s to contribute revenue to the central government. The amount requested was $3 million, four times larger than the previous year's requisition. Of this sum, 30 percent was needed for the operating costs of the government. Another 30 percent was earmarked to pay debts owed to foreign lenders, who insisted on payment in gold or silver. The remaining 40 percent was to go to Americans who owned government bonds, the IOUs of the Revolutionary years. A significant slice of that 40 percent represented the interest (but not the principal) owed to army officers for their recently issued "commutation certificates." This was a tax that, if collected, was going to hurt.

At this time, states were struggling under state tax levies. Several states without major ports (and the import duties that ports generated) were already asking a great deal of their farmer citizens in order to retire state debts from the Revolution. New Jersey and Connecticut fit this profile, and both state legislatures voted to ignore the requisition. In other states, like New Hampshire, town meetings voted to refuse to pay, on the grounds that the towns didn't have the money. In late 1786, a group of two hundred armed insurgents surrounded the New Hampshire capitol to protest the taxes but were driven off by a hastily called and armed militia. The shocked assemblymen pulled back from an earlier order to haul delinquent taxpayers into courts. Some states (Rhode Island, North Carolina, and Georgia) responded to their constituents' protests by issuing abundant amounts of paper money and allowing taxes to be paid in greatly depreciated currency.

Nowhere were the tensions so extreme as in Massachusetts. For four years in a row, a fiscally conservative legislature, dominated by the coastal commercial centers, had passed tough tax laws to pay state creditors who required payment in hard money, not cheap paper. Then in March 1786, the legislature in Boston loaded the federal requisition onto the bill. In June, farmers in southeastern Massachusetts marched on a courthouse in an effort to close it down, and petitions of complaint about oppressive taxation poured in from the western two-thirds of the state. In July 1786, when the legislature adjourned, having yet again ignored their complaints, dissidents held a series of conventions and called for revisions to the state constitution to promote democracy, eliminate the elite upper house, and move the capital farther west in the state.

Still unheard in Boston, the dissidents in six counties targeted the county courts, the local symbol of state authority. In the fall of 1786, several thousand armed men in each protest event forced bewildered judges to close their courts until the state constitution was revised. Sympathetic local militias did not intervene. The insurgents were not predominantly poor or debt-ridden farmers; they included veteran soldiers and officers in the Continental army as well as town leaders. One was a farmer and onetime army captain, Daniel Shays.

The governor of Massachusetts, James Bowdoin, once a protester against British taxes, now characterized the western dissidents as illegal rebels. He vilified Shays as the chief leader (he was not), and a Boston newspaper claimed that Shays planned to burn Boston to the ground and overthrow the government, a report that created panic. Another former radical, Samuel Adams, took the extreme position that "the man who dares rebel against the laws of a republic ought to suffer death." Those aging revolutionaries had little considered that representatives in a state legislature could seem to be as oppressive as monarchs. The dissidents challenged the assumption that popularly elected governments would always be fair and just.

Members of the Continental Congress had much to worry about. In nearly every state, the requisition of 1785 spawned some combination of crowd protests, threats to state authorities, demands for inflationary paper money, and emotional diatribes about greedy money speculators. The Massachusetts insurgency was the worst episode, and it seemed to be spinning out of control. In October 1786, the congress began to anticipate the need for armed intervention. But

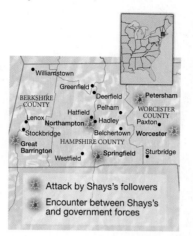

Shays's Rebellion, 1786–1787

Attack by Shays's followers

Encounter between Shays's and government forces

when it called for enlistments to triple the size of the federal army, fewer than 100 men responded. So Governor Bowdoin raised a private army, gaining the services of some 3,000 men with pay provided by wealthy and fearful Boston merchants.

In January 1787, the insurgents learned of the private army marching west from Boston, and 1,500 of them moved swiftly to capture a federal armory in Springfield to obtain weapons. But a militia band loyal to the state government beat them to the weapons facility and met their attack with gunfire; 4 rebels were killed and another 20 wounded. The final and bloodless encounter came at Petersham, where Bowdoin's army surprised the rebels on a freezing February morning and took 150 prisoners; the others fled into the woods, but most were soon rounded up and jailed. Daniel Shays escaped capture by fleeing to the self-declared independent republic of Vermont.

In the end, 2 men were executed for rebellion; 16 more sentenced to hang were reprieved at the last moment on the gallows. Some 4,000 men gained leniency by confessing their misconduct and swearing an oath of allegiance to the state. A special Disqualification Act prohibited the penitent rebels from voting, holding public office, serving on juries, working as schoolmasters, or operating taverns for up to three years.

Shays's Rebellion caused leaders throughout the country to worry about the confederation's ability to handle civil disorder. Inflammatory Massachusetts newspapers wrote about bloody mob rule; perhaps, some feared, similar "combustibles" in other states were awaiting the spark that would set off a dreadful political conflagration. New York lawyer John Jay wrote to George Washington, "Our affairs seem to lead to some crisis, some revolution — something I cannot foresee or conjecture. I am uneasy and apprehensive; more so than during the war." Benjamin Franklin, in his eighties, shrewdly observed that in 1776 Americans had feared "an excess of power in the rulers" but now the problem was perhaps "a defect of obedience" in the subjects. Among such leaders, the sense of crisis in the confederation had greatly deepened.

REVIEW   Why did farmers in western Massachusetts revolt against the state legislature?

Two Rebel Leaders and a Silver Bowl for an Anti-Shays General
A Boston almanac of 1787 yields the only rough depiction of Daniel Shays in existence. Shays is standing with another rebel leader, Job Shattuck, from the town of Groton. This particular almanac series was quite pro-Constitution in 1788, so very likely this picture was intended to mock the rebels by showing them in fancy uniforms and armed with swords, trappings beyond their presumed lowly means. The silver bowl was a present to an official general, William Shepard of Springfield, from his militiamen, who honored his victory over the insurgents. Presentational silver conveyed a double message: It announced gratitude and praise in engraved words, and it transmitted considerable monetary value in the silver itself. General Shepard could display his trophy on a shelf, use it as a punch bowl, will it to descendants to keep his moment of fame alive, or melt it down in hard times.
Bowl: Yale University Art Gallery, Mabel Brady Garvan Collection; illustration: National Portrait Gallery, Smithsonian Institution/Art Resource, NY.

▶ The United States Constitution

Shays's Rebellion provoked an odd mixture of fear and hope that the government under the Articles of Confederation was losing its grip on power. A small circle of Virginians decided to try one last time to augment the powers granted to the government by the Articles. Their call for a meeting to discuss trade regulation led, more quickly than they could have imagined in 1786, to a total reworking of the national government.

From Annapolis to Philadelphia

Led by James Madison, the Virginians convinced the confederation congress to allow a September 1786 meeting of delegates at Annapolis, Maryland, to try again to revise the trade regulation powers of the Articles. Only five states participated, and the delegates rescheduled the meeting for Philadelphia in May 1787. The congress reluctantly endorsed the Philadelphia meeting and limited its scope to "the sole and express purpose of revising the Articles of Confederation." But at least one representative at the Annapolis meeting had more ambitious plans. **Alexander Hamilton** of New York hoped the Philadelphia meeting would do whatever was necessary to strengthen the federal government. Young Hamilton was suited for such bold steps. Born in impoverished circumstances in the West Indies, he had made his way into the elite circles of New York society (via talent, hard work, and a well-connected marriage) and now fully identified with the elite and their fear of democratic disorder.

The fifty-five men who assembled at Philadelphia in May 1787 for the **constitutional convention** were generally those who had already concluded that there were weaknesses in the Articles of Confederation. Few attended who were opposed to revising the Articles. Patrick Henry, author of the Virginia Resolves in 1765 and more recently state governor, refused to go to the con-

vention, saying he "smelled a rat." Rhode Island declined to send delegates. Two men sent by New York's legislature to check the influence of fellow-delegate Alexander Hamilton left in dismay in the middle of the convention, leaving Hamilton as the sole representative of the state.

This gathering of white men included no artisans, day laborers, or ordinary farmers. Two-thirds of the delegates were lawyers. Half had been officers in the Continental army. The majority had served in the confederation congress and knew its strengths and weaknesses. Seven men had been governors of their states and knew firsthand the frustrations of thwarted executive power. A few elder statesmen attended, such as Benjamin Franklin and George Washington, but on the whole the delegates were young, like Madison and Hamilton.

The Pennsylvania Statehouse

The constitutional convention assembled at the Pennsylvania statehouse to sweat out the summer of 1787. Despite the heat, the delegates nailed the windows shut to eliminate the chance of being heard by eavesdroppers, so intent were they on secrecy. The statehouse, built in the 1740s to house the colony's assembly, accommodated the Continental Congress at various times in the 1770s and 1780s. The building is now called Independence Hall in honor of the signing of the Declaration of Independence there in 1776. Historical Society of Pennsylvania.

The Virginia and New Jersey Plans

The convention worked in secrecy, which enabled the men to freely explore alternatives without fear that their honest opinions would come back to haunt them. The Virginia delegation first laid out a fifteen-point plan for a complete restructuring of the government. This **Virginia Plan** was a total repudiation of the principle of a confederation of states. Largely the work of Madison, the plan set out a three-branch government composed of a two-chamber legislature, a powerful executive, and a judiciary. It practically eliminated the voices of the smaller states by pegging representation in both houses of the congress to population. The theory was that government operated directly on people, not on states. Among the breathtaking powers assigned to the congress were the rights to veto state legislation and to coerce states militarily to obey national laws. To prevent the congress from having absolute power, the executive and judiciary could jointly veto its actions.

In mid-June, delegates from New Jersey, Connecticut, Delaware, and New Hampshire — all small states — unveiled an alternative proposal. The **New Jersey Plan**, as it was called, maintained the existing single-house congress of the Articles of Confederation in which each state had one vote. Acknowledging the need for an executive, it created a plural presidency to be shared by three men elected by the congress from among its membership. Where it sharply departed from the existing government was in the sweeping powers it gave to the new congress: the right to tax, regulate trade, and use force on unruly state governments. In favoring national power over states' rights, it aligned itself with the Virginia Plan. But the New Jersey Plan retained the confederation principle that the national government was to be an assembly of states, not of people.

For two weeks, delegates debated the two plans, focusing on the key issue of representation. The small-state delegates conceded that one house in a two-house legislature could be apportioned by population, but they would never agree that both houses could be. Madison was equally vehement about bypassing representation by state, which he viewed as the fundamental flaw in the Articles.

The debate seemed deadlocked, and for a while the convention was "on the verge of dissolution, scarce held together by the strength of a hair," according to one delegate. Only in mid-July did the so-called **Great Compromise** break the stalemate and produce the basic structural features of the emerging **United States Constitution**. Proponents of the competing plans agreed on a bicameral legislature. Representation in the lower house, the House of Representatives, would be apportioned by population, and representation in the upper house, the Senate, would come from all the states equally. Instead of one vote per state in the upper house, as in the New Jersey Plan, the compromise provided two senators who voted independently.

Representation by population turned out to be an ambiguous concept once it was subjected to rigorous discussion. Who counted? Were slaves, for example, people or property? As people, they would add weight to the southern delegations in the House of Representatives, but as property they would add to the tax burdens of those states. What emerged was the compromise known as the **three-fifths clause**: All free persons plus "three-fifths of all other Persons" constituted the numerical base for the apportionment of representatives.

Using "all other Persons" as a substitute for "slaves" indicates the discomfort delegates felt in acknowledging in the Constitution the existence of slavery. The words *slave* and *slavery* appear nowhere in the document, but slavery figured in two places besides the three-fifths clause. Government power over trade regulation naturally included the slave trade, which the Constitution euphemistically described as "the Migration or Importation of such Persons as any of the States now shall think proper to admit." Another provision contrived to guarantee the return of fugitive slaves using awkward, lawyer-like prose: "No person, held to Service or Labour in one State, under the Laws thereof, escaping into another, shall, in Consequence of any Law or Regulation therein, be discharged from such Service or Labour but shall be delivered up on Claim of the party to whom such Service or Labour may be due." Although slavery was nowhere named, it was nonetheless recognized, protected, and thereby perpetuated by the U.S. Constitution.

Democracy versus Republicanism

The delegates in Philadelphia made a distinction between *democracy* and *republicanism* new to the American political vocabulary. Pure democracy was now taken to be a dangerous thing. As a Massachusetts delegate put it, "The evils we experience flow from the excess of democracy." The delegates still favored republican institutions, but they created a government that gave direct voice to the people only in

> "The evils we experience flow from the excess of democracy."
> — A Massachusetts delegate

the House and that granted a check on that voice to the Senate, a body of men elected not by direct popular vote but by the state legislatures. Senators served for six years, with no limit on reelection; they were protected from the whims of democratic majorities, and their long terms fostered experience and maturity in office.

Similarly, the presidency evolved into a powerful office out of the reach of direct democracy. The delegates devised an electoral college whose only function was to elect the president and vice president. Each state's legislature would choose the electors, whose number was the sum of representatives and senators for the state, an interesting blending of the two principles of representation. The president thus would owe his office not to the Congress, the states, or the people, but to a temporary assemblage of distinguished citizens who could vote their own judgment on the candidates. His term of office was four years, but he could be reelected without limitation.

The framers had developed a far more complex form of federal government than that provided by the Articles of Confederation. To curb the excesses of democracy, they devised a government with limits and checks on all three of its branches. They set forth a powerful president who could veto legislation passed in Congress, but they gave Congress the power to override presidential vetoes. They set up a national judiciary to settle disputes between states and citizens of different states. They separated the branches of government not only by functions and by reciprocal checks but also by deliberately basing the election of each branch on different universes of voters — voting citizens (the House), state legislators (the Senate), and the electoral college (the presidency).

The convention carefully listed the powers of the president and of Congress. The president could initiate policy, propose legislation, and veto acts of Congress; he could command the military and direct foreign policy; and he could appoint the entire judiciary, subject to Senate approval. Congress held the purse strings: the power to levy taxes, to regulate trade, and to coin money and control the currency. States were expressly forbidden to issue paper money. Two more powers of Congress — to "provide for the common defence and general Welfare" of the country and "to make all laws which shall be necessary and proper" for carrying out its powers — provided elastic language that came closest to Madison's wish to grant sweeping powers to the new government.

While no one was entirely satisfied with every line of the Constitution, only three dissenters refused to sign the document. The Constitution specified a mechanism for ratification that avoided the dilemma faced earlier by the confederation government: Nine states, not all thirteen, had to ratify it, and special ratifying conventions elected only for that purpose, not state legislatures, would make the crucial decision.

> **REVIEW**   Why did the government proposed by the constitutional convention employ multiple checks on each branch?

▶ Ratification of the Constitution

Had a popular vote been taken on the Constitution in the fall of 1787, it probably would have been rejected. In populous Virginia, Massachusetts, and New York, substantial majorities opposed a powerful new national government. North Carolina and Rhode Island refused to call ratifying conventions. Seven states were easy victories for the Constitution, but securing the approval of the nine required for ratification proved difficult. Pro-Constitution forces, called Federalists, had to strategize very shrewdly to defeat anti-Constitution forces, called Antifederalists.

The Federalists

Proponents of the Constitution moved into action swiftly. To silence the criticism that they had gone beyond their charge, they submitted the document to the congress. The congress withheld explicit approval but resolved to send the Constitution to the states for their consideration. The pro-Constitution forces shrewdly secured another advantage by calling themselves **Federalists**. By all logic, this label was more suitable for the backers of the confederation concept, because the Latin root of the word *federal* means "league." Their opponents thus became known as Antifederalists, a label that made them sound defensive and negative, lacking a program of their own.

To gain momentum, the Federalists targeted the states most likely to ratify quickly. Delaware provided unanimous ratification by early December, before the Antifederalists had even begun to campaign. Pennsylvania, New Jersey, and Georgia followed within a month (Map 8.3). Delaware and New Jersey were small states

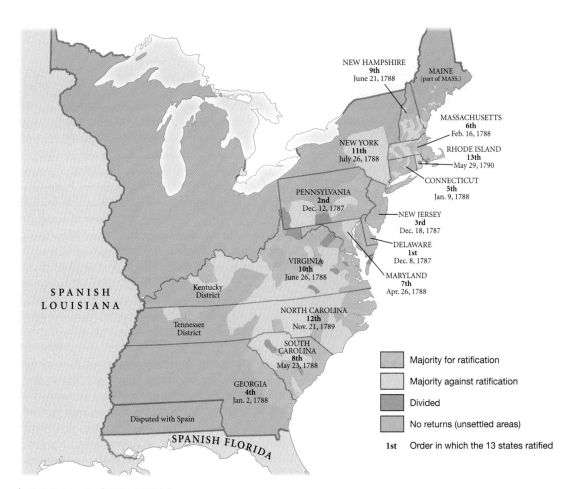

NEW HAMPSHIRE
9th
June 21, 1788

MAINE
(part of MASS.)

MASSACHUSETTS
6th
Feb. 16, 1788

RHODE ISLAND
13th
May 29, 1790

NEW YORK
11th
July 26, 1788

CONNECTICUT
5th
Jan. 9, 1788

PENNSYLVANIA
2nd
Dec. 12, 1787

NEW JERSEY
3rd
Dec. 18, 1787

DELAWARE
1st
Dec. 8, 1787

SPANISH
LOUISIANA

Kentucky
District

VIRGINIA
10th
June 26, 1788

MARYLAND
7th
Apr. 26, 1788

Tennessee
District

NORTH CAROLINA
12th
Nov. 21, 1789

SOUTH
CAROLINA
8th
May 23, 1788

GEORGIA
4th
Jan. 2, 1788

Disputed with Spain

SPANISH FLORIDA

Majority for ratification

Majority against ratification

Divided

No returns (unsettled areas)

1st   Order in which the 13 states ratified

MAP ACTIVITY

Map 8.3   Ratification of the Constitution, 1788–1790

Populated areas cast votes for delegates to state ratification conventions. This map shows Antifederalist strength generally concentrated in backcountry, noncoastal, and non-urban areas, but with significant exceptions (for example, Rhode Island).

READING THE MAP: Where was Federalist strength concentrated? How did the distribution of Federalist and Antifederalist sentiment affect the order of state ratifications of the Constitution?

CONNECTIONS: What objections did Antifederalists have to the new United States Constitution? How did their locations affect their view of the Federalist argument?

surrounded by more powerful neighbors; a government that would regulate trade and set taxes according to population was an attractive proposition. Georgia sought the protection that a stronger national government would afford against hostile Indians and Spanish Florida to the south. "If a weak State with the Indians on its back and the Spaniards on its flank does not see the necessity of a General Government there must I think be wickedness or insanity in the way," said Federalist George Washington.

Another three easy victories came in Connecticut, Maryland, and South Carolina. As in Pennsylvania, merchants, lawyers, and urban artisans in general favored the new Constitution,

as did large landowners and slaveholders. This tendency for the established political elite to be Federalist enhanced the prospects of victory, for Federalists already had power and influence disproportionate to their number. Antifederalists in these states tended to be rural, western, and noncommercial, men whose access to news was limited and whose participation in state government was tenuous.

Massachusetts was the first state to give the Federalists serious difficulty. The vote to select the ratification delegates decidedly favored the Antifederalists, whose strength lay in the western areas of the state, home to Shays's Rebellion. One rural delegate from Worcester County voiced widely

Mercy Otis Warren

The sister of James Otis and the wife of James Warren, both prominent leaders in the pre-revolutionary movement in Massachusetts, Mercy Otis Warren was well positioned to learn about revolutionary politics from the ground up. An ardent advocate for independence, she counted Abigail and John Adams among her close friends but broke with them in the late 1780s when she took up the Antifederalist cause. In 1788 Warren published a pamphlet explaining her well-argued objections to the Constitution. She declined to put her name on the publication, choosing instead to give "Columbian Patriot" as a pseudonym. Why might she have done that? Photograph © 2012 Museum of Fine Arts, Boston, Bequest of Winslow Warren, 31.212.

shared suspicions: "These lawyers and men of learning and money men that talk so finely, and gloss over matters so smoothly, to make us poor illiterate people swallow down the pill, expect to get into Congress themselves; they expect to be the managers of the Constitution and get all the power and all the money into their own hands, and then they will swallow up all us little folks." Nevertheless, the Antifederalists' lead was slowly eroded by a vigorous newspaper campaign. In the end, the Federalists won in Massachusetts by a very slim margin and only with promises that amendments to the Constitution would be taken up in the first Congress.

By May 1788, eight states had ratified; only one more was needed. North Carolina and Rhode Island were hopeless for the Federalist cause, and New Hampshire seemed nearly as bleak. More worrisome was the failure to win over the largest and most economically critical states, Virginia and New York.

The Antifederalists

The **Antifederalists** were a composite group, united mainly in their desire to block the Constitution. Although much of their strength came from back-country areas long suspicious of eastern elites, many Antifederalist leaders came from the same well-connected social background as Federalist leaders; economic class alone did not differentiate them. The Antifederalists also drew strength in states such as New York that were already on sure economic footing and could afford to remain independent. Probably the biggest appeal of the Antifederalists' position lay in the long-nurtured fear that distant power might infringe on people's liberties. The language of the earlier Revolutionary movement was not easily forgotten.

But by the time eight states had ratified the Constitution, the Antifederalists faced a far harder task than they had once imagined. First, they were no longer defending the status quo now that the momentum lay with the Federalists. Second, it was difficult to defend the confederation government with its admitted flaws. Even so, they remained genuinely fearful that the new government would be too distant from the people and could thus become corrupt or tyrannical. "The difficulty, if not impracticability, of exercising the equal and equitable powers of government by a single legislature over an extent of territory that reaches from the Mississippi to the western lakes, and from them to the Atlantic ocean, is an insuperable objection to the adoption of the new system," wrote one articulate Antifederalist in a compelling and much-read political pamphlet. The author, "A Columbia Patriot," was an alias for Mercy Otis Warren, a Massachusetts woman whose father, brother, and husband had all been active leaders in the Revolutionary movement in Boston.

The new government was indeed distant. In the proposed House of Representatives, the only directly democratic element of the Constitution, one member represented some 30,000 people. How could that member really know or communicate with his whole constituency, Antifederalists worried. One Antifederalist essayist contrasted the proposed model with the personal character of state-level representation: "The members of our state legislature are annually elected — they are subject to instructions — they are chosen within small circles — they are sent but a small distance from their respective homes. Their conduct is constantly known to their constituents. They frequently see, and are seen, by the men whose servants they are."

Antifederalists also feared that representatives would always be elites and thus "ignorant of the sentiments of the middling and much more of the lower class of citizens, strangers to their ability, unacquainted with their wants, difficulties, and distress," a Maryland man worried. None of this would be a problem under a confederation system, according to the Antifederalists, because real power would continue to reside in the state governments.

The Federalists generally agreed that the elite would be favored for national elections. Indeed, Federalists wanted power to reside with intelligent, virtuous leaders like themselves. They did not envision a government constituted of every class of people. "Fools and knaves have voice enough in government already," quipped one Federalist, without being guaranteed representation in proportion to their total population. Alexander Hamilton claimed that mechanics and laborers preferred to have their social betters represent them. Antifederalists disagreed: "In reality, there will be no part of the people represented, but the rich.... It will literally be a government in the hands of the few to oppress and plunder the many." (See "Historical Question," page 252.)

Antifederalists fretted over many specific features of the Constitution. It prohibited state-issued paper money. It regulated the time and place of congressional elections, leading to fears that only one inconvenient polling place might be authorized, disfranchising rural voters. The most widespread objection was the Constitution's glaring omission of any guarantees of individual liberties in a bill of rights like those contained in many state constitutions.

Despite Federalist campaigns in the large states, it was a small state — New Hampshire — that

> **"Fools and knaves have voice enough in government already."**
> — A Federalist

Silk Banner of the New York Society of Pewterers

As soon as nine states ratified the Constitution, the Federalists held spectacular victory celebrations meant to demonstrate national unity behind the new government. New York City's parade, coming three days before the state's own ratification vote in July 1788, involved five thousand participants marching under seventy-six occupational banners representing farmers, brewers, tobacconists, lawyers, and others. This banner was carried by the Society of Pewterers, metalsmiths who made household utensils. Despite the broad spectrum of male workers represented in the parade, many of whom could not vote, no working women participated. Why? © Collection of the New-York Historical Society.

Was the New United States a Christian Country?

Rebecca Samuel, a Jewish resident of Virginia, conveyed her excitement about the new U.S. Constitution when she wrote her German parents in 1791 that finally "Jew and Gentile are as one" in the realm of politics and citizenship. Other voices were distinctly less approving. An Antifederalist pamphlet warned that the pope could become president; another feared that "a Turk, a Jew, a Roman Catholic, and what is worse than all, a Universalist, may be President."

The document that produced such wildly different reactions was indeed remarkable for the conspicuous absence of religion. The Constitution did not invoke Christianity as a state religion. It made no reference to an almighty being, and it specifically promised, in Article 6, section 3, that "no religious test shall ever be required as a qualification to any office or public trust under the United States."

More than a few Christian leaders were stunned at the Constitution's near silence on religion, a clear turnabout from state constitutions of the 1770s and 1780s. A New Yorker warned that "should the Citizens of America be as Irreligious as her Constitution, we will have reason to tremble, lest the Governor of the universe . . . crush us to atoms." A delegate to North Carolina's ratifying convention predicted that the Constitution was "an invitation for Jews and pagans of every kind to come among us." A concerned Presbyterian minister asked Alexander Hamilton why religion was

not in the Constitution. Hamilton reportedly quipped, "Indeed, Doctor, we forgot it."

Measured against the practices of state governments, Hamilton's observation is hardly credible. The men who wrote the state constitutions actively debated principles of inclusion and exclusion for voting rights and officeholding. Along with factors like property ownership, race, gender, and age, many also argued for religious qualifications.

Most leaders of the 1780s took for granted that Christianity was the one true faith and the essential foundation of morality. All but two state constitutions assumed the primacy of Protestantism, and one-third of them collected public taxes to support Christian churches. Every state but one required officeholders to take a Christian oath. For example, every member of Pennsylvania's legislature swore to "acknowledge the Scripture of the Old and New Testament to be given by divine inspiration."

Other common political practices affirmed Christian practice. Governors proclaimed fast days and public thanksgivings in the name of the Holy Trinity. Chaplains led legislatures in Christian prayer. Jurors and witnesses swore Christian oaths. New England states passed Sabbath laws prohibiting all work or travel on Sunday. Blasphemy laws punished people who cursed the Christian God or Jesus.

Although close to half the state constitutions did include freedom of

religious conscience as an explicit right, this right promised nothing about political equality. How then did the U.S. Constitution come to be such a break from the immediate past? Had the Constitution's writers really just forgotten about religion?

Not James Madison of Virginia. Madison arrived at the constitutional convention fresh from a hard-fought battle in Virginia to establish religious liberty free from all state interference. Opponents sponsored a bill to support Christian ministers with tax money; Madison instead secured passage in 1786 of the Virginia Statute for Religious Freedom, a document written several years earlier by Thomas Jefferson. The statute guaranteed freedom of conscience and prohibited any distinctions in "civil capacities" based on religion. In Jefferson's distinctive formulation, the statute asserted "that our civil rights have no dependence on our religious opinions any more than our opinions in physics or geometry." There could be no religious tests for officeholding thereafter in that state and no state funding of ministers.

The Virginia Statute expressed Madison's ideal, but on practical grounds he thought it best for the U.S. Constitution to say as little as possible about religion, since state laws reflected a variety of positions. When Antifederalists demanded a bill of rights, Madison drew up a list for the first Congress to consider. Two on his list dealt with religion, but only one was approved by Congress to become part of the First Amendment: "Congress shall make no law respecting an establishment of religion, or prohibiting the free exercise thereof." In a stroke, Madison placed religious worship and the privileging of any one church beyond Congress's power. Significantly, his second proposal

provided the decisive ninth vote for ratification on June 21, 1788. Federalists there succeeded in getting the convention postponed from February to June and conducted an intense and successful lobbying effort on specific delegates in the interim.

The Big Holdouts: Virginia and New York

With nine states voting in favor, the Constitution was ensured passage, but four states still opposed ratification. A glance at a map demonstrated

Touro Synagogue
A Jewish community inhabited the coastal shipping city of Newport, Rhode Island, as early as the 1650s. In 1759, the thriving group built a synagogue, the oldest Jewish house of worship still standing in the United States. It is sited diagonally on its property so that worshippers face east, the direction of Jerusalem. President Washington visited Newport in 1790 and wrote to "the Hebrew Congregation" a few days later: "It is now no more that toleration is spoken of, as if it was by the indulgence of one class of people, that another enjoyed the exercise of their inherent natural rights." Touro Synagogue/photo John T. Hopf.

failed to gain traction in congressional debate: "No State shall violate the equal rights of conscience." Evidently, the states wanted to be able to keep their Christian-only rules — rules that would violate dissenters' consciences and thus keep them out of office.

Gradually, states deleted restrictive laws, but as late as 1840 Jews still could not hold public office in four states; even into the twentieth century, Sunday laws in some states forced business closings on the Christian Sabbath, creating economic hardship for both owners and workers whose religion prohibited work on Saturday. The guarantee of freedom of conscience in religion was implanted in various founding documents in the 1770s and 1780s, but it has taken many years to fulfill Jefferson's and Madison's larger vision of what true religious liberty means: the freedom for religious belief to be independent of civil status.

Thinking about Beliefs and Attitudes

1. Why do you think so many state constitutions allowed only Protestants to hold political office?

2. What point was Jefferson making when he compared opinions about religion to opinions about physics or geometry as relevant factors for officeholding?

3. Why did Madison's language guaranteeing that Congress would not establish a federal religion appeal to Antifederalists? Why did other representatives in Congress reject Madison's additional proposal that states be prohibited from violating "the equal rights of conscience"?

the necessity of pressing the Federalist case in the two largest, Virginia and New York (see Map 8.3). Although Virginia was home to Madison and Washington, an influential Antifederalist group led by Patrick Henry and George Mason made the outcome uncertain. The Federalists finally but barely won ratification in Virginia by proposing twenty specific amendments that the new government would promise to consider.

New York voters tilted toward the Antifederalists out of a sense that a state so large and powerful need not relinquish so much authority to the new federal government. But New York was also home to some of the most persuasive Federalists. Starting in October 1787, Alexander Hamilton collaborated with James Madison and New York lawyer John Jay on a series of eighty-five essays on the political philosophy of the new Constitution. Published in New York newspapers and later republished as *The Federalist Papers*, the essays brilliantly set out the failures of the Articles of Confederation and offered an analysis of the complex nature of the Federalist position. In one of the most compelling essays, number 10, Madison challenged the Antifederalists' heartfelt conviction that republican government had to be small-scale. Madison argued that a large and diverse population was itself a guarantee of liberty. In a national government, no single faction could ever be large enough to subvert the freedom of other groups. "Extend the sphere, and you take in a greater variety of parties and interests; you make it less probable that a majority of the whole will have a common motive to invade the rights of other citizens," Madison asserted. He called it "a republican remedy for the diseases most incident to republican government."

At New York's ratifying convention, Antifederalists predominated, but impassioned debate and lobbying — plus the dramatic news of Virginia's ratification — finally tipped the balance to the Federalists. Still, the Antifederalists' approval of the document was delivered with a list of twenty-four individual rights they hoped would be protected and thirty-three structural changes they hoped to see in the Constitution. New York's ratification ensured the legitimacy of the new government, yet it took another year and a half for Antifederalists in North Carolina to come around. Fiercely independent Rhode Island held out until May 1790, and even then it ratified by only a two-vote margin.

In less than twelve months, the U.S. Constitution was both written and ratified. (See appendix I, page A-1.) An amazingly short time by twenty-first-century standards, it is even more remarkable for the late eighteenth century, with its horse-powered transportation and hand-printed communications. The Federalists had faced a formidable task, but by building momentum and ensuring consideration of a bill of rights, they did indeed carry the day.

REVIEW Why did Antifederalists oppose the Constitution?

▶ Conclusion: The "Republican Remedy"

Thus ended one of the most intellectually tumultuous and creative periods in American history. American leaders experimented with ideas and drew up plans to embody their evolving and conflicting notions of how a society and a government ought to be formulated. There was widespread agreement that government should derive its power and authority from the people, but a narrow vision of "the people" prevailed. With limited exceptions — New Jersey, for example — free blacks and women were excluded from government. Indians, even when dubiously called "members" of a state, were never considered political participants, and neither were slaves. Even taking free white males as "the people," men disagreed fiercely over the degree of democracy — the amount of direct control of government by the people — that would be workable in American society.

The period began in 1775 with a confederation government that could barely be ratified because of its requirement of unanimity for approval. Amendments also required unanimity, which proved impossible to achieve on questions dealing with western lands, an impost, and the proper way to respond to unfair taxation in a republican state. The new Constitution offered a different approach to these problems by loosening the grip of impossible unanimity and by embracing the ideas of a heterogeneous public life and a carefully balanced government that together would prevent any one part of the public from tyrannizing another. The genius of James Madison was to anticipate that diversity of opinion was not only an unavoidable reality but also a hidden strength of the new society beginning to take shape. This is what he meant in *Federalist* essay number 10 when he spoke of the "republican remedy" for the troubles most likely to befall a government in which the people are the source of authority.

Despite Madison's optimism, political differences remained keen and worrisome to many. The Federalists still hoped for a society in which leaders of exceptional wisdom would discern the best path for public policy. They looked backward to a society of hierarchy, rank, and benevolent rule by an aristocracy of talent, but they created a government with forward-looking checks and balances as a guard against corruption, which they figured would most likely emanate from the people. The Antifederalists also looked backward, but to an old order of small-scale direct democracy and local control, in which virtuous people kept a close eye on potentially corruptible rulers. The Antifederalists feared a national government led by distant, self-interested leaders who needed to be held in check. In the 1790s, these two conceptions of republicanism and of leadership would be tested in real life. And to a degree, these competing visions of leadership, diversity, democracy, and corruption still animate American public life today.

▶ Selected Bibliography

General Works

Lance Banning, *The Sacred Fire of Liberty: James Madison and the Founding of the Federal Republic* (1995).
Gary B. Nash, *The Unknown American Revolution: The Unruly Birth of Democracy and the Struggle to Create America* (2006).
Peter S. Onuf and Cathy D. Matson, *A Union of Interests: Political and Economic Thought in Revolutionary America* (1990).
Jack Rakove, *Revolutionaries: A New History of the Invention of America* (2010).
Robert E. Shalhope, *The Roots of Democracy: American Thought and Culture, 1760–1800* (2004).
Alan Taylor, *The Divided Ground: Indians, Settlers, and the Northern Borderland of the American Revolution* (2006).
Gordon Wood, *The Creation of the American Republic, 1776–1787* (1969).
Alfred F. Young, ed., *Beyond the American Revolution: Explorations in the History of American Radicalism* (1993).

The Confederation Government and the States

Daniel M. Friedenberg, *Life, Liberty, and the Pursuit of Land: The Plunder of Early America* (1992).
Marc W. Kruman, *Between Authority and Liberty: State Constitution Making in Revolutionary America* (1997).
Peter S. Onuf, *Statehood and Union: A History of the Northwest Ordinance* (1987).
Charles Rappleye, *Robert Morris, Financier of the American Revolution* (2010).
Jack N. Rakove, *The Beginnings of National Politics: An Interpretive History of the Continental Congress* (1979).

Citizenship

Ira Berlin, *Many Thousands Gone: The First Two Centuries of Slavery in North America* (1998).
Linda K. Kerber, *Women of the Republic: Intellect and Ideology in Revolutionary America* (1980).
Joanne Pope Melish, *Disowning Slavery: Gradual Emancipation and "Race" in New England, 1780–1860* (1998).
Gary B. Nash and Jean R. Sonderlund, *Freedom by Degrees: Emancipation in Pennsylvania and Its Aftermath* (1991).
Leonard L. Richards, *Shays's Rebellion: The American Revolution's Final Battle* (2002).
Marylynn Salmon, *Women and the Law of Property in Early America* (1986).
Rosemarie Zagarri, *A Woman's Dilemma: Mercy Otis Warren and the American Revolution* (1995).

The Constitution and Ratification

John K. Alexander, *The Selling of the Constitutional Convention: A History of News Coverage* (1990).
Richard Beeman, *Plain, Honest Men: The Making of the American Constitution* (2010).
Carol Berkin, *A Brilliant Solution: Inventing the American Constitution* (2003).
Richard Brookhiser, *Gentleman Revolutionary: Gouverneur Morris, the Rake Who Wrote the Constitution* (2003).
Saul Cornell, *The Other Founders: Anti-Federalism and the Dissenting Tradition in America, 1788–1828* (1999).
Michael Allen Gillespie and Michael Lienesch, eds., *Ratifying the Constitution* (1989).
Woody Holton, *Unruly Americans and the Origins of the Constitution* (2007).
John P. Kaminski and Richard Leffler, *Federalists and Antifederalists: The Debate over the Constitution* (1998).
Cecelia M. Kenyon, *Men of Little Faith: Selected Writings by Cecelia Kenyon* (2003).
Leonard W. Levy, *The Establishment Clause: Religion and the First Amendment* (1994).
Jackson Turner Main, *The Antifederalists: Critics of the Constitution, 1781–1788* (2006).
William Lee Miller, *The First Liberty: Religion and the American Republic* (1986).
Richard B. Morris, *Witnesses at the Creation: Hamilton, Madison, Jay, and the Constitution* (1985).
Jack N. Rakove, *Original Meanings: Politics and Ideas in the Making of the Constitution* (1996).

▶ **FOR MORE BOOKS ABOUT TOPICS IN THIS CHAPTER,** see the Online Bibliography at **bedfordstmartins.com/roark.**

▶ **FOR ADDITIONAL PRIMARY SOURCES FROM THIS PERIOD,** see Michael Johnson, ed., *Reading the American Past,* Fifth Edition.

▶ **FOR WEB SITES, IMAGES, AND DOCUMENTS RELATED TO TOPICS AND PLACES IN THIS CHAPTER,** visit Make History at **bedfordstmartins.com/roark.**

Reviewing Chapter 8

KEY TERMS

Explain each term's significance.

The Articles of Confederation
> Articles of Confederation (p. 229)
> requisition (p. 229)

The Sovereign States
> republicanism (p. 232)
> bills of rights (p. 232)
> Elizabeth Freeman (Mum Bett) (p. 234)
> gradual emancipation (p. 234)

The Confederation's Problems
> Robert Morris (p. 238)
> impost (p. 238)
> Newburgh Conspiracy (p. 238)
> Iroquois Confederacy (p. 239)
> Treaty of Fort Stanwix (p. 240)
> Northwest Territory (p. 240)
> Northwest Ordinance (p. 241)
> Shays's Rebellion (p. 244)

The United States Constitution
> James Madison (p. 245)
> Alexander Hamilton (p. 245)
> constitutional convention (p. 246)
> Virginia Plan (p. 247)
> New Jersey Plan (p. 247)
> Great Compromise (p. 247)
> United States Constitution (p. 247)
> three-fifths clause (p. 247)

Ratification of the Constitution
> Federalists (p. 248)
> Antifederalists (p. 250)
> *The Federalist Papers* (p. 254)

REVIEW QUESTIONS

Use key terms and dates to support your answer.

1. Why was the confederation government's authority so limited? (pp. 229–231)

2. How did states determine who would be allowed to vote? (pp. 232–236)

3. Why did farmers in western Massachusetts revolt against the state legislature? (pp. 237–244)

4. Why did the government proposed by the constitutional convention employ multiple checks on each branch? (pp. 245–248)

5. Why did Antifederalists oppose the Constitution? (pp. 248–254)

MAKING CONNECTIONS

Draw on key terms, the timeline, and review questions.

1. Leaders in the new nation held that voting should be restricted to citizens who possessed independence of mind. What did they mean by "independence of mind," and why did they provide for this restriction? How did this principle limit voters in the early Republic?

2. Why did many Revolutionary leaders shaping the government of the new nation begin to find the principle of democracy troubling? How did they attempt to balance democracy with other concerns in the new government?

3. Twenty-first-century Americans see a profound tension between the Revolutionary ideals of liberty and equality and the persistence of American slavery. Did Americans in the late eighteenth century see a tension? How do the official documents cited in this chapter reflect their feelings on the topic of slavery? In your answer, be sure to discuss factors that might have shaped varied responses, such as region, race, and class.

4. The Northwest Territory was the confederation's greatest asset. Discuss the proposals to manage settlement of the new territory. How did they shape the nation's expansion? Which proposals succeeded, and which ones failed?

LINKING TO THE PAST

Link events in this chapter to earlier events.

1. Compare and contrast the complaints against taxation connected with the Stamp Act in 1765 and those resulting from the congressional requisition of 1785. What were the principal arguments in each case? In either case, was it simply a matter of people refusing to pay to support government functions? Why do you think anti–Stamp Act activists like Samuel Adams took a negative view of the 1786 tax protests? (See chapter 6.)

2. Thomas Paine's pamphlet *Common Sense*, which sharply criticized the monarchy, was widely circulated and hailed by rebellious colonists in 1776. In light of the colonists' negative view toward monarchical power leading up to the Revolutionary War, how do you explain the powerful presidency that the victorious Americans set up in 1787? (See chapter 7.)

▶ FOR PRACTICE QUIZZES AND OTHER STUDY TOOLS, visit the Online Study Guide at bedfordstmartins.com/roark.

TIMELINE 1775–1804

1775	• Second Continental Congress begins to meet.
1776	• Declaration of Independence adopted.
	• Virginia adopts state bill of rights.
1777	• Articles of Confederation sent to states.
1778	• State constitutions completed.
1780	• Pennsylvania institutes gradual emancipation.
1781	• Articles of Confederation ratified.
	• Creation of executive departments.
	• Slaves Mum Bett and Quok Walker successfully sue for freedom in Massachusetts.
1782	• Virginia relaxes state manumission law.
1783	• Newburgh Conspiracy exposed.
	• Treaty of Paris signed, ending the Revolutionary War.
	• Massachusetts extends suffrage to taxpaying free blacks.
1784	• Gradual emancipation laws passed in Rhode Island and Connecticut.
	• Treaty of Fort Stanwix.
1785	• Treaty of Fort McIntosh.
	• Congress issues requisition for $3 million to the states.
1786	• Shays's Rebellion begins.
1787	• Shays's Rebellion crushed.
	• Northwest Ordinance.
	• Delaware provides manumission law.
	• Constitutional convention meets in Philadelphia.
	• *The Federalist Papers* begin to appear in New York newspapers.
1788	• U.S. Constitution ratified.
1789	• Slavery ended in Massachusetts by judicial decision.
1790	• Maryland provides manumission law.
1799	• Gradual emancipation law passed in New York.
1804	• Gradual emancipation law passed in New Jersey.

INAUGURAL BALUSTRADE
This gold-painted iron railing graced the balcony of Federal Hall in New York City, where George Washington took the president's oath of office in 1789 (pictured here in a contemporary engraving). Thirteen arrows, distinct yet united, form the centerpiece of the ornate balustrade. Frenchman Pierre l'Enfant designed it for the inauguration, symbolically turning the much older building into the home of the new Federal Congress. L'Enfant came to revolutionary America with Lafayette, wintered at Valley Forge with Washington, and fought in the southern campaign. His major assignment of the 1790s was the design and planning of an entire city, Washington, D.C.

9

The New Nation Takes Form
1789–1800

ALEXANDER HAMILTON, THE NATION'S FIRST SECRETARY OF THE treasury, exercised vast influence over the economic and domestic policy of the new government. Heralded as a brilliant unifier of the pro-Constitution Federalists of 1788, Hamilton in his new role soon proved to be the most polarizing figure of the 1790s.

Determination marked his disadvantaged childhood. Hamilton grew up on a small West Indies island. His parents never married. His father, the impoverished fourth son of a Scottish lord, disappeared when Alexander was nine, and his mother, a woman with a checkered past, died two years later. Jeered as a "whore child," Hamilton developed a fierce ambition to make good. He clerked for a merchant who was so impressed with the lad that he sent him to the mainland colonies for an education. Hamilton started at King's College (now Columbia University) in 1773, but the war intruded. Political articles he wrote for a New York newspaper brought him to the attention of General George Washington, who made the nineteen-year-old his close aide and an officer. After the war, Hamilton practiced law in New York and participated in the constitutional convention in Philadelphia. His astute *Federalist* essays — he produced more than fifty in just a few months — helped secure the ratification of the Constitution.

Hamilton's private life was similarly upwardly mobile. Handsome and now well connected, he married Betsey Schuyler, daughter of a very wealthy New Yorker. Hamilton's magnetic charm attracted both men and women at dinner parties and social gatherings. Late-night socializing, however, never interfered with Hamilton's prodigious capacity for work.

As secretary of the treasury, Hamilton quickly moved into high gear. "If a Government appears to be confident of its own powers, it is the surest way to inspire the same confidence in others," he once remarked. He immediately secured big loans from two banks and started to track tax revenues from trade, the government's main source of income. Most trade was with Britain, so Hamilton sought ways to protect Anglo-American relations. Next he tackled the country's unpaid Revolutionary War debt, writing in three months a forty-thousand-word report for Congress explaining how to fund the debt and pump millions of dollars into the U.S. economy. His bold plan for a national banking system aimed to enhance and control the money supply. Finally, he wrote a richly detailed analysis of ways to promote manufacturing via government subsidies and tariff policies.

Hamilton was both visionary and practical. No one could deny that he was a gifted man with remarkable political intuitions. Yet this magnetic man made enemies in the 1790s, as the "founding fathers" of the Revolution and Constitution became competitors and even bitter rivals. To some extent, jealousy over Hamilton's talents and his access to President Washington explains the chill, but serious differences in political philosophy drove the divisions deeper.

Personalities clashed. Hamilton's charm no longer worked with James Madison, now a representative in Congress and an opponent of all of Hamilton's plans. His charm had never worked with John Adams, the new vice president, who privately called him "the bastard brat of a Scotch pedlar" motivated by "disappointed Ambition and unbridled malice and revenge." Years later, when asked why he had deserted Hamilton, Madison coolly replied, "Colonel Hamilton deserted me." Hamilton assumed that government was safest when in the hands of "the rich, the wise, and the good" — words he used to describe America's commercial elite. For Hamilton, economic and political power naturally belonged together, creating an energetic force for economic growth. By contrast, agrarian values ran deep with Jefferson and Madison, and they were suspicious of get-rich-quick speculators, financiers, and manufacturing development. Differing views of European powers also loomed large in the rivalries. Hamilton admired everything British, while Jefferson was enchanted by France, where he had lived in the 1780s. These loyalties governed foreign relations in the late 1790s, when the United States tangled with both overseas rivals.

The personal and political antagonisms of this first generation of American leaders left their mark on the young country. Leaders generally agreed on Indian policy in the new republic — peace when possible, war when necessary — but on little else. No one was prepared for the intense and passionate polarization over economic and foreign policy. The disagreements were articulated around particular events and policies: taxation and the public debt, a new farmers' rebellion in a western region, policies favoring commercial development, a treaty with Britain, a rebellion in Haiti, and the Quasi-War with France, which led to severe strictures on sedition and free speech. But at their heart, these disagreements sprang from opposing ideologies on the value of democracy, the nature of leadership, and the limits of federal power.

By 1800, the oppositional politics ripening between Hamiltonian and Jeffersonian politicians would begin to crystallize into political parties, the Federalists and the Republicans. To the citizens of that day, this was an unhappy development.

***Alexander Hamilton*, by John Trumbull**
Hamilton was confident, handsome, audacious, brilliant, and very hardworking. Ever slender, in marked contrast to the more corpulent leaders of his day, he posed for this portrait in 1792, at the age of thirty-seven and at the height of his power. CSFB Collection of Americana, NYC.

▶ The Search for Stability

After the struggles of the 1780s, the most urgent task in establishing the new government was to secure stability. Leaders sought ways to heal old divisions, and the first presidential election offered the means to do that in the person of George Washington, who enjoyed widespread veneration. People trusted him to exercise the untested and perhaps elastic powers of the presidency.

Congress had important work as well in initiating the new government. Congress quickly agreed on the Bill of Rights, which answered the concerns of many Antifederalists. In the cultural realm, the private virtue of women was mobilized to bolster the public virtue of male citizens and to enhance political stability. Republicanism was forcing a rethinking of women's relation to the state.

Washington Inaugurates the Government

The unanimous election of George Washington in February 1789 was quick work, the tallying of the 69 votes by the electoral college a mere formality. (By contrast, John Adams became vice president with just 34 electoral votes, with the remaining 35 votes split among a variety of candidates; Adams's pride was wounded.) Washington perfectly embodied the republican ideal of disinterested, public-spirited leadership. Indeed, he cultivated that image through astute ceremonies such as the dramatic surrender of his sword to the Continental Congress at the end of the war, symbolizing the subservience of military power to the law, a point he had made previously during the Newburgh Conspiracy (see chapter 8).

Once in office, Washington calculated his moves, knowing that every step set a precedent and that any misstep could be dangerous for the fragile government. Congress debated a title for Washington, ranging from "His Highness, the President of the United States of America and Protector of Their Liberties" to "His Majesty, the President"; Washington favored "His High Mightiness." But in the end, republican simplicity prevailed. The final title was simply "President of the United States of America," and the established form of address became "Mr. President," a subdued

yet dignified title in a society where only property-owning adult white males could presume to be called "Mister."

Washington's genius in establishing the presidency lay in his capacity for implanting his own reputation for integrity into the office itself. He was not a brilliant thinker or a shrewd political strategist. He was not even a particularly congenial man. In the political language of the day, he was "virtuous," meaning that he took pains to elevate the public good over private interest and projected honesty and honor over ambition. He remained aloof, resolute, and dignified, to the point of appearing wooden at times. He encouraged pomp and ceremony to create respect for the office, traveling with six horses to pull his coach, hosting formal balls, and surrounding himself with uniformed servants. He even held weekly "levees," as European monarchs did, hour-long audiences granted to distinguished visitors (including women), at which Washington appeared attired in black velvet, with a feathered hat and a polished sword. The president and his guests bowed, avoiding the egalitarian familiarity of a handshake. But he always managed, perhaps just barely, to avoid the extreme of royal splendor.

Liverpool Souvenir Pitcher, 1789
A British pottery manufacturer produced this commemorative pitcher for the American market to capture sales at the time of George Washington's inauguration in 1789. The design shows Liberty as a woman dressed in a golden gown, her liberty cap on a pole. She is holding a laurel wreath (signifying classical honors) over Washington's head. Fifteen labeled links encircle the scene, representing the states, although in 1789 Rhode Island and North Carolina had not yet ratified the Constitution, and Vermont and Kentucky were merely anticipated states. The Liverpool manufacturer was looking ahead; commemorative pitchers, jugs, and mugs were commonplace articles of consumer culture produced in Britain for the American market. Smithsonian Institution, Washington, D.C.

How Did America's First Congress Address the Question of Slavery?

In its opening months, the First Congress had an ambitious agenda. It established executive departments, the judiciary, and a federal postal system. It crafted the Bill of Rights, debated Alexander Hamilton's *Report on Public Credit*, and ratified its first Indian treaty. Tackling slavery was nowhere on its agenda. Congressmen assumed that key North-South compromises embedded in the Constitution had resolved the issue. But they were wrong: An angry debate over slavery burst forth in early 1790.

In mid-February, citizens of Pennsylvania and New York petitioned Congress to "exercise justice and mercy" and to end the "trafficking in the persons of fellow-men" — that is, the slave trade. The petitioners were Quakers, members of a religion with a long-standing moral objection to slavery. The pragmatic James Madison urged the representatives to refer the petitions to a congressional committee, thus keeping them out of public view. Representatives from South Carolina and Georgia instead urged immediate dismissal, citing the Constitution's ban on interference with the slave trade before 1808. Reaching no agreement, the Congress postponed discussion for a day.

But the next day brought another petition, not coincidentally. Drawn up by a largely Quaker group called the Pennsylvania Abolition Society, it asked Congress "to discourage every species of traffic in the persons of our fellow-men" and to "countenance the restoration of liberty" to slaves. The petition quoted the Constitution to prove the government's duty to "promote the general welfare, and secure the blessings of liberty" for all. That Benjamin Franklin's signature topped the list of petitioners gave it significant political clout.

This second petition was not just about the Atlantic slave trade, which was indeed protected for twenty years by the Constitution. It called for Congress to legislate on the domestic buying and selling of slaves, about which the Constitution was silent. Further, restoring liberty to slaves required an emancipation law, again something not barred by the Constitution. No method was specified "for removing this inconsistency from the character of the American people," but the petitioners expressed confidence in a merciful Congress.

The petitions touched off an explosive debate in the House. Several northern representatives tried to use them to reopen up the contentious issue; representatives from the deep South were adamantly opposed. A rare moment of humor surfaced when a South Carolina member asserted that during ratification, "We took each other, with our mutual bad habits and respective evils, for better, for worse; the Northern States adopted us with our slaves, and we adopted them with their Quakers." No other levity was to be heard. Southerners cited biblical justifications for slavery, argued that slavery civilized slaves, predicted economic collapse if slavery ended, and called the petitioners fanatics. Madison finally got his way: The petitions were referred to a committee, amid mounting concern that newspaper coverage of the debate would create rebelliousness among slaves.

A month later, that committee's report defined a middle road in clarifying the powers of Congress over slavery. As expected, the report affirmed that Congress could not end the slave trade before 1808, but it also concluded that Congress could neither force emancipation nor deny it. And while the report held that Congress had no authority to regulate slave treatment, it urged southern legislatures to pass humanitarian laws regulating the provision of food and housing and the protection of slave women and families. Southern representatives strongly objected to this third pronouncement, touching off yet another bitter public debate in Congress.

Washington chose talented and experienced men to preside over the newly created Departments of War, Treasury, and State. For the Department of War, Washington selected General **Henry Knox**, former secretary of war in the confederation government. For the Treasury — an especially tough job in view of revenue conflicts during the confederation (see chapter 8) — the president appointed **Alexander Hamilton**, known for his general brilliance and financial astuteness. To lead the Department of State, the foreign policy arm of the executive branch, Washington chose **Thomas Jefferson**, a master of diplomatic relations and the current minister to France. For attorney general, Washington picked Edmund Randolph, a Virginian who had attended the

Benjamin Franklin
In 1789 a Philadelphia scientific society hired Charles Willson Peale to paint Franklin as scientist (hence the lightning). Franklin was quite ill at that time, so Peale copied a portrait he had painted in 1785 and then visited the bedridden man to update the image. "His pain was so great that he could sit only ¼ hour," reported Peale. Whatever his illness, Franklin no doubt would have appreciated the healing powers of hot tea all the more had it been served to him in this decorated British teapot: "Health to the Sick, Honour to the Brave, Success to the Lover, Freedom to the Slave." Portrait: Courtesy of the Historical Society of Pennsylvania Collection Atwater Kent Museum of Philadelphia; teapot: Winterthur Museum, Teapot, Gift of S. Robert Teitelman, 2009.21.15.

In the end, a shorter report was hammered out in debate as the formal reply to the petitioners, in which the key provision read: "The Congress have no authority to interfere in the emancipation of slaves, or in the treatment of them within any of the States; it remaining with the several States alone to provide any regulation therein, which humanity and true policy may require." The final vote on this amended report was a squeaker, with 29 ayes to 25 nays.

The Quaker groups conceded and ceased filing petitions, but a discouraged Benjamin Franklin made one last attempt to shape public opinion by writing a satirical essay for a Philadelphia newspaper. In it, the elder statesman ridiculed the proslavery speeches by transposing their exact arguments into a bogus document by a purported North African Muslim leader explaining why his country's fifty thousand Christian slaves were better off enslaved than free. It was vintage Franklin — funny, smart, and cutting. It was also Franklin's final public pronouncement; he died suddenly three weeks later, at the age of eighty-four. The congressional report launched by his 1790 petition stood for more than four decades as the silencing mechanism against any attempt at the federal level to disrupt slavery.

Thinking about Cause and Effect

1. Why did Congress answer the Quaker petitioners? Did it have to?

2. What was the result of the Quakers' efforts to abolish slavery? Do you think they were astute political strategists?

3. What was the South Carolina representative implying when he ironically referred to southern slaves and northern Quakers as "mutual bad habits and respective evils"? Do you think he was talking about slavery as an institution, or slaves as people, in this statement?

constitutional convention but who had turned Antifederalist during ratification. For chief justice of the Supreme Court, Washington designated **John Jay**, a New York lawyer who, along with Madison and Hamilton, had vigorously defended the Constitution in *The Federalist Papers*.

Soon Washington began to hold regular meetings with these men, thereby establishing the precedent of a presidential cabinet. (Vice President John Adams was not included; his only official duty, to preside over the Senate, he found "a punishment." To his wife he complained, "My country has in its wisdom contrived for me the most insignificant office.") No one anticipated that two decades of party turbulence would emerge from the brilliant but explosive mix of Washington's first cabinet.

The Bill of Rights

An important piece of business for the First Congress, meeting in 1789, was the passage of the **Bill of Rights**. Seven states had ratified the Constitution on the condition that guarantees of individual liberties and limitations to federal power be swiftly incorporated. The Federalists of 1787 had thought an enumeration of rights unnecessary, but in 1789 Congressman James Madison understood that healing the divisions of the 1780s was of prime importance. He said, "It will be a desirable thing to extinguish from the bosom of every member of the community, any apprehensions that there are those among his countrymen who wish to deprive them of the liberty for which they valiantly fought and honorably bled."

Madison pulled much of his wording of rights directly from various state constitutions with bills of rights. He enumerated guarantees of freedom of speech, press, and religion; the right to petition and assemble; and the right to be free from unwarranted searches and seizures. One amendment asserted the right to keep and bear arms in support of a "well-regulated militia," to which Madison added, "but no person religiously scrupulous of bearing arms, shall be compelled to render military service in person." That provision for what a later century would call "conscientious objector" status failed to gain acceptance in Congress.

In September 1789, Congress approved a set of twelve amendments and sent them to the states for approval. The process of state ratification took another two years, but there was no serious doubt about the outcome. By 1791, ten amendments were eventually ratified. The First through Eighth Amendments dealt with individual liberties, and the Ninth and Tenth concerned the boundary between federal and state authority. (See the amendments to the U.S. Constitution in appendix I, page A-12.)

Still, not everyone was entirely satisfied. State ratifying conventions had submitted some eighty proposed amendments. Congress never considered proposals to change structural features of the new government, and Madison had no intention of reopening debates about the length of the president's term or the power to levy excise taxes. He also had no thought to use the Bill of Rights to address the status of enslaved people. But others capitalized on the First Amendment's right to petition to force the First Congress into a bitter debate over slavery (see "Historical Question," page 262).

Significantly, no one complained about one striking omission in the Bill of Rights: the right to vote. Only much later was voting seen as a fundamental liberty requiring protection by constitutional amendment — indeed, by four amendments. The Constitution deliberately left the definition of eligible voters to the states because of the existing wide variation in local voting practices. Most of these practices were based on property qualifications, but some touched on religion and, in one unusual case (New Jersey), on sex and race (see chapter 8).

The Republican Wife and Mother

The exclusion of women from political activity did not mean they had no civic role or responsibility. A flood of periodical articles in the 1790s by both male and female writers reevaluated courtship, marriage, and motherhood in light of republican ideals. Tyrannical power in the ruler, whether king or husband, was declared a thing of the past. Affection, not duty, bound wives to their husbands and citizens to their government. In republican marriages, the writers claimed, women had the capacity to reform the morals and manners of men. One male author promised women that "the solidity and stability of the liberties of your country rest with you; since Liberty is never sure, 'till Virtue reigns triumphant. . . . While you thus keep our country virtuous, you maintain its independence."

Until the 1790s, public virtue was strictly a masculine quality. But another sort of virtue enlarged in importance: sexual chastity, a private asset prized as a feminine quality. Essayists of the 1790s explicitly advised young women to use sexual virtue to increase public virtue in men. "Love and courtship . . . invest a lady with more authority than in any other situation that falls to the lot of human beings," one male essayist proclaimed. If women spurned selfish suitors, they could promote good morals more than any social institution could, essayists promised.

Republican ideals also cast motherhood in a new light. Throughout the 1790s, advocates for female education, still a controversial proposition, argued that education would produce better mothers, who in turn would produce better citizens, a concept historians call **republican motherhood**. Benjamin Rush, a Pennsylvania physician and educator, called for female education because "our ladies should be qualified . . . in instructing their sons in the principles of liberty and government." A woman speaker at a Fourth of July picnic in Connecticut in 1799 articulated family duty in service to the state to her all-female audience: "As mothers, wives, sisters, and daughters, we may all be important, [and] teach our little boys, the inestimable value of Freedom, how to blend and harmonize the natural and social rights of man, and as early impressions are indelible, thus assist our dear country, to be as glorious in maintaining, as it was great in gaining her immortal independence." A Massachusetts essayist named **Judith Sargent Murray** favored education that would remake women into self-confident, rational beings. Her first essay of 1790 was boldly titled "On the Equality of the Sexes," but a subsequent essay on education reassured readers that educated women would retain their "characteristic trait" of sweetness. Even Murray had to justify female education in the context of family duty.

This shift in understanding about women's relation to the state was subtle but profoundly important. Politics was still a masculine preserve, but now women's domestic obligations were infused with political meaning, and a few women became so bold as to claim an expanded scope for women's intellectual development as well. But nothing about this shift altered traditional gender relations. The analogy between marriage and civil society worked precisely because of the self-subordination inherent in the term *virtue*. Men should put the public good first, before selfish desires, just as women must put their husbands and families first, before themselves. Women might gain literacy and knowledge, but only in the service of improved domestic duty. In Federalist America, wives and citizens alike should feel affection for and trust in their rulers; neither should ever rebel.

> **REVIEW**   How did political leaders in the 1790s attempt to overcome the divisions of the 1780s?

▶ Hamilton's Economic Policies

The new government had the luck to be launched in flush economic times. Compared to the severe financial instability of the 1780s, the 1790s brimmed with opportunity, as seen in increased agricultural trade and improvements in transportation and banking. In 1790, the federal government moved from New York City to Philadelphia, a more central location with a substantial mercantile class. There, Alexander Hamilton, secretary of the treasury, embarked

Republican Womanhood: Judith Sargent Murray
The young woman in this 1772 portrait became known in the 1790s as America's foremost spokeswoman for woman's equality. Judith Sargent Murray wrote essays for the *Massachusetts Magazine* under the pen name "Constantia." Her 1790 essay, "On the Equality of the Sexes," asserted that women had "natural powers" of mind fully the equal of men's. In 1798, she published her collected "Constantia" essays in a book titled *The Gleaner*, George Washington and John Adams each bought a copy. John Singleton Copley, Terra Foundation for American, Chicago/Art Resource, NY.

on his innovative plan to solidify the government's economic base. But controversy arose at every turn. Hamilton's plan to combine the large national debt with unpaid state debts produced a crisis in the First Congress. And his plan to raise revenues via taxation on whiskey brought on the country's first domestic rebellion.

Agriculture, Transportation, and Banking

Dramatic increases in international grain prices motivated American farmers to boost agricultural production for the export trade. Europe's rising population needed grain, and the French Revolutionary and Napoleonic Wars, which engulfed Europe after 1793 for a dozen years, severely compromised production there. From the Connecticut River valley to the Chesapeake, farmers planted more wheat, generating new

jobs for millers, coopers, dockworkers, and ship and wagon builders.

Cotton production also underwent a boom, spurred by market demand and a mechanical invention. Limited amounts of smooth-seed cotton had long been grown in the coastal areas of the South, but this variety of cotton did not thrive in the drier inland regions. Greenseed cotton grew well inland, but its rough seeds stuck to the cotton fibers and were labor-intensive to remove. In 1793, Yale graduate Eli Whitney devised a machine called a gin that easily separated out the seeds; cotton production soared, giving a boost to transatlantic trade with Britain, whose factories eagerly processed the raw cotton into cloth.

A surge of road building further stimulated the economy. Before 1790, one bumpy road connected Maine to Georgia, but with the establishment of the U.S. Post Office in 1792, road mileage increased sixfold to facilitate the transport of mail. Private companies also built toll roads, such as the Lancaster Turnpike west of Philadelphia, the Boston-to-Albany turnpike, and a third road from Virginia to Tennessee. By 1800, a dense network of dirt, gravel, and plank roadways connected towns in southern New England and the Middle Atlantic states, spurring commercial stage companies to regularize and speed up passenger traffic. A trip from New York to Boston took four days; from New York to Philadelphia, less than two (Map 9.1). In 1790, Boston had only three stagecoach companies; by 1800, there were twenty-four.

> "A national debt if not excessive will be to us a national blessing; it will be a powerful cement of our union."
>
> — ALEXANDER HAMILTON

A third development signaling economic resurgence was the growth of commercial banking. During the 1790s, the number of banks nationwide multiplied tenfold, from three to twenty-nine in 1800. Banks drew in money chiefly through the sale of stock. They then made loans in the form of banknotes, paper currency backed by the gold and silver that stockholders paid in. Because banks issued two or three times as much money in banknotes as

they held in hard money, they were creating new money for the economy.

The U.S. population expanded along with economic development, propelled by large average family size and better than adequate food and land resources. As measured by the first two federal censuses in 1790 and 1800, the population grew from 3.9 million to 5.3 million, an increase of 35 percent.

The Public Debt and Taxes

The upturn in the economy, plus the new taxation powers of the government, suggested that the government might soon repay its wartime debt, amounting to more than $52 million owed to foreign and domestic creditors. But Hamilton had a different plan. He issued a *Report on Public Credit* in January 1790, recommending that the debt be funded — but not repaid immediately — at full value. This meant that old certificates of debt would be rolled over into new bonds, which would earn interest until they were retired several years later. There would still be a public debt, but it would be secure, giving its holders a direct financial stake in the new government. The bonds would circulate, injecting millions of dollars of new money into the economy. "A **national debt** if not excessive will be to us a national blessing; it will be a powerful cement of our union," Hamilton wrote to a financier. The debt was the "price of liberty," he further argued, and had to be honored, not repudiated. But it would not paid off either: Hamilton's goal was to make the new country creditworthy, not debt-free.

Funding the debt in full was controversial because speculators had already bought up debt certificates cheaply, and Hamilton's report touched off further speculation. (Hamilton himself held no certificates, but his father-in-law held some with a face value of $60,000.) Philadelphia and New York speculators sent agents into backcountry regions looking for certificates of debt whose unwary owners were ignorant about the proposed face-value funding.

Hamilton compounded controversy with his proposal to add to the federal debt another $25 million that some state governments still owed to individuals. During the war, states had obtained supplies by issuing

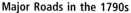

Major Roads in the 1790s

Montreal

St. Lawrence R.

MAINE (part of MASS.)

Champlain

VT.   Portland

N.Y.   N.H.

Mohawk R.   Albany   Boston

MASS.

Providence

CONN.

R.I.

PA.   N.J.   New York

Trenton   ATLANTIC OCEAN

Lancaster   Philadelphia

MD.

Baltimore

DEL.

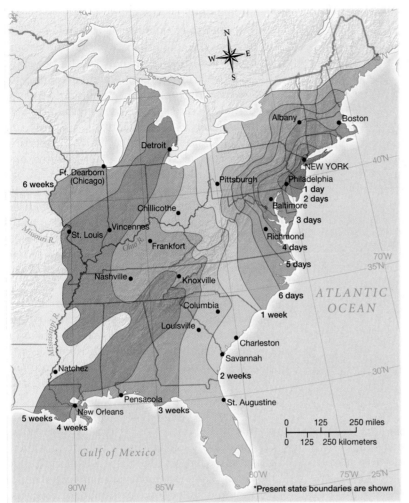

MAP ACTIVITY

Map 9.1 Travel Times from New York City in 1800
Notice that travel out of New York extends over a much greater distance in the first week than in subsequent weeks. River corridors in the West and East speeded up travel — but only if one were going downriver. Also notice that travel by sea (north and south along the coast) was much faster than land travel.

READING THE MAP: Compare this map to the map "Major Roads in the 1790s" (page 266) and to Map 9.2 (page 273). What physical and cultural factors account for the slower travel times west of Pittsburgh?
CONNECTIONS: Why did Americans in the 1790s become so interested in traveling long distances? How did travel times affect the U.S. economy?

IOUs to farmers, merchants, and moneylenders. Some states, such as Virginia and New York, had paid off these debts entirely. Others, such as Massachusetts, had partially paid them off through heavy taxation of the people. About half the states had made little headway. Hamilton called for the federal government to assume these state debts and combine them with the federal debt, in effect consolidating federal power over the states.

Congressman James Madison strenuously objected to putting windfall profits in the pockets of speculators. He instead proposed a complex scheme to pay both the original holders of the federal debt and the speculators, each at fair fractions of the face value. Hamilton countered that tracking the history of traded certificates would be impossible, and further, each prior sale at a devalued price was the correct market price at that moment and could not be undone by the government. Madison also strongly objected to assumption of all the states' debts. A large debt

was dangerous, Madison warned, especially because it would lead to high taxation. Secretary of State Jefferson also was fearful of Hamilton's proposals: "No man is more ardently intent to see the public debt soon and sacredly paid off than I am. This exactly marks the difference between Colonel Hamilton's views and mine, that I would wish the debt paid tomorrow; he wishes it never to be paid, but always to be a thing where with to corrupt and manage the legislature."

A solution to this impasse arrived when Jefferson invited Hamilton and Madison to dinner. Over good food and wine, Hamilton secured the reluctant Madison's promise to restrain his opposition. In return, Hamilton pledged to back efforts to locate the nation's new capital city in the South, along the Potomac River, an outcome that was sure to please Virginians. In early July 1790, Congress voted for the Potomac site, and in late July Congress passed the debt package, assumption and all.

RATE OF TOLL

	Cts
E...oot pafsenger†	3
Hor. rider	8
T...eled Pleasure carriage	20
Fo...eeled do. do.	50
Cu..cle	90
Cart or waggon by one beast	10
Drawn by two beasts	15
Loaded do.	25
By three do. empty	20
Loaded do.	30
By four do. empty	25
Loaded do.	37½
Each additional beast	5
Sleigh drawn by one beast	10
By two do.	15
Sled by one do.	6½
By two do.	12½
By four do.	25
Each additional beast	5
Horfe jack or mule	4
Neat cattle	3
Sheep & swine each	1

Bridge Toll Sign, 1796
This sign lists an amazing variety of tolls charged for crossing a bridge over the Connecticut River between Cornish, New Hampshire, and Windsor, Vermont, in 1796. Owners of bridges and toll roads collected fees from users of their privately built rights-of-way. Can you deduce any principle of pricing in this list? Is the list exhaustive? What if a boy with a dog attempted to cross the bridge? Do you imagine there were traffic jams at the tollgate? New Hampshire Historical Society.

The First Bank of the United States and the *Report on Manufactures*

The second and third major elements of Hamilton's economic plan were his proposal to create a national **Bank of the United States** and his program to encourage domestic manufacturing. Arguing that banks were the "nurseries of national wealth," Hamilton modeled his bank plan on European central banks, such as the Bank of England, a private corporation that used the government's money to invigorate the British economy. According to Hamilton's plan, the central bank was to be capitalized at $10 million, a sum larger than all the hard money in the entire nation. The federal government would hold 20 percent of the bank's stock, making the bank in effect the government's fiscal agent, holding its revenues derived from import duties, land sales, and various other taxes. The other 80 percent of the bank's capital would come from private investors, who could buy stock in the bank with either hard money (silver or gold) or the recently funded and thus sound federal securities. Because of its size and the privilege of being the only national bank, the central bank would help stabilize the economy by exerting prudent control over credit, interest rates, and the value of the currency.

Concerned that a few rich bankers might have undue influence over the economy, Madison tried but failed to stop the plan in Congress. Jefferson advised President Washington that the Constitution did not permit Congress to charter banks. Hamilton, however, pointed out that the Constitution gave Congress specific powers to regulate commerce and a broad right "to make all laws which shall be necessary and proper for carrying into execution the foregoing powers." Washington sided with Hamilton and signed the Bank of the United States into law in February 1791, with a charter allowing it to operate for twenty years.

When the bank's privately held stock went on sale in Philadelphia, Boston, and New York City in July, it sold out in a few hours, touching off an immediate mania of speculation in resale that lasted a month and drew in many hundreds of urban merchants and artisans. A discouraged Madison reported that in New York "the Coffee House is an eternal buzz with the gamblers," some of them self-interested congressmen intent on "public plunder." Stock prices shot upward and then plunged in mid-August, causing Jefferson to fret about the risk to morality inherent in gambling in stocks: "The spirit of gaming, once it has seized a subject, is incurable. The tailor who has made thousands in one day, tho' he has lost them the next, can never again be content with the slow and moderate earnings of his needle."

The third component of Hamilton's plan was issued in December 1791 in the **Report on Manufactures**, a proposal to encourage the production of American-made goods. Domestic manufacturing was in its infancy, and Hamilton aimed to mobilize the new powers of the federal government to grant subsidies to manufacturers and to impose moderate tariffs on those same products from overseas. Hamilton's plan targeted manufacturing of iron goods, arms and ammunition, coal, textiles, wood products, and glass. Among the blessings of manufacturing, he counted the new employment opportunities that would open to children and unmarried young women, who he assumed were under-utilized in agricultural societies. The *Report on Manufactures*, however, was never approved by Congress, and indeed never even voted on. Many confirmed agriculturalists in Congress feared that manufacturing was a curse rather than a blessing. Madison and Jefferson in particular were alarmed by stretching the "general welfare" clause of the Constitution to include public subsidies to private businesses.

The Whiskey Rebellion

Hamilton's plan to restore public credit required new taxation to pay the interest on the large national debt. In deference to the merchant class, Hamilton did not propose a general increase in import duties, nor did he propose land taxes, which would have fallen hardest on the nation's wealthiest landowners. Instead, he convinced Congress in 1791 to pass a 25 percent excise tax on whiskey, to be paid by farmers when they brought their grain to the distillery, then passed on to individual whiskey consumers in the form of higher prices. Members of Congress from eastern states favored the tax — especially New Englanders, where the favorite drink was rum. A New Hampshire representative observed that the country would be "drinking down the national debt," an idea he evidently found acceptable. More seriously, Virginia representative James Madison hoped that the tax might promote "sobriety and thereby prevent disease and untimely deaths."

Not surprisingly, the new excise tax proved unpopular with grain farmers in the western regions and whiskey drinkers everywhere. In 1791, farmers in Kentucky and the western parts of Pennsylvania, Virginia, Maryland, and the Carolinas forcefully conveyed to Congress their resentment of Hamilton's tax. One farmer complained that he had already paid half his grain to the local distillery for distilling his rye, and now the distiller was taking the new whiskey tax out of the farmer's remaining half. This "reduces the balance to less than one-third of the original quantity. If this is not an oppressive tax, I am at a loss to describe what is so," the farmer wrote. Congress responded with modest modifications to the tax in 1792, but even so, discontent was rampant.

Simple evasion of the law was the most common response. In some places, crowds threatened to tar and feather federal tax collectors, and distilleries underreported their production. Four counties in Pennsylvania established committees of correspondence and held assemblies

The Return for SOUTH CAROLINA having been made since the foregoing Schedule was originally printed, the whole Enumeration is here given complete, except for the N. Western Territory, of which no Return has yet been published.

DISTICTS	Free white Males of 16 years and upwards, including heads of families.	Free white Males under sixteen years.	Free white Females, including heads of families.	All other free persons.	Slaves.	Total.
Vermont	22435	22328	40505	255	16	85539
N. Hampshire	36086	34851	70160	630	158	141885
Maine	24384	24748	46870	538	NONE	96540
Massachusetts	95453	87289	190582	5463	NONE	378787
Rhode Island	16019	15799	32652	3407	948	68825
Connecticut	60523	54403	117448	2808	2764	237946
New York	83700	78122	152320	4654	21324	340120
New Jersey	45251	41416	83287	2762	11423	184139
Pennsylvania	110788	106948	206363	6537	3737	434373
Delaware	11783	12143	22384	3899	8887	59094
Maryland	55915	51339	101395	8043	103036	319728
Virginia	110936	116135	215046	12866	292627	747610
Kentucky	15154	17057	28922	114	12430	73677
N. Carolina	69988	77506	140710	4975	100572	393751
S. Carolina	35576	37722	66880	1801	107094	249073
Georgia	13103	14044	25739	398	29264	82548
	807094	791850	1541263	59150	694280	3893635

Total number of Inhabitants of the United States exclusive of S. Western and N. Territory.	Free white Males of 21 years and upwards.	Free Males under 21 years of age.	Free white Females.	All other persons.	Slaves.	Total.
S. W. territory N. Ditto	6271	10277	15365	361	3417	35691

VISUAL ACTIVITY

1790 Census Page

This page displays the final tally of the first federal census in 1790, mandated by the U.S. Constitution as the means to determine both representation in Congress and proportional taxation of the states. Notice the choice of five classifications for the count: free white males age sixteen or older, free white males under age sixteen, free white females, all other free persons, and slaves. To implement the Constitution's three-fifths clause (counting slaves as three-fifths of a person), slaves had to be counted separately from all free persons. Separating white males into two broad age groups at sixteen provided a measure of military strength, important to know in times of Indian (or other) wars. U.S. Census Bureau.

READING THE IMAGE: Which northern states still had slaves? Which state had the largest population? Which had the largest white population?

CONNECTIONS: Why did the census separate males from females? Who might "all other free persons" include? Since women, children, and "all other free persons" counted for purposes of apportionment, could it be said that those groups were represented in the new government?

to carry their message to Congress. Hamilton admitted to Congress that the revenue was far less than anticipated. But rather than abandon the law, he tightened up the prosecution of tax evaders.

This will make the 'Squire ... he our fill of grog.

come friend burn. I'll take thee to thy master.

for thou art our old friend the long noled pensioner.

Just where he hung the people meet.
To see him swing was music sweet.

AN EXCISEMAN.

An Exciseman, 1792
This rough cartoon threatens the hated figure of the whiskey tax collector, shown making off with two barrels of the drink. An evil spirit hooks him by the nose to deliver him to the gallows where is he roasted over a flaming barrel of whiskey. The ghoulish poem under the gallows begins: "Just where he hung the people meet/To see him swing was music sweet." Text below the cartoon (not shown here) explains that "Distillers and Farmers pay all due deference and respect to Congress" and will "contribute amply" to government, but they hate harassment by a tax collector. Courtesy of the Historical Society of Pennsylvania Collection Atwater Kent Museum of Philadelphia.

In western Pennsylvania, Hamilton had one ally, a stubborn tax collector named John Neville who refused to quit even after a group of spirited farmers burned him in effigy. In May 1794, Neville filed charges against seventy-five farmers and distillers for tax evasion. His action touched off the **Whiskey Rebellion**. In July, he and a federal marshal were ambushed in Allegheny County by a group of forty men. Neville's house was then burned to the ground by a crowd estimated at five hundred, and one man in the crowd was killed. At the end of July, seven thousand Pennsylvania farmers planned a march — or perhaps an attack, some thought — on Pittsburgh to protest the hated tax.

In response, President Washington nationalized the Pennsylvania militia and set out, with Hamilton at his side, at the head of thirteen thousand soldiers. A worried Philadelphia newspaper criticized the show of force: "Shall Pennsylvania be converted into a human slaughterhouse because the dignity of the United States will not admit of conciliatory measures? Shall torrents of blood be spilled to support an odious excise system?" But in the end, no blood was spilled. By the time the army arrived in late September, the demonstrators had dispersed. No battles were fought, and no shots were exchanged. Twenty men were rounded up as rebels and charged with high treason, but only two were convicted, and both were soon pardoned by Washington.

Had the federal government overreacted? Thomas Jefferson thought so; he saw the event as a replay of Shays's Rebellion of 1786, when a protest against government taxation had been met with unreasonable government force (see chapter 8). The rebel farmers agreed; they felt entitled to protest oppressive taxation. Hamilton

and Washington, however, thought that laws passed by a republican government must be obeyed. To them, the Whiskey Rebellion presented an opportunity for the new federal government to flex its muscles and stand up to civil disorder.

REVIEW   Why were Hamilton's economic policies controversial?

▶ Conflict on America's Borders and Beyond

While the whiskey rebels challenged federal leadership from within the country, disorder threatened the United States from external sources as well. From 1789 onward, serious trouble brewed in four directions. To the southwest, the loosely confederated Creek Indians pushed back against the western thrust of the white southern population, which gave George Washington the opportunity to test the use of diplomacy and avoid costly war. To the northwest, a powerful confederation of Indian tribes in the Ohio Country went to formidable lengths to scare away white settlers, resulting in six years of brutal warfare. At the same time, conflicts between the major European powers forced Americans to take sides and nearly thrust the country into another war, this time across the Atlantic. And to the south, a Caribbean slave rebellion raised fears that racial war could arise in the United States. Despite these conflicts and the grave threats they posed to the young country, Washington won reelection to the presidency unanimously in the fall of 1792.

Creeks in the Southwest

An urgent task of the new government was to take charge of Indian affairs, ending the ambiguous divided authority between state and confederation government that had characterized the 1780s. Washington and his secretary of war, Henry Knox, hoped to secure peace with the Indians, partly out of a sense of fair play but also over worries about the expense of warfare. Some twenty thousand Indians affiliated with the Creeks occupied lands extending from Georgia into what is now Mississippi, and border skirmishes with land-hungry Georgians were becoming a frequent occurrence. Knox and Washington singled out one Creek chief, **Alexander McGillivray**, and sent a delegation to Georgia for preliminary treaty negotiations.

McGillivray, the son of a Scottish trader and a French-Creek mother, had an unusual history that prepared him to be a major cultural broker. His maternal line conferred a legitimate claim to Creek leadership; his paternal line afforded him access to the literacy and numeracy taught in American schools. Fluent in English and near fluent in Spanish, McGillivray spoke several Creek languages and had even studied Greek and Latin. In the 1770s, he worked for the British distributing gifts to various southern tribes; in the 1780s, he gained renown for brokering negotiations with the Spanish in Florida. The chief agreed to meet with Knox's delegates with some reluctance, since the Creeks' military strength at that point was quite sufficient to keep Georgia settlers at bay.

The American negotiators offered substantial terms to McGillivray, most notably a guarantee of the Creeks' extensive tribal lands and a promise to protect their borders from white settlers. In return, they asked him to cede a disputed tract of land where settlers already lived. But McGillivray sent the negotiators away, enjoying, as he wrote to a Spanish trader, the spectacle of the self-styled "masters of the new world" having "to bend and supplicate for peace at the feet of a people whom shortly before they despised."

A year later, Secretary Knox renewed efforts for a treaty. Georgia settlers and land speculators continued to push onto Creek land. Because of the war brewing north of the Ohio River with the much more belligerent tribes of the Northwest, the federal government had no military resources to spare. To coax McGillivray to the treaty table, Knox invited him to New York City to meet with the president himself. McGillivray arrived in a triumphal procession, joined by twenty-seven lesser chiefs and their entourages. The Creek leader was accorded the honors of a head of state.

The negotiations stretched out for a month in the capital city. In the end, the 1790 **Treaty of New York** incorporated Knox's original plan: Creek tribal lands were guaranteed, with a promise of boundary protection by federal troops against land-seeking settlers. The Creeks were assured of annual payments in money and trade goods, including "domestic animals and implements of husbandry" — words that hinted at a future time when the Creeks would become more agricultural and thus less in need of expansive hunting grounds. The Creeks promised to accept the United States alone as its trading partner, shutting out Spain. At the signing ceremony, Washington read the treaty aloud, with a translator repeating each article to the assembled

Alexander McGillivray, 1790
When the Creek delegation came to New York City to negotiate a treaty, artist Jonathan Trumball was on hand. He showed the guests a portrait he had just completed of George Washington; the Indians professed amazement. "I had been desirous of obtaining portraits of some of the principal men, who possessed a dignity of manner, form, countenance and expression, worthy of Roman Senators," Trumball recalled, but all declined to sit for him. So the artist made five drawings "by stealth." McGillivray is shown wearing an American military coat, a present from Washington, with epaulettes of the rank of brigadier general. Charles Allen Munn Collection, Fordham University Library, Bronx, New York.

chiefs. But both sides had made promises they could not keep. McGillivray thought that the Creeks' interests were best served by maintaining creative tension between the American and Spanish authorities, and by 1792, he had signed an agreement with the Spanish governor of New Orleans, in which each side offered mutual pledges to protect against encroachments by Georgia settlers. By the time Alexander McGillivray died in 1793, his purported leadership of the Creeks was in serious question, and the Treaty of New York joined the list of treaties never fully implemented. Its promise of federal border protection of Creek boundaries was unrealistic from the start, and its pledge of full respect for Creek sovereignty also was only a promise on paper.

At the very start of the new government, in dealing with the Creeks, Washington and Knox tried to find a different way to approach Indian affairs, one rooted more in British than in American experience. But in the end, the demographic imperative of explosive white population growth and westward-moving, land-seeking settlers, together with the economic imperative of land speculation, meant that confrontation with the native population was nearly inevitable. As Washington wrote in 1796, "I believe scarcely any thing short of a Chinese Wall, or line of Troops will restrain Land Jobbers, and the encroachment of Settlers, upon Indian Territory."

Ohio Indians in the Northwest

In the 1783 Treaty of Paris, Britain had yielded all land east of the Mississippi River to the United States without regard to the resident Indian population. The 1784 Treaty of Fort Stanwix (see chapter 8) had attempted to solve that omission by establishing terms between the new confederation government and native peoples, but the various key tribes of the Ohio Valley — the Shawnee, Delaware, and Miami — had not been involved in those negotiations. To confuse matters further, British troops still occupied half a dozen forts in the northwest, protecting an ongoing fur trade between British traders and Indians and thereby sustaining Indians' claims to that land.

"I have always been of the opinion that we never should have a permanent peace with those Indians until they were made to experience our superiority."
—General ANTHONY WAYNE

The doubling of the American population from two million in 1770 to nearly four million in 1790 greatly intensified the pressure for western land. Several thousand settlers a year moved down the Ohio River in the mid-1780s. Most headed for Kentucky on the south bank of the river, but some eyed the forests to the north, in Indian country. By the late 1780s, government land sales in eastern Ohio had commenced, although actual settlement lagged.

Meanwhile, the U.S. Army entered the western half of Ohio, where white settlers did not dare to go. Fort Washington, built on the Ohio River in 1789 at the site of present-day Cincinnati, became the command post for three major invasions of Indian country (Map 9.2). General Josiah Harmar, under orders to subdue the Indians of western Ohio, marched with 1,400 men into Ohio's northwest region in the fall of 1790, burning Indian villages. His inexperienced troops were ambushed by Miami and Shawnee Indians led by their chiefs, **Little Turtle** and **Blue Jacket**. Harmar lost one-eighth of his soldiers.

Harmar's defeat spurred efforts to clear Ohio for permanent American settlement. General **Arthur St. Clair**, the military governor of the Northwest Territory, had pursued peaceful tactics in the 1780s, signing treaties with Indians for land in eastern Ohio — dubious treaties, as it happened, since the Indian negotiators were not authorized to yield land. In the wake of Harmar's bungled operation, St. Clair geared up for military action, and in the fall of 1791 he led two thousand men (accompanied by two hundred women camp followers) north from Fort Washington to claim Ohio territory from the Miami and Shawnee tribes. Along the route, St. Clair's men quickly built two forts, named for Hamilton and Jefferson. However, when the Indians attacked at daybreak on November 4 at the headwaters of the Wabash River, St. Clair's army was not protected by fortifications.

Before noon, 55 percent of the Americans were dead or wounded; only three of the women escaped alive. "The savages seemed not to fear anything we could do," wrote an officer afterward. "The ground was literally covered with the dead." The Indians captured valuable weaponry, scalped and dismembered the dying, and pursued fleeing survivors for miles. With more than nine hundred lives lost, this was the most stunning American loss in the history of the U.S.-Indian wars. Grisly tales of St. Clair's defeat became instantly infamous, increasing the level of terror that Americans brought to their confrontations with the Indians.

Washington doubled the U.S. military presence in Ohio and appointed a new commander, General Anthony Wayne of Pennsylvania, nicknamed "Mad Anthony" for his headstrong, hard-drinking style of leadership. About the Ohio natives, Wayne wrote, "I have always been of the opinion that we never should have a permanent peace

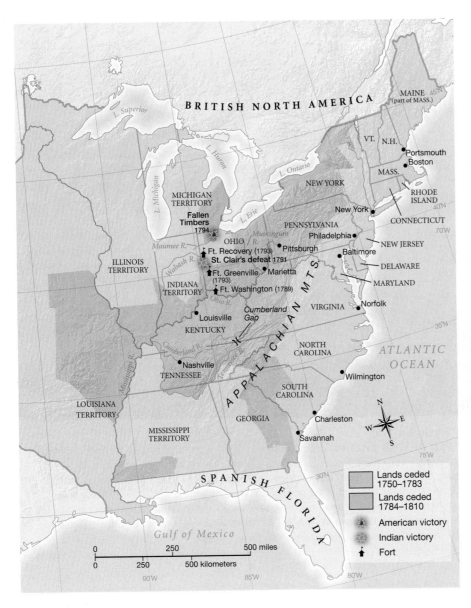

MAP ACTIVITY

Map 9.2 Western Expansion and Indian Land Cessions to 1810
By the first decade of the nineteenth century, intense Indian wars had resulted in significant cessions of land to the U.S. government by treaty.

READING THE MAP: Locate the Appalachians. The Proclamation Line of 1763 that ran along these mountains forbade colonists to settle west of the line. How well was that purpose met?

CONNECTIONS: How much did the population of the United States grow between 1750 and 1790? How did this growth affect western settlement?

with those Indians until they were made to experience our superiority." Throughout 1794, Wayne's army engaged in skirmishes with Shawnee, Delaware, and Miami Indians. Chief Little Turtle of the Miami tribe advised negotiation; in his view, Wayne's large army looked overpowering. But Blue Jacket of the Shawnees counseled continued warfare, and his view prevailed.

The decisive action came in August 1794 at the **battle of Fallen Timbers**, near the Maumee River where a recent tornado had felled many trees. The confederated Indians — mainly Ottawas, Potawatomis, Shawnees, and Delawares numbering around eight hundred — ambushed the Americans but were underarmed, and Wayne's troops made effective use of their guns and bayonets. The Indians withdrew and sought refuge at nearby Fort Miami, still held by the British, but their former allies locked the gate and refused

protection. The surviving Indians fled to the woods, their ranks decimated.

Fallen Timbers was a major defeat for the Indians. The Americans had destroyed cornfields and villages on the march north, and with winter approaching, the Indians' confidence was sapped. They reentered negotiations in a much less powerful bargaining position. In 1795, about a thousand Indians representing nearly a dozen tribes met with Wayne and other American emissaries to work out the **Treaty of Greenville**. The Americans offered treaty goods (calico shirts, axes, knives, blankets, kettles, mirrors, ribbons, thimbles, and abundant wine and liquor casks) worth $25,000 and promised additional shipments every year. The government's idea was to create a dependency on American goods to keep the Indians friendly. In exchange, the Indians ceded most of Ohio to the Americans;

Treaty of Greenville, 1795
This painting of the 1790s purports to depict the signing of the Treaty of Greenville. An American officer kneels and writes—not a likely posture for drafting a treaty. One Indian gestures emphatically, as if to dictate terms, but in fact the treaty was completely favorable to the United States. Although Indians from a dozen Ohio tribes gathered at the signing ceremony, this picture shows unrealistically open spaces and very few Indians. The treaty medal—one of dozens distributed to Indian participants by U.S. officials—commemorates the event. Why might "E Pluribus Unum"—"Out of many, one"—appear on the medal? Painting: Chicago Historical Society; medal: Indiana Historical Society.

only the northwest part of the territory was reserved solely for the Indians.

The treaty brought temporary peace to the region, but it did not restore a peaceful life to the Indians. The annual allowance from the United States too often came in the form of liquor. "More of us have died since the Treaty of Greenville than we lost by the years of war before, and it is all owing to the introduction of liquor among us," said Chief Little Turtle in 1800. "This liquor that they introduce into our country is more to be feared than the gun and tomahawk."

France and Britain

While Indian battles engaged the American military in the west, another war overseas to the east was also closely watched. Since 1789, revolution had been raging in France. At first, the general American reaction was positive, for it was flattering to think that the American

Revolution had inspired imitation in France. As monarchy and privilege were overthrown in France, towns throughout America celebrated the victory of the French people with civic feasts and public festivities. Dozens of pro-French political clubs, called democratic or republican societies, sprang up around the country.

Many American women exhibited solidarity with revolutionary France by donning tricolor cockades, decorative knots of red, white, and blue ribbons. Pro-French headgear for committed women included an elaborate turban, leading one horrified Federalist newspaper editor to chastise the "fiery frenchified dames" thronging Philadelphia's streets. In Charleston, South Carolina, a pro-French pageant in 1793 united two women as partners, one representing France and the other America. The women repudiated their husbands "on account of ill treatment" and "conceived the design of living together in the strictest union and friendship," while a gun salute

Revolutionary Solidarity

In the early 1790s, those Americans enthused by the French Revolution might accessorize with a tricolor cockade — a distinctive bow made from red, white, and blue ribbons. American newspapers avidly reported details of Parisian revolutionary fashions for women, as shown in this French picture. Another short-lived, pro-French fad appeared in marriage announcements in Boston, Hartford, and Philadelphia newspapers in the early months of 1793, in which grooms adopted *Citizen* as their title of address, with the corresponding term *Citess* for brides. (*Citess* was invented on the spot and spelled eighteenth-century style with a character shaped like the letter *f*.) In France, *Citoyen* and *Citoyenne* enjoyed widespread use as egalitarian titles of address. Outfit: Bibliothèque Nationale de France; Announcement: Courtesy, American Antiquarian Society.

MARRIED, By Citizen *Thacher*, Citizen FREDERICK W. GEYER, jun. to Citess REBECCA, daughter to Citizen NATHAN FRAZER.——On Thursday Evening last, by Citizen *Lathrop*, Citizen JONATHAN WILD, to Citess MARY, daughter to Citizen SAMUEL RIDGWAY.

sealed the pledge. Most likely, this ceremony was not the country's first civil union but instead a richly metaphorical piece of street theater in which the spurned husbands represented the French and British monarchies. In addition to these purely symbolic actions, the growing exchange of political and intellectual ideas across the Atlantic helped plant the seeds of a woman's rights movement in America (see "Beyond America's Borders," page 276).

Anti–French Revolution sentiments also ran deep. Vice President John Adams, who lived in France in the 1780s, trembled to think of radicals in France or America. "Too many Frenchmen, after the example of too many Americans, pant for the equality of persons and property," Adams said. "The impracticability of this, God Almighty has decreed, and the advocates for liberty, who attempt it, will surely suffer for it."

Support for the French Revolution remained a matter of personal conviction until 1793, when Britain and France went to war and French versus British loyalty became a critical foreign policy debate. France had helped America substantially during the American Revolution, and the confederation government had signed an alliance in 1778 promising aid if France were ever under attack. Americans optimistic about the eventual outcome of the French Revolution wanted to deliver on that promise. But those shaken by the report of the guillotining of thousands of French people — including the king and queen — as well as those with strong commercial ties to Britain sought ways to stay neutral.

In May 1793, President Washington issued the Neutrality Proclamation, which contained friendly assurances to both sides, in an effort to stay out of European wars. Yet American ships continued to trade between the French West Indies and France. In late 1793 and early 1794, the British expressed their displeasure by capturing more than three hundred of these vessels near the West Indies. Clearly, something had to be done to assert American power.

President Washington sent John Jay, the chief justice of the Supreme Court and a man of strong pro-British sentiments, to England in 1794 to negotiate commercial relations in the British West Indies and secure compensation for the seizure of American ships. In addition, Jay was supposed to resolve several long-standing problems. Southern planters wanted reimbursement for the slaves lured away by the British army during the war, and western settlers wanted Britain to vacate the frontier

France, Britain, and Woman's Rights in the 1790s

During the 1770s and 1780s, no one in America wondered publicly about rights for women. Boycotts by the Daughters of Liberty before the Revolution did not challenge gender hierarchy, nor did New Jersey's handful of women voters (see chapter 8). It took radical ideas from France and Britain to spark new ideas challenging women's subordinate status in American society.

In France between 1789 and 1793, the revolution against monarchy enlarged ideas about citizenship and led some women to call themselves *citoyennes*, female citizens. Women's political clubs, such as the Society of Republican Revolutionary Women in Paris, sent petitions and gave speeches to the National Assembly, demanding education, voting rights, and a curbing of patriarchal powers of men over women. In 1791, Frenchwoman Olympe de Gouges rewrote the male revolutionaries' document *The Declaration of the Rights of Man* into *The Rights of Woman*, a manifesto asserting that "all women are born free and remain equal to men in rights." Another prominent woman, Anne Josèphe Théroigne de Méricourt, maintained a political *salon* (intellectual gathering), marched around Paris in masculine riding attire, and addressed crowds engaged in violent street actions. Her vision went beyond political rights to the social customs that dictated women's subordination: "It is time for women to break out of the shameful incompetence in which men's ignorance, pride, and injustice have so long held us captive."

Although the male National Assembly never approved voting rights for French women in that era, it did reform French civil and family law in the early 1790s. Marriage was removed from the control of the church, divorce was legalized, and the age of majority for women was lowered. A far-reaching change in inheritance law required division of a patriarch's estate among all his children, regardless of age, sex, and even legitimacy. By contrast, most American states adopted traditional English family law virtually unchanged.

French feminism traveled across the Channel to Britain and directly inspired a talented woman named Mary Wollstonecraft. Born into a respectable but downwardly mobile family, the self-educated Wollstonecraft took work as a governess before establishing herself as a writer in London. There she met the radical Thomas Paine and the philosopher William Godwin, along with other leading artists and intellectuals. In 1792, she published *A Vindication of the Rights of Woman*, offering a contrast to Paine's 1791 book *The Rights of Man*. Where Paine talked about property and politics as fundamental rights and never considered women, Wollstonecraft argued that women, as humans, also had inherent rights. She spoke forcefully about the intellectual equality of the sexes that would become evident once women could get an equal education. She championed female economic independence and, most radically, suggested that traditional marriage at its worst was legalized prostitution.

Wollstonecraft's book created an immediate sensation in America. Excerpts appeared in periodicals, bookstores stocked the London edition, and by 1795 there were three American reprints. Some women readers were cautious. A sixty-year-old Philadelphian, Elizabeth Drinker, reflected in her diary, "In very many of her sentiments, she, as some of our friends say, speaks my mind; in some others, I do not altogether coincide with her. I am not for quite so much independence." Others embraced Wollstonecraft's ideas. In 1794, a youthful Priscilla Mason delivered a biting commencement address at a Philadelphia girls' academy, inspired by Wollstonecraft to condemn "the high and mighty

forts still occupied because of their proximity to the Indian fur trade.

Jay returned from his diplomatic mission with a treaty that no one could love. First, the **Jay Treaty** failed to address the captured cargoes or the lost property in slaves. Second, it granted the British a lenient eighteen months to withdraw from the frontier forts, as well as continued rights in the fur trade. (This provision disheartened the Indians just then negotiating the Treaty of Greenville in Ohio. It was a significant factor in their decision to make peace.) Finally, the treaty called for repayment with interest of the debts that some American planters still owed to British firms dating from the Revolutionary War. In exchange for such generous terms, Jay secured limited trading rights in the West Indies and agreement that some issues — boundary disputes with Canada and the damage and loss claims of shipowners — would be decided later by arbitration commissions.

When newspapers published the terms of the treaty, powerful opposition emerged from Maine to Georgia. In Massachusetts, graffiti

FRONTISPIECE.

Publish'd at Philad.ª Dec.ʳ 1.ˢᵗ 1792.

Woman's Rights in the *Lady's Magazine,* **1792**
A new Philadelphia publication aimed at women readers commissioned this engraving to accompany excerpts from Mary Wollstonecraft's *A Vindication of the Rights of Woman.* Lady Liberty, on the left in Greek dress, shares a paper titled "Rights of Woman" with a young woman in eighteenth-century garb. Notice the objects arranged below Liberty: a book, a musical instrument, an artist's palette, a globe, and a page of geometrical shapes. The kneeling figure seems to gesture toward them. What do they suggest about the nature of the "rights of woman" that this picture endorses? Library Company of Philadelphia.

that same July Fourth rejected Wollstonecraft with the claim that woman's rights really meant a woman's duty "to submit to the control of that government she has voluntarily chosen" — namely, the government of a husband.

The interest in the rights of woman faded fast, however. The unhappy fate of de Gouges, guillotined in France in 1794 for her criticism of French leaders, was soon followed by the news of Wollstonecraft's death in childbirth in 1797. Soon thereafter, William Godwin, father of her infant daughter, revealed details of her unconventional personal life, including news of love affairs, two children conceived out of wedlock, and two suicide attempts. "Her licentious practice renders her memory odious to every friend of virtue," declared a prominent American minister in 1801, shutting down nearly all possibility for continued public admiration of Wollstonecraft and her ideas about women.

America in a Global Context

1. Contrast the radical ideas of Mary Wollstonecraft with the more moderate concept of "republican motherhood," which summarizes American women's contributions to civil society and family life.

2. Why might Wollstonecraft's unconventional personal life cast doubt on the value of her ideas about the rights of woman?

lords" (men) who denied women education and professional opportunities. "Happily, a more liberal way of thinking begins to prevail. . . . Let us by suitable education, qualify ourselves for those high departments," Mason said.

Male readers' responses were varied as well. Aaron Burr, a senator from New York, called Wollstonecraft's book "a work of genius." A Fourth of July speaker in New Jersey in 1793 proclaimed that "the Rights of Woman are no longer strange sounds to an American ear" and called for revisions in state law codes. Critics of Wollstonecraft's ideas were not in short supply. A New York orator on

appeared on walls: "Damn John Jay! Damn every one who won't damn John Jay! Damn everyone who won't stay up all night damning John Jay!" Bonfires in many places burned effigies of Jay and copies of the treaty. Nevertheless, the treaty passed the Senate in 1795 by a vote of 20 to 10. Some representatives in the House, led by Madison, tried to undermine the Senate's approval by insisting on a separate vote on the funding provisions of the treaty, on the grounds that the House controlled all spending bills. Finally, in 1796, the House approved funds to implement

the various commissions mandated by the treaty, but by only a three-vote margin. The bitter vote in both houses of Congress divided along the same lines as the Hamilton-Jefferson split on economic policy.

The Haitian Revolution

In addition to the Indian troubles and the European wars across the Atlantic, yet another bloody conflict to the south polarized and even terrorized many Americans in the 1790s. The French colony of Saint Domingue, in the western third of the large Caribbean island of Hispaniola, became engulfed in revolution starting in 1791. Bloody war raged for more than a decade, resulting in 1804 in the birth of the Republic of Haiti, the first and only independent black state to arise out of a successful slave revolution.

The **Haitian Revolution** was a complex event involving many participants, including the diverse local population and, eventually, three European countries. Some 30,000 whites dominated the island in 1790, running sugar and coffee plantations with the enslaved labor of close to half a million blacks, two-thirds of them of African birth. The white French colonists were not the only plantation owners, however. About 28,000 free mixed-race people (*gens de couleur*) owned one-third of the island's plantations and nearly a quarter of the slave labor force. Despite their economic status, these mixed-race planters were barred from political power, but they aspired to it.

The French Revolution of 1789 was the immediate catalyst for rebellion in this already tense society. First, white colonists challenged the white royalist government in an effort to link Saint Domingue with the new revolutionary government in France. Next, the mixed-race planters rebelled in 1791, demanding equal civil rights with the whites. No sooner was this revolt viciously suppressed than another part of the island's population rose up; thousands of slaves armed with machetes and torches wreaked devastation and slaughter. In 1793, the civil war escalated to include French, Spanish, and British troops fighting the inhabitants and also one another. Led by former slave Toussaint L'Ouverture, slaves and free blacks in alliance with Spain occupied the northern

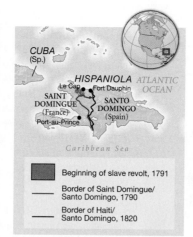

Haitian Revolution, 1791–1804

regions of the island, leaving a thousand plantations in ruins and tens of thousands of people dead. Thousands of white and mixed-race planters, along with some of their slaves, fled to Spanish Louisiana and southern cities in the United States. Charleston alone accepted so many refugees that the city's population was one-sixth French in the early nineteenth century.

White Americans followed the revolution in fascinated horror through newspapers and refugees' accounts. A few sympathized with the impulse for liberty, but others feared that violent black insurrection might spread to the United States. White refugees were welcomed in Charleston, Norfolk, and Richmond, but French-speaking blacks, whether free or slave, were eventually barred from entry to all southern states except Virginia. Many black American slaves also fastened on news of the

Toussaint L'Ouverture
This French engraving made around 1800 depicts the Haitian leader in full military dress and feathered hat commandingly issuing a document to French officers. Library of Congress.

revolution, hearing about it from dockworkers, black sailors, and refugees and through oral networks in taverns and shops. The amazing news of the success of a first-ever massive revolution by slaves traveled quickly in this oral culture. Whites complained of behaviors that might prefigure plots and conspiracies, such as increased insolence and higher runaway rates among slaves.

The Haitian Revolution provoked naked fear of a race war in white southerners. Jefferson, agonizing over the contagion of liberty in 1797, wrote another Virginia slaveholder that "if something is not done, and soon done, we shall be the murderers of our own children . . . ; the revolutionary storm, now sweeping the globe, will be upon us, and happy if we make timely provision to give it an easy passage over our land. From the present state of things in Europe and America, the day which brings our combustion must be near at hand; and only a single spark is wanting to make that day to-morrow."

Jefferson's cataclysmic fears were not shared by New Englanders. Timothy Pickering of Massachusetts, in Washington's cabinet since 1795, chastised the inconsistent Jefferson for supporting French revolutionaries while condemning black Haitians fighting for freedom just because they had "a skin not colored like our own." Not that Pickering supported either type of violent revolutionary — he did not. But he and his political allies, soon to be called the Federalists, were far more willing to contemplate trade and diplomatic relations with the emerging black republic of Haiti.

REVIEW Why did the United States feel vulnerable to international threats in the 1790s?

► Federalists and Republicans

By the mid-1790s, polarization over the French Revolution, Haiti, the Jay Treaty, and Hamilton's economic plans had led to two distinct and consistent rival political groups: **Federalists** and **Republicans**. Politicians and newspapers adopted these labels, words that summarized conflicting political positions. Federalist leaders supported Britain in foreign policy and commercial interests at home, while Republicans rooted for liberty in France and worried about monarchical Federalists at home. The labels did not yet describe full-fledged political parties; such division was still thought to be a sign of failure of the experiment in government. Even so, Washington's decision not to seek a third term led to serious partisan electioneering in the presidential and congressional elections of 1796. Federalist John Adams won the presidency, but party strife accelerated over failed diplomacy in France, bringing the United States to the brink of war. Pro-war and antiwar antagonism created a major crisis over political free speech, militarism, and fears of sedition and treason.

The Election of 1796

Washington struggled to appear to be above party politics, and in his farewell address he stressed the need to maintain a "unity of government" reflecting a unified body politic. He also urged the country to "steer clear of permanent alliances with any portion of the foreign world." The leading contenders for his position, John Adams of Massachusetts and Thomas Jefferson of Virginia, in theory agreed with him, but around them raged a party contest split along pro-British versus pro-French lines.

Adams and Jefferson were not adept politicians in the modern sense, skilled in the arts of persuasion and intrigue. Bruised by his conflicts with Hamilton, Jefferson had resigned as secretary of state in 1793 and retreated to Monticello, his home in Virginia. Adams's job as vice president kept him closer to the political action, but his personality often put people off. He was temperamental, thin-skinned, and quick to take offense.

The leading Federalists informally caucused and chose Adams as their candidate, with Thomas Pinckney of South Carolina to run with him. The Republicans settled on Aaron Burr of New York to pair with Jefferson. The Constitution did not anticipate parties and tickets. Instead, each electoral college voter could cast two votes for any two candidates, but on only one ballot. The top vote-getter became president, and the next-highest assumed the vice presidency. (This procedural flaw was corrected by the Twelfth Amendment, adopted in 1804.) With only one ballot, careful maneuvering was required to make sure that the chief rivals for the presidency did not land in the top two spots.

Into that maneuverable moment stepped Alexander Hamilton. No longer in the cabinet, Hamilton had returned to his law practice in 1795, but he kept a firm hand on political developments. Hamilton did not trust Adams; he preferred Pinckney, and he tried to influence southern electors to switch from Jefferson to the slave-owning Pinckney by publishing a series of anonymous biting satires directed against Jefferson. But his plan failed: Adams was elected president with 71 electoral votes; Jefferson came in second with 68 and thus became vice president. Pinckney got 59 votes, while Burr trailed with 30.

Adams's inaugural speech pledged neutrality in foreign affairs and respect for the French people, based on his several years of residence there, which made Republicans hopeful. To please Federalists, Adams retained three cabinet members from Washington's administration — the secretaries of state, treasury, and war. But the three were Hamilton loyalists, passing off Hamilton's judgments and advice as their own to the unwitting Adams. Vice President Jefferson extended a conciliatory hand to Adams when the two old friends met in Philadelphia, still the capital. They even took temporary lodging in the same boardinghouse, as if expecting to work closely together. But the Hamiltonian cabinet ruined the honeymoon. Jefferson's advice was spurned, and he withdrew from active counsel of the president.

The XYZ Affair

From the start, Adams's presidency was in crisis. France retaliated for the British-friendly Jay Treaty by abandoning its 1778 alliance with the United States. In 1796, it refused to recognize the U.S. minister sent by President Washington to France. Next, French privateers — armed private vessels — started detaining American ships carrying British goods; by March 1797, more than three hundred American vessels had been seized. To avenge these insults, Federalists started murmuring openly about war with France. Adams preferred negotiations and dispatched a three-man commission to France in the fall of 1797. But at the same time, the president recommended new expenditures for military defense. Negotiations, it appeared, would be backed by the muscle of military preparedness. Congress approved money for building three new naval frigates, for arming merchant vessels, and for reinforcing and improving defenses in coastal cities.

When the three American commissioners arrived in Paris, French officials would not receive them. Finally, the French minister of foreign affairs, Talleyrand, sent three French agents — unnamed and soon known to the American public as X, Y, and Z — to the American commissioners with the information that $250,000 might grease the wheels of diplomacy and that a $12 million loan to the French government would be the price of a peace treaty. Incensed, the commissioners brought news of the bribery attempt to the president.

Americans reacted to the **XYZ affair** with shock and anger. Even staunch pro-French Republicans began to reevaluate their allegiance. The Federalist-dominated Congress appropriated money for an army of ten thousand soldiers and repealed all prior treaties with France. In 1798, twenty naval warships launched the United States into its first undeclared war, called the **Quasi-War** by historians to underscore its uncertain legal status. The main scene of action was the Caribbean, where more than one hundred French ships were captured.

There was no home-front unity in this time of undeclared war; antagonism only intensified between Federalists and Republicans. Because there seemed to be very little chance of a land invasion by France, leading Republicans feared, with some justification, that the Federalists' real aim might be to raise the army to threaten domestic dissenters. Some claimed that Hamilton had

John and Abigail Adams
The artist Gilbert Stuart began painting these companion portraits in 1800; Adams was 65 and his wife was 56. A friend once listed Adams's shortcomings as a politician: "He can't dance, drink, game, flatter, promise, dress, swear with gentlemen, and small talk and flirt with the ladies." But, luckily, Adams had a secret weapon to keep him resilient: Abigail, his wife, a woman of astute intellect and wisdom. National Gallery of Art, Washington, D.C.

masterminded the army buildup and was lobbying to be second in command, behind the aging ex-president Washington, presumed to be the man to lead the army. President Adams was increasingly mistrustful of members of his cabinet, but they backed the military buildup, and Adams was too weak politically to prevail. He was, moreover, beginning to suspect that his cabinet was more loyal to Hamilton than to the president.

Antagonism spiraled out of control between Federalists and Republicans. Republican newspapers heaped abuse on Adams. One denounced him as "a person without patriotism, without philosophy, and a mock monarch." Pro-French mobs roamed the streets of Philadelphia, the capital, and Adams, fearing for his personal safety, stocked weapons in his presidential quarters. Federalists, too, went on the offensive. In Newburyport, Massachusetts, they lit a huge bonfire and burned issues of the state's Republican newspapers. Officers in a New York militia unit drank a menacing toast on July 4, 1798: "One and but one party in the United States." A Federalist editor ominously declared that "he who is not for us is against us."

The Alien and Sedition Acts

With tempers so dangerously high and fears that political dissent was perhaps akin to treason, Federalist leaders moved to muffle the opposition.

In mid-1798, Congress hammered out the Sedition Act, which not only made conspiracy and revolt illegal but also penalized speaking or writing anything that defamed the president or Congress. Criticizing government leaders became a criminal offense. One Federalist in Congress justified his vote for the law this way: "Let gentlemen look at certain papers printed in this city and elsewhere, and ask themselves whether an unwarrantable and dangerous combination does not exist to overturn and ruin the government by publishing the most shameless falsehoods against the representatives of the people." In all, twenty-five men, almost all Republican newspaper editors, were charged with sedition; twelve were convicted. (See "Documenting the American Promise," page 282.)

Congress also passed two Alien Acts. The first extended the waiting period for an alien to achieve citizenship from five to fourteen years and required all aliens to register with the federal government. The second empowered the president in time of war to deport or imprison without trial any foreigner suspected of being a danger to the United States. The clear intent of these laws was to harass French immigrants already in the United States and to discourage others from coming.

Republicans strongly opposed the **Alien and Sedition Acts** on the grounds that they were in conflict with the Bill of Rights, but they did not have the votes to revoke the acts in Congress,

Cartoon of the Lyon-Griswold Fight in Congress
The political tensions of 1798 were not merely intellectual; two men brawled on the floor of Congress. Roger Griswold, a Connecticut Federalist, called Matthew Lyon, a Vermont Republican, a coward. Lyon responded with some well-aimed spit, the first departure from the gentleman's code of honor. Griswold responded by raising his cane to Lyon, whereupon Lyon grabbed nearby fire tongs to beat back his assailant. Madison wrote to Jefferson that the two should have dueled, the honorable way to avenge insults. But Lyon, a recent Scots-Irish immigrant, preferred rough-and-tumble fighting as the best response to insult.
Library of Congress.

The Crisis of 1798: Sedition

As President John Adams inched toward an undeclared war with France, criticism of his foreign policy reached an all-time high. Newspaper editors and politicians favorable to France blasted him with such intemperate language that his supporters feared that the United States could be pushed to the brink of civil war. Federalists in Congress tried to muffle the opposition by criminalizing seditious words, believing it to be the only way to preserve the country. Republicans just redoubled their opposition.

DOCUMENT 1
Abigail Adams Complains of Sedition, 1798

Throughout the spring of 1798, a beleaguered Abigail Adams complained repeatedly in confidential letters to her sister Mary Cranch about the need for a sedition law to put a stop to the political criticisms of her husband, the president, by Benjamin Bache, the pro-French editor of the Philadelphia Aurora.

(April 26): . . . Yet dairingly do the vile incendaries keep up in Baches paper the most wicked and base, voilent & calumniating abuse—It was formerly considerd as leveld against the Government, but now it . . . insults the Majesty of the Sovereign People. But nothing will have an Effect until Congress passes a Sedition Bill. . . . (April 28): . . . We are now wonderfully popular except with Bache & Co who in his paper calls the President old, querilous, Bald, blind, cripled, Toothless Adams. (May 10): . . . This Bache is cursing & abusing daily. If that fellow . . . is not surpressd, we shall come to a civil war. (May 26): . . . I wish the Laws of our Country were competant to punish the stirer up of sedition, the writer and Printer of base and unfounded calumny. This would contribute as much to the Peace and harmony of our Country as any measure. . . . (June 19): . . . In any other Country Bache & all his papers would have been seazd and ought to be here, but congress are dilly dallying about passing a Bill enabling the President to seize suspisious persons, and their papers. (June 23): . . . I wish our Legislature would set the example & make a sedition act, to hold in order the base Newspaper calumniators. In this State, you could not get a verdict, if a prosecution was to be commenced.

SOURCE: *New Letters of Abigail Adams, 1788–1801,* edited by Stewart Mitchell, pp. 165, 167, 172, 179, 193, 196. Copyright © 1974 by The American Antiquarian Society. Reprinted by permission of Houghton Mifflin Company. All rights reserved.

DOCUMENT 2
The Sedition Act of 1798

On July 14, 1798, Congress approved a bill making sedition with malicious intent a crime.

SECTION 1. . . . if any persons shall unlawfully combine or conspire together, with intent to oppose any measure or measures of the government of the United States . . . , or to impede the operation of any law of the United States, or to intimidate or prevent any person holding . . . office in or under the government of the United States, from undertaking, performing or executing his trust or duty, and if any person or persons, with intent as aforesaid, shall counsel, advise or attempt to procure any insurrection, riot, unlawful assembly, or combination . . . , he or they shall be deemed guilty of a high misdemeanor, and on conviction . . . shall be punished by a fine not exceeding five thousand dollars, and by imprisonment during a term not less than six months nor exceeding five years. . . .

SEC. 2. . . . If any person shall write, print, utter or publish, or shall cause or procure to be written, printed, uttered or published . . . , any false, scandalous and malicious writing or writings against the government of the United States, or either house of the Congress of the United States, or the President of the United States, with intent to defame the said government . . . or to bring them . . . into contempt or disrepute; or to excite against them . . . the hatred of the good people of the United States . . . , or to aid, encourage or abet any hostile designs of any foreign nation against the United States . . . , then such person, being thereof convicted . . . shall be punished by a fine not exceeding two thousand dollars, and by imprisonment not exceeding two years.

SOURCE: Excerpted text from congressional bill, July 14, 1798.

DOCUMENT 3
Matthew Lyon Criticizes John Adams, 1798

Matthew Lyon, a member of Congress from Vermont, published this criticism of President Adams in a letter to the editor of Spooner's Vermont Journal *(July 31, 1798). It became the first of three counts against him in a sedition trial. Lyon drew a four-month sentence and a fine of $1,000. From jail, he ran for reelection to Congress — and won.*

As to the Executive, when I shall see the efforts of that power bent on the promotion of the comfort, the happiness, and the accommodation of the people, that Executive shall have my zealous and uniform support. But when I see every consideration of the public welfare swallowed up in a continual grasp for power, in an unbounded thirst for ridiculous pomp, foolish adulation, or selfish avarice; when I shall behold men of real merit daily turned out of office for no other cause but independence of sentiment; when I shall see men of firmness, merit, years, abilities, and experience, discarded on their application for office, for fear they possess that independence; and men of meanness preferred for the ease with which they take up and advocate opinions, the consequence of which they know but little of; when I shall see the sacred name of religion employed as a State engine to make mankind hate and persecute one another, I shall not be their humble advocate.

SOURCE: Matthew Lyon, Letter in *Spooner's Vermont Journal,* July 31, 1798. Quoted in *Matthew Lyon: New Man of the Democratic Revolution, 1749–1822* by Aleine Austin, pp. 108–9. Copyright © 1981 Aleine Austin. Reprinted with permission of Pennsylvania State University Press.

DOCUMENT 4
The Virginia Resolution, December 24, 1798

James Madison drafted the Virginia Resolution and had a trusted ally present it to the Virginia legislature, which was dominated by Republicans. (Jefferson did the same for Kentucky.) The Virginia document denounces the Alien and Sedition Acts and declares that states have the right to "interpose" to stop unconstitutional actions by the federal government.

RESOLVED . . . That this assembly most solemnly declares a warm attachment to the Union of the States, to maintain which it pledges all its powers; and that for this end, it is their duty to watch over and oppose every infraction of those principles which constitute the only basis of that Union, because a faithful observance of them, can alone secure its existence and the public happiness.

That this Assembly doth explicitly and peremptorily declare, that it views the powers of the federal government, as resulting from the compact, to which the states are parties; as limited by the plain sense and intention of the instrument constituting the compact; as no further valid that they are authorized by the grants enumerated in that compact; and that in case of a deliberate, palpable, and dangerous exercise of other powers, not granted by the said compact, the states who are parties thereto, have the right, and are in duty bound, to interpose for arresting the progress of the evil, and for maintaining within their respective limits, the authorities, rights and liberties appertaining to them. . . .

That the General Assembly doth particularly protest against the palpable and alarming infractions of the Constitution, in the two late cases of the "Alien and Sedition Acts" . . . ; the first of which exercises a power no where delegated to the federal government . . . ; and the other of which acts, exercises in like manner, a power not delegated by the constitution, but on the contrary, expressly and positively forbidden by one of the amendments thereto; a power, which more than any other, ought to produce universal alarm, because it is levelled against that right of freely examining public characters and measures, and of free communication among the people thereon, which has ever been justly deemed, the only effectual guardian of every other right.

SOURCE: Avalon Project, Yale Law School, 1996. www.yale.edu. © 1996–2007 The Avalon Project at Yale Law School. Reprinted with permission.

Questions for Analysis and Debate

1. Why did the Federalists believe that the Sedition Act was necessary? What exactly was the threat, according to Abigail Adams? What threat is implied by the wording of the act?

2. Does Matthew Lyon's criticism of President Adams rise to the level of threat that the Federalists feared? How do you explain Lyon's guilty verdict? His reelection to Congress?

3. What might Madison have meant by "interpose" as the desired action by states? What could states actually do?

4. Which side had the stronger argument in 1798–1799? Do you think there should be limits on what can be said publicly about high government officials? Why or why not?

nor could the federal judiciary, dominated by Federalist judges, be counted on to challenge them. Jefferson and Madison turned to the state legislatures, the only other competing political arena, to press their opposition. Each man anonymously drafted a set of resolutions condemning the acts and had the legislatures of Virginia and Kentucky present them to the federal government in late fall 1798. The **Virginia and Kentucky Resolutions** put forth the decidedly novel argument that state legislatures have the right to judge the constitutionality of federal laws and even to nullify them. These were amazing assertions of state power, in view of Madison's role in 1787 in creating a federal government that superseded the states, and in view of Jefferson's position as the vice president. By their action, both men ran the risk of being charged with sedition. The resolutions made little dent in the Alien and Sedition Acts, but the idea of a state's right to nullify federal law did not disappear. It would resurface several times in decades to come, most notably in a major tariff dispute in 1832 and in the sectional arguments that led to the Civil War.

> **"We are all republicans, we are all federalists."**
> —President THOMAS JEFFERSON

Amid all the war hysteria and sedition fears in 1798, President Adams regained his balance. He was uncharacteristically restrained in pursuing opponents under the Sedition Act, and he finally refused to declare war on France, as extreme Federalists wished. No doubt he was beginning to realize how much he had been the dupe of Hamilton. He also shrewdly realized that France was not eager for war and that a peaceful settlement might be close at hand. In January 1799, a peace initiative from France arrived in the form of a letter assuring Adams that diplomatic channels were open again and that new peace commissioners would be welcomed in France.

Adams accepted this overture and appointed new negotiators. By late 1799, the Quasi-War with France had subsided, and in 1800 the negotiations resulted in a treaty declaring "a true and sincere friendship" between the United States and France. But Federalists were not pleased; Adams lost the support of a significant part of his own party and sealed his fate as the first one-term president of the United States.

The election of 1800 was openly organized along party lines. The self-designated national leaders of each group met to handpick their candidates for president and vice president. Adams's chief opponent was Thomas Jefferson. When the election was finally over, President Jefferson mounted the inaugural platform to announce, "We are all republicans, we are all federalists," an appealing rhetoric of harmony appropriate to an inaugural address. But his formulation perpetuated a denial of the validity of party politics, a denial that ran deep in the founding generation of political leaders.

> **REVIEW**   Why did Congress pass the Alien and Sedition Acts in 1798?

▶ Conclusion: Parties Nonetheless

American political leaders began operating the new government in 1789 with great hopes of unifying the country and overcoming selfish factionalism. The enormous trust in President Washington was the central foundation for those hopes, and Washington did not disappoint, becoming a model Mr. President with a blend of integrity and authority. Stability was further aided by easy passage of the Bill of Rights (to appease Antifederalists) and by attention to cultivating a virtuous citizenry of upright men supported and rewarded by republican womanhood. Diplomatic attempts were made to secure a peace treaty with the Creeks in the southwest and to offer them protection. (Overtures to the Indians in the northwest were less successful.) Yet the hopes of the honeymoon period soon turned to worries and then fears as major political disagreements flared up.

At the core of the conflict was a group of talented men — Hamilton, Madison, Jefferson, and Adams — so recently allies but now opponents. They diverged over Hamilton's economic program, over relations with the British and the Jay Treaty, over the French and Haitian revolutions, and over preparedness for war abroad and free speech at home. Hamilton was perhaps the driving force in these conflicts, but the antagonism was not about mere personality. Parties were taking shape not around individuals, but around principles, such as ideas about what constituted enlightened leadership, how powerful the federal government should be, who was the best ally in Europe, and when oppositional political speech turned into treason. The Federalists were pro-British, pro-commerce, and ever alarmed about the potential excesses of democracy. The Republicans celebrated, up to a point, the radical republicanism of France and opposed the Sedition Act as an alarming example of an overbearing government cutting off freedom of speech.

When Jefferson in his inaugural address of 1800 offered his conciliatory assurance that Americans were at the same time "all republicans" and "all federalists," he probably mystified some listeners. Possibly, he meant to suggest that both groups shared two basic ideas — the value of republican government, in which power derived from the people, and the value of the unique federal system of shared governance structured by the Constitution. But by 1800, *Federalist* and *Republican* defined competing philosophies of government. To at least some of his listeners, Jefferson's assertion of harmony across budding party lines could only have seemed bizarre. For the next two decades, these two groups would battle each other, each fearing that the success of the other might bring about the demise of the country. And meanwhile, leaders continued to worry that partisan spirit itself was a bad thing.

▶ Selected Bibliography

Politics

Bernard Bailyn, *To Begin the World Anew: The Genius and Ambiguities of the American Founders* (2003).
Ron Chernow, *Alexander Hamilton* (2004).
Ron Chernow, *Washington: A Life* (2010).
Jerry A. Clouse, *The Whiskey Rebellion: Southwestern Pennsylvania's Frontier People Test the American Constitution* (1995).
Stanley Elkins and Eric McKitrick, *The Age of Federalism: The Early American Republic, 1788–1800* (1993).
Joseph J. Ellis, *American Creation: Triumphs and Tragedies in the Founding of the Republic* (2008).
Joseph J. Ellis, *Founding Brothers: The Revolutionary Generation* (2000).
John E. Ferling, *Adams vs. Jefferson: The Tumultuous Election of 1800* (2005).
John E. Ferling, *The Ascent of George Washington: The Hidden Political Genius of an American Icon* (2010).
David P. Geggus, ed., *The Impact of the Haitian Revolution in the Atlantic World* (2002).
David Patrick Geggus and Norman Fiering, eds., *The World of the Haitian Revolution* (2008).
Peter P. Hill, *French Perceptions of the Early American Republic, 1783–1793* (1988).
Ralph Ketcham, *Presidents above Party: The First American Presidency, 1789–1829* (1984).
David McCullough, *John Adams* (2001).
Jeffrey L. Pasley, *The Tyranny of Printers: Newspaper Politics in the Early American Republic* (2001).
Thomas P. Slaughter, *The Whiskey Rebellion: Frontier Epilogue to the American Revolution* (1986).
Larry E. Tise, *The American Counterrevolution: A Retreat from Liberty, 1783–1800* (1999).
Richard J. Twomey, *Jacobins and Jeffersonians: Anglo-American Radicalism in the United States, 1790–1820* (1989).
Henry Wiencek, *An Imperfect God: George Washington, His Slaves, and the Creation of America* (2003).

Society and Culture

Susan Branson, *These Fiery Frenchified Dames: Women and Political Culture in Early National Philadelphia* (2001).
Richard D. Brown, *Knowledge Is Power: The Diffusion of Information in Early America, 1700–1865* (1989).
Nancy Cott, *The Bonds of Womanhood: Women's Sphere in New England, 1780–1835* (1997).
Joanne B. Freeman, *Affairs of Honor: National Politics in the New Republic* (2001).
Richard R. John, *Spreading the News: The American Postal System from Franklin to Morse* (1996).
Linda Kerber, *Women of the Republic: Intellect and Ideology in Revolutionary America* (1997).
Clare A. Lyons, *Sex among the Rabble: An Intimate History of Gender and Power in the Age of Revolution, Philadelphia, 1730–1830* (2006).
Bruce H. Mann, *Republic of Debtors: Bankruptcy in the Age of American Independence* (2002).
Simon P. Newman, *Parades and the Politics of the Street: Festive Culture in the Early American Republic* (2000).
Sheila L. Skemp, *Judith Sargent Murray: A Brief Biography with Documents* (1998).
Rosemarie Zagarri, *Revolutionary Backlash: Women and Politics in the Early American Republic* (2007).

Indians and the Frontier

Andrew R. L. Cayton, *Frontier Republic: Ideology and Politics in the Ohio Country, 1780–1825* (1989).
Gregory E. Dowd, *A Spirited Resistance: The North American Indian Struggle for Unity, 1745–1815* (1992).
R. Douglas Hurt, *The Ohio Frontier: Crucible of the Old Northwest, 1720–1830* (1998).
Claudio Saunt, *A New Order of Things: Property, Power, and the Transformation of the Creek Indians, 1733–1816* (1999).
Wiley Sword, *President Washington's Indian War: The Struggle for the Old Northwest, 1790–1795* (1993).

▶ **FOR MORE BOOKS ABOUT TOPICS IN THIS CHAPTER,** see the Online Bibliography at **bedfordstmartins.com/roark.**

▶ **FOR ADDITIONAL PRIMARY SOURCES FROM THIS PERIOD,** see Michael Johnson, ed., *Reading the American Past*, Fifth Edition.

▶ **FOR WEB SITES, IMAGES, AND DOCUMENTS RELATED TO TOPICS AND PLACES IN THIS CHAPTER,** visit Make History at **bedfordstmartins.com/roark.**

Reviewing Chapter 9

KEY TERMS

Explain each term's significance.

The Search for Stability
Henry Knox (p. 262)
Alexander Hamilton (p. 262)
Thomas Jefferson (p. 262)
John Jay (p. 263)
Bill of Rights (p. 264)
republican motherhood (p. 264)
Judith Sargent Murray (p. 265)

Hamilton's Economic Policies
Report on Public Credit (p. 266)
national debt (p. 266)
Bank of the United States (p. 268)
Report on Manufactures (p. 268)
Whiskey Rebellion (p. 270)

Conflict on America's Borders and Beyond
Alexander McGillivray (p. 271)
Treaty of New York (p. 271)
Little Turtle (p. 272)
Blue Jacket (p. 272)
Arthur St. Clair (p. 272)
battle of Fallen Timbers (p. 273)
Treaty of Greenville (p. 273)
Jay Treaty (p. 276)
Haitian Revolution (p. 278)

Federalists and Republicans
Federalists (p. 279)
Republicans (p. 279)
XYZ affair (p. 280)
Quasi-War (p. 280)
Alien and Sedition Acts (p. 281)
Virginia and Kentucky Resolutions (p. 284)

REVIEW QUESTIONS

Use key terms and dates to support your answer.

1. How did political leaders in the 1790s attempt to overcome the divisions of the 1780s? (pp. 261–265)

2. Why were Hamilton's economic policies controversial? (pp. 265–270)

3. Why did the United States feel vulnerable to international threats in the 1790s? (pp. 270–279)

4. Why did Congress pass the Alien and Sedition Acts in 1798? (pp. 279–284)

MAKING CONNECTIONS

Draw on key terms, the timeline, and review questions.

1. Why did the Federalist alliance of the late 1780s fracture in the 1790s? Why was this development troubling to the nation? In your answer, cite specific ideological and political developments that hindered cooperation.

2. What provoked the Whiskey Rebellion? How did the government respond? In your answer, discuss the foundations and precedents of the conflict, as well as the significance of the government's response.

3. Americans held that virtue was pivotal to the success of their new nation. What did they mean by *virtue*? How did they hope to ensure that their citizens and their leaders possessed virtue?

4. The domestic politics of the new nation were profoundly influenced by conflicts beyond the nation's borders. Discuss how conflicts abroad contributed to domestic political developments in the 1790s.

LINKING TO THE PAST

Link events in this chapter to earlier events.

1. Americans fought against the French in the Seven Years' War but welcomed them as allies during the Revolutionary War. Did either or both of those earlier experiences with France have any bearing on the sharp division in the 1790s between pro-French and anti-French political leaders in the United States? (See chapters 6 and 7.)

2. Shays's Rebellion appeared to some in 1786 to underscore the need for a stronger national government. Compare the Whiskey Rebellion to Shays's Rebellion. How were they similar, and how were they different? Did the Constitution of 1787 make a difference in the authorities' response to rebellion? (See chapter 8.)

▶ FOR PRACTICE QUIZZES AND OTHER STUDY TOOLS, see the Online Study Guide at bedfordstmartins.com/roark.

TIMELINE 1789–1800

1789
- George Washington inaugurated first president.
- French Revolution begins.
- First Congress meets.
- Fort Washington erected in western Ohio.

1790
- Congress approves Hamilton's debt plan.
- Judith Sargent Murray publishes "On the Equality of the Sexes."
- National capital moved from New York City to Philadelphia.
- Shawnee and Miami Indians in Ohio defeat General Josiah Harmar.

1791
- States ratify Bill of Rights.
- Congress and president charter Bank of the United States.
- Ohio Indians defeat General Arthur St. Clair.
- Congress passes whiskey tax.
- Haitian Revolution begins.
- Hamilton issues *Report on Manufactures*.

1793
- Anglo-French Wars commence in Europe.
- Washington issues Neutrality Proclamation.
- Eli Whitney invents cotton gin.

1794
- Whiskey Rebellion.
- Battle of Fallen Timbers.

1795
- Treaty of Greenville.
- Jay Treaty.

1796
- Federalist John Adams elected second president.

1797
- XYZ affair.

1798
- Quasi-War with France erupts.
- Alien and Sedition Acts.
- Virginia and Kentucky Resolutions.

1800
- Republican Thomas Jefferson elected third president.

PATRIOTIC PITCHER, 1800
This earthenware pitcher celebrates American military readiness. A militia officer strikes a springy pose near a cannon that juts out aggressively. Martial words frame the picture and provide a toast. "Success to America Whose Militia Is Better Than Standing Armies." The picture's swagger implies a military preparedness that was in fact woefully off the mark in 1800. Thousands of American-themed pitchers — with eagles and flags, Miss Liberty and George Washington — were marketed by British manufacturers. Pitchers saw daily use wherever people gathered to eat or drink, as in this country tavern scene painted by Philadelphia artist John Lewis Krimmel.

Pitcher: Kahn Fine Antiques/photo courtesy of Antiques and Fine Arts; background: Toledo Museum of Art.

(on pitcher) Success to AMERICA whose MILITIA is better than Standing ARMIES

May its Citizens Emulate Soldiers And its Soldiers Heroes

While Justice is the Throne to which we are bound for ever
Our Country's Rights and Laws we ever will defend

10

Republicans in Power
1800–1824

THE NAME TECUMSEH TRANSLATES AS "SHOOTING STAR," A FITTING name for the Shawnee chief who reached meteoric heights of fame among Indians during Thomas Jefferson's presidency. From Canada to Georgia and west to the Mississippi, Tecumseh was accounted a charismatic leader, for which white Americans praised (and feared) him. Graceful, eloquent, compelling, astute: Tecumseh was all these and more, a gifted natural commander, equal parts politician and warrior.

The Ohio Country, where Tecumseh was born in 1768, was home to some dozen Indian tribes, including the Shawnee, recently displaced from the South. During the Revolutionary War, the region became a battleground with the "Big Knives," as the Shawnee people called the Americans. Tecumseh's childhood was marked by repeated violence and the loss of his father and two brothers in battle. The Revolution's end in 1783 brought no peace to Indian country. American settlers pushed west, and the youthful Tecumseh honed his warrior skills by ambushing pioneers flatboating down the Ohio River. He fought at the battle of Fallen Timbers, a major Indian defeat, but avoided the 1795 negotiations of the Treaty of Greenville, in which half a dozen dispirited tribes ceded much of Ohio to the Big Knives. In frustration, he watched as seven treaties between 1802 and 1805 whittled away more Indian land.

Some Indians, resigned and tired, looked for ways to accommodate, taking up farming, trade, and even intermarriage with the Big Knives. Others spent their treaty payments on alcohol. Tecumseh's younger brother Tenskwatawa led an embittered life of idleness and drink. But Tecumseh rejected accommodation and instead campaigned for a return to ancient ways. Donning traditional animal-skin garb, he traveled around the Great Lakes region after 1805 persuading tribes to join his pan-Indian confederacy. The territorial governor of Indiana, William Henry Harrison, reported, "For four years he has been in constant motion. You see him today on the Wabash, and in a short time hear of him on the shores of Lake Erie or Michigan, or on the banks of the Mississippi, and wherever he goes he makes an impression favorable to his purpose."

Even Tecumseh's dissolute brother was born anew. After a near-death experience in 1805, Tenskwatawa revived and recounted a startling vision of meeting the Master of Life. Renaming himself the Prophet, he urged

Indians everywhere to regard whites as children of the Evil Spirit, destined to be destroyed.

Tecumseh and the Prophet established a new village called Prophetstown, located in present-day Indiana, offering a potent blend of spiritual regeneration and political unity that attracted thousands of followers. Governor Harrison admired and feared Tecumseh, calling him "one of those uncommon geniuses which spring up occasionally to produce revolutions."

President Thomas Jefferson worried about an organized Indian confederacy and its potential for a renewed alliance with the British in Canada. Those worries became a reality during Jefferson's second term in office (1805–1809). Although his first term (1801–1805) brought notable successes, such as the Louisiana Purchase and the Lewis and Clark expedition, his second term was consumed by the threat of war with either Britain or France, in a replay of the late-1790s tensions. When war came in 1812, the enemy was Britain, bolstered by a reenergized Indian-British alliance. Among the causes of the war were insults over international shipping rights and the capture of U.S. vessels. But the war also derived compelling strength from Tecumseh's confederacy. Significant battles pitted U.S. soldiers against Indians in the Great Lakes, Tennessee, and Florida.

In the end, the War of 1812 settled little between the United States and Britain, but it was tragically conclusive for the Indians. Eight hundred warriors led by Tecumseh helped defend Canada against U.S. attacks, but the British did not reciprocate when the Indians were under threat. Tecumseh died on Canadian soil at the battle of the Thames in the fall of 1813. No Indian leader with his star power would emerge again east of the Mississippi.

The briefly unified Indian confederacy under Tecumseh had no counterpart in the young Republic's confederation of states, where widespread unity behind a single leader proved impossible to achieve. Republicans did battle with Federalists during the Jefferson and Madison administrations, but then Federalists doomed their party by opposing the War of 1812. After 1815, they ceased to be a major force in political life. The next two presidents, James Monroe and John Quincy Adams, congratulated themselves on the Federalists' demise and Republican unity, but in fact divisions within their own party were extensive. Wives of politicians increasingly inserted themselves into this dissonant mix, managing their husbands' politicking and enabling them to appear above the fray and maintain the fiction of a nonpartisan state. That it was a fiction became sharply apparent in the most serious political crisis of this period, the Missouri Compromise of 1820.

Tecumseh

Several portraits of Tecumseh exist, but they all present a different visage, and none of them enjoys verified authenticity. This one perhaps comes closest to how Tecumseh actually looked. It is an 1848 engraving adapted from an earlier drawing that no longer exists, sketched by a French trader in Indiana named Pierre Le Dru in a live sitting with the Indian leader in 1808. The engraver has given Tecumseh a British army officer's uniform, showing that he fought on the British side in the War of 1812. Notice the head covering and the medallion around Tecumseh's neck, marking his Indian identity. Library of Congress.

▶ Jefferson's Presidency

The nerve-wracking election of 1800, decided in the House of Representatives, stoked fears that party divisions would ruin the country. A panicky Federalist newspaper in Connecticut predicted that a victory by **Thomas Jefferson** would produce a bloody civil war and usher in an immoral reign of "murder, robbery, rape, adultery and incest." Similar fears were expressed in the South, where a frightful slave uprising seemed a possible outcome of Jefferson's victory. But nothing nearly so dramatic occurred. Jefferson later called his election the "revolution of 1800," referring to his repudiation of Federalist practices and his cutbacks in military spending and taxes. While he cherished a republican simplicity in governance, he inevitably encountered events that required decisive and sometimes expensive government action. One early example came when pirates repeatedly threatened American ships off the north coast of Africa.

Turbulent Times: Election and Rebellion

The result of the election of 1800 (Map 10.1) remained uncertain from polling times in the late fall to repeated roll call votes in the House of Representatives in February 1801. Federalist John Adams, never secure in his leadership of the Federalist Party, was no longer in the presidential race once it reached the House. Instead, the contest was between Jefferson and his running mate, Senator **Aaron Burr** of New York. Republican voters in the electoral college slipped up, giving Jefferson and Burr an equal number of votes, an outcome possible because of the single balloting to choose both president and vice president. (To fix this problem, the Twelfth Amendment to the Constitution, adopted in 1804, provided for distinct ballots for the two offices.) The vain and ambitious Burr declined to concede, so the sitting Federalist-dominated House of Representatives got to choose the president.

Each state delegation had one vote, and nine were needed to win. Some Federalists preferred Burr, believing that his character flaws made him susceptible to Federalist pressure. But the influential Alexander Hamilton, though no friend of Jefferson, recognized that the high-strung Burr would be more dangerous in the presidency. Jefferson was a "contemptible hypocrite" in Hamilton's opinion, but at least he

was not corrupt. Jefferson received the votes of eight states on the first ballot. Thirty-six ballots and six days later, he got the critical ninth vote, as well as a tenth. This election demonstrated a remarkable feature of the new government: No matter how hard fought the campaign, the leadership of the nation could shift from one group to its rivals in a peaceful transfer of power effected by ballots, not bullets.

As the country struggled over its white leadership crisis, a twenty-four-year-old blacksmith named Gabriel, the slave of Thomas Prossor, plotted rebellion in Virginia. Inspired by the Haitian Revolution (see chapter 9), and perhaps directly informed of it by French slaves new to the Richmond area, Gabriel was said to be organizing a thousand slaves to march on the state capital of Richmond and take the governor, James Monroe, hostage. On the appointed day, however, a few nervous slaves went to the authorities with news of **Gabriel's rebellion**, and within days scores of implicated conspirators were jailed and brought to trial.

> **"I have nothing more to offer than what General Washington would have had to offer, had he been taken by the British and put to trial by them."**
>
> — A jailed slave accused of contemplating rebellion

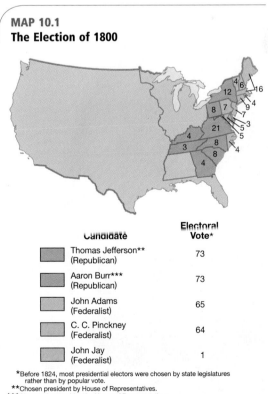

MAP 10.1
The Election of 1800

Candidate	Electoral Vote*
Thomas Jefferson** (Republican)	73
Aaron Burr*** (Republican)	73
John Adams (Federalist)	65
C. C. Pinckney (Federalist)	64
John Jay (Federalist)	1

*Before 1824, most presidential electors were chosen by state legislatures rather than by popular vote.
**Chosen president by House of Representatives.
***Chosen vice president by House of Representatives.

Pistols from the Burr-Hamilton Duel

In 1804, Vice President Aaron Burr shot and killed Alexander Hamilton with a .54-caliber pistol. Hamilton had long scorned Burr, and when a newspaper published Hamilton's disdain, Burr felt obliged to avenge his honor. Dueling, fully accepted in the South as an extralegal remedy for insult, had recently been outlawed in northern states. Burr was charged with a misdemeanor in New York, where the challenge was issued, and with homicide in New Jersey, where the duel was fought. After four months as a fugitive in the South, Burr resumed his official duties in Washington. He was never arrested. Courtesy of Chase Manhattan Archives.

One of the jailed rebels compared himself to the most venerated icon of the early Republic: "I have nothing more to offer than what General Washington would have had to offer, had he been taken by the British and put to trial by them." Such talk invoking the specter of a black George Washington worried white Virginians, and in the fall of 1800 twenty-seven black men were hanged for allegedly contemplating rebellion. Finally, Jefferson advised Governor Monroe to halt the hangings. "The world at large will forever condemn us if we indulge a principle of revenge," Jefferson wrote.

The Jeffersonian Vision of Republican Simplicity

Once elected, Thomas Jefferson turned his attention to establishing his administration in clear contrast to the Federalists. For his inauguration, held in the village called Washington City, he dressed in everyday clothing to strike a tone of republican simplicity, and he walked to the Capitol for the modest swearing-in ceremony. As president, he scaled back Federalist building plans for Washington and cut the government budget.

Martha Washington and Abigail Adams had received the wives of government officials at weekly teas, thereby cementing social relations in the governing class. But Jefferson, a longtime widower, disdained female gatherings and avoided the women of Washington City. He abandoned George Washington's practice of holding weekly formal receptions, limiting these drop-in gatherings to just two a year. His preferred social event was the small dinner party with carefully chosen politicos, either all Republicans or all Federalists (and all male). At these intimate dinners, the president exercised influence and strengthened informal relationships that would help him govern.

Thomas Jefferson, **by John Trumbull**

This miniature portrait of Jefferson was made in the late 1780s, when the young widower lived with his two daughters and their attendant, the slave Sally Hemings. In 1802, a scandal erupted when a journalist charged that Jefferson had fathered several children by Hemings. DNA evidence from 1998, combined with historical evidence about Jefferson's whereabouts at the start of Hemings's six pregnancies, makes a powerful case that Jefferson fathered at least some of her children. Jefferson never commented about Hemings in his writings, and the written record on her side is entirely mute. Two of her four surviving children were allowed to slip away to freedom in the 1820s; the other two were freed in Jefferson's will. Monticello/Thomas Jefferson Memorial Foundation, Inc.

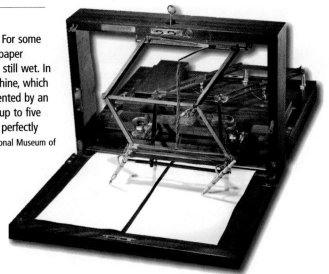

Jefferson was no Antifederalist. He had supported the Constitution in 1788, despite his concern about the unrestricted reelection allowed to the president. But events of the 1790s had caused him to worry about the stretching of powers in the executive branch. Jefferson had watched with distrust as Hamiltonian policies refinanced the public debt, established a national bank, and secured commercial ties with Britain (see chapter 9). These policies seemed to Jefferson to promote the interests of money-hungry speculators and profiteers at the expense of the rest of the country. Financial schemes that seemed merely to allow rich men to become richer were corrupt and worthless, he believed, and their promotion by the federal government was not authorized by the Constitution. In Jefferson's vision, the source of true liberty in America was the independent farmer, someone who owned and worked his land both for himself and for the market.

Jefferson set out to dismantle Federalist innovations. He reduced the size of the army by a third, preferring "a well-disciplined militia" for defense, and he cut back the navy to just half a dozen ships. With the consent of Congress, he abolished all federal taxes based on population or whiskey. Government revenue would now derive solely from customs duties and the sale of western land. This strategy benefited the South, where three-fifths of the slaves counted for representation but not for taxation now. By the end of his first term, Jefferson had deeply reduced Hamilton's cherished national debt.

A properly limited federal government, according to Jefferson, was responsible merely for running a postal system, maintaining the federal courts, staffing lighthouses, collecting customs duties, and conducting a census once every ten years. The president had one private secretary, a young man named Meriwether Lewis, to help with his correspondence, and Jefferson paid him out of his own pocket. The Department of State employed only 8 people: Secretary James Madison, 6 clerks, and a messenger. The Treasury Department was by far the largest unit, with 73 revenue commissioners, auditors, and clerks, plus 2 watchmen. The entire payroll of the executive branch amounted to a mere 130 people in 1801.

However, one large set of government workers lay beyond Jefferson's command. His predecessor, John Adams, had made 217 last-minute appointments of Federalists to various judicial and military posts. Jefferson refused to honor those "midnight judges" who had not yet been fully processed. One disappointed job seeker, William Marbury, sued the new secretary of state, James Madison, for failure to make good on the appointment. This action gave rise to a landmark Supreme Court case, **_Marbury v. Madison_**, decided in 1803. The Court ruled that although Marbury's commission was valid and the new president should have delivered it, the Court could not compel him to do so. What made the case significant was little noted at the time: The Court found that the grounds of Marbury's suit, resting in the Judiciary Act of 1789, were in conflict with the Constitution. For the first time, the Court acted to disallow a law on the grounds that it was unconstitutional.

Dangers Overseas: The Barbary Wars

Jefferson's desire to keep government and the military small met a severe test in the western Mediterranean Sea, where U.S. trading interests ran afoul of local Muslim states, leading to the first formal declaration of war against the United States by a foreign power. For well over a cen-

The Burning of the Frigate *Philadelphia* in Tripoli Harbor, 1804
After losing the warship *Philadelphia* to Tripolitan forces in 1803, American naval leaders decided to destroy it to prevent its use by the so-called pirates of North Africa. Commander Stephen Decatur engineered the daring nighttime raid. With his men concealed below decks of a modest trading vessel, Decatur entered the harbor and had his Arabic-speaking pilot secure permission to tie up next to the *Philadelphia*. The American raiding party quickly boarded, sending the Tripolitan guards into the water to swim to shore. In twenty minutes the warship was ablaze; Decatur departed with only one injured man and no fatalities. The Mariners Museum, Newport News, Virginia.

hundred-man crew was captured along with the ship. In retaliation, a U.S. naval ship commanded by Lieutenant Stephen Decatur sailed into the harbor after dark, guided by an Arabic-speaking pilot to fool harbor sentries. Decatur's crew set the *Philadelphia* on fire, rendering the ship useless to its hijackers and making Decatur an instant hero in America. A later foray into the harbor to try to blow up the entire Tripoli fleet with a bomb-laden boat failed when the explosives detonated prematurely, killing eleven Americans.

In 1804, William Eaton, an American officer stationed in Tunis, felt the humiliation of his country's ineffectiveness. He requested a thousand Marines to invade Tripoli, but Secretary of State James Madison rejected the plan and another scheme to ally with the pasha's exiled brother to effect regime change. On his own, Eaton contacted the brother, assembled a force of four hundred men (mostly Greek and Egyptian mercenaries plus his Marines), and marched them over five hundred miles of desert for a surprise attack on Derne, Tripoli's second-largest city. Amazingly, he succeeded. The pasha of Tripoli yielded, released — for a fee — the prisoners taken from the *Philadelphia*, and negotiated a treaty with the United States that terminated tribute. One significant clause of the treaty stipulated that the United States "has in itself no character of enmity against the Laws, Religion or Tranquility of Musselmen [Muslims]" and that "no pretext arising from Religious Opinions, shall ever produce an interruption of the Harmony existing between the two Nations." Peace with the other Barbary States came in a second treaty in 1812.

tury, four Muslim states on the northern coast of Africa — Morocco, Algiers, Tunis, and Tripoli, called the Barbary States by Americans — controlled all Mediterranean shipping traffic by demanding large annual payments (called "tribute") for safe passage. Countries electing not to pay found their ships at risk for seizure, with cargoes plundered and crews captured and sold into slavery. By the mid-1790s, the United States was paying $50,000 a year. About a hundred American merchant ships annually traversed the Mediterranean, trading lumber, tobacco, sugar, and rum for regional delicacies such as raisins, figs, capers, and medicinal opium.

In May 1801, when the pasha (military head) of Tripoli failed to secure a large increase in his tribute, he declared war on the United States. Jefferson had long considered such payments extortion, and he sent four warships to the Mediterranean to protect U.S. shipping. From 1801 to 1803, U.S. frigates engaged in skirmishes with Barbary privateers.

Then, in late 1803, the USS *Philadelphia* ran aground near Tripoli's harbor. Its three-

The **Barbary Wars** of 1801–1805 cost Jefferson's government more money than the tribute demanded. But the honor of the young country was thought to be at stake. At political gatherings, the slogan "Millions for defense, but not a cent for tribute" became a popular toast.

REVIEW   How did Jefferson attempt to undo the Federalist innovations of earlier administrations?

▶ Opportunities and Challenges in the West

While Jefferson remained cautious about exercising federal power, he quickly learned that circumstances sometimes required him to enlarge the authority of the presidency. Shifting politics in Europe in 1803 opened an unexpected door to the spectacular purchase from France of the Louisiana Territory. To explore the largely unmarked boundaries of this huge acquisition, Jefferson sent four separate expeditions into the prairie and mountains. The powerful Osage of the Arkansas River valley responded to overtures for an alliance and were soon lavishly welcomed by Jefferson in Washington City, but the even more powerful Comanche of the southern Great Plains stood their ground against all invaders. Meanwhile, the expedition by Lewis and Clark, the longest and northernmost trek of the four launched by Jefferson, mapped U.S. terrain all the way to the Pacific Ocean, giving a boost to expansionist aspirations.

The Louisiana Purchase

When the map of North America was redrawn in 1763, at the end of the Seven Years' War, a large expanse of the territory west of the Mississippi River shifted from France to Spain (see Map 6.2, page 164). Spain never controlled or settled the area centered on the Great Plains, which was already peopled by many Indian tribes, most notably the powerful and expansionist Comanche nation. New Orleans was Spain's principal stronghold in the region, a onetime French city strategically sited on the Mississippi River near its outlet to the Gulf of Mexico. Spain profited modestly from trade taxes it imposed on the small but growing flow of agricultural products shipped down the river from American farms in the western parts of Kentucky and Tennessee (to be sold at New Orleans or Caribbean destinations).

The biggest concern of the Spanish governor of New Orleans was that the sparse population of lower Louisiana was insufficient to ward off an anticipated westward movement of Americans. Spanish officials took steps to encourage European immigration, but only small numbers of Germans and French came. Up the river at St. Louis, the Spanish governor happily welcomed Native American refugees from the Northwest Territory who had been pushed out by what was termed a "plague of locusts" — American settlers — in the 1790s. Hoping that a Spanish-Indian alliance might be able to stop the expected demographic wave, he promised that the Spanish would "receive you in their homes as if you all belonged to our nation." Still, defending many hundreds of miles of the river against Americans on the move was a daunting prospect. "You can't put doors on open country," said an adviser to the Spanish king.

Thus, in 1800 Spain struck a secret deal to return this trans-Mississippi territory to France, in the hopes that a French Louisiana would provide a buffer zone between Spain's more valuable holdings in Mexico and the land-hungry Americans. The French emperor Napoleon accepted the transfer and agreed to Spain's condition that France could not sell Louisiana to anyone without Spain's permission.

From the U.S. perspective, Spain had proved a weak western neighbor, but France was another story. Jefferson was so alarmed by the rumored transfer that he instructed Robert R. Livingston, America's minister in France, to approach the French and offer to buy New Orleans. At first, the French denied they owned the city. But when Livingston hinted that the United States might seize it if buying was not an option, the French negotiator asked him to name his price for the entire Louisiana Territory from the Gulf of Mexico north to Canada. Livingston stalled, and the Frenchman made suggestions: $125 million? $60 million? Livingston shrewdly stalled some more and within days accepted the bargain price of $15 million (Map 10.2).

> "You can't put doors on open country."
> — An advisor to the Spanish king

On the verge of war with Britain, France needed both money and friendly neutrality from the United States, and it got both from the quick sale of the Louisiana Territory. In addition, the recent and costly loss of Haiti as a colony made a French presence in New Orleans less feasible as well. But in selling Louisiana to the United States, France had broken its agreement with Spain, which protested that the sale was illegal.

Moreover, there was no consensus on the western border of this land transfer. Spain claimed that the border was about one hundred miles west of the Mississippi River, while in Jefferson's eyes it was some eight hundred miles farther west, defined by the crest of the Rocky Mountains. When Livingston pressured the French negotiator to clarify his country's understanding of the

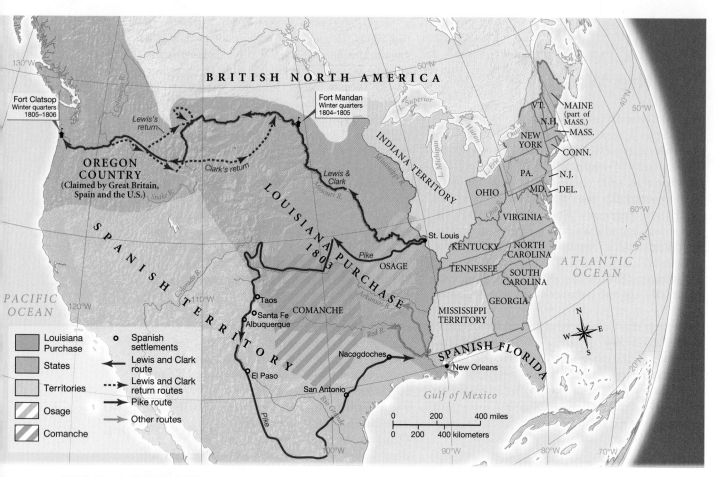

MAP ACTIVITY

Map 10.2   Jefferson's Expeditions in the West, 1804–1806
The Louisiana Purchase of 1803 brought the U.S. a large territory without clear boundaries. Jefferson sent off four scientific expeditions to take stock of the land's possibilities and to assess the degree of potential antagonism from Indian and Spanish inhabitants.

READING THE MAP: How did the size of the newly acquired territory compare to the land area of the existing American states and territories? What natural features of the land might have suggested boundaries for the Louisiana Purchase? Did those natural features coincide with actual patterns of human habitation already in place?

CONNECTIONS: What political events in Europe created the opportunity for the Jefferson administration to purchase Louisiana? How did the acquisition of Louisiana affect Spain's hold on North America?

boundary, the negotiator replied, "I can give you no direction. You have made a noble bargain for yourself, and I suppose you will make the most of it."

Jefferson and most members of Congress were delighted with the **Louisiana Purchase**. In late 1803, the American army took formal control of the Louisiana Territory, and the United States nearly doubled in size — at least on paper. The Spanish inhabitants of New Orleans had relinquished the city to a few French officials just a month before the Americans arrived to claim it, and now many of the Spaniards left for Texas or West Florida (along the

Gulf coast), lands still in Spanish hands. One departing Spanish officer expressed his loathing for the "ambitious, restless, lawless, conniving, changeable, and turbulent" Americans, writing, "I am so disgusted with hearing them that I can hardly wait to leave them behind me."

The Lewis and Clark Expedition

Jefferson quickly launched four government-financed expeditions up the river valleys of the new territory to establish relationships with Indian tribes and to determine Spanish influence and presence. The first set out in 1804 to explore the upper reaches of the Missouri River. Jefferson appointed twenty-eight-year-old Meriwether Lewis, his secretary, to head the expedition and instructed him to investigate Indian cultures, to collect plant and animal specimens, and to chart the geography of the West, with particular attention to locating the headwaters of the rivers "running southwardly" to Spain's settlements. (See "Visualizing History," page 298.) The expedition was also charged with scouting locations for military posts, negotiating fur trade agreements, and identifying river routes to the West (see Map 10.2).

For his co-leader, Lewis chose Kentuckian William Clark, a veteran of the 1790s Indian wars. Together, they handpicked a crew of forty-five, including expert rivermen, gunsmiths, hunters, interpreters, a cook, and Clark's slave named York. The explorers left St. Louis in the spring of 1804, working their way northwest up the Missouri River. They camped for the winter at a Mandan village in what is now central North Dakota. The Mandan Indians were familiar with British and French traders from Canada, but the black man York created a sensation. Reportedly, the Indians rubbed moistened fingers over the man's skin to see if the color was painted on.

The following spring, the explorers headed west, accompanied by a sixteen-year-old Shoshoni woman named **Sacajawea**. Kidnapped by Mandans at about age ten, she had been sold to a French trapper as a slave/wife. Hers was not a unique story among Indian women, and such women knew several languages, making them valuable translators and mediators. Further, Sacajawea and her new baby allowed the American expedition to appear peaceful to suspicious tribes. As Lewis wrote in his journal, "No woman ever accompanies a war party of Indians in this quarter."

The **Lewis and Clark expedition** reached the Pacific Ocean at the mouth of the Columbia River in November 1805. When the two leaders returned home the following year, they were greeted as national heroes. They had established favorable relations with dozens of Indian tribes; they had collected invaluable information on the peoples, soils, plants, animals, and geography of the West; and they had inspired a nation of restless explorers and solitary imitators.

Osage and Comanche Indians

The three additional U.S. expeditions set forth between 1804 and 1806 from the Mississippi River to probe the contested southwestern border of the Louisiana Purchase. The first exploring

Comanche Feats of Horsemanship, 1834
Pennsylvania artist George Catlin toured the Great Plains and captured Comanche equestrian warfare in training. "Every young man," Catlin wrote, learned "to drop his body upon the side of his horse at the instant he is passing, effectually screened from his enemies' weapons. . . . [H]e will hang whilst his horse is at fullest speed, carrying with him his bow and his shield, and also his long lance . . . which he will wield upon his enemy as he passes; rising and throwing his arrows over the horse's back, or with equal ease and equal success under the horse's neck." Smithsonian American Art Museum, Washington, DC/Art Resource, NY.

Cultural Exchange on the Lewis and Clark Trail

Lewis and Clark carried many gifts for the Indians they anticipated meeting as they traveled up the Missouri River toward the Rocky Mountains. Intended to signal goodwill and respect, some of the gifts held other subtle meanings as well.

Upon encountering new tribes, the explorers presented high-ranking Indian leaders with silver medals bearing the likeness of President Jefferson, in two, three-, or four-inch sizes. Imagine the Indian recipients' reactions. What specific message might the image of the president convey? On what basis do you think the explorers chose to distribute the various sizes?

Thomas Jefferson's Peace Medal, 1801

The explorers traveled with ornamental trinkets ("ear bobs," silk handkerchiefs, ivory combs, ribbons) as well as practical goods (brass buttons, needles and thread, blankets, calico shirts) that demonstrated

American manufacturing and handcraft. They carried a few small mirrors and magnifying glasses but on one occasion found that making fire with the latter engendered suspicion, not goodwill. Blue glass beads — portable and inexpensive — were a sought-after gift, leading Clark to observe that beads "may be justly compared to gold and Silver among civilized nations."

Blue Trade Beads

party left from Natchez, Mississippi, and ascended the Red River to the Ouachita River, ending at a hot springs in present-day Arkansas. Two years later, the second group of explorers followed the Red River west into eastern Texas, and the third embarked from St. Louis and traveled west, deep into the Rockies. This third group, led by Zebulon Pike, had gone too far, in the view of the Spaniards: Pike and his men were arrested, taken to northern Mexico, and soon released.

Of the scores of Indian tribes in this lower Great Plains region, two enjoyed reputations for territorial dominance. The **Osage** ruled the land between the Missouri and the lower Arkansas rivers, while the trading and raiding grounds of the **Comanche** stretched from the upper Arkansas River to the Rockies and south into Texas, a vast area called Comanchería. Both were formidable tribes that proved equal to the Spaniards. The Osage accomplished this through careful diplomacy and periodic shows of strength. The Comanche cemented their dominance by expert horsemanship; a brisk trade in guns, captives, and goods; and a constant readiness to employ strong-arm tactics and violence.

Jefferson turned his attention to cultivating the Osage, whose attractive lands (in present-day southern Missouri) beckoned as farmland

in America's future. He directed Meriwether Lewis, on his way west, to invite the Osage to Washington City. When the delegation of eleven Osage leaders arrived in 1804, Jefferson greeted them as heads of state, with elaborate ceremonies and generous gifts. He positioned the Osage as equals of the Americans: "The great spirit has given you strength & has given us strength, not that we might hurt one another, but to do each other all the good in our power." Jefferson's goal was to make the Osage a strong trading partner, but he also had firm notions about what items to offer for trade: hoes and ploughs for the men; spinning wheels and looms for the women. These highly gendered tools signified a departure from the native gender system in which women tended crops while men hunted game. As Jefferson saw it, such equipment would bring the Indians the blessings of an agricultural civilization. Diminished reliance on the hunt would reduce the amount of land that tribes needed to sustain their communities. Jefferson expressed his hope that "commerce is the great engine by which we are to coerce them, & not war."

For their part, the Osage wanted Jefferson primarily to provide protection against Indian refugees displaced by American settlers east of the Mississippi. Jefferson's Osage alliance soon

Jefferson pointedly urged Lewis to take small hand-cranked corn mills, to acculturate the native women to American household technology. Indian women, with full charge of corn agriculture and its preparation as food, used mortars and pestles to pulverize dried kernels. Each time Lewis and Clark presented tribal chiefs with a corn mill and demonstrated its use, the recipients professed to be "highly pleased." Yet a year later, a fur trader visiting the Mandan nation wrote, "I saw the remains of an excellent large corn mill, which the foolish fellows had demolished to barb their arrows." Did the explorers perhaps fail in their mission by giving the mill to male leaders instead of to

Corn Mill Grinder

women? Or could this repurposing of the food grinder be read as a rejection by the women themselves of Americans' gendered practices?

The explorers received gifts as well. The most impressive was the necklace shown here, made of thirty-five four-inch grizzly bear claws. The explorers encountered a number of Indian men wearing bear claw "collars" (Lewis's term for it). For many tribes, bears were sacred animals, and their claws embodied spiritual power. Grizzlies are large (up to nine hundred pounds) and aggressive, so acquiring so many claws without firearms clearly took extraordinary courage. Can you imagine the impact of wearing such an ornament when meeting visitors from a distant and unknown society? Was it a forceful show of courage and power? Why might Indians bestow this rare necklace on the explorers? Did it honor their manly

Grizzly Bear Claw Necklace

courage? Or promote a spiritual brotherhood? Or might it have been intended to discourage further shootings of the sacred bears?

SOURCE: Jefferson's medal: Research Division of the Oklahoma Historical Society; trade beads: Ralph Thompson Collection of the North Dakota Lewis & Clark Bicentennial Foundation, Washburn, ND; corn mill: The Colonial Williamsburg Foundation; bear claw necklace: Peabody Museum, Harvard University, Photo 99-12-10/99700.

proved to be quite expensive, with costs arising from ransoming prisoners, providing defense, brokering treaties, and giving gifts all around. In 1806, a second ceremonial visit to Washington and other eastern cities by a dozen Osage leaders cost the federal government $10,000.

These promising peace initiatives were short-lived. By 1808, intertribal warfare was on the rise, and the governor of the Louisiana Territory declared that the U.S. government no longer had an obligation to protect the Osage. Jefferson's presidency was waning, and soon the practice of whittling away Indian lands through coercive treaties, so familiar to men like Tecumseh, reasserted itself. A treaty in 1808, followed by others in 1818, 1825, and 1839, shrank the Osage lands, and by the 1860s they were forced onto a small region in present-day Oklahoma.

By contrast, the Comanche managed to resist attempts to dominate them. For nearly a century, several branches of the tribe extended control over other tribes and over the Spaniards, holding the latter in check in small settlements clustered around Santa Fe in New Mexico and a few locations in Texas. Maps drawn in Europe marking Spanish ownership of vast North American lands simply did not correspond

to the reality on the ground. One sign of Comanche success was their demographic surge during the mid- to late eighteenth century, owing both to their ability to take captives and blend them into their tribe and to their superior command of food resources, especially buffalo.

In 1807, a Comanche delegation arrived at Natchitoches in Louisiana, where a newly appointed U.S. Indian agent entertained them lavishly to demonstrate American power and wealth. In a highly imaginative speech, the agent proclaimed an improbable solidarity with the Comanche: "It is now so long since our Ancestors came from beyond the great Water that we have no remembrance of it. We ourselves are Natives of the Same land that you are, in other words white Indians, we therefore Should feel & live together like brothers & Good Neighbours."

The Comanche welcomed the United States as a new trading partner and invited traders to travel into Comanchería to their market fairs. Into the late 1820s, this trade flourished on an extensive scale, with Americans selling weapons, cloth, and household metal goods in exchange for horses, mules, bison, and furs. And despite maps of the United States that showed the Red River just inside the southwestern border of the Louisiana

Purchase, the land from the Red north to the Arkansas River, west of Arkansas, remained under Indian control and thus off-limits to settlement by white Americans until the late nineteenth century (see Map 10.2).

> **REVIEW** Why was Spain concerned that France sold the Louisiana Territory to the United States?

► Jefferson, the Madisons, and the War of 1812

Jefferson easily retained the presidency in the election of 1804, with his 162 electoral votes trouncing the 14 won by Federalist Charles Cotesworth Pinckney of South Carolina. Jefferson faced seriously escalating tensions with both France and Britain, leading him to try a novel tactic, an embargo, to stave off war. His Republican secretary of state, James Madison, followed Jefferson as president in 1808, again defeating Pinckney but by a much narrower margin.

Madison continued with a modified embargo, but he broke from Jefferson's all-male style of social networking by involving his gregarious wife, Dolley Madison, in serious politics. Under James Madison's leadership, the country declared war in 1812 on Britain and on Tecumseh's Indian confederacy. The two-year war cost the young nation its White House and its Capitol, but victory was proclaimed at the end nonetheless.

Impressment and Embargo

In 1803, France and Britain went to war, and both repeatedly warned the United States not to ship arms to the other. Britain acted on these threats in 1806, stopping U.S. ships to inspect cargoes for military aid to France and seizing suspected deserters from the British navy, along with many Americans. Ultimately, 2,500 U.S. sailors were "impressed" (taken by force) by the British, who needed them for their war with France.

In retaliation against the **impressment** of American sailors, Jefferson convinced Congress to pass a nonimportation law banning a variety of British-made goods, such as leather products, window glass, and beer.

One incident made the usually cautious Jefferson nearly belligerent. In June 1807, the American ship *Chesapeake*, harboring some British deserters, was ordered to stop by the British frigate *Leopard*. The *Chesapeake* refused, and the *Leopard* opened fire, killing three Americans and capturing four alleged deserters—right at the mouth of the Chesapeake Bay, well within U.S. territorial waters. In response, Congress passed the **Embargo Act of 1807**, banning all importation of British goods into the country. Though a drastic measure, the embargo was meant to forestall war and make Britain suffer. All foreign ports were declared off-limits to American merchants to discourage illegal trading through secondary ports. Jefferson was convinced that Britain needed America's agricultural products far more than America needed British goods.

The Embargo Act of 1807 was a disaster. From 1790 to 1807, U.S. exports had increased fivefold, but the embargo brought commerce to a standstill. In New England, the heart of the shipping industry, unemployment rose. Grain plummeted in value, river traffic halted, tobacco rotted in the South, and cotton went unpicked. Protest petitions flooded Washington. The federal government suffered, too, for import duties were a significant source of revenue. Jefferson paid political costs as well and decided not to run for a third term. The Federalist Party, in danger of fading away after its weak showing in the election of 1804, began to revive.

James Madison was chosen to be the Republican candidate by party caucuses — informal political groups that orchestrated the selection of candidates for state and local elections. The Federalist caucuses again chose Pinckney, and in the election he secured 47 electoral votes, compared to 14 in 1804; Madison's total was 122. Support for the Federalists remained centered in New England, whose shipping industry suffered heavy losses in the embargo. The Republicans still held the balance of power nationwide.

The *Chesapeake* Incident, June 22, 1807

Dolley Madison, by Gilbert Stuart
The "presidentress" of the Madison administration sat for this official portrait in 1804. She wears an empire-style dress, at the height of French fashion in 1804 and a style worn by many women at the coronation of the emperor Napoleon in Paris. The hallmarks of such a dress were a light fabric (muslin or chiffon), short sleeves, a high waistline from which the fabric fell straight to the ground, and usually a low, open neckline, as shown here. © White House Historical Association.

Dolley Madison and Social Politics

As wife of the highest-ranking cabinet officer, **Dolley Madison** developed elaborate social networks during her first eight years in Washington. Hers constituted the top level of female politicking in the highly political city, since Jefferson had no First Lady. Although women could not vote and supposedly left politics to men, the female relatives of Washington politicians took on several overtly political functions that greased the wheels of the affairs of state. They networked through dinners, balls, receptions, and the intricate custom of "calling," in which men and women paid brief visits and left calling cards at each other's homes. Webs of friendship and influence in turn facilitated female political lobbying. It was not uncommon for women in this social set to write letters of recommendation for men seeking government work. Hostessing was no trivial or leisured business; it significantly influenced the federal government's patronage system.

When James Madison became president, Dolley Madison, called by some the "presidentress," struck a balance between queenliness and republican openness. She dressed the part in resplendent clothes, choosing a plumed velvet turban for her headdress at her husband's inauguration. She opened three elegant rooms in the executive mansion for a weekly open-house party called "Mrs. Madison's crush" or "squeeze." In contrast to George and Martha Washington's stiff, brief receptions, the Madisons' parties went on for hours, with scores or even hundreds of guests milling about, talking, and eating. Members of Congress, cabinet officers, distinguished guests, envoys from foreign countries, and their womenfolk attended with regularity. The affable and generous Mrs. Madison made her guests comfortable with small talk, but a female partygoer reported that "Mr. Madison had no leisure for the ladies; every moment of his time is engrossed by the crowd of male visitors who court his notice, and after passing the first complimentary salutations, his attention is unavoidably withdrawn to more important objects." His wife's weekly squeeze established informal channels of information and provided crucial political access, a key element of smooth governance.

In 1810–1811, the Madisons' house acquired its present name, the White House, probably in reference to its white-painted sandstone exterior. The many guests at the weekly parties experienced simultaneously the splendor of the executive mansion and the atmosphere of republicanism that made it accessible to so many. Dolley Madison, ever an enormous political asset to her rather shy husband, understood well the symbolic function of the White House to enhance the power and legitimacy of the presidency.

> **"Mr. Madison had no leisure for the ladies; every moment of his time is engrossed by the crowd of male visitors who court his notice."**
> — A female guest at Mrs. Madison's "squeeze"

Tecumseh and Tippecanoe

While the Madisons cemented alliances at home, difficulties with Britain and France overseas and with Indians in the old Northwest continued to increase. The Shawnee chief **Tecumseh** (see pages 289–90) actively solidified his confederacy, while the more northern tribes renewed their ties with supportive British agents and fur traders in Canada, a potential source of food and weapons. If the United States went to war with Britain, there would clearly be serious repercussions on the frontier.

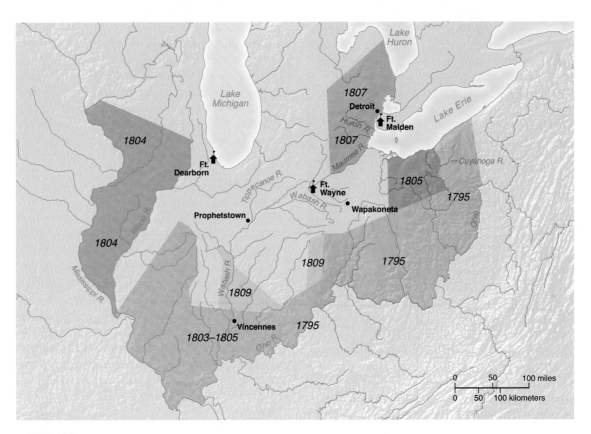

MAP 10.3

Indian Lands Ceded by Treaties in the Northwest Territory, 1795–1809

The Treaty of Greenville (1795) transferred two-thirds of Ohio to the Americans. For more than a decade thereafter, officials such as William Henry Harrison managed to acquire for the United States vast tracts along the Ohio and Mississippi rivers by negotiating with Indians whose authority to speak for their tribes was often unclear or dubious. "Land Cessions in the Old Northwest, 1795–1809." From *Tecumseh: A Life* by John Sugden. Copyright 1997 by John Sugden. Reprinted with the permission of Henry Holt and Company LLC.

Shifting demographics raised the stakes for both sides. The 1810 census counted some 230,000 Americans in Ohio only seven years after it achieved statehood. Another 40,000 Americans inhabited the territories of Indiana, Illinois, and Michigan. The Indian population of the entire region (the old Northwest Territory) was much smaller, probably about 70,000, a number unknown to the Americans but certainly gauged by Tecumseh during his extensive travels.

Up to 1805, Indiana's territorial governor, William Henry Harrison, had negotiated a series of treaties in a divide-and-conquer strategy aimed at extracting Indian lands for paltry payments (Map 10.3). But with the rise to power of Tecumseh and his brother **Tenskwatawa**, the Prophet, Harrison's strategy faltered. A fundamental part of Tecumseh's message was the assertion that all Indian lands were held in common by all the tribes. "No tribe has the right to sell [these lands],

even to each other, much less to strangers . . . ," Tecumseh said. "Sell a country! Why not sell the air, the great sea, as well as the earth? Didn't the Great Spirit make them all for the use of his children?" In 1809, while Tecumseh was away on a recruiting trip, Harrison assembled the leaders of the Potawatomi, Miami, and Delaware tribes to negotiate the Treaty of Fort Wayne. After promising (falsely) that this was the last cession of land the United States would seek, Harrison secured three million acres at about two cents per acre.

When he returned, Tecumseh was furious with both Harrison and the tribal leaders. Leaving his brother in charge at Prophetstown on the Tippecanoe River, the Shawnee chief left to seek alliances with tribes in the South. In November 1811, Harrison decided to attack Prophetstown with a thousand men. The two-hour battle resulted in the deaths of sixty-two Americans and forty

Indians before the Prophet's forces fled the town, which Harrison's men set on fire. The **battle of Tippecanoe** was heralded as a glorious victory for the Americans, but Tecumseh was now more ready than ever to make war on the United States.

The War of 1812

The Indian conflicts in the old Northwest soon merged into the wider conflict with Britain, now known as the War of 1812. In 1809, Congress replaced Jefferson's stringent embargo with the Non-Intercourse Act, which prohibited trade only with Britain and France and their colonies, thus restoring trade with other European countries to alleviate somewhat the anguish of shippers, farmers, and planters. By 1811, the country was seriously divided and on the verge of war.

The new Congress seated in March 1811 contained several dozen young Republicans eager to avenge the insults from abroad. Thirty-four-year-old **Henry Clay** from Kentucky and twenty-nine-year-old John C. Calhoun from South Carolina became the center of a group informally known as the **War Hawks**. Mostly lawyers by profession, they came from the West and South and welcomed a war with Britain both to justify attacks on the Indians and to bring an end to impressment. Many were also expansionists, looking to occupy Florida and threaten Canada. Clay was elected Speaker of the House, an extraordinary honor for a newcomer. Calhoun won a seat on the Foreign Relations Committee. The War Hawks approved major defense expenditures, and the army soon quadrupled in size.

In June 1812, Congress declared war on Great Britain in a vote divided along sectional lines: New England and some Middle Atlantic states opposed the war, fearing its effect on commerce, while the South and West were strongly for it. Ironically, Britain had just announced

Battle of Tippecanoe, 1811

that it would stop the search and seizure of American ships, but the war momentum would not be slowed. The Foreign Relations Committee issued an elaborate justification titled *Report on the Causes and Reasons for War*, written mainly by Calhoun and containing extravagant language about Britain's "lust for power," "unbounded tyranny," and "mad ambition." These were fighting words in a war that was in large measure about insult and honor.

The War Hawks proposed an invasion of Canada, confidently predicting victory in four weeks. Instead, the war lasted two and a half years, and Canada never fell. The northern invasion turned out to be a series of blunders that revealed America's grave unpreparedness for war against the unexpectedly powerful British and Indian forces. Detroit quickly fell, as did Fort Dearborn, site

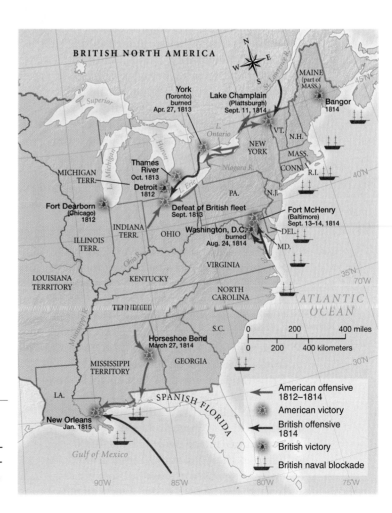

MAP 10.4
The War of 1812
During the War of 1812, battles were fought along the Canadian border and in the Chesapeake region. The most important American victory came in New Orleans two weeks after a peace agreement had been signed in England.

The Burning of Washington City
On August 24, 1814, the British army entered the nation's capital and set government buildings ablaze. This British line engraving celebrates that victory, showing disciplined troops armed with torches. To the left behind the soldiers, the White House burns, as does the round dome of the Capitol in the distance. Some soldiers plundered for trophies of war that night. Shown here is James Madison's personal medicine chest, taken back to England by a British soldier. One of the soldier's descendants returned the souvenir to President Franklin D. Roosevelt in 1939.
Engraving: Anne S. K. Brown Military Collection, Brown University Library; medicine chest: FDR Library.

of the future Chicago (Map 10.4). By the fall of 1812, the outlook was grim.

Worse, the New England states dragged their feet in raising troops, and some New England merchants carried on illegal trade with Britain. While President Madison fumed about Federalist disloyalty, Bostonians drank East India tea in Liverpool cups. The fall presidential election pitted Madison against DeWitt Clinton of New York, nominally a Republican but able to attract the Federalist vote. Clinton picked up all of New England's electoral votes, with the exception of Vermont's, and also took New York, New Jersey, and part of Maryland. Madison won in the electoral college, 128 to 89, but his margin of victory was considerably smaller than in 1808.

In late 1812 and early 1813, the tide began to turn in the Americans' favor. First came some reassuring victories at sea. Then the Americans attacked York (now Toronto) and burned it in April 1813. A few months later, Commodore Oliver Hazard Perry defeated the British fleet at the western end of Lake Erie. Emboldened, General Harrison drove an army into Canada from Detroit and in October 1813 defeated the British and Indians at the battle of the Thames, where Tecumseh was killed.

Creek Indians in the South who had allied with Tecumseh's confederacy were also plunged into all-out war. Some 10,000 living in the Mississippi Territory put up a spirited fight against U.S. forces for ten months in 1813–1814. Even without Tecumseh's recruitment trip of 1811 or the War of 1812, the Creeks had grievances aplenty, sparked by American settlers moving into their territory. Using guns obtained from Spanish Florida, the Creeks mounted a strong defense. But the **Creek War** ended suddenly in March 1814 when a general named Andrew Jackson led 2,500 Tennessee militiamen in a bloody attack called the Battle of Horseshoe Bend. More than 550 Indians were killed, and several hundred more died trying to escape across a river. Later that year, General Jackson extracted from the defeated tribe a treaty relinquishing thousands of square miles of their land to the United States.

Washington City Burns: The British Offensive

In August 1814, British ships sailed into the Chesapeake Bay, landing 5,000 troops and throwing the capital into a panic. Families evacuated, banks hid their money, and government clerks carted away boxes of important papers. Dolley Madison, with dinner for guests cooking over the fire, fled with her husband's papers, leaving several struggling servants to rescue a portrait of George Washington. As the cook related, "When the British did arrive, they ate up the very dinner, and drank the wines, &c.,

that I had prepared for the President's party." Then they torched the White House. They also burned the Capitol, a newspaper office, and a well-stocked arsenal. Instead of trying to hold the city, the British headed north and attacked Baltimore, but a fierce defense by the Maryland militia thwarted that effort.

In another powerful offensive that same month, British troops marched from Canada into New York State, but a series of mistakes cost them a naval skirmish at Plattsburgh on Lake Champlain, and they retreated to Canada. Five months later, another large British army landed in lower Louisiana and, in early January 1815, encountered General Andrew Jackson and his militia just outside New Orleans. Jackson's forces dramatically carried the day. The British suffered between 2,000 and 3,000 casualties, the Americans fewer than 80. Jackson became an instant hero. The **battle of New Orleans** was the most glorious victory the Americans had experienced, allowing some Americans to boast that the United States had won a second war of independence from Britain. No one in the United States knew that negotiators in Europe had signed a peace agreement two weeks earlier.

The Treaty of Ghent, signed in December 1814, settled few of the surface issues that had led to war. Neither country could claim victory, and no land changed hands. Instead, the treaty reflected a mutual agreement to give up certain goals. The Americans dropped their plea for an end to impressments, which in any case subsided as soon as Britain and France ended their war in 1815. They also gave up any claim to Canada. The British agreed to stop all aid to the Indians. Nothing was said about shipping rights. The most concrete result was a plan for a commission to determine the exact boundary between the United States and Canada.

Antiwar Federalists in New England could not gloat over the war's ambiguous conclusion because of an ill-timed and seemingly unpatriotic move on their part. The region's leaders had convened a secret meeting in Hartford, Connecticut, in December 1814 to discuss dramatic measures to curb the South's power. They proposed abolishing the Constitution's three-fifths clause as a basis of representation; requiring a two-thirds vote instead of a simple majority for imposing embargoes, admitting states, or declaring war; limiting the president to one term; and prohibiting the election of successive presidents from the same state. The cumulative aim of these proposals was to reduce the South's political power and break Virginia's lock on the presidency. New England wanted to make sure that no sectional party could again lead the country into war against the clear interests of another. The Federalists at Hartford even discussed secession from the Union but rejected that path. Coming just as peace was achieved, however, the **Hartford Convention** looked very unpatriotic. The Federalist Party never recovered its grip, and within a few years it was reduced to a shadow of its former self, even in New England.

No one really won the War of 1812; however, Americans celebrated as though they had, with parades and fireworks. The war gave rise to a new spirit of nationalism. The paranoia over British tyranny evident in the 1812 declaration of war was laid to rest, replaced by pride in a more equal relationship with the old mother country. Indeed, in 1817 the two countries signed the Rush-Bagot disarmament treaty (named after its two negotiators), which limited each country to a total of four naval vessels, each with just a single cannon, to patrol the vast watery border between them. The Rush-Bagot treaty was perhaps the most successful disarmament treaty for a century to come.

The biggest winners in the War of 1812 were the young men, once called War Hawks, who took up the banner of the Republican Party and carried it in new, expansive directions. These young politicians favored trade, western expansion, internal improvements, and the energetic development of new economic markets. The biggest losers of the war were the Indians. Tecumseh was dead, his brother the Prophet was discredited, the prospects of an Indian confederacy were dashed, the Creeks' large homeland was seized, and the British protectors were gone.

REVIEW Why did Congress declare war on Great Britain in 1812?

► Women's Status in the Early Republic

Dolley Madison's pioneering role as "presidentress" showed that at the pinnacles of power, elite women could assume an active presence in civic affairs. But, as with the 1790s cultural compromise that endorsed female education to make women into better wives and mothers (see chapter 9), Mrs. Madison and her female circle practiced politics to further their husbands' careers. There was little talk of the "rights of woman."

From 1800 to 1825, key institutions central to the shaping of women's lives — the legal system, marriage, and religion — proved fairly resistant to change. State legislatures and the courts maintained the legal dependency of married white women in a country whose defining characteristic for men was independence. Marriage laws for whites continued to support unequal power between men and women, while religious organizations reconsidered the role of women in church governance in the face of rising church membership rates for women. The most dramatic opportunity for women came with the flowering of female academies whose rigorous curricula fostered high-level literacy and rational thought. Even when advertised as institutions to prepare girls to be intelligent mothers, many academies built up their students' self-confidence and implanted expectations that their mental training would find a use beyond the kitchen and nursery.

Women and the Law

The Anglo-American view of women, embedded in English common law, was that wives had no independent legal or political personhood. The legal doctrine of *feme covert* (covered woman) held that a wife's civic life was completely subsumed by her husband's. A wife was obligated to obey her husband; her property was his, her domestic and sexual services were his, and even their children were legally his. Women had no right to keep their wages, to make contracts, or to sue or be sued.

State legislatures generally passed up the opportunity to rewrite the laws of domestic relations even though they redrafted other British laws in light of republican principles. Lawyers never paused to defend, much less to challenge, the assumption that unequal power relations lay at the heart of marriage.

The one aspect of family law that changed in the early Republic was divorce. Before the Revolution, only New England jurisdictions recognized a limited right to divorce; by 1820, every state except South Carolina did so. However, divorce was uncommon and in many states could be obtained only by petition to the state's legislature, a daunting obstacle for many ordinary people. A mutual wish to terminate a marriage was never sufficient grounds for a legal divorce. A New York judge affirmed that "it would be aiming a deadly blow at public morals to decree a dissolution of the marriage contract merely because the parties requested it.

Divorces should never be allowed, except for the protection of the innocent party, and for the punishment of the guilty." States upheld the institution of marriage both to protect persons they thought of as naturally dependent (women and children) and to regulate the use and inheritance of property. (Unofficial self-divorce, desertion, and bigamy were remedies that ordinary people sometimes chose to get around the law, but all were socially unacceptable.) Legal enforcement of marriage as an unequal relationship played a major role in maintaining gender inequality in the nineteenth century.

Single adult women could own and convey property, make contracts, initiate lawsuits, and pay taxes. They could not vote (except in New Jersey before 1807), serve on juries, or practice law, so their civil status was limited. Single women's economic status was often limited as well, by custom as much as by law. Job prospects were few and low-paying. Unless they had inherited adequate property or could live with married siblings, single adult women in the early Republic very often were poor.

None of the legal institutions that structured white gender relations applied to black slaves. As property themselves, under the jurisdiction of slave owners, they could not freely consent to any contractual obligations, including marriage. The protective features of state-sponsored unions were thus denied to black men and women in slavery. But this also meant that slave unions did not establish unequal power relations between partners backed by the force of law, as did marriages among the free.

Women and Church Governance

In most Protestant denominations around 1800, white women made up the majority of congregants. Yet church leadership of most denominations rested in men's hands. There were some exceptions, however. In Baptist congregations in New England, women served along with men on church governance committees, deciding on the admission of new members, voting on hiring ministers, and even debating doctrinal points. Quakers, too, had a history of recognizing women's spiritual talents. Some were accorded the status of minister, capable of leading and speaking in Quaker meetings.

Between 1790 and 1820, a small and highly unusual set of women actively engaged in open preaching. Most were from Freewill Baptist

in men's clothes, wore her hair in a masculine style, shunned gender-specific pronouns, and preached openly in Rhode Island and Philadelphia. In the early nineteenth century, Wilkinson established a town called New Jerusalem in western New York with some 250 followers. Her fame was sustained by periodic newspaper articles that fed public curiosity about her lifelong transvestism and her unfeminine forcefulness.

The decades from 1790 to the 1820s marked a period of unusual confusion, ferment, and creativity in American religion. New denominations blossomed, new styles of religiosity gripped adherents, and an extensive periodical press devoted to religion popularized all manner of theological and institutional innovations. In such a climate, the age-old tradition of gender subordination came into question here and there among the most radically democratic of the churches. But the presumption of male authority over women was deeply entrenched in American culture. Even denominations that had allowed women to participate in church governance began to pull back, and most churches reinstated patterns of hierarchy along gender lines.

Female Education

First in the North and then in the South, states and localities began investing in public schools to foster an educated citizenry deemed essential to the healthy functioning of a republic. Young girls attended district schools, sometimes along with boys or, in rural areas, more often in separate summer sessions. Basic literacy and numeracy formed the curriculum taught to white children aged roughly six to eleven. By 1830, girls had made rapid gains, in many places approaching male literacy rates. (Far fewer schools addressed the needs of free black children, whether male or female.)

More advanced female education came from a growing number of private academies. Judith Sargent Murray, the Massachusetts author who had called for equality of the sexes around 1790 (see chapter 9), predicted in 1800 that "a new era in female history" would emerge because "**female academies** are everywhere establishing." Some dozen female academies were established in the 1790s, and by 1830 that number had grown to nearly two hundred. Candidates for admission were primarily daughters of elite families as well as those of middling families with elite or intellectual aspirations, such as ministers' daughters.

Women and the Church: Jemima Wilkinson
In this early woodcut, Jemima Wilkinson, "the Publick Universal Friend," wears a clerical collar and body-obscuring robe, in keeping with the claim that the former Jemima was now a person without gender. With hair pulled back tight on the head and curled at the neck in a masculine style of the 1790s, was Wilkinson masculinized, or did the "Universal Friend" truly transcend gender? Rhode Island Historical Society.

groups centered in New England and upstate New York. Others came from small Methodist sects, and yet others rejected any formal religious affiliation. Probably fewer than a hundred such women existed, but several dozen traveled beyond their local communities, creating converts and controversy. They spoke from the heart, without prepared speeches, often exhibiting trances and claiming to exhort (counsel or warn) rather than to preach.

The best-known exhorting woman was **Jemima Wilkinson**, who called herself "the Publick Universal Friend." After a near-death experience from a high fever, Wilkinson proclaimed her body no longer female or male but the incarnation of the "Spirit of Light." She dressed

One Woman's Quest to Provide Higher Education for Women

Talented young men seeking the mental enrichment and career boost of higher education saw their opportunities expand rapidly in the early Republic. By 1830, six dozen private and state-chartered institutions offered them training in science, history, religion, literature, and philosophy. Yet not a single one admitted females.

With the spread of district schools and female academies, however, the number of girls trained for advanced study was on the rise. The winning rationale for female education — that mothers molded the character of rising generations — worked well to justify basic schooling. But a highly intellectual woman, negatively termed a "bluestocking," was thought to put her very femininity at risk. Some critics sounded a more practical note: "When girls become scholars, who is to make the puddings and pies?"

The academic aspirations of Emma Hart — born in Connecticut in 1787 as the sixteenth in a farm family of seventeen children — were encouraged by her father, who read Shakespeare at night to his large brood. After graduating from the local district school and then an academy for girls, Emma taught for a term at the district school before moving to Vermont to head the Middlebury Female Academy, founded in 1800. There, she taught sixty adolescents in an underheated building.

Emma ran the academy for two years until her marriage in 1809 to an established Middlebury physician and banker named John Willard. Marriage for white women usually brought an end to employment outside the home. Yet despite caring for a baby and attending to her domestic duties, Emma found time to read books from her husband's well-stocked library. She read widely, from political philosophy to medical treatises, physiology texts, and even Euclid's geometry.

Four years into their marriage, John Willard suffered severe financial losses. This turn of events led Emma Willard to open an advanced girls' school in her home. She patterned her courses on those at nearby Middlebury College for men, and her rigorous curriculum soon drew students from all over the Northeast. One satisfied father with political connections persuaded the Willards to relocate to his home state of New York with the promise to help them secure state funding for a school.

Emma drew up a formal proposal in 1819, arguing that advanced female education would both enhance motherhood and supply excellent teachers needed for a projected state-supported school system. Though her proposal was endorsed by Governor DeWitt Clinton, John Adams, and Thomas Jefferson, the New York assembly failed to fund Willard's school. Local citizens in Troy supplied Willard with a building, however, and in 1821 the Troy Female Seminary opened with students coming from many states. Willard deliberately chose the modest term "seminary" instead of "college," which was "the province of the men." Yet her rigorous curriculum did include "masculine" subjects such as Latin, Greek, mathematics, and science in addition to modern languages and

The three-year curriculum included both ornamental arts and solid academics. The former strengthened female gentility: drawing, needlework, music, and French conversation. The academic subjects included English grammar, literature, history, the natural sciences, geography, and elocution (the art of effective public speaking). Academy catalogs show that, by the 1820s, the courses and reading lists at the top female academies equaled those at male colleges such as Harvard, Yale, Dartmouth, and Princeton. The girls at these academies studied Latin, rhetoric, logic, theology, moral philosophy, algebra, geometry, and even chemistry and physics.

Two of the best-known female academies were the Troy Female Seminary in New York, founded by Emma Willard in 1821, and the Hartford Seminary in Connecticut, founded by Catharine Beecher in 1822. (See "Seeking the American Promise," page 308.) Unlike theological seminaries that trained men for the clergy, Troy and Hartford prepared their female students to teach, on the grounds that women made better teachers than did men. Author Harriet Beecher Stowe, educated at her sister's school and then a teacher there, agreed: "If men have more knowledge they have less talent at communicating it. Nor have they the patience, the long-suffering, and gentleness necessary to superintend the formation of character."

literature. Willard taught geometry and trigonometry herself and hired other teachers for classes in astronomy, botany, geology, chemistry, and zoology. She soon forged a cooperative alliance with the neighboring Rensselaer Polytechnic Institute. In direct emulation of Harvard and Princeton, her seminary also offered a required course in moral philosophy, which Willard herself taught to all senior students using the same texts employed at the male colleges.

Willard invited the public to weeklong examinations, where students solved algebra problems and geometry proofs on chalkboards and gave twenty-minute discourses on history and philosophy. Educated men were particularly encouraged to question the students, to put to rest any "lurking suspicion, that the learning which a female possesses must be superficial." One minister was astonished, and pleased, to see "Euclid discussed by female lips." By emphasizing geometry, Willard vindicated her claim that women could equal men in logic. But she took pains to make sure her students preserved "feminine delicacy" and avoided "the least indelicacy of language or behavior, such as too much exposure of the person."

More than the rigorous curriculum inspired these young women. Willard was an exemplary role model, beloved by many of her students for her dedication and confidence. A student named Elizabeth Cady, who attended the seminary in the 1830s and later became an important figure in the woman's rights movement, recalled that Willard had a "profound self respect (a rare quality in a woman) which gave her a dignity truly regal." Willard graciously gave much of the credit to her unusually supportive husband: "He entered into the full spirit of my views, with a disinterested zeal for the sex whom, as he had come to believe, his own had unjustly neglected."

The Troy Female Seminary flourished; it still exists today as the Emma Willard School. From 1821 to 1871, more than 12,000 girls attended; it was larger than most men's colleges. Ministers' daughters received a discount on tuition, and many girls were allowed to defer payment until they were wage-earning teachers. Nearly 5,000 graduates in the first fifty years became teachers, and some 150 directed their own schools scattered across the nation. When the marquis de Lafayette, aging hero of the American Revolution, visited Willard's school in 1824, he pronounced it a "Female University." Surely, Willard took pleasure in his recognition of her success.

Portrait of Emma Willard
Emma Hart Willard's calm composure shines through in this portrait. Emma Willard School.

Questions for Consideration

1. How did Emma Willard's own life demonstrate the importance of female education for a family's financial security?

2. Compare the occupation of Emma Willard with that of Dolley Madison. In what ways were these women similar? How did they differ?

The most immediate value of advanced female education lay in the self-cultivation and confidence it provided. Following the model of male colleges, female graduation exercises showcased speeches and recitations performed in front of a mixed-sex audience of family, friends, and local notables. Here, the young women's elocution studies paid off; they had learned the art of persuasion along with correct pronunciation and the skill of fluent speaking. Academies also took care to promote a pleasing female modesty. Female pedantry or intellectual immodesty triggered the stereotype of the "bluestocking," a British term of hostility for a too-learned woman doomed to fail in the marriage market.

By the mid-1820s, the total annual enrollment at the female academies and seminaries equaled enrollment at the near six dozen male colleges in the United States. Both groups accounted for only about 1 percent of their age cohorts in the country at large, indicating that advanced education was clearly limited to a privileged few. Among the men, this group disproportionately filled the future rosters of ministers, lawyers, judges, and political leaders. Most female graduates in time married and raised families, but first many of them became teachers at academies and district schools. A large number also became authors, contributing essays and poetry to newspapers,

Many factors promoted increased partisanship. Monroe and his aloof wife, Elizabeth, sharply curtailed social gatherings at the White House, driving the hard work of social networking into competing channels. Ill feelings were stirred by a sectional crisis over the admission of Missouri to the Union, and foreign policy questions involving European claims to Latin America animated sharp disagreements as well. The election of 1824 brought forth an abundance of candidates, all claiming to be Republicans. The winner was John Quincy Adams in an election decided by the House of Representatives and, many believed, a backroom bargain. Put to the test of practical circumstances, the one-party political system failed and then fractured.

From Property to Democracy

Up to 1820, presidential elections occurred in the electoral college, at a remove from ordinary voters. The excitement generated by state elections, however, created an insistent pressure for greater democratization of presidential elections.

In the 1780s, twelve of the original thirteen states enacted property qualifications based on the time-honored theory that only male freeholders — landowners, as distinct from tenants or servants — had sufficient independence of mind to be entrusted with the vote. Of course, not everyone accepted that restricted idea of the people's role in government (see chapter 8). In the 1790s, Vermont became the first state to enfranchise all adult males, and four other states soon broadened suffrage considerably by allowing all male taxpayers to vote, a status that could be triggered simply by owning a cow, since local property taxes were an ever-present and generally nonburdensome reality. Between 1800 and 1830, greater democratization became a lively issue both in established states and in new states emerging in the West.

In the established states, lively newspaper exchanges and petition campaigns pushed state after state to hold constitutional conventions, where questions of suffrage, balloting procedures, apportionment, and representation were hotly debated. Both political philosophy and practical politics were entwined in these debates: Who are "the people" in a government founded on popular sovereignty, and whose party or interest group gains the most from expanded suffrage?

In new states, small populations together with yet smaller numbers of large property owners meant that few men could vote under typical restrictive property qualifications. Congress initially set a fifty-acre freehold as the threshold

An Academy Student's Embroidery
Girls in the burgeoning female academies studied grammar, history, geography, arithmetic, French, and sometimes Greek, Latin, and geometry, although study of ancient languages and abstruse math was sometimes criticized as an intrusion into male domains. Female students also learned ornamental sewing. This work of silk embroidery comes from South Carolina and probably dates from around 1800–1810, judging from the high-waisted dress style. It shows an accomplished student, with map and globe on the table. What do you think would be more challenging for a 14-year-old girl: to learn basic arithmetic or to embroider so expertly? Rivers Collection, Charleston.

editing periodicals, and publishing novels. The new attention to the training of female minds laid the foundation for major changes in the gender system as girl students of the 1810s matured into adult women of the 1830s.

> **REVIEW** How did the civil status of American women and men differ in the early Republic?

▶ Monroe and Adams

With the elections of 1816 and 1820, Virginians continued their hold on the presidency. In 1816, **James Monroe** beat Federalist Rufus King of New York, garnering 183 electoral votes to King's 34. In 1820, the Republican Monroe was reelected with all but one electoral vote. The collapse of the Federalist Party ushered in an apparent period of one-party rule, but politics remained highly contentious. At the state level, increasing voter engagement sparked a drive for universal white male suffrage.

Painting on a patriotic motif by John A. Woodside of Philadelphia, in the early 1800s

VISUAL ACTIVITY

"We Owe Allegiance to No Crown"

John A. Woodside, a Philadelphia sign painter, made his living creating advertisements and ornamental pictures for hotels, taverns, and city fire engines. He specialized in promotional paintings conveying a booster spirit, especially heroic scenes on banners to be carried in parades. At some point in his decades-long career, which ran from about 1815 to 1850, he created this scene of a youthful sailor being crowned with a laurel wreath, the ancient Greek symbol of victory, by a breezy Miss Liberty (identified by the liberty cap she carries on a stick).

READING THE IMAGE: : What might the chain at the sailor's feet indicate? What do you think the slogan on the banner means? What do you see in the picture that would help date it? (Hint: examine the flag. And for the truly curious, consider the history of men's facial hair styles.)

CONNECTIONS: How and why does the painting reference the War of 1812? Regardless of the painting's date, what message do you think Woodside is trying to convey here?

Picture Research Consultants & Archives.

for voting, but in Illinois fewer than three hundred men met that test at the time of statehood. When Indiana, Illinois, and Mississippi became states, their constitutions granted suffrage to all taxpayers. Five additional new western states abandoned property and taxpayer qualifications altogether.

The most heated battles over suffrage occurred in eastern states, where expanding numbers of commercial men, renters, and mortgage holders of all classes contended with entrenched landed elites who, not surprisingly, favored the status quo. Still, by 1820, half a dozen states passed suffrage reform. Some stopped short of complete male suffrage, instead tying the vote to tax status or militia service. In the remainder of the states, the defenders of landed property qualifications managed to delay expanded suffrage for two more decades. But it was increasingly hard to persuade the disfranchised that landowners alone had a stake in government. Proponents of the status quo began to argue instead that the "industry and good habits" necessary to achieve a propertied status in life were what gave landowners the right character to vote. Opponents fired back blistering attacks. One delegate to New York's constitutional convention said, "More integrity and more patriotism are generally found in the labouring class of the community than in the higher orders."

Owning land was no more predictive of wisdom and good character than it was of a person's height or strength, said another observer.

Both sides of the debate generally agreed that character mattered, and many ideas for ensuring an electorate of proper wisdom came up for discussion. The exclusion of paupers and felons convicted of "infamous crimes" found favor in legislation in many states. Literacy tests and raising the voting age to a figure in the thirties were debated but ultimately discarded. The exclusion of women required no discussion in the constitutional conventions, so firm was the legal power of *feme covert*. But in one exceptional moment, at the Virginia convention in 1829, a delegate wondered aloud why unmarried women over the age of twenty-one could not vote; he was quickly silenced with the argument that all women lacked the "free agency and intelligence" necessary for wise voting.

Free black men's enfranchisement was another story, generating much discussion at all the conventions. Under existing freehold qualifications, a small number of propertied black men could vote; universal or taxpayer suffrage would inevitably enfranchise many more. Many delegates at the various state conventions spoke against that extension, claiming that blacks as a race lacked prudence, independence, and knowledge. With the exception of New York, which

^^H^H^H

The House of Representatives, by Samuel F. B. Morse, 1822
In this large chamber, arising in 1815–1819 from the ashes of the old Capitol, Congress debated the various Missouri statehood bills. Built in a grand classical style, the room had towering marble columns and a cast-steel dome. A window in the dome provided natural light; the oil chandelier, lowered and lighted by hand, permitted evening sessions. Unfortunately, echoes bouncing off the smooth dome ruined the room's acoustics. Various fixes were tried — hanging draperies, rearranging the desks. In 1850 Congress finally authorized a bigger chamber. The room shown here is now called Statuary Hall, where Capitol visitors can experience for themselves the poor acoustics. Samuel F. B. Morse, *The House of Representatives*, completed 1822; probably reworked 1823; oil on canvas, 86-7/8 x 130-5/8 inches. The Corcoran Gallery of Art, Washington, D.C., Museum Purchase, Gallery Fund 11.14.

retained the existing property qualification for black voters as it removed it for whites, the general pattern was one of expanded suffrage for whites and a total eclipse of suffrage for blacks.

The Missouri Compromise

The politics of race produced the most divisive issue during Monroe's term. In February 1819, Missouri—so recently the territory of the powerful Osage Indians—applied for statehood. Since 1815, four other states had joined the Union (Indiana, Mississippi, Illinois, and Alabama) following the blueprint laid out by the Northwest Ordinance of 1787. But Missouri posed a problem. Although much of its area was on the same latitude as the free state of Illinois, its territorial population included ten thousand slaves brought there by southern planters.

Missouri's unusual combination of geography and demography led a New York congressman, James Tallmadge Jr., to propose two amendments to the statehood bill. The first stipulated that slaves born in Missouri after statehood would be free at age twenty-five, and the second declared that no new slaves could be imported

into the state. Tallmadge's model was New York's gradual emancipation law of 1799 (see chapter 8). It did not strip slave owners of their current property, and it allowed them full use of the labor of newborn slaves well into their prime productive years. Still, southern congressmen objected because in the long run the amendments would make Missouri a free state, presumably no longer allied with southern economic and political interests. Just as southern economic power rested on slave labor, southern political power drew extra strength from the slave population because of the three-fifths rule. In 1820, the South owed seventeen of its seats in the House of Representatives to its slave population.

Tallmadge's amendments passed in the House by a close and sharply sectional vote of North against South. The ferocious debate led a Georgia representative to observe that the question had started "a fire which all the waters of the ocean could not extinguish. It can be extinguished only in blood." The Senate, with an even number of slave and free states, voted down the amendments, and Missouri statehood was postponed until the next congressional term.

In 1820, a compromise emerged. Maine, once part of Massachusetts, applied for statehood as a free state, balancing against Missouri as a slave state. The Senate further agreed that the southern boundary of Missouri — latitude 36°30' — extended west, would become the permanent line dividing slave from free states, guaranteeing the North a large area where slavery was banned (Map 10.5). The House also approved the **Missouri Compromise**, thanks to expert deal brokering by Kentucky's Henry Clay, who earned the nickname "the Great Pacificator" for his superb negotiating skills. The whole package passed because seventeen northern congressmen decided that minimizing sectional conflict was the best course and voted with the South.

President Monroe and former president Jefferson at first worried that the Missouri crisis would reinvigorate the Federalist Party as the party of the North. But even ex-Federalists agreed that the split between free and slave states was too dangerous a fault line to be permitted to become a shaper of national politics. When new parties did develop in the 1830s, they

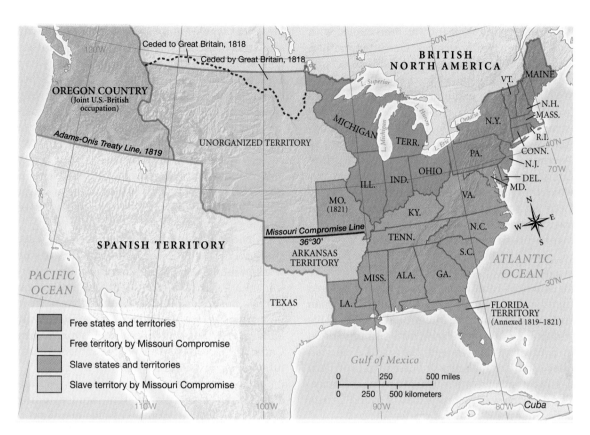

MAP ACTIVITY

Map 10.5   The Missouri Compromise, 1820

After a difficult battle in Congress, Missouri entered the Union in 1821 as part of a package of compromises. Maine was admitted as a free state to balance slavery in Missouri, and a line drawn at latitude 36°30' put most of the rest of the Louisiana Territory off-limits to slavery in the future.

READING THE MAP: How many free and how many slave states were there prior to the Missouri Compromise? What did the admission of Missouri as a slave state threaten to do?

CONNECTIONS: Who precipitated the crisis over Missouri, what did he propose, and where did the idea come from? Who proposed the Missouri Compromise, and who benefited from it?

took pains to bridge geography, each party developing a presence in both North and South. Monroe and Jefferson also worried about the future of slavery. Both understood slavery to be deeply problematic, but, as Jefferson said, "we have the wolf by the ears, and we can neither hold him, nor safely let him go. Justice is in one scale, and self-preservation in the other."

The Monroe Doctrine

As Congress struggled with the slavery issue, new foreign policy challenges also arose. In 1816, U.S. troops led by General Andrew Jackson invaded Spanish Florida in search of Seminole Indians harboring escaped slaves. Once there, Jackson declared himself the commander of northern Florida, demonstrating his power in

1818 by executing two British men who he claimed were dangerous enemies. In asserting rule over the territory, and surely in executing the two British subjects on Spanish land, Jackson had gone too far. Privately, President Monroe was distressed and pondered court-martialing Jackson, prevented only by Jackson's immense popularity as the hero of the battle of New Orleans. Instead, John Quincy Adams, the secretary of state, negotiated with Spain the Adams-Onís Treaty, which delivered all of Florida to the United States in 1819 and finally settled the disputed borders of the Louisiana Purchase. In exchange, the Americans agreed to abandon any claim to Texas or Cuba. Southerners viewed this as a large concession, having eyed both places as potential acquisitions for future slave states.

Spain at that moment was preoccupied with its colonies in South America. One after another, Chile, Colombia, Peru, and finally Mexico declared themselves independent in the early 1820s. To discourage Spain and other European countries from reconquering these colonies, Monroe in 1823 formulated a declaration of principles on South America, known in later years as the **Monroe Doctrine**. The president warned that "the American Continents, by the free and independent condition which they have assumed and maintain, are henceforth not to be considered as subjects for future colonization by any European power." Any attempt to interfere in the Western Hemisphere would be regarded as "the manifestation of an unfriendly disposition towards the United States." In exchange for noninterference by Europeans, Monroe pledged that the United States would stay out of European struggles. At that time, Monroe did not intend his statement to lay a foundation for U.S. intervention in South America. Indeed, the small American navy could not realistically defend Chile or Peru against a major power such as Spain or France. The doctrine was Monroe's idea of sound foreign policy, but it did not have the force of law.

The Election of 1824

Monroe's nonpartisan administration was the last of its kind, a throwback to eighteenth-century ideals, as was Monroe, with his powdered wig and knee breeches. Monroe's cabinet contained men of sharply different philosophies, all calling themselves Republicans. Secretary of State **John Quincy Adams** represented the urban Northeast; South Carolinian John C. Calhoun spoke for the planter aristocracy as secretary of war; and William H. Crawford of Georgia, secretary of the treasury, was a proponent of Jeffersonian states' rights and limited federal power. Even before the end of Monroe's first term, these men and others began to maneuver for the election of 1824.

Crucially helping them to maneuver were their wives, who accomplished some of the work of modern campaign managers by courting men — and women — of influence. The parties not thrown by Elizabeth Monroe were now given all over town by women whose husbands were jockeying for political favor. Louisa Catherine Adams had a weekly party for guests numbering in the hundreds.

The somber Adams lacked charm — "I am a man of reserved, cold, austere, and forbidding manners," he once wrote — but his abundantly charming (and hardworking) wife made up for that. She attended to the etiquette of social calls, sometimes making two dozen in a morning, and counted sixty-eight members of Congress as her regular guests. This was smart politics, in case

Election Sewing or Trinket Boxes from 1824
Women could express their support for a presidential candidate by purchasing a sewing box emblazoned with his face. On the left is a box with John Quincy Adams's picture inside the cover; the top of the box (not visible here) has a velvet pincushion printed with the slogan "Be Firm for Adams." The competing box on the right features Andrew Jackson's likeness under glass on top of the cover. The lithographic portrait was hand-colored with watercolors. Notice that Jackson is shown in his military uniform, with the title of general and a rather younger-looking face than he actually had in 1824. Collection of Janice L. and David J. Frent.

Candidate*	Electoral Vote	Popular Vote	Percent of Popular Vote
John Q. Adams	84	108,740	30.5
Andrew Jackson	99	153,544	43.1
Henry Clay	37	47,136	13.2
W. H. Crawford	41	46,618	13.1

*No distinct political parties

Note: Because no candidate garnered a majority in the electoral college, the election was decided in the House of Representatives. Although Clay was eliminated from the running, as Speaker of the House he influenced the final decision in favor of Adams.

MAP 10.6
The Election of 1824

the House of Representatives wound up deciding the 1824 election — which it did.

John Quincy Adams (as well as Louisa Catherine) was ambitious for the presidency, but so were others. Candidate Henry Clay, Speaker of the House and negotiator of the Treaty of Ghent with Britain in 1814, promoted a new "American System," a package of protective tariffs to encourage manufacturing and federal expenditures for internal improvements such as roads and canals. Treasurer William Crawford was a favorite of Republicans from Virginia and New York, even after he suffered an incapacitating stroke in mid-1824. Calhoun was another serious contender, having served in Congress and in several cabinets. A southern planter, he attracted northern support for his backing of internal improvements and protective tariffs.

The final candidate was an outsider and a latecomer: General **Andrew Jackson** of Tennessee. Jackson had far less national political experience than the others, but he enjoyed great celebrity from his military career. In 1824, on the anniversary of the battle of New Orleans, the Adamses threw a spectacular ball in his honor, hoping that some of Jackson's charisma would rub off on Adams, who was not yet think-

ing of Jackson as a rival for office. Not long after, Jackson's supporters put his name forward for the presidency, and voters in the West and South reacted with enthusiasm. Adams was dismayed, while Calhoun dropped out of the race and shifted his attention to winning the vice presidency.

Along with democratizing the vote, eighteen states (out of the full twenty-four) had put the power to choose members of the electoral college directly in the hands of voters, making the 1824 election the first one to have a popular vote tally for the presidency. Jackson proved by far to be the most popular candidate, winning 153,544 votes. Adams was second with 108,740, Clay won 47,136 votes, and the debilitated Crawford garnered 46,618. This was not a large turnout, probably amounting to just over a quarter of adult white males. Nevertheless, the election of 1824 marked a new departure in choosing presidents. Partisanship energized the electorate; apathy and a low voter turnout would not recur until the twentieth century.

In the electoral college, Jackson received 99 votes, Adams 84, Crawford 41, and Clay 37 (Map 10.6). Jackson lacked a majority, so the House of Representatives stepped in for the second time in U.S. history. Each congressional delegation had one vote; according to the Constitution's Twelfth Amendment, passed in 1804, only the top three candidates joined the runoff. Thus Henry Clay was out of the race and in a position to bestow his support on another candidate.

Jackson's supporters later characterized the election of 1824 as the "corrupt bargain." Clay backed Adams, and Adams won by one vote in the House in February 1825. Clay's support made sense on several levels. Despite strong mutual dislike, he and Adams agreed on issues such as federal support to build roads and canals. Moreover, Clay was uneasy with Jackson's volatile temperament and unstated political views and with Crawford's diminished capacity. What made Clay's decision look "corrupt" was that immediately after the election, Adams offered to appoint Clay secretary of state — and Clay accepted.

In fact, there probably was no concrete bargain; Adams's subsequent cabinet appointments demonstrated his lack of political astuteness. But Andrew Jackson felt that the election had been stolen from him, and he wrote bitterly that "the Judas of the West [Clay] has closed the contract and will receive the thirty pieces of silver."

The Adams Administration

John Quincy Adams, like his father, was a one-term president. His career had been built on diplomacy, not electoral politics, and despite his wife's deftness in the art of political influence, his own political horse sense was not well developed. With his cabinet choices, he welcomed his opposition into his inner circle. He asked Crawford to stay on in the Treasury. He retained an openly pro-Jackson postmaster general even though that position controlled thousands of nationwide patronage appointments. He even asked Jackson to become secretary of war. With Calhoun as vice president (elected without opposition by the electoral college) and Clay at the State Department, the whole argumentative crew would have been thrust into the executive branch. Crawford and Jackson had the good sense to decline the appointments.

Adams had lofty ideas for federal action during his presidency, and the plan he put before Congress was so sweeping that it took Henry Clay aback. Adams called for federally built roads, canals, and harbors. He proposed a national university in Washington as well as government-sponsored scientific research. He wanted to build observatories to advance astronomical knowledge and to promote precision in timekeeping, and he backed a decimal-based system of weights and measures. In all these endeavors, Adams believed he was continuing the legacy of Jefferson and Madison, using the powers of government to advance knowledge. But his opponents feared he was too Hamiltonian, using federal power inappropriately to advance commercial interests.

Whether he was more truly Federalist or Republican was a moot point. Lacking the give-and-take political skills required to gain congressional support, Adams was unable to implement much of his program. He scorned the idea of courting voters to gain support and using the patronage system to enhance his power. He often made appointments (to posts such as customs collectors) to placate enemies rather than to reward friends. A story of a toast offered to the president may well have been mythical, but as humorous folklore it made the rounds during his term and came to summarize Adams's precarious hold on leadership. A dignitary raised a glass and said, "May he strike confusion to his foes," to which another voice scornfully chimed in, "as he has already done to his friends."

REVIEW How did the collapse of the Federalist Party influence the administrations of James Monroe and John Quincy Adams?

▶ Conclusion: Republican Simplicity Becomes Complex

The Jeffersonian Republicans at first tried to undo much of what the Federalists had created in the 1790s, but their promise of a simpler government gave way to the complexities of domestic and foreign issues. The sudden acquisition of the Louisiana Purchase promised land and opportunity to settlers but first required intricate federal-level dealings with powerful western Indians. British impressments of American sailors challenged Jefferson and Madison to stand up to the onetime mother country, culminating in the War of 1812. Fighting both the British and their Indian allies, the Americans engaged in two years of inconclusive battles, mostly on American soil. Their eventual triumph at the battle of New Orleans allowed them the illusion that they had fought a second war of independence.

The War of 1812 was the Indians' second lost war for independence. Tecumseh's vision of an unprecedentedly large confederacy of Indian tribes that would halt westward expansion by white Americans was cut short by the war and by his death. When Canada was under attack, the British valued its defense more than they valued their promises to help the Indians.

The war elevated to national prominence General Andrew Jackson, whose popularity with voters in the 1824 election surprised traditional politicians (and their politically astute wives) and threw the one-party rule of Republicans into a tailspin. New western states with more lenient voter qualifications and eastern states with reformed suffrage laws further eroded the old political elite. Appeals to the mass of white male voters would be the hallmark of all nineteenth-century elections after 1824. In such a system, John Quincy Adams and men like him were at a great disadvantage.

Ordinary American women, whether white or free black, had no place in government. Male legislatures maintained women's *feme covert* status, keeping wives dependent on husbands. A few women claimed greater personal autonomy through religion, while many others benefited from expanded female schooling in schools and academies. These increasingly substantial gains in education would blossom into a major transformation of gender starting in the 1830s and 1840s.

Amid the turmoil of the early Republic, two events in particular sparked developments that would prove momentous in later decades. The bitter debate over slavery that surrounded the Missouri Compromise accentuated the serious divisions between northern and southern states — divisions that would only widen in the decades to come. And Jefferson's long embargo and Madison's wartime trade stoppage gave a big boost to American manufacturing by removing competition with British factories. When peace returned in 1815, the years of independent development burst forth into a period of sustained economic growth that continued nearly unabated into the mid-nineteenth century.

▶ Selected Bibliography

Politics

Andrew Burstein and Nancy Isenberg, *Madison and Jefferson* (2010).
Saul Cornell, *The Other Founders: Anti-Federalism and the Dissenting Tradition in America, 1788–1828* (1999).
Joseph J. Ellis, *American Sphinx: The Character of Thomas Jefferson* (1997).
Joanne B. Freeman, *Affairs of Honor: National Politics in the New Republic* (2001).
Nancy Isenberg, *Fallen Founder: The Life of Aaron Burr* (2008).
Alexander Keyssar, *The Right to Vote: The Contested History of Democracy in the United States* (2000).
Jon Kukla, *A Wilderness So Immense: The Louisiana Purchase and the Destiny of America* (2003).
Jeffrey L. Pasley, Andrew W. Robertson, and David Waldstreicher, *Beyond the Founders: New Approaches to the Political History of the Early American Republic* (2003).
Stephen Watts, *The Republic Reborn: War and the Making of Liberal America, 1790–1820* (1987).
Sean Wilentz, *The Rise of American Democracy: Jefferson to Lincoln* (2005).
Richard Zacks, *The Pirate Coast: Thomas Jefferson, the First Marines, and the Secret Mission of 1805* (2006).

Indians, the War of 1812, and the West

Stephen E. Ambrose, *Undaunted Courage: Meriwether Lewis, Thomas Jefferson, and the Opening of the American West* (1996).
Carl Benn, *The Iroquois in the War of 1812* (1998).
James F. Brooks, *Captives and Cousins: Slavery, Kinship, and Community in the Southwest Borderlands* (2002).
Kathleen DuVal, *The Native Ground: Indians and Colonists in the Heart of the Continent* (2007).
R. David Edmunds, *Tecumseh and the Quest for Indian Leadership* (1984).
Albert Furtwangler, *Acts of Discovery: Visions of America in the Lewis and Clark Journals* (1993).
Pekka Hämäläinen, *The Comanche Empire* (2009).

John Sugden, *Tecumseh: A Life* (1997).
Alan Taylor, *The Civil War of 1812: American Citizens, British Subjects, Irish Rebels, and Indian Allies* (2010).
Richard White, *The Middle Ground: Indians, Empires, and Republics in the Great Lakes Region, 1650–1815* (1991).

Slavery

Douglas Egerton, *Gabriel's Rebellion* (1993).
Annette Gordon-Reed, *The Hemingses of Monticello: An American Family* (2009).
James Oliver Horton and Lois E. Horton, *In Hope of Liberty: Culture, Community, and Protest among Northern Free Blacks, 1700–1860* (1997).
Gary B. Nash, *Forging Freedom: The Formation of Philadelphia's Black Community, 1720–1840* (1988).
Shane White, *Somewhat More Independent: The End of Slavery in New York City, 1710–1810* (1991).

Women, Marriage, and Religion

Catherine Allgor, *Parlor Politics: In Which the Ladies of Washington Help Build a City and a Government* (2000).
Norma Basch, *Framing American Divorce: From the Revolutionary Generation to the Victorians* (1999).
Norma Basch, *In the Eyes of the Law: Women, Marriage, and Property in Nineteenth-Century New York* (1982).
Catherine A. Brekus, *Strangers and Pilgrims: Female Preaching in America, 1740–1845* (1998).
Nancy Cott, *Public Vows: A History of Marriage and the Nation* (2001).
Susan Juster, *Disorderly Women: Sexual Politics and Evangelicalism in Revolutionary New England* (1994).
Mary Kelley, *Learning to Stand and Speak: Women, Education, and Public Life in America's Republic* (2006).
Susan E. Klepp, *Revolutionary Conceptions: Women, Fertility, and Family Limitation in America, 1760–1820* (2009).
Mary Beth Sievens, *Stray Wives: Marital Conflict in Early National New England* (2005).

▶ **FOR MORE BOOKS ABOUT TOPICS IN THIS CHAPTER,** see the Online Bibliography at **bedfordstmartins.com/roark.**

▶ **FOR ADDITIONAL PRIMARY SOURCES FROM THIS PERIOD,** see Michael Johnson, ed., *Reading the American Past,* Fifth Edition.

▶ **FOR WEB SITES, IMAGES, AND DOCUMENTS RELATED TO TOPICS AND PLACES IN THIS CHAPTER,** visit Make History at **bedfordstmartins.com/roark.**

Reviewing Chapter 10

KEY TERMS

Explain each term's significance.

Jefferson's Presidency
    Thomas Jefferson (p. 291)
    Aaron Burr (p. 291)
    Gabriel's rebellion (p. 291)
    Marbury v. Madison (p. 293)
    Barbary Wars (p. 294)

Opportunities and Challenges in the West
    Louisiana Purchase (p. 296)
    Sacajawea (p. 297)
    Lewis and Clark expedition (p. 297)
    Osage (p. 298)
    Comanche (p. 298)

Jefferson, the Madisons, and the War of 1812
    Impressment (p. 300)
    Embargo Act of 1807 (p. 300)
    Dolley Madison (p. 301)
    Tecumseh (p. 301)
    Tenskwatawa (p. 302)
    battle of Tippecanoe (p. 303)
    Henry Clay (p. 303)
    War Hawks (p. 303)
    Creek War (p. 304)
    battle of New Orleans (p. 305)
    Hartford Convention (p. 305)

Women's Status in the Early Republic
    feme covert (p. 306)
    Jemima Wilkinson (p. 307)
    female academies (p. 307)

Monroe and Adams
    James Monroe (p. 310)
    Missouri Compromise (p. 312)
    Monroe Doctrine (p. 314)
    John Quincy Adams (p. 314)
    Andrew Jackson (p. 315)

REVIEW QUESTIONS

Use key terms and dates to support your answer.

1. How did Jefferson attempt to undo the Federalist innovations of earlier administrations? (pp. 291–294)

2. Why was Spain concerned that France sold the Louisiana Territory to the United States? (pp. 295–300)

3. Why did Congress declare war on Great Britain in 1812? (pp. 300–305)

4. How did the civil status of American women and men differ in the early Republic? (pp. 305–310)

5. How did the collapse of the Federalist Party influence the administrations of James Monroe and John Quincy Adams? (pp. 310–316)

MAKING CONNECTIONS

Draw on key terms, the timeline, and review questions.

1. When Jefferson assumed the presidency following the election of 1800, he expected to transform the national government. Describe his republican vision and his successes and failures in implementing it. Did subsequent Republican presidents advance the same objectives?

2. How did the United States expand and strengthen its control of territory in North America in the early nineteenth century? In your answer, discuss the roles of diplomacy, military action, and political leadership in contributing to this development.

3. Regional tensions emerged as a serious danger to the American political system in the early nineteenth century. Discuss specific conflicts that had regional dimensions. How did Americans resolve, or fail to resolve, these tensions?

4. Although the United States denied its female citizens equality in public life, some women were able to exert considerable influence. How did they do so? In your answer, discuss the legal, political, and educational status of women in the early Republic.

LINKING TO THE PAST

Link events in this chapter to earlier events.

1. Compare the British-Indian alliance in the Revolutionary War with the British-Indian alliance in the War of 1812. Were there any reasons for men like Tecumseh to think that the alliance might work out better the second time? (See chapter 7.)

2. How do you think the Federalist supporters of the Constitution in 1787–1788 felt about the steady decline in states' property qualifications for male voters that occurred between 1800 and 1824? Did the democratization of voting necessarily undermine the Constitution's restrictions on direct democracy in the federal government? (See chapter 8.)

▶ **For practice quizzes and other study tools,** visit the Online Study Guide at **bedfordstmartins.com/roark.**

TIMELINE 1800–1825

1800	• Republicans Thomas Jefferson and Aaron Burr tie in electoral college.
	• Fears of slave rebellion led by Gabriel in Virginia result in twenty-seven executions.
1801	• House of Representatives elects Thomas Jefferson president after thirty-six ballots.
	• Pasha of Tripoli declares war on United States.
1803	• *Marbury v. Madison.*
	• Britain and France each warn United States not to ship war-related goods to the other.
	• United States purchases Louisiana Territory.
1804	• U.S. Marines and foreign mercenaries under William Eaton take Derne, Tripoli.
	• President Jefferson meets with Osage leaders in Washington City.
1804–1806	• Lewis and Clark expedition travels from St. Louis to Pacific Ocean.
1807	• British attack and search *Chesapeake.*
	• Embargo Act.
	• United States establishes trade with Comanche Indians.
1808	• Republican James Madison elected president; Dolley Madison soon dubbed "presidentress."
1809	• Treaty of Fort Wayne.
	• Non-Intercourse Act.
1811	• Battle of Tippecanoe.
1812	• United States declares war on Great Britain.
1813	• Tecumseh dies at battle of the Thames.
1814	• British attack Washington City.
	• Treaty of Ghent.
	• New England Federalists meet at Hartford Convention.
1815	• Battle of New Orleans.
1816	• Republican James Monroe elected president.
1819	• Adams-Onís Treaty.
1820	• Missouri Compromise.
1823	• Monroe Doctrine asserted.
1825	• John Quincy Adams elected president by House of Representatives.

Appendix Directory

THE DECLARATION OF INDEPENDENCE

In Congress, July 4, 1776,

THE UNANIMOUS DECLARATION OF THE THIRTEEN UNITED STATES OF AMERICA

When in the course of human events, it becomes necessary for one people to dissolve the political bands which have connected them with another, and to assume, among the powers of the earth, the separate and equal station to which the laws of nature and of nature's God entitle them, a decent respect to the opinions of mankind requires that they should declare the causes which impel them to the separation.

We hold these truths to be self-evident, that all men are created equal; that they are endowed by their Creator with certain unalienable rights; that among these, are life, liberty, and the pursuit of happiness. That, to secure these rights, governments are instituted among men, deriving their just powers from the consent of the governed; that, whenever any form of government becomes destructive of these ends, it is the right of the people to alter or to abolish it, and to institute a new government, laying its foundation on such principles, and organizing its powers in such form, as to them shall seem most likely to effect their safety and happiness. Prudence, indeed, will dictate that governments long established, should not be changed for light and transient causes; and, accordingly, all experience hath shown, that mankind are more disposed to suffer, while evils are sufferable, than to right themselves by abolishing the forms to which they are accustomed. But, when a long train of abuses and usurpations, pursuing invariably the same object, evinces a design to reduce them under absolute despotism, it is their right, it is their duty, to throw off such government and to provide new guards for their future security. Such has been the patient sufferance of these colonies, and such is now the necessity which constrains them to alter their former systems of government. The history of the present King of Great Britain is a history of repeated injuries and usurpations, all having, in direct object, the establishment of an absolute tyranny over these States. To prove this, let facts be submitted to a candid world: He has refused his assent to laws the most wholesome and necessary for the public good.

He has forbidden his governors to pass laws of immediate and pressing importance, unless suspended in their operation till his assent should be obtained; and, when so suspended, he has utterly neglected to attend to them.

He has refused to pass other laws for the accommodation of large districts of people, unless those people would relinquish the right of representation in the legislature; a right inestimable to them, and formidable to tyrants only.

He has called together legislative bodies at places unusual, uncomfortable, and distant from the depository of their public records, for the sole purpose of fatiguing them into compliance with his measures.

He has dissolved representative houses repeatedly for opposing, with manly firmness, his invasions on the rights of the people.

He has refused, for a long time after such dissolutions, to cause others to be elected; whereby the legislative powers, incapable of annihilation, have returned to the people at large for their exercise; the state remaining in the mean-time exposed to all the danger of invasion from without, and convulsions within.

He has endeavoured to prevent the population of these States; for that purpose, obstructing the laws for naturalization of foreigners, refusing to pass others to encourage their migration hither, and raising the conditions of new appropriations of lands.

He has obstructed the administration of justice, by refusing his assent to laws for establishing judiciary powers.

He has made judges dependent on his will alone, for the tenure of their offices, and the amount and payment of their salaries.

He has erected a multitude of new offices, and sent hither swarms of officers to harass our people, and eat out their substance.

He has kept among us, in times of peace, standing armies, without the consent of our legislature.

He has affected to render the military independent of, and superior to, the civil power.

He has combined, with others, to subject us to a jurisdiction foreign to our Constitution, and unacknowledged by our laws; giving his assent to their acts of pretended legislation:

For quartering large bodies of armed troops among us:

For protecting them by a mock trial, from punishment, for any murders which they should commit on the inhabitants of these States:

For cutting off our trade with all parts of the world:

For imposing taxes on us without our consent:

For depriving us, in many cases, of the benefit of trial by jury:

For transporting us beyond seas to be tried for pretended offences:

For abolishing the free system of English laws in a neighboring province, establishing therein an arbitrary government, and enlarging its boundaries, so as to render it at once an example and fit instrument for introducing the same absolute rule into these colonies:

For taking away our charters, abolishing our most valuable laws, and altering, fundamentally, the powers of our governments:

For suspending our own legislatures, and declaring themselves invested with power to legislate for us in all cases whatsoever.

He has abdicated government here, by declaring us out of his protection, and waging war against us.

He has plundered our seas, ravaged our coasts, burnt our towns, and destroyed the lives of our people.

He is, at this time, transporting large armies of foreign mercenaries to complete the works of death, desolation, and tyranny, already begun, with circumstances of cruelty and perfidy scarcely paralleled in the most barbarous ages, and totally unworthy the head of a civilized nation.

He has constrained our fellow citizens, taken captive on the high seas, to bear arms against their country, to become the executioners of their friends, and brethren, or to fall themselves by their hands.

He has excited domestic insurrections amongst us, and has endeavored to bring on the inhabitants of our frontiers, the merciless Indian savages, whose known rule of warfare is an undistinguished destruction of all ages, sexes, and conditions.

In every stage of these oppressions, we have petitioned for redress; in the most humble terms; our repeated petitions have been answered only by repeated injury. A prince, whose character is thus marked by every act which may define a tyrant, is unfit to be the ruler of a free people.

Nor have we been wanting in attention to our British brethren. We have warned them, from time to time, of attempts made by their legislature to extend an unwarrantable jurisdiction over us. We have reminded them of the circumstances of our emigration and settlement here. We have appealed to their native justice and magnanimity, and we have conjured them, by the ties of our common kindred, to disavow these usurpations, which would inevitably interrupt our connections and correspondence. They, too, have been deaf to the voice of justice and consanguinity. We must, therefore, acquiesce in the necessity which denounces our separation, and hold them as we hold the rest of mankind, enemies in war, in peace, friends.

We, therefore, the representatives of the United States of America, in general Congress assembled, appealing to the Supreme Judge of the world for the rectitude of our intentions, do, in the name, and by authority of the good people of these colonies, solemnly publish and declare, that these united colonies are, and of right ought to be, free and independent states: that they are absolved from all allegiance to the British Crown, and that all political connection between them and the state of Great Britain is, and ought to be, totally dissolved; and that, as free and independent states, they have full power to levy war, conclude peace, contract alliances, establish commerce, and to do all other acts and things which independent states may of right do. And, for the support of this declaration, with a firm reliance on the protection of Divine Providence, we mutually pledge to each other our lives, our fortunes, and our sacred honor.

The foregoing Declaration was, by order of Congress, engrossed, and signed by the following members:

JOHN HANCOCK

New Hampshire
Josiah Bartlett
William Whipple
Matthew Thornton

Massachusetts Bay
Samuel Adams
John Adams
Robert Treat Paine
Elbridge Gerry

Rhode Island
Stephen Hopkins
William Ellery

Connecticut
Roger Sherman
Samuel Huntington
William Williams
Oliver Wolcott

New York
William Floyd
Phillip Livingston
Francis Lewis
Lewis Morris

New Jersey
Richard Stockton
John Witherspoon
Francis Hopkinson
John Hart
Abraham Clark

Pennsylvania
Robert Morris
Benjamin Rush
Benjamin Franklin
John Morton
George Clymer

James Smith
George Taylor
James Wilson
George Ross
Caesar Rodney
George Read
Thomas M'Kean

Maryland
Samuel Chase
William Paca
Thomas Stone
Charles Carroll,
   of Carrollton

North Carolina
William Hooper
Joseph Hewes
John Penn

South Carolina
Edward Rutledge
Thomas Heyward, Jr.
Thomas Lynch, Jr.
Arthur Middleton

Virginia
George Wythe
Richard Henry Lee
Thomas Jefferson
Benjamin Harrison
Thomas Nelson, Jr.
Francis Lightfoot Lee
Carter Braxton

Georgia
Button Gwinnett
Lyman Hall
George Walton

Resolved, That copies of the Declaration be sent to the several assemblies, conventions, and committees, or councils of safety, and to the several commanding officers of the continental troops; that it be proclaimed in each of the United States, at the head of the army.

THE ARTICLES OF CONFEDERATION AND PERPETUAL UNION

Agreed to in Congress, November 15, 1777.
Ratified March 1781.

BETWEEN THE STATES OF NEW HAMPSHIRE, MASSACHUSETTS BAY, RHODE ISLAND AND PROVIDENCE PLANTATIONS, CONNECTICUT, NEW YORK, NEW JERSEY, PENNSYLVANIA, DELAWARE, MARYLAND, VIRGINIA, NORTH CAROLINA, SOUTH CAROLINA, GEORGIA.*

Article 1

The stile of this confederacy shall be "The United States of America."

Article 2

Each State retains its sovereignty, freedom and independence, and every power, jurisdiction, and right, which is not by this confederation expressly delegated to the United States, in Congress assembled.

Article 3

The said states hereby severally enter into a firm league of friendship with each other for their common defence, the security of their liberties and their mutual and general welfare; binding themselves to assist each other against all force offered to, or attacks made upon them, or any of them, on account of religion, sovereignty, trade, or any other pretence whatever.

Article 4

The better to secure and perpetuate mutual friendship and intercourse among the people of the different states in this union, the free inhabitants of each of these states, paupers, vagabonds, and fugitives from justice excepted, shall be entitled to all privileges and immunities of free citizens in the several states; and the people of each State shall have free ingress and regress to and from any other State, and shall enjoy therein all the privileges of trade and commerce, subject to the same duties, impositions, and restrictions, as the inhabitants thereof respectively; provided, that such restrictions shall not extend so far as to prevent the removal of property, imported into any State, to any other State of which the owner is an inhabitant; provided also, that no imposition, duties, or restriction, shall be laid by any State on the property of the United States, or either of them. If any person guilty of, or charged with treason, felony, or other high misdemeanor in any State, shall flee from justice and be found in any of the United States, he shall, upon demand of the governor or executive power of the State from which he fled, be delivered up and removed to the State having jurisdiction of his offence. Full faith and credit shall be given in each of these states to the records, acts, and judicial proceedings of the courts and magistrates of every other State.

Article 5

For the more convenient management of the general interests of the United States, delegates shall be annually appointed, in such manner as the legislature of each State shall direct, to meet in Congress, on the 1st Monday in November in every year, with a power reserved to each State to recall its delegates, or any of them, at any time within the year, and to send others in their stead for the remainder of the year.

No State shall be represented in Congress by less than two, nor by more than seven members; and no person shall be capable of being a delegate for more than three years in any term of six years; nor shall any person, being a delegate, be capable of holding any office under the United States, for which he, or any other for his benefit, receives any salary, fees, or emolument of any kind.

Each State shall maintain its own delegates in a meeting of the states, and while they act as members of the committee of the states.

In determining questions in the United States, in Congress assembled, each State shall have one vote.

Freedom of speech and debate in Congress shall not be impeached or questioned in any court or place out of Congress: and the members of Congress shall be protected in their persons from arrests and imprisonments, during the time of their going to and from, and attendance on Congress, except for treason, felony, or breach of the peace.

---

*This copy of the final draft of the Articles of Confederation is taken from the Journals, 9:907–925, November 15, 1777.

Article 6

No State, without the consent of the United States, in Congress assembled, shall send any embassy to, or receive any embassy from, or enter into any conference, agreement, alliance, or treaty with any king, prince, or state; nor shall any person, holding any office of profit or trust under the United States, or any of them, accept of any present, emolument, office or title, of any kind whatever, from any king, prince, or foreign state; nor shall the United States, in Congress assembled, or any of them, grant any title of nobility.

No two or more states shall enter into any treaty, confederation, or alliance, whatever, between them, without the consent of the United States, in Congress assembled, specifying accurately the purposes for which the same is to be entered into, and how long it shall continue.

No state shall lay any imposts or duties which may interfere with any stipulations in treaties entered into by the United States, in Congress assembled, with any king, prince, or state, in pursuance of any treaties already proposed by Congress to the courts of France and Spain.

No vessels of war shall be kept up in time of peace by any State, except such number only as shall be deemed necessary by the United States, in Congress assembled, for the defence of such State or its trade; nor shall any body of forces be kept up by any State, in time of peace, except such number only as, in the judgment of the United States, in Congress assembled, shall be deemed requisite to garrison the forts necessary for the defence of such State; but every State shall always keep up a well regulated and disciplined militia, sufficiently armed and accoutred, and shall provide, and constantly have ready for use, in public stores, a due number of field pieces and tents, and a proper quantity of arms, ammunition and camp equipage.

No State shall engage in any war without the consent of the United States, in Congress assembled, unless such State be actually invaded by enemies, or shall have received certain advice of a resolution being formed by some nation of Indians to invade such State, and the danger is so imminent as not to admit of a delay till the United States, in Congress assembled, can be consulted; nor shall any State grant commissions to any ships or vessels of war, nor letters of marque or reprisal, except it be after a declaration of war by the United States, in Congress assembled, and then only against the kingdom or state, and the subjects thereof, against which war has been so declared, and under such regulations as shall be established by the United States, in Congress assembled, unless such State be infested by pirates, in which case vessels of war may be fitted out for that occasion, and kept so long as the danger shall continue, or until the United States, in Congress assembled, shall determine otherwise.

Article 7

When land forces are raised by any State for the common defence, all officers of or under the rank of colonel, shall be appointed by the legislature of each State respectively, by whom such forces shall be raised, or in such manner as such State shall direct; and all vacancies shall be filled up by the State which first made the appointment.

Article 8

All charges of war and all other expences, that shall be incurred for the common defence or general welfare, and allowed by the United States, in Congress assembled, shall be defrayed out of a common treasury, which shall be supplied by the several states, in proportion to the value of all land within each State, granted to or surveyed for any person, as such land and the buildings and improvements thereon shall be estimated according to such mode as the United States, in Congress assembled, shall, from time to time, direct and appoint.

The taxes for paying that proportion shall be laid and levied by the authority and direction of the legislatures of the several states, within the time agreed upon by the United States, in Congress assembled.

Article 9

The United States, in Congress assembled, shall have the sole and exclusive right and power of determining on peace and war, except in the cases mentioned in the 6th article; of sending and receiving ambassadors; entering into treaties and alliances, provided that no treaty of commerce shall be made, whereby the legislative power of the respective states shall be restrained from imposing such imposts and duties on foreigners as their own people are subjected to, or from prohibiting the exportation or importation of any species of goods or commodities whatsoever; of establishing rules for deciding, in all cases, what captures on land or water shall be legal, and in what manner prizes, taken by land or naval forces in the service of the United States, shall be divided or appropriated; of granting letters of marque and reprisal in times of peace; appointing courts for the trial of piracies and felonies committed on the high seas, and establishing courts for receiving and determining, finally, appeals in all cases of captures; provided, that no member of Congress shall be appointed a judge of any of the said courts.

The United States, in Congress assembled, shall also be the last resort on appeal in all disputes and differences now subsisting, or that hereafter may arise between two or more states concerning boundary, jurisdiction or any other cause whatever; which authority shall always be exercised in the manner following: whenever the legislative or executive authority, or lawful agent of any State, in controversy with another, shall present a petition to Congress, stating the matter in question, and praying for a hearing, notice thereof shall be given, by order of Congress, to the legislative or executive authority of the other State in controversy, and a day assigned for the appearance of the parties by their lawful agents, who shall then be directed to appoint, by joint consent, commissioners or judges to constitute a court for hearing and determining the matter in question; but, if they cannot agree, Congress shall name three persons out of each of the United States, and from the list of such persons each party shall alternately strike out one, the petitioners beginning, until the number shall be reduced to thirteen; and from that number not less than seven, nor more than nine names, as Congress shall direct, shall, in the presence of Congress, be drawn out by lot; and the persons whose names shall be so drawn, or any five of them, shall be commissioners or judges to hear and finally determine the controversy, so always as a major part of the judges who shall hear the cause shall agree in the determination; and if either party shall neglect to attend at the day appointed, without shewing reasons which Congress shall judge sufficient, or, being present, shall refuse to strike, the Congress shall proceed to nominate three persons out of each State, and the secretary of Congress shall strike in behalf of such party absent or refusing; and the judgment and sentence of the court to be appointed, in the manner before prescribed, shall be final and conclusive; and if any of the parties shall refuse to submit to the authority of such court, or to appear or defend their claim or cause, the court shall nevertheless proceed to pronounce sentence or judgment, which shall, in like manner, be final and decisive, the judgment or sentence and other proceedings begin, in either case, transmitted to Congress, and lodged among the acts of Congress for the security of the parties concerned: provided, that every commissioner, before he sits in judgment, shall take an oath, to be administered by one of the judges of the supreme or superior court of the State where the cause shall be tried, "well and truly to hear and determine the matter in question, according to the best of his judgment, without favour, affection, or hope of reward:" provided, also, that no State shall be deprived of territory for the benefit of the United States.

All controversies concerning the private right of soil, claimed under different grants of two or more states, whose jurisdictions, as they may respect such lands and the states which passed such grants, are adjusted, the said grants, or either of them, being at the same time claimed to have originated antecedent to such settlement of jurisdiction, shall, on the petition of either party to the Congress of the United States, be finally determined, as near as may be, in the same manner as is before prescribed for deciding disputes respecting territorial jurisdiction between different states.

The United States, in Congress assembled, shall also have the sole and exclusive right and power of regulating the alloy and value of coin struck by their own authority, or by that of the respective states; fixing the standard of weights and measures throughout the United States; regulating the trade and managing all affairs with the Indians not members of any of the states; provided that the legislative right of any State within its own limits be not infringed or violated; establishing and regulating post offices from one State to another throughout all the United States, and exacting such postage on the papers passing through the same as may be requisite to defray the expences of the said office; appointing all officers of the land forces in the service of the United States, excepting regimental officers; appointing all the officers of the naval forces, and commissioning all officers whatever in the service of the United States; making rules for the government and regulation of the said land and naval forces, and directing their operations.

The United States, in Congress assembled, shall have authority to appoint a committee to sit in the recess of Congress, to be denominated "a Committee of the States," and to consist of one delegate from each State, and to appoint such other committees and civil officers as may be necessary for managing the general affairs of the United States, under their direction; to appoint one of their number to preside; provided that no person be allowed to serve in the office of president more than one year in any term of three years; to ascertain the necessary sums of money to be raised for the service of the United States, and to appropriate and apply the same for defraying the public expences; to borrow money or emit bills on the credit of the United States, transmitting, every half year, to the respective states, an account of the sums of money so borrowed or emitted; to build and equip a navy; to agree upon the number of land forces, and to make requisitions from each State for its quota, in proportion to the number of white inhabitants in such State; which requisitions shall be binding; and thereupon, the legislature of each State shall appoint the regimental officers, raise the men, and cloathe, arm, and equip them in a soldier-like manner, at the expence of the United States; and the officers and men so cloathed, armed, and equipped, shall march to the place appointed and within the time agreed on by the United States, in Congress assembled; but if the United States, in Congress assembled, shall, on consideration of circumstances, judge proper that any State should not raise men, or should raise a smaller number than its quota, and that any other State should raise a greater number of men than the quota thereof, such extra number shall be raised, officered, cloathed, armed, and equipped in the same manner as the quota of such State, unless the legislature of such State shall judge that such extra number cannot be safely spared out of the same, in which case they shall raise, officer, cloathe, arm, and equip as many of such extra number as they judge can be safely spared. And the officers and men so cloathed, armed, and equipped, shall march to the place appointed and within the time agreed on by the United States, in Congress assembled.

The United States, in Congress assembled, shall never engage in a war, nor grant letters of marque and reprisal in time of peace, nor enter into any treaties or alliances, nor coin money, nor regulate the value thereof, nor ascertain the sums and expences necessary for the defence and welfare of the United States, or any of them: nor emit bills, nor borrow money on the credit of the United States, nor appropriate money, nor agree upon the number of vessels of war to be built or purchased, or the number of land or sea forces to be raised, nor appoint a commander in chief of the army or navy, unless nine states assent to the same; nor shall a question on any other point, except for adjourning from day to day, be determined, unless by the votes of a majority of the United States, in Congress assembled.

The Congress of the United States shall have power to adjourn to any time within the year, and to any place within the United States, so that no period of adjournment be for a longer duration than the space of six months, and shall publish the journal of their proceedings monthly, except such parts thereof, relating to treaties, alliances or military operations, as, in their judgment, require secrecy; and the yeas and nays of the delegates of each State on any question shall be entered on the journal, when it is desired by any delegate; and the delegates of a State, or any of them, at his, or their request, shall be furnished with a transcript of the said journal, except such parts as are above excepted, to lay before the legislatures of the several states.

Article 10

The committee of the states, or any nine of them, shall be authorized to execute, in the recess of Congress, such of the powers of Congress as the United States, in Congress assembled, by the consent of nine states, shall, from time to time, think expedient to vest them with; provided, that no power be delegated to the said committee, for the exercise of which, by the articles of confederation, the voice of nine states, in the Congress of the United States assembled, is requisite.

Article 11

Canada acceding to this confederation, and joining in the measures of the United States, shall be admitted into and entitled to all the advantages of this union; but no other colony shall be admitted into the same, unless such admission be agreed to by nine states.

Article 12

All bills of credit emitted, monies borrowed and debts contracted by, or under the authority of Congress before the assembling of the United States, in pursuance of the present confederation, shall be deemed and considered as a charge against the United States, for payment and satisfaction whereof the said United States and the public faith are hereby solemnly pledged.

Article 13

Every State shall abide by the determinations of the United States, in Congress assembled, on all questions which, by this confederation, are submitted to them. And the articles of this confederation shall be inviolably observed by every State, and the union shall be perpetual; nor shall any alteration at any time hereafter be made in any of them, unless such alteration be agreed to in a Congress of the United States, and be afterwards confirmed by the legislatures of every State.

These articles shall be proposed to the legislatures of all the United States, to be considered, and if approved of by them, they are advised to authorize their delegates to ratify the same in the Congress of the United States; which being done, the same shall become conclusive.

THE CONSTITUTION OF THE UNITED STATES*

Agreed to by Philadelphia Convention, September 17, 1787. Implemented March 4, 1789.

Preamble

We the people of the United States, in order to form a more perfect union, establish justice, insure domestic tranquility, provide for the common defense, promote the general welfare, and secure the blessings of liberty to ourselves and our posterity, do ordain and establish this Constitution for the United States of America.

Article I

Section 1 All legislative powers herein granted shall be vested in a Congress of the United States, which shall consist of a Senate and a House of Representatives.

Section 2 The House of Representatives shall be composed of members chosen every second year by the people of the several States, and the electors in each State shall have the qualifications requisite for electors of the most numerous branch of the State Legislature.

No person shall be a Representative who shall not have attained to the age of twenty-five years, and been seven years a citizen of the United States, and

---

*Passages no longer in effect are in italic type.

who shall not, when elected, be an inhabitant of that State in which he shall be chosen.

Representatives and direct taxes shall be apportioned among the several States which may be included within this Union, according to their respective numbers, *which shall be determined by adding to the whole number of free persons, including those bound to service for a term of years and excluding Indians not taxed, three-fifths of all other persons.* The actual enumeration shall be made within three years after the first meeting of the Congress of the United States, and within every subsequent term of ten years, in such manner as they shall by law direct. The number of Representatives shall not exceed one for every thirty thousand, but each State shall have at least one Representative; *and until such enumeration shall be made, the State of New Hampshire shall be entitled to choose three, Massachusetts eight, Rhode Island and Providence Plantations one, Connecticut five, New York six, New Jersey four, Pennsylvania eight, Delaware one, Maryland six, Virginia ten, North Carolina five, South Carolina five, and Georgia three.*

When vacancies happen in the representation from any State, the Executive authority thereof shall issue writs of election to fill such vacancies.

The House of Representatives shall choose their Speaker and other officers; and shall have the sole power of impeachment.

Section 3 The Senate of the United States shall be composed of two Senators from each State, *chosen by the legislature thereof,* for six years; and each Senator shall have one vote.

Immediately after they shall be assembled in consequence of the first election, they shall be divided as equally as may be into three classes. The seats of the Senators of the first class shall be vacated at the expiration of the second year, of the second class at the expiration of the fourth year, and of the third class at the expiration of the sixth year, so that one-third may be chosen every second year; *and if vacancies happen by resignation or otherwise, during the recess of the legislature of any State, the Executive thereof may make temporary appointments until the next meeting of the legislature, which shall then fill such vacancies.*

No person shall be a Senator who shall not have attained to the age of thirty years, and been nine years a citizen of the United States, and who shall not, when elected, be an inhabitant of that State for which he shall be chosen.

The Vice-President of the United States shall be President of the Senate, but shall have no vote, unless they be equally divided.

The Senate shall choose their other officers, and also a President pro tempore, in the absence of the Vice-President, or when he shall exercise the office of President of the United States.

The Senate shall have the sole power to try all impeachments. When sitting for that purpose, they shall be on oath or affirmation. When the President of the United States is tried, the Chief Justice shall preside: and no person shall be convicted without the concurrence of two-thirds of the members present.

Judgment in cases of impeachment shall not extend further than to removal from the office, and disqualification to hold and enjoy any office of honor, trust or profit under the United States: but the party convicted shall nevertheless be liable and subject to indictment, trial, judgment and punishment, according to law.

Section 4 The times, places and manner of holding elections for Senators and Representatives shall be prescribed in each State by the legislature thereof; but the Congress may at any time by law make or alter such regulations, except as to the places of choosing Senators.

The Congress shall assemble at least once in every year, and such meeting *shall be on the first Monday in December, unless they shall by law appoint a different day.*

Section 5 Each house shall be the judge of the elections, returns and qualifications of its own members, and a majority of each shall constitute a quorum to do business; but a smaller number may adjourn from day to day, and may be authorized to compel the attendance of absent members, in such manner, and under such penalties, as each house may provide.

Each house may determine the rules of its proceedings, punish its members for disorderly behavior, and with the concurrence of two-thirds, expel a member.

Each house shall keep a journal of its proceedings, and from time to time publish the same, excepting such parts as may in their judgment require secrecy; and the yeas and nays of the members of either house on any question shall, at the desire of one-fifth of those present, be entered on the journal.

Neither house, during the session of Congress, shall, without the consent of the other, adjourn for more than three days, nor to any other place than that in which the two houses shall be sitting.

Section 6 The Senators and Representatives shall receive a compensation for their services, to be ascertained by law and paid out of the treasury of the United States. They shall in all cases except treason, felony and breach of the peace, be privileged from arrest during their attendance at the session of their respective houses, and in going to and returning from the same; and for any speech or debate in either house, they shall not be questioned in any other place.

No Senator or Representative shall, during the time for which he was elected, be appointed to any civil office under the authority of the United States, which shall have been created, or the emoluments whereof shall have been increased, during such time; and no person holding any office under the United States shall be a member of either house during his continuance in office.

Section 7 All bills for raising revenue shall originate in the House of Representatives; but the Senate may propose or concur with amendments as on other bills.

Every bill which shall have passed the House of Representatives and the Senate, shall, before it become a law, be presented to the President of the United States; if he approve he shall sign it, but if not he shall return it with objections to that house in which it shall have originated, who shall enter the objections at large on their journal, and proceed to reconsider it. If after such reconsideration two-thirds of that house shall agree to pass the bill, it shall be sent, together with the objections, to the other house, by which it shall likewise be reconsidered, and, if approved by two-thirds of that house, it shall become a law. But in all such cases the votes of both houses shall be determined by yeas and nays, and the names of the persons voting for and against the bill shall be entered on the journal of each house respectively. If any bill shall not be returned by the President within ten days (Sundays excepted) after it shall have been presented to him, the same shall be a law, in like manner as if he had signed it, unless the Congress by their adjournment prevent its return, in which case it shall not be a law.

Every order, resolution, or vote to which the concurrence of the Senate and House of Representatives may be necessary (except on a question of adjournment) shall be presented to the President of the United States; and before the same shall take effect, shall be approved by him, or being disapproved by him, shall be repassed by two-thirds of the Senate and House of Representatives, according to the rules and limitations prescribed in the case of a bill.

Section 8 The Congress shall have power

To lay and collect taxes, duties, imposts, and excises, to pay the debts and provide for the common defense and general welfare of the United States; but all duties, imposts and excises shall be uniform throughout the United States;

To borrow money on the credit of the United States;

To regulate commerce with foreign nations, and among the several States, and with the Indian tribes;

To establish an uniform rule of naturalization, and uniform laws on the subject of bankruptcies throughout the United States;

To coin money, regulate the value thereof, and of foreign coin, and fix the standard of weights and measures;

To provide for the punishment of counterfeiting the securities and current coin of the United States;

To establish post offices and post roads;

To promote the progress of science and useful arts by securing for limited times to authors and inventors the exclusive right to their respective writings and discoveries;

To constitute tribunals inferior to the Supreme Court;

To define and punish piracies and felonies committed on the high seas and offences against the law of nations;

To declare war, grant letters of marque and reprisal, and make rules concerning captures on land and water;

To raise and support armies, but no appropriation of money to that use shall be for a longer term than two years;

To provide and maintain a navy;

To make rules for the government and regulation of the land and naval forces;

To provide for calling forth the militia to execute the laws of the Union, suppress insurrections and repel invasions;

To provide for organizing, arming, and disciplining the militia, and for governing such part of them as may be employed in the service of the United States, reserving to the States respectively the appointment of the officers, and the authority of training the militia according to the discipline prescribed by Congress;

To exercise exclusive legislation in all cases whatsoever, over such district (not exceeding ten miles square) as may, by cession of particular States, and the acceptance of Congress, become the seat of the government of the United States, and to exercise like authority over all places purchased by the consent of the legislature of the State, in which the same shall be, for erection of forts, magazines, arsenals, dockyards, and other needful buildings;—and

To make all laws which shall be necessary and proper for carrying into execution the foregoing powers, and all other powers vested by this Constitution in the government of the United States, or in any department or officer thereof.

Section 9 *The migration or importation of such persons as any of the States now existing shall think proper to admit shall not be prohibited by the Congress prior to the year one thousand eight hundred and eight; but a tax or duty may be imposed on such importation, not exceeding ten dollars for each person.*

The privilege of the writ of habeas corpus shall not be suspended, unless when in cases of rebellion or invasion the public safety may require it.

No bill of attainder or ex post facto law shall be passed.

No capitation, or other direct, tax shall be laid, unless in proportion to the census or enumeration herein before directed to be taken.

No tax or duty shall be laid on articles exported from any State.

No preference shall be given by any regulation of commerce or revenue to the ports of one State over those of another; nor shall vessels bound to, or from, one State be obliged to enter, clear, or pay duties in another.

No money shall be drawn from the treasury, but in consequence of appropriations made by law; and a regular statement and account of the receipts and expenditures of all public money shall be published from time to time.

No title of nobility shall be granted by the United States: and no person holding any office of profit or trust under them, shall, without the consent of the Congress, accept of any present, emolument, office, or title, of any kind whatever, from any king, prince, or foreign state.

Section 10 No State shall enter into any treaty, alliance, or confederation; grant letters of marque and reprisal; coin money; emit bills of credit; make anything but gold and silver coin a tender in payment of debts; pass any bill of attainder, ex post facto law, or law impairing the obligation of contracts, or grant any title of nobility.

No State shall, without the consent of Congress, lay any imposts or duties on imports or exports, except what may be absolutely necessary for executing its inspection laws: and the net produce of all duties and imposts, laid by any State on imports or exports, shall be for the use of the treasury of the United States; and all such laws shall be subject to the revision and control of the Congress.

No State shall, without the consent of Congress, lay any duty of tonnage, keep troops, or ships of war in time of peace, enter into any agreement or compact with another State, or with a foreign power, or engage in war, unless actually invaded, or in such imminent danger as will not admit of delay.

Article II

Section 1 The executive power shall be vested in a President of the United States of America. He shall hold his office during the term of four years, and, together with the Vice-President, chosen for the same term, be elected as follows:

Each State shall appoint, in such manner as the legislature thereof may direct, a number of electors, equal to the whole number of Senators and Representatives to which the State may be entitled in the Congress; but no Senator or Representative, or person holding an office of trust or profit under the United States, shall be appointed an elector.

The electors shall meet in their respective States, and vote by ballot for two persons, of whom one at least shall not be an inhabitant of the same State with themselves. And they shall make a list of all the persons voted for, and of the number of votes for each; which list they shall sign and certify, and transmit sealed to the seat of government of the United States, directed to the President of the Senate. The President of the Senate shall, in the presence of the Senate and House of Representatives, open all the certificates, and the votes shall then be counted. The person having the greatest number of votes shall be the President, if such number be a majority of the whole number of electors appointed; and if there be more than one who have such majority, and have an equal number of votes, then the House of Representatives shall immediately choose by ballot one of them for President; and if no person have a majority, then from the five highest on the list said house shall in like manner choose the President. But in choosing the President the votes shall be taken by States, the representation from each State having one vote; a quorum for this purpose shall consist of a member or members from two-thirds of the States, and a majority of all the States shall be necessary to a choice. In every case, after the choice of the President, the person having the greatest number of votes of the electors shall be the Vice-President. But if there should remain two or more who have equal votes, the Senate shall choose from them by ballot the Vice-President.

The Congress may determine the time of choosing the electors, and the day on which they shall give their votes; which day shall be the same throughout the United States.

No person except a natural-born citizen, *or a citizen of the United States at the time of the adoption of this Constitution,* shall be eligible to the office of President; neither shall any person be eligible to that office who shall not have attained to the age of thirty-five years, and been fourteen years a resident within the United States.

In cases of the removal of the President from office or of his death, resignation, or inability to discharge the powers and duties of the said office, the same shall devolve on the Vice-President, and the Congress may by law provide for the case of removal, death, resignation, or inability, both of the President and Vice-President, declaring what officer shall then act as President, and such officer shall act accordingly, until the disability be removed, or a President shall be elected.

The President shall, at stated times, receive for his services a compensation, which shall neither be increased nor diminished during the period for which he shall have been elected, and he shall not receive within that period any other emolument from the United States, or any of them.

Before he enter on the execution of his office, he shall take the following oath or affirmation:—"I do solemnly swear (or affirm) that I will faithfully execute the office of the President of the United States, and will to the best of my ability preserve, protect and defend the Constitution of the United States."

Section 2 The President shall be commander in chief of the army and navy of the United States, and of the militia of the several States, when called into the actual service of the United States; he may require the opinion, in writing, of the principal officer in each of the executive departments, upon any subject relating to the duties of their respective offices, and he shall have power to grant reprieves and pardons for offenses against the United States, except in cases of impeachment.

He shall have power, by and with the advice and consent of the Senate, to make treaties, provided two-thirds of the Senators present concur; and he shall nominate, and by and with the advice and consent of the Senate, shall appoint ambassadors, other public ministers and consuls, judges of the Supreme Court, and all other officers of the United States, whose appointments are not herein otherwise provided for, and which shall be established by law: but Congress may by law vest the appointment of such inferior officers, as they think proper, in the President alone, in the courts of law, or in the heads of departments.

The President shall have power to fill up all vacancies that may happen during the recess of the Senate, by granting commissions which shall expire at the end of their next session.

Section 3 He shall from time to time give to the Congress information of the state of the Union, and recommend to their consideration such measures as he shall judge necessary and expedient; he may, on extraordinary occasions, convene both houses, or either of them, and in case of disagreement between them, with respect to the time of adjournment, he may adjourn them to such time as he shall think proper; he shall receive ambassadors and other public ministers; he shall take care that the laws be faithfully executed, and shall commission all the officers of the United States.

Section 4 The President, Vice-President and all civil officers of the United States shall be removed from office on impeachment for, and on conviction of, treason, bribery, or other high crimes and misdemeanors.

Article III

Section 1 The judicial power of the United States shall be vested in one Supreme Court, and in such inferior courts as the Congress may from time to time ordain and establish. The judges, both of the Supreme and inferior courts, shall hold their offices during good behavior, and shall, at stated times, receive for their services a compensation which shall not be diminished during their continuance in office.

Section 2 The judicial power shall extend to all cases, in law and equity, arising under this Constitution, the laws of the United States, and treaties made, or which shall be made, under their authority;—to all cases affecting ambassadors, other public ministers and consuls;—to all cases of admiralty and maritime jurisdiction;—to controversies to which the United States shall be a party;—to controversies between two or more States;—*between a State and citizens of another State*;—between citizens of different States;—between citizens of the same State claiming lands under grants of different States, and between a State, or the citizens thereof, and foreign states, citizens or subjects.

In all cases affecting ambassadors, other public ministers and consuls, and those in which a State shall be party, the Supreme Court shall have original jurisdiction. In all the other cases before mentioned, the Supreme Court shall have appellate jurisdiction, both as to law and fact, with such exceptions, and under such regulations, as the Congress shall make.

The trial of all crimes, except in cases of impeachment, shall be by jury; and such trial shall be held in the State where said crimes shall have been committed; but when not committed within any State, the trial shall be at such place or places as the Congress may by Law have directed.

Section 3 Treason against the United States shall consist only in levying war against them, or in adhering to their enemies, giving them aid and comfort. No person shall be convicted of treason unless on the testimony of two witnesses to the same overt act, or on confession in open court.

The Congress shall have power to declare the punishment of treason, but no attainder of treason shall work corruption of blood, or forfeiture except during the life of the person attainted.

Article IV

Section 1 Full faith and credit shall be given in each State to the public acts, records, and judicial proceedings of every other State. And the Congress may by general laws prescribe the manner in which such acts, records, and proceedings shall be proved, and the effect thereof.

Section 2 The citizens of each State shall be entitled to all privileges and immunities of citizens in the several States.

A person charged in any State with treason, felony, or other crime, who shall flee from justice, and be found in another State, shall on demand of the executive authority of the State from which he fled, be delivered up, to be removed to the State having jurisdiction of the crime.

No Person held to service or labor in one State, under the laws thereof, escaping into another, shall, in consequence of any law or regulation therein, be discharged from such service or labor, but shall be delivered up on claim of the party to whom such service or labor may be due.

Section 3 New States may be admitted by the Congress into this Union; but no new State shall be formed or erected within the jurisdiction of any other State; nor any State be formed by the junction of two or more States, or parts of States, without the consent of the legislatures of the States concerned as well as of the Congress.

The Congress shall have power to dispose of and make all needful rules and regulations respecting the territory or other property belonging to the United States; and nothing in this Constitution shall be so construed as to prejudice any claims of the United States, or of any particular State.

Section 4 The United States shall guarantee to every State in this Union a republican form of government, and shall protect each of them against invasion; and on application of the legislature, or of the executive (when the legislature cannot be convened), against domestic violence.

Article V

The Congress, whenever two-thirds of both houses shall deem it necessary, shall propose amendments to this Constitution, or, on the application of the legislatures of two-thirds of the several States, shall call a convention for proposing amendments, which, in either case, shall be valid to all intents and purposes, as part of this Constitution, when ratified by the legislatures of three-fourths of the several States, or by conventions in three-fourths thereof, as the one or the other mode of ratification may be proposed by the Congress; provided *that no amendments which may be made prior to the year one thousand eight hundred and eight shall in any manner affect the first and fourth clauses in the ninth section of the first article*; and that no State, without its consent, shall be deprived of its equal suffrage in the Senate.

Article VI

All debts contracted and engagements entered into, before the adoption of this Constitution, shall be as valid against the United States under this Constitution, as under the Confederation.

This Constitution, and the laws of the United States which shall be made in pursuance thereof; and all treaties made, or which shall be made, under the authority of the United States, shall be the supreme law of the land; and the judges in every State shall be bound thereby, anything in the Constitution or laws of any State to the contrary notwithstanding.

The Senators and Representatives before mentioned, and the members of the several State legislatures, and all executive and judicial officers, both of the United States and of the several States, shall be bound by oath or affirmation to support this Constitution; but no religious test shall ever be required as a qualification to any office or public trust under the United States.

Article VII

The ratification of the conventions of nine States shall be sufficient for the establishment of this Constitution between the States so ratifying the same.

Done in convention by the unanimous consent of the States present, the seventeenth day of September in the year of our Lord one thousand seven hundred and eighty-seven and of the Independence of the United States of America the twelfth. In witness whereof we have hereunto subscribed our names.

GEORGE WASHINGTON
PRESIDENT AND DEPUTY FROM VIRGINIA

New Hampshire
John Langdon
Nicholas Gilman

Massachusetts
Nathaniel Gorham
Rufus King

Connecticut
William Samuel
   Johnson
Roger Sherman

New York
Alexander Hamilton

New Jersey
William Livingston
David Brearley
William Paterson
Jonathan Dayton

Pennsylvania
Benjamin Franklin
Thomas Mifflin
Robert Morris
George Clymer
Thomas FitzSimons
Jared Ingersoll
James Wilson
Gouverneur Morris

Delaware
George Read
Gunning Bedford, Jr.
John Dickinson
Richard Bassett
Jacob Broom

Maryland
James McHenry
Daniel of St. Thomas
   Jenifer
Daniel Carroll

Virginia
John Blair
James Madison, Jr.

North Carolina
William Blount
Richard Dobbs Spaight
Hugh Williamson

South Carolina
John Rutledge
Charles Cotesworth
   Pinckney
Charles Pinckney
Pierce Butler

Georgia
William Few
Abraham Baldwin

AMENDMENTS TO THE CONSTITUTION WITH ANNOTATIONS (including the six unratified amendments)

▶ IN THEIR EFFORT TO GAIN Antifederalists' support for the Constitution, Federalists frequently pointed to the inclusion of Article 5, which provides an orderly method of amending the Constitution. In contrast, the Articles of Confederation, which were universally recognized as seriously flawed, offered no means of amendment. For their part, Antifederalists argued that the amendment process was so "intricate" that one might as easily roll "sixes an hundred times in succession" as change the Constitution.

The system for amendment laid out in the Constitution requires that two-thirds of both houses of Congress agree to a proposed amendment, which must then be ratified by three-quarters of the legislatures of the states. Alternatively, an amendment may be proposed by a convention called by the legislatures of two-thirds of the states. Since 1789, members of Congress have proposed thousands of amendments. Besides the seventeen amendments added since 1789, only the six "unratified" ones included here were approved by two-thirds of both houses and sent to the states for ratification.

Among the many amendments that never made it out of Congress have been proposals to declare dueling, divorce, and interracial marriage unconstitutional as well as proposals to establish a national university, to acknowledge the sovereignty of Jesus Christ, and to prohibit any person from possessing wealth in excess of $10 million.*

Among the issues facing Americans today that might lead to constitutional amendment are efforts to balance the federal budget, to limit the number of terms elected officials may serve, to limit access to or prohibit abortion, to establish English as the official language of the United States, and to prohibit flag burning. None of these proposed amendments has yet garnered enough support in Congress to be sent to the states for ratification.

Although the first ten amendments to the Constitution are commonly known as the Bill of Rights, only Amendments 1–8 actually provide guarantees of individual rights. Amendments 9 and 10 deal with the structure of power within the constitutional system. The Bill of Rights was promised to appease Antifederalists who refused to ratify the Constitution without guarantees of individual liberties and limitations to federal power. After studying more than two hundred amendments recommended by the ratifying conventions of the states, Federalist James Madison presented a list of seventeen to Congress, which used Madison's list as the founda-

tion for the twelve amendments that were sent to the states for ratification. Ten of the twelve were adopted in 1791. The first on the list of twelve, known as the Reapportionment Amendment, was never adopted (see page A-15). The second proposed amendment was adopted in 1992 as Amendment 27 (see page A-24).

Amendment I

Congress shall make no law respecting an establishment of religion, or prohibiting the free exercise thereof; or abridging the freedom of speech, or of the press; or the right of the people peaceably to assemble, and to petition the government for a redress of grievances.

◆ ◆ ◆

▶ The First Amendment is a potent symbol for many Americans. Most are well aware of their rights to free speech, freedom of the press, and freedom of religion and their rights to assemble and to petition, even if they cannot cite the exact words of this amendment.

The First Amendment guarantee of freedom of religion has two clauses: the "free exercise clause," which allows individuals to practice or not practice any religion, and the "establishment clause," which prevents the federal government from discriminating against or favoring any particular religion. This clause was designed to create what Thomas Jefferson referred to as "a wall of separation between church and state." In the 1960s, the Supreme Court ruled that the First Amendment prohibits prayer (see Engel v. Vitale, online) and Bible reading in public schools.

Although the rights to free speech and freedom of the press are established in the First Amendment, it was not until the twentieth century that the Supreme Court began to explore the full meaning of these guarantees. In 1919, the Court ruled in Schenck v. United States (online) that the government could suppress free expression only where it could cite a "clear and present danger." In a decision that continues to raise controversies, the Court ruled in 1990, in Texas v. Johnson, that flag burning is a form of symbolic speech protected by the First Amendment.

Amendment II

A well-regulated militia being necessary to the security of a free State, the right of the people to keep and bear arms shall not be infringed.

◆ ◆ ◆

*Richard B. Bernstein, *Amending America* (New York: Times Books, 1993), 177–81.

▶ *Fear of a standing army under the control of a hostile government made the Second Amendment an important part of the Bill of Rights. Advocates of gun ownership claim that the amendment prevents the government from regulating firearms. Proponents of gun control argue that the amendment is designed only to protect the right of the states to maintain militia units.*

In 1939, the Supreme Court ruled in United States v. Miller *that the Second Amendment did not protect the right of an individual to own a sawed-off shotgun, which it argued was not ordinary militia equipment. Since then, the Supreme Court has refused to hear Second Amendment cases, while lower courts have upheld firearms regulations. Several justices currently on the bench seem to favor a narrow interpretation of the Second Amendment, which would allow gun control legislation. The controversy over the impact of the Second Amendment on gun owners and gun control legislation will certainly continue.*

Amendment III

No soldier shall, in time of peace, be quartered in any house without the consent of the owner, nor in time of war, but in a manner to be prescribed by law.

◆ ◆ ◆

▶ *The Third Amendment was extremely important to the framers of the Constitution, but today it is nearly forgotten. American colonists were especially outraged that they were forced to quarter British troops in the years before and during the American Revolution. The philosophy of the Third Amendment has been viewed by some justices and scholars as the foundation of the modern constitutional right to privacy. One example of this can be found in Justice William O. Douglas's opinion in* Griswold v. Connecticut *(online).*

Amendment IV

The right of the people to be secure in their persons, houses, papers, and effects, against unreasonable searches and seizures, shall not be violated, and no warrants shall issue but upon probable cause, supported by oath or affirmation, and particularly describing the place to be searched, and the persons or things to be seized.

◆ ◆ ◆

▶ *In the years before the Revolution, the houses, barns, stores, and warehouses of American colonists were ransacked by British authorities under "writs of assistance" or general warrants. The British, thus empowered, searched for seditious material or smuggled goods that could then be used as evidence against colonists who were charged with a crime only after the items were found. The first part of the Fourth Amendment protects citizens from "unreasonable" searches and seizures.*

The Supreme Court has interpreted this protection as well as the words search and seizure *in different ways at different times. At one time, the Court did not recognize electronic eavesdropping as a form of search and seizure, though it does today. At times, an "unreasonable" search has been almost any search carried out without a warrant, but in the two decades before 1969, the Court sometimes sanctioned warrantless searches that it considered reasonable based on "the total atmosphere of the case."*

The second part of the Fourth Amendment defines the procedure for issuing a search warrant and states the requirement of "probable cause," which is generally viewed as evidence indicating that a suspect has committed an offense.

The Fourth Amendment has been controversial because the Court has sometimes excluded evidence that has been seized in violation of constitutional standards. The justification is that excluding such evidence deters violations of the amendment, but doing so may allow a guilty person to escape punishment.

Amendment V

No person shall be held to answer for a capital, or otherwise infamous crime, unless on a presentment or indictment of a grand jury, except in cases arising in the land or naval forces, or in the militia, when in actual service in time of war or public danger; nor shall any person be subject for the same offence to be twice put in jeopardy of life or limb; nor shall be compelled in any criminal case to be a witness against himself, nor be deprived of life, liberty, or property, without due process of law; nor shall private property be taken for public use without just compensation.

◆ ◆ ◆

▶ *The Fifth Amendment protects people against government authority in the prosecution of criminal offenses. It prohibits the state, first, from charging a person with a serious crime without a grand jury hearing to decide whether there is sufficient evidence to support the charge and, second, from charging a person with the same crime twice. The best-known aspect of the Fifth Amendment is that it prevents a person from being "compelled . . . to be a witness against himself." The last clause, the "takings clause," limits the power of the government to seize property.*

Although invoking the Fifth Amendment is popularly viewed as a confession of guilt, a person may be innocent yet still fear prosecution. For example, during the Red-baiting era of the late 1940s and 1950s, many people who had participated in legal activities that were associated with the Communist Party claimed the Fifth Amendment privilege rather than testify before the House Un-American Activities Committee because the mood of the times cast those activities in a negative light. Since "taking the Fifth" was viewed as an admission of guilt, those people often lost their jobs or became unemployable. (See chapter 26.) Nonetheless, the right to protect oneself against self-incrimination plays an important role in guarding against the collective power of the state.

Amendment VI

In all criminal prosecutions, the accused shall enjoy the right to a speedy and public trial, by an impartial jury of the State and district wherein the crime shall have been committed, which district shall have been previously ascertained by law, and to be informed of the nature and cause of the accusation; to be confronted with the witnesses against him; to have compulsory process for obtaining witnesses in his favor, and to have the assistance of counsel for his defence.

◆ ◆ ◆

▶ *The original Constitution put few limits on the government's power to investigate, prosecute, and punish crime. This process was of great concern to the early Americans, however, and of the twenty-eight rights specified in the first eight amendments, fifteen have to do with it. Seven rights are specified in the Sixth Amendment. These include the right to a speedy trial, a public trial, a jury trial, a notice of accusation, confrontation by opposing witnesses, testimony by favorable witnesses, and the assistance of counsel.*

Although this amendment originally guaranteed these rights only in cases involving the federal government, the adoption of the Fourteenth Amendment began a process of applying the protections of the Bill of Rights to the states through court cases such as Gideon v. Wainwright *(online).*

Amendment VII

In suits at common law, where the value in controversy shall exceed twenty dollars, the right of trial by jury shall be preserved, and no fact tried by a jury shall be otherwise reexamined in any court of the United States, than according to the rules of the common law.

◆ ◆ ◆

▶ *This amendment guarantees people the same right to a trial by jury as was guaranteed by English common law in 1791. Under common law, in civil trials (those involving money damages) the role of the judge was to settle questions of law and that of the jury was to settle questions of fact. The amendment does not specify the size of the jury or its role in a trial, however. The Supreme Court has generally held that those issues be determined by English common law of 1791, which stated that a jury consists of twelve people, that a trial must be conducted before a judge who instructs the jury on the law and advises it on facts, and that a verdict must be unanimous.*

Amendment VIII

Excessive bail shall not be required, nor excessive fines imposed, nor cruel and unusual punishments inflicted.

◆ ◆ ◆

▶ *The language used to guarantee the three rights in this amendment was inspired by the English Bill of Rights of 1689. The Supreme Court has not had a lot to say about "excessive fines." In recent years it has agreed that, despite the provision against "excessive bail," persons who are believed to be dangerous to others can be held without bail even before they have been convicted.*

Although opponents of the death penalty have not succeeded in using the Eighth Amendment to achieve the end of capital punishment, the clause regarding "cruel and unusual punishments" has been used to prohibit capital punishment in certain cases (see Furman v. Georgia, *online) and to require improved conditions in prisons.*

Amendment IX

The enumeration in the Constitution, of certain rights, shall not be construed to deny or disparage others retained by the people.

◆ ◆ ◆

▶ *Some Federalists feared that inclusion of the Bill of Rights in the Constitution would allow later generations of interpreters to claim that the people had surrendered any rights not specifically enumerated there. To guard against this, Madison added language that became the Ninth Amendment. Interest in this heretofore largely ignored amendment revived in 1965 when it was used in a concurring opinion in* Griswold v. Connecticut *(online). While Justice William O. Douglas called on the Third Amendment to support the right to privacy in deciding that case, Justice Arthur Goldberg, in the concurring opinion, argued that the right to privacy regarding contraception was an unenumerated right that was protected by the Ninth Amendment.*

In 1980, the Court ruled that the right of the press to attend a public trial was protected by the Ninth Amendment. While some scholars argue that modern judges cannot identify the unenumerated rights that the framers were trying to protect, others argue that the Ninth Amendment should be read as providing a constitutional "presumption of liberty" that allows people to act in any way that does not violate the rights of others.

Amendment X

The powers not delegated to the United States by the Constitution, nor prohibited by it to the States, are reserved to the States respectively, or to the people.

♦ ♦ ♦

▶ *The Antifederalists were especially eager to see a "reserved powers clause" explicitly guaranteeing the states control over their internal affairs. Not surprisingly, the Tenth Amendment has been a frequent battleground in the struggle over states' rights and federal supremacy. Prior to the Civil War, the Democratic Republican Party and Jacksonian Democrats invoked the Tenth Amendment to prohibit the federal government from making decisions about whether people in individual states could own slaves. The Tenth Amendment was virtually suspended during Reconstruction following the Civil War. In 1883, however, the Supreme Court declared the Civil Rights Act of 1875 unconstitutional on the grounds that it violated the Tenth Amendment. Business interests also called on the amendment to block efforts at federal regulation.*

The Court was inconsistent over the next several decades as it attempted to resolve the tension between the restrictions of the Tenth Amendment and the powers the Constitution granted to Congress to regulate interstate commerce and levy taxes. The Court upheld the Pure Food and Drug Act (1906), the Meat Inspection Acts (1906 and 1907), and the White Slave Traffic Act (1910), all of which affected the states, but struck down an act prohibiting interstate shipment of goods produced through child labor. Between 1934 and 1935, a number of New Deal programs created by Franklin D. Roosevelt were declared unconstitutional on the grounds that they violated the Tenth Amendment. (See chapter 24.) As Roosevelt appointees changed the composition of the Court, the Tenth Amendment was declared to have no substantive meaning. Generally, the amendment is held to protect the rights of states to regulate internal matters such as local government, education, commerce, labor, and business, as well as matters involving families such as marriage, divorce, and inheritance within the state.

Unratified Amendment

Reapportionment Amendment (proposed by Congress September 25, 1789, along with the Bill of Rights)

After the first enumeration required by the first article of the Constitution, there shall be one Representative for every thirty thousand, until the number shall amount to one hundred, after which the proportion shall be so regulated by Congress, that there shall be not less than one hundred Representatives, nor less than one Representative for every forty thousand persons, until the number of Representatives shall amount to two hundred; after which the proportion shall be so regulated by Congress, that there shall not be less than two hundred Representatives, nor more than one Representative for every fifty thousand persons.

♦ ♦ ♦

▶ *If the Reapportionment Amendment had passed and remained in effect, the House of Representatives today would have more than 5,000 members rather than 435.*

Amendment XI
[Adopted 1798]

The judicial power of the United States shall not be construed to extend to any suit in law or equity, commenced or prosecuted against one of the United States by citizens of another State, or by citizens or subjects of any foreign state.

♦ ♦ ♦

▶ *In 1793, the Supreme Court ruled in favor of Alexander Chisholm, executor of the estate of a deceased South Carolina merchant. Chisholm was suing the state of Georgia because the merchant had never been paid for provisions he had supplied during the Revolution. Many regarded this Court decision as an error that violated the intent of the Constitution.*

Antifederalists had long feared a federal court system with the power to overrule a state court.

When the Constitution was being drafted, Federalists had assured worried Antifederalists that section 2 of Article 3, which allows federal courts to hear cases "between a State and citizens of another State," did not mean that the federal courts were authorized to hear suits against a state by citizens of another state or a foreign country. Antifederalists and many other Americans feared a powerful federal court system because they worried that it would become like the British courts of this period, which were accountable only to the monarch. Furthermore, Chisholm v. Georgia prompted a series of suits against state governments by creditors and suppliers who had made loans during the war.

In addition, state legislators and Congress feared that the shaky economies of the new states, as well as the country as a whole, would be destroyed, especially if loyalists who had fled to other countries sought reimbursement for land and property that had been seized. The day after the Supreme Court announced its decision, a resolution proposing the Eleventh Amendment, which overturned the decision in Chisholm v. Georgia, *was introduced in the U.S. Senate.*

Amendment XII
[Adopted 1804]

The electors shall meet in their respective States, and vote by ballot for President and Vice-President, one of whom, at least, shall not be an inhabitant of the same State with themselves; they shall name in their ballots the person voted for as President, and in distinct ballots the person voted for as Vice-President, and they shall make distinct lists of all persons voted for as President, and of all persons voted for as Vice-President, and of the number of votes for each, which lists they shall sign and certify, and transmit sealed to the seat of government of the United States, directed to the President of the Senate;—the President of the Senate shall, in the presence of the Senate and House of Representatives, open all the certificates and the votes shall then be counted;—the person having the greatest number of votes for President shall be the President, if such number be a majority of the whole number of electors appointed; and if no person have such majority, then from the persons having the highest numbers not exceeding three on the list of those voted for as President, the House of Representatives shall choose immediately, by ballot, the President. But in choosing the President, the votes shall be taken by States, the representation from each State having one vote; a quorum for this purpose shall consist of a member or members from two-thirds of the States, and a majority of all the States shall be necessary to a choice. And if the House of Representatives shall not choose a President whenever the right of choice shall devolve upon them, before the fourth day of March next following, then the Vice-President shall act as President, as in the case of the death or other constitutional disability of the President.

The person having the greatest number of votes as Vice-President shall be the Vice-President, if such number be a majority of the whole number of electors appointed; and if no person have a majority, then from the two highest numbers on the list the Senate shall choose the Vice-President; a quorum for the purpose shall consist of two-thirds of the whole number of Senators, and a majority of the whole number shall be necessary to a choice. But no person constitutionally ineligible to the office of President shall be eligible to that of Vice-President of the United States.

◆ ◆ ◆

▶ *The framers of the Constitution disliked political parties and assumed that none would ever form. Under the original system, electors chosen by the states would each vote for two candidates. The candidate who won the most votes would become president, while the person who won the second-highest number of votes would become vice president. Rivalries between Federalists and Antifederalists led to the formation of political parties, however, even before George Washington had left office. Though Washington was elected unanimously in 1789 and 1792, the elections of 1796 and 1800 were procedural disasters because of party maneuvering (see chapters 9 and 10). In 1796, Federalist John Adams was chosen as president, and his great rival, the Antifederalist Thomas Jefferson (whose party was called the Republican Party), became his vice president. In 1800, all the electors cast their two votes as one of two party blocs. Jefferson and his fellow Republican nominee, Aaron Burr, were tied with 73 votes each. The contest went to the House of*

Representatives, which finally elected Jefferson after 36 ballots. The Twelfth Amendment prevents these problems by requiring electors to vote separately for the president and vice president.

Unratified Amendment

Titles of Nobility Amendment (proposed by Congress May 1, 1810)

If any citizen of the United States shall accept, claim, receive or retain any title of nobility or honor or shall, without the consent of Congress, accept and retain any present, pension, office or emolument of any kind whatever, from any emperor, king, prince or foreign power, such person shall cease to be a citizen of the United States, and shall be incapable of holding any office of trust or profit under them or either of them.

◆ ◆ ◆

▶ *This amendment would have extended Article 1, section 9, clause 8 of the Constitution, which prevents the awarding of titles by the United States and the acceptance of such awards from foreign powers without congressional consent. Historians speculate that general nervousness about the power of the emperor Napoleon, who was at that time extending France's empire throughout Europe, may have prompted the proposal. Though it fell one vote short of ratification, Congress and the American people thought the proposal had been ratified, and it was included in many nineteenth-century editions of the Constitution.*

The Civil War and Reconstruction Amendments (Thirteenth, Fourteenth, and Fifteenth Amendments)

▶ *In the four months between the election of Abraham Lincoln and his inauguration, more than 200 proposed constitutional amendments were presented to Congress as part of a desperate attempt to hold the rapidly dissolving Union together. Most of these were efforts to appease the southern states by protecting the right to own slaves or by disfranchising African Americans through constitutional amendment. None were able to win the votes required from Congress to send them to the states. The relatively innocuous Corwin Amendment seemed to be the only hope for preserving the Union by amending the Constitution.*

The northern victors in the Civil War tried to restructure the Constitution just as the war had restructured the nation. Yet they were often divided in their goals. Some wanted to end slavery; others hoped for social and economic equality regardless of race; others hoped that extending the power of the ballot box to former slaves would help create a new political order. The debates over the Thirteenth, Fourteenth, and Fifteenth Amendments were bitter. Few of those who fought for these changes were satisfied with the amendments themselves; fewer still were satisfied with their interpretation. Although the amendments put an end to the legal status of slavery, it took nearly a hundred years after the amendments' passage before most of the descendants of former slaves could begin to experience the economic, social, and political equality the amendments had been intended to provide.

Unratified Amendment
Corwin Amendment (proposed by Congress March 2, 1861)

No amendment shall be made to the Constitution which will authorize or give to Congress the power to abolish or interfere, within any State, with the domestic institutions thereof, including that of persons held to labor or service by the laws of said State.

♦ ♦ ♦

▶ *Following the election of Abraham Lincoln, Congress scrambled to try to prevent the secession of the slaveholding states. House member Thomas Corwin of Ohio proposed the "unamendable" amendment in the hope that by protecting slavery where it existed, Congress would keep the southern states in the Union. Lincoln indicated his support for the proposed amendment in his first inaugural address. Only Ohio and Maryland ratified the Corwin Amendment before it was forgotten.*

Amendment XIII
[Adopted 1865]

Section 1 Neither slavery nor involuntary servitude, except as a punishment for crime whereof the party shall have been duly convicted, shall exist within the United States, or any place subject to their jurisdiction.

Section 2 Congress shall have power to enforce this article by appropriate legislation.

♦ ♦ ♦

▶ *Although President Lincoln had abolished slavery in the Confederacy with the Emancipation Proclamation of 1863, abolitionists wanted to rid the entire country of slavery. The Thirteenth Amendment did this in a clear and straightforward manner. In February 1865 when the proposal was approved by the House, the gallery of the House was newly opened to black Americans who had a chance at last to see their government at work. Passage of the proposal was greeted by wild cheers from the gallery as well as tears on the House floor, where congressional representatives openly embraced one another.*

The problem of ratification remained, however. The Union position was that the Confederate states were part of the country of thirty-six states. Therefore, twenty-seven states were needed to ratify the amendment. When Kentucky and Delaware rejected it, backers realized that without approval

from at least four former Confederate states, the amendment would fail. Lincoln's successor, President Andrew Johnson, made ratification of the Thirteenth Amendment a condition for southern states to rejoin the Union. Under those terms, all the former Confederate states except Mississippi accepted the Thirteenth Amendment, and by the end of 1865 the amendment had become part of the Constitution and slavery had been prohibited in the United States.

Amendment XIV
[Adopted 1868]

Section 1 All persons born or naturalized in the United States, and subject to the jurisdiction thereof, are citizens of the United States and of the State wherein they reside. No State shall make or enforce any law which shall abridge the privileges or immunities of citizens of the United States; nor shall any State deprive any person of life, liberty, or property, without due process of law; nor deny to any person within its jurisdiction the equal protection of the laws.

Section 2 Representatives shall be appointed among the several States according to their respective numbers, counting the whole number of persons in each State, excluding Indians not taxed. But when the right to vote at any election for the choice of Electors for President and Vice-President of the United States, Representatives in Congress, the executive and judicial officers of a State, or the members of the legislature thereof, is denied to any of the male inhabitants of such State, being twenty-one years of age and citizens of the United States, or in any way abridged, except for participation in rebellion, or other crime, the basis of representation therein shall be reduced in the proportion which the number of such male citizens shall bear to the whole number of male citizens twenty-one years of age in such State.

Section 3 No person shall be a Senator or Representative in Congress, or Elector of President and Vice-President, or hold any office, civil or military, under the United States, or under any State, who, having previously taken an oath, as a member of Congress, or as an officer of the United States, or as a member of any State legislature, or as an executive or judicial officer of any State, to support the Constitution of the United States, shall have engaged in insurrection or rebellion against the same, or given aid or comfort to the enemies thereof. Congress may, by a vote of two-thirds of each house, remove such disability.

Section 4 The validity of the public debt of the United States, authorized by law, including debts incurred for payment of pensions and bounties for services in suppressing insurrection or rebellion, shall not be questioned. But neither the United States nor any State shall assume or pay any debt or obligation incurred in aid of insurrection or rebellion against the United States, or any claim for the loss or emancipation of any slave; but all such debts, obligations, and claims shall be held illegal and void.

Section 5 The Congress shall have power to enforce, by appropriate legislation, the provisions of this article.

◆ ◆ ◆

▶ *Without Lincoln's leadership in the reconstruction of the nation following the Civil War, it soon became clear that the Thirteenth Amendment needed additional constitutional support. Less than a year after Lincoln's assassination, Andrew Johnson was ready to bring the former Confederate states back into the Union with few changes in their governments or politics. Anxious Republicans drafted the Fourteenth Amendment to prevent that from happening. The most important provisions of this complex amendment made all native-born or naturalized persons American citizens and prohibited states from abridging the "privileges or immunities" of citizens; depriving them of "life, liberty, or property, without due process of law"; and denying them "equal protection of the laws." In essence, it made all ex-slaves citizens and protected the rights of all citizens against violation by their own state governments.*

As occurred in the case of the Thirteenth Amendment, former Confederate states were forced to ratify the amendment as a condition of representation in the House and the Senate. The intentions of the Fourteenth Amendment, and how those intentions should be enforced, have been the most debated point of constitutional history. The terms due process and equal protection have been especially troublesome. Was the amendment designed to outlaw racial segregation? Or was the goal simply to prevent the leaders of the rebellious South from gaining political power?

The framers of the Fourteenth Amendment hoped Article 2 would produce black voters who would increase the power of the Republican Party. The federal government, however, never used its power to punish states for denying blacks their right to vote. Although the Fourteenth Amendment had an immediate impact in giving black Americans citizenship, it did nothing to protect blacks from the vengeance of whites once Reconstruction ended. In the late nineteenth and early twentieth centuries, section 1 of the Fourteenth Amendment was often used to protect business interests and strike down laws protecting workers on the grounds that the rights of "persons," that is, corporations, were protected by "due process." More recently, the Fourteenth Amendment has been used to justify school desegregation and affirmative action programs, as well as to dismantle such programs.

Amendment XV
[Adopted 1870]

Section 1 The right of citizens of the United States to vote shall not be denied or abridged by the United States or by any State on account of race, color, or previous condition of servitude.

Section 2 The Congress shall have power to enforce this article by appropriate legislation.

◆ ◆ ◆

▶ *The Fifteenth Amendment was the last major piece of Reconstruction legislation. While earlier Reconstruction acts had already required black suffrage in the South, the Fifteenth Amendment extended black voting rights to the entire nation. Some Republicans felt morally obligated to do away with the double standard between North and South since many northern states had stubbornly refused to enfranchise blacks. Others believed that the freedman's ballot required the extra protection of a constitutional amendment to shield it from white counterattack. But partisan advantage also played an important role in the amendment's passage, since Republicans hoped that by giving the ballot to northern blacks, they could lessen their political vulnerability.*

Many women's rights advocates had fought for the amendment. They had felt betrayed by the inclusion of the word "male" in section 2 of the Fourteenth Amendment and were further angered when the proposed Fifteenth Amendment failed to prohibit denial of the right to vote on the grounds of sex as well as "race, color, or previous condition of servitude." In this amendment, for the first time, the federal government claimed the power to regulate the franchise, or vote. It was also the first time the Constitution placed limits on the power of the states to regulate access to the franchise. Although ratified in 1870, the amendment was not enforced until the twentieth century.

The Progressive Amendments (Sixteenth–Nineteenth Amendments)

▶ *No amendments were added to the Constitution between the Civil War and the Progressive Era. America was changing, however, in fundamental ways. The rapid industrialization of the United States after the Civil War led to many social and economic problems. Hundreds of amendments were proposed, but none received enough support in Congress to be sent to the states. Some scholars believe that regional differences and rivalries were so strong during this period that it was almost impossible to gain a consensus on a constitutional amendment. During the Progressive Era, however, the Constitution was amended four times in seven years.*

Amendment XVI

[Adopted 1913]

The Congress shall have power to lay and collect taxes on incomes, from whatever source derived, without apportionment among the several States, and without regard to any census or enumeration.

♦ ♦ ♦

▶ *Until passage of the Sixteenth Amendment, most of the money used to run the federal government came from customs duties and taxes on specific items, such as liquor. During the Civil War, the federal government taxed incomes as an emergency measure. Pressure to enact an income tax came from those who were concerned about the growing gap between rich and poor in the United States. The Populist Party began campaigning for a graduated income tax in 1892, and support continued to grow. By 1909, thirty-three proposed income tax amendments had been presented in Congress, but lobbying by corporate and other special interests had defeated them all. In June 1909, the growing pressure for an income tax, which had been endorsed by Presidents Roosevelt and Taft, finally pushed an amendment through the Senate. The required thirty-six states had ratified the amendment by February 1913.*

Amendment XVII

[Adopted 1913]

Section 1 The Senate of the United States shall be composed of two Senators from each State, elected by the people thereof, for six years; and each Senator shall have one vote. The electors in each State shall have the qualifications requisite for electors of [voters for] the most numerous branch of the State legislatures.

Section 2 When vacancies happen in the representation of any State in the Senate, the executive authority of such State shall issue writs of election to fill such vacancies: Provided, that the Legislature of any State may empower the executive thereof to make temporary appointments until the people fill the vacancies by election as the Legislature may direct.

Section 3 This amendment shall not be so construed as to affect the election or term of any Senator chosen before it becomes valid as part of the Constitution.

♦ ♦ ♦

▶ *The framers of the Constitution saw the members of the House as the representatives of the people and the members of the Senate as the representatives of the states. Originally senators were to be chosen by the state legislators. According to reform advocates, however, the growth of private industry and transportation conglomerates during the Gilded Age had created a network of corruption in which wealth and power were exchanged for influence and votes in the Senate. Senator Nelson Aldrich, who represented Rhode Island in the late nineteenth and early twentieth centuries, for example, was known as "the senator from Standard Oil" because of his open support of special business interests.*

Efforts to amend the Constitution to allow direct election of senators had begun in 1826, but since any proposal had to be approved by the Senate, reform seemed impossible. Progressives tried to gain influence in the Senate by instituting party caucuses and primary elections, which gave citizens the chance to express their choice of a senator who could then be officially elected by the state legislature. By 1910, fourteen of the country's thirty senators received popular votes through a state primary before the state legislature made its selection. Despairing of getting a proposal through the Senate, supporters of a direct election amendment had begun in 1893 to seek a convention of representatives from two-thirds of the states to propose an amendment that could then be ratified. By 1905, thirty-one of forty-five states had endorsed such an amendment. Finally, in 1911, despite extraordinary opposition, a proposed amendment passed the Senate; by 1913, it had been ratified.

Amendment XVIII

[Adopted 1919; repealed 1933 by Amendment XXI]

Section 1 After one year from the ratification of this article the manufacture, sale, or transportation of intoxicating liquors within, the importation thereof into, or the exportation thereof from the United States and all territory subject to the jurisdiction thereof, for beverage purposes, is hereby prohibited.

Section 2 The Congress and the several States shall have concurrent power to enforce this article by appropriate legislation.

Section 3 This article shall be inoperative unless it shall have been ratified as an amendment to the Constitution by the legislatures of the several States, as provided by the Constitution, within seven years from the date of the submission thereof to the States by the Congress.

♦ ♦ ♦

▶ *The Prohibition Party, formed in 1869, began calling for a constitutional amendment to outlaw alcoholic beverages in 1872. A prohibition amendment was first proposed in the Senate in 1876 and was revived eighteen times before 1913. Between 1913 and 1919, another thirty-nine attempts were made to prohibit liquor in the United States through a constitutional amendment. Prohibition became a key element of the progressive agenda as reformers linked alcohol and drunkenness to numerous social problems, including the corruption of immigrant voters. While opponents of such an amendment argued that it was undemocratic, supporters claimed that their efforts had widespread public support. The admission of twelve "dry" western states to the Union in the early twentieth century and the spirit of sacrifice during World War I laid the groundwork for passage and ratification of the Eighteenth Amendment in 1919. Opponents added a time limit to the amendment in the hope that they could thus block ratification, but this effort failed. (See also Amendment XXI.)*

Amendment XIX
[Adopted 1920]

Section 1 The right of citizens of the United States to vote shall not be denied or abridged by the United States or by any State on account of sex.

Section 2 Congress shall have the power to enforce this article by appropriate legislation.

♦ ♦ ♦

▶ *Advocates of women's rights tried and failed to link woman suffrage to the Fourteenth and Fifteenth Amendments. Nonetheless, the effort for woman suffrage continued. Between 1878 and 1912, at least one and sometimes as many as four proposed amendments were introduced in Congress each year to grant women the right to vote. While over time women won very limited voting rights in some states, at both the state and federal levels opposition to an amendment for woman suffrage remained very strong. President Woodrow Wilson and other officials felt that the federal government should not interfere with the power of the states in this matter. Others worried that granting suffrage to women would encourage ethnic minorities to exercise their own right to vote. And many were concerned that giving women the vote would result in their abandoning traditional gender roles. In 1919, following a protracted and often bitter campaign of protest in which women went on hunger strikes and chained themselves to fences, an amendment was introduced with the backing of President Wilson. It narrowly passed the Senate (after efforts to limit the suffrage to white women failed) and was adopted in 1920 after Tennessee became the thirty-sixth state to ratify it.*

Unratified Amendment
Child Labor Amendment (proposed by Congress June 2, 1924)

Section 1 The Congress shall have power to limit, regulate, and prohibit the labor of persons under eighteen years of age.

Section 2 The power of the several States is unimpaired by this article except that the operation of State laws shall be suspended to the extent necessary to give effect to legislation enacted by Congress.

♦ ♦ ♦

▶ *Throughout the late nineteenth and early twentieth centuries, alarm over the condition of child workers grew. Opponents of child labor argued that children worked in dangerous and unhealthy conditions, that they took jobs from adult workers, that they depressed wages in certain industries, and that states that allowed child labor had an economic advantage over those that did not. Defenders of child labor claimed that children provided needed income in many families, that working at a young age developed character, and that the effort to prohibit the practice constituted an invasion of family privacy.*

In 1916, Congress passed a law that made it illegal to sell goods made by children through interstate commerce. The Supreme Court, however, ruled that the law violated the limits on the power of Congress to regulate interstate commerce. Congress then tried to penalize industries that used child labor by taxing such goods. This measure was also thrown out by the courts. In response, reformers set out to amend the Constitution. The proposed amendment was ratified by twenty-eight states, but by 1925, thirteen states had rejected it. Passage of the Fair Labor Standards Act in 1938, which was upheld by the Supreme Court in 1941, made the amendment irrelevant.

Amendment XX
[Adopted 1933]

Section 1 The terms of the President and Vice-President shall end at noon on the 20th day of January, and the terms of Senators and Representatives at noon on the 3rd day of January, of the years in which such terms would have ended if this article had not been ratified; and the terms of their successors shall then begin.

Section 2 The Congress shall assemble at least once in every year, and such meeting shall begin at noon on the 3rd day of January, unless they shall by law appoint a different day.

Section 3 If, at the time fixed for the beginning of the term of the President, the President-elect shall have died, the Vice-President-elect shall become President. If a President shall not have been chosen before the time fixed for the beginning of his term, or if the President-elect shall have failed to qualify, then the Vice-President-elect shall act as President until a President shall have qualified; and the Congress may by law provide for the case wherein neither a President-elect nor a Vice-President-elect shall have qualified, declaring who shall then act as President, or the manner in which one who is to act shall be selected, and such person shall act accordingly until a President or Vice-President shall have qualified.

Section 4 The Congress may by law provide for the case of the death of any of the persons from whom the House of Representatives may choose a President whenever the right of choice shall have devolved upon them, and for the case of the death of any of the persons from whom the Senate may choose a Vice-President whenever the right of choice shall have devolved upon them.

Section 5 Sections 1 and 2 shall take effect on the 15th day of October following the ratification of this article.

Section 6 This article shall be inoperative unless it shall have been ratified as an amendment to the Constitution by the Legislatures of three-fourths of the several States within seven years from the date of its submission.

◆ ◆ ◆

▶ *Until 1933, presidents took office on March 4. Since elections are held in early November and electoral votes are counted in mid-December, this meant that more than three months passed between the time a new president was elected and when he took office. Moving the inauguration to January shortened the transition period and allowed Congress to begin its term closer to the time of the president's inauguration. Although this seems like a minor change, an amendment was required because the Constitution specifies terms of office. This amendment also deals with questions of succession in the event that a president- or vice president-elect dies before assuming office. Section 3 also clarifies a method for resolving a deadlock in the electoral college.*

Amendment XXI
[Adopted 1933]

Section 1 The eighteenth article of amendment to the Constitution of the United States is hereby repealed.

Section 2 The transportation or importation into any State, Territory, or Possession of the United States for delivery or use therein of intoxicating liquors, in violation of the laws thereof, is hereby prohibited.

Section 3 This article shall be inoperative unless it shall have been ratified as an amendment to the Constitution by conventions in the several States, as provided in the Constitution, within seven years from the date of the submission thereof to the States by the Congress.

◆ ◆ ◆

▶ *Widespread violation of the Volstead Act, the law enacted to enforce prohibition, made the United States a nation of lawbreakers. Prohibition caused more problems than it solved by encouraging crime, bribery, and corruption. Further, a coalition of liquor and beer manufacturers, personal liberty advocates, and constitutional scholars joined forces to challenge the amendment. By 1929, thirty proposed repeal amendments had been introduced in Congress, and the Democratic Party made repeal part of its platform in the 1932 presidential campaign. The Twenty-first Amendment was proposed in February 1933 and ratified less than a year later. The failure of the effort to enforce prohibition through a constitutional amendment has often been cited by opponents to subsequent efforts to shape public virtue and private morality.*

Amendment XXII
[Adopted 1951]

Section 1 No person shall be elected to the office of the President more than twice, and no person who has held the office of President, or acted as President, for more than two years of a term to which some other person was elected President shall be elected to the office of President more than once. But this article shall not apply to any person holding the office of President when this Article was proposed by the Congress, and shall not prevent any person who may be holding the office of President, or acting as President, during the term within which this Article becomes operative from holding the office of President or acting as President during the remainder of such term.

Section 2 This article shall be inoperative unless it shall have been ratified as an amendment to the Constitution by the legislatures of three-fourths of the several States within seven years from the date of its submission to the States by the Congress.

◆ ◆ ◆

▶ *George Washington's refusal to seek a third term of office set a precedent that stood until 1912, when former president Theodore Roosevelt sought, without success, another term as an independent candidate. Democrat Franklin Roosevelt was the only president to seek and win a fourth term, though he did so amid great controversy. Roosevelt died in April 1945, a few months after the beginning of his fourth term. In 1946, Republicans won control of the House and the Senate, and early in 1947 a proposal for an amendment to limit future presidents to two four-year terms was offered to the states for ratification. Democratic critics of the Twenty-second Amendment charged that it was a partisan posthumous jab at Roosevelt.*

Since the Twenty-second Amendment was adopted, however, the only presidents who might have been able to seek a third term, had it not existed, were Republicans Dwight Eisenhower, Ronald Reagan, and George W. Bush, and Democrat Bill Clinton. Since 1826, Congress has entertained 160 proposed amendments to limit the president to one six-year term. Such amendments have been backed by fifteen presidents, including Gerald Ford and Jimmy Carter.

Amendment XXIII

[Adopted 1961]

Section 1 The District constituting the seat of Government of the United States shall appoint in such manner as the Congress may direct: A number of electors of President and Vice-President equal to the whole number of Senators and Representatives in Congress to which the District would be entitled if it were a State, but in no event more than the least populous State; they shall be in addition to those appointed by the States, but they shall be considered for the purposes of the election of President and Vice-President, to be electors appointed by a State; and they shall meet in the District and perform such duties as provided by the twelfth article of amendment.

Section 2 The Congress shall have the power to enforce this article by appropriate legislation.

♦ ♦ ♦

▶ *When Washington, D.C., was established as a federal district, no one expected that a significant number of people would make it their permanent and primary residence. A proposal to allow citizens of the district to vote in presidential elections was approved by Congress in June 1960 and was ratified on March 29, 1961.*

Amendment XXIV

[Adopted 1964]

Section 1 The right of citizens of the United States to vote in any primary or other election for President or Vice-President, for electors for President or Vice-President, or for Senator or Representative in Congress, shall not be denied or abridged by the United States or any State by reason of failure to pay any poll tax or other tax.

Section 2 The Congress shall have the power to enforce this article by appropriate legislation.

♦ ♦ ♦

▶ *In the colonial and Revolutionary eras, financial independence was seen as necessary to political independence, and the poll tax was used as a requirement for voting. By the twentieth century, however, the poll tax was used mostly to bar poor people, especially southern blacks, from voting. While conservatives complained that the amendment interfered with states' rights, liberals thought that the amendment did not go far enough because it barred the poll tax only in national elections and not in state or local elections. The amendment was ratified in 1964,*

however, and two years later, the Supreme Court ruled that poll taxes in state and local elections also violated the equal protection clause of the Fourteenth Amendment.

Amendment XXV

[Adopted 1967]

Section 1 In case of the removal of the President from office or of his death or resignation, the Vice-President shall become President.

Section 2 Whenever there is a vacancy in the office of the Vice-President, the President shall nominate a Vice-President who shall take office upon confirmation by a majority vote of both Houses of Congress.

Section 3 Whenever the President transmits to the President pro tempore of the Senate and the Speaker of the House of Representatives his written declaration that he is unable to discharge the powers and duties of his office, and until he transmits to them a written declaration to the contrary, such powers and duties shall be discharged by the Vice-President as Acting President.

Section 4 Whenever the Vice-President and a majority of either the principal officers of the executive departments or of such other body as Congress may by law provide, transmit to the President pro tempore of the Senate and the Speaker of the House of Representatives their written declaration that the President is unable to discharge the powers and duties of his office, the Vice-President shall immediately assume the powers and duties of the office as Acting President.

Thereafter, when the President transmits to the President pro tempore of the Senate and the Speaker of the House of Representatives his written declaration that no inability exists, he shall resume the powers and duties of his office unless the Vice-President and a majority of either the principal officers of the executive department[s] or of such other body as Congress may by law provide, transmit within four days to the President pro tempore of the Senate and the Speaker of the House of Representatives their written declaration that the President is unable to discharge the powers and duties of his office. Thereupon Congress shall decide the issue, assembling within forty-eight hours for that purpose if not in session. If the Congress, within twenty-one days after receipt of the latter written declaration, or, if Congress is not in session, within twenty-one days after Congress is required to assemble, determines by two-thirds vote of both Houses that the President is unable to discharge the powers and duties of his office, the Vice-President shall continue to discharge the same as Acting President; otherwise, the President shall resume the powers and duties of his office.

♦ ♦ ♦

▶ *The framers of the Constitution established the office of vice president because someone was needed to preside over the Senate. The first president to die in office was William Henry Harrison, in 1841. Vice President John Tyler had himself sworn in as president, setting a precedent that was followed when seven later presidents died in office. The assassination of President James A. Garfield in 1881 posed a new problem, however. After he was shot, the president was incapacitated for two months before he died; he was unable to lead the country, while his vice president, Chester A. Arthur, was unable to assume leadership. Efforts to resolve questions of succession in the event of a presidential disability thus began with the death of Garfield.*

In 1963, the assassination of President John F. Kennedy galvanized Congress to action. Vice President Lyndon Johnson was a chain smoker with a history of heart trouble. According to the 1947 Presidential Succession Act, the two men who stood in line to succeed him were the seventy-two-year-old Speaker of the House and the eighty-six-year-old president of the Senate. There were serious concerns that any of these men might become incapacitated while serving as chief executive. The first time the Twenty-fifth Amendment was used, however, was not in the case of presidential death or illness, but during the Watergate crisis. When Vice President Spiro T. Agnew was forced to resign following allegations of bribery and tax violations, President Richard M. Nixon appointed House Minority Leader Gerald R. Ford vice president. Ford became president following Nixon's resignation eight months later and named Nelson A. Rockefeller as his vice president. Thus, for more than two years, the two highest offices in the country were held by people who had not been elected to them.

Amendment XXVI
[Adopted 1971]

Section 1 The right of citizens of the United States, who are eighteen years of age or older, to vote shall not be denied or abridged by the United States or by any State on account of age.

Section 2 The Congress shall have power to enforce this article by appropriate legislation.

◆ ◆ ◆

▶ *Efforts to lower the voting age from twenty-one to eighteen began during World War II. Recognizing that those who were old enough to fight a war should have some say in the government policies that involved them in the war, Presidents Eisenhower, Johnson, and Nixon endorsed the idea. In 1970, the combined pressure of the antiwar movement and the demographic pressure*

of the baby boom generation led to a Voting Rights Act lowering the voting age in federal, state, and local elections.

In Oregon v. Mitchell (1970), the state of Oregon challenged the right of Congress to determine the age at which people could vote in state or local elections. The Supreme Court agreed with Oregon. Since the Voting Rights Act was ruled unconstitutional, the Constitution had to be amended to allow passage of a law that would lower the voting age. The amendment was ratified in a little more than three months, making it the most rapidly ratified amendment in U.S. history.

Unratified Amendment
Equal Rights Amendment (proposed by Congress March 22, 1972; seven-year deadline for ratification extended to June 30, 1982)

Section 1 Equality of rights under the law shall not be denied or abridged by the United States or by any State on account of sex.

Section 2 The Congress shall have the power to enforce, by appropriate legislation, the provisions of this article.

Section 3 This amendment shall take effect two years after the date of ratification.

◆ ◆ ◆

▶ *In 1923, soon after women had won the right to vote, Alice Paul, a leading activist in the woman suffrage movement, proposed an amendment requiring equal treatment of men and women. Opponents of the proposal argued that such an amendment would invalidate laws that protected women and would make women subject to the military draft. After the 1964 Civil Rights Act was adopted, protective workplace legislation was removed anyway.*

The renewal of the women's movement, as a byproduct of the civil rights and antiwar movements, led to a revival of the Equal Rights Amendment (ERA) in Congress. Disagreements over language held up congressional passage of the proposed amendment, but on March 22, 1972, the Senate approved the ERA by a vote of 84 to 8, and it was sent to the states. Six states ratified the amendment within two days, and by the middle of 1973 the amendment seemed well on its way to adoption, with thirty of the needed thirty-eight states having ratified it. In the mid-1970s, however, a powerful "Stop ERA" campaign developed. The campaign portrayed the ERA as a threat to "family values" and traditional relationships between men and women. Although thirty-five states ultimately ratified the ERA, five of those state legislatures voted to rescind ratification, and the amendment was never adopted.

Unratified Amendment

D.C. Statehood Amendment (proposed by Congress August 22, 1978)

Section 1 For purposes of representation in the Congress, election of the President and Vice-President, and article V of this Constitution, the District constituting the seat of government of the United States shall be treated as though it were a State.

Section 2 The exercise of the rights and powers conferred under this article shall be by the people of the District constituting the seat of government, and as shall be provided by Congress.

Section 3 The twenty-third article of amendment to the Constitution of the United States is hereby repealed.

Section 4 This article shall be inoperative, unless it shall have been ratified as an amendment to the Constitution by the legislatures of three-fourths of the several states within seven years from the date of its submission.

◆ ◆ ◆

▶ *The 1961 ratification of the Twenty-third Amendment, giving residents of the District of Columbia the right to vote for a president and vice president, inspired an effort to give residents of the district full voting rights. In 1966, President Lyndon Johnson appointed a mayor and city council; in 1971, D.C. residents were allowed to name a nonvoting delegate to the House; and in 1981, residents were allowed to elect the mayor and city council. Congress retained the right to overrule laws that might affect commuters, the height of federal buildings, and selection of judges and prosecutors. The district's nonvoting delegate to Congress, Walter Fauntroy, lobbied fiercely for a congressional amendment granting statehood to the district. In 1978, a proposed amendment was approved and sent to the states. A number of states quickly ratified the amendment, but, like the ERA, the D.C. Statehood Amendment ran into trouble.*

Opponents argued that section 2 created a separate category of "nominal" statehood. They argued that the federal district should be eliminated and that the territory should be reabsorbed into the state of Maryland. Although these theoretical arguments were strong, some scholars believe that racist attitudes toward the predominantly black population of the city were also a factor leading to the defeat of the amendment.

Amendment XXVII

[Adopted 1992]

No law, varying the compensation for the services of the Senators and Representatives, shall take effect, until an election of Representatives shall have intervened.

◆ ◆ ◆

▶ *While the Twenty-sixth Amendment was the most rapidly ratified amendment in U.S. history, the Twenty-seventh Amendment had the longest journey to ratification. First proposed by James Madison in 1789 as part of the package that included the Bill of Rights, this amendment had been ratified by only six states by 1791. In 1873, however, it was ratified by Ohio to protest a massive retroactive salary increase by the federal government. Unlike later proposed amendments, this one came with no time limit on ratification.*

In the early 1980s, Gregory D. Watson, a University of Texas economics major, discovered the "lost" amendment and began a single-handed campaign to get state legislators to introduce it for ratification. In 1983, it was accepted by Maine. In 1984, it passed the Colorado legislature. Ratifications trickled in slowly until May 1992, when Michigan and New Jersey became the thirty-eighth and thirty-ninth states, respectively, to ratify. This amendment prevents members of Congress from raising their own salaries without giving voters a chance to vote them out of office before they can benefit from the raises.

THE CONSTITUTION OF THE CONFEDERATE STATES OF AMERICA

▶ *In framing the Constitution of the Confederate States, the authors adopted, with numerous small but significant changes and additions, the language of the Constitution of the United States, and followed the same order of arrangement of articles and sections. The revisions that they made to the original Constitution are shown here. The parts stricken out are enclosed in brackets, and the new matter added in framing the Confederate Constitution is printed in italics.*

Adopted March 11, 1861

WE, the People of the [United States] *Confederated States, each State acting in its sovereign and independent character,* in order to form a [more perfect

Union] *permanent Federal government*, establish Justice, insure domestic Tranquillity [provide for the common defense, promote the general Welfare], and secure the Blessings of Liberty to ourselves and our Posterity, *invoking the favor and guidance of Almighty God*, do ordain and establish this Constitution for the [United] *Confederate* States of America.

Article I

Section I All legislative Powers herein [granted] *delegated*, shall be vested in a Congress of the [United] *Confederate* States, which shall consist of a Senate and House of Representatives.

Section II The House of Representatives shall be composed of Members chosen every second Year by the People of the several States, and the Electors in each State shall *be citizens of the Confederate States, and* have the Qualifications requisite for Electors of the most numerous Branch of the State Legislature; *but no person of foreign birth, and not a citizen of the Confederate States, shall be allowed to vote for any officer, civil or political, State or federal.*

No Person shall be a Representative who shall not have attained to the Age of twenty-five Years, and [been seven Years a Citizen of the United] *be a citizen of the Confederate States*, and who shall not, when elected, be an Inhabitant of that State in which he shall be chosen.

Representatives and direct Taxes shall be apportioned among the several States which may be included within this [Union] *Confederacy*, according to their respective Numbers, which shall be determined by adding to the whole Number of free Persons, including those bound to Service for a Term of Years, and excluding Indians not taxed, three-fifths of all [other Persons] *slaves*. The actual Enumeration shall be made within three Years after the first Meeting of the Congress of the [United] *Confederate States*, and within every subsequent Term of ten Years, in such Manner as they shall by Law direct. The Number of Representatives shall not exceed one for every [thirty] *fifty* Thousand, but each State shall have at Least one Representative; and until such enumeration shall be made, the State of [New Hampshire shall be entitled to choose three, Massachusetts eight, Rhode Island and Providence Plantations one, Connecticut five, New York six, New Jersey four, Pennsylvania eight, Delaware one, Maryland six, Virginia ten, North Carolina five, South Carolina five, and Georgia three] *South Carolina shall be entitled to choose six, the State of Georgia ten, the State of Alabama nine, the State of Florida two, the State of Mississippi seven, the State of Louisiana six, and the State of Texas six.*

When vacancies happen in the Representation from any State, the Executive Authority thereof shall issue Writs of Election to fill such Vacancies.

The House of Representatives shall choose their Speaker and other Officers; and shall have the sole Power of Impeachment; *except that any judicial or other federal officer resident and acting solely within the limits of any State, may be impeached by a vote of two-thirds of both branches of the Legislature thereof.*

Section III The Senate of the [United] *Confederate* States shall be composed of two Senators from each State, chosen by the Legislature thereof, for six Years, *at the regular session next immediately preceding the commencement of the term of service*; and each Senator shall have one Vote.

Immediately after they shall be assembled in Consequence of the first Election, they shall be divided as equally as may be into three Classes. The Seats of the Senators of the first Class shall be vacated at the Expiration of the second Year, of the second Class at the Expiration of the fourth Year, and of the third Class at the Expiration of the sixth Year, so that one-third may be chosen every second Year; and if Vacancies happen by Resignation, or otherwise, during the Recess of the Legislature of any State, the Executive thereof may make temporary Appointments until the next Meeting of the Legislature, which shall then fill such Vacancies.

No Person shall be a Senator who shall not have attained to the Age of thirty Years, and [been nine Years a Citizen of the United] *be a citizen of the Confederate* States, and who shall not, when elected, be an Inhabitant of that State for which he shall be chosen.

The Vice President of the [United] *Confederate* States shall be President of the Senate, but shall have no Vote, unless they be equally divided.

The Senate shall choose their other Officers, and also a President pro tempore, in the Absence of the Vice President, or when he shall exercise the Office of President of the United States.

The Senate shall have the sole Power to try all Impeachments. When sitting for that Purpose, they shall be on Oath or Affirmation. When the President of the [United] *Confederate* States is tried, the Chief Justice shall preside: And no Person shall be convicted without the Concurrence of two-thirds of the Members present.

Judgment in Cases of Impeachment shall not extend further than to removal from Office, and Disqualification to hold and enjoy any Office of honour, Trust or Profit under the [United] *Confederate* States; but the Party convicted shall nevertheless be liable and subject to Indictment, Trial, Judgment and Punishment, according to Law

Section IV The Times, Places and Manner of holding Elections for Senators and Representatives, shall be prescribed in each State by the Legislature thereof, *subject to the provisions of this Constitution*; but the Congress may at any time by Law make or alter such Regulations, except as to the *times and* places of choosing Senators.

The Congress shall assemble at least once in every Year, and such Meeting shall be on the first Monday in December, unless they shall by Law appoint a different Day.

Section V Each House shall be the Judge of the Elections, Returns and Qualifications of its own Members, and a Majority of each shall constitute a Quorum to do Business; but a smaller Number may adjourn from day to day, and may be authorized to compel the Attendance of absent Members, in such Manner, and under such Penalties as each House may provide.

Each House may determine the Rules of its Proceedings, punish its Members for disorderly Behaviour, and, with the Concurrence of two-thirds *of the whole number* expel a Member.

Each House shall keep a Journal of its Proceedings, and from time to time publish the same, excepting such Parts as may in their Judgment require Secrecy; and the Yeas and Nays of the Members of either House on any question shall, at the Desire of one-fifth of those Present, be entered on the Journal.

Neither House, during the Session of Congress, shall, without the Consent of the other, adjourn for more than three days, nor to any other Place than that in which the two Houses shall be sitting.

Section VI The Senators and Representatives shall receive a Compensation for their Services, to be ascertained by Law, and paid out of the Treasury of the [United] *Confederate* States. They shall in all Cases, except Treason [Felony] and Breach of the Peace, be privileged from Arrest during their Attendance at the Session of their respective Houses, and in going to and returning from the same; and for any Speech or Debate in either House, they shall not be questioned in any other Place.

No Senator or Representative shall, during the Time for which he was elected, be appointed to any civil Office under the Authority of the [United] *Confederate* States, which shall have been created, or the Emoluments whereof shall have been increased during such time; and no Person holding any Office under the [United] *Confederate* States, shall be a Member of either House during his Continuance in Office. *But Congress may, by law, grant to the principal officers in each of the executive departments a seat upon the floor of either House, with the privilege of discussing any measures appertaining to his department.*

Section VII All Bills for raising Revenue shall originate in the House of Representatives; but the Senate may propose or concur with Amendments as on other Bills.

Every Bill which shall have passed [the House of Representatives and the Senate] *both Houses*, shall, before it become a Law, be presented to the President of the [United] *Confederate* States; If he approve he shall sign it, but if not he shall return it, with his Objections to that House in which it shall have originated, who shall enter the Objections at large on their Journal, and proceed to reconsider it. If after such Reconsideration two-thirds of that House shall agree to pass the Bill, it shall be sent, together with the

Objections, to the other House, by which it shall likewise be reconsidered, and if approved by two-thirds of that House, it shall become a Law. But in all *such* Cases the Votes of both Houses shall be determined by Yeas and Nays, and the Names of the Persons voting for and against the Bill shall be entered on the Journal of each House respectively. If any Bill shall not be returned by the President within ten Days (Sundays excepted) after it shall have been presented to him, the Same shall be a law, in like Manner as if he had signed it, unless the Congress by their Adjournment prevent its return, in which Case it shall not be a Law. *The President may approve any appropriation and disapprove any other appropriation in the same bill. In such case he shall, in signing the bill, designate the appropriation disapproved, and shall return a copy of such appropriation, with his objections, to the House in which the bill shall have originated; and the same proceedings shall then be had as in case of other bills disapproved by the President.*

Every Order, Resolution, or Vote to which the Concurrence of [the Senate and House of Representatives] *both Houses* may be necessary (except on a question of Adjournment), shall be presented to the President of the [United] *Confederate* States; and before the Same shall take Effect, shall be approved by him, or being disapproved by him, [shall] *may* be repassed by two-thirds of [the Senate and House of Representatives] *both Houses*, according to the Rules and Limitations prescribed in the Case of a Bill.

Section VIII The Congress shall have Power.

To lay and collect Taxes, Duties, Imposts and *Excises, for revenue necessary* to pay the Debts [and], provide for the common Defense [and general Welfare of the United States; but], *and carry on the government of the Confederate States; but no bounties shall be granted from the treasury, nor shall any duties, or taxes, or importation from foreign nations be laid to promote or foster any branch of industry; and* all Duties, Imposts and Excises shall be uniform throughout the [United] Confederate States;

To borrow Money on the credit of the [United] Confederate States;

To regulate Commerce with foreign Nations, and among the several States, and with the Indian Tribes; *but neither this, nor any other clause contained in this Constitution, shall ever be construed to delegate the power to Congress to appropriate money for any internal improvement intended to facilitate commerce; except for the purpose of furnishing lights, beacons, and buoys, and other aids to navigation upon the coasts, and the improvement of harbors, and the removing of obstructions in river navigation; in all such cases such duties shall be laid on the navigation facilitated thereby, as may be necessary to pay the costs and expenses thereof;*

To establish an uniform Rule of Naturalization, and uniform Laws on the subject of Bankruptcies throughout the [United] *Confederate* States; *but no law of Congress shall discharge any debt contracted before the passage of the same;*

To coin Money, regulate the Value thereof, and of foreign Coin, and fix the Standard of Weights and Measures;

To provide for the Punishment of counterfeiting the Securities and current Coin of the [United] *Confederate* States;

To establish Post Offices and post [Roads] *routes; but the expenses of the Postoffice Department, after the first day of March, in the year of our Lord eighteen hundred and sixty-three, shall be paid out of its own revenues;*

To promote the progress of Science and useful Arts, by securing for limited Times to Authors and Inventors the exclusive Right to their respective Writings and Discoveries;

To constitute Tribunals inferior to the supreme Court;

To define and punish Piracies and Felonies committed on the high Seas, and Offences against the Law of Nations;

To declare War, grant Letters of Marque and Reprisal, and make Rules concerning Captures on Land and Water;

To raise and support Armies, but no Appropriation of Money to that Use shall be for a longer Term than two Years;

To provide and maintain a Navy;

To make Rules for the Government and Regulation of the land and naval Forces;

To provide for calling forth the Militia to execute the Laws of the [Union] *Confederate States,* suppress Insurrections and repel Invasions;

To provide for organizing, arming, and disciplining the Militia and for governing such Part of them as may be employed in the Service of the [United] *Confederate* States, reserving to the States respectively, the Appointment of the Officers, and the Authority of training the Militia according to the Discipline prescribed by Congress;

To exercise exclusive Legislation in all Cases whatsoever, over such District (not exceeding ten Miles square) as may, by Cession of particular States, and the Acceptance of Congress, become the Seat of the Government of the [United] *Confederate* States, and to exercise like Authority over all Places purchased by the Consent of the Legislature of the State in which the Same shall be, for the Erection of Forts, Magazines, Arsenals, Dock Yards, and other needful Buildings;—And

To make all Laws which shall be necessary and proper for carrying into Execution the foregoing Powers, and all other Powers vested by this Constitution in the Government of the [United] *Confederate* States or in any Department or Officer thereof.

Section IX [The Migration or Importation of such Persons as any of the States now existing shall think proper to admit, shall not be prohibited by the Congress prior to the Year one thousand eight hundred and eight, but a Tax or Duty may be imposed on such Importation, not exceeding ten dollars for each Person.] *The importation of negroes of the African race from any foreign country other than the slaveholding States or territories of the United States of America, is hereby forbidden; and Congress is required to pass such laws as shall effectually prevent the same. Congress shall also have power to prohibit the introduction of slaves from any State not a member of, or territory not belonging to, this Confederacy.*

The Privilege of the Writ of Habeas Corpus shall not be suspended, unless when in Cases of Rebellion or Invasion the public Safety may require it. No Bill of Attainder or ex post facto Law, *or law denying or impairing the right of property in negro slaves,* shall be passed.

No Capitation, or other direct, Tax shall be laid, unless in Proportion to the Census or Enumeration herein before directed to be taken.

No Tax or Duty shall be laid on Articles exported from any State, *except by a vote of two-thirds of both Houses.*

No Preference shall be given by any Regulation of Commerce or Revenue to the Ports of one State over those of another; nor shall Vessels bound to, or from, one State, be obliged to enter, clear, or pay Duties in another.

No Money shall be drawn from the Treasury, but in Consequence of Appropriations made by Law; and a regular Statement and Account of the Receipts and Expenditures of all public Money shall be published from time to time.

Congress shall appropriate no money from the Treasury except by a vote of two-thirds of both Houses, taken by yeas and nays, unless it be asked and estimated for by some one of the heads of departments and submitted to Congress by the President; or for the purpose of paying its own expenses and contingencies; or for the payment of claims against the Confederate States, the justice of which shall have been officially declared by a tribunal for the investigation of claims against the Government, which it is hereby made the duty of Congress to establish.

All bills appropriating money shall specify in Federal currency the exact amount of each appropriation and the purposes for which it is made; and Congress shall grant no extra compensation to any public contractor, officer, agent or servant, after such contract shall have been made or such service rendered.

No Title of Nobility shall be granted by the [United] *Confederate States*; and no Person holding any Office of Profit or Trust under them, shall, without the Consent of the Congress, accept of any present, Emolument, Office, or Title, of any kind whatever, from any King, Prince or foreign State.

[*Here the framers of the Confederate Constitution insert the U.S. Bill of Rights.*] Congress shall make no law respecting an establishment of religion, or prohibiting the free exercise thereof; or abridging the freedom of speech, or of the press; or the right of the people peaceably to assemble, and to petition the Government for a redress of grievances.

A well-regulated Militia, being necessary to the security of a free State, the right of the people to keep and bear Arms shall not be infringed.

No Soldier shall, in time of peace, be quartered in any house, without the consent of the Owner, nor in time of war, but in a manner to be prescribed by law.

The right of the people to be secure in their persons, houses, papers, and effects, against unreasonable searches and seizures, shall not be violated, and no Warrants shall issue, but upon probable cause, supported by Oath or affirmation, and particularly describing the place to be searched, and the persons or things to be seized.

No person shall be held to answer for a capital, or otherwise infamous crime, unless on a presentment or indictment of a Grand Jury, except in cases arising in the land or naval forces, or in the Militia, when in actual service in time of War or public danger; nor shall any person be subject for the same offence to be twice put in jeopardy of life or limb; nor shall be compelled in any Criminal Case to be a witness against himself, nor be deprived of life, liberty or property without due process of law; nor shall private property be taken for public use, without just compensation.

In all criminal prosecutions, the accused shall enjoy the right to a speedy and public trial, by an impartial jury of the State and district wherein the crime shall have been committed, which district shall have been previously ascertained by law, and to be informed of the nature and cause of the accusation; to be confronted with the witnesses against him; to have Compulsory process for obtaining Witnesses in his favour, and to have the Assistance of Counsel for his defence.

In Suits at common law, where the value in controversy shall exceed twenty dollars, the right of trial by jury shall be preserved, and no fact tried by a jury shall be otherwise reexamined in any Court of the [United] *Confederate* States, than according to the rules of the common law.

Excessive bail shall not be required, nor excessive fines imposed, nor cruel and unusual punishments inflicted.

Every law or resolution having the force of law, shall relate to but one subject, and that shall be expressed in the title.

Section X No State shall enter into any Treaty, Alliance, or Confederation; grant Letters of Marque and Reprisal; coin Money; [emit Bills of Credit;] make any Thing but gold and silver Coin a Tender in Payment of Debts; pass any Bill of Attainder, or ex post facto Law, or Law impairing the Obligation of Contracts, or grant any Title of Nobility.

No State shall, without the consent of the Congress, lay any Imposts or Duties on Imports or Exports, except what may be absolutely necessary for executing its inspection Laws: and the net Produce of all Duties and Imposts, laid by any State on Imports or Exports, shall be for the Use of the Treasury of the [United] *Confederate* States; and all such Laws shall be subject to the Revision and Control of the Congress.

No State shall, without the Consent of Congress, lay any Duty of Tonnage, *except on seagoing vessels, for the improvement of its rivers and harbors navigated by the said vessels; but such duties shall not conflict with any treaties of the Confederate States with foreign nations; and any surplus of revenue thus derived shall, after making such improvement, be paid into the common treasury; nor shall any State* keep Troops, or Ships of War in time of Peace, enter into any Agreement or Compact with another State, or with a foreign Power, or engage in War, unless actually invaded, or in such imminent Danger as will not admit of Delay. *But when any river divides or flows through two or more States, they may enter into compacts with each other to improve the navigation thereof.*

Article II

Section I [The executive Power shall be vested in a President of the United States of America. He shall hold his Office during the Term of four Years, and, together with the Vice President, chosen for the same Term, be elected, as follows:] *The executive power shall be vested in a President of the Confederate States of America. He and the Vice President shall hold their offices for the term of six years; but the President shall not be reeligible.*

The President and Vice President shall be elected as follows: Each State shall appoint in such Manner as the Legislature thereof may direct, a Number of Electors, equal to the whole Number of Senators and Representatives to which the State may be entitled in the Congress; but no Senator or Representative, or Person holding an Office of Trust or Profit under the [United] *Confederate* States, shall be appointed an Elector.

The Electors shall meet in their respective States, and vote by ballot for President and Vice President, one of whom, at least, shall not be an inhabitant of the same State with themselves; they shall name in their ballots the person voted for as President, and in distinct ballots the person voted for as Vice President, and they shall make distinct lists of all persons voted for as President, and of all persons voted for as Vice President, and of the number of votes for each, which lists they shall sign and certify, and transmit sealed to the seat of the government of the [United] *Confederate* States, directed to the President of the Senate;— The President of the Senate shall, in the presence of the Senate and House of Representatives, open all the certificates and the votes shall then be counted;—The person having the greatest number of votes for President shall be the President, if such number be a majority of the whole number of Electors appointed; and if no person have such majority, then from the persons having the highest numbers not exceeding three on the list of those voted for as President, the House of Representatives shall choose immediately, by ballot, the President. But in choosing the President, the votes shall be taken by States, the representation from each State having one vote; a quorum for this purpose shall consist of a member or members from two-thirds of the States, and a majority of all the States shall be necessary to a choice. And if the House of Representatives shall not choose a President whenever the right of choice shall devolve upon them, before the fourth day of March next following, then the Vice President shall act as President, as in the case of the death or other constitutional disability of the President. The person having the greatest number of votes as Vice President shall be the Vice President, if such number be a majority of the whole number of Electors appointed, and if no person have a majority, then from the two highest numbers on the list the Senate shall choose the Vice President; a quorum for the purpose shall consist of two-thirds of the whole number of Senators, and a majority of the whole number shall be necessary to a choice. But no person constitutionally ineligible to the office of President shall be eligible to that of Vice President of the [United] *Confederate* States.

The Congress may determine the Time of choosing the Electors, and the Day on which they shall give their Votes; which Day shall be the same throughout the [United] *Confederate* States.

No Person except a natural-born Citizen [or a Citizen of the United States] *of the Confederate States, or a citizen thereof,* at the time of the Adoption of this Constitution, *or a citizen thereof born in the United States prior to the 20th of December, 1860,* shall be eligible to the Office of President; neither shall any Person be eligible to that Office who shall not have attained to the Age of thirty-five Years, and been fourteen Years a Resident within the [United States] *limits of the Confederate States, as they may exist at the time of his election.*

In Cases of the Removal of the President from Office, or of his Death, Resignation, or Inability to discharge the Powers and Duties of the said Office, the same shall devolve on the Vice President, and the Congress may by Law provide for the Case of Removal, Death, Resignation, or Inability, both of the President and Vice President, declaring what Officer shall then act as President, and such Officer shall act accordingly, until the Disability be removed, or a President shall be elected.

The President shall, at stated Times, receive for his Services, a Compensation, which shall neither be increased nor diminished during the Period for which he shall have been elected, and he shall not receive within that Period any other Emolument from the [United] *Confederate* States or any of them.

Before he enters on the Execution of his Office, he shall take the following Oath or Affirmation—"I do solemnly swear (or affirm) that I will faithfully execute the Office of President of the [United] *Confederate* States, and will to the best of my Ability, preserve, protect and defend the Constitution [of the United States] *thereof.*"

Section II The President shall be Commander in Chief of the Army and Navy of the [United] *Confederate* States, and of the Militia of the several States, when called into the actual Service of the [United] *Confederate* States; he may require the Opinion, in writing, of the principal Officer in each of the executive Departments, upon any Subject relating to the Duties of their respective Offices, and he shall have Power to grant Reprieves and Pardons for Offenses against the [United] *Confederate* States, except in Cases of Impeachment.

He shall have Power, by and with the Advice and Consent of the Senate, to make Treaties, provided two-thirds of the Senators present concur; and he shall nominate, and by and with the Advice and Consent of the Senate, shall appoint Ambassadors, other public Ministers and Consuls, Judges of the supreme Court, and all other Officers of the [United] *Confederate* States, whose Appointments are not herein otherwise provided for, and which shall be established by Law: but the Congress may by Law vest the Appointment of such inferior Officers, as they think proper, in the President alone, in the Courts of Law, or in the Heads of Departments. *The principal officer in each of the executive departments, and all persons connected with the diplomatic service, may be removed from office at the pleasure of the President. All other civil officers of the executive department may be removed at any time by the President, or other appointing power, when their services are unnecessary, or for dishonesty, incapacity, inefficiency, misconduct, or neglect of duty; and when so removed, the removal shall be reported to the Senate, together with the reasons therefor.*

The President shall have Power to fill [up] all Vacancies that may happen during the Recess of the Senate, by granting Commissions which shall expire at the End of their next Session.

Section III [He] *The President* shall from time to time give to the Congress Information of the State of the [Union] *Confederacy,* and recommend to their Consideration such Measures as he shall judge necessary and expedient; he may, on extraordinary Occasions, convene both Houses, or either of them, and in Case of Disagreement between them, with Respect to the Time of Adjournment, he may adjourn them to such Time as he shall think proper; he shall receive Ambassadors and other public Ministers; he shall take Care that the Laws be faithfully executed, and shall Commission all the officers of the [United] *Confederate* States.

Section IV The President, Vice President and all civil Officers of the [United] *Confederate* States, shall be removed from Office or Impeachment for, and Conviction of, Treason, Bribery, or other high Crimes and Misdemeanors.

Article III

Section I The judicial Power of the [United] *Confederate* States shall be vested in one [supreme] *Superior* Court, and in such inferior Courts as the Congress may from time to time ordain and establish. The Judges, both of the supreme and inferior Courts, shall hold their Offices during good Behavior, and shall, at stated Times, receive for their Services a Compensation, which shall not be diminished during their Continuance in Office.

Section II The judicial Power shall extend to all cases [in Law and Equity, arising under this Constitution], *arising under this Constitution, in law and equity,* the Laws of the [United] *Confederate* States, and Treaties made, or which shall be made, under their Authority;—to all Cases affecting Ambassadors, other public Ministers, and Consuls;—to all Cases of admiralty and maritime Jurisdiction;—to Controversies to which the [United] *Confederate* States shall be a Party;—to Controversies between two or more States;— between a State and Citizens of another State *where the State is plaintiff;—between* Citizens *claiming lands under grants* of different States,—[between Citizens of the same State claiming Lands under Grants of different States,] and between a State, or the Citizens thereof, and foreign States, Citizens or Subjects; *but no State shall be sued by a citizen or subject of any foreign State.*

In all Cases affecting Ambassadors, other public Ministers and Consuls, and those in which a State shall be Party, the supreme Court shall have original Jurisdiction. In all the other Cases before mentioned, the supreme Court shall have appellate Jurisdiction, both as to Law and Fact, with such Exceptions, and under such Regulations as the Congress shall make.

The Trial of all Crimes, except in Cases of Impeachment, shall be by Jury; and such Trial shall be held in the State where the said Crime[s] shall have been committed; but when not committed within any State, the Trial shall be at such Place or Places as the Congress may by Law have directed.

Section III Treason against the [United] *Confederate* States shall consist only in levying War against them, or in adhering to their Enemies, giving them Aid and Comfort. No Person shall be convicted of Treason unless on the Testimony of two Witnesses to the same overt Act, or on Confession in open Court.

The Congress shall have Power to declare the Punishment of Treason, but no Attainder of Treason shall work Corruption of Blood, or Forfeiture except during the Life of the Person attainted.

Article IV

Section I Full Faith and Credit shall be given in each State to the public Acts, Records, and judicial Proceedings of every other State. And the Congress may by general Laws prescribe the Manner in which such Acts, Records and Proceedings shall be proved, and the Effect thereof.

Section II The Citizens of each State shall be entitled to all Privileges and Immunities of Citizens in the several States, *and shall have the right of transit and sojourn in any State of this Confederacy, with their slaves and other property; and the right of property in such slaves shall not be impaired.*

A Person charged in any State with Treason, Felony, or other Crime, who shall flee from Justice, and be found in another State, shall on Demand of the executive Authority of the State from which he fled, be delivered up, to be removed to the State having Jurisdiction of the Crime.

No *slave* or Person held to Service or Labor in [one State] *any State or Territory of the Confederate States* under the Laws thereof, escaping *or unlawfully carried* into another, shall, in Consequence of any Law or Regulation therein, be discharged from such Service or Labor, but shall be delivered up on Claim of the Party to whom such *slave belongs, or to whom such* Service or Labor may be due.

Section III [New States may be admitted by the Congress into this Union;] *Other States may be admitted into this Confederacy by a vote of two-thirds of the whole House of Representatives and two-thirds of the Senate, the Senate voting by States;* but no new State shall be formed or erected within the Jurisdiction of any other State; nor any State be formed by the Junction of two or more States, or Parts of States, without the Consent of the Legislatures of the States concerned as well as of the Congress.

The Congress shall have Power to dispose of and make all needful Rules and Regulations [respecting the Territory or other Property belonging to the United States; and nothing in this Constitution shall be so construed as to Prejudice any Claims of the United States, or of any particular State] *concerning the property of the Confederate States, including the lands thereof.*

The Confederate States may acquire new territory, and Congress shall have power to legislate and provide governments for the inhabitants of all territory belonging to the Confederate States lying without the limits of the several States, and may permit them, at such times and in such manner as it may by law provide, to form States to be admitted into the Confederacy. In all such territory the institution of negro slavery as it now exists in the Confederate States shall be recognized and protected by Congress and by the territorial government, and the inhabitants of the several Confederate States and territories shall have the right to take to such territory any slaves lawfully held by them in any of the States or Territories of the Confederate States.

Section IV The [United] *Confederate* States shall guarantee to every State [in this Union] *that now is, or hereafter may become, a member of this Confederacy,* a Republican Form of Government, and shall protect each of them against Invasion; and on Application of the Legislature, or of the Executive (when the Legislature [cannot be convened] *is not in session*) against domestic Violence.

Article V

[The Congress, whenever two-thirds of both Houses shall deem it necessary, shall propose Amendments to this Constitution, or on the Application of the Legislatures of two-thirds of the several States, shall call a Convention for proposing Amendments, which, in either Case, shall be valid to all Intents and Purposes, as Part of this Constitution, when ratified by the Legislatures of three-fourths of the several States, or by Conventions in three-fourths thereof, as the one or the other Mode of Ratification may be proposed by the Congress; Provided that no Amendment which may be made prior to the Year one thousand eight hundred and eight shall in any Manner affect the first and fourth Clauses in the Ninth Section of the first Article; and that no State, without its Consent, shall be deprived of its equal Suffrage in the Senate.] *Upon the demand of any three States, legally assembled in their several Conventions, the Congress shall summon a Convention of all the States, to take into consideration such amendments to the Constitution as the said States shall concur in suggesting at the time when the said demand is made; and should any of the proposed amendments to the Constitution be agreed on by the said Convention—voting by States—and the same be ratified by the Legislatures of two-thirds of the several States, or by Conventions in two-thirds thereof—as the one or the other mode of ratification may be proposed by the general Convention—they shall henceforward form a part of this Constitution. But no State shall, without its consent, be deprived of its equal representation in the Senate.*

Article VI

The Government established by this Constitution is the successor of the Provisional Government of the Confederate States of America, and all laws passed by the latter shall continue in force until the same shall be repealed or modified; and all the officers appointed by the same shall remain in office until their successors are appointed and qualified or the offices abolished.

All Debts contracted and Engagements entered into, before the Adoption of this Constitution, shall be as valid against the [United] *Confederate* States under this Constitution, as under the [Confederation] *Provisional Government.*

This Constitution and the Laws of the [United] *Confederate* States [which shall be] made in Pursuance thereof; and all Treaties made, or which shall be made, under the authority of the [United] *Confederate* States,

shall be the supreme Law of the Land; and the Judges in every State shall be bound thereby, any Thing in the Constitution or Laws of any State to the Contrary notwithstanding.

The Senators and Representatives before mentioned, and the Members of the several State Legislatures, and all executive and judicial Officers, both of the [United] *Confederate* States and of the several States, shall be bound by Oath or Affirmation, to support this Constitution; but no religious Test shall ever be required as a Qualification to any Office or public Trust under the [United] *Confederate* States.

The enumeration in the Constitution, of certain rights, shall not be construed to deny or disparage others retained by the people *of the several States.*

The powers not delegated to the [United] *Confederate* States by the Constitution, nor prohibited by it to the States, are reserved to the States respectively, or to the people.

Article VII

The Ratification of the Conventions of [nine] *five* States shall be sufficient for the Establishment of this Constitution between the States so ratifying the same.

When five States shall have ratified this Constitution, in the manner before specified, the Congress under the Provisional Constitution shall prescribe the time for holding the election of President and Vice President; and for the meeting of the electoral college; and for counting the votes and inaugurating the President. They shall also prescribe the time for holding the first election of members of Congress under this Constitution, and the time for assembling the same. Until the assembling of such Congress, the Congress under the Provisional Constitution shall continue to exercise the legislative powers granted them, not extending beyond the time limited by the Constitution of the Provisional Government.

[Done in Convention by the Unanimous Consent of the States present, the Seventeenth Day of September in the Year of our Lord one thousand seven hundred and eighty-seven and of the Independence of the United States of America the Twelfth.] *Adopted unanimously March 11, 1861.*

U.S. Politics and Government

PRESIDENTIAL ELECTIONS

Year	Candidates	Parties	Popular Vote	Percentage of Popular Vote	Electoral Vote	Percentage of Voter Participation
1789	GEORGE WASHINGTON (Va.)*				69	
	John Adams				34	
	Others				35	
1792	GEORGE WASHINGTON (Va.)				132	
	John Adams				77	
	George Clinton				50	
	Others				5	
1796	JOHN ADAMS (Mass.)	Federalist			71	
	Thomas Jefferson	Democratic-Republican			68	
	Thomas Pinckney	Federalist			59	
	Aaron Burr	Dem.-Rep.			30	
	Others				48	
1800	THOMAS JEFFERSON (Va.)	Dem.-Rep.			73	
	Aaron Burr	Dem.-Rep.			73	
	John Adams	Federalist			65	
	C. C. Pinckney	Federalist			64	
	John Jay	Federalist			1	
1804	THOMAS JEFFERSON (Va.)	Dem.-Rep.			162	
	C. C. Pinckney	Federalist			14	
1808	JAMES MADISON (Va.)	Dem.-Rep.			122	
	C. C. Pinckney	Federalist			47	
	George Clinton	Dem.-Rep.			6	
1812	JAMES MADISON (Va.)	Dem.-Rep.			128	
	De Witt Clinton	Federalist			89	
1816	JAMES MONROE (Va.)	Dem.-Rep.			183	
	Rufus King	Federalist			34	
1820	JAMES MONROE (Va.)	Dem.-Rep.			231	
	John Quincy Adams	Dem.-Rep.			1	
1824	JOHN Q. ADAMS (Mass.)	Dem.-Rep.	108,740	30.5	84	26.9
	Andrew Jackson	Dem.-Rep.	153,544	43.1	99	
	William H. Crawford	Dem.-Rep.	46,618	13.1	41	
	Henry Clay	Dem.-Rep.	47,136	13.2	37	
1828	ANDREW JACKSON (Tenn.)	Democratic	647,286	56.0	178	57.6
	John Quincy Adams	National Republican	508,064	44.0	83	
1832	ANDREW JACKSON (Tenn.)	Democratic	687,502	55.0	219	55.4
	Henry Clay	National Republican	530,189	42.4	49	
	John Floyd	Independent			11	
	William Wirt	Anti-Mason	33,108	2.6	7	

*State of residence when elected president.

Year	Candidates	Parties	Popular Vote	Percentage of Popular Vote	Electoral Vote	Percentage of Voter Participation
1836	**MARTIN VAN BUREN (N.Y.)**	Democratic	765,483	50.9	170	57.8
	W. H. Harrison	Whig			73	
	Hugh L. White	Whig	739,795	49.1	26	
	Daniel Webster	Whig			14	
	W. P. Mangum	Independent			11	
1840	**WILLIAM H. HARRISON (Ohio)**	Whig	1,274,624	53.1	234	78.0
	Martin Van Buren	Democratic	1,127,781	46.9	60	
	J. G. Birney	Liberty	7,069	—		
1844	**JAMES K. POLK (Tenn.)**	Democratic	1,338,464	49.6	170	78.9
	Henry Clay	Whig	1,300,097	48.1	105	
	J. G. Birney	Liberty	62,300	2.3	—	
1848	**ZACHARY TAYLOR (La.)**	Whig	1,360,099	47.4	163	72.7
	Lewis Cass	Democratic	1,220,544	42.5	127	
	Martin Van Buren	Free-Soil	291,263	10.1	—	
1852	**FRANKLIN PIERCE (N.H.)**	Democratic	1,601,117	50.9	254	69.6
	Winfield Scott	Whig	1,385,453	44.1	42	
	John P. Hale	Free-Soil	155,825	5.0	—	
1856	**JAMES BUCHANAN (Pa.)**	Democratic	1,832,995	45.3	174	78.9
	John C. Frémont	Republican	1,339,932	33.1	114	
	Millard Fillmore	American	871,731	21.6	8	
1860	**ABRAHAM LINCOLN (Ill.)**	Republican	1,866,452	39.8	180	81.2
	Stephen A. Douglas	Democratic	1,375,157	29.4	12	
	John C. Breckinridge	Democratic	847,953	18.1	72	
	John Bell	Union	590,631	12.6	39	
1864	**ABRAHAM LINCOLN (Ill.)**	Republican	2,213,665	55.1	212	73.8
	George B. McClellan	Democratic	1,805,237	44.9	21	
1868	**ULYSSES S. GRANT (Ill.)**	Republican	3,012,833	52.7	214	78.1
	Horatio Seymour	Democratic	2,703,249	47.3	80	
1872	**ULYSSES S. GRANT (Ill.)**	Republican	3,597,132	55.6	286	71.3
	Horace Greeley	Democratic; Liberal Republican	2,834,125	43.9	66	
1876	**RUTHERFORD B. HAYES (Ohio)**	Republican	4,036,298	48.0	185	81.8
	Samuel J. Tilden	Democratic	4,288,590	51.0	184	
1880	**JAMES A. GARFIELD (Ohio)**	Republican	4,454,416	48.5	214	79.4
	Winfield S. Hancock	Democratic	4,444,952	48.1	155	
1884	**GROVER CLEVELAND (N.Y.)**	Democratic	4,874,986	48.5	219	77.5
	James G. Blaine	Republican	4,851,981	48.3	182	
1888	**BENJAMIN HARRISON (Ind.)**	Republican	5,439,853	47.9	233	79.3
	Grover Cleveland	Democratic	5,540,309	48.6	168	
1892	**GROVER CLEVELAND (N.Y.)**	Democratic	5,555,426	46.1	277	74.7
	Benjamin Harrison	Republican	5,182,690	43.0	145	
	James B. Weaver	People's	1,029,846	8.5	22	
1896	**WILLIAM McKINLEY (Ohio)**	Republican	7,104,779	51.1	271	79.3
	William J. Bryan	Democratic-People's	6,502,925	47.7	176	
1900	**WILLIAM McKINLEY (Ohio)**	Republican	7,207,923	51.7	292	73.2
	William J. Bryan	Dem.-Populist	6,358,133	45.5	155	
1904	**THEODORE ROOSEVELT (N.Y.)**	Republican	7,623,486	57.9	336	65.2
	Alton B. Parker	Democratic	5,077,911	37.6	140	
	Eugene V. Debs	Socialist	402,283	3.0	—	
1908	**WILLIAM H. TAFT (Ohio)**	Republican	7,678,908	51.6	321	65.4
	William J. Bryan	Democratic	6,409,104	43.1	162	
	Eugene V. Debs	Socialist	420,793	2.8	—	

Year	Candidates	Parties	Popular Vote	Percentage of Popular Vote	Electoral Vote	Percentage of Voter Participation
1912	WOODROW WILSON (N.J.)	Democratic	6,293,454	41.9	435	58.8
	Theodore Roosevelt	Progressive	4,119,538	27.4	88	
	William H. Taft	Republican	3,484,980	23.2	8	
	Eugene V. Debs	Socialist	900,672	6.1	—	
1916	WOODROW WILSON (N.J.)	Democratic	9,129,606	49.4	277	61.6
	Charles E. Hughes	Republican	8,538,221	46.2	254	
	A. L. Benson	Socialist	585,113	3.2	—	
1920	WARREN G. HARDING (Ohio)	Republican	16,143,407	60.5	404	49.2
	James M. Cox	Democratic	9,130,328	34.2	127	
	Eugene V. Debs	Socialist	919,799	3.4	—	
1924	CALVIN COOLIDGE (Mass.)	Republican	15,725,016	54.0	382	48.9
	John W. Davis	Democratic	8,386,503	28.8	136	
	Robert M. La Follette	Progressive	4,822,856	16.6	13	
1928	HERBERT HOOVER (Calif.)	Republican	21,391,381	57.4	444	56.9
	Alfred E. Smith	Democratic	15,016,443	40.3	87	
	Norman Thomas	Socialist	881,951	2.3	—	
	William Z. Foster	Communist	102,991	0.3	—	
1932	FRANKLIN D. ROOSEVELT (N.Y.)	Democratic	22,821,857	57.4	472	56.9
	Herbert Hoover	Republican	15,761,841	39.7	59	
	Norman Thomas	Socialist	881,951	2.2	—	
1936	FRANKLIN D. ROOSEVELT (N.Y.)	Democratic	27,751,597	60.8	523	61.0
	Alfred M. Landon	Republican	16,679,583	36.5	8	
	William Lemke	Union	882,479	1.9	—	
1940	FRANKLIN D. ROOSEVELT (N.Y.)	Democratic	27,244,160	54.8	449	62.5
	Wendell Willkie	Republican	22,305,198	44.8	82	
1944	FRANKLIN D. ROOSEVELT (N.Y.)	Democratic	25,602,504	53.5	432	55.9
	Thomas E. Dewey	Republican	22,006,285	46.0	99	
1948	HARRY S. TRUMAN (Mo.)	Democratic	24,105,695	49.5	303	53.0
	Thomas E. Dewey	Republican	21,969,170	45.1	189	
	J. Strom Thurmond	States'-Rights Democratic	1,169,021	2.4	38	
	Henry A. Wallace	Progressive	1,156,103	2.4	—	
1952	DWIGHT D. EISENHOWER (N.Y.)	Republican	33,936,252	55.1	442	63.3
	Adlai Stevenson	Democratic	27,314,992	44.4	89	
1956	DWIGHT D. EISENHOWER (N.Y.)	Republican	35,575,420	57.6	457	60.6
	Adlai Stevenson	Democratic	26,033,066	42.1	73	
	Other	—	—		1	
1960	JOHN F. KENNEDY (Mass.)	Democratic	34,227,096	49.9	303	62.8
	Richard M. Nixon	Republican	34,108,546	49.6	219	
	Other	—	—		15	
1964	LYNDON B. JOHNSON (Texas)	Democratic	43,126,506	61.1	486	61.7
	Barry M. Goldwater	Republican	27,176,799	38.5	52	
1968	RICHARD M. NIXON (N.Y.)	Republican	31,770,237	43.4	301	60.9
	Hubert H. Humphrey	Democratic	31,270,533	42.7	191	
	George Wallace	American Indep.	9,906,141	13.5	46	
1972	RICHARD M. NIXON (N.Y.)	Republican	47,169,911	60.7	520	55.2
	George S. McGovern	Democratic	29,170,383	37.5	17	
	Other	—	—		1	
1976	JIMMY CARTER (Ga.)	Democratic	40,830,763	50.0	297	53.5
	Gerald R. Ford	Republican	39,147,793	48.0	240	
	Other	—	1,575,459	2.1	—	
1980	RONALD REAGAN (Calif.)	Republican	43,901,812	51.0	489	54.0
	Jimmy Carter	Democratic	35,483,820	41.0	49	
	John B. Anderson	Independent	5,719,722	7.0	—	
	Ed Clark	Libertarian	921,188	1.1	—	

Year	Candidates	Parties	Popular Vote	Percentage of Popular Vote	Electoral Vote	Percentage of Voter Participation
1984	**RONALD REAGAN (Calif.)**	Republican	54,455,075	59.0	525	53.1
	Walter Mondale	Democratic	37,577,185	41.0	13	
1988	**GEORGE H. W. BUSH (Texas)**	Republican	47,946,422	54.0	426	50.2
	Michael S. Dukakis	Democratic	41,016,429	46.0	112	
1992	**WILLIAM J. CLINTON (Ark.)**	Democratic	44,908,254	43.0	370	55.9
	George H. W. Bush	Republican	39,102,282	38.0	168	
	H. Ross Perot	Independent	19,721,433	19.0	—	
1996	**WILLIAM J. CLINTON (Ark.)**	Democratic	47,401,185	49.2	379	49.0
	Robert Dole	Republican	39,197,469	40.7	159	
	H. Ross Perot	Independent	8,085,294	8.4	—	
2000	**GEORGE W. BUSH (Texas)**	Republican	50,456,062	47.8	271	51.2
	Al Gore	Democratic	50,996,862	48.4	267	
	Ralph Nader	Green Party	2,858,843	2.7	—	
	Patrick J. Buchanan	—	438,760	0.4	—	
2004	**GEORGE W. BUSH (Texas)**	Republican	61,872,711	50.7	286	60.3
	John F. Kerry	Democratic	58,894,584	48.3	252	
	Other	—	1,582,185	1.3	—	
2008	**BARACK OBAMA (Illinois)**	Democratic	69,456,897	52.9	365	56.8
	John McCain	Republican	59,934,314	45.7	173	

PRESIDENTS, VICE PRESIDENTS, AND SECRETARIES OF STATE

The Washington Administration (1789–1797)
Vice President	John Adams	1789–1797
Secretary of State	Thomas Jefferson	1789–1793
	Edmund Randolph	1794–1795
	Timothy Pickering	1795–1797

The John Adams Administration (1797–1801)
Vice President	Thomas Jefferson	1797–1801
Secretary of State	Timothy Pickering	1797–1800
	John Marshall	1800–1801

The Jefferson Administration (1801–1809)
Vice President	Aaron Burr	1801–1805
	George Clinton	1805–1809
Secretary of State	James Madison	1801–1809

The Madison Administration (1809–1817)
Vice President	George Clinton	1809–1813
	Elbridge Gerry	1813–1817
Secretary of State	Robert Smith	1809–1811
	James Monroe	1811–1817

The Monroe Administration (1817–1825)
Vice President	Daniel Tompkins	1817–1825
Secretary of State	John Quincy Adams	1817–1825

The John Quincy Adams Administration (1825–1829)
Vice President	John C. Calhoun	1825–1829
Secretary of State	Henry Clay	1825–1829

The Jackson Administration (1829–1837)
Vice President	John C. Calhoun	1829–1833
	Martin Van Buren	1833–1837
Secretary of State	Martin Van Buren	1829–1831
	Edward Livingston	1831–1833
	Louis McLane	1833–1834
	John Forsyth	1834–1837

The Van Buren Administration (1837–1841)
Vice President	Richard M. Johnson	1837–1841
Secretary of State	John Forsyth	1837–1841

The William Harrison Administration (1841)
Vice President	John Tyler	1841
Secretary of State	Daniel Webster	1841

The Tyler Administration (1841–1845)
Vice President	None	
Secretary of State	Daniel Webster	1841–1843
	Hugh S. Legaré	1843
	Abel P. Upshur	1843–1844
	John C. Calhoun	1844–1845

The Polk Administration (1845–1849)
Vice President	George M. Dallas	1845–1849
Secretary of State	James Buchanan	1845–1849

The Taylor Administration (1849–1850)
Vice President	Millard Fillmore	1849–1850
Secretary of State	John M. Clayton	1849–1850

The Fillmore Administration (1850–1853)

Vice President	None	
Secretary of State	Daniel Webster	1850–1852
	Edward Everett	1852–1853

The Pierce Administration (1853–1857)

Vice President	William R. King	1853–1857
Secretary of State	William L. Marcy	1853–1857

The Buchanan Administration (1857–1861)

Vice President	John C. Breckinridge	1857–1861
Secretary of State	Lewis Cass	1857–1860
	Jeremiah S. Black	1860–1861

The Lincoln Administration (1861–1865)

Vice President	Hannibal Hamlin	1861–1865
	Andrew Johnson	1865
Secretary of State	William H. Seward	1861–1865

The Andrew Johnson Administration (1865–1869)

Vice President	None	
Secretary of State	William H. Seward	1865–1869

The Grant Administration (1869–1877)

Vice President	Schuyler Colfax	1869–1873
	Henry Wilson	1873–1877
Secretary of State	Elihu B. Washburne	1869
	Hamilton Fish	1869–1877

The Hayes Administration (1877–1881)

Vice President	William A. Wheeler	1877–1881
Secretary of State	William M. Evarts	1877–1881

The Garfield Administration (1881)

Vice President	Chester A. Arthur	1881
Secretary of State	James G. Blaine	1881

The Arthur Administration (1881–1885)

Vice President	None	
Secretary of State	F. T. Frelinghuysen	1881–1885

The Cleveland Administration (1885–1889)

Vice President	Thomas A. Hendricks	1885–1889
Secretary of State	Thomas F. Bayard	1885–1889

The Benjamin Harrison Administration (1889–1893)

Vice President	Levi P. Morton	1889–1893
Secretary of State	James G. Blaine	1889–1892
	John W. Foster	1892–1893

The Cleveland Administration (1893–1897)

Vice President	Adlai E. Stevenson	1893–1897
Secretary of State	Walter Q. Gresham	1893–1895
	Richard Olney	1895–1897

The McKinley Administration (1897–1901)

Vice President	Garret A. Hobart	1897–1901
	Theodore Roosevelt	1901
Secretary of State	John Sherman	1897–1898
	William R. Day	1898
	John Hay	1898–1901

The Theodore Roosevelt Administration (1901–1909)

Vice President	Charles Fairbanks	1905–1909
Secretary of State	John Hay	1901–1905
	Elihu Root	1905–1909
	Robert Bacon	1909

The Taft Administration (1909–1913)

Vice President	James S. Sherman	1909–1913
Secretary of State	Philander C. Knox	1909–1913

The Wilson Administration (1913–1921)

Vice President	Thomas R. Marshall	1913–1921
Secretary of State	William J. Bryan	1913–1915
	Robert Lansing	1915–1920
	Bainbridge Colby	1920–1921

The Harding Administration (1921–1923)

Vice President	Calvin Coolidge	1921–1923
Secretary of State	Charles E. Hughes	1921–1923

The Coolidge Administration (1923–1929)

Vice President	Charles G. Dawes	1925–1929
Secretary of State	Charles E. Hughes	1923–1925
	Frank B. Kellogg	1925–1929

The Hoover Administration (1929–1933)

Vice President	Charles Curtis	1929–1933
Secretary of State	Henry L. Stimson	1929–1933

The Franklin D. Roosevelt Administration (1933–1945)

Vice President	John Nance Garner	1933–1941
	Henry A. Wallace	1941–1945
	Harry S. Truman	1945
Secretary of State	Cordell Hull	1933–1944
	Edward R. Stettinius Jr.	1944–1945

The Truman Administration (1945–1953)

Vice President	Alben W. Barkley	1949–1953
Secretary of State	Edward R. Stettinius Jr.	1945
	James F. Byrnes	1945–1947
	George C. Marshall	1947–1949
	Dean G. Acheson	1949–1953

The Eisenhower Administration (1953–1961)

Vice President	Richard M. Nixon	1953–1961
Secretary of State	John Foster Dulles	1953–1959
	Christian A. Herter	1959–1961

The Kennedy Administration (1961–1963)

Vice President	Lyndon B. Johnson	1961–1963
Secretary of State	Dean Rusk	1961–1963

The Lyndon Johnson Administration (1963–1969)

Vice President	Hubert H. Humphrey	1965–1969
Secretary of State	Dean Rusk	1963–1969

The Nixon Administration (1969–1974)

Vice President	Spiro T. Agnew	1969–1973
	Gerald R. Ford	1973–1974
Secretary of State	William P. Rogers	1969–1973
	Henry A. Kissinger	1973–1974

The Ford Administration (1974–1977)

Vice President	Nelson A. Rockefeller	1974–1977
Secretary of State	Henry A. Kissinger	1974–1977

The Carter Administration (1977–1981)

Vice President	Walter F. Mondale	1977–1981
Secretary of State	Cyrus R. Vance	1977–1980
	Edmund Muskie	1980–1981

The Reagan Administration (1981–1989)

Vice President	George H. W. Bush	1981–1989
Secretary of State	Alexander M. Haig	1981–1982
	George P. Shultz	1982–1989

The George H. W. Bush Administration (1989–1993)

Vice President	J. Danforth Quayle	1989–1993
Secretary of State	James A. Baker III	1989–1992
	Lawrence S. Eagleburger	1992–1993

The Clinton Administration (1993–2001)

Vice President	Albert Gore	1993–2001
Secretary of State	Warren M. Christopher	1993–1997
	Madeleine K. Albright	1997–2001

The George W. Bush Administration (2001–2009)

Vice President	Richard Cheney	2001–2009
Secretary of State	Colin Powell	2001–2005
	Condoleezza Rice	2005–2009

The Barack Obama Administration (2009–)

Vice President	Joseph Biden	2009–
Secretary of State	Hillary Clinton	2009–

ADMISSION OF STATES TO THE UNION

State	Date of Admission	State	Date of Admission
Delaware	December 7, 1787	Rhode Island	May 29, 1790
Pennsylvania	December 12, 1787	Vermont	March 4, 1791
New Jersey	December 18, 1787	Kentucky	June 1, 1792
Georgia	January 2, 1788	Tennessee	June 1, 1796
Connecticut	January 9, 1788	Ohio	March 1, 1803
Massachusetts	February 6, 1788	Louisiana	April 30, 1812
Maryland	April 28, 1788	Indiana	December 11, 1816
South Carolina	May 23, 1788	Mississippi	December 10, 1817
New Hampshire	June 21, 1788	Illinois	December 3, 1818
Virginia	June 25, 1788	Alabama	December 14, 1819
New York	July 26, 1788	Maine	March 15, 1820
North Carolina	November 21, 1789	Missouri	August 10, 1821

ADMISSION OF STATES TO THE UNION

State	Date of Admission	State	Date of Admission
Arkansas	June 15, 1836	Colorado	August 1, 1876
Michigan	January 16, 1837	North Dakota	November 2, 1889
Florida	March 3, 1845	South Dakota	November 2, 1889
Texas	December 29, 1845	Montana	November 8, 1889
Iowa	December 28, 1846	Washington	November 11, 1889
Wisconsin	May 29, 1848	Idaho	July 3, 1890
California	September 9, 1850	Wyoming	July 10, 1890
Minnesota	May 11, 1858	Utah	January 4, 1896
Oregon	February 14, 1859	Oklahoma	November 16, 1907
Kansas	January 29, 1861	New Mexico	January 6, 1912
West Virginia	June 19, 1863	Arizona	February 14, 1912
Nevada	October 31, 1864	Alaska	January 3, 1959
Nebraska	March 1, 1867	Hawaii	August 21, 1959

SUPREME COURT JUSTICES

Name	Service	Appointed by	Name	Service	Appointed by
John Jay*	1789–1795	Washington	Philip P. Barbour	1836–1841	Jackson
James Wilson	1789–1798	Washington	John Catron	1837–1865	Van Buren
John Blair	1789–1796	Washington	John McKinley	1837–1852	Van Buren
John Rutledge	1790–1791	Washington	Peter V. Daniel	1841–1860	Van Buren
William Cushing	1790–1810	Washington	Samuel Nelson	1845–1872	Tyler
James Iredell	1790–1799	Washington	Levi Woodbury	1845–1851	Polk
Thomas Johnson	1791–1793	Washington	Robert C. Grier	1846–1870	Polk
William Paterson	1793–1806	Washington	Benjamin R. Curtis	1851–1857	Fillmore
John Rutledge†	1795	Washington	John A. Campbell	1853–1861	Pierce
Samuel Chase	1796–1811	Washington	Nathan Clifford	1858–1881	Buchanan
Oliver Ellsworth	1796–1799	Washington	Noah H. Swayne	1862–1881	Lincoln
Bushrod Washington	1798–1829	J. Adams	Samuel F. Miller	1862–1890	Lincoln
Alfred Moore	1799–1804	J. Adams	David Davis	1862–1877	Lincoln
John Marshall	1801–1835	J. Adams	Stephen J. Field	1863–1897	Lincoln
William Johnson	1804–1834	Jefferson	**Salmon P. Chase**	1864–1873	Lincoln
Henry B. Livingston	1806–1823	Jefferson	William Strong	1870–1880	Grant
Thomas Todd	1807–1826	Jefferson	Joseph P. Bradley	1870–1892	Grant
Gabriel Duval	1811–1836	Madison	Ward Hunt	1873–1882	Grant
Joseph Story	1811–1845	Madison	**Morrison R. Waite**	1874–1888	Grant
Smith Thompson	1823–1843	Monroe	John M. Harlan	1877–1911	Hayes
Robert Trimble	1826–1828	J. Q. Adams	William B. Woods	1880–1887	Hayes
John McLean	1829–1861	Jackson	Stanley Matthews	1881–1889	Garfield
Henry Baldwin	1830–1844	Jackson	Horace Gray	1882–1902	Arthur
James M. Wayne	1835–1867	Jackson	Samuel Blatchford	1882–1893	Arthur
Roger B. Taney	1836–1864	Jackson	Lucius Q. C. Lamar	1888–1893	Cleveland
			Melville W. Fuller	1888–1910	Cleveland
			David J. Brewer	1889–1910	B. Harrison
			Henry B. Brown	1890–1906	B. Harrison
			George Shiras	1892–1903	B. Harrison
			Howell E. Jackson	1893–1895	B. Harrison

*Chief Justices appear in bold type.
†Acting Chief Justice; Senate refused to confirm appointment.

Name	Service	Appointed by	Name	Service	Appointed by
Edward D. White	1894–1910	Cleveland	**Frederick M. Vinson**	1946–1953	Truman
Rufus W. Peckham	1896–1909	Cleveland	Tom C. Clark	1949–1967	Truman
Joseph McKenna	1898–1925	McKinley	Sherman Minton	1949–1956	Truman
Oliver W. Holmes	1902–1932	T. Roosevelt	**Earl Warren**	1953–1969	Eisenhower
William R. Day	1903–1922	T. Roosevelt	John Marshall Harlan	1955–1971	Eisenhower
William H. Moody	1906–1910	T. Roosevelt	William J. Brennan Jr.	1956–1990	Eisenhower
Horace H. Lurton	1910–1914	Taft	Charles E. Whittaker	1957–1962	Eisenhower
Charles E. Hughes	1910–1916	Taft	Potter Stewart	1958–1981	Eisenhower
Willis Van Devanter	1910–1937	Taft	Byron R. White	1962–1993	Kennedy
Edward D. White	1910–1921	Taft	Arthur J. Goldberg	1962–1965	Kennedy
Joseph R. Lamar	1911–1916	Taft	Abe Fortas	1965–1969	L. Johnson
Mahlon Pitney	1912–1922	Taft	Thurgood Marshall	1967–1991	L. Johnson
James C. McReynolds	1914–1941	Wilson	**Warren E. Burger**	1969–1986	Nixon
			Harry A. Blackmun	1970–1994	Nixon
Louis D. Brandeis	1916–1939	Wilson	Lewis F. Powell Jr.	1972–1988	Nixon
John H. Clarke	1916–1922	Wilson	William H. Rehnquist	1972–1986	Nixon
William H. Taft	1921–1930	Harding	John Paul Stevens	1975–	Ford
George Sutherland	1922–1938	Harding	Sandra Day O'Connor	1981–2006	Reagan
Pierce Butler	1923–1939	Harding			
Edward T. Sanford	1923–1930	Harding	**William H. Rehnquist**	1986–2005	Reagan
Harlan F. Stone	1925–1941	Coolidge			
Charles E. Hughes	1930–1941	Hoover	Antonin Scalia	1986–	Reagan
Owen J. Roberts	1930–1945	Hoover	Anthony M. Kennedy	1988–	Reagan
Benjamin N. Cardozo	1932–1938	Hoover	David H. Souter	1990–2009	G. H. W. Bush
Hugo L. Black	1937–1971	F. Roosevelt			
Stanley F. Reed	1938–1957	F. Roosevelt	Clarence Thomas	1991–	G. H. W. Bush
Felix Frankfurter	1939–1962	F. Roosevelt			
William O. Douglas	1939–1975	F. Roosevelt	Ruth Bader Ginsburg	1993–	Clinton
Frank Murphy	1940–1949	F. Roosevelt	Stephen Breyer	1994–	Clinton
Harlan F. Stone	1941–1946	F. Roosevelt	John G. Roberts Jr.	2005–	G. W. Bush
James F. Byrnes	1941–1942	F. Roosevelt	Samuel Anthony Alito Jr.	2006–	G. W. Bush
Robert H. Jackson	1941–1954	F. Roosevelt			
Wiley B. Rutledge	1943–1949	F. Roosevelt	Sonia Sotomayor	2009–	Obama
Harold H. Burton	1945–1958	Truman	Elena Kagan	2010–	Obama

SIGNIFICANT SUPREME COURT CASES

Marbury v. Madison (1803)

This case established the right of the Supreme Court to review the constitutionality of laws. The decision involved judicial appointments made during the last hours of the administration of President John Adams. Some commissions, including that of William Marbury, had not yet been delivered when President Thomas Jefferson took office. Infuriated by the last-minute nature of Adams's Federalist appointments, Jefferson refused to send the undelivered commissions out, and Marbury decided to sue. The Supreme Court, presided over by John Marshall, a Federalist who had assisted Adams in the judicial appointments, ruled that although Marbury's commission was valid and the new president should have delivered it, the Court could not compel him to do so. The Court based its reasoning on a finding that the grounds of Marbury's suit, resting in the Judiciary Act of 1789, were in conflict with the Constitution.

For the first time, the Court had overturned a national law on the grounds that it was unconstitutional. John Marshall had quietly established the concept of judicial review: The Supreme Court had given itself the authority to nullify acts of the other branches of the federal government. Although the Constitution provides for judicial review, the Court had not exercised this power before and did not use it again until 1857. It seems likely that if the Court had waited until 1857 to use this power, it would have been difficult to establish.

McCulloch v. Maryland (1819)

In 1816, Congress authorized the creation of a national bank. To protect its own banks from competition with a branch of the national bank in Baltimore, the state legislature of Maryland placed a tax of 2 percent on all notes issued by any bank operating in Maryland that was not chartered by the state. McCulloch, cashier of the Baltimore branch of the Bank of the United States, was convicted for refusing to pay the tax. Under the leadership of Chief Justice John Marshall, the Court ruled that the federal government had the power to establish a bank, even though that specific authority was not mentioned in the Constitution.

Marshall maintained that the authority could be reasonably implied from Article 1, section 8, which gives Congress the power to make all laws that are necessary and proper to execute the enumerated powers. Marshall also held that Maryland could not tax the national bank because in a conflict between federal and state laws, the federal law must take precedence. Thus he established the principles of implied powers and federal supremacy, both of which set a precedent for subsequent expansion of federal power at the expense of the states.

Scott v. Sandford (1857)

Dred Scott was a slave who sued for his own and his family's freedom on the grounds that, with his master, he had traveled to and lived in free territory that did not allow slavery. When his case reached the Supreme Court, the justices saw an opportunity to settle once and for all the vexing question of slavery in the territories. The Court's decision in this case proved that it enjoyed no special immunity from the sectional and partisan passions of the time. Five of the nine justices were from the South and seven were Democrats.

Chief Justice Roger B. Taney hated Republicans and detested racial equality; his decision reflects those prejudices. He wrote an opinion not only declaring that Scott was still a slave but also claiming that the Constitution denied citizenship or rights to blacks, that Congress had no right to exclude slavery from the territories, and that the Missouri Compromise was unconstitutional. While southern Democrats gloated over this seven-to-two decision, sectional tensions were further inflamed, and the young Republican Party's claim that a hostile "slave power" was conspiring to destroy northern liberties was given further credence. The decision brought the nation closer to civil war and is generally regarded as the worst decision ever rendered by the Supreme Court.

Butchers' Benevolent Association of New Orleans v. Crescent City Livestock Landing and Slaughterhouse Co. (1873)

The *Slaughterhouse* cases, as the cases docketed under the *Butchers'* title were known, were the first legal test of the Fourteenth Amendment. To cut down on cases of cholera believed to be caused by contaminated water, the state of Louisiana prohibited the slaughter of livestock in New Orleans except in one slaughterhouse, effectively giving that slaughterhouse a monopoly. Other New Orleans butchers claimed that the state had deprived them of their occupation without due process of law, thus violating the Fourteenth Amendment.

In a five-to-four decision, the Court upheld the Louisiana law, declaring that the Fourteenth Amendment protected only the rights of federal citizenship, like voting in federal elections and interstate travel. The federal government thus was not obliged to protect basic civil rights from violation by state governments. This decision would have significant implications for African Americans and their struggle for civil rights in the twentieth century.

United States v. E. C. Knight Co. (1895)

Also known as the *Sugar Trust* case, this was among the first cases to reveal the weakness of the Sherman Antitrust Act in the hands of a pro-business Supreme Court. In 1895, American Sugar Refining Company purchased four other sugar producers, including the E. C. Knight Company, and thus took control of more than 98 percent of the sugar refining in the United States. In an effort to limit monopoly, the government brought suit against all five of the companies for violating the Sherman Antitrust Act, which outlawed trusts and other business combinations in restraint of trade. The Court dismissed the suit, however, arguing that the law applied only to commerce and not to manufacturing, defining the latter as a local concern and not part of the interstate commerce that the government could regulate.

Plessy v. Ferguson (1896)

African American Homer Plessy challenged a Louisiana law that required segregation on trains passing through the state. After ensuring that the railroad and the conductor knew that he was of mixed race (Plessy appeared to be white but under the racial code of Louisiana was classified as "colored" because he was one-eighth black), he refused to move to the "colored only" section of the coach. The Court ruled against Plessy by a vote of seven to one, declaring that "separate but equal" facilities were permissible according to section 1 of the Fourteenth Amendment, which calls upon the states to provide "equal protection of the laws" to anyone within their jurisdiction. Although the case was viewed as relatively insignificant at the time, it cast a long shadow over several decades.

Initially, the decision was viewed as a victory for segregationists, but in the 1930s and 1940s civil rights advocates referred to the doctrine of "separate but equal" in their efforts to end segregation. They argued that segregated institutions and accommodations were often not equal to those available to whites, and finally succeeded in overturning *Plessy* in *Brown v. Board of Education* in 1954 (see below).

Lochner v. New York (1905)

In this case, the Court ruled against a New York state law that prohibited employees from working in bakeries more than ten hours a day or sixty hours a week. The purpose of the law was to protect the health of workers, but the Court ruled that it was unconstitutional because it violated "freedom of contract" implicitly protected by the due process clause of the Fourteenth Amendment. Most of the justices believed strongly in a laissez-faire economic system that favored survival of the fittest. They felt that government protection of workers interfered with this system. In a dissenting opinion, Justice Oliver Wendell Holmes accused the majority of distorting the Constitution and of deciding the case on "an economic theory which a large part of the country does not entertain."

Muller v. Oregon (1908)

In 1905, Curt Muller, owner of a Portland, Oregon, laundry, demanded that one of his employees, Mrs. Elmer Gotcher, work more than the ten hours allowed as a maximum workday for women under Oregon law. Muller argued that the law violated his "freedom of contract" as established in prior Supreme Court decisions.

Progressive lawyer Louis D. Brandeis defended the Oregon law by arguing that a state could be justified in abridging freedom of contract when the health, safety, and welfare of workers was at issue. His innovative strategy drew on ninety-five pages of excerpts from factory and medical reports to substantiate his argument that there was a direct connection between long hours and the health of women and thus the health of the nation. In a unanimous decision, the Court upheld the Oregon law, but later generations of women fighting for equality would question the strategy of arguing that women's reproductive role entitled them to special treatment.

Schenck v. United States (1919)

During World War I, Charles Schenck and other members of the Socialist Party printed and mailed out flyers urging young men who were subject to the draft to oppose the war in Europe. In upholding the conviction of Schenck for publishing a pamphlet urging draft resistance, Justice Oliver Wendell Holmes established the "clear and present danger" test for freedom of speech. Such utterances as Schenck's during a time of national peril, Holmes wrote, could be considered the equivalent of shouting "Fire!" in a crowded theater. Congress had the right to protect the public against such an incitement to panic, the Court ruled in a unanimous decision. But the analogy was a false one. Schenck's pamphlet had little power to provoke a public firmly opposed to its message. Although Holmes later modified his position to state that the danger must relate to an immediate evil and a specific action, the "clear and present danger" test laid the groundwork for those who later sought to limit First Amendment freedoms.

Schechter Poultry Corp. v. United States (1935)

During the Great Depression, the National Industrial Recovery Act (NIRA), which was passed under President Franklin D. Roosevelt, established fair competition codes that were designed to help businesses. The Schechter brothers of New York City, who sold chickens, were convicted of violating the codes. The Supreme Court ruled that the NIRA unconstitutionally conferred legislative power on an administrative agency and overstepped the limits of federal power to regulate interstate commerce. The decision was a significant blow to the New Deal recovery program, demonstrating both historic American resistance to economic planning and the refusal of the business community to yield its autonomy unless it was forced to do so.

Brown v. Board of Education (1954)

In 1950, the families of eight Topeka, Kansas, children sued the Topeka Board of Education. The children were blacks who lived within walking distance of a whites-only school. The segregated school system required them to take a time-consuming, inconvenient, and dangerous route to get to a black school, and their parents argued that there was no reason their children should not be allowed to attend the nearest school. By the time the case reached the Supreme Court, it had been joined with similar cases regarding segregated schools in other states and the District of Columbia. A team of lawyers from the National Association for the Advancement of Colored People (NAACP), led by Thurgood Marshall (who would later be appointed to the Supreme Court), urged the Court to overturn the fifty-eight-year-old precedent established in *Plessy v. Ferguson*, which had enshrined "separate but equal" as the law of the land. A unanimous Court, led by Chief Justice Earl Warren, declared that "separate educational facilities are inherently unequal" and thus violate the Fourteenth Amendment. In 1955, the Court called for desegregation "with all deliberate speed" but established no deadline.

Roth v. United States (1957)

In 1957, New Yorker Samuel Roth was convicted of sending obscene materials through the mail in a case that ultimately reached the Supreme Court. With a six-to-three vote, the Court reaffirmed the historical view that obscenity is not protected by the First Amendment. Yet it broke new ground by declaring that a work could be judged obscene only if, "taken as a whole," it appealed to the "prurient interest" of "the average person."

Prior to this case, work could be judged obscene if portions were thought able to "deprave and corrupt" the most susceptible part of an audience (such as children). Thus, serious works of literature such as Theodore Dreiser's *An American Tragedy*, which was banned in Boston when first published, had received no protection. Although this decision continued to pose problems of definition, it did help to protect most works that attempt to convey ideas, even if those ideas have to do with sex, from the threat of obscenity laws.

Engel v. Vitale (1962)

In 1959, five parents with ten children in the New Hyde Park, New York, school system sued the school board. The parents argued that the so-called Regents' Prayer that public school students in New York recited at the start of every school day violated the doctrine of separation of church and state outlined in the First Amendment. In 1962, the Supreme Court voted six to one in favor of banning the Regents' Prayer.

The decision threw the religious community into an uproar. Many religious leaders expressed dismay and even shock; others welcomed the decision. Several efforts to introduce an amendment allowing school prayer have failed. Subsequent Supreme Court decisions have banned reading of the Bible in public schools. The Court has also declared mandatory flag saluting to be an infringement of religious and personal freedoms.

Gideon v. Wainwright (1963)

When Clarence Earl Gideon was tried for breaking into a poolroom, the state of Florida rejected his demand for a court-appointed lawyer as guaranteed by the Sixth Amendment. In 1963, the Court upheld his demand in a unanimous decision that established the obligation of states to provide attorneys for indigent defendants in felony cases. Prior to this decision, the right to an attorney had applied only to federal cases, not state cases. In its ruling in *Gideon v. Wainwright*, the Supreme Court applied the Sixth through the Fourteenth Amendments to the states. In 1972, the Supreme Court extended the right to legal representation to all cases, not just felony cases, in its decision in *Argersinger v. Hamlin*.

Griswold v. Connecticut (1965)

With a vote of seven to two, the Supreme Court reversed an "uncommonly silly law" (in the words of Justice Potter Stewart) that made it a crime for anyone in the state of Connecticut to use any drug, article, or instrument to prevent conception. *Griswold* became a landmark case because here, for the first time, the Court explicitly invested with full constitutional status "fundamental personal rights," such as the right to privacy, that were not expressly enumerated in the Bill of Rights. The majority opinion in the case held that the law infringed on the constitutionally protected right to privacy of married persons.

Although the Court had previously recognized fundamental rights not expressly enumerated in the Bill of Rights (such as the right to procreate in *Skinner v. Oklahoma* in 1942), *Griswold* was the first time the Court had justified, at length, the practice of investing such unenumerated rights with full constitutional status. Writing for the majority, Justice William O. Douglas explained that the First, Third, Fourth, Fifth, and Ninth Amendments imply "zones of privacy" that are the foundation for the general right to privacy affirmed in this case.

Miranda v. Arizona (1966)

In 1966, the Supreme Court, by a vote of five to four, upheld the case of Ernesto Miranda, who appealed a murder conviction on the grounds that police had gotten him to confess without giving him access to an attorney. The *Miranda* case was the culmination of the Court's efforts to find a meaningful way of determining whether police had used due process in extracting confessions from people accused of crimes. The *Miranda* decision upholds the Fifth Amendment protection against self-incrimination outside the courtroom and requires that suspects be given what came to be known as the "Miranda warning," which advises them of their right to remain silent and warns them that anything they say might be used against them in a court of law. Suspects must also be told that they have a right to counsel.

New York Times Co. v. United States (1971)

With a six-to-three vote, the Court upheld the right of the *New York Times* and the *Washington Post* to print materials from the so-called *Pentagon Papers*, a secret government study of U.S. policy in Vietnam, leaked by dissident Pentagon official Daniel Ellsberg. Since the papers revealed deception and secrecy in the conduct of the Vietnam War, the Nixon administration had quickly obtained a court injunction against their further publication, claiming that suppression was in the interests of national security. The Supreme Court's decision overturning the injunction strengthened the First Amendment protection of freedom of the press.

Furman v. Georgia (1972)

In this case, the Supreme Court ruled five to four that the death penalty for murder or rape violated the cruel and unusual punishment clause of the Eighth Amendment because the manner in which the death penalty was meted out was irregular, "arbitrary," and "cruel." In response, most states enacted new statutes that allow the death penalty to be imposed only after a postconviction hearing at which evidence must be presented to show that "aggravating" or "mitigating" circumstances were factors in the crime. If the post-conviction hearing hands down a death sentence, the case is automatically reviewed by an appellate court.

In 1976, the Court ruled in *Gregg v. Georgia* that these statutes were not unconstitutional. In 1977, the Court ruled in *Coker v. Georgia* that the death penalty for rape was "disproportionate and excessive," thus allowing the death penalty only in murder cases. Between 1977 and 1991, some 150 people were executed in the United States. Public opinion polls indicate that about 70 percent of Americans favor the death penalty for murder. Capital punishment continues to generate controversy, however, as opponents argue that there is no evidence that the death penalty deters crime and that its use reflects racial and economic bias.

Roe v. Wade (1973)

In 1973, the Court found, by a vote of seven to two, that state laws restricting access to abortion violated a woman's right to privacy guaranteed by the due process clause of the Fourteenth Amendment. The decision was based on the cases of two women living in Texas and Georgia, both states with stringent antiabortion laws. Upholding the individual rights of both women and physicians, the Court ruled that the Constitution protects the right to abortion and that states cannot prohibit abortions in the early stages of pregnancy.

The decision stimulated great debate among legal scholars as well as the public. Critics argued that since abortion was never addressed in the Constitution, the Court could not claim that legislation violated fundamental values of the Constitution. They also argued that since abortion was a medical procedure with an acknowledged impact on a fetus, it was inappropriate to invoke the kind of "privacy" argument that was used in *Griswold v. Connecticut* (see page A-43), which was about contraception. Defenders suggested that the case should be argued as a case of gender discrimination, which did violate the equal protection clause of the Fourteenth Amendment. Others said that the right to privacy in sexual matters was indeed a fundamental right.

Regents of the University of California v. Bakke (1978)

When Allan Bakke, a white man, was not accepted by the University of California Medical School at Davis, he filed a lawsuit alleging that the admissions program, which set up different standards for test scores and grades for members of certain minority groups, violated the Civil Rights Act of 1964, which outlawed racial or ethnic preferences in programs supported by federal funds. Bakke further argued that the university's practice of setting aside spaces for minority applicants denied him equal protection as guaranteed by the Fourteenth Amendment. In a five-to-four decision, the Court ordered that Bakke be admitted to the medical school, yet it sanctioned affirmative action programs to attack the results of past discrimination as long as strict quotas or racial classifications were not involved.

Webster v. Reproductive Health Services (1989)

By a vote of five to four, the Court upheld several restrictions on the availability of abortions as imposed by Missouri state law. It upheld restrictions on the use of state property, including public hospitals, for abortions. It also upheld a provision requiring physicians to perform tests to determine the viability of a fetus that a doctor judged to be twenty weeks of age or older. Although the justices did not go so far as to overturn the decision in *Roe v. Wade* (see at left), the ruling galvanized interest groups on both sides of the abortion issue. Opponents of abortion pressured state legislatures to place greater restrictions on abortions; those who favored availability of abortion tried to mobilize public action by presenting the decision as a major threat to the right to choose abortion.

Cipollone v. Liggett (1992)

In a seven-to-two decision, the Court ruled in favor of the family of Rose Cipollone, a woman who died of lung cancer after smoking for forty-two years. The Court rejected arguments that health warnings on cigarette packages protected tobacco manufacturers from personal injury suits filed by smokers who contract cancer and other serious illnesses.

Miller v. Johnson (1995)

In a five-to-four decision, the Supreme Court ruled that voting districts created to increase the voting power of racial minorities were unconstitutional. The decision threatens dozens of congressional, state, and local voting districts that were drawn to give minorities more representation as had been required by the Justice Department under the Voting Rights Act. If states are required to redraw voting districts, the number of black members of Congress could be sharply reduced.

Romer v. Evans (1996)

In a six-to-three decision, the Court struck down a Colorado amendment that forbade local governments from banning discrimination against homosexuals. Writing for the majority, Justice Anthony Kennedy said that forbidding communities from taking action to protect the rights of homosexuals and not of other groups unlawfully deprived gays and lesbians of opportunities that were available to others. Kennedy based the decision on the guarantee of equal protection under the law as provided by the Fourteenth Amendment.

Bush v. Palm Beach County Canvassing Board (2000)

In a bitterly argued five-to-four decision, the Court reversed the Florida Supreme Court's previous order for a hand recount of contested presidential election ballots in several counties of that battleground state, effectively securing the presidency for Texas Republican governor George W. Bush. The ruling ended a protracted legal dispute between presidential candidates Bush and Vice President Al Gore while inflaming public opinion: For the first time since 1888, a president who failed to win the popular vote took office. Critics charged that the Supreme Court had applied partisanship rather than objectivity to the case, pointing out that the decision went against this Court's customary interpretation of the Constitution to favor state over federal authority.

Lawrence v. Texas (2003)

In the 1986 case *Bowers v. Hardwick*, the Supreme Court upheld the constitutionality of a Georgia law that outlawed sodomy, ruling that sexual privacy was not protected by the Constitution. This decision came into question, however, when *Lawrence v. Texas* arrived at the Supreme Court in 2002, challenging the constitutionality of a Texas anti-sodomy statute. In this case, the Court voted six to three to strike down the statute, asserting that the 1986 decision was based on an interpretation of constitutional liberties that was too narrow. This decision thus overruled *Bowers v. Hardwick*, with the majority holding that the Texas law violated the Fourteenth Amendment's declaration that no state shall "deprive any person of life, liberty, or property, without due process of law." The decision in *Lawrence v. Texas* was hailed as a legal victory for the gay and lesbian community. It was landmark in its implication that laws cannot be made on the basis of morality, without proof of harm.

Hamdan v. Rumsfeld (2005)

In 2001, Salim Ahmed Hamdan, driver for al-Qaeda leader Osama bin Laden, was arrested in Afghanistan as a suspected terrorist. He was charged with conspiracy to commit terrorist offenses after being held in the U.S. military base in Guantanamo Bay, Cuba, for two years. It was decided that Hamdan would be tried by a military commission under an order from President George W. Bush that commissions be established for express non-citizens, including those with connections to al-Qaeda. Hamdan, however, claimed that trial by military commission was unlawful under the Geneva Conventions and Uniform Code of Military Justice (UCMJ).

In the case's first round through the courts, the U.S. District Court of the District of Columbia ruled in Hamdan's favor. Upon appeal, the decision was reversed, the new court ruling that the military commission was indeed lawful, and that the Geneva Conventions could not be enforced by the U.S. judicial systems. The Supreme Court issued a writ of certiorari in 2005 and ultimately upheld Hamdan's case by a vote of five to three, stating that the military commission was unlawful under both the Geneva Conventions and the UCMJ. This decision put a halt to all Guantanamo Bay tribunals, and was praised by human rights activists and lawyers.

Citizens United v. Federal Election Commission (2010)

In 2010, the Supreme Court overruled a ban on political spending by corporations in a vote of five to four. The case went to court after Citizens United, a conservative nonprofit organization, tried to air its critical documentary on Hillary Clinton, *Hillary: The Movie*, during the 2008 presidential campaign. *Citizens United v. Federal Election Commission* quickly became a matter of free speech and raised the sensitive question of whether corporations should be viewed as individuals under the First Amendment.

The Court's decision overturned two precedents and divided the nation in an already heated time in the political sphere. Advocates for the ruling felt that the previous ban would have given the Supreme Court power to prohibit other political outlets, such as newspapers and television programs. Dissenters, including President Barack Obama, believed that the vote created an opening for wealthy corporations to take advantage of the democratic system. In reversing years of policy, the ruling left all to speculate on its possible impact not only on the 2008 election, but also on American politics as a whole.

THE AMERICAN ECONOMY

THESE SIX "SNAPSHOTS" OF THE U.S. ECONOMY show significant changes over the past century and a half. In 1849, the agricultural sector was by far the largest contributor to the economy. By the turn of the century, with advances in technology and an abundance of cheap labor and raw materials, the country had experienced remarkable industrial expansion, and the manufacturing industries dominated. By 1950, the service sector had increased significantly, fueled by the consumerism of the 1920s and the post–World War II years, and the economy was becoming more diversified. Note that by 1990, the government's share in the economy had grown to more than 10 percent and activity in both the trade and manufacturing sectors had declined, partly as a result of competition from Western Europe and Asia. Manufacturing continued to decline, and by 2008 the service and finance, real estate, and insurance sectors had all grown steadily to eclipse it.

Main Sectors of the U.S. Economy: 1849, 1899, 1950, 1990, 2001, 2008

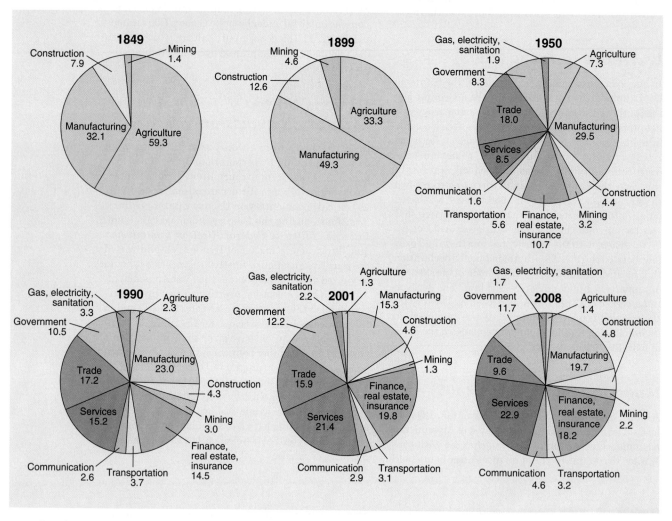

SOURCE: Data from *Historical Statistics of the United States, Colonial Times to 1970* (1975); *Statistical Abstract of the United States, 2010;* U.S. Bureau of Economic Analysis, *Industry Accounts Data, 2010.*

FEDERAL SPENDING AND THE ECONOMY, 1790–2009

Year	Gross Domestic Product (in billions)	Foreign Trade (in billions)		Federal Federal Budget (in billions)	Surplus/Deficit (in billions)	Federal Debt (in billions)
		Exports	Imports			
1790	4.03	0.43	0.50	0.09	0.0032	1.64
1800	7.40	1.10	1.41	0.17	0.0010	1.29
1810	10.6	1.02	1.29	0.12	0.0187	0.81
1820	14.4	1.44	1.52	0.37	−0.0078	1.87
1830	22.2	1.62	1.55	0.33	0.2120	1.07
1840	31.5	2.66	2.16	0.48	−0.0977	0.08
1850	49.6	2.95	3.45	0.78	0.0788	1.24
1860	82.1	7.56	6.84	1.19	−0.1340	1.23
1870	112	6.54	6.70	4.50	1.47	34.8
1880	192	15.8	14.1	4.96	1.22	38.9
1890	319	19.3	17.5	6.73	1.80	23.3
1900	423	30.8	19.1	10.7	0.95	26.7
1910	534	30.6	26.2	11.1	−0.29	17.6
1920	688	67.4	45.0	49.8	2.27	189
1930	893	39.3	34.3	33.7	7.22	159
1940	1,167	46.4	85.6	104	−41.50	495
1950	2,006	94.3	82.1	294	−14.30	257
1960	2,831	145	125	629	2.10	291
1970	4,270	270	246	983	−14.30	381
1980	5,839	470	513	1,369	−171	909
1990	8,034	545	686	1,832	−323	3,206
2000	11,226	1,071	1,449	2,041	270	5,269
2009	12,703	1,571	1,946	3,186	−1,280	11,876

NOTE: All Figures are in 2005 dollars.

SOURCE: *Historical Statistics of the U.S., 1789–1945* (1949), *Statistical Abstract of the U.S., 1965* (1965), *Statistical Abstract of the U.S., 1990* (1990), *Statistical Abstract of the U.S., 2011* (2011), and Louis Johnston and Samuel H. Williamson, "What Was the U.S. GDP Then?" MeasuringWorth, 2011, www.measuringworth.org/usgdp.

A DEMOGRAPHIC PROFILE OF THE UNITED STATES AND ITS PEOPLE

Population

FROM AN ESTIMATED 4,600 white inhabitants in 1630, the country's population grew to a total of more than 308 million in 2010. It is important to note that the U.S. census, first conducted in 1790 and the source of these figures, counted blacks, both free and slave, but did not include American Indians until 1860. The years 1790 to 1900 saw the most rapid population growth, with an average increase of 25 to 35 percent per decade. In addition to "natural" growth—birthrate exceeding death rate—immigration was also a factor in that rise, especially between 1840 and 1860, 1880 and 1890, and 1900 and 1910 (see table on page A-51). The twentieth century witnessed slower growth, partly a result of 1920s immigration restrictions and a decline in the birthrate, especially during the depression era and the 1960s and 1970s. The U.S. population is expected to pass 340 million by the year 2020.

POPULATION GROWTH, 1630–2010

Year	Population	Percent Increase	Year	Population	Percent Increase
1630	4,600	—	1830	12,866,020	33.5
1640	26,600	473.3	1840	17,069,453	32.7
1650	50,400	89.1	1850	23,191,876	35.9
1660	75,100	49.0	1860	31,443,321	35.6
1670	111,900	49.1	1870	39,818,449	26.6
1680	151,500	35.4	1880	50,155,783	26.0
1690	210,400	38.9	1890	62,947,714	25.5
1700	250,900	19.3	1900	75,994,575	20.7
1710	331,700	32.2	1910	91,972,266	21.0
1720	466,200	40.5	1920	105,710,620	14.9
1730	629,400	35.0	1930	122,775,046	16.1
1740	905,600	43.9	1940	131,669,275	7.2
1750	1,170,800	30.0	1950	150,697,361	14.5
1760	1,593,600	36.1	1960	179,323,175	19.0
1770	2,148,100	34.8	1970	203,302,031	13.4
1780	2,780,400	29.4	1980	226,542,199	11.4
1790	3,929,214	41.3	1990	248,718,302	9.8
1800	5,308,483	35.1	2000	281,422,509	13.1
1810	7,239,881	36.4	2010	308,745,538	9.7
1820	9,638,453	33.1			

SOURCE: *Historical Statistics of the U.S.* (1960), *Historical Statistics of the U.S., Colonial Times to 1970* (1975), *Statistical Abstract of the U.S., 1996* (1996), *Statistical Abstract of the U.S., 2003* (2003), and United States Census (2010).

Birthrate, 1820–2007

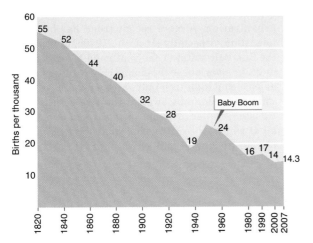

SOURCE: Data from *Historical Statistics of the U.S., Colonial Times to 1970* (1975) and *Statistical Abstract of the U.S., 2007* (2007).

Death Rate, 1900–2007

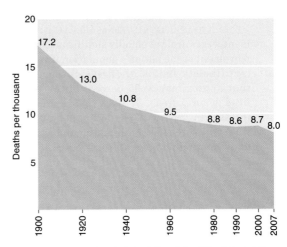

SOURCE: Data from *Historical Statistics of the U.S., Colonial Times to 1970* (1975) and *Statistical Abstract of the U.S., 2007* (2007).

Life Expectancy, 1900–2007

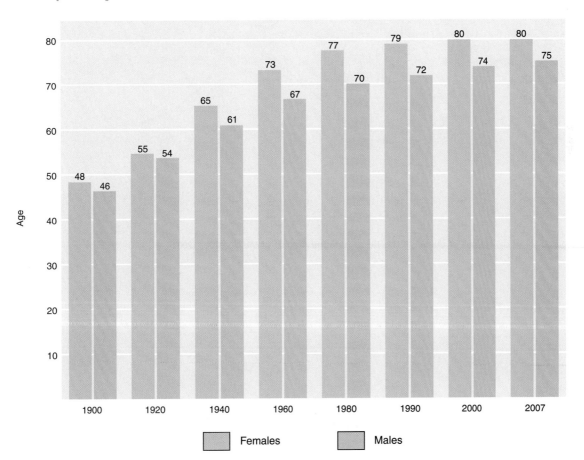

SOURCE: Data from *Historical Statistics of the U.S., Colonial Times to 1970* (1975) and *Statistical Abstract of the U.S., 2007* (2007).

MIGRATION AND IMMIGRATION

WE TEND TO ASSOCIATE INTERNAL MIGRATION with movement westward, yet equally significant has been the movement of the nation's population from the country to the city. In 1790, the first U.S. census recorded that approximately 95 percent of the population lived in rural areas. By 1990, that figure had fallen to less than 25 percent. The decline of the agricultural way of life, late-nineteenth-century industrialization, and immigration have all contributed to increased urbanization. A more recent trend has been the migration, especially since the 1970s, of people to the Sun Belt states of the South and West, lured by factors as various as economic opportunities in the defense and high-tech industries and good weather. This migration has swelled the size of cities like Houston, Dallas, Tucson, Phoenix, and San Diego, all of which in recent years ranked among the top ten most populous U.S. cities.

Rural and Urban Population, 1750–2000

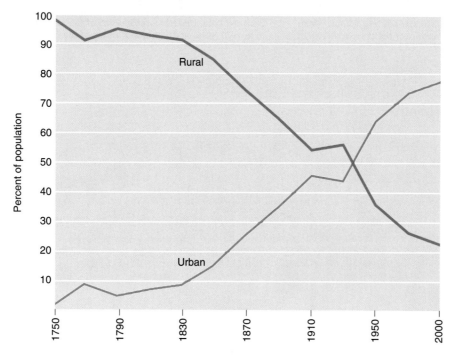

SOURCE: *Statistical Abstract of the U.S., 1991* (1991), *Statistical Abstract of the U.S., 2002* (2002).

THE QUANTITY AND CHARACTER OF IMMIGRATION to the United States has varied greatly over time. During the first major influx, between 1840 and 1860, newcomers hailed primarily from northern and western Europe. From 1880 to 1915, when rates soared even more dramatically, the profile changed, with 80 percent of the "new immigration" coming from central, eastern, and southern Europe. Following World War I, strict quotas reduced the flow considerably. Note also the significant falloff during the years of the Great Depression and World War II. The sources of immigration during the last half century have changed significantly, with the majority of people coming from Latin America, the Caribbean, and Asia. The latest surge during the 1980s and 1990s brought more immigrants to the United States than in any decade except 1901–1910.

RATES OF IMMIGRATION, 1821–2009

Year	Number	Rate per Thousand of Total Resident Population
1821–1830	151,824	1.6
1831–1840	599,125	4.6
1841–1850	1,713,521	10.0
1851–1860	2,598,214	11.2
1861–1870	2,314,824	7.4
1871–1880	2,812,191	7.1
1881–1890	5,246,613	10.5
1891–1900	3,687,546	5.8
1901–1910	8,795,386	11.6
1911–1920	5,735,811	6.2
1921–1930	4,107,209	3.9
1931–1940	528,431	0.4
1941–1950	1,035,039	0.7
1951–1960	2,515,479	1.6
1961–1970	3,321,677	1.8
1971–1980	4,493,300	2.2
1981–1990	7,338,100	3.0
1991	1,827,167	7.2
1992	973,977	3.8
1993	904,292	3.5
1994	804,416	3.1
1995	720,461	2.7
1996	915,900	3.4
1997	798,378	2.9
1998	654,451	2.4
1999	646,568	2.3
2000	849,807	3.0
2001	1,064,318	3.7
2002	1,063,732	3.7
2003	704,000	2.4
2004	958,000	3.3
2005	1,122,000	3.8
2006	1,266,129	4.2
2007	1,052,415	3.5
2008	1,107,126	3.6
2009	1,130,818	3.7

SOURCE: *Historical Statistics of the U.S., Colonial Times to 1970* (1975), *2002 Yearbook of Immigration Statistics* (2002), and *Statistical Abstract of the U.S., 1996, 1999, 2003, 2005,* and *2011* (1996, 1999, 2003, 2005, 2011).

Major Trends In Immigration, 1820–2010

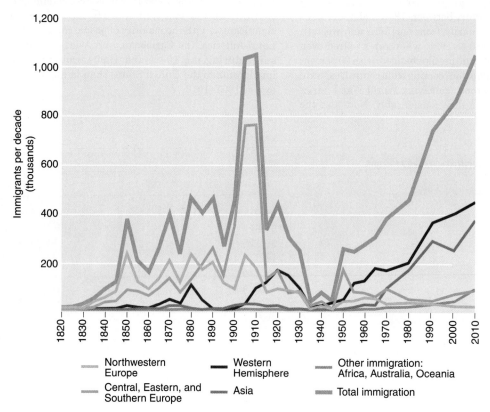

SOURCE: Data from *Historical Statistics of the U.S., Colonial Times to 1970* (1975), *Statistical Abstract of the U.S., 1999* (1999), and *Statistical Abstract of the U.S., 2011* (2011).

Glossary of Historical Vocabulary

antinomian A person who does not obey societal or religious laws. In colonial Massachusetts, Puritan authorities accused Anne Hutchinson of antinomianism because she believed that Christians could achieve salvation by faith alone. They further asserted, incorrectly, that Hutchinson also held the belief that it was not necessary to follow God's laws as set forth in the Bible. (p. 103)

archaeology A social science devoted to learning about people who lived in the past through the study of physical artifacts created by humans. Most but not all archaeological study focuses on the history of people who lived before the use of the written word. (p. 5)

Archaic A term applied to various hunting and gathering cultures that descended from Paleo-Indians. The term also refers to the period of time when these cultures dominated ancient America, roughly from 8000 BP to between 2000 and 1000 BP. (p. 11)

artifacts Material remains studied and used by archaeologists and historians to support their interpretations of human history. Examples of artifacts include bones, pots, baskets, jewelry, furniture, tools, clothing, and buildings. (p. 5)

artisan A term commonly used prior to 1900 to describe a skilled craftsman, such as a cabinetmaker. (pp. 50, 124)

Bill of Rights The commonly used term for the first ten amendments to the U.S. Constitution. The Bill of Rights (the last of which was ratified in 1791) guarantees individual liberties and defines limitations to federal power. Many states made the promise of the prompt addition of a bill of rights a precondition for their ratification of the Constitution. (pp. 261, 262, 263, 264)

Calvinism The religious doctrine of which the primary tenet is that salvation is predestined by God. Founded by John Calvin of Geneva during the Protestant Reformation, Calvinism required its adherents to live according to a strict religious and moral code. The Puritans who settled in colonial New England were devout Calvinists. (p. 98) *See also* predestination.

checks and balances A system in which the executive, legislative, and judicial branches of the government curb each other's power. Checks and balances were written into the U.S. Constitution during the Constitutional Convention of 1787. (p. 254)

Columbian exchange The transatlantic exchange of goods, peoples, and ideas that began when Columbus arrived in the Caribbean in 1492, ending the age-old separation of the hemispheres. (pp. 39, 40, 52, 53, 56)

covenant An agreement or pact; in American history, this refers to a religious agreement. The Pilgrims used this term in the Mayflower Compact to refer to the agreement among themselves to establish a law-abiding community in which all members would work together for the common good. Later, New England Puritans used this term to refer to the agreement they made with God and each other to live according to God's will as revealed through Scripture. (pp. 98, 105) *See also* Halfway Covenant.

culture A term used here to connote what is commonly called "way of life." It refers not only to how a group of people supplied themselves with food and shelter but also to their family relationships, social groupings, religious ideas, and other features of their lives. (pp. 3, 13, 14, 16, 139, 298)

democracy A system of government in which the people have the power to rule, either directly or indirectly, through their elected representatives. Believing that direct democracy was dangerous, the framers of the Constitution created a government that gave direct voice to the people only in the House of Representatives and that placed a check on that voice in the Senate by offering unlimited six-year terms to senators, elected by the state legislatures to protect them from the whims of democratic majorities. The framers further curbed the perceived dangers of democracy by giving each of the three branches of government (legislative, executive, and judicial) the ability to check the power of the other two. (pp. 247, 248, 254, 255, 331, 332, 333) *See also* checks and balances.

English Reformation *See* Reformation.

Enlightenment An eighteenth-century philosophical movement that emphasized the use of reason to reevaluate previously accepted doctrines and traditions. (p. 144)

evangelicalism The trend in Protestant Christianity stressing salvation through conversion, repentance of sin, adherence to Scripture, and the importance of preaching over ritual. During the Second Great Awakening in the 1830s, evangelicals worshipped at camp meetings and religious revivals led by exuberant preachers. (p. 322) *See also* Second Great Awakening.

franchise The right to vote. The franchise was gradually widened in the United States to include groups such as women and African Americans, who had no vote when the Constitution was ratified. (p. 310) *See also* suffrage.

frontier A borderland area. In U.S. history, this refers to the borderland between the areas primarily inhabited by Europeans or their descendants and the areas solely inhabited by Native Americans. (pp. 132, 147, 156, 164, 165)

Great Awakening The widespread movement of religious revitalization in the 1730s and 1740s that emphasized vital religious faith and personal choice. It was characterized by large, open-air meetings at which emotional sermons were given by itinerant preachers. (p. 145)

Halfway Covenant A Puritan compromise that allowed the unconverted children of the "visible saints" to become "halfway" members of the church and to baptize their own children even though they were not full members of the church themselves because they had not experienced full conversion. Massachusetts ministers accepted this compromise in 1662, but the compromise remained controversial throughout the seventeenth century. (p. 105)

hard currency (hard money) Money coined directly from, or backed in full by, precious metals (particularly gold). (p. 266)

indentured servitude A system that committed poor immigrants to four to seven years of labor in exchange for passage to the colonies and food and shelter after they arrived. An indenture is a type of contract. (pp. 71, 73)

land grant A gift of land from a government, usually intended to encourage settlement or development. The British government issued several land grants to encourage development in the American colonies. In the mid-nineteenth century, the U.S. government issued land grants to encourage railroad development and, through the passage of the Land-Grant College Act (also known as the Morrill Act) in 1862, set aside public land to support universities. (p. 209)

liberty The condition of being free or enjoying freedom from control. This term also refers to the possession of certain social, political, or economic rights, such as the right to own and control property. Eighteenth-century American colonists invoked the principle to argue for strict limitations on government's ability to tax its subjects. (pp. 158, 170, 171, 172, 173, 174, 264)

mercantilism A set of policies that regulated colonial commerce and manufacturing for the enrichment of the mother country. Mercantilist policies ensured that the American colonies in the mid-seventeenth century produced agricultural goods and raw materials to be shipped to Britain, where they would increase wealth in the mother country through reexportation or manufacture into finished goods that would then be sold to the colonies and elsewhere. (p. 77)

Middle Passage The crossing of the Atlantic (as a slave destined for auction) in the hold of a slave ship in the eighteenth and nineteenth centuries. Conditions were unimaginably bad, and many slaves died during these voyages. (p. 124)

Monroe Doctrine President James Monroe's 1823 declaration that the Western Hemisphere was closed to any further colonization or interference by European powers. In exchange, Monroe pledged that the United States would not become involved in European struggles. Although Monroe could not back his policy with action, it was an important formulation of national goals. (pp. 313, 314, 316)

Navigation Acts British acts of 1650, 1651, and 1660 that, together with a 1663 law (the Staple Act), set forth three fundamental regulations governing colonial trade. First, all colonial goods imported into England had to be transported on English ships using primarily English crews. Second, specific colonial products could be shipped only to England or to other English colonies. Third, all goods imported into the colonies had to pass through England. The 1660 Navigation Act assessed an explicit import tax of two pence on every pound of colonial tobacco; these tobacco taxes yielded about a quarter of all English customs revenues in the 1660s. The Navigation Acts fueled tension between the colonies and the monarchy in the century leading up to the Revolutionary War (1775–1783). (pp. 77, 112, 168)

nullification The idea that states can disregard federal laws when those laws represent an overstepping of congressional powers. The controversial idea was first proposed by opponents of the Alien and Sedition Acts of 1798 and later by South Carolina politicians in 1828 as a response to the Tariff of Abominations. (p. 337)

predestination The idea that individual salvation or damnation is determined by God at, or just prior to, a person's birth. The concept of predestination invalidated the idea that salvation could be obtained through either faith or good works. (p. 98) *See also* Calvinism.

Protestantism A powerful Christian reform movement that began in the sixteenth century with Martin Luther's critiques of the Roman Catholic Church. Over the centuries, Protestantism has taken many different forms, branching into numerous denominations with differing systems of worship. (pp. 54–56, 86, 93, 94)

Protestant Reformation *See* Reformation.

Puritanism The ideas and religious principles held by dissenters from the Church of England, including the belief that the church needed to be purified by eliminating the elements of Catholicism from its practices. (pp. 91–92, 93–97, 101)

Reformation The reform movement that began in 1517 with Martin Luther's critiques of the Roman Catholic Church, which led to the formation of Protestant Christian groups. The English Reformation began with Henry VIII's break with the Roman Catholic Church, which established the Protestant Church of England. Henry VIII's decision was politically motivated; he had no particular quarrel with Catholic theology and remained an orthodox Catholic in most matters of religious practice. (pp. 430–431, 437)

republicanism The belief that the unworkable model of European-style monarchy should be replaced with a form of government in which supreme power resides in the hands of citizens with the right to vote and is exercised by a representative government answerable to this electorate. In Revolutionary-era America, republicanism became a social philosophy that embodied a sense of community and called individuals to act for the public good. (pp. 232, 247–248)

suffrage The right to vote. The term *suffrage* is most often associated with the efforts of American women to secure voting rights. (pp. 233, 311–312) *See also* franchise.

virtual representation The notion, propounded by the British Parliament in the eighteenth century, that the House of Commons represented all British subjects—wherever they lived and regardless of whether they had directly voted for their representatives. Prime Minister George Grenville used this idea to argue that the Stamp Act and other parliamentary taxes on British colonists did not constitute taxation without representation. The American colonists rejected this argument, insisting that political representatives derived authority only from explicit citizens' consent (indicated by elections), and that members of a distant government body were incapable of adequately representing their interests. (p. 169)

War Hawks Young Republicans elected to the U.S. Congress in the fall of 1810 who were eager for war with Britain in order to legitimize attacks on Indians, end impressment, and avenge foreign insults. (p. 303) *See also* hawks.

yeoman A farmer who owned a small plot of land that was sufficient to support a family and was tilled by family members and perhaps a few servants. (pp. 77, 140)

Index

ATLAS OF THE TERRITORIAL GROWTH OF THE UNITED STATES

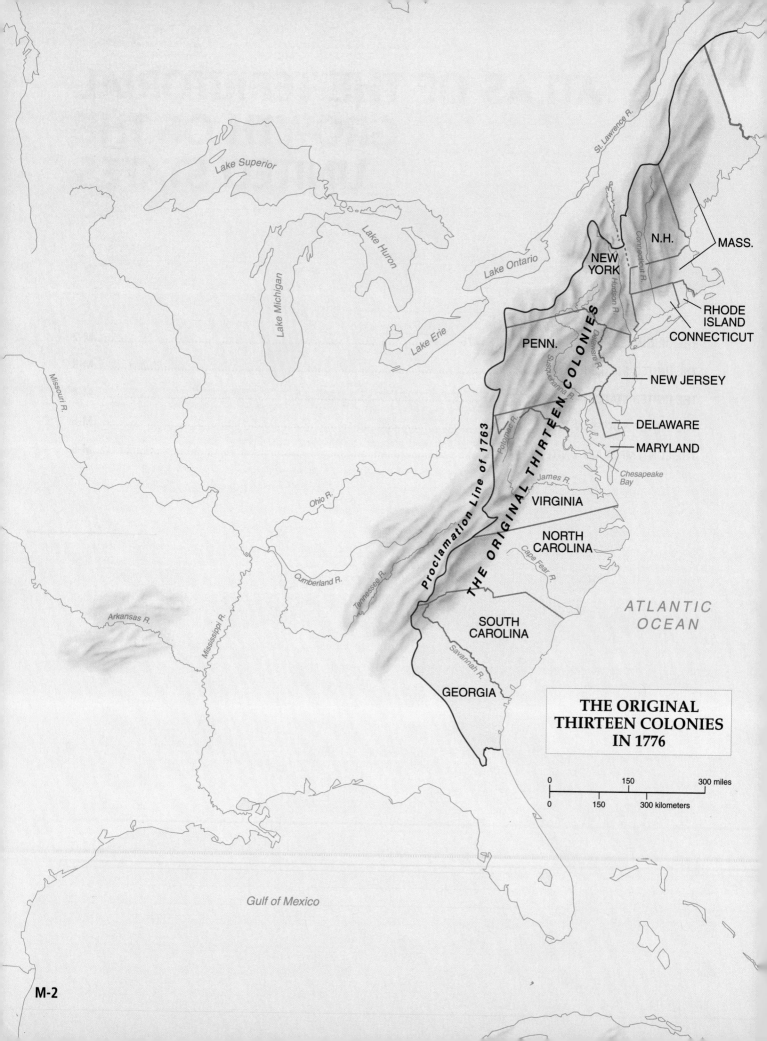

Lake Superior

Lake Michigan

Lake Huron

Lake Ontario

Lake Erie

St. Lawrence R.

Missouri R.

Ohio R.

Cumberland R.

Tennessee R.

Arkansas R.

Mississippi R.

Proclamation Line of 1763

THE ORIGINAL THIRTEEN COLONIES

N.H.

MASS.

NEW YORK

RHODE ISLAND

CONNECTICUT

Connecticut R.

Hudson R.

PENN.

Delaware R.

Susquehanna R.

NEW JERSEY

DELAWARE

MARYLAND

Potomac R.

Chesapeake Bay

James R.

VIRGINIA

NORTH CAROLINA

Cape Fear R.

SOUTH CAROLINA

Savannah R.

GEORGIA

ATLANTIC OCEAN

Gulf of Mexico

THE ORIGINAL
THIRTEEN COLONIES
IN 1776

0	150	300 miles
0	150	300 kilometers

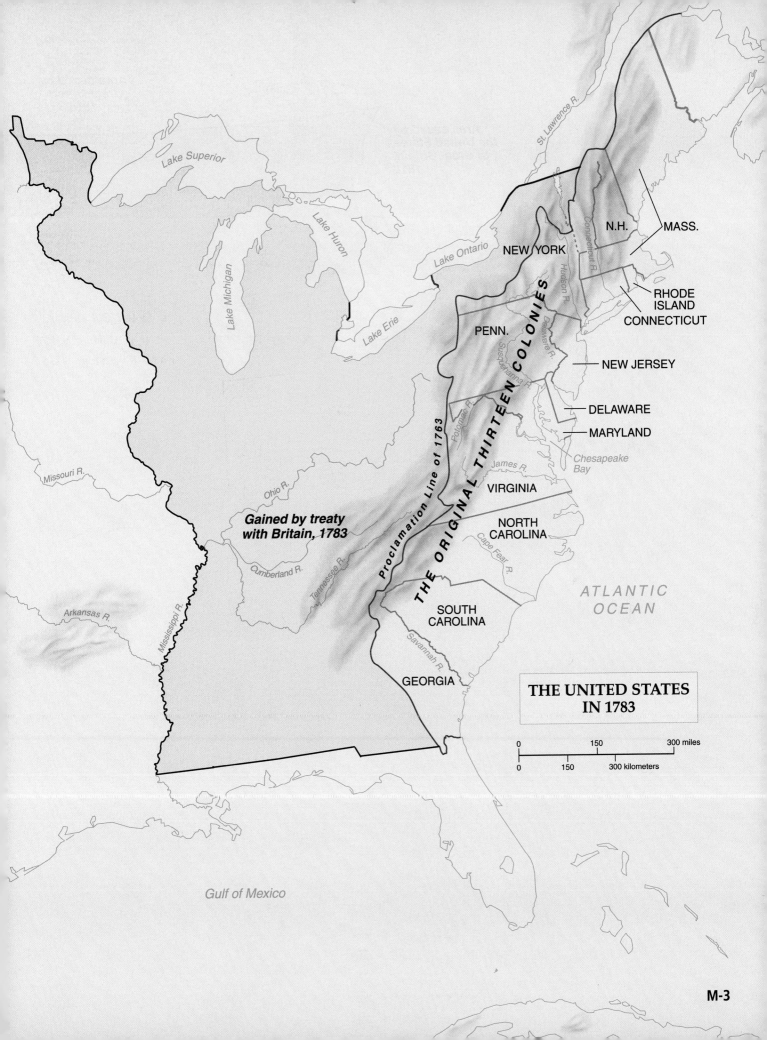

Lake Superior

Lake Huron

Lake Michigan

Lake Ontario

Lake Erie

St. Lawrence R.

N.H.

MASS.

NEW YORK

RHODE ISLAND

CONNECTICUT

Connecticut R.

Hudson R.

PENN.

Susquehanna R.

Delaware R.

NEW JERSEY

DELAWARE

MARYLAND

Potomac R.

Chesapeake Bay

James R.

VIRGINIA

THE ORIGINAL THIRTEEN COLONIES

Proclamation Line of 1763

NORTH CAROLINA

Cape Fear R.

Missouri R.

Ohio R.

Gained by treaty with Britain, 1783

Cumberland R.

Tennessee R.

SOUTH CAROLINA

Arkansas R.

Mississippi R.

Savannah R.

GEORGIA

ATLANTIC OCEAN

THE UNITED STATES IN 1783

0   150   300 miles

0   150   300 kilometers

Gulf of Mexico

M-3

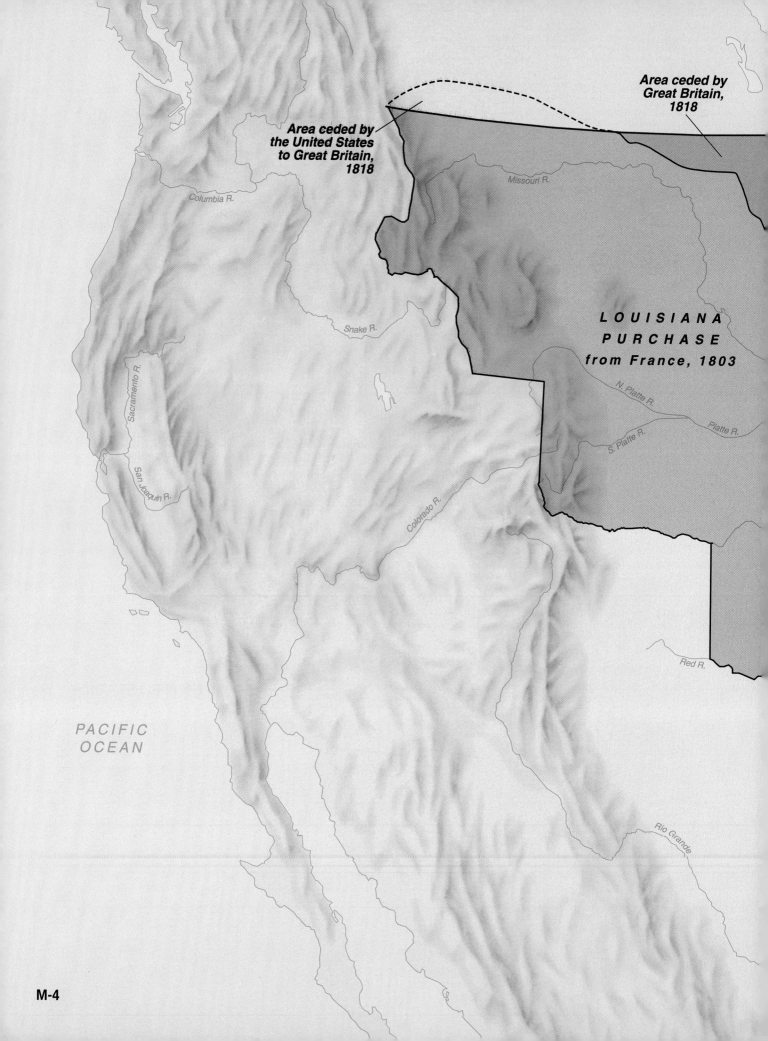

Area ceded by
Great Britain,
1818

Area ceded by
the United States
to Great Britain,
1818

Missouri R.

Columbia R.

Snake R.

*LOUISIANA
PURCHASE
from France, 1803*

N. Platte R.

Platte R.

S. Platte R.

Sacramento R.

San Joaquin R.

Colorado R.

Red R.

PACIFIC
OCEAN

Rio Grande

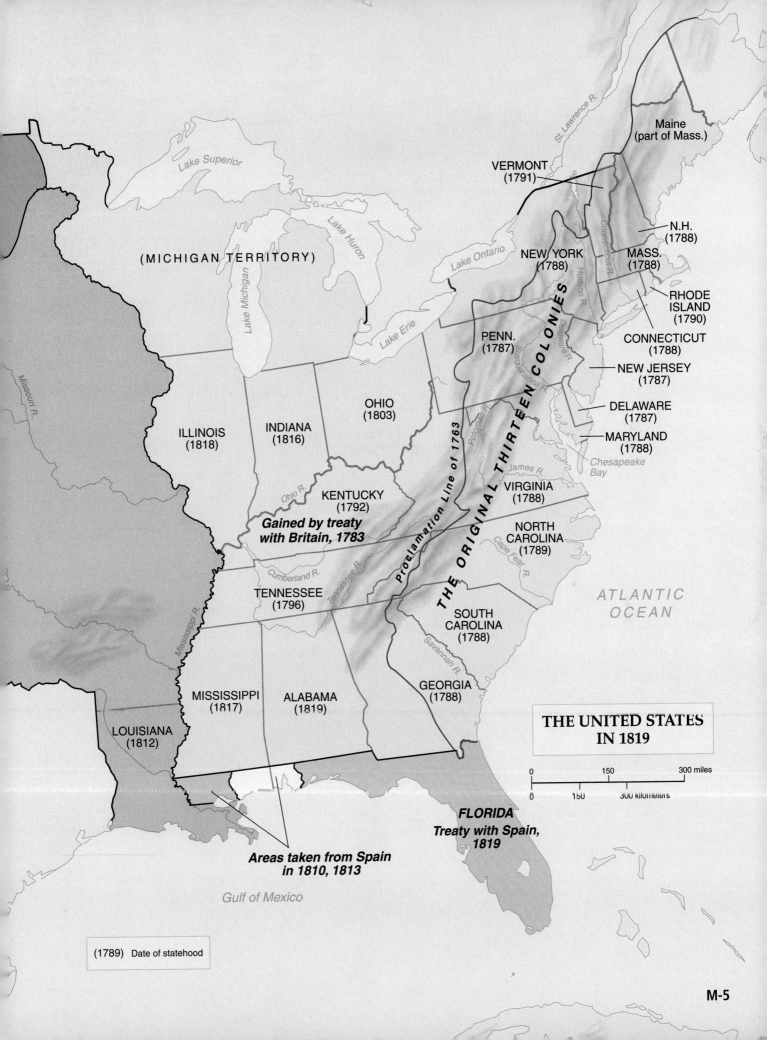

Maine
(part of Mass.)

St. Lawrence R.

Lake Superior

VERMONT
(1791)

(MICHIGAN TERRITORY)

Lake Huron

Lake Michigan

Lake Ontario

NEW YORK
(1788)

N.H.
(1788)

MASS.
(1788)

Connecticut R.

RHODE
ISLAND
(1790)

CONNECTICUT
(1788)

Lake Erie

Hudson R.

PENN.
(1787)

Delaware R.

NEW JERSEY
(1787)

Missouri R.

OHIO
(1803)

DELAWARE
(1787)

ILLINOIS
(1818)

INDIANA
(1816)

Potomac R.

MARYLAND
(1788)

Chesapeake
Bay

Ohio R.

KENTUCKY
(1792)

**Gained by treaty
with Britain, 1783**

Proclamation Line of 1763

James R.

VIRGINIA
(1788)

THE ORIGINAL THIRTEEN COLONIES

NORTH
CAROLINA
(1789)

Cumberland R.

Tennessee R.

Cape Fear R.

ATLANTIC
OCEAN

Mississippi R.

TENNESSEE
(1796)

SOUTH
CAROLINA
(1788)

Savannah R.

MISSISSIPPI
(1817)

ALABAMA
(1819)

GEORGIA
(1788)

LOUISIANA
(1812)

**THE UNITED STATES
IN 1819**

0   150   300 miles

0   150   300 kilometers

**FLORIDA
Treaty with Spain,
1819**

**Areas taken from Spain
in 1810, 1813**

Gulf of Mexico

(1789)   Date of statehood

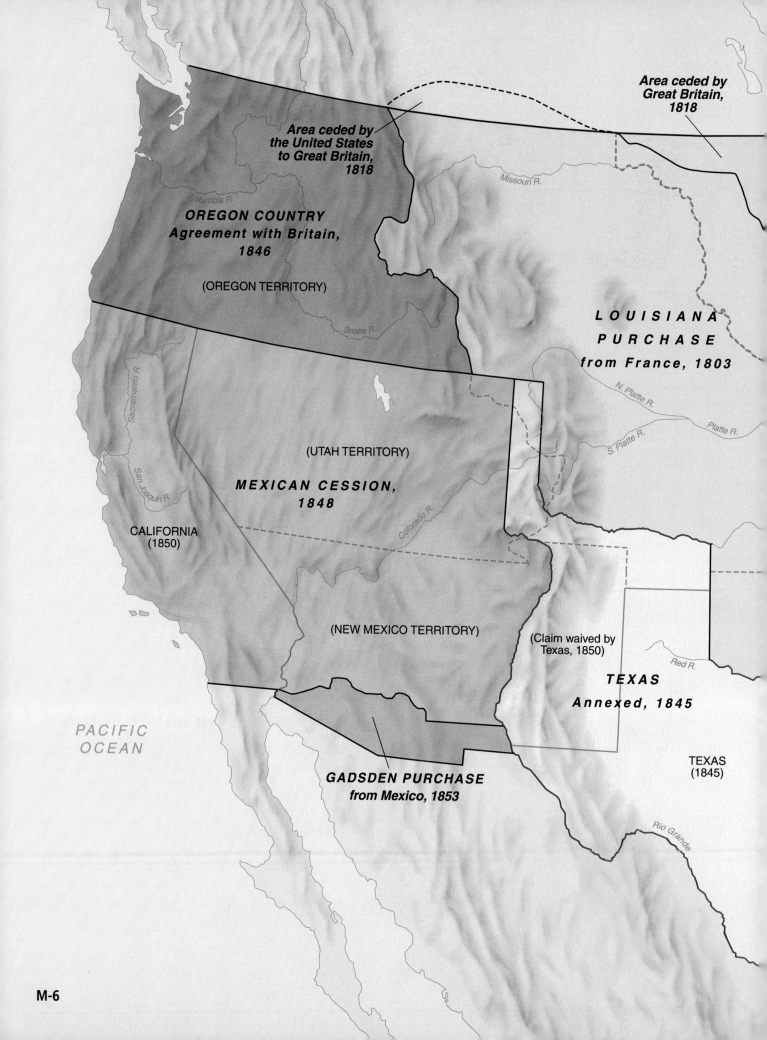

Area ceded by Great Britain, 1818

Area ceded by the United States to Great Britain, 1818

Missouri R.

OREGON COUNTRY
Agreement with Britain, 1846

(OREGON TERRITORY)

Columbia R.

Snake R.

LOUISIANA PURCHASE
from France, 1803

N. Platte R.

Platte R.

Sacramento R.

S. Platte R.

(UTAH TERRITORY)

San Joaquin R.

MEXICAN CESSION, 1848

CALIFORNIA (1850)

Colorado R.

(NEW MEXICO TERRITORY)

(Claim waived by Texas, 1850)

Red R.

TEXAS
Annexed, 1845

TEXAS (1845)

PACIFIC OCEAN

GADSDEN PURCHASE
from Mexico, 1853

Rio Grande

Areas ceded by Britain, 1842
(Webster-Ashburton Treaty)

Lake Superior

(MINNESOTA TERRITORY)

WISCONSIN
(1848)

Lake Huron

Lake Michigan

MICHIGAN
(1837)

Lake Ontario

Lake Erie

VERMONT
(1791)

MAINE
(1820)

St. Lawrence R.

NEW YORK
(1788)

N.H.
(1788)

MASS.
(1788)

Connecticut R.

Hudson R.

RHODE ISLAND
(1790)

PENN.
(1787)

Susquehanna R.

Delaware R.

CONNECTICUT
(1788)

NEW JERSEY
(1787)

DELAWARE
(1787)

IOWA
(1846)

Missouri R.

OHIO
(1803)

ILLINOIS
(1818)

INDIANA
(1816)

MARYLAND
(1788)

Chesapeake Bay

Potomac R.

James R.

Proclamation Line of 1763

MISSOURI
(1821)

Ohio R.

KENTUCKY
(1792)

Gained by treaty
with Britain, 1783

VIRGINIA
(1788)

THE ORIGINAL THIRTEEN COLONIES

NORTH CAROLINA
(1789)

Cape Fear R.

Cumberland R.

Tennessee R.

TENNESSEE
(1796)

ATLANTIC
OCEAN

ARKANSAS
(1836)

SOUTH CAROLINA
(1788)

(INDIAN TERRITORY)

Mississippi R.

MISSISSIPPI
(1817)

ALABAMA
(1819)

GEORGIA
(1788)

Savannah R.

LOUISIANA
(1812)

**THE UNITED STATES
IN 1853**

FLORIDA
(1845)

0   150   300 miles

0   150   300 kilometers

Areas taken from Spain
in 1810, 1813

FLORIDA
Treaty with Spain,
1819

Gulf of Mexico

(1789)   Date of statehood

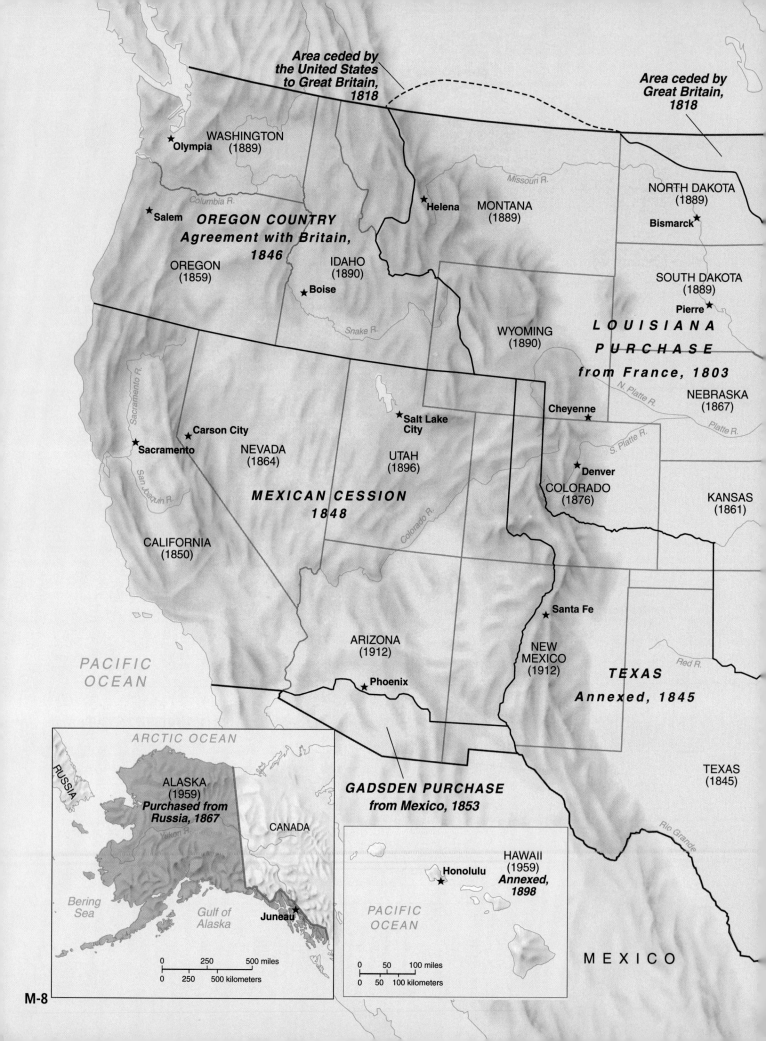

Area ceded by
the United States
to Great Britain, 1818

Area ceded by
Great Britain, 1818

WASHINGTON
(1889)
★ Olympia

★ Salem

OREGON COUNTRY
Agreement with Britain,
1846

OREGON
(1859)

★ Helena   MONTANA
(1889)

IDAHO
(1890)
★ Boise

NORTH DAKOTA
(1889)
Bismarck ★

SOUTH DAKOTA
(1889)
Pierre ★

WYOMING
(1890)

LOUISIANA
PURCHASE
from France, 1803

NEBRASKA
(1867)

Columbia R.
Missouri R.
Snake R.
N. Platte R.
Platte R.

★ Salt Lake
City

Cheyenne ★

★ Carson City

★ Sacramento

NEVADA
(1864)

UTAH
(1896)

MEXICAN CESSION
1848

CALIFORNIA
(1850)

★ Denver
COLORADO
(1876)

KANSAS
(1861)

S. Platte R.
Colorado R.
Sacramento R.
San Joaquin R.

★ Santa Fe

ARIZONA
(1912)

NEW
MEXICO
(1912)

TEXAS
Annexed, 1845

PACIFIC
OCEAN

★ Phoenix

Red R.

GADSDEN PURCHASE
from Mexico, 1853

TEXAS
(1845)

Rio Grande

ARCTIC OCEAN

RUSSIA

ALASKA
(1959)
Purchased from
Russia, 1867

CANADA

Yukon R.

Bering
Sea

Gulf of
Alaska

Juneau ★

| 0 | 250 | 500 miles |
| 0 | 250 | 500 kilometers |

HAWAII
(1959)
Annexed,
1898

★ Honolulu

PACIFIC
OCEAN

| 0 | 50 | 100 miles |
| 0 | 50 | 100 kilometers |

MEXICO

M-8

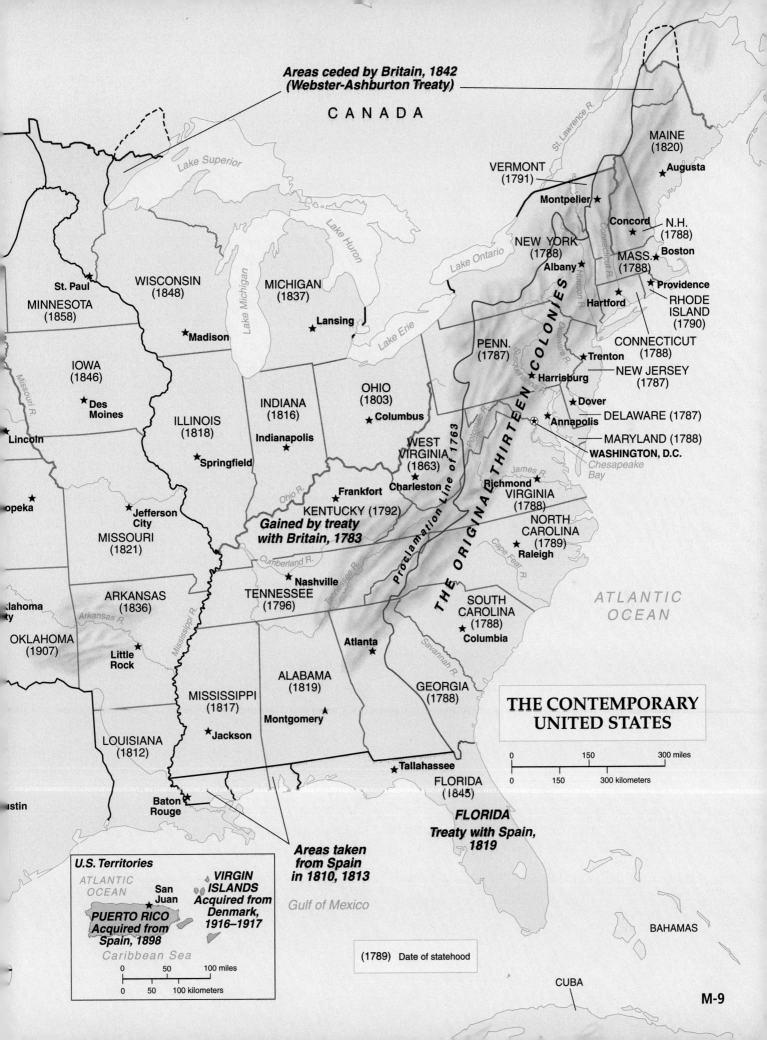

Areas ceded by Britain, 1842
(Webster-Ashburton Treaty)

C A N A D A

St. Lawrence R.

MAINE
(1820)
★ Augusta

VERMONT
(1791)
Montpelier ★

Concord ★   N.H.
(1788)

NEW YORK
(1788)
Albany ★

MASS.
(1788)   Boston ★

Lake Superior

Lake Huron

Lake Ontario

★ Hartford   Providence ★
RHODE
ISLAND
(1790)

CONNECTICUT
(1788)

NEW JERSEY
(1787)

Connecticut R.

Hudson R.

Delaware R.

WISCONSIN
(1848)

St. Paul ★
MINNESOTA
(1858)

MICHIGAN
(1837)

Lake Michigan

Lake Erie

PENN.
(1787)

★ Trenton
Harrisburg ★

★ Dover   DELAWARE (1787)

★ Madison

Lansing ★

IOWA
(1846)

OHIO
(1803)

WASHINGTON, D.C.

★ Des
Moines

INDIANA
(1816)

Columbus ★

Susquehanna R.

⊗ Annapolis   MARYLAND (1788)

Chesapeake Bay

ILLINOIS
(1818)

Indianapolis ★

WEST
VIRGINIA
(1863)

Potomac R.

★ Lincoln

Springfield ★

Frankfort ★

Charleston ★

Richmond ★

James R.

★opeka

KENTUCKY (1792)

VIRGINIA
(1788)

Jefferson
City ★

**Gained by treaty
with Britain, 1783**

Ohio R.

Cumberland R.

NORTH
CAROLINA
(1789)
Raleigh ★

MISSOURI
(1821)

Missouri R.

Nashville ★

Tennessee R.

ATLANTIC
OCEAN

ARKANSAS
(1836)

TENNESSEE
(1796)

SOUTH
CAROLINA
(1788)

Columbia ★

Cape Fear R.

lahoma
ty

Arkansas R.

OKLAHOMA
(1907)

Little
Rock ★

Atlanta ★

Savannah R.

ALABAMA
(1819)

MISSISSIPPI
(1817)

GEORGIA
(1788)

Montgomery ★

LOUISIANA
(1812)

Jackson ★

Mississippi R.

★ Tallahassee

FLORIDA
(1845)

Baton
Rouge ★

**Areas taken
from Spain
in 1810, 1813**

**FLORIDA
Treaty with Spain,
1819**

stin

Gulf of Mexico

THE CONTEMPORARY
UNITED STATES

| 0 | | 150 | | 300 miles |
| 0 | | 150 | 300 kilometers | |

U.S. Territories

ATLANTIC
OCEAN

San
Juan ★

*VIRGIN
ISLANDS
Acquired from
Denmark,
1916–1917*

**PUERTO RICO
Acquired from
Spain, 1898**

Caribbean Sea

| 0 | 50 | 100 miles |
| 0 | 50 | 100 kilometers |

(1789)   Date of statehood

BAHAMAS

CUBA

Proclamation Line of 1763

THE ORIGINAL THIRTEEN COLONIES

About the authors

JAMES L. ROARK (Ph.D., Stanford University) is Samuel Candler Dobbs Professor of American History at Emory University. In 1993, he received the Emory Williams Distinguished Teaching Award, and in 2001–2002 he was Pitt Professor of American Institutions at Cambridge University. He has written *Masters without Slaves: Southern Planters in the Civil War and Reconstruction* and coauthored *Black Masters: A Free Family of Color in the Old South* with Michael P. Johnson.

MICHAEL P. JOHNSON (Ph.D., Stanford University) is professor of history at Johns Hopkins University. His publications include *Toward a Patriarchal Republic: The Secession of Georgia*; *Abraham Lincoln, Slavery, and the Civil War: Selected Speeches and Writings*; and *Reading the American Past: Selected Historical Documents*, the documents reader for *The American Promise*. He has also coedited *No Chariot Let Down: Charleston's Free People of Color on the Eve of the Civil War* with James L. Roark.

PATRICIA CLINE COHEN (Ph.D., University of California, Berkeley) is professor of history at the University of California, Santa Barbara, where she received the Distinguished Teaching Award in 2005–2006. She has written *A Calculating People: The Spread of Numeracy in Early America* and *The Murder of Helen Jewett: The Life and Death of a Prostitute in Nineteenth-Century New York*, and she has coauthored *The Flash Press: Sporting Male Weeklies in 1840s New York*.

SARAH STAGE (Ph.D., Yale University) has taught U.S. history at Williams College and the University of California, Riverside, and she was visiting professor at Beijing University and Szechuan University. Currently she is professor of women's studies at Arizona State University. Her books include *Female Complaints: Lydia Pinkham and the Business of Women's Medicine* and *Rethinking Home Economics: Women and the History of a Profession*.

SUSAN M. HARTMANN (Ph.D., University of Missouri) is Arts and Humanities Distinguished Professor of History at Ohio State University. In 1995 she won the university's Exemplary Faculty Award in the College of Humanities. Her publications include *Truman and the 80th Congress*; *The Home Front and Beyond: American Women in the 1940s*; *From Margin to Mainstream: American Women and Politics since 1960*; and *The Other Feminists: Activists in the Liberal Establishment*.

About the cover image

Frank Blackwell Mayer, *The Continentals*, 1875

Frank Blackwell Mayer submitted this painting, *The Continentals*, to the 1876 Philadelphia Centennial Exhibition, in commemoration of the one hundredth anniversary of the Battle of Bunker Hill, one of the first battles of the Revolutionary War. The uplifting scene depicts two soldiers leading their fellow troops with the sounds of drum and flute. In the aftermath of the Civil War, a conflict that bitterly divided the country, this painting inspired in many Americans a renewed sense of patriotism and national pride.